COMPUTER APPLICATIONS FOR HANDLING LEGAL EVIDENCE,
POLICE INVESTIGATION AND CASE ARGUMENTATION

Law, Governance and Technology Series

VOLUME 5

Series Editors:

POMPEU CASANOVAS, *Institute of Law and Technology, UAB, Spain*

GIOVANNI SARTOR, *University of Bologna (Faculty of Law-CIRSFID) and European University Institute of Florence, Italy*

Scientific Advisory Board:

GIANMARIA AJANI, *University of Turin, Italy*; KEVIN ASHLEY, *University of Pittsburgh, USA*; KATIE ATKINSON, *University of Liverpool, UK*; TREVOR J.M. BENCH-CAPON, *University of Liverpool, UK*; V. RICHARDS BENJAMINS, *Telefonica, Spain*; GUIDO BOELLA, *Universita' degli Studi di Torino, Italy*; JOOST BREUKER, *Universiteit van Amsterdam, The Netherlands*; DANIÈLE BOURCIER, *CERSA, France*; TOM BRUCE, *Cornell University, USA*; NURIA CASELLAS, *Institute of Law and Technology, UAB, Spain*; CRISTIANO CASTELFRANCHI, *ISTC-CNR, Italy*; JACK G. CONRAD, *Thomson Reuters, USA*; ROSARIA CONTE, *ISTC-CNR, Italy*; FRANCESCO CONTINI, *IRSIG-CNR, Italy*; JESÚS CONTRERAS, *iSOCO, Spain*; JOHN DAVIES, *British Telecommunications plc, UK*; JOHN DOMINGUE, *The Open University, UK*; JAIME DELGADO, *Universitat Politècnica de Catalunya, Spain*; MARCO FABRI, *IRSIG-CNR, Italy*; DIETER FENSEL, *University of Innsbruck, Austria*; ENRICO FRANCESCONI, *ITTIG-CNR, Italy*; FERNANDO GALINDO, *Universidad de Zaragoza, Spain*; ALDO GANGEMI, *ISTC-CNR, Italy*; MICHAEL GENESERETH, *Stanford University, USA*; ASUNCIÓN GÓMEZ-PÉREZ, *Universidad Politécnica de Madrid, Spain*; THOMAS F. GORDON, *Fraunhofer FOKUS, Germany*; GUIDO GOVERNATORI, *NICTA, Australia*; GRAHAM GREENLEAF, *The University of New South Wales, Australia*; MARKO GROBELNIK, *Josef Stefan Institute, Slovenia*; JAMES HENDLER, *Rensselaer Polytechnic Institute, USA*; RINKE HOEKSTRA, *Universiteit van Amsterdam, The Netherlands*; ETHAN KATSH, *University of Massachusetts Amherst, USA*; MARC LAURITSEN, *Capstone Practice Systems, Inc., USA*; RONALD LEENES, *Tilburg Institute for Law, Technology, and Society, Tilburg University, The Netherlands*; PHILIP LIETH, *Queen's University Belfast, UK*; ARNO LODDER, *VU University Amsterdam, The Netherlands*; JOSÉ MANUEL LÓPEZ COBO, *Playence, Austria*; PIERRE MAZZEGA, *LMTG - UMR5563 CNRS/IRD/UPS, France*; MARIE-FRANCINE MOENS, *Katholieke Universiteit Leuven, Belgium*; PABLO NORIEGA, *IIIA - CSIC, Spain*; ANJA OSKAMP, *Open Universiteit, The Netherlands*; SASCHA OSSOWSKI, *Universidad Rey Juan Carlos, Spain*; UGO PAGALLO, *Università degli Studi di Torino, Italy*; MONICA PALMIRANI, *Università di Bologna, Italy*; ABDUL PALIWALA, *University of Warwick, UK*; ENRIC PLAZA, *IIIA - CSIC, Spain*; MARTA POBLET, *Institute of Law and Technology, UAB, Spain*; DANIEL POULIN, *University of Montreal, Canada*; HENRY PRAKKEN, *Universiteit Utrecht and The University of Groningen, The Netherlands*; HAIBIN QI, *Huazhong University of Science and Technology, P.R. China*; DORY REILING, *Amsterdam District Court, The Netherlands*; PIER CARLO ROSSI, *Italy*; EDWINA L. RISSLAND, *University of Massachusetts, Amherst, USA*; COLIN RULE, *University of Massachusetts, USA*; MARCO SCHORLEMMER, *IIIA-CSIC, Spain*; CARLES SIERRA, *IIIA-CSIC, Spain*; MIGEL ANGEL SICILIA, *Universidad de Alcalá, Spain*; RONALD W. STAUDT, *Chicago-Kent College of Law, USA*; RUDI STUDER, *Karlsruhe Institute of Technology, Germany*; DANIELA TISCORNIA, *ITTIG-CNR, Italy*; JOAN-JOSEP VALLBÉ, *Institute of Law and Technology, UAB, Spain*; TOM VAN ENGERS, *Universiteit van Amsterdam, The Netherlands*; FABIO VITALI, *Università di Bologna, Italy*; MARY-ANNE WILLIAMS, *The University of Technology, Sydney, Australia*; RADBOUD WINKELS, *University of Amsterdam, The Netherlands*; ADAM WYNER, *University of Liverpool, UK*; HAJIME YOSHINO, *Meiji Gakuin University, Japan*; HAJIME YOSHINO, *Meiji Gakuin University, Japan*; JOHN ZELEZNIKOW, *Victoria University, Australia*

For further volumes:
http://www.springer.com/series/8808

COMPUTER APPLICATIONS FOR HANDLING LEGAL EVIDENCE, POLICE INVESTIGATION AND CASE ARGUMENTATION

Volume 1

by

Ephraim Nissan

Goldsmiths' College, University of London, UK

with a chapter
by the VIRTOPSY team;

a chapter by Richard Leary;

sections by Jonathan Yovel;
by John Zeleznikow with Andrew Stranieri and John
Yearwood, or with Richard Leary and Wim Vandenberghe;
by Louis Akin; and by Jeroen Keppens;

and sections co-authored
by S. Eyal Shimony and E. Nissan;
by Aldo Franco Dragoni and E. Nissan; and by
Carmelo Asaro, E. Nissan, and Antonio A. Martino.

Foreword by John Zeleznikow

Dr. Ephraim Nissan
Department of Computing
Goldsmiths' College
University of London
London, SE14 6NW
England
ephraimnissan@hotmail.com

Printed in 2 volumes
ISBN 978-90-481-8989-2   ISBN 978-90-481-8990-8 (eBook)
DOI 10.1007/978-90-481-8990-8
Springer Dordrecht Heidelberg London New York

Library of Congress Control Number: 2011940957

© Springer Science+Business Media Dordrecht 2012
This work is subject to copyright. All rights are reserved by the Publisher, whether the whole or part of the material is concerned, specifically the rights of translation, reprinting, reuse of illustrations, recitation, broadcasting, reproduction on microfilms or in any other physical way, and transmission or information storage and retrieval, electronic adaptation, computer software, or by similar or dissimilar methodology now known or hereafter developed. Exempted from this legal reservation are brief excerpts in connection with reviews or scholarly analysis or material supplied specifically for the purpose of being entered and executed on a computer system, for exclusive use by the purchaser of the work. Duplication of this publication or parts thereof is permitted only under the provisions of the Copyright Law of the Publisher's location, in its current version, and permission for use must always be obtained from Springer. Permissions for use may be obtained through RightsLink at the Copyright Clearance Center. Violations are liable to prosecution under the respective Copyright Law.
The use of general descriptive names, registered names, trademarks, service marks, etc. in this publication does not imply, even in the absence of a specific statement, that such names are exempt from the relevant protective laws and regulations and therefore free for general use.
While the advice and information in this book are believed to be true and accurate at the date of publication, neither the authors nor the editors nor the publisher can accept any legal responsibility for any errors or omissions that may be made. The publisher makes no warranty, express or implied, with respect to the material contained herein.

Printed on acid-free paper

Springer is part of Springer Science+Business Media (www.springer.com)

This book is dedicated to the memory of Marco Somalvico (1941–2002). The thematic connection to the subject of this paper is provided by his encouragement – after a talk on ALIBI which as being his guest, I gave at my alma mater, the Technical University of Milan – to persist and further develop this direction of research, which on the evidence of the talk he considered very promising.[1] What I owe to Marco Somalvico is much more than that.[2]

---

[1] The next step in my actual induction into the discipline of AI & Law was the warm reception that Prof. Antonio Martino gave a talk of mine on ALIBI in Lisbon in 1989. I had originally been thinking of it mainly as an AI planning system for the generation of explanations; the latter also still is a thriving area of research in artificial intelligence.

[2] Cf. Nissan (2003i, 2007d); Colombetti, Gini, and Nissan (2007, 2008a, 2008b); Nissan, Gini, and Colombetti (2008 [2009], 2009a, 2009b).

Foreword

As a thirteen year old boy, the only articles I would read were the sporting columns of Melbourne daily newspapers. My mother was exasperated, how could she get her son to read books. Then she hit upon an excellent idea – *may be he would read novels by Sherlock Holmes.*

From that day in 1963, I became a voracious reader of stories about Sherlock Holmes – not only the countless short stories and four long stories, but also anything the author of the Holmes' stories, Sir Arthur Conan Doyle had written. And my interest included books about other detectives (such as Poirot and Maigret) and related movies.

But despite my interest in detective stories, for the next thirty-seven years I did not exhibit any interest in forensic science.[3] Then, in late 2000, Colin Aitken, then a reader in statistics at the University of Edinburgh, offered me the position as research director of a new centre for forensic statistics and legal reasoning. Having accepted the exciting position, I needed to explore the domain of forensic statistics and legal reasoning. And what an exciting trip it was.

When I arrived at the University of Edinburgh, I realised that Sir Arthur Conan Doyle had been a medical student there. One of his professors was Dr. Joseph Bell, a forensic pathologist. Bell was the man who inspired the character of Sherlock Holmes and shared many qualities with the famous detective. Thus we opened the Joseph Bell Centre for Forensic Statistics and Legal Reasoning. Its remit was to analyse, evaluate, interpret and present evidence using the skills in artificial intelligence, law and statistics from the University of Edinburgh, Glasgow Caledonian University and the Lothian and Borders Police Force Forensic Science Laboratory. Our goal was to develop software for the mathematically sound and legally permissible interpretation of scientific evidence. Then we needed to communicate and represent this knowledge to lawyers and juries at the trial stage. This requires interactions between different agencies – many police forces, forensic science laboratories, procurators fiscal, judges, advocates and juries.

The first areas of research at the Joseph Bell Centre for Forensic Statistics and legal reasoning were:

---

[3] As opposed to artificial intelligence for law (AI & Law).

- the definition and description of legal procedures for building a case based on evidence;
- the identification and application of mathematically acceptable techniques for interpreting and drawing conclusions from forensic evidence;
- the determination of the validity of conclusions drawn from analogous data or from a particular data sample;
- the investigation of the possibility of a common source for several samples of forensic significance;
- the identification and analysis of risk factors as part of the European anti-fraud initiative;
- the representation and implementation of all the above on a computer in an accessible format;
- the development of legal decision support systems.

The construction of such computer systems is a daunting task. Our initial approach has been to build small-scale knowledge-based systems in specific domains. Projects undertaken were:

(1) the value of trace evidence in linking a scene to a suspect, or a scene to a scene;
(2) the assessment of cross-transfer evidence;
(3) protocols for determination of sample size in criminal investigations;
(4) the reliability of eyewitness testimony;
(5) the examination of trends in European financial fraud;
(6) the role of statistical evidence in cases of suspected excess deaths in a medical context;
(7) the role of statistical evidence in cases of suspected credit card fraud; and
(8) the distinction between homicide, suicide and lawful deaths.

But the most daunting question was how could we integrate the vast multitude of knowledge required to undertake such a gigantic task. In his monumental book, *Computer Applications for Handling Legal Evidence, Police Investigation, and Case Argumentation,* Dr. Ephraim Nissan addresses this task. Rather than investigate biology, chemistry, law or statistics, Nissan focuses upon using computer techniques to organise the evidence and to enhance the analysis of forensic evidence. But even this is a major task, as can be seen by the size of his monograph.

Dr. Nissan's book of about one thousand three hundred pages investigates large areas of law, computer science, and some statistics, also addressing topics in the forensic disciplines, but mostly leaving the significant biological and forensic science topics to other treatises. See however the important Chapter 9 by the VIRTOPSY team in Bern. As Dr. Nissan states in his preface, his book provides an overview of computer techniques and tools for handling legal evidence, police intelligence, crime analysis or detection, and forensic testing, as well as investigating the modelling of argumentation and narratives. Whilst, over the past decade, there have been numerous publications discussing how computers can be used to evaluate legal evidence, Dr. Nissan's monograph is the first book to attempt this task. We are very grateful for the monumental book he has produced.

Dr. Nissan commences by investigating how one can reason with evidence. He looks at both logical and statistical models for modelling evidence and conducts an in depth investigation of his ALIBI system and Paul Thagard's work on the Claus von Bülow Trials, using ECHO, a Coherence Network, and Bayesian networks. He also informs readers about the Bayesian controversy among legal scholars. Becoming aware of the arguments put forth by Ron Allen is crucial, for readers entering the field covered by this book, whether one sides with the Bayesians, or accepts the critique. It is important to realise the reference-class problem, itself a source of disagreement among forensic statisticians.

Chapter 3 involves a detailed investigation of argumentation. Argumentation has been used in knowledge engineering in two distinct ways; with a focus on the use of argumentation to structure knowledge (i.e. non-dialectical emphasis) and with a focus on the use of argumentation to model discourse (i.e. dialectical emphasis). Dialectical approaches typically automate the construction of an argument and counter arguments normally with the use of a non-monotonic logic where operators are defined to implement discursive primitives such as *attack, rebut,* or *accept.*

In applications of argumentation to model dialectical reasoning, argumentation is used specifically to model discourse and only indirectly used to structure knowledge. The concepts of conflict and of argument preferences map directly onto a discursive situation where participants are engaged in dispute. In contrast, many uses of argumentation for knowledge engineering application do not model discourse. This corresponds more closely to a non-dialectical perspective. The analysis of argument advanced by Toulmin (1958) does not distinguish dialectical argumentation from non-dialectical argumentation. By illustrating that logic can be viewed as a kind of generalised jurisprudence rather than as a science, Toulmin (1958) advanced a structure of rhetoric that captures the layout of arguments. Jurisprudence focuses attention on procedures by which legal claims are advanced and attacked. Toulmin (1958) sought to identify procedures by which any claim is advanced. He identified a layout of arguments that was constant regardless of the content of the argument.

As well as the important argumentation theory of Toulmin, Dr. Nissan also devotes as much attention to the early work of analysis evidence of John Henry Wigmore. Wigmore developed a graphical method for evidence analysis. Wigmore's evidence rules are still used by many U.S. courts. His graphical method is used by some scholars, such as Dave Schum, Terence Anderson, and William Twining. Dr. Nissan also considers the argumentation schemes of Doug Walton, Katia Sycara (Persuader) and Tom Gordon (Carneades). Chapter 5 discusses in detail the related topic of narratives, considering what artificial intelligence offers for their treatment, as well as related legal scholarship.

Chapter 4 involves a lengthy examination of appropriate decision support systems (it concludes with a section about relevance and formalism, by Jonathan Yovel). As Oatley, Ewart and Zeleznikow (2006) say 'there exists very little literature about predictive models for police decision support'. Early work included the use of neural networks for the prediction of repeat victimisation (Oatley et al., 2002). This research predicted the occurrence of the next crime, and the expected time interval for this perpetration. The best neural network models trained on this data for predicting the next crime achieved an average performance, and it was impossible to find a neural network model for predicting the time interval without either obvious over-training, or extremely poor performance and it is unfortunate that in that earlier study there was no time to use a dataset where the time intervals were not left as single point values.

Until recently, very few computer systems have attempted to make decisions using evidence sources. Tillers and Schum (1998) and Schum (1994) discussed Wigmore's pioneering approach (Wigmore, 1913) to proof in litigation. Wigmore's method of diagramming the body of evidence in a case is the central method behind Walton's (2002) treatise on legal argumentation and evidence. Schum and Tillers (1991) examined marshalling legal evidence. Kadane and Schum (1996) used probability and Wigmore's diagrams of evidence to analyse the trial of the American anarchists Sacco and Vanzetti.[4] There is a controversy about Bayesianism in law. It should not be ignored. Some applications are less controversial; these are not about the judicial decision, or about strength claimed for the evidence in court, but rather for costs/benefits analysis, for the prosecutor to evaluate whether to prosecute, and for subservient tasks that do not affect the evaluation of the evidence (e.g., statistics inside tools for data mining is unlikely to be controversial among legal scholars). The real challenge for the application of artificial intelligence to legal evidence is to produce accounts of plausibility (ones that would take into account narrative coherence) that would not be the irritant that Bayesian accounts are within legal scholarship of evidence.

Various techniques have been used to construct criminal investigation decision support systems. Statistics has been used to analyse evidence (Aitken, 1995; Schum, 1994). Areas investigated include DNA testing, fingerprints, footwear and ballistics.

Chapter 6 involves a very thorough examination of crime data mining. In investigating the topic, Oatley, Ewart, and Zeleznikow stated (2006, p. 24):

> In 2003/2004, approximately 5.9 million crimes were notified to 43 Police Services in England and Wales. Property crimes such as theft and burglary account for 78% of recorded crimes and over 430,000 (14%) of these involve the burglary of a domestic dwelling.
>
> Once notified, the Police must investigate. Sometimes this will constitute only the recording of the details of the offence from the victim. More often, the investigation will comprise a detailed examination of the crime scene, the collection of forensic material and recording of witness and victim statements. This level of process is not just reserved for serious crimes, but is routine practice even for relatively minor ones.
>
> It is apparent that regardless of the level of investigation, a single recorded crime will generate a considerable amount and diversity of information. The challenge is not only to

---

[4] Combining Bayesianism and Wigmore Charts is also what is done in Dawid, Hepler, and Schum's (2011) "Inference Networks: Bayes and Wigmore". Also see Hepler et al. (2007).

store this information, but to use it to facilitate the investigative process. The features of one case at a particular point in time may have little value but the ability to retrospectively interrogate such a comprehensive crime database is a powerful investigative tool.

The value of this technological challenge is best understood through considering the task of the investigator. In general terms, it is worth noting that the detection of crime in many Police Services will involve not just Police Officers, but civilian crime analysts and scene of crimes officers (SOCOs). In respect of crime detection, Canter (2000) describes the nature of forensic decision making. It is how the investigators draw inferences and conclusions from the data they have available in order to embark upon the most appropriate way forward in order to identify and prosecute the culprit.

However, there is an established literature on the problems of information processing and inference that may beset human decision making. It should be evident that decision making with the forensic domain is problematic. This may be a contributory factor in the detection rate for a volume crime such as burglary is as low as 13% of recorded incidents.

Computer Science methodologies have the ability to select and display such information to the investigator. In this way, the salience of crime features is revealed. These are aspects of the crime which have most potential to assist the investigation in a number of ways, including the identification of crime patterns, linking offences and the identification of suspects.

Chapter 7, by Richard Leary, is about the FLINTS software for link analysis. That chapter enables a closer look at one of the kinds of tools that were discussed in Chapter 6. Chapter 8 looks at forensic techniques. Here and elsewhere in the book, one finds coverage of work by my former colleagues at the Joseph Bell Centre for Forensic Statistics and Legal Reasoning. Chapter 8 begins with coverage of research by Jeroen Keppens into the use of model based reasoning to evaluate possible scenarios at crime scenes, whilst a section inside Chapter 4 is concerned with Michael Bromby's ADVOKATE, a system developed to evaluate eye-witness identification. Chapter 8 also discusses the contexts of processing human faces, such as the generation of facial composites. A number of forensic disciplines are covered more concisely, before discussing fingerprint research more extensively. Controversies concerning both fingerprints and DNA are mentioned. Chapter 9 is about virtual autopsies by means of computer imaging, and was authored by a team in Bern.

Dr. Nissan's treatise offers a panoramic view of topics, techniques and tools. It is understandable to forensic scientists, statisticians and practitioners of Artificial Intelligence and Computer Science. Also legal scholars and practitioners will be interested. So will an audience within police science. Appropriate tools for legal professionals and law enforcement agencies are investigated in detail.

In order to deal with hypotheses, representations and tools for the organisation of arguments are useful; therefore research into argumentation is cited, and argumentation tools or methods that are useful for reasoning about the evidence are surveyed. The final part of the book is devoted to data mining and to a variety of forensic techniques. There is a useful glossary (a few of the entries are like brief sections providing additional discussion), and of course the bibliography is very large.

Dr. Nissan has compiled a monumental book. I strongly commend it as a book to be both read and referenced.

Melbourne, Victoria, Australia   John Zeleznikow

Acknowledgements

I am grateful to Ron Allen, Peter Tillers, and Bernard Jackson for specific comments on earlier drafts, to two extremely perceptive anonymous referees of the book the way it was submitted, as well as to an anonymous referee (of a related work) who provided a useful critique from the Bayesian camp (even though I have been trying to be neutral in the Bayesianism controversy among legal scholars or forensic statisticians). I am grateful to John Zeleznikow for sustained encouragement in this project, to Lars Ebert and his co-authors from the VIRTOPSY project in Bern, and to Richard Leary, to Jonathan Yovel, to John Zeleznikow, Andrew Stranieri, John Yearwood, and Wim Vanderberghe, to Louis Akin, and to Jeroen Keppens for their respective efforts in contributing to this volume the texts that appear under their names. Moreover, one of the sections in this book appears under Solomon Eyal Shimony's and my own names, the result of fruitful collaboration years ago. Another section is jointly authored by Aldo Franco Dragoni and myself, also based on a joint project of ours. The section on DAEDALUS, a tool developed by Carmelo Àsaro, is partly based on previous work I co-authored with him and Antonio Martino.

Charlie Frowd kindly provided an explanation about EvoFIT, as well as two screenshots reproduced in this book. Deirdre Hogan of Aprilage in Toronto kindly provided images generated by their age-progression software. Moreover, my gratitude goes to Laurance Donnelly and Alastair Ruffell, for enabling me to find out more about forensic geology. "Polo" Chau, his team leader Christos Faloutsos, and the latter's executive assistant Marilyn Walgora from Carnegie Mellon University generously enabled the reproduction of several images describing the team's NetProbe and Polonium systems. Louis Akin, a crime scene analyst from Austin, Texas, contributed a brief section, as well as several photographs. Richard Leary's chapter also comprises photographs from crime scene analysis, as well as many screenshots of the software he describes. From Milan, Mario Arrigoni Neri of Nova Semantics kindly drew a graph expressly for this book; it appears as Figure 6.1.7.3.2, and is intended in order to clarify a detail from a screenshot from software of his, appearing as 6.1.7.3.1 (for the permission to reproduce this, I also thank Marco Colombetti).

John Zeleznikow wrote the Foreword. Others provided encouraging comments on drafts. As to co-investigators, I am especially grateful to Aldo Franco Dragoni and Eyal Shimony: I present some of the results of joint research with each in turn, previously published as articles. The section about *Daedalus* is mostly based on Asaro, Martino, and Nissan (2001), and is indebted to Carmelo Àsaro's input to that article of ours, apart from *Daedalus* having been programmed by Judge Asaro himself, and all screen snapshots in that section having been made by him. Much reading went into the making of this book, but in particular, reading an excellent book by Jesús Mena (2003) gave me an idea not of replication, but of how to arrange the presentation in my chapter on data mining for criminal investigation or intelligence. Amina Memon's course handouts at her website helped me to better understand how to present the literature about eyewitness psychology.

Attending the workshop on Archaeology and Forensic Science, held at the British Academy in London on 27 February 2007, was very useful. Prof. Aron Vecht's explanations about the chemistry of a forensic application are gratefully acknowledged. Over the years, contacts with other scholars have helped me to improve specific parts of this book as it was taking shape. They include forensic geologists Laurance Donnelly and Alastair Ruffell, as well as Jeimy Cano, whose field of expertise is digital anti-forensics. I gratefully acknowledge extensive help from Mrs. Ann Aldridge, at the Inter-Library Loans Department of the Library at Goldsmiths' College of the University of London. Besides, I am grateful to Yaakov HaCohen-Kerner in Jerusalem for signalling to me a few articles.

Within my own family, this work would not have been possible without my mother's patience and abnegation. Words could not capture a "thank you" big enough. On one dramatic occasion in the early second century C.E., the renowned Rabbi Akiva, in fortuitous circumstances when coming home, introduced to his many pupils the lady to whom, rather than to him – he acknowledged – they owed what he had been able to teach them.[5]

On a very different plane, I acknowledge with gratitude the patience of Nachum Dershowitz, the joint editor with me of a jubilee volume, also published with Springer: that other project, also in its very final phases, had to queue as this one was getting its final touches. Eamonn Martin, a technician, recovered my file system in early 2011, when for weeks it wasn't clear whether the files of this and other projects were affected, which would have required reconstituting much of the work.

At Springer in Dordrecht in the Netherlands, my thanks go to Neil Olivier and Diana Nijenhuijzen. My contacts were initially especially with the former, and afterwards especially with the latter. Their role and patient support have been crucial in respectively the earlier phase and final phase of the process of getting this book accepted and then into shape. At Integra in Pondicherry in India, I thank Manoj

---

[5] There is no reason not to start giving proper citations already in the Acknowledgement section. Accounts of that episode were given in both the *Babylonian Talmud* (in two of its tractates: *Ketubbot* 62b; *Nedarim* 50a; cf. *Shabbat* 59a–b), and the *Jerusalem Talmud* (again, in two tractates: *Shabbat* 6:1, 7d; and *Sotah* 9:15, 24c), as well as in *Avot de-Rabbi Nathan* (in Version A, chapter 6, and in Version B, chapter 12). See however Tal Ilan's (2005) summary of current scholarly interpretations of that story.

Raju, Sangeetha Sathiamurthy, and Gandhimathi Ganesan, who in turn were assiduously in contact with me, during the quite demanding production process. There surely also were, among the typesetters, (to me) anonymous clever hands for whom I do not have a name by which to thank them.

Many persons have contributed to this book, and I had the benefit of advice from several scholars; I am responsible for any conceptual imperfections which remain in this work. Between the undertaking of this writing project, and the submission of the revised manuscript of over 1,500 pages in large type in late May, early June 2011, five years had elapsed. In January and February I was blocked by a computer crash, and it wasn't until February that I was relieved to hear that my file system could be recovered. Even after the recovery, large Word files with many figures belonging to my other writing projects, and which I was checking upon recovery, kept crashing at the press of the 'Save' button, and had to be recovered again from the burnt computer.

Miraculously I would say, the huge file of this book was recovered in good shape, and augmenting it (imagine the apprehension) did not result in the file being damaged by further crashes, even though separate small files had to be provided afterwards, especially footnotes. Needless to say, Since the recovery from the crash I was keeping backups of this book's main file on a very frequent basis. During the autumn of 2011, upon the instructions from the typesetters, I had to redraw many of the figures of this book, to ensure better reproduction. Then during the winter until the early spring, my task of correcting the proofs and providing index entries was very exacting, more exacting than any proof correction I had ever done in decades. It swallowed a huge amount of work in daylight and by night, on occasion into the little hours of the morning.

Come March, I only allowed the festival of Purim the half hour it took me to read aloud the Scroll of Esther in the original Hebrew with the traditional cantillation, as customarily required, and meanwhile, the huge reams of paper never left my kitchen table, except on Friday late afternoons for the entry of the Sabbath (in which case they remained stacked away until the end of the same). On the day after (the normatively joyful festival of) Purim, I was chagrined to find in an email that I was sternly given one more week with weekends at both ends to complete this project. Hardly the 'Thank you' I expected. Even though I tried to obtain a reprieve (a futile attempt), the correction process being curtailed means that typos or instances of misformatting from Chapter 6 to Chapter 9 and beyond (in the Glossary and Bibliography) could not be as thoroughly eliminated as from Chapters 1 to 5 and 10. I beg the benevolence and leniency of the reader for such typos and perhaps instances of misformatting that are left. At least, I hope I managed to catch broken cross-references. Meanwhile, a jubilee volume I had to complete for the Berlin offices of Springer had to wait one year, and I am thankful to my joint editor in that other project, to its many authors, and to the Jubilaris of that book for their patience.

Admittedly, the scope of the book you are now reading is very wide, so ideally there should have been more than one author; the participation of other authors for specific topics responds to this need. Even though the book is large, there still are various things that could be fleshed out. I have tried to take on board all the advice

I was given, within the timescales that this publication project required. Citations could be even more numerous, and the field keeps growing.

Along with the detailed, four-level table of contents, and with the cross-references in many of the entries of the Glossary, also this Subject Index is an important point of entry for accessing information in this book. Making it so detailed was indispensable. A thorough, detailed index is a crucial need for very long books with a broad scope such as this one. The rule of adequacy of the indexing is a linear function,[6] not a constant proportion: the longer the book, the more a thorough subject index becomes absolutely indispensable (obviously, also depending upon the kind of the book: a telephone directory needs no indexing...).[7]

The indexing of Chapters 2 to 5 is especially meticulous. Had I been allowed more time, I would have indexed as thoroughly – which was my intention to do - also Chapter 6 (the longest of this book: it takes about 200 pages), and Chapter 8. Hopefully also the indexing of Chapters 6 to 9 will be found to be adequate by the benevolent reader. Some sketchy indexing is also provided for the Glossary. Even just browsing the Subject Index will hopefully awaken the curiosity of those giving it a try. Try 'Forest spotted owlet', 'Walrus', and 'Whale'. Or then try and 'Footwear'. What do they do in an AI & Law book? Check in the index, to find out.

---

[6] The general formula $y = a + bx$ expresses a linear function. Let y be the percentage of a book length to be allocated to adequate indexing.

[7] The formula $y = 0 + 0x$ expresses the particular case of a phone directory.

Contents

Volume 1

1 A Preliminary Historical Perspective 1
2 Models of Forming an Opinion 13
   2.1 Modelling Adjudicators' Shifts of Opinion 13
      2.1.1 Preliminaries 13
      2.1.2 Distributed Belief Revision for Modelling
           the Dynamics of Adjudicators' Opinion 16
           by Aldo Franco Dragoni and Ephraim Nissan
      2.1.3 Further Considerations, and Suggestions
           of Possible Refinements 26
      2.1.4 Devices of Manipulation of Incoming
           Information in Court 28
      2.1.5 Remarks About Procedures and Jurisdictions 29
      2.1.6 A Taxonomy of Quantitative Models 31
      2.1.7 An Excessive Focus on Juries? 36
   2.2 Reasoning About a Charge and Explanations: Seminal
      Tools from the Late 1980s and Their Aftermath 39
      2.2.1 ECHO, and PEIRCE's Remake of the Peyer Case . . 39
           2.2.1.1 Thagard's 1989 Simulation of the
                 Jury at the Peyer Case 39
           2.2.1.2 Thagard's Principles of
                 Explanatory Coherence 40
           2.2.1.3 Thagard's Neural Network
                 Algorithm in ECHO 41
           2.2.1.4 Thagard's Greedy Algorithm for
                 Simulating a Trial 43
           2.2.1.5 Josephson's Abducer, PEIRCE-IGTT . . . 44
           2.2.1.6 Abductive Reasoning, and
                 Inference to the Best Explanation 47
           2.2.1.7 The von Bülow Trials 49

		2.2.1.8	Thagard's Treatment of the von Bülow Trials: Using ECHO and a Coherence Network, vs. Producing a Bayesian Network with JavaBayes	51
	2.2.2	ALIBI, a Planner for Exoneration		53
		2.2.2.1	1989: An *Annus Mirabilis*?	53
		2.2.2.2	Workings and Structure of ALIBI	54
		2.2.2.3	Examples of ALIBI's Output	57
		2.2.2.4	Knowledge Representation in ALIBI . . .	61
		2.2.2.5	An Illustration of the Conceptual Factors Involved in Common Sense About the Jeweller's Example . . .	69
		2.2.2.6	An Afterlife of Some ALIBI Sessions . .	75
		2.2.2.7	Extension with the *Dramatis Personae* Approach	79
		2.2.2.8	Wells and Olson's Taxonomy of Alibis . .	95
2.3	A Quick Survey of Some Bayesian and Naive Bayesian Approaches in Law			99
	by Andrew Stranieri and John Zeleznikow			
	2.3.1	Underlying Concepts		99
	2.3.2	Some Applications in Law		104
2.4	The Controversy Concerning the Probabilistic Account of Juridical Proof			107
2.5	A Quick Sampling of Some Probabilistic Applications			111
	2.5.1	Poole's Independent Choice Logic and Reasoning About Accounts of a Crime		111
	2.5.2	Dynamic Uncertain Inference Concerning Criminal Cases, and Snow and Belis's Recursive Multidimensional Scoring		115
2.6	Kappa Calculus in the Service of Legal Evidence			117
	by Solomon Eyal Shimony and Ephraim Nissan			
	2.6.1	Preliminary Considerations		117
	2.6.2	A Review of Åqvist's Scheme		119
	2.6.3	A Review of Kappa Calculus		120
	2.6.4	A Comparison of the Schemes		121
		2.6.4.1	Equivalence of Kappa-Calculus to Grading Mechanisms	121
		2.6.4.2	Reintroducing the Probabilities	124
	2.6.5	Suggested Solution		125
	2.6.6	Contextual Assessment of the Method		126
	2.6.7	An Application to Relative Plausibility? Considerations About a Role for the Formalism . . .		126

3	Argumentation			129
	3.1	Types of Arguments		129
	3.2	Wigmore Charts vs. Toulmin Structure for Representing Relations Among Arguments		130
		3.2.1	Preliminaries	130
		3.2.2	The Notation of Wigmore Charts	132
		3.2.3	A Wigmorean Analysis of an Example	133
			3.2.3.1 The Case, the Propositions, and the Wigmore Chart	133
			3.2.3.2 Considerations About the Situation at Hand	136
		3.2.4	Another Example: An Embarrassing Situation in Court	137
			3.2.4.1 An Episode During a Trial	137
			3.2.4.2 The Propositions and Their Wigmore Charts	139
	3.3	Pollock's Inference Graphs and Degrees of Justification		146
	3.4	Beliefs		149
		3.4.1	Beliefs, in Some Artificial Intelligence Systems	149
		3.4.2	Dispositional Beliefs vs. Dispositions to Believe	152
		3.4.3	Common Knowledge, and Consequentialism	153
		3.4.4	Commitment vs. Belief: Walton's Approach	154
			3.4.4.1 The Problem of Recognising Belief, Based on Commitment	154
			3.4.4.2 Walton's Argument Schemes and Critical Questions for Argument from Commitment	156
			3.4.4.3 Walton's Argument Scheme and Critical Questions for Telling Out Belief Based on Commitment	157
			3.4.4.4 Another Approach to Critical Questions	159
	3.5	Arguments in PERSUADER		161
	3.6	Representing Arguments in *Carneades*		164
		3.6.1	*Carneades* vs. Toulmin	164
		3.6.2	Proof Standards in *Carneades*	165
		3.6.3	The Notation of *Carneades*	165
	3.7	Some Computer Tools that Handle Argumentation		166
	3.8	Four Layers of Legal Arguments		168
	3.9	A Survey of the Literature on Computational Models of Argumentation		169
		3.9.1	Within AI & Law	169
		3.9.2	Within Other Research Communities	171
	3.10	Computational Models of Legal Argumentation About Evidence		174
		3.10.1	Some Early and Ongoing Research	174
		3.10.2	*Stevie*	176

3.11 Argumentation for Dialectical Situations,
vs. for Structuring Knowledge Non-dialectically,
and an Integration of the Two 177
by Andrew Stranieri, John Zeleznikow, and John Yearwood
    3.11.1 Three Categories of Concepts Grouping
Concepts of Argumentation 177
    3.11.2 From the Toulmin Argument Structure,
to the Generic Actual Argument Model 178
    3.11.3 Dialectical vs. Non-Dialectical Argumentation 179
    3.11.4 Variations of Toulmin's Structure 181
        3.11.4.1 Johnson's Variation of the
Toulmin Layout 183
        3.11.4.2 The Freeman and Farley Variation
on Toulmin Warrants 184
        3.11.4.3 Bench-Capon's Variation of the
Toulmin Layout 186
        3.11.4.4 Considerations Concerning
Toulmin Variations 187
    3.11.5 A Generic Non-dialectical Model of
Argumentation: The *Generic Actual Argument
Model (GAAM)*....................... 187
        3.11.5.1 The Argument Template 187
        3.11.5.2 Discussion 191
        3.11.5.3 Representing Actual Arguments 192
    3.11.6 Applications of the Generic/Actual Argument Model . 195
        3.11.6.1 The *Split Up* System for
Negotiating a Divorce 195
        3.11.6.2 The *Embrace* System for
Assessing Refugee Status 200
        3.11.6.3 The *GetAid* System for Legal Aid
Eligibility 202
        3.11.6.4 An Application Outside Law: *eTourism* . 203
    3.11.7 Envoi 205

4 **Computer Assistance for, or Insights into, Organisational Aspects** ... 207
  4.1 Computer Help for Organising 207
    4.1.1 Procedural-Support Systems for Organising
the Evidence: *CaseNote*, *MarshalPlan*, *Daedalus* ... 207
    4.1.2 The Lund Procedure 210
    4.1.3 *Daedalus*, a Procedural-Support Tool for the
Italian Examining Magistrate and Prosecutor 212
by Carmelo Asaro, Ephraim Nissan,
and Antonio A. Martino
        4.1.3.1 Background of the Project, and Its Users . 212
        4.1.3.2 General Remarks About Italian
Procedural Law 213

		4.1.3.3	The Phases of an Inquiry in Italy	215
		4.1.3.4	The Criteria of an Inquiry	218
		4.1.3.5	Once the Decision to Prosecute is Taken .	221
		4.1.3.6	A Sample Session: The Bindi Extortion Case	222
		4.1.3.7	Effects of the Jurisdiction: Why Is *Daedalus'* Emphasis on Step-by-Step Validation So Important in Italy? And Why Is the Statute of Limitations So Important in *Itaca*? . . . . by Ephraim Nissan	236
		4.1.3.8	Further Considerations About *Daedalus*, and About Select Aspects of the Human Process It Subserves by Ephraim Nissan	237
4.2	On Some Criminal Justice Information Systems or Other Tools			239
	4.2.1	Tools for Decision Support, vs. Tools for Applying a Procedure			239
	4.2.2	Risks of Too High Data Concentration			240
	4.2.3	Support from User Communities, vs. Tools Bestowed from Above			241
	4.2.4	Past Cases, New Cases, and Using the Former for the Latter			243
	4.2.5	Prosecutorial Discretion and Judicial Discretion . . .			246
4.3	Evaluating Costs and Benefits				249
	4.3.1	Evaluating Costs and Benefits While Preparing a Case			249
		4.3.1.1	Ways Economics and Evidence Meet: The Rules of Evidence in Terms of Economic Rationality	249
		4.3.1.2	Alvin Goldman's Concept of Epistemic Paternalism	250
		4.3.1.3	The Litigation Risk Analysis Method . . .	252
		4.3.1.4	Bargaining, and Game Theory	253
	4.3.2	Evaluating the Effects of Obtaining or Renouncing a Piece of Evidence			255
	4.3.3	Benefits, Costs, and Dangers of Argumentation			256
	4.3.4	Costs and Benefits of Digital Forensic Investigations .			260
4.4	ADVOKATE, and Assessing Eyewitness Suitability and Reliability				263
	4.4.1	The Turnbull Rules			263
	4.4.2	The ADVOKATE Project			266
	4.4.3	More on Taxonomies of Factors			270

	4.5	Policing: Organisational Aspects of Intelligence, and the Handling of Suspects	273
		4.5.1 Organisational Problems of Police Intelligence Systems	273
		4.5.2 Handling the Suspects: Equipment, Techniques, and Crucial Problems	281
		4.5.2.1 Polygraph Tests: A Deeply Controversial Tool	281
		4.5.2.2 A Caution Against Unquestioned Assumptions: A Digression on Juridic Cultures and the Evidentiary Value of Self-Incriminating Confessions	287
		4.5.2.3 Computerised Identity Parades (Lineups) .	290
	4.6	Relevance	298
		4.6.1 Definitions	298
		4.6.2 Legal Formalism, Artificial Intelligence and the Indeterminacy of Relevance .... by Jonathan Yovel	301
		4.6.2.1 Relevance, Within Law as Being a System for Processing Information	301
		4.6.2.2 Relevance: Why It Is Difficult for Formal Systems	302
		4.6.2.3 Relevance and Legal Formalism	305
		4.6.2.4 Relevance, Evidence and Beyond: Three Theoretical Approaches	308
		4.6.2.5 Considerations About Applying Relevance Logic	314
		4.6.2.6 A Refutation of the Argument from the Distinction Between Relevance and Admissibility	315
		4.6.2.7 Conclusion of the Section About Relevance	316
		4.6.3 Relevance Logic	317
		4.6.3.1 A Gentle Introduction to the Main Concepts	317
		4.6.3.2 Any Potential for Application in Automated Tools for Law?	321
5	The Narrative Dimension		323
	5.1	Legal Narratives	323
		5.1.1 Overall Narrative Plausibility: Preliminaries	323
		5.1.2 Approaches to Narratives from the "New Evidence Scholarship"	324
		5.1.3 Background Generalisations	328
		5.1.4 The Impact of Modes of Communication	334

	5.1.5	Pitfalls to Avoid: There Is No Shortcut for the Practically Minded, and No Alternative to Reading the Legal Literature on Evidence	335
5.2	An Overview of Artificial Intelligence Approaches to Narratives		336
	5.2.1	What Is in a Narrative?	336
	5.2.2	A Fable Gone Awry: An Example of Story-Generation with TALE-SPIN	337
	5.2.3	A Few Challenges	339
	5.2.4	The Task of Reconstructing the Facts	342
	5.2.5	Grammar-Driven vs. Goal-Driven Processing of Stories: Propp's Precedent	344
	5.2.6	Let Us Not Simplify the 1970s: A More Populated Pool of Approaches, and More Nuanced Distinctions	349
	5.2.7	Some Computational Narrative Processing Projects from the 1970s, 1980s, 1990s, and Later	351
	5.2.8	Primitive Acts in the Conceptual Dependency Approach	357
	5.2.9	Scripts, Goals, Plans, MOPs, and TAUs in the Conceptual Dependency Approach	358
		5.2.9.1 Goals	358
		5.2.9.2 Scripts in Cullingford's SAM	359
		5.2.9.3 I-Links and MOPS (Memory Organization Packages) in Dyer's BORIS	361
		5.2.9.4 Evidence for a Divorce Case, in BORIS	363
		5.2.9.5 Thematic Abstraction Units (TAUs) in Dyer's BORIS	364
		5.2.9.6 Other Kinds of Knowledge Sources in BORIS	365
		5.2.9.7 Contractual Situations and Shady Deals in STARE	371
	5.2.10	SWALE and Related Systems for Generating Explanations from Precedents	373
	5.2.11	Input from Earlier Research into More Recent Research in Automated Story Understanding	376
	5.2.12	Other Systems for Automated Story Understanding	378
	5.2.13	Automated or Interactive Story Generation	380
	5.2.14	eChronicle Systems	389
	5.2.15	Virtual Embodied Agents	394
	5.2.16	Story-Generation with MINSTREL	397
	5.2.17	Environments For Storytelling	399
	5.2.18	Bias in Narrative Reporting, and Nonlinear Retelling	403
	5.2.19	Self-Exoneration with ALIBI, in the Perspective of Narrative Inventiveness	404

		5.2.20	Crime Stories, Mediation by the Media, and Crime Fiction: Any Lesson to Be Learnt in Computer Models?	406

                 5.2.20   Crime Stories, Mediation by the Media, and Crime Fiction: Any Lesson to Be Learnt in Computer Models? 406

                       5.2.20.1   Criminal Investigation and Criminal Trials Within the Remit of Literary Studies 406

                       5.2.20.2   When Life Imitates Art 410

                       5.2.20.3   The *JAMA* Model: Modelling an Outcry for Failing to Prosecute. On the Impinging Cultural Effects of a Repertoire of Former Narratives ... 411

                       5.2.20.4   Episodic Similarities vs. Character Similarities 417

                 5.2.21   Mathematical Logic and Crime Stories from *CSI: Crime Scene Investigation*™: Löwe, Pacuit and Saraf's Representation, Building Blocks, and Algorithm 418

                 5.2.22   Other Approaches 427

       5.3   Episodic Formulae 428

                 5.3.1   Instances of a Method of Representation for Narratives and Legal Narratives 428

                 5.3.2   The Notation of Episodic Formulae 435

                 5.3.3   An Example: From Suspects and Allegations to Forensic Testing of the Stuffed Birds of the Meinertzhagen Collection 444

                       5.3.3.1   The Background, and the Narrative Represented 444

                       5.3.3.2   Preliminaries of the Formal Representation for the Stuffed Birds Case: Formulae About Meinertzhagen and His Bird Collection . 454

                       5.3.3.3   A Notation for Biographies 458

                       5.3.3.4   Formalising the Allegations About Meinertzhagen's Stuffed Birds .. 464

       5.4   Bex's Approach to Combining Stories and Arguments in Sense-Making Software for Crime Investigation 476

       5.5   Persuasion Stories vs. Arguments 481

Volume 2

6   Accounting for Social, Spatial, and Textual Interconnections 483

       6.1   Methods 483

                 6.1.1   An Introduction 483

                 6.1.2   Social Networks, and Link Analysis 494

                       6.1.2.1   Social Networks and Their Visualisation . 494

                       6.1.2.2   Link Analysis 504

		6.1.2.3	Link Analysis Tools for Criminal Investigation	508

6.1.2.3 Link Analysis Tools for Criminal Investigation 508
6.1.2.4 Various Tools Applied to Criminal Intelligence 511
6.1.2.5 Gianluigi Me's Investigation Strategy for Tackling Internet Child Pornography 511
6.1.3 Assessing the Risk of Crimes 512
6.1.4 Geographic Information Systems for Mapping Crimes 513
6.1.5 Detection 518
    6.1.5.1 General Considerations 518
    6.1.5.2 Complex Tools' Vulnerability to Manipulation by Perpetrators 520
6.1.6 Autonomous Agents 524
    6.1.6.1 From Blackboard to Multiagent Systems . 524
    6.1.6.2 Multiagent Systems, Simulation and Geographic Space, in Tools for Training Police Officers 534
6.1.7 The Challenge of Handling a Disparate Mass of Data 536
    6.1.7.1 Data Warehousing 536
    6.1.7.2 XML for Interoperability Between Data Sources 537
    6.1.7.3 Ontologies 544
    6.1.7.4 Legal Ontologies 553
           by Andrew Stranieri and John Zeleznikow
    6.1.7.5 An Application of Ontologies to Eliminating Sensitive Information While Declassifying Documents: The Case of Accounts of Crime Investigation 559
    6.1.7.6 A Digression – *Maurice v. Judd* (New York, 1818): Is Whale Oil a Kind of Fish Oil? When the Jury Had to Decide About Ontology 561
    6.1.7.7 Legal Modelling, and Financial Fraud Ontology Transnational Online Investment Fraud 566
           by Richard Leary, Wim Vandenberghe, and John Zeleznikow
6.1.8 Automatic Text (and Multimedia) Summarisation . . 587
    6.1.8.1 An Overview 587
    6.1.8.2 Text Summarisation Projects for Law . . . 595
           by Andrew Stranieri and John Zeleznikow

6.1.9	Text Mining		598
	6.1.9.1	General Considerations	598
	6.1.9.2	Examples of text Mining as Applied to Law	602
		by Andrew Stranieri and John Zeleznikow	
	6.1.9.3	Support Vector Machines, and Their Use for Information Retrieval, Text Classification and Matching	603
		by Andrew Stranieri, John Zeleznikow, and Ephraim Nissan	
6.1.10	Stylometrics, Determining Authorship, Handwriting, and Questioned Documents Evidence		611
6.1.11	Classification, Clustering, Series Analysis, and Association in Knowledge Discovery from Legal Databases		618
	by Andrew Stranieri and John Zeleznikow		
	6.1.11.1	Classification	618
	6.1.11.2	Clustering	621
	6.1.11.3	Series Analysis	622
	6.1.11.4	Detecting Association Rules	623
	6.1.11.5	On Interestingness. Commonplace Cases, Rather Than Leading (Interesting, Landmark) Cases, Are Suitable in Training Sets for Legal Knowledge Discovery Algorithms	625
6.1.12	Inconsistent Data		628
	by Andrew Stranieri and John Zeleznikow		
	6.1.12.1	Reasons for Inconsistency	628
	6.1.12.2	Noise and Outliers	628
	6.1.12.3	Judicial Error as a Source of Inconsistency	630
	6.1.12.4	Dealing with Contradictory Data: An Example from *Split Up*	633
	6.1.12.5	Inconsistencies Due to New Legislation or Precedents	635
	6.1.12.6	How to Deal with Inconsistent Data	636
6.1.13	Rule Induction		637
	by Andrew Stranieri and John Zeleznikow		
	6.1.13.1	Preliminaries	637
	6.1.13.2	Pattern Interestingness	638
	6.1.13.3	Features of, and Difficulties with, Rule Induction Systems	639
	6.1.13.4	Examples of Rule Induction in Law	642

Contents   xxvii

	6.1.14	Using Neural Networks	643
		by Andrew Stranieri and John Zeleznikow	
		6.1.14.1 Historical Background	643
		6.1.14.2 Feed Forward Networks	645
		6.1.14.3 Back Propagation of Errors	650
		6.1.14.4 Setting Up a Neural Network	650
		6.1.14.5 Training a Neural Network	652
		6.1.14.6 Learning Rate	653
		6.1.14.7 Momentum and Bias	654
		6.1.14.8 Training Stopping Criteria	654
		6.1.14.9 Application to Law of Neural Networks .	656
		6.1.14.10 Application to Classification	658
		6.1.14.11 Application to Rule Defeasibility	659
		6.1.14.12 Vagueness	661
		6.1.14.13 Application to Modelling Discretionary Legal Domains	662
		6.1.14.14 Unsupervised Neural Networks	663
		6.1.14.15 Text Clustering with Self-Organising Maps (Kohonen Neural Networks)	664
	6.1.15	Using Fuzzy Logic	666
		by Andrew Stranieri and John Zeleznikow	
	6.1.16	Using Genetic Algorithms in Data Mining	668
		by Andrew Stranieri, John Zeleznikow, and Ephraim Nissan	
		6.1.16.1 Evolutionary Computing and Genetic Algorithms	668
		6.1.16.2 Genetic and Other Methods as Applied to Transforming Pre-processed Data Upstream of the Data Mining Phase	671
		6.1.16.3 Nearest Neighbours Approaches and Their Integration with Genetic Algorithms	674
6.2	Case Studies of Link Analysis and Data Mining		675
	6.2.1	Digital Resources and Uncovering Perpetration: Email Mining, Computer Forensics, and Intrusion Detection	675
		6.2.1.1 Email Mining	675
		6.2.1.2 The Enron Email Database as an Opportunity for Research	677
		6.2.1.3 Discovering Social Coalitions with the SIGHTS Text Mining System ...	679
		6.2.1.4 Recursive Data Mining	682

		6.2.1.5	The Disciplinary Context: A Brief Introduction to Computer Forensics . . .	685
		6.2.1.6	Digital Steganography	689
		6.2.1.7	Digital Forensics and Bayesian Networks	692
		6.2.1.8	Intrusion Detection in Computer Resources A Glimpse of an Intruder's Modus Operandi	695
		6.2.1.9	A Classification of Intrusion Detection Systems	697
		6.2.1.10	Intrusion Detection by Means of Various Learning Techniques	701
		6.2.1.11	Masquerading and Its Detection	703
		6.2.1.12	Honeypots for Trapping Intruders	706
	6.2.2	The United States' Anti-Drug Network (ADNET) . .		712
	6.2.3	Investigating Internet Auction Fraud		714
		6.2.3.1	What the Problem Is	714
		6.2.3.2	Data Mining and Online Auction Fraud: Techniques in the Background of NetProbe	721
		6.2.3.3	How NetProbe Works	730
		6.2.3.4	A Non-Mining Model for Reasoning on the Evidence of Online Auction Fraud	736
	6.2.4	Graph Mining for Malware Detection, Using *Polonium*		740
		6.2.4.1	Preliminaries About Graph Mining	740
		6.2.4.2	The *Polonium* System	742
	6.2.5	Link Analysis with *Coplink*		748
	6.2.6	The EDS Project for the U.S. Federal Defense Financial Accounting Service		752
	6.2.7	Information Extraction Tools for Integration with a Link Analysis Tool, Developed in the Late 1990s by Sterling Software		754
	6.2.8	The Poznan Ontology Model for the Link Analysis of Fuel Fraud		758
	6.2.9	Fiscal Fraud Detection with the Pisa SNIPER Project		762

7 FLINTS, a Tool for Police Investigation and Intelligence Analysis: A project by Richard Leary explained by its author 767
  7.1 Introduction: Motivations and History of the Project 767
  7.2 Early Beginnings 769
  7.3 FLINTS 1 771
  7.4 Identifying "Unknown" Offenders 773
  7.5 Systemising the Identification of Unknown Offenders 774
  7.6 Link Detection 778

7.7	The First Generation of FLINTS	780
7.8	Integration, Linking and Analysis Tools	781
7.9	Expanding FLINTS to Other Police Areas	783
7.10	Volume Crimes and Volume Suspects: Not *Single* Events and *Single* Suspects	785
7.11	Performance Monitoring and System Identification	785
7.12	Using FLINTS: A Tour of the System as the User Sees It	787
7.13	The Intellectual Foundations of FLINTS	800
7.14	What Is It About FLINTS That Makes It Different?	801
7.15	A Case Study in Linked Burglary	802
7.16	Forensic Decision-Making	808
7.17	Second-Generation FLINTS	815
7.18	Access to the System: Searching or Surfing?	817
7.19	Asking Questions About People and Suspects	820
7.20	Asking Questions About Crimes and Events	820
7.21	Displaying Modified Wigmorean Charts: Graphical Results in FLINTS	821
7.22	Geographical Analysis	824
7.23	Temporal Analysis	826
7.24	Prolific (Volume) Offenders Search	827
7.25	Using Geography to Identify Prolific Offenders	828
7.26	Hot Spot Searches	833
7.27	Vehicle Searching	835
7.28	Analytical Audit Trails	836

8 The Forensic Disciplines: Some Areas of Actual or Potential Application 841
   8.1 Crime Scenario Modelling: The Dead Bodies Project, and a Scenario Space Generated Using an ATMS 841
      8.1.1 Generating Crime Scenarios Automatically 841
      8.1.2 The Structure of ATMS Inference in the Scenario Space Builder 850
      8.1.3 An Extension with Bayesian Networks, Entropy, and Returned Evidence Collection Strategies 852
      8.1.4 Further Research 855
          by Jeroen Keppens
   8.2 Processing Human Faces: A Panoply of Contexts 858
      8.2.1 Computer Tools for Face Processing: Preliminary Considerations 858
      8.2.2 Face Recognition Tools for Identification 859
         8.2.2.1 Facial Recognition Classification, from a Database of Mug Shots 859

		8.2.2.2	Reconstructing a Face from Verbal Descriptions: Mug Shots, vs. Sketches and Composites	861
		8.2.2.3	*FacePrints* for Generating Facial Composites	864
		8.2.2.4	The CRIME-VUs and EvoFIT Projects . .	864
	8.2.3	Age-Progression Software and Post-Surgery Face Recognition		868
	8.2.4	Facial Expression Recognition		871
	8.2.5	Digital Image Forensics		871
	8.2.6	Facial Reconstruction from Skeletal Remains		874
	8.2.7	Considerations about Socio-Cultural Factors in Portraiture That Have Been Analysed with Episodic Formulae		877
8.3	The Burgeoning Forensic Disciplines of Expert Opinion			879
	8.3.1	General Considerations, and Some of the Specialties		879
	8.3.2	Statistics Comes into the Picture		886
	8.3.3	Some More Forensic Disciplines		890
8.4	The Contribution to Forensic Science of Anthropology and Archaeology			893
	8.4.1	Forensic Archaeology and Anthropology		893
	8.4.2	Factors Involved in Forensic Anthropology		896
		8.4.2.1	Preliminaries	896
		8.4.2.2	Ante-mortem Skeletal Pathology, and Para-, Peri-, and Post-mortem Traumas	897
		8.4.2.3	A Digression on Formal Models of Time .	898
		8.4.2.4	Software Tools for Human Anatomy . . .	901
8.5	Aspects of the Contribution to Forensic Science of Geology, Geophysics, and Botany			905
	8.5.1	Forensic Geology		905
	8.5.2	Techniques from Geophysics in Forensic Archaeology vs. in Archaeology		908
	8.5.3	A Clarification About Time Slicing		913
	8.5.4	From Soil to Scent: Between Current Practice and Imagining the Digital Potential		915
		8.5.4.1	Scent-Detection, Odorology, Cadaver Dogs, and Gas Soil Surveying: The Detection of the Scent of an Individual, vs. the Detection of a Kind (Graves)	915
		8.5.4.2	Electronic Noses	916
	8.5.5	Forensic Palynology		924
	8.5.6	Computing in Environmental Forensics		928

	8.6	Forensic Engineering		935
	8.7	Individual Identification		937
		8.7.1	The Cultural Context: The History of Identification Methods	937
		8.7.2	DNA and Fingerprints	943
			8.7.2.1 DNA Evidence: A Brief Introduction	943
			8.7.2.2 Statisticians' Disagreements About How to Evaluate DNA Samples	946
			8.7.2.3 Human Fingerprints	948
			8.7.2.4 Fingerprints from Dead Bodies	952
			8.7.2.5 The Problem of Assessing Fingerprint Sufficient Similarity	952
		8.7.3	Computational Techniques for Fingerprint Recognition	957
			8.7.3.1 General Considerations	957
			8.7.3.2 Bistarelli, Santini, and Vaccarelli's Algorithm, Suiting the Hardware Constraints of a Smartcard Architecture	963
			8.7.3.3 The Tohoku Algorithm for Fingerprint Matching Based on Band-Limited Phase-Only Correlation	967
	8.8	Bloodstain Pattern Analysis, and the Use of Software for Determining the Angle of Impact of Blood Drops		973
		8.8.1	The Basics	973
		8.8.2	Software	977
		8.8.3	Point or Area of Origin	978
		8.8.4	More Concerning Software	981
		8.8.5	Effects of Velocity on Blood Drops and Blood Spatter	983
			by Louis Akin	
			8.8.5.1 Introduction	983
			8.8.5.2 Photography, and Traditional Determination of Velocities of Blood Spatter	985
			8.8.5.3 Blood Spatter Flight Characteristics	987
			8.8.5.4 Point of Convergence (POC)	988
			8.8.5.5 Determining the Angle of Impact (AOI), and the Point of Origin	989
9	Virtopsy: The Virtual Autopsy			991
	by Lars C. Ebert, Thomas Ruder, David Zimmermann, Stefan Zuber, Ursula Buck, Antoine Roggo, Michael Thali, and Gary Hatch			
	9.1	Introduction		991

	9.1.1	Preliminary Considerations	991
	9.1.2	Indications for Virtopsy	992
9.2	Technical Aspects of Virtopsy: Imaging Modalities and Techniques		993
	9.2.1	The Virtobot System	993
	9.2.2	Photogrammetry and Surface Scanning	994
	9.2.3	Post-mortem Computer Tomography (PMCT)	995
		9.2.3.1 CT Scanners	995
		9.2.3.2 Identification by Means of CT Scanning	996
	9.2.4	Magnetic Resonance Imaging (MRI)	996
	9.2.5	Post-mortem CT Angiography	998
	9.2.6	Tissue/Liquid Sampling	999
	9.2.7	Virtopsy Workflow	1000
9.3	Visualisation: The Main Concepts for Storage, Processing and Visualization of Medical Image Data		1002
	9.3.1	Data Storage	1002
	9.3.2	Imaging in Two Dimensions (2D Imaging)	1002
	9.3.3	Imaging in Three Dimensions (3D Imaging)	1003
	9.3.4	Animation	1005
	9.3.5	Segmentation	1006
	9.3.6	Image Fusion	1007
	9.3.7	Rapid Prototyping	1007
	9.3.8	Post-mortem vs. Ante-mortem Imaging	1008
	9.3.9	Medical Image Data for Radiologists and Pathologists	1008
	9.3.10	Medical Image Data for Medical Laypersons	1010
9.4	Virtopsy and the Swiss Justice System		1011
	9.4.1	Advantages of Virtopsy in Court	1011
	9.4.2	Virtopsy in the Current Legal System and Practice of Switzerland	1012
	9.4.3	Criminal Procedure in Switzerland: The Legal Basis for Virtopsy Imaging Methods?	1012
		9.4.3.1 Background	1012
		9.4.3.2 Legal Basis for Virtopsy in Switzerland	1013
		9.4.3.3 Evidence Law in Switzerland	1013
10	Concluding Remarks		1017
Appendix: Glossary			1021
References			1123
Author Index			1269
Subject Index			1301

Abstract

This book caters to a broad audience, and provides an overview of computer techniques and tools for handling legal evidence, police intelligence, crime analysis or detection, and forensic testing, with a chapter on the modelling of argumentation and its application to these, as well as with a chapter on how to handle narratives by computer. We also briefly address costs and benefits of obtaining more evidence while preparing a case, as a factor in deciding whether to prosecute or to litigate. Notwithstanding a few seminal precursors from the late 1980s, it is only with the new century that the modelling of reasoning on legal evidence has emerged as a significant area within the well-established field of AI & Law (active since the 1970s). An overview such as this one has never been attempted before between two covers. It offers a panoramic view of topics, techniques and tools. It is intended to clarify the broader picture for the specialist, as well as to introduce practitioners of AI or other computer scientists into this subject. For its newcomers, it is essential not to simplistically blunder into such design choices that would results in flaws making the tools unusable by legal professionals, so it is important to be aware of ongoing controversies. Other tools are appropriate for law enforcement, e.g., tools assisting in crime analysis. In order to deal with hypotheses, representations and tools for the organisation of arguments are useful; therefore, research into argumentation is cited, and argumentation tools or methods that are useful for reasoning about the evidence are surveyed. The final part of the book is devoted to data mining, and next, to a panoply of forensic techniques. For example, the book includes a chapter from the VIRTOPSY team in Bern, about how computer imaging can be used in order to plan autopsies by making them less invasive. The large bibliography is preceded by an extensive glossary, being a useful resource for many of the subjects covered in this book. Several of the entries afford an opportunity for further discussion of select topics.

Abstracts of the Chapters

Chapter 1 A Preliminary Historical Perspective
This introductory chapter makes considerations about the thematics, the organisation of the book, and (along very broad lines) the state of the art, the latter's historical development, and its publication forums. The book is organised around three poles: the modelling of reasoning, the modelling of argumentation and its application to narratives, and a cluster of data mining techniques and the specifics of forensic science disciplines. We mention the controversy, among legal scholars, among those willing to accept probabilistic models, and those who want instead a ranking of the relative plausibility of alternative accounts of a legal narratives, without committing to a Bayesian framework. Artificial intelligence is able to contribute to both camps, and has already done so. Bayesian networks are often applied to causality also in the legal domain, but those arguing against probabilistic quantification are at present vindicated by the rise of the plausibility ranking of legal narratives (Section 5.4) within argumentation research (Chapter 3). AI practitioners need to exercise care, lest methodological flaws vitiate their tools in the domain with some legal scholars, let alone opponents in litigation. There would be little point for computer scientists to develop tools for legal evidence, if legal scholars would find them vitiated ab initio. This is especially true of tools that would reason about the evidence in criminal cases, in view of fact-finding in the courtroom: whether to convict or not – this being different from the situation of the police, whose aim is to detect crime and to find suspects, without having the duty of proving their guilt beyond reasonable doubt, which is the task of the prosecutors. Tools helping the prosecutor to predict an outcome and choose whether to prosecute are not as central to the Bayesian controversy, as prescriptive models of judicial decision-making. This chapter also says something about the communities of users that may benefit from advances in AI & Law technology. In particular, we devote some discussion to computer assistance in policing.

Chapter 2 Models of Forming an Opinion
This chapter is concerned with models of reasoning about the evidence. We consider, in turn, "metre models" of the shifts of opinion in the adjudicators' mind as items of information come in, and a distributed belief revision model for such

dynamics. We discuss the weight given jury research in North America. Then we consider some seminal computer tools modelling the reasoning about a charge and explanations: Thagard's ECHO (and its relation to Josephson's PEIRCE-IGTT), and Nissan's ALIBI, a planner seeking exoneration and producing explanations minimising liability. A quick survey of Bayesian approaches in law is followed with a discussion of the controversy concerning applications of Bayesianism to modelling juridical decision-making. We quickly sample some probabilistic applications (Poole's Independent Choice Logic and reasoning about accounts of a crime, and next, dynamic uncertain inference concerning criminal cases, and Snow and Belis's recursive multidimensional scoring). Finally, we consider Shimony and Nissan's application of the kappa calculus to grading evidential strength, and then argue for trying to model relative plausibility.

Chapter 3 Argumentation

We begin this chapter about argumentation, by considering types of arguments, and contrast Wigmore Charts to Toulmin's structure of argument. We develop two examples in detail, and then turn to Pollock's inference graphs and degrees of justification. We then discuss beliefs. From Walton's approach to commitment vs. belief and to argument schemes, we turn to Bench-Capon & Atkinson's approach to critical questions concerning a story of alleged crime. We consider arguments in PERSUADER, in *Carneades*, and in *Stevie*. We survey computer tools for argumentation, and computational models of argumentation, especially as far as they relate to legal argument. We distinguish between argumentation for dialectical situations, vs. for structuring knowledge non-dialectically: a section by Stranieri, Zeleznikow, and Yearwood discusses an integration of those two uses of argumentation in a legal context, in the Generic Actual Argument Model (GAAM), also considering a few applications of the latter.

Chapter 4 Computer Assistance for, or Insights into, Organisational Aspects

We first consider computer help for organising tasks relevant for managing the evidence. We consider the Lund procedure, as well as a few tools: *CaseNote*, *MarshalPlan*, and from Italy's judiciary, *Daedalus*. We develop in particular a discussion of the latter, which is a tool for the examining magistrate and then the prosecution. We then turn to criminal justice information systems, and discuss prosecutorial vs. judiciary discretion. We discuss facets of evaluating costs and benefits, beginning with the costs and benefits while preparing a case (discussing, in turn, the rules of evidence in terms of economic rationality, Alvin Goldman's concept of epistemic paternalism, the Litigation Risk Analysis method, and bargaining in relation to game theory). We then turn to evaluating the effects of obtaining or renouncing a piece of evidence, then to the benefits, costs, and dangers of argumentation, and finally to the costs and benefits of digital forensic investigations. Next, we discuss Bromby's ADVOKATE, for assessing eyewitness suitability and reliability (we also consider the Turnbull rules, and further elaborate on taxonomies of factors). In the section about policing, we consider organisational aspects of intelligence, and the handling of suspects, and deal in turn with organisational problems of police intelligence systems, with handling the suspects (equipment, techniques, and crucial problems), with polygraph tests and their controversial status, with the evidentiary value of self-incriminating confessions being culture-bound rather than universal in juridical cultures, and with computerised identity parades (lineups) and concerns about identity parades. This chapter concludes with a section (by Jonathan Yovel) on relevance, in relation to legal formalism as well as to logic formalism and artificial intelligence. A refutation is proposed, of the argument from the distinction between relevance and admissibility.

Chapter 5 The Narrative Dimension

We begin by discussing legal narratives, and overall narrative plausibility. We consider approaches from the New Evidence scholarship, discuss background generalisations, as well as the impact of modes of communication (the pragmatics of the delivery in court of a legal narrative), and then warn about pitfalls to avoid, in consideration of what controversy within legal scholarship implies about the need for the modelling of legal narratives with artificial intelligence techniques to meet with approval from legal scholars. We then undertake a long overview (in over twenty subsections) of artificial intelligence approaches to narratives. Historically, a legal context for narratives was involved in tools such as BORIS and STARE. Among the other things, we consider the JAMA model, and then conclude the overview with a project from quarters different from those traditionally associated with story-processing in the artificial intelligence research community: namely, Löwe, Pacuit and Saraf's application of mathematical logic to crime stories. We then explain episodic formulae, and develop an example: the controversy concerning a collection of stuffed birds amid allegations that items were stolen and restuffed. We finally consider Bex's approach to combining stories and arguments in sense-making software for crime investigation, and then Bex and Bench-Capon's undertaken project concerning persuasion stories vs. arguments.

Chapter 6 Accounting for Social, Spatial, and Textual Interconnections Link Analysis and Data Mining for Criminal Investigation

This is a chapter about what link analysis and data mining can do for criminal investigation. It is a long and complex chapter, in which a variety of techniques and topics are accommodated. It is divided in two parts, one about methods, and the other one about real-case studies. We begin by discussing social networks and their visualisation, as well as what unites them with or distinguishes them from link analysis (which itself historically arose from the disciplinary context of ergonomics). Having considered applications of link analysis to criminal investigation, we turn to crime risk assessment, to geographic information systems for mapping crimes, to detection, and then to multiagent architectures and their application to policing. We then turn to the challenge of handling a disparate mass of data, and introduce the reader to data warehousing, XML, ontologies, legal ontologies, and financial fraud ontology. A section about automated summarisation and its application to law is followed by a discussion of text mining and its application to law, and by a section on support vector machines for information retrieval, text classification, and matching. A section follows, about stylometrics, determining authorship, handwriting identification and its automation, and questioned documents evidence. We next discuss classification, clustering, series analysis, and association in knowledge discovery from legal databases; then, inconsistent data; rule induction (including in law); using neural networks in the legal context; fuzzy logic; and genetic algorithms. Before turning to case studies of link analysis and data mining, we take a broad view of digital resources and uncovering perpetration: email mining, computer forensics, and intrusion detection. We consider the Enron email database; the discovery of social coalitions with the SIGHTS text mining system, and recursive data mining. We discuss digital forensics, digital steganography, and intrusion detection (the use of learning techniques, the detection of masquerading, and honeypots for trapping intruders). Case studies include, for example: investigating Internet auction fraud with *NetProbe*; graph mining for malware detection with *Polonium*; link analysis with *Coplink*; a project of the U.S. Federal Defense Financial Accounting Service; information extraction tools for integration with a link analysis tool; the Poznan ontology model for the link analysis of fuel fraud; and fiscal fraud detection with the Pisa SNIPER project.

Chapter 7 FLINTS, a Tool for Police Investigation and Intelligence Analysis
This chapter presents and discusses, in 28 sections, a link analysis tool for the British police, FLINTS. The chapter considers, in turn, the motivations and history of the project; the early beginning resulting in FLINTS 1; identifying "unknown" offenders, and systemising it; link detection; more about the first generation of FLINTS; integrations, linking and analysis tools; expanding FLINTS to other police areas; volume crimes and volume suspects; performance monitoring and system identification; a tour of FLINTS as the user sees it; the intellectual foundations; and what stands out in FLINTS. We turn to a case study in linked burglary. We then discuss forensic decision-making; second-generation FLINTS; access to the system (searching vs. surfing); asking questions about people and suspects; asking questions about crimes and events; displaying modified Wigmore Charts, and the graphical results in FLINTS; geographical analysis; temporal analysis; prolific (volume) offenders search; using geography to identify prolific offenders; hot spot searches; vehicle searching; and analytical audit trails.

Chapter 8 The Forensic Disciplines: Some Areas of Actual or Potential Application
We first begin with an artificial intelligence approach to crime scenario modelling once a dead body has been found. We then turn to a panoply of contexts and approaches to the processing of human faces: face recognition methods and tools for identification; foreseeing how aging would affect a face (e.g., of a child who went missing); facial expression recognition; digital image forensics (with doctored photographs); facial reconstruction from skeletal remains; and factors in portraiture analysed in the TIMUR episodic formulae model. Having begun with these two major areas (crime scenario modelling, and face processing), we take a broad view

of the forensic disciplines of expert opinion, and the sometimes controversial role of statistics in them. We then consider the contribution to forensic science of anthropology and archaeology, as well as software tools for human anatomy. Next, we turn to forensic geology and techniques from geophysics; scent-detection and electronic noses; forensic palynology and its databases; computing in environmental forensics; and forensic engineering. Two large sections, each internally subdivided into nine units, conclude this chapter: "Individual Identification", and "Bloodstain Pattern Analysis, and the Use of Software for Determining the Angle of Impact of Blood Drops". The former begins with a history of identification methods, and continues with DNA evidence, and a controversy among statisticians concerning this; we then discuss human fingerprints, and growing skepticism concerning reliability of identification by fingerprints. We then turn to computational techniques for fingerprint recognition, and having surveyed these, we proceed to describe in detail two such techniques.

Chapter 9 Virtopsy: The Virtual Autopsy
This chapter provides an overview of the Virtopsy procedure, a computerised approach to autopsy, lessening the need for invasive examination. Invasiveness results in the loss of evidence, and of the structural integrity of organs; it is also offensive to some worldviews. At the Institute of Forensic Medicine of the University of Bern, the Virtopsy project has unfolded during the 2000s, its aim being the application of high tech methods from the fields of measurement engineering, automation and medical imaging to create a complete, minimally invasive, reproducible and objective forensic assessment method. The data generated can be digitally stored or quickly sent to experts without a loss of quality. If new questions arise, the data can be revised even decades after the incident. This chapter describes technical aspects of the Virtopsy procedure, including imaging modalities and techniques (the Virtobot system, photogrammetry and surface scanning, post-mortem computer tomography, magnetic resonance imaging, post-mortem CT angiography, tissue/liquid sampling), then turning to the workflow of Virtopsy, and to a technical discussion of visualisation. Medical image data are for either radiologists and pathologists, or medical laypersons (such as in a courtroom situation). The final part of this chapter discusses Virtopsy in relation to the Swiss justice system.

Chapter 10 Concluding Remarks
This chapter briefly recapitulates which chapter discussed which topics. Then, in a few diagrams, an overarching view is taken of part of the broad set of domains we have been considering in this book. The themes in the book up to the conclusions chapters are supplemented with a Glossary following Chapter 10, and whose entries are often substantial and contain discussion. The bibliography is very large, as could be expected given the broad scope of the book, along with the latter often delving into details.

Call for Information

Future editions will hopefully appear in due course. I would appreciate it if readers will inform me about their research as it progresses, or their tools as they become available, and would provide me with copy of publications as they appear, in view of possible coverage in a future edition. I can be contacted by email (ephraimnissan@hotmail.com). Readers wishing to use the graphic files or the Latex code for the symbols of episodic formulae (see Section 5.3) are welcome to ask for them; I would be glad to provide copy of such files, and would like to learn about the applications.

List of Section Authors

Louis L. Akin Crime Scene Analyst, Austin, TX, USA, ai@akininc.com

Carmelo Asaro Tribunale della Libertà, Rome, Italy

Ursula Buck Center of Forensic Imaging and Virtopsy, Institute of Forensic Medicine, University of Bern, 3012 Bern, Switzerland

Aldo Franco Dragoni Dipartimento di Ingegneria Informatica, Gestionale e dell'Automazione, Università Politecnica delle Marche, Ancona, Italy

Lars C. Ebert Center of Forensic Imaging and Virtopsy, Institute of Forensic Medicine, University of Bern, 3012 Bern, Switzerland

Gary Hatch Center of Forensic Imaging and Virtopsy, Institute of Forensic Medicine, University of Bern, 3012 Bern, Switzerland

Jeroen Keppens King's College, London, England

Richard Leary Forensic Pathways Ltd.[8], Tamworth, Staffordshire, England, rleary@forensic-pathways.com

Antonio A. Martino Universidad del Salvador, Buenos Aires, Argentina, (emeritus of the University of Pisa, Pisa, Italy)

Ephraim Nissan Department of Computing, Goldsmiths' College, University of London, London, England, ephraimnissan@hotmail.com

Antoine Roggo Center of Forensic Imaging and Virtopsy, Institute of Forensic Medicine, University of Bern, 3012 Bern, Switzerland

Thomas Ruder Center of Forensic Imaging and Virtopsy, Institute of Forensic Medicine, University of Bern, 3012 Bern, Switzerland

Solomon E. Shimony Ben-Gurion University of the Negev, Beer-Sheva, Israel

Andrew Stranieri University of Ballarat, Ballarat, VIC, Australia

---

[8] See for example http://www.forensic-pathways.com/PDFs/FPL_Overview_of_Analytics.pdf

Michael Thali Center of Forensic Imaging and Virtopsy, Institute of Forensic Medicine, University of Bern, 3012 Bern, Switzerland

Wim Vandenberghe Dechert LLP, B-1050 Brussels, Belgium

John Yearwood University of Ballarat, Ballarat, VIC, Australia

Jonathan Yovel Law School, University of Haifa, Haifa, Israel; Yale Law School, Yale University, New Haven, CT, USA

John Zeleznikow Victoria University, Melbourne, VIC, Australia

David Zimmermann Center of Forensic Imaging and Virtopsy, Institute of Forensic Medicine, University of Bern, 3012 Bern, Switzerland

Stefan Zuber Center of Forensic Imaging and Virtopsy, Institute of Forensic Medicine, University of Bern, 3012 Bern, Switzerland

Chapter 1
A Preliminary Historical Perspective

Basically, this book is organised around three poles:

- Artificial intelligence applications to the modelling of reasoning about legal evidence, as well as to the handling of narratives;
- The modelling of argumentation, especially as applied to law, and computer tools for that purpose; and
- The specifics of disciplines within forensic science, especially in relation to actual or potential applications of computing.

The organisation of this book, by thematic clusters, is reflected accurately by the detailed table of contents. Apart from the chapters in this book, also several of the entries in the "Glossary" are substantial, and in some cases (e.g., s.vv. "mens rea", "examination", "time", and "hearsay") they can be considered as short sections providing further important information on given subjects. These are things that any practitioner of computing and in particular artificial intelligence, if setting to develop an application to legal evidence, other than by mere implementation of an extant design, ought to know. This is all the more the case if for the requirements analysis, the input from legal professionals is not articulate. A project leader should be very careful with such issues, lest he or she should be sorry later. In fact, it will not be enough to obtain functioning software; this software will have to be acceptable to strict scrutiny, to either law enforcement, or legal professional practice. The incentive for finding fault is that during litigation, if a procedural or substantive legal inadequacy can be apportioned (and this objection is upheld) to the use made of a given piece of software, then this may have an even major impact on the outcome of the judicial case at hand.

That we should be able to offer such a caveat, depends on a state of affairs in which information technology, as well as the pool of techniques from artificial intelligence, already have results to show, in the domain of legal evidence or of police investigations. The story of how we got there, is something that by itself deserves to be told. In the 1990s, AI applications to legal evidence were at most a desideratum, apart from some pioneering projects whose results catered to scholars in artificial intelligence or in cognitive science, yet were not operational in the application domain. There used to be computer tools for disparate kinds of forensic testing, but in all likelihood the first time that the several disciplines within forensic science are brought together with AI modelling of reasoning about legal evidence and with AI modelling of argumentation, is in the present treatment in this book. This was a good reason to have a unified treatment.

Popular perceptions of trials, through printed or cinematic whodunit stories, emphasise evidence. Undeniably, evidence plays a major role in law.[1] It is by no means the case that research in legal computing, or even more specifically in artificial intelligence and law (AI & Law), has been mainly concerned with legal evidence. Quite on the contrary, until the early 2000s evidence has been a surprisingly inconspicuous subject within AI & Law. Strangely, it took AI & Law three decades for Evidence to emerge conspicuously. In the 1970s, much work in AI & Law was on *deontic logics,* which are *modal logics* of *obligation* and *permission.*

Even as impressive practical tools emerged, with an array of topics active in AI & Law, still evidence was, in a sense, the unseen Cinderella. Some reference to evidence may have occurred, within treatments of other subjects within AI & Law. It can be safely stated that the turning point, for the status of evidence on the stage of AI & Law, was my own first initiative for a journal special issue on the subject, the proposal for which was accepted by the late Donald Berman *qua* regular editor of *Artificial Intelligence and Law,* as early as 1996. That initiative was not intended to record the state of the art as available at the time. Rather, it was about bootstrapping a pool of research and papers into existence, where these had been sorely absent. The initiative involved bringing together scholars from different disciplinary compartments, and this spurred interest and collaboration before we went to press. By-products included a conference session I co-chaired in Amsterdam in December 1999: whereas the audience was of legal scholars, some of the speakers were from AI, not necessarily previously associated with AI & Law. Eventually, several journal special issues resulted, and other people who hadn't been among the authors started their own projects, or even undertook initiatives such as workshops.

Already in a guest editorial (Nissan & Martino, 2003b) of a special issue published in 2003 (namely, Nissan & Martino, 2003a), I was able to plot a graph (See Fig. 1.1), in which themes each appeared inside a circle, and showing the sundry thematic relations of the papers (identified by the authors' names) that had appeared in the journal special issues in AI & Law which I had guest-edited up to that point, including the issue whose editorial it was (and for which, the thematic relations in Fig. 1.2 hold). Already at the time, I felt able to state that Fig. 1.1, "due to its intricacy, may look perhaps like a dish of pasta" (Nissan & Martino, 2003b, p. 239).

---

[1] For evidence in legal scholarship, see, e.g., Twining (1985, 1989, 1990), Stein (2005), Nicolson (1994). A textbook on Evidence in England and Wales is Templeman and Reay (1999). From outside Anglo-Saxon jurisdictions, see, e.g., Tonini (1997).

1 A Preliminary Historical Perspective

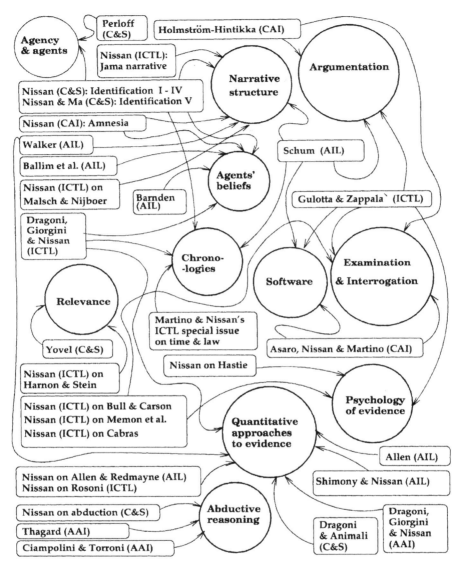

Fig. 1.1 Thematic relations of the articles that appeared in the journal special issues *Artificial Intelligence and Law* (*AIL*), 9(2/3), in 2001; *Computing and Informatics* (*CAI*), 20(6), in 2001; *Cybernetics & Systems* (*C&S*), 34(4/5) and 34(6/7), in 2003; in *Applied Artificial Intelligence* (*AAI*), 18(3/4), in 2004; in *Information and Communications Technology Law* (*ICTL*),10(1), and also on pp. 231–264, ibid., 10(2), in 2001. Also included are the papers on the representation of time in legal contexts, in the special issue of *Information and Communications Technology Law*, 7(3), in 1998. All those journal issues were guest-edited by Antonio Martino and Ephraim Nissan, except *Information and Communications Technology Law*, 10(2), whose scope was more broadly in AI & Law, and whose guest-editors were Donald Peterson, John Barnden, and Ephraim Nissan

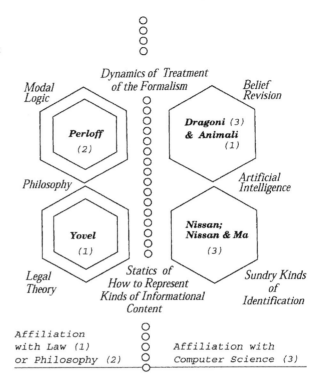

Fig. 1.2 Thematic relations of the articles that appeared in the special issue (Nissan & Martino, 2003a) on legal evidence, in *Cybernetics & Systems*, 34(4/5)

At present, Evidence is a viable, pursued, subdomain within AI & Law. Even some AI & Law scholars who had chosen not to take part in the journal special issues initiative, typically and admittedly because of being at a remove from a concern with evidence, eventually turned to working on such projects in which evidence features conspicuously. The trend leaked into other areas pursued in AI & Law, mainly the modelling of legal argumentation. Moreover, contacts and even joint initiatives unfolded and continue to take place between such scholars and legal evidence scholars, who in turn had started to move in that direction after I turned to them (of course initially mainly for advice) with Don Berman's agreement to the special issue in my hand. That the new trend keeps going now in such a sustained manner is an unmistakable indicator of successful emergence of the theme within AI & Law.

Let us turn to argumentation, which since the 1990s has been a very active field within AI & Law. It is definitely not the case that historically, all computational techniques for handling argumentation have been necessarily applied to legal arguments, let alone to legal evidence. Until the mid-1990s it would have been strange to combine treatment of computer tools for handling arguments (at the time, an emerging field within AI & Law, yet not about evidence), with a discussion of formal, computational approaches to legal evidence, as until that time formalisms for evidence used to be a hot topic among some legal scholars and statisticians, whereas within

1 A Preliminary Historical Perspective

AI & Law the field had yet to emerge. Emerging trends make it cogent and stimulating to treat argumentation as well as other kinds of models of reasoning about the evidence within the same compass. Current developments in both fields are such that there is some synergism in dealing with both of them in the same overview.

AI & Law is more specific than the field of legal computing. Zeleznikow (2004) discussed the construction of intelligent legal decision-support systems in over fifty pages. Within AI & Law, with some seminal work from the end of the 1980s and then organically from the late 1990s, a new area has been developing, which applies AI techniques to how to reason on legal evidence, which requires also capturing within a formal setting at least some salient aspects of the legal narrative at hand. In turn, the subdomain of AI & Law that is mainly concerned with evidence is distinct from the application of computing, and of AI techniques in particular, in the various individual forensic disciplines, e.g., computer imaging or computer graphic techniques for reconstructing from body remains a set of faces in three dimensions, practically fleshing out a skull, which show what a dead person may have looked like – a method that is not without its critics, by comparison to photographs of the dead person once this has been identified. By way of exemplification from the forensic sciences, chapters or sections devoted to a few of them are included in this book: see Chapters 8 and 9, and Sections 6.1.10 and 6.2.1.5.

AI & Law is a field that is either the sole specialty of its typical journals, or a specialty along with law for information and computing technology. *Artificial Intelligence and Law* (Kluwer/Springer) is the standard journal of the former category, whereas both areas are hosted by *Information and Communications Technology Law* (Taylor & Francis), a journal whose previous title used to be *Law, Computers, and Artificial Intelligence* (Carfax). An older journal than both is *Informatica e Diritto* (in Florence). Oxford University Press publishes the *International Journal of Law and Information Technology*. In Australia, the University of Tasmania publishes the *Journal of Law and Information Science*. The website of the University of Warwick (England) hosts an e-journal called *Journal of Information Law & Technology*.[2] In 2010, Taylor and Francis launched the journal *Argument & Computation,* whose scope is important for the domain of AI & Law. As to *Law, Probability and Risk: A Journal for Reasoning Under Uncertainty,* launched by Oxford University Press in 2002, it is a journal of legal scholars and statisticians that also publishes relevant papers in AI & Law: "The journal is intended mainly for academic lawyers, mathematicians and statisticians. The journal seeks to publish papers that deal with topics on the interface of law and probabilistic reasoning" (from its blurb when launched). There exists as well the Kluwer journal, edited in Florence, *Information Technology and the Law: An International Bibliography*. "Artificial intelligence and legal reasoning" is category 023 in that journal.

It is important to understand that vis-à-vis artificial intelligence in general, applications to law have not been only at the receiving end: there has also been a flow of

---

[2] http://elj.warwick.ac.uk/jilt

techniques which, once they proved effective in as fine-textured, "soft" and complex a field as law is, have become available within AI for an array of other applications. Basic research in AI has benefited from there being research ongoing in AI & Law. Another thing of which one should be aware, it that in the process by which the modelling of reasoning on legal evidence has begun to emerge within AI & Law, and then to move from the periphery to the mainstream of AI & Law, it was not the latter which contributed techniques to the new subdomain; rather, the new subdomain used techniques from the general field of AI, and insights from legal evidence scholarship concerned with probability and plausibility,[3] before techniques which are conspicuous within the pool of tools that had already been developed within AI & Law also came to fruition.

In a sense, it could have been expected that in order to make progress, one should look for AI techniques outside AI & Law: the latter had been rather neglecting evidence for the very reason that its tools had not been adequate as yet for dealing with evidence thoroughly. In contrast, AI in general had been much concerned with evidentiary reasoning. It stands to reason that such results from AI could have been promptly applied, if only (and this is the crux of the matter) the status of quantitative models for decision-making in criminal cases (as opposed to civil cases) weren't a hotly disputed topic among legal scholars.

AI practitioners need to exercise care, lest methodological flaws vitiate their tools in the domain with some legal scholars, let alone opponents in litigation. There would be little point for computer scientists to develop tools for legal evidence, if legal scholars would find them vitiated ab initio. This is especially true of tools that would reason about the evidence in criminal cases, in view of fact-finding in the courtroom: whether to convict or not; this being different from the situation of the police, whose aim is to detect crime and to find suspects, without having the duty of proving their guilt beyond reasonable doubt, which is the task of the prosecutors.

It was crucial to get legal scholars of evidence on board, or at least sympathetically interested, and to obtain their input and feedback when steering the new direction of research within AI & Law, in trying to promote the development of credible computer tools or abstract techniques to deal with legal evidence. Besides, legal scholars and statisticians fiercely supporting or opposing Bayesianism in handling probabilities in judicial contexts (e.g., Allen & Redmayne, 1997; Nissan, 2001a; Tillers & Green, 1988) had come to realise the desirability of models of plausibility, rather than of just (strictly) probability. The participants in the debate about Bayesianism in law or more in general, about probabilities in law, are in practice continuing a controversy that started in the early modern period (Nissan, 2001b), with Voltaire being sceptical of probabilities in judicial decision-making, whereas

---

[3] *Plausibility* may be understood to be either more general than *probability*, or something different altogether. "Polya developed a formal characterisation of qualitative human reasoning as an alternative to probabilistic methods for performing commonsense reasoning. He identified four patterns of plausible inference: inductive patterns, successive verification of several consequences, verification of improbable consequences and inference from analogy" (Stranieri & Zeleznikow, 2005a, Glossary, s.v. *plausible inference*).

in the 19th century Boole, of Boolean algebra fame, believed in the formalism's potential applicability to law. An anonymous referee for an article by the present author has remarked: "This particular intellectual battle should also be better placed in the broader context [...]. The fight has raged, and at least still burns, across the disciplines of statistics, philosophy, artificial intelligence and rather more derivatively in medicine and law". It is true that also in epistemology, i.e., the philosophy of knowledge, there is a controversy about Bayesianism. In Dragoni and Nissan (2004, p. 297), we remarked[4]:

> In the literature of epistemology, objections and counterobjections have been expressed concerning the adequacy of Bayesianism. One well-known critic is Alvin Plantinga (1993a, Chap. 7; 1993b, Chap. 8). In a textbook, philosopher Adam Morton (2003, Chap. 10) gave these headings to the main objections generally made by some epistemologists: "Beliefs cannot be measured in numbers", "Conditionalization gives the wrong answers", "Bayesianism does not define the strength of evidence", and, most seriously, "Bayesianism needs a fixed body of propositions" (ibid., pp. 158–159). One of the Bayesian responses to the latter objection about "the difficulty of knowing what probabilities to give novel propositions" (ibid., p. 160), "is to argue that we can rationally give a completely novel proposition any probability we like. Some probabilities may be more convenient or more normal, but if the proposition is really novel, then no probability is forbidden. Then we can consider evidence and use it, via Bayes' theorem, to change these probabilities. Given enough evidence, many differences in the probabilities that are first assigned will disappear, as the evidence forces them to a common value" (ibid.). For specific objections to Bayesian models of judicial decision making, the reader is urged to see the ones made in Ron Allen's lead article [(1997)] in Allen and Redmayne (1997).

We shall come back to this topic, not as superficially as here in the introduction. Among the "Bayesian enthusiasts" concerning legal evidence, perhaps none is more so than Robertson and Vignaux[5]; whereas Ron Allen is prominent, and cogently articulate,[6] among the "Bayesio-skeptics"; see e.g. Allen (2001a) on his desiderata vis-à-vis artificial intelligence modelling of the plausibility of legal narratives (cf. Allen, 2008a, 2008b). Such charged labels are on occasion objected to, and the denotationally yet not connotationally equivalent labels, respectively "Bayesians" and "skeptics", appear to be preferable. No application of statistics to the evaluation of evidence has won as much acclaim, even from Bayesio-skeptics, as Kadane and Schum's[7] (1996) evaluation of the evidence in the Sacco and Vanzetti case from the 1920s, but in a sense the Bayesio-skeptics could afford to be generous, because that

---

[4] Some readers may feel that throughout this long book, the exposition is somewhat marred by overquotation, but I preferred to take this risk, or rather considered this an acceptable cost: I adopted, in a sense, a documentaristic approach, and often quote verbatim. The scope of the topics touched upon in this book is so vast, as to make it necessary to give readers direct access to some passages in which relevant notions have already been well formulated by other authors.

[5] E.g., Robertson and Vignaux (1995); cf. Aitken (1995), Taroni, Aitken, Garbolino, and Biedermann (2006).

[6] Also see e.g. Jonathan Cohen's (1977) *The Probable and the Provable*.

[7] By Dave Schum, see also, e.g., 'Probability and the processes of discovery, proof, and choice' (Schum, 1986), and *Evidential Foundations of Probabilistic Reasoning* (Schum, 1994). On cascaded inference, see Schum and Martin (1982).

project had taken years to develop, and therefore is of little "real time" practical use in ongoing judicial settings.[8]

It was in this context, that it took a systematic, organic effort in order to promote the new subdomain of modelling the reasoning on evidence within AI & Law. This was mainly done through several editorial initiatives, as well as workshops, of the present writer and of others (Martino & Nissan, 2001; Nissan & Martino,[9] 2001, 2003a, 2004a; MacCrimmon & Tillers, 2002, on which see Nissan, 2004),[10] and this in turn involved spurring scholars from disparate disciplinary quarters to develop some piece of research to specification, and then to have referees from different specialties evaluate the resulting papers again and again.

For example, such practitioners of AI or of logic who had never before been concerned with legal applications, contributed some important applied techniques to a pool, until there was a critical mass of research visible enough to spur scholars within AI & Law the way it had been before, to enter the new subdomain and contribute their own techniques. Among the latter, it was perhaps argumentation techniques, a hotly pursued area of research within AI & Law during the 1990s, which constitute the most spectacular contribution.

Let us say something about the communities of users that may benefit from advances in AI & Law technology. Most often, computer tools used by legal professionals are technologically unambitious (at any rate, this is the case from the viewpoints of scholars in artificial intelligence, and in particular of AI & Law): legal professionals are likely to be using tools for document processing, and legal databases. Even simple tools for organising the evidence and the structure of how to argue a case may make a difference, in terms of work facilitation.

As to police officers, while in the office they may be using standard office tools, as well as (in Britain) the Police National Computer. Some police stations use computer tools for the way identity parades are carried out (see Section 4.5.2.3), but also intelligence and crime analysts use specialist tools (see Section 4.5.1 and Chapters 6 and 7).

Yet here, too, there are tools that may be of much help when carrying out investigations, e.g., Richard Leary's FLINTS (Force Linked Intelligence System), a tool for criminal intelligence analysis, performing *network link analysis;* it was originally applied it in the West Midlands Police (see Chapter 7). There is considerable

---

[8] The statistics of identification of perpetrators from DNA samples is the one area in which the statisticians could be thought, on the face of it, to prevail upon the sceptics, were it not for the contradictions of the several ways in which DNA samples can be interpreted statistically, quite a worrying problem that that has been popularised by Geddes (2010). See Section 8.7.2 below.

[9] Another journal special issue on AI & Law, but one in which only part of the papers are on evidence, is Peterson, Barnden, and Nissan (2001). Meanwhile, Kaptein, Prakken, and Verheij have published (2009) the paper-collection *Legal Evidence and Proof: Statistics, Stories, Logic*.

[10] I published about select topics in legal evidence as a challenge for AI in Nissan (2008a). Nissan (2009a) is a survey that served me as a blueprint for the present book. Brief encyclopaedic entries on AI for legal evidence or on computer tools for argumentation that I published include Nissan (2008b, 2008c, 2008d, 2008e). That material is either expanded, or incorporated in the present book.

1 A Preliminary Historical Perspective

research ongoing into the use of data mining techniques assisting with criminal link analysis (see Chapter 6).

There exists a body of research into the general organisational problems that have occurred on the ground when police forces adopted computer technology as part of *intelligence-led policing*.[11] There are socio-legal studies that deal with this. See Section 4.5.1. Let us just cite here a few articles by James Sheptycki (2004) and by his collaborator Jerry Ratcliffe (2005, 2007). For example, concerning intelligence-led policing, Ratcliffe writes (2005, p. 437):

> The ability to employ new methods of information management to better understand and respond to the criminal environment is not the sole domain of intelligence-led policing. There is overlap with the way that crime analysis is used within problem-oriented policing (Scott, 2000; Tilley, 2003), both for problem definition and evaluation analysis. High volume crime analysis, including the use of mapping, has become a core activity of crime analysts (Cope, 2003) and is central to CompStat. CompStat is an operational management process and is much more than just maps of crime, however, the mapping of volume crime patterns does form an integral part of the overall strategy (McGuire, 2000). CompStat combines computer technology, operational strategy, and managerial accountability, and is inherently data-driven (Walsh, 2001).

Ratcliffe described as follows some organisational problems arising from having to copy paper records into digital format (2005, pp. 442–443):

> Interpretation of the criminal environment does not just require a suitable intelligence structure; it also requires appropriate data sources and analytical tools. One district commander mentioned that his officers had 'done an internal audit and found a 50% error rate in data recording.' Clearly any intelligence is only as good as the data it originates from, and a 50% error rate is a serious cause for concern. For example, computer simulation of crime mapping scenarios suggests that 85% is a minimum acceptable geocoding rate for basic crime mapping (Ratcliffe, 2004), placing significant doubts about a 50% error rate in basic recording. The practice of entering paper records onto the local computer system was not only error-prone, it was also time-consuming and limited to two offense categories: burglary and vehicle crime. There was no time to record other offense categories.
>
> As there is no requirement of patrol officers to enter data onto a computer, considerable time was spent on data entry in order to digitally transcribe paper records. At least one person in every intelligence office mentioned, during interviews, problems with data entry. The main issues were the lack of personnel, and the content of data entry training that had been available to those analysts who had received training. These individuals complained that the training had not covered hard skills such as those required to operate the various mapping and record management platforms operated by the NZP [i.e., New Zealand Police]. As a result, data entry was slow and hindered the ability of the organization to identify timely intelligence. An Inspector in charge of a district-level intelligence office pointed out that in an internal study it had been shown to take sixteen minutes to enter the details of a burglary on to the records management system, and that while they record data on modus operandi and the property stolen, 'nobody has time to analyze the stuff.'

---

[11] Intelligence led policing is the subject of Ratcliffe (2002, 2003, 2005). Cf. Cope's article (2004) entitled "Intelligence led policing or policing led intelligence?". "Where intelligence-led policing differs from other strategies is in the focus on recidivist offenders, and the encouragement given to surveillance and the use of informants to gather intelligence that might not otherwise come to the attention of police [...]" (Ratcliffe, 2005, p. 437).

There also is a down-to-earth manner of noticing the impact of computer technology in law enforcement, on the pool of skills (including computer literacy) as expected from candidates for specific roles. Let us consider an advert from England, of the Kent Police in a local newspaper. The post advertised (in December 2007) is *Criminal Justice Unit Supervisor*. The pay is not impressive. What are the skills required? And which computer skills are required? The ad reads as follows:

> You will be responsible for supervising the day-to-day work of the criminal justice unit, together with another supervisor, to ensure case papers are properly prepared and submitted to the prosecuting authorities within tight timescales, responding to inquiries quickly and efficiently.
>
> You must have well developed communication skills to tactfully, but assertively, deal with witnesses and victims who can be angry and abusive in cases where they have received no compensation from the courts or feel let down by the justice system, distressed at having to attend court or just reluctant witnesses who do not feel that they have time to attend court.
>
> An ability to communicate at all levels within the unit and as part of the wider inter-agency approach involving the court, CPS (Crown Prosecution Service), probation and other criminal justice partners is essential.

The ability to manage office work, supervising caseworkers to whom particular criminal cases are entrusted, plays an important part. One would expect some ability to exploit technology, but that will only come later on, in the ad:

> You must evidence your ability to work under pressure and drive through change, which is essential for the role, as all work passed to the office is subject to strict time limits. The ability to prioritise and allocate work to Caseworkers and to plan ahead is also essential for the smooth running of the unit.
>
> The nature of this work is often distressing and sensitive as the unit deals with cases involving rape, child abuse and other sexual offences, road traffic collisions, as well as murder and offences against the person. You must have the ability to keep the caseworkers motivated, complete regular performance reviews with staff and be aware of signs of stress. You have to be fully dedicated to the role, as the unit has no control over the amount of work that has to be produced during any given week. You must also demonstrate flexibility and be prepared to stay as required at the end of the day, in oder to ensure that all witnesses are warned for crown court the next day and any problems are resolved.

It is at this point in the advert, that information technology skills are mentioned. This is something similar to what is found in ads for other jobs with the police. Whereas a wide range of application is mentioned, this mainly pertains to standard office software. Also police databases are mentioned, though:

> Proven evidence in the ability to utilise a full range of Microsoft Office applications is essential. Experience in the use of Genesis and Police National Computer, together with knowledge of the criminal justice procedures would be an advantage.

For a post of *Restorative Justice Administrator*, coordinating a young offenders' programme, and involving "reviewing case files from officers, checking that the relevant documents have been completed", and so forth, the ad stated: "Good IT skills are essential, with previous experience of the force's and national databases. You should be educated to at least GCSE standards or equivalent, including English Language and Mathematics". Realising that much is important and sobering. Fancy tools should not be such that would become a burden to often overburdened police staff, and for one thing, in the U.K. it is well-known that office work is taking an inordinate percentage of time spent by the force, sometimes at the expense of patrolling. But sometimes it is the tasks that intelligence or crime analysts are given that are inappropriate for their skills, and they may be using software in order to produce inappropriate output (such as management statistics), just as they use software for what is their proper pool of skills. See Section 4.5.1. Some other computer tools for the police are intended for training.[12]

Now let us consider a Kent Police ad for a *Training Officer:* "an enthusiastic and self-motivated Area Training Officer to work within the Personnel and Training Unit". That one carries a better salary that the post of Criminal Justice Unit Supervisor. The Area Training Officer has to work with a police college "in the arranging of centralising training courses", and is "required to identify and analyse local training needs, arrange and deliver appropriate training, whilst prioritising the demands placed on the area". "You should be able to co-ordinate, design and deliver training in a range of styles, as well as having the ability to demonstrate practical experience of various training techniques". Some statistics skills are required of the post-holder:

> You will be required to undertake training needs analysis on an individual or group basis and provide management reports and statistical information. This is seen by the area to be a key element of the role, as the link between performance management and training is key to the area business.

And here come the IT skills, in the ad considered:

> You must be flexible in your working hours as there may be a requirement for you to work approximately one evening per week for ongoing training of staff. Strong IT skills are essential, along with excellent communication skills and the ability to negotiate with senior managers, supervisors and outside organisations. An understanding of police roles is desirable.

Again, there are IT skills and IT skills. There are such IT skills that it would be reasonable to require of staffs, and IT skills that would be, quite unhelpfully, an unreasonable burden, if imposed as a requirement. If we are to develop useful tools at the forefront of what the state of technology affords, it is essential that the new tools will not be resented, and will not complicate the life of users.

Lawyers and policemen have different educational backgrounds. Their attitudes to technology and to numerate skills may also be different, and are certainly different from those of academic computer scientists. It is essential to calibrate the intended use of tools we may conceive of, according to the real-world features and professional cultures of the communities of users. As a matter of fact, there is an array of several professional communities who are being addressed in this book as a readership, and there is an array of several professional communities that are the intended users of both extant and potential tools within the scope of this book.

---

[12] We are going to see (in Section 6.1.6.2) that some AI computer tools with a graphic (actually, geographic) interface are intended for training at the police academy, such as *ExpertCop,* a tool developed by Vasco Furtado's team in Brazil (Furtado & Vasconcelos, 2007).

This book-form presentation was preceded by a less ambitious attempt at synthesis, in a couple of articles by this author (Nissan, 2008a, 2009a). They represent a preparatory stage in what was to become this book. The domain is mature for a volume such as the one you are reading now.

The range of techniques and tools explained, hopefully in an accessible manner, in this book is not presented in an overly technical manner. It is mainly an introduction, with indications of how (what to access in order) to pursue specific technical directions. Reading this book will hopefully result, for professionals in the fields concerned, in an ability to define requirements and perhaps commission a project; or then it will result in an ability for designers who are computer scientists, to see how to usefully direct their talents in this array of application domains.

Chapter 2
Models of Forming an Opinion

2.1 Modelling Adjudicators' Shifts of Opinion

2.1.1 Preliminaries

It is far from being the case that trial by jury is universal, in criminal cases. Even in England and Wales there is an incipient shift away, in some circumstances, towards *bench trials*, i.e., such trials that the adjudicator is one or more trained judges. There are jurisdictions in Continental Europe that make room for a lay jury, and yet the reins are in the hands of professional judges to an extent one would not expect in the Anglo-American system.

Jury research is a domain, one of whose subdomain is *mathematical modelling of judicial decision-making*, presented as though it is the decision-making of a jury. Nevertheless, some of the mathematical research that has emerged from jury research especially in North America is arguably of interest also to scholars from such countries that their respective jurisdiction only has bench trials, because actually such mathematical models confine themselves to describe shifts of opinion on the part of the adjudicator, thus, possibly of a trained judge.

In fact, typically such mathematical models do not account for deliberations among jurors when they retire, and account instead for the impression that exposure to incoming items of evidence, or to arguments made by lawyers, makes on the cognition of the adjudicator (a lay juror, or a trained judge), to the extent that this impression is reduced to a measurable parameter that shifts between "not guilty" and "guilty". Such models are known as *metre-models* (*meter-models*).

For such readers who are not conversant with Law, it may be useful to point out the succession of events at the criminal trial in Anglo-Saxon countries:

Indictment;
The accused is asked to plea guilty or not guilty:
    If the defendant pleas guilty — plea-bargain:
        The court hears the facts from the prosecution
            (with no need to present evidence);
        Defence may intervene;
        Sentence.

If the defendant pleas not guilty, the case will have to be prosecuted;
  Adjournment to an agreed date;
  Adjournment hearing (following adversarial lines);
  Prosecution opening speech;
  Prosecution calls witnesses;
    Examination in chief;
    Cross-examination;
    (sometimes) re-examination;
  Close of the prosecution case;
  (The defence may submit that there is no call to answer.
  If the court accepts this, the defendant is discharged.
  Otherwise:)
  Defence calls witnesses:
    Examination in chief;
    Cross-examination;
    (sometimes) re-examination;
  Defence's closing speech to the bench;
    (Prosecution may have one more speech,
    but then defence must have the last word.)
  The magistrates retire to consider their decision
    (the decision is taken either by a bench of lay
    magistrates, i.e., a jury, or a stipendiary magistrate,
    i.e., a trained judge);
  The magistrates return and give a verdict (and state no reason);
    If the verdict is 'not guilty',
      then the defendant is discharged;
    If the verdict is 'guilty', then:
      The court hears the facts from the prosecution
        (with no need to present evidence);
      Defence may intervene;
      Sentence.

The descriptive modelling of the decision-making process of jurors is an active area of research in psychology in North America. Sometimes, computer tools have been involved in simulations, most often with very strong simplifications. Apparently the first article published in an AI forum, and presenting a model simulating quantitatively how the opinion of a jury is shaped, was Gaines, Brown, and Doyle (1996), based on a BSc project by Gaines (1994).

Hastie (1993) is the standard reference about *metre-models* of juror decision-making, i.e., such quantitative models that are not themselves concerned with specific narrative details, even though these can be reduced to propositions and used as data when testing the models. Even though arguably it is unrealistic to disregard the details of the legal narrative at hand and how it is delivered in court, still the

2.1 Modelling Adjudicators' Shifts of Opinion

metre-models are a valuable pool of techniques which arguably could be used in combination with narrative models.

When we say "valuable", this is (alas) blue sky research. It is valuable for scholars, and it is not the case that anybody in the courtroom or in lawyers' offices is expected, or hoped, or desired to use those models. As we are going to see in this book, tools for legal professionals are something different. Starting with when we'll get to Paul Thagard's ECHO model (which measures strength of conviction on the part of a jury, in terms of how explanatorily coherent competing explanations are, for the criminal case being tried), it will make sense that even though past trials have been successfully simulated, such a tool could also be used by lawyers or prosecutors when evaluating the evidence they have, and the arguments they intend to use. That is to say, with a tool such as Thagard's ECHO, they could experiment with the degree of explanatory coherence[1] of what they provisionally have on their hands, and adjust their presentation of the evidence accordingly.

Hastie (1994, figure 1.1 on p. 7) describes trial events "in terms of the types of information presented to the juror." These include: indictment, defendant's plea, prosecution opening statement, defense opening statement, witnesses (comprising the sequence: statements of witness and judge, observations of witnesses, observations of judge), defense closing arguments, prosecution closing arguments, judge's instructions on procedures (the procedures being: presumption of innocence, determination of facts, admissibility, credibility, reasonable inference, and standard of proof), and judge's instructions on verdicts (where verdict categories have these features: identity, mental state, actions, and circumstances).

For the juror's task, Hastie proposes a flowchart of its tentative structure (Hastie, 1994, p. 8, figure 1.2), notwithstanding the differences of opinions that admittedly exist in the literature about how this takes place in the juror's cognition. Given inputs from the trial (witnesses, exhibits, and so forth), the juror has to encode meaning, the next step being (A) "Select admissible evidence". Later on in the trial events, given the judge's procedural instructions, the juror has to encode the meaning of the procedures (presumption of innocence, and so forth, as listed earlier), and this in turn has three outgoing arcs, to: (B) "Evaluate for credibility" (into which, an arc comes from A as well), (C) "Evaluate for implications", and (Z), for which see in the following.

There is a loop by which (B) "Evaluate for credibility" leads into (C) "Evaluate for implications", and then into (D) "Construct sequence of events", which in turn provides a feedback which affects B. Besides, D leads to a test: (T) "More evidence?" If there is indeed, one goes to A; otherwise, one goes to Z. Given the judge's instructions on verdicts, the juror has to learn verdict categories, and this in turn leads to (Z) "Predeliberation judgment". The flowchart from Hastie is redrawn here, with some simplification, in Fig. 2.1.1.1.

---

[1] *Coherence* is crucial for how cogent legal narratives are. But *coherence* is also a crucial factor in argumentation, and coherence in this other sense has been formally modelled in Henry Prakken's (2005) "Coherence and flexibility in dialogue games for argumentation".

Fig. 2.1.1.1 A flowchart for the juror's task

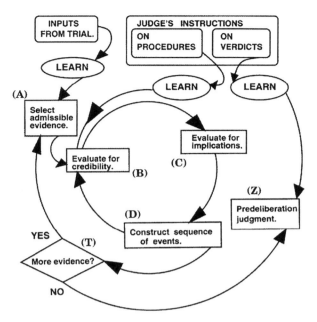

2.1.2 Distributed Belief Revision for Modelling the Dynamics of Adjudicators' Opinion

Aldo Franco Dragoni and Ephraim Nissan

Delivery of the evidence in court conforms with *dynamic uncertain inference*. "Dynamic uncertain inference is the formation of opinions based upon evidence or argument whose availability is neither disclosed to the analyst in advance nor disclosed all at once" (Snow & Belis, 2002, p. 397).[2] The present Section 2.1.2 presents a model for dealing with belief revision because of incoming information.

Belief revision is a well researched area within artificial intelligence. It studies, in terms of formal logic, the impact of the acquisition of incoming items of information. Let us consider what it may offer application to the modelling of how the opinions and beliefs of an adjudicator evolve as the trial goes on. New information and evidence integrate and corroborate the cognisance of the court, but other testimonies might cause conflicts. In this case, it seems natural that the acquisition of the new evidences should be accompanied by a reduction of the credibility of the

---

[2] Reasoning on that kind of situation is also modelled in a project described in Section 2.5.2 below.

2.1 Modelling Adjudicators' Shifts of Opinion

conflicting pieces of knowledge. If the juror's corpus of evidence is not a flat set of facts but contains rules, finding such conflicts and determining all the sentences involved in the contradictions can be hard. In dealing with these "changes of mind", if we are to adopt a formalism for belief revision, we have to heavily rely on symbolic logic, since as much as it contributed to the history of "thinking", logic could as well solve the problem of "thinking over". Generally speaking, AI researchers call this cognitive process *belief revision*.

Benferhat, Dubois, and Prade (2001) pointed out the similarities between belief revision and *database merging* (or *data fusion*): "Fusion and revision are closely related because revision can be viewed as a fusion process where the input information has priority over a priori beliefs, while fusion is basically considered as a symmetric operation. Both fusion and revision involve inconsistency handling".

Since the seminal, influential philosophical work of Alchourrón, Gärdenfors, and Makinson (1985), ideas on belief revision have been progressively refined (Gärdenfors, 1988) towards normative, effective and computable paradigms (Benferhat, Cayrol, Dubois, Lang, & Prade, 1993; Nebel, 1994). They introduced three rational principles which belief revision should obey.

AGM1 *Consistency*: revision must yield a consistent knowledge space.
AGM2 *Minimal Change*: revision should alter as little as possible the knowledge space.
AGM3 *Priority to the Incoming Information*: incoming information always belongs to the revised knowledge space.

Aldo Franco Dragoni replaced the *principle of priority* of the incoming information with a *principle of recoverability* (also called *principle of persistence*), i.e., it should be possible to backtrack from how belief was revised, in case such backtracking is warranted by the arrival of new items of evidence. It was this new principle that made their model of belief revision interesting for application to modelling of a judicial context.

It is important, for belief revision models for such an application,

- to enable *iterating* the revision,
- to enable *combining* such items of evidence that are concomitant and consistent,
- to keep track of the *source* of an item of information, and to make use of the association between the information and its source,
- and not to throw away anything: alternative multiple context should be kept, and compared when this is suitable.

The model presented in Dragoni and Nissan (2004) builds upon Dragoni, Giorgini, and Nissan (2001), and fits among the metre-models as known from jury research, but is more sophisticated in that it applies a belief revision formalism, rather than the simpler formalisms previously used by jury research psychologists. Dragoni and Nissan (2004), being concerned with modelling the dynamics of how judicial factfinders (judges or jurors) propend to either verdict, have incorporated in the architecture they describe a component which modifies (by feedback) the credibility of the source from which an item of information comes, according to how the credibility[3] of that item of information is currently faring. Their model takes into account how the degree of credibility of the different persons who provide different items of information is dynamically affected by how some information they supplied comes to be evaluated.[4]

That system works as follows (see Fig. 2.1.2.1, from Dragoni & Nissan, 2004, p. 290). Upon the arrival of a new {source, information} pair into the knowledge base (i.e., a set of extant {source, information} pairs), a truth-maintenance mechanism is applied, which finds all minimally inconsistent subsets, finds all maximally consistent subsets, and generates a set of maximally consistent subsets.

From this set and from a set of pairs {information source, source reliability score}, a statistical technique is applied (it may be Dempster-Shafer),[5] and a set

---

[3] In distributed AI, dealing with societies of artificial agents, the topic of an agent's *reputation* has tended to be underresearched, but it ought to be an important topic for distributed AI just as it is for social psychology. A book on the subject is Conte and Paolucci (2002). The same considerations apply to trust among agents, also an important subject for AI modelling, just the way it is for social psychology, and which is the subject of a book by Castelfranchi and Falcone (2010). See a survey in Sabater and Sierra (2005).

[4] In psychological research about detecting deception (e.g., Vrij, 2000; Porter & Yuille, 1995, 1996; Colwell, Hiscock-Anisman, Memon, Woods, & Yaeger, 2006) – a subject to which we are going to return (see fn 81 below) – "The Statement Validity Analysis (SVA), a memory-based approach, is the most widely used system of credibility assessment to date" (Colwell et al., 2006). It is traced back to Undeutsch's (1982) statement reality analysis. The latter became known as the Undeutch Hypothesis. It "which posits that memory for an actual event will differ from fabrication in structure, content, and quality; and that these systematic differences will be measurable. Recall of a genuine memory is expected to demonstrate a richness of detail, logical structure, and spontaneity or 'unstructured production' " (Colwell et al., 2006). "The cognitive approach to credibility/deception is based on the Information Manipulation Theory (IMT) [McCornack, 1992]. Maintaining deception in an interrogative atmosphere can be a cognitively demanding task. A deceiver must deal with his/her conflicting goals of disclosing enough information to please the interrogator while retaining sufficient control over the facts conveyed to avoid detection" (Colwell et al., 2006). According to IMT, which "highlights the complex and interactional nature of deception, emphasizing impression management and the deceiver's control over the information" (Colwell et al., 2006): "Deceivers usually convey less information than truth-tellers (less quantity), reply in a more irrelevant manner (less relevance), provide incoherent information (lower quality), and rarely engage in sarcasm (different manner of responding [(Porter & Yuille, 1995)]). These specific mechanisms, as well as others, can provide a multitude of channels for a deceiver to utilize." (Colwell et al., 2006).

[5] "Dempster-Shafer theory [(Shafer, 1976)] has been developed to handle partially specified domains. It distinguishes between uncertainty and ignorance by creating belief functions. Belief functions allow the user to bound the assignment of probabilities to certain events, rather than give events specific probabilities. Belief functions satisfy axioms that are weaker than those for probability theory. When the probabilistic values of the beliefs that a certain event occurred are exact, then the belief value is exactly the probability that the event occurred. In this case, Dempster-Shafer theory and probability theory provide the same conclusions" (Stranieri & Zeleznikow, 2005a).

2.1 Modelling Adjudicators' Shifts of Opinion

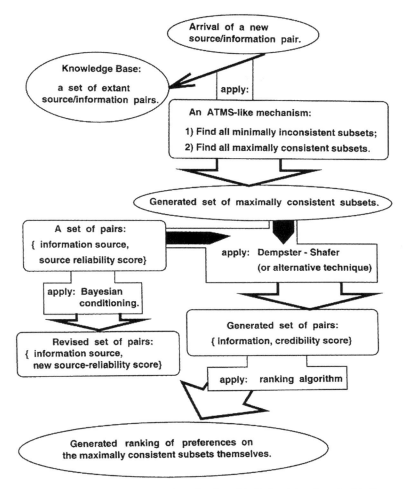

Fig. 2.1.2.1 Control flow in the approach to distributed belief revision described in Dragoni and Nissan (2004)

is generated of {information source, source reliability score} pairs. A ranking algorithm is applied, and a ranking of preferences is generated for the maximally consistent subsets themselves.

Moreover, by applying Bayesian conditioning, the reliability scores of the information sources are revised (Dragoni & Nissan, 2004; also see Dragoni & Animali, 2003). On credibility and probability, see Schum (1989).

The overall schema of the multi-agent belief revision system we proposed in Dragoni and Nissan (2004), as whown here in Fig. 2.1.2.1, incorporates the basic ideas, current in artificial intelligence, of:

- Assumption-based Truth Maintenance System (ATMS)[6] to keep different scenarios.
- Bayesian probability to recalculate the a-posteriori reliability of the sources of information.
- The Dempster-Shafer Theory of Evidence to calculate the credibility of the various pieces of information.

In Fig. 2.1.2.2, on the left side, one can see an incoming information, β (whose source, U, is identified), further to the set of beliefs already found in the knowledge base, namely, informations α and χ, which both come from source W, and moreover an information being a rule ("If α, then not β"), which comes from source T.

The latter could, for example, be an expert witness, or then a fictitious character such as common sense. In the parlance of Anglo-American legal evidence

---

[6] An ATMS is a mechanism that enables a problem solver to make inferences under different hypothetical conditions, by maintaining the assumptions on which each piece of information and each inference depends (de Kleer, 1986, 1988). An ATMS maintains how each piece of inferred information depends on presumed information and facts, and how inconsistencies arise. "A *Truth maintenance system* (TMS) may be employed to protect the logical integrity of the conclusions of an inferencing system" (Luger & Stubblefield, 1998, section 7.2.3, p. 275).

"Jon Doyle (1979) created one of the earliest truth maintenance systems, called a *justification based truth maintenance system* or JTMS. Doyle was the first researcher to explicitly separate the truth maintenance system, a network of propositions and their justifications, from the reasoning system operating in some domain. The result of this split is that the JTMS communicates with the problem solver, perhaps an automated theorem prover, receiving information about new propositions and justifications and in turn supplying the problem solver with information about which propositions should be believed based on the current existing justifications. There are three main operations that are performed by the JTMS. First, the JTMS inspects the network of justifications. This inspection can be triggered by queries from the problem solver such as: Should I believe in proposition p? Why should I believe proposition p? What assumptions underlie proposition p? The second operation of the JTMS is to modify the dependency network, where modifications are driven by information supplied by the problem solver. Modifications include adding new propositions, adding or removing premises, adding contradictions, and justifying the belief in a proposition. The final operation of the JTMS is to update the network. This operation is executed whenever a change is made in the dependency network. The update operation recomputes the labels of all propositions in a manner that is consistent with existing justifications" (Luger & Stubblefield, 1998, section 7.2.3, pp. 276–277).

"A second type [of] truth maintenance system is the *assumption-based truth maintenance system* (ATMS). The term *assumption-based* was first introduced by de Kleer (1984), although similar ideas may be found in Martins and Shapiro (1983). [Cf. Martins and Shapiro (1988), Martins (1990).] In these systems, the labels for nodes in the network are no longer IN and OUT but rather the sets of premises (assumptions) underlying their derivation. de Kleer also makes a distinction between premise nodes that hold universally and nodes that can be assumptions made by the problem solver and that may later be retracted. [...] The communication between the ATMS and the problem solver is similar to that between JTMS and its problem solver with operators for *inspection, modification*, and *updating*. The only difference is that with ATMS there is no longer a single state of belief but rather subsets of potential supporting premises. The goal of computation with the ATMS is to find minimal sets of premises sufficient for the support of each node. This computation is done by propagating and combining labels, beginning with labels for the premises" (Luger & Stubblefield, 1998, section 7.2.3, pp. 278–279).

2.1 Modelling Adjudicators' Shifts of Opinion

Fig. 2.1.2.2 The arrival of a new information item

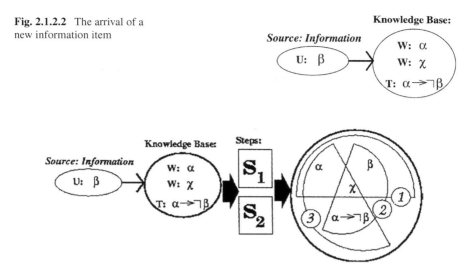

Fig. 2.1.2.3 The second step: the generation of all the maximally consistent subsets of KB (i.e., the knowledge base), plus the incoming information

theory, common sense is called "background generalizations", "common-sense generalizations", or "general experience" (see Twining, 1999).

Once past the knowledge base in the flowchart of Fig. 2.1.2.2, in order to revise the set of beliefs with the new information β coming from source U, two steps are undertaken. Refer to Fig. 2.1.2.3. The ATMS-like mechanism is triggered; it executes steps S1 and S2.

These are dual operations, respectively, as follows:

- Find all minimally inconsistent subsets (NOGOODSs).
- Find all maximally consistent subsets (GOODSs).

In the notation of set theory, the Venn diagram on the right side of Fig. 2.1.2.3 is intended to capture the following concept. Three GOODSs have been generated; the one labelled 1 includes α, β, and χ; the one labelled 2 includes B, χ, and the rule "If α, then not β"; whereas yet another GOODS, labeled 3, includes: α, χ, and the same rule "If α, then not β".

Each one out of these three GOODSs is a candidate for being the preferred new cognitive state (rather than the only new cognitive state). The decision as to which cognitive state to select is taken based on Dempster-Shafer (see Table 2.1.2.1). Refer to Fig. 2.1.2.4.

Dempster-Shafer is resorted to in order to select the new preferred cognitive state, which consists of an assignment of degrees of credibility to the three competing GOODSs. Dempster-Shafer takes as input values of a priori source-reliability (this degree being set a priori is possibly a limitation), and translates them into a

Table 2.1.2.1 The role of the Dempster-Shafer theory of evidence

Ω:	models of the finite language $\mathcal{L}$ adopted in the trial under consideration
S_i:	a source of information
K_i:	information received from S_i expressed through $\mathcal{L}$
$[K_i] \subseteq \Omega$:	models of K_i
R_i:	a priori reliability of S_i (i.e., probability that S_i is reliable)

From the testimony of each S_i a basic probability assigment on 2^Ω can be extracted:

$$m_i(X) = \begin{cases} R_i & X = [K_i] \\ 1 - R_i & X = \Omega \\ 0 & \text{otherwise} \end{cases}$$

Dempster Rule of Combination of multiple evidence:

$$m(X) = \frac{\sum_{X_1 \cap ... \cap X_n = X} m_1(X_1) \cdot ... \cdot m_n(X_n)}{\sum_{X_1 \cap ... \cap X_n \neq \emptyset} m_1(X_1) \cdot ... \cdot m_n(X_n)}$$

Belief Function Bel(X): it assesses a degree of credibility for each formula of $\mathcal{L}$ from the combined evidence $m(X)$:

$$\text{Bel}(X) = \sum_{X' \subseteq X} m(X')$$

---

ranking in terms of credibility of the items of information given by those sources. Yet, Dempster-Shafer could instead directly weigh the three GOODS, whereas we make it weigh the formulae instead. This choice stems from Dragoni's feeling that the behavior of Dempster-Shafer is unsatisfactory when evaluating the GOOD in its entirety. (In fact, as the GOOD is a formula, Dempster-Shafer could conceivably assign a weight to it directly.)

Next, from the ranking of credibility on the individual formulae, we can obtain (by means of algorithms not discussed here) a ranking of preferences on the GOODSs themselves. In the example, this highest ranking is for the GOOD with: α, β, and χ. (Thus, provisionally discarding the contribution of source T, which here was said to be "common sense".) Nevertheless, our system generates a different output. The output actually generated by the system is obtained downstream of a recalculation of source reliability, achieved by trivially applying Bayes' theorem. In our example, it can be seen how it is source T ("common sense") which is most penalised by the contradiction that occurred. Thus, in output B′, the rule which precludes β was replaced with β itself. Note that the selection of B′ is merely a suggestion: the user of the system could make different choices, by suitably activating search functions, or then by modifying the reliability values of the sources.

2.1 Modelling Adjudicators' Shifts of Opinion

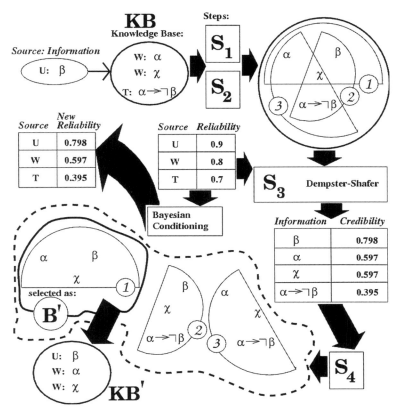

Fig. 2.1.2.4 The complete process of belief revision according to the approach proposed in Dragoni and Nissan (2004)

Once the next information arrives, everything will be triggered anew from the start, but with a new knowledge base, which will be the old knowledge base revised with the information. It is important to realise that the new knowledge base is not to be confused with B'. Therefore, any information provisionally discarded is recoverable later on, and if it will be recovered indeed, it will be owing to the maximal consistency of the GOODSs.

The Dempster-Shafer Theory of Evidence is a simple and intuitive way to transfer the sources' reliability to the information's credibility, and to combine the evidences of multiple sources. Notwithstanding these advantages there are shortcomings, including the requirement that the degrees of reliability of the sources be established a priori, as well as computational complexity, and also disadvantages stemming from epistemological considerations from legal theory. At any rate, the adoption of Dempster-Shafer in the present framework is a choice that could perhaps be called into question. A refinement is called for, because as it stands, the system requires (as said) associating with the sources an a priori degree of reliability and, moreover, application other than approximated of Dempster-Shafer is computationally very complex.

A few remarks of evaluation follow, first about consistency. Of course, we want to enforce or restore consistency: judiciary acts cannot stem from an inconsistent set of hypotheses. Yet, we want to avoid unduly dismissing any possibility altogether. Therefore we contrast all such GOODSs that are obtained from the set of information items (which are globally inconsistent) provided by the various sources involved. Sometimes the same source may be found in contradiction, or provide inconsistent information (self-inconsistency).

In 1981, Marvin Minsky, one of the founding fathers of artificial intelligence, stated: "I do not believe that consistency is necessary or even desirable in developing an intelligent system". "What is important is how one handles paradoxes or conflicts". Enforcing consistency produces limitations: "I doubt the feasibility of representing ordinary knowledge in the form of many small independently true propositions (context-free truths)". In our own approach, we have a single, global, never forgetting, inconsistent knowledge background, upon which many, specific, competitive, ever changing, consistent cognitive contexts are acting.

An important thing to bear in mind, concerning the model from Dragoni and Nissan (2004), is that the principle of *recoverability* only applies to *revision*, but not to *updating*. In fact, if I see an object in a position Y, I can no longer believe it to be in a position A. If then I am told that it is *not* in Y, this does not imply that it went back to position X. Perhaps the object went from position Y to position Z.

Another way to state this is as follows. If observation (or information item) β caused the removal of information item α, this does not imply that if there is a further notification γ of change, that removes β, then we must recover and restore the information item α.

In the words of Dragoni and Nissan (2004, p. 286):

> An important follow-up of research [into belief revision] has been the sharp distinction made between "revision" and "updating". If the new information reports of some modification in the current state of a dynamic world, then the consequent change in the representation of the world is called "updating". If the new information reports of new evidence regarding a static world whose representation was approximate, incomplete, or erroneous, then the corresponding change is called "revision". With revision, the items of information which gradually arrive all refer to the same situation, which is fixed in time: such is the case of a criminal event whose narrative circumstances have to be reconstructed by an investigative team or by fact finders (a judge or a jury). In contrast, with updating, the items of information which gradually arrive refer to situations which keep changing dynamically: the use for such items of information is to make the current representation as corresponding as possible to the current state of the situation represented.
>
> This applies, for example, to a flow of information on a serial killer still on the loose. For example, Cabras (1996) considers the impact of the construal in the mass media in Italy of a criminal case, on the investigation itself, and on the "giudici popolari" to whom the case could have gone (this is the "domesticated" version of a jury at criminal trials at a "Corte d'Assise" [the Assizes] in Italy, where trained judges are in control anyway). The case she selected is that of the so-called "Monster of Foligno", a serial killer who used to leave messages between crimes. A man eventually implicated himself by claiming that he

2.1 Modelling Adjudicators' Shifts of Opinion

was the killer. He was released in due course, and later on, the real culprit was found. We didn't try our formalism on this case, yet arguably investigations on serial killers are a good example of updating instead of revision,[7] vis-à-vis recoverability in the sense we explained [...].

The issue of sources of information (or indeed of prediction) with different degrees of reliability has been discussed by Pollock (2010, p. 12), concerning defeasible reasoning[8] as being represented in *inference-graphs*:

> For example, let P be "Jones says that it is going to rain", R be "Smith says that it is not going to rain", and Q be "It is going to rain". Given P and Q, and supposing you regard Smith and Jones as equally reliable, what should you believe about the weather? It seems clear that you should withhold belief, accepting neither Q nor ∼Q.
>
> But now, suppose we do not regard Jones and Smith as equally reliable. E.g., Jones is a professional weatherman, with an enviable track record of successfully predicting whether it is going to rain. Suppose his predictions are correct 90% of the time. On the other hand, Smith predicts the weather on the basis of whether his bunion hurts, and although his predictions are surprisingly reliable, they are still only correct 80% of the time. Given just one of these predictions, we would be at least weakly justified in believing it. But given the pair of predictions, it seems clear that an inference on the basis of Jones' prediction would be defeated outright. What about the inference from Smith's prediction. Because Jones is significantly more reliable than Smith, we might still regard ourselves as weakly justified in believing that it is going to rain, but the degree of justification we would have for that conclusion seems significantly less than the degree of justification we would have in the absence of Smith's contrary prediction, even if Smith's predictions are only somewhat reliable. On the other hand, if Smith were almost as reliable as Jones, e.g., if Smith were right 89% of the time, then it does not seems that we would be even weakly justified in accepting Jones' prediction. The upshot is that in cases of rebutting defeat, if the argument for the defeater is almost as strong as the argument for the defeatee, then the defeatee should be regarded as defeated. This is not to say that its degree of justification should be 0, but it should be low enough that it could never been justified simpliciter.[9] On the other hand, if the strength of the argument for the defeater is significantly less than that for the defeatee, then the degree of justification of the defeatee should be lowered significantly, even if it is not rendered 0. In other words, the weakly justified defeaters acts as diminishers. So this

---

[7] Another example that befits updating, rather than revision, is when, in the series of messages from the Red Brigades while they were holding prisoner the Italian politician Aldo Moro (who was abducted on 16 March 1978 from his car in Rome, the five men of his escort having been killed), there was a rather abnormal message which stated that Moro's body had been dumped in a lake in the mountains of central Italy, Lago della Duchessa. The bottom of the lake was searched by law enforcement staff, who found instead the body of a shepherd (it was an unrelated crime). But then the series of messages from the Red Brigades started again, with no reference to their prank of sending law enforcement agents scuttling to Lago della Duchessa.

[8] "Nonmonotonic reasoning, because conclusions must sometimes be reconsidered, is called *defeasible*; that is, new information may sometimes invalidate previous results. Representation and search procedures that keep track of the reasoning steps of a logic system are called *truth maintenance systems* or TMS. In defeasible reasoning, the TMS preserves the consistency of the knowledge base, keeping track of conclusions that might later need be questioned" (Luger & Stubblefield, 1998, p. 270).

[9] In Latin *simpliciter* means "simply", but here it has the following technical sense: "Justification simpliciter requires the degree of justification to pass a threshold, but the threshold is contextually determined and not fixed by logic alone." (Pollock, 2010, p. 8).

seems to be a fairly non-controversial case in which varying degrees of justification affect the defeat statuses of conclusions in inference-graphs.

2.1.3 Further Considerations, and Suggestions of Possible Refinements

An epistemologist, Laurence BonJour (1998, originally 1985), introduced five conditions for coherence, the first one being: "A system of beliefs is coherent only if it is logically consistent" (ibid., p. 217 as reprinted in 1998). While introducing the first condition, he remarked in note 7: "It may be questioned whether it is not an oversimplification to make logical consistency in this way an absolutely necessary condition for coherence. In particular, some proponents of relevance logics may want to argue that in some cases a system of beliefs which was sufficiently rich and complex but which contained some trivial inconsistency might be preferable to a much less rich system which was totally consistent..." (BonJour, ibid., p. 230). *Relevance logics* in this context are not necessarily very relevant to the concept of "relevance" in the judiciary parlance (in which sense, the term has to do with the admissibility of evidence as a matter of policy). See Section 4.6.3 on relevance logics.

Among the requirements or desiderata for a distributed belief revision framework, in Dragoni and Nissan (2004) we listed the desirability of the mechanism also displaying sensitivity to the syntax. Consider Fig. 2.1.3.1. Is it really necessary to consider different, yet logically equivalent formulations of set of propositions, to be equivalent when the syntactic difference represents a difference in presentation? How you present information in court may make or break your case. You do not want the information to be introduced in a clumsy manner. Are redundancies of information of no value at all?

Moreover, is even a local, peripheral inconsistency enough to invariably ditch a witness statement? The discovery of a pair of items of information in contradiction inside a rich-textured, articulate witness, should not necessarily invalidate the informational content of the entire deposition. That is to say: a set of propositions is not equivalent to their logic conjunction. This is a critique of what in belief revision research is known as "Dalal's Principle", by which two logically equivalent pieces of information should produce exactly the same revision. Arguably, Dalal's Principle is unworkable in practice, if we are to apply belief revision to the modelling of reasoning in court on incoming evidence, because it takes cognitive

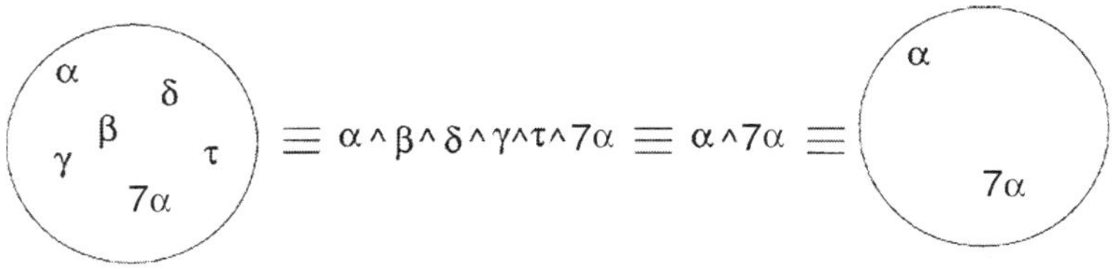

$$\left(\begin{array}{c} \alpha \quad \delta \\ \beta \\ \gamma \quad \tau \\ 7\alpha \end{array} \right) \equiv \alpha \wedge \beta \wedge \delta \wedge \gamma \wedge \tau \wedge 7\alpha \equiv \alpha \wedge 7\alpha \equiv \left(\begin{array}{c} \alpha \\ \\ 7\alpha \end{array} \right)$$

Fig. 2.1.3.1 An example of syntactic equivalence. (Based on a drawing by Aldo Franco Dragoni.)

2.1 Modelling Adjudicators' Shifts of Opinion

arbitrariness to delimit the set. How fine-grained are the details to be? What about cross-examination tactics?

Desiderata include criteria for deciding about inconsistency containedness. How local is it to be? When can we just cut off the NOGOODSs and retain the rest? Within the architecture described earlier in Section 2.1.2, this would belong in the phases of recalculation of source reliability and information credibility. One more problem is *confabulation* in depositions (i.e., witnesses infer rather than merely reporting; this may be because, e.g., witnesses discussed their recollections, and this had an effect on what they later think they remember). In particular, if it was two eyewitnesses who saw the same event and they then discussed it, this may influence what they later claim to remember; this is sometimes referred to as *memory conformity*.

Whereas our present framework is too abstract to take narrative aspects into account, arguably our system could be a building block in an architecture with a complementary component to deal with narratives. In particular, a witness who reconstructs by inference instead of just describing what was witnessed is confabulating; this is precisely what traditional AI systems from the 1980s, whose function was to answer questions about an input narrative text, do when information does not explicitly appear in the text they analyse. Within the compass of this paper, we cannot address these issues. Nevertheless, in Dragoni and Nissan (2004, p. 296) we claimed that the formal framework described is as good as other metre-based formal approaches to modeling juror decision making, to the extent that such models do not explicitly handle narrative structure.

Yet a major problem stemming from the adoption of Dempster-Shafer is that it is apparently tilted towards *confirmationism* instead of *falsificationism*. Confirmationism[10] is also referred to sometimes as *cognitive dissonance*,[11] and what is meant is a bias of human decision-makers in favour of learning such information that confirms their preconceptions, over information that contradicts these.

Take the case of a terrorist or organised crime "supergrass" informing about accomplices and testifying in court. In Italy, such "pentiti" or "superpentiti" are not considered to be reliable until further proof is obtained; the supergrasses reliability is taken to be greater to the extent that greater is the extent to which the deposition matches further evidence. A shortcoming of this is that part of the deposition may be false and unaffected by such further proof. Dempster-Shafer, as described in the framework of the architecture introduced in Dragoni and Nissan (2004), falls short of not being tricked into unduly increasing the reliability of such an untruthful witness. Dempster-Shafer also tends to believe information from a source until contrary evidence is obtained. Such epistemological considerations affect not only

---

[10] On *confirmation bias* as occurring in the police interrogation rooms, see e.g. Kassin, Goldstein, and Savitsky (2003), Meissner and Kassin (2002), and Hill, Memon, and McGeorge (2008).

[11] This name for the concept was spread by a book by Leon Festinger (1919–1989), *A Theory of Cognitive Dissonance* (Festinger, 1957).

formal representations; they also affect the way, for example, the mass media may convey a criminal case or the proceedings in court. They may also affect what justice itself makes of witness statements made by children (i.e., child testimony). None of these issues is addressed in the formalism presented in Section 2.1.2.

The multi-agent approach described is appropriate when a flow of new items of information arrives from several sources, and each {information, source} pair has an unknown credibility degree. This befits the gradual delivery of the evidence in court, when a juror's opinion (or the opinion of the judges in a bench trial) is shaped concerning evidentiary strength. A formalism for dealing with evidentiary strength has been presented in Shimony and Nissan (2001); see Section 2.6 below.

2.1.4 Devices of Manipulation of Incoming Information in Court

The approach to incoming information could be refined, with respect to the idealised conditions of Dragoni and Nissan (2004), presented in Section 2.1.2 above. In the present Section 2.1.4, we suggest factors to take into account, such as rhetorical devices affecting the timing at which information arrives, in the courtroom.

Let us point out first of all that the acceptance of, or resistance to, incoming information (and attempts at persuasion)[12] is of course a wider topic than the trial by jury. Consider this assessment of the character of Charles I, King of England (the one who was beheaded, which was in 1649). In some respects he was a sound strategist during the Civil War. Yet he had flaws "which had a detrimental effect upon his generalship". Namely: "He was a bad judge of men, the readiness with which he listened to the accusations against Rupert is ample evidence of this". Moreover: "He compounded this weakness with a habit of agreeing with whoever last spoke to him – a fatal tendency, bearing in mind the poor quality of many of his advisers" (Young & Holmes, 1974, p. 336 in the 2000 edn.). This shows the influence of the makeup of the rationality and temperament of an individual decision-maker.

In a treatise on persuasion in the courtroom, Guglielmo Gulotta (one of Italy's leading forensic psychologists, who also intervenes in court in his capacity as a barrister) discusses the tactics of *inoculation*, which aims at making the recipient of the message resistant beforehand to the attempts at persuasion which the other side may be expected to enact (Gulotta, 2004, section 18.4, pp. 135–136). The following is quoted in my own translation:

---

[12] In psychology, studies of *persuasion* include, e.g., Chaiken (1987), Chaiken, Liberman, and Eagly (1989), Chaiken, Wood, and Eagly (1996), Clark and Delia (1976). In the given disciplinary context of psychology, "the study of persuasion concerns the variables and processes that govern the formation and change of attitudes" (Chaiken et al., 1996, p. 702). *Message-based persuasion* is one strand of such research. Other traditions of persuasion research include "the influence of individuals' own behaviors and messages on their attitudes, social influence effects in group contexts and, to a lesser extent, the attitudinal effects of mere or repeated exposure to attitude objects and the selective effects of attitudes on information processing" (ibid.). Also see Cialdini (1993) about *influence*. Papageorgis and McGuire (1961) discussed *immunity to persuasion* produced by pre-exposure to weakened counterarguments. Persuasion is also the subject of, e.g., Stiff (1994), Sawyer (1981), Petty and Cacioppo (1986) and Petty, Wegener, and White (1998).

2.1 Modelling Adjudicators' Shifts of Opinion

[Inoculation] suggests to anticipate, in an mitigated form, the theses which one's adversary will presumably develop, and to facilitate the elaboration of objections in such a way that, once the attempts at persuasion will be carried out, the recipient of the message will already possess elements to repel them. Research indicates that this effect is not merely due to warning the audience about forthcoming persuasory manoeuvres, but depends on the fact that the subject is enabled to anticipate his own reflections on the matter. This tends to neutralize the *recency* effect, by privileging the *primacy* effect.

Another way to manipulate primacy and recency is by *stealing thunder*, and in particular *revealing the worst first* is one way to accomplish this (Williams & Dolnik, 2001; Dolnik, Case, & Williams, 2003). "Sometimes, in order to cause 'immunity', a defence counsel would say things which discredit his client. This may be done, for example, by being the first one to reveal something negative for one's client, knowing that the other side may use this later. With mock juries, this technique appeared to be especially useful, as it mitigates, in the eyes of factfinders, its negative meaning, based on the principle that old news are no news" (Gulotta, 2004, p. 136, fn. 4 [my translation], citing Williams & Dolnik, 2001; Dolnik et al., 2003).

What does this mean, in respect of AI modelling? Rhetorical devices that, short of lying, manipulate perception have already come to the attention of AI research by the early 1980s. A program, IMP, was devised (Jameson, 1983), that was explicitly concerned with the relation between truth and manipulative presentation. IMP may try to mislead on purpose, without actually lying. A dialogue system, it impersonates a real estate agent, trying to rent moderately priced furnished rooms on the Hamburg market. Well-informed about the market, IMP assumes that the customer possesses the same general information, against which the customer assesses the qualities of the room considered. The program tries to convey a good impression about the goods, and about itself as well. It would not volunteer damaging information, unless a direct, specific relevant question is made. IMP has a goal of maintaining a neutral image of itself and an impression of completeness for its own answers; on occasion, it reportedly simulated insulted surprise if an intervening question by the customer seems to imply (by detailed questioning) that IMP is concealing information.

Having closed this digression, let us make some considerations about procedures and jurisdictions, before we turn to an encompassing view of attempts at devising a formal account of juror's decision-making, within jury research.

2.1.5 Remarks About Procedures and Jurisdictions

In this book, we are going to make the occasional comment about procedural issues. As these are not central to the thrust of this book, we do not really delve into these, but then the risk arises that what we do say about procedural issues would be overly simplistic. For example, take the rules of hearsay. It is essential to realise the difference among jursidictions, because the rules of admissibility of hearsay evidence vary substantially between the United Kingdom and the United States, and even between Scotland and England.

Therefore, readers should realise that whenever we do broach procedural issues, such statements are not to be applied sweepingly: such matters are jurisdiction specific. The consequences of this for AI development is that oftentimes, applications will not be portable across jurisdictions. A project whose end-product is realistically expected to be used by legal professionals will need to focus on a specific jurisdiction, and if anything it will be useful to find out beforehand whether and how choices made will affect usefulness in some other jurisdiction, if this is of interest.

In his introduction to Hastie (1993), Hastie points out: "One development in traditional jurisprudential scholarship is a candidate for the role of a general theory of juror decision making; namely the utilitarian model of rational decision making that has been imported into jurisprudence from economics" (p. 4). Optimal decision making has been modelled, in the literature, not just for the role of the juror, but for the judge, attorney, police, and perpetrators of criminal behaviour, as well as the general principles of the legislator or of a judicial system.

For example, for the purpose of explaining why, according to economic rationality, it makes sense that hearsay be not admitted as evidence in court – incidentally, an expert system dealing with the hearsay rule is the *Hearsay Rule Advisor* (Blackman, 1988; MacCrimmon, 1989) – legal scholars Shapira (2002) and Callen (2002) discuss what went wrong in the reasoning of Shakespeare's character of Othello, when Othello believed rumours about Desdemona having supposedly betrayed him. Also see Stein (2001). By the way: the *hearsay rule* (in English and American law) "requires a court to exclude any written or oral statement not made in the course of the proceedings which is offered *as evidence of the correctness of the matter asserted*. A statement which is relevant independently of the real intention of the speaker [e.g., a contractually binding statement] or the truth of what is stated [e.g., an allegedly libellous statement] is not adduced for a testimonial purpose and is therefore outside the scope of the rule" (Pattenden, 1993, p. 138). This is not to say that in some jurisdictions hearsay is inadmissible; e.g., McNeal (2007) discusses hearsay at the Iraqi High Tribunal, in consideration of the legacy of international tribunals for war crimes or crimes against humanity. "The IHT allowed hearsay evidence and the reading of ex parte affidavits as evidence, two of the most criticized practices of the Nuremberg Tribunal. The IHT also allowed the admission of testimony by anonymous witnesses, a legacy of the Yugoslavia Tribunal which has since been rejected by that same court" (ibid., from the abstract).

Unlike the typical situation in the jurisdictions of Continental Europe, which expect the judge to provide a motivation for the adjudication and thereby rationalises his or her intimate conviction about how to find in the case at hand,[13] juries in Anglo-Saxon jurisdictions do not provide a motivation,[14] and therefore the rationale for the finding is not made explicit. By contrast, in Anglo-American jurisdiction there is an emphasis on abiding by the rules about how the evidence is acquired.

---

[13] For example, Iacoviello's book (1997) discussed how the Court of Cassation in Italy check the motivation of the sentence given in criminal trials heard by the lower courts in Italy. Iacoviello (2006) invoked clearer rules about flaws in the motivation, and the effect they have in terms of mistrial.

[14] It is sometimes said that this is because the jury replaces the medieval ordeal, in which the adjudication was taken to be supernatural.

Alex Stein's *Foundations of Evidence Law* (2000) provides a systematic examination of the underlying theory of evidence law (i.e., which evidence is admissible, and how the risk of error is apportioned) in Anglo-American legal systems. Stein adopted an interdisciplinary approach, which combines probability theory, epistemology, economic analysis, and moral philosophy. In Stein's Chapter 5, an economic analysis of evidence law is introduced:

> This analysis makes an unqualified utilitarian assumption (subsequently softened in Chapters 6 and 7) that evidential rules and doctrines are geared towards cost-efficiency. Cost-efficiency requires adjudicators to minimize the aggregate cost of accuracy-enhancing procedures and fact-finding errors. Chapter 5 examines the evidential mechanisms to attain this goal. These mechanisms enhance cost-efficiency by eliminating the problem of private information and the misalignment between the private litigants' incentives and the social good. These mechanisms include decision rules that determine the burdens and the standards of proof,[15] as well as different process rules that determine what evidence is admissible and what fact-finding methodologies are allowed. Decision rules minimize the aggregate cost of accuracy and errors by applying a different technique. These rules attach fact-finding methodologies that are more meticulous and more expensive to adjudication in which the cost of error is relatively high. Adjudication in which the cost of error is relatively low is equipped with more rudimentary and correspondingly inexpensive fact-finding methodologies. Mechanisms geared towards cost-efficiency also include credibility rules. These special rules elicit credible signalling from litigants with private information through adjustment of penalties and rewards.
>
> Chapters 6 and 7 shift from utility to fairness and, correspondingly, from economics to morality. They examine the apportionment of the risk of fact-finding error in criminal and civil adjudication, respectively. These chapters identify and analyse two fundamental precepts: the equality principle that controls the apportionment of the risk of error in civil litigation; and the 'equal best' standard that needs to be satisfied in every criminal case in order to convict the accused. These precepts derive from political morality. [...] (Stein, ibid., p. xii).

2.1.6 A Taxonomy of Quantitative Models

Optimality for judicial decision making is too strong an assumption (Hastie, 1993, p. 5). The research in Hastie (1993) "focuses on the manner in which jurors behave before they enter the social context of deliberation in criminal felony cases" (ibid., p. 5), with "at least four competing approaches represented" among behavioural scientists' descriptive models of decision making (ibid., p. 10), namely, such that are "based on probability theory, 'cognitive' algebra, stochastic processes, and information processing theory" (ibid., pp. 10–11). Bayes' theorem is involved, in the former, for descriptive purposes in Hastie (1993) – being applied to the psychological processes in which a juror is engaged – rather than in prescribing how to evaluate evidence to reach a verdict, "or to evaluate and improve jurors' performance" (ibid., p. 12).

"The second class of approaches to juror's decision making fits among such psychological theories of mental processes that are couched in the form of algebraic

---

[15] Cf. Bex and Walton's (2010) "Burdens and Standards of Proof for Inference to the Best Explanation". Also see Atkinson and Bench-Capon (2007a).

equations (Hastie, 1993, p. 17), with evidence being combined according to a weighted average equation" (Nissan, 2003f). "As in the Bayesian model, we are dealing with a single meter in which the results of all the subprocesses are summarized in a current belief and in which the ultimate 'categorical' verdict decision is based on the comparison of the final belief meter reading to a threshold to convict" (Hastie, 1993, p. 19), but belief updating in the algebraic approach is additive instead of multiplicative as in Bayesian models, and moreover extreme judgments are adjustable instead of final. "Stochastic process models are the third family; they differ from the previous two in that the larger process is assumed to behave in a random fashion, and what is probabilistic is state transitions over time. The fourth family adopts the information processing paradigm from cognitive psychology; they are typified by the room they make for mental representations, memory activation, elementary information processes, an executive monitor, and a specific cognitive architecture" (Nissan, 2003f).

Such categories of models are concerned with evaluating evidential strength (e.g., Shimony & Nissan, 2001; see Section 2.6 below). The following is quoted from Michon and Pakes (1995):

> One key factor in the criminal justice procedure is the assessment of the 'strength of evidence'. Traditionally this has been a major topic in legal psychology (Pennington and Hastie, 1981; Holstein, 1985; Hastie, 1993). Strength of evidence is obviously involved in assessing likelihoods of the outcome of criminal trials and demands for pre-trial custody.[16]
>
> Several models have been proposed for describing how judges and jurors represent and evaluate the complex and often ambiguous information that is presented in a criminal trial. [...] A useful distinction can be made between bottom-up and top-down approaches.

Namely (Michon & Pakes, 1995):

> Bottom-up approaches take the evidence as piece-by-piece information. Each piece of information may cause the decision-maker to adjust his or her belief in the guilt or innocence of the suspect. In this case judgement formation is treated as a discrete, step-by-step process that can be logically described. Several models of this sort have been proposed (Schum and Martin, 1982; Thomas and Hogue, 1976). They can be characterised as 'fact-driven' because the actor in these models is supposed to be passive when it comes to the structuring and interpretation of the information presented. The actor performs a series of belief adjustments on the basis of factual information alone.

By contrast to such *fact-driven* models, there is a category of models that are driven by a hypothesis about the most likely narrative scenario (Michon & Pakes, 1995):

> In contrast, top-down models can be characterised as 'hypothesis-driven'. In the latter models, the decision-maker attempts to build a cognitive representation of what happened. This representation is assumed to have the structure of a narrative (Bennett and Feldman, 1981). Pieces of evidence are selected and weighed in such a fashion that they support the most likely scenario of what may have actually happened. Judgements in these models

---

[16] An example of the fallacies associated with subjective estimates of the likelihood of future things, is more clearly seen when it comes to how *post factum* one reports one's own evaluation of the likelihood beforehand. See Fischhoff and Beyth's (1975) ' "I Knew It Would Happen": Remembered Probabilities of Once-Future Things', as well as Merton's (1948) 'The Self-Fulfilling Prophecy'.

2.1 Modelling Adjudicators' Shifts of Opinion

are not formed by weighing each piece of information separately, but come about when a substantial proportion of all the evidence is processed and represented in a coherent explanatory framework (Schank, 1986). The judgement is then based on this representation of the body of evidence as a whole.

Bayesian models are typical among *probabilistic* models, as being part of *belief updating* models, and these in turn are a quite conspicuous class of fact-driven models (ibid.):

> A major example of the bottom-up or fact-driven approach is the Bayesian framework. [...] A decision-maker starts out with a prior probability that a certain event — a criminal action by a certain defendant — occurred. This probability is expressed as a likelihood ratio — that is, the ratio between the likelihood that the suspect is guilty divided by the likelihood that the suspect is innocent. When a new piece of evidence is presented, it may alter the prior likelihood ratio into a posterior probability concerning the event. When all the information is processed, a final likelihood concerning the occurrence of the event is obtained. The Bayesian approach is one particular instance of a class of belief updating models. Other models of this kind use weighed averages which determine the impact of pieces of evidence. Each new piece of evidence is assigned a value. The sign of this value is dependent on whether it implies guilt or innocence of the suspect and its weight is dependent on how much importance the piece of evidence is given. The main difference between Bayesian models (such as Schum and Martin, [1982]) and weighed average models is that in the Bayesian approach the revision of beliefs is modelled by a multiplicative computation. In the weighed average models, this computation is additive. Both models have been criticised as incomplete and incorrect (Pennington and Hastie, 1981; Einhorn and Hogarth, 1985). Both have, however, inspired a great deal of research concerning judgement formation in social and cognitive psychology, not only in the legal context but in many other contexts as well.

In Table 2.1.6.1, we contrast the Bayesian updating model, the algebraic sequential averaging model, and the stochastic Poissonian process model. Remember that in the latter, what is probabilistic is the state transitions in time.

The parameter's range is between "not guilty" and "guilty", and because of the presumption of innocence, the initial value of the parameter must initially be on the former value. There is then a cycle by which new items of evidences are presented in court, and later on, the lawyers present their arguments. At each such step of new

Table 2.1.6.1 "Traditional" metre models

Which model	Bayesian updating model	Algebraic sequential averaging model	Stochastic Poissonian[17] process model
Which parameter	Probability of guilt	Opinion	Weight of the evidence
Initial value	Prior probability	Initial "anchor"[18]	Initial opinion
Main operator	Multiplication	Sum	Weight adjustment

---

[17] An intuitive explanation of the term is that, e.g., bus arrivals are Poissonian.
[18] By "anchor", in the algebraic sequential averaging model, opinion is meant.

Fig. 2.1.6.1 Presumption of innocence constrains the initial value of the parameter in metre-models, as a function of time and of incoming information

information arriving, there is the possibility that the value of the parameter be modified. Therefore, it can be said that the parameter we have been considering varies along the axis of time. See Fig. 2.1.6.1. The flowcharts in Figs. 2.1.6.2, 2.1.6.3, 2.1.6.4, and 2.1.6.5 contrast the metre-models.

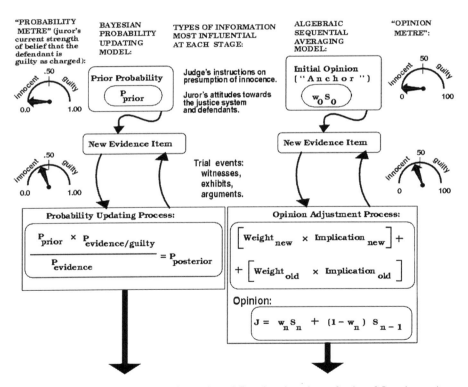

Fig. 2.1.6.2 Redrawn initial part of a coalesced flowchart based on of pairs of flowcharts given in Hastie's introduction in Hastie (1993) for the Bayesian probability updating model, and the algebraic sequential averaging model of how jurors supposedly make their mind gradually, as the evidence is being delivered in court

2.1 Modelling Adjudicators' Shifts of Opinion

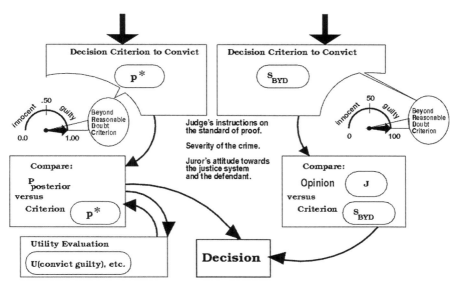

Fig. 2.1.6.3 Redrawn final part of a coalesced flowchart based on of pairs of flowcharts given in Hastie's introduction in Hastie (1993) for the Bayesian probability updating model, and the algebraic sequential averaging model of how jurors supposedly make their mind gradually, as the evidence is being delivered in court

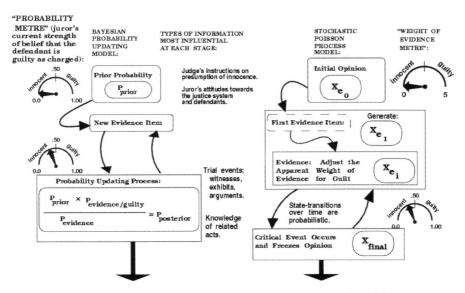

Fig. 2.1.6.4 Redrawn initial part of a coalesced flowchart based on of pairs of flowcharts given in Hastie's introduction in Hastie (1993) for the Bayesian probability updating model, and and the stochastic Poisson process model of how jurors supposedly make their mind gradually, as the evidence is being delivered in court

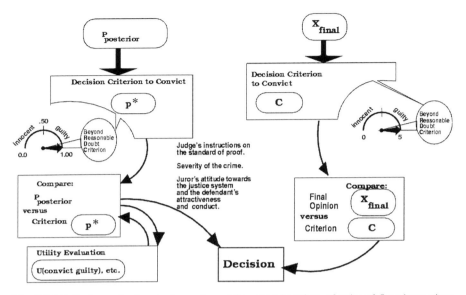

Fig. 2.1.6.5 Redrawn final part of a coalesced flowchart based on of pairs of flowcharts given in Hastie's introduction in Hastie (1993) for the Bayesian probability updating model, and and the stochastic Poisson process model of how jurors supposedly make their mind gradually, as the evidence is being delivered in court

2.1.7 An Excessive Focus on Juries?

There is a caveat, apart from the limitations of quantitative models of jury decision-making. The excessive focus on juries is itself problematic. "Modelling judicial decision-making applies to both trained factfinders (trained judges in bench trials), and – in countries where there is a jury system – lay factfinders, i.e., jurors. Yet, there is much more that deserves attention, than trial by jury" (Nissan & Martino, 2004b).

Bench trials are such trials that it is the judge or judges, not a jury, who return a verdict. In the words of a British legal scholar, William Twining (1997): "[P]roblems of proof, information handling, and 'evidence' arise at all stages of legal processes" (ibid., p. 443). "There is also growing realisation that it is misleading to treat the contested trial, especially the contested jury trial, as the only or the main or even the paradigm arena in which decisions about questions of fact are taken, even in the United States. 'The jury model' still dominates much American evidentiary discourse and has an unfortunate effect on satellite fields, such as the agenda for psychological research into evidentiary problems" (ibid., p. 444).

"A striking example is the recent empirical work on the role of stories in fact-finding, which treats contested jury trials as the paradigm: e.g. [Bennett & Feldman (1981)]; and the important 'story model' of Nancy Pennington and Reid

2.1 Modelling Adjudicators' Shifts of Opinion

Hastie (1986, 1988, 1992, 1993),[19] which is a by-product of jury research [in Hastie et al. (1983), Hastie (1993)]; *cf.* the distorting effect of the jury model on

---

[19] Pennington and Hastie showed people a movie of a trial. They found that in order to make sense of the wealth of detail, the participants constructed stories about what happened. In another experiment, they found that when evidence was given in an order which made the story easy to construct, the participants were more likely to construct the same story. When the evidence was in story order, 78% of participants found the defendant guilty. Yet when the evidence was out of order, only 31% voted for the guilty verdict.

Emplotting items of information into an explanatory narrative is also a subject of debate concerning historical explanation. In the journal *History and Theory*, David Carr's (2008) 'Narrative Explanation and Its Malcontents' gives this general example about how we figure out narrative explanations (ibid., pp. 19–20):

> Suppose that on a busy city street we see a young man carrying a large potted plant that almost obscures his view, running so fast that he risks colliding with other pedestrians, and shouting the name of a woman in a very loud voice. When someone like this attracts our attention, his action puzzles us. We want to know why he's behaving in this strange way. We seek an explanation.
>
> We learn that he has returned home to find a note from his girlfriend with whom he shared his apartment, but with whom he had been quarreling; indeed she had decided to leave him and move out, and in fact had removed her belongings and is gone. The man was shaken and distraught. Then he noticed that she left behind her favorite plant, and learned from a neighbor that she had left only a few minutes ago and is walking in the direction of a friend's apartment. Seizing on the plant as a pretext to find her and beg her to return, he picks it up and runs into the street, hoping to catch up with her.
>
> Most of us would be satisfied with this account as an explanation of the man's action. We might ask for more details, but we don't really need them. Our perplexity goes away; our question has been answered. We now know why he did what he did.
>
> What we have given is a typical narrative account. We have explained an action by telling a story about it. The narrative has all the standard elements of a good story: it has a central subject or protagonist. It has a beginning: we need not go any further back than his return to the empty apartment, though it helps to learn that the two had been quarreling before that. That sets the scene. The story has a middle, in which our hero reacts emotionally to the opening scene, assesses the situation with the help of some new information (that she had just left), and decides to take action. What he does then, running with the plant through the street and shouting his girlfriend's name, is where we came in, as it were. There is an element of suspense here: will he succeed? And the story has an end, even though we don't yet know exactly what it will be. He'll catch up with her or he won't. If he does, he'll be successful in winning her back, or he won't. But this range of alternatives, even though we don't know which of them will occur, is determined by the story so far. They belong to the story.
>
> One thing to be noted about this explanation is that it is probably the same one that the man himself would give for his own action. Though we could have gotten this explanation from someone else, we could also have gotten it from him, if we had occasion to ask. This rather obvious fact suggests that the narrative mode is very close in form to the structure of action itself, from the agent's point of view. [...]

However (Carr, 2008, p. 21):

> Of course, questions might arise about whether the man was telling the truth, especially if his story conflicted with another story — say, his girlfriend's story — of the same events. Here we would indeed have a legitimate reason to question the agent's narrative account of his own action. If it became important for some reason to settle the discrepancy, we might have to call in other witnesses and ask for their accounts of the same action.

eyewitness identification research" (Twining, 1997, p. 444, fn. 16). In an edited volume published in Britain and entitled *The Jury Under Attack* (Findlay & Duff, 1988), McCabe felt able to ask, in the very title of an article: "Is Jury Research Dead?" (McCabe, 1988).

Juries may be swayed by a witness (typically, the alleged victim) that unwittingly recovers false memories,[20] with or without the help of a (misguided) psychotherapist; this danger is being increasingly recognised by legal psychologists, and the internationally most famous scholar carrying out such research is Elizabeth Loftus.[21] Over the years, results similar to hers have been obtained by independent teams, and she appears to be right in claiming that in various ways, human memory appears to be fluid. Whereas such a realisation may be troubling for the

---

This could take us from the everyday into the world of legal or juridical institutions, where someone — a judge or jury — would have to decide which account of the action to believe. A journalist might have similar concerns, wanting to reconstruct "what really happened" out of the varying accounts of the original events. Historians, too, often see their task as reconstruction of the past along these lines. Here the value of hindsight is that from its perspective it can reveal elements that augment the original story.

[20] *False memories* of events that actually never happened in an individual's lifetime, and are nevertheless retrieved by that individual, have been researched by various scholars (especially concerning the susceptibility of children to the development of false memories), but are especially associated with research conducted by Elizabeth Loftus (http://www.seweb.uci.edu/faculty/loftus/). See, e.g., Brainerd and Reyna (2004), Garven, Wood, Malpass, and Shaw (1998), Howe (2005), Johnson, Hashtroudi, and Lindsay (1993), Lane and Zaragoza (2007), Strange, Sutherland, and Garry (2006), and Wade, Garry, Read, and Lindsay (2002), Wade, Sharman, Garry, Memon, Merckelbach, and Loftus (2007). In the late 2000s, Henry Otgaar has produced a steady flow of publications on false memories, especially in children (http://www.personeel.unimaas.nl/henry.otgaar/#Publications), e.g., Otgaar, Candel, and Merckelbach (2008), Otgaar, Candel, Merckelbach, and Wade (2009), Otgaar, Candel, Memon, and Almerigogna (2010), Otgaar et al. (2010), Otgaar, Candel, Scoboria, and Merckelbach (2010), Otgaar, Candel, Smeets, and Merckelbach (2010), Otgaar and Smeets (2010), Howe, Candel, Otgaar, Malone, and Wimmer (2010), and Otgaar (2009).

[21] E.g., Loftus and Doyle (1997), Loftus (1979, 1981a, 1981b, 1987, 1997, 1998, 2002, 2003a, 2003b, 2005); cf. Loftus (1974, 1975, 1976, 1980, 1983, 1986a, 1986b, 1991, 1993a, 1993b); and see: Loftus and Greene (1980), Loftus and Ketcham (1994), Loftus and Pickrell (1995), Loftus and Rosenwald (1993), Loftus and Palmer (1974), Loftus and Hoffman (1989), Loftus and Loftus (1980), Loftus, Miller, and Burns (1978), Loftus, Weingardt, and Wagenaar (1985), Loftus, Loftus, and Messo (1987), Loftus, Donders, Hoffman, and Schooler (1989), Penrod, Loftus, and Winkler (1982), Garry, Manning, Loftus, and Sherman (1996), Mazzoni, Loftus, and Kirsch (2001), Wells and Loftus (1991), Schooler, Gerhard, and Loftus (1986), Bell and Loftus (1988, 1989), Deffenbacher and Loftus (1982), Monahan and Loftus (1982), Castella and Loftus (2001), Nourkova, Bernstein, and Loftus (2004), and Harley, Carlsen, and Loftus (2004).

Neimark (1996) has written about Loftus. After teaching for 29 years at the University of Washington at Seattle, she moved to the University of California at Irvine. Nevertheless, her debunking the myth of "repressed memories" (cf., e.g., McNally, 2003) in relation to child abuse as alleged in the Jane Doe case had unpleasant consequences for the scholar (Tavris, 2002). She is much admired, while also controversial. Her results cannot be safely ignored.

justice system, its being inconvenient does not exempt from awareness and caution when accepting testimony.[22]

2.2 Reasoning About a Charge and Explanations: Seminal Tools from the Late 1980s and Their Aftermath

2.2.1 ECHO, and PEIRCE's Remake of the Peyer Case

2.2.1.1 Thagard's 1989 Simulation of the Jury at the Peyer Case

The year 1989 saw the earliest publication of two projects, very different from each other, but which within a decade would prove to have been seminal for the modelling of reasoning about legal evidence. They are ECHO, and ALIBI. Let us start with ECHO. We point out right away that whereas the respective immediate purposes of both projects were theoretical, nevertheless a tool such as ECHO could be conceivably useful for lawyers or the prosecution using it while preparing a trial, in order to carry out a simulation of jury behaviour, based on the provisional state of the evidence and of the arguments intended or expected to be used.[23]

The input for ECHO simulations of a trial is constituted by sets of simple propositions, and these propositions include items of evidence, prosecution hypotheses, and defence hypotheses. Some other possible statements are identified as contradictions. Some other statements are instances of an *explains* function, followed by its parameter instances.[24] Such statements include prosecution explanations, defence explanations, and motives. Moreover, data are declared, within the input code, these data being testimonies uttered by the witnesses, thus being observed by everyone inside the courtroom.

The philosopher and cognitivist Paul Thagard first presented his ECHO project in a paper entitled 'Explanatory Coherence' (Thagard, 1989). He then went on using and refining ECHO, exemplifying it on different legal cases; e.g., see Thagard

---

[22] A psychologist of law, Amina Memon, in her 2008 course handouts on *Psychology, Law and Eyewitness Testimony* at the University of Aberdeen in Scotland, stated: "The last 20 years has seen an explosion of research in the Psychology and Law field. The area that has grown more than any other is research on perceptions of credibility and accuracy of participants in the legal system. Psychologists have asked questions that have direct relevance in the legal arena: Are there reliable indicators of deception? Is it possible to persuade an innocent person that they may have committed a crime? Are juries biased? Can social pressure to remember result in false memory creation? [...]"

[23] Code in the LISP programming language for ECHO is available at its originator's website. That is the website (http://cogsci.uwaterloo.ca) of Paul Thagard's computational epistemology laboratory.

[24] The syntax (explains (H1 H2) E1) means that hypotheses H1 and H2 together explain evidence E1. Coding this in LISP is straightforward. "The relation *explains* is asymmetrical, but ECHO establishes a symmetrical link between a hypothesis and what it explains" (Thagard, 2004, p. 237).

(2004). In ECHO, neural computing[25] was (and is) resorted to, in order to model the reasoning of a jury on a murder case against California Highway police officer Craig Peyer, who was tried in San Diego for the murder of Cara Knott on 27 December 1986. The trial ended on 27 February 1988, in a hung jury.

Twenty-two young and attractive women (who therefore were like the victim) testified that Peyer had pulled them over. And it was known that Peyer had pulled the victim over, on the night of her death. The witnesses who had been pulled over by Peyer, also testified that Peyer talked to them longer than was necessary for just a ticket. Moreover, they were all pulled over near the stretch of road where the victim's body was found.

Thagard's ECHO is a tool which applies *abductive* reasoning. See, e.g., Walton (2004, 2010) about abductive reasoning. That in ECHO the modelling is of the reasoning of a jury, fits in the framework of jury research, a domain which, as mentioned earlier, is very active in North America. Using the Peyer case as his example in Thagard (1989), "Thagard encoded the problem into his ECHO system by treating each hypothesis and finding as a node in a neural network, with links connecting each hypothesis node to nodes corresponding to explained findings. Incompatible hypotheses were connected by inhibitory links. Thagard assigned each hypothesis the same initial confidence value, so we treated them similarly, giving each an initial confidence value of LIKELY" (Fox & Josephson, 1994, pp. 218–219).

2.2.1.2 Thagard's Principles of Explanatory Coherence

Let us consider the technical aspects of using ECHO. ECHO is based on Thagard's theory of explanatory coherence, which consists of the following principles, quoted here from Thagard (2004, pp. 234–235):

Principle E1. Symmetry. Explanatory coherence is a symmetric relation, unlike, say, conditional probability. That is, two propositions, p and q, cohere each other equally.

Principle E2. Explanation. (a) A hypothesis coheres with what it explains, which can either be evidence or another hypothesis; (b) hypotheses that together explain some other proposition cohere with each other; and (c) the more hypotheses it takes to explain something, the lower the degree of coherence.

Principle E3. Analogy. Similar hypotheses that explain similar pieces of evidence cohere.

Principle E4. Data priority. Propositions that describe the results of observations have a degree of acceptability on their own.

Principle E5. Contradiction. Contradictory propositions are incoherent with each other.

Principle E6. Competition. If P and Q both explain a proposition, and if P and Q are not explanatorily connected, then P and Q are incoherent with each other. (P and Q are explanatorily connected if one explains the other or if together they explain something.)

Principle E7. Acceptance. The acceptability of a proposition in a system of propositions depends on its coherence with them.

---

[25] Neural networks are the subject of Section 6.1.14 in this book.

2.2 Reasoning About a Charge and Explanations: Seminal Tools

How to determine coherence-based acceptance is not fully specified in those seven principles. There are various algorithmic solutions available (alternative to each other) that, along with those seven principles, can compute acceptance and rejection of propositions, on the basis of coherence relations.

2.2.1.3 Thagard's Neural Network Algorithm in ECHO

If the algorithm uses an artificial neural network (which is the case with ECHO), propositions are represented as *units*, i.e., artificial neurons. Pairs of these are linked by excitatory or inhibitory links. (Figure 2.2.1.3.1 shows an example of neural network. Neural networks are the subject of Section 6.1.14 in this book.)

- Coherence relations are represented by excitatory links.
- Inhibitory relations are represented by inhibitory links.

Explanatory coherence is dealt with as a constraint satisfaction problem to be solved. Positive constraints are the coherence relations established by explanation relations. Relations of contradiction or incompatibility between propositions are negative constraints. In the words of Thagard (2004, p. 235):

> Acceptance or rejection of a proposition is represented by the degree of activation of the unit. The program ECHO spreads activation among all units in a network until some units are activated and others are inactivated, in a way that maximizes the coherence of all the propositions represented by the units.

In Fig. 2.2.1.3.2, I drew a flowchart showing Thagard's neural network construction algorithm. This phase is followed by the initial activation and then by a cycle

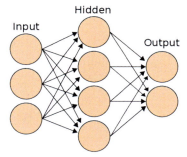

Fig. 2.2.1.3.1 An example of artificial neural network.[26] The network shown has one *hidden layer*. It is sandwiched between the input layer of nodes, and the output layer of nodes. Such nodes that are neither input nor oputput are called *hidden nodes*. In this example, all nodes of a given layer are connected to all nodes of the next layer (if any) and of the preceding layer (if any). Generally speaking, this need not be the case. In ECHO, only some of the possible connections are present, and the links are either inhibitory or excitatory

---

[26] This image (http://en.wikipedia.org/wiki/File:Artificial_neural_network.svg) was made by C. Burnett and is in the public domain under the terms of the GNU Free Documentation License.

Fig. 2.2.1.3.2 The neural network construction stage in Thagard's ECHO algorithm

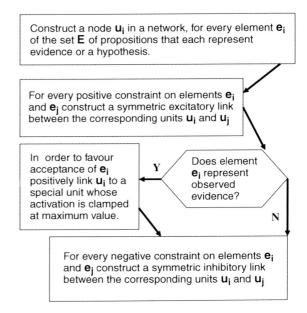

of activations (these are called *propagations* of the neural networks, as shown in Fig. 2.2.1.3.3.

Thagard (2004, p. 236) explained the formulae of the cycle of activation in his neural network, according to one of the algorithms he has been using:

> A number of equations are available for specifying how this updating is done (McClelland and Rumelhart, 1989). For example, on each cycle the activation of a unit j, a_j, can be updated according to the following equation:

$$a_j(t+1) = a_j(t)(1-d) + net_j \left(max - a_j(t)\right) \quad \text{if } net_j > 0,$$

otherwise

$$net_j \left(a_j(t) - min\right).$$

Here d is a decay parameter (say, .05) that decrements each unit at every cycle, *min* is a minimum activation (−1), and *max* is maximum activation (1). Based on the weight w_{ij} between each unit i and j, we can calculate net_j, the net input to a unit, by:

$$net_j = \sum_i w_{ij} a_i(t).$$

Although all links in coherence networks are symmetrical, the flow of activation is not, because a special unit with activation clamped at the maximum value spreads activation to favored units linked to it, such as units representing evidence in the explanatory coherence model ECHO. Typically, activation is constrained to remain between a minimum (e.g., −1) and a maximum (e.g., 1).

Fig. 2.2.1.3.3 The neural network activation cycle in Thagard's ECHO algorithm

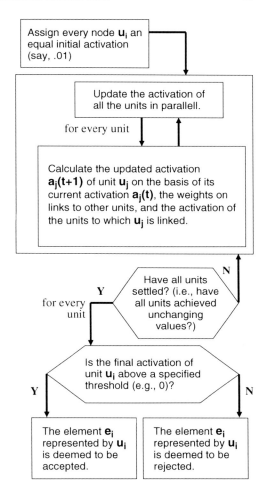

2.2.1.4 Thagard's Greedy Algorithm for Simulating a Trial

Thagard (2000a, p. 35) introduced a different algorithm for carrying out simulations by means of ECHO. This alternative algorithm does not require a neural network. It is quoted here from Thagard (2004, pp. 236–237); bear in mind that E is the set of elements each being a proposition, either evidence or a hypothesis. This algorithm belongs to the class of so-called *greedy* algorithms: this search algorithm is greedy because it never backtracks to reconsider its previous choices.

1. Randomly assign the elements of E into A (accepted) or R (rejected).
2. For each element e in E, calculate the gain (or loss) in the weight of satisfied constraints that would result from flipping e, i.e., moving it from A to R if it is in A, or moving it from R to A otherwise.

3. Produce a new solution by flipping the element that most increases coherence, i.e., move it from A to R or from R to A. In case of ties, choose randomly.
4. Repeat 2 and 3 until either a maximum number of tries have taken place or until there is no flip that increases coherence.

2.2.1.5 Josephson's Abducer, PEIRCE-IGTT

A team led by John Josephson reimplemented the Peyer case, using a different inference engine, PEIRCE-IGTT, also being an *abducer*, i.e., an engine for abductive reasoning.[27] "One point of comparison is that PEIRCE-IGTT can trace its reasoning process, and this reasoning process makes sense at every step. In contrast ECHO works by repeated cycles of propagating activations, and even if each spread of activation can be explained as a reasoning step that makes sense, ECHO took 78 cycles to settle, so its reasoning was much less direct. PEIRCE formed its conclusions quickly, and, in effect, produced an argument for innocence given the evidence. (In contrast ECHO leaned toward guilt, although it resisted complete rejection of the innocence hypothesis.)" (Fox & Josephson, 1994, p. 222).

Commenting on this passage in a previous draft of the present work, a legal scholar, Ron Allen, remarked about the "comparison of ECHO and PEIRCE-IGTT, one of which concludes the guy is innocent and the other guilty. The legal analyst, of course, wants to know which is right and why we should believe it" (in an e-mail of 14 April 2006).

Fox and Josephson (1994) go on explaining the workings of the tools: "It might be suggested that ECHO engages in a complex weighing of evidence in its attempt to maximize explanatory coherence, whereas PEIRCE makes too much of a small number of findings. We submit that PEIRCE's behaviour for the case was entirely reasonable. It considered all the evidence" (ibid., p. 222). "It could have found the case to be ambiguous and, like the jury, refused to come to a conclusion; but it did not. Instead it produced a conclusion, with a clear chain of reasoning leading to it" (ibid., p. 223).

According to the developers of PEIRCE (ibid., p. 223), the Peyer case used as an example

> demonstrates that the fifth-generation [i.e., Machine 5] abductive-assembly strategy can generate chains of reasoning, and arrive at conclusions, even if all the hypotheses are given identical initial confidence values. The strategy makes good use of confidence differences if they are available, but it does not absolutely require them. It is able to solve a problem categorically, based on explanatory relationships and incomparabilities alone, or with the assistance of additional hypothesis interactions such as soft implications.

Moreover (Fox & Josephson, 1994, p. 223):

> The Peyer example also illustrates how explanatory relationships can work synergistically with incompatibility relationships to reduce residual ambiguity. This is the phenomenon of *uncovered essentials*. What happens is that eliminating a hypothesis, based

---

[27] Clearly the system PEIRCE was named after the philosopher Charles Sanders Peirce (1839–1914), with whom the theory of abductive reasoning is mainly associated. An architecture for abductive reasoning was also described by Poole (1989).

2.2 Reasoning About a Charge and Explanations: Seminal Tools

on incompatibility with some proposition already accepted, eliminates a potential explainer for some finding, thereby allowing a rival explainer to stand up as superior. (This happens similarly for uncovered clear-bests and bests, where confidence is reduced, instead of the hypothesis being eliminated.) Thus, at a point in the processing where a finding is ambiguous (it has alternative explainers with no confident way to decide between them), the ambiguity may be broken or reduced by eliminating or downgrading of some of the rival explainers. [...] Moreover, the process of acceptance, leading to ambiguity reduction, followed by further acceptance and further ambiguity reduction, can potentially continue for many cycles, leading to a kind of spreading wave of ambiguity reduction as islands of high confidence are extended to cover data newly made unambiguous. We call this process *spreading disambiguation*.

The contribution of PEIRCE is to abductive reasoning within AI. This in turn is useful for modelling reasoning on judicial cases, as seen from exemplification on the Peyer case. The same case was used as an example by Ciampolini and Torroni (2004), who modelled it by using abductive logic-based agents and their ALIAS multi-agent architecture. "Agent behaviour in ALIAS can be expressed by means of the *Language for Abductive Logic Agents*, LAILA. This language [enables the modelling of] agent actions and interactions in a logic programming style" (ibid., p. 260).[28]

Let us consider the steps of the default algorithm of PEIRCE-IGTT, which "presupposes that there is a means of generating or obtaining the findings for the case and a means of generating hypotheses to explain the findings" (Fox & Josephson, 1994, p. 216). Such "generated hypotheses must have initial confidence values, and they must have associations with the findings that each can explain" (ibid.). At the end of the algorithm, "either all findings have been accounted for, or there are no more hypotheses available to explain findings, or the only remaining hypotheses are too close in plausibility and explanatory power to decide between them" (ibid., p. 217).

Because of how the hytpotheses are categorised, "each pass through the loop portion of the algorithm further limits the confidence in any hypothesis newly included into the composite"[29] (Fox & Josephson, 1994, pp. 217–218). "Hypotheses may be

---

[28] On abduction and logic programming, see Kakas, Kowalski, and Toni (1992, 1998), Toni and Kowalski (1995), Fung and Kowalski (1997), Eshghi and Kowalski (1989). On abductive logical models, also see sections 3.1 and 4 in Prakken and Renooij (2001), whereas Section 5 in that same paper is about argument-based reconstruction of a given case about a car accident. In MacCrimmon and Tillers (2002), Part Five comprises four articles on abductive inference as applied to fact investigation in law.

[29] With reference to the RED-2 tool for abduction, the Josephsons' book states: "Logically, the composite hypothesis is a conjunction of little hypotheses, so, if we remove one of the conjuncts, the resulting hypothesis is distinctly more likely to be true because it makes fewer commitments. Superfluous hypothesis parts make factual commitments, expose themselves to potential falsity, with no compensating gain in explanatory power. To put it more classically: if hypothesis parts are treated as logical conjuncts, then an additional part introduces an additional truth condition to satisfy. Thus the hypothesis that is simpler (in not including an unneeded part) is more likely to be true. Thus the sense of parsimony we use here is such that *the more parsimonious hypothesis is more likely to be true.*" (quoted from p. 84 in the same book: Josephson & Josephson, 1994).

Confirmed, Essential,[30] Clear-Best, Weak-Best, Guessed, Disbelieved (because of incompatibility), or Ruled-Out (because of a low confidence rating), and these judgments may be relative to Confirmeds, Essentials, Clear-Best, Weak-Best, or Guessed hypotheses" (ibid.). See the definitions in the following. The steps of the algorithm are quoted from Fox and Josephson (ibid., pp. 216–217):

1. Generate or obtain findings to be explained and generate hypotheses (with their confidence values and coverages).
2. Initialize the composite with any hypotheses predetermined to be in the composite (set up by the tool user who has decided to always include certain hypotheses or by the system user interactively while he or she explores alternative hypotheses).
3. When this algorithm is used in a layered-abduction machine,[31] expand expectations from higher levels (if a higher layer abductive conclusion has implications either positively or negatively for hypotheses at the current level). The expectations will cause the confidence values of the hypotheses in question to be adjusted. [...]
4. Propagate the effects of hypotheses initially accepted into the composite. This may rule out other hypotheses that are incompatible with those in the composite, or it may alter confidence values or other hypotheses that are implied by hypotheses in the composite.
5. Loop on the following, either until all findings are accounted for or until no more progress is made in extending the explanatory coverage.

---

[30] Cf. in RED-2: "After parsimony criticism, a second process of criticism begins in which each hypothesis in the composite is examined to see if it is essential, that is, to see if part of what it explains can be explained in no other way. There are two ways to find essentials. The first is during the initial assembly process. If only one hypothesis offers to explain a finding on which attention is focused, that hypothesis is a *discovered essential*. The second way to discover essentials is that an attempt is made for each part of the composite hypothesis, not already known to be essential, to assemble a complete alternative hypothesis not including that part. If the attempt succeeds, it shows that there are other ways of explaining the same things, even though they may not be as good as the original. But if the attempt fails, it shows that there is something that has *no other plausible explanation* other than by using the hypothesis part in question [...] Note the distinction between hypothesis parts that are nonsuperfluous relative to a particular composite, that is they cannot be removed without explanatory loss, and essentials without which no complete explanations can be found in the whole hypothesis space. An essential hypothesis is very probably correct, especially if it was rated as highly plausible by its specialist" (Josephson & Josephson, 1994, pp. 84–85).

[31] John R. Josephson, in the same book on p. 238, begins a chapter which "develops the hypothesis that perception is abduction in layers and that understanding spoken language is a special case"; it "present[s] a layered-abduction computational model of perception that unifies bottom-up and top-down processing in a single logical and information-processing framework. In this model the processes of interpretation are broken down into discrete layers where at each layer a best-explanation composite hypothesis is formed of the data presented by the layer or layers below, with the help of information from above. The formation of such a hypothesis is an abductive inference process, similar to diagnosis or scientific theory formation."

2.2 Reasoning About a Charge and Explanations: Seminal Tools

a. Find all Confirmed hypotheses and include them in the composite. A Confirmed hypothesis is (here) one that receives the highest possible confidence score (this is an optional feature that can be turned off by the system builder if top-scoring hypotheses should not be automatically included in the composite).
If Confirmed hypotheses are found, then propagate the effects to the latest inclusions and go back to the loop beginning, else continue.
b. Find all Essential hypotheses[32] and include them in the composite.
If Essential hypotheses are found, then propagate the effects of including them in the composite, and go back to the loop beginning, else continue.
c. Find all Clear-Best hypotheses. To be a Clear-Best, a hypothesis must have a score higher than a given threshold and must surpass all other explanations for some finding by another given threshold. (Thresholds are established by the tool user at the time the system is built; they can be easily modified during or between cases; the tool provides defaults if no thresholds are specified.)
If Clear-Best hypotheses are found, then propagate the effects of including them in the composite, and go back to the loop beginning, else continue.
d. Find and include all the Weak-Bests. Here we may relax the criteria set for the Clear-Bests. This step is optional.
If Weak-Best hypotheses are included in the composite, then propagate the effects and go back to the loop beginning, else continue.
End loop.

6. (Optional extended-guessing step) If there are still some unaccounted findings, attempt to guess among the remaining hypotheses that have not been ruled out. Guessing is accomplished by letting each unexplained finding vote for the highest rated hypotheses offering to explain it. This voting allows hypotheses to stand out from alternatives according to their power to help explain the unexplained remainder, if in no other way.
If any guessed hypotheses are included, then propagate the effects and go back to the loop beginning, else end.

2.2.1.6 Abductive Reasoning, and Inference to the Best Explanation

"In general, legal reasoning in trials such as those of Claus von Bülow's" – for which, see Section 2.2.1.7 – "can be characterized as inference to the best overall causal story" (Thagard, 2004, p. 231). Talking about "inference to the best overall

---

[32] "In PEIRCE-IGTT, each pass through the loop leads to conclusions whose proper confidence is relative to the previous passes. A hypothesis judged to be Essential because a competing hypothesis was ruled out as a result of its being incompatible with a Clear-Best, is only an Essential hypothesis *relative* to Clear-Bests. An Essential from the first pass through the loop is more confidently an Essential than an Essential that is relative to Clear-Bests is. Similarly, any newly included hypothesis that is relative to guessing (that is, a hypothesis is included as a result of the effects of the inclusion of a guessed hypothesis) must be regarded as less confident than any hypothesis included before guessing began." (Fox & Josephson, 1994, p. 217).

causal story" is talking about a particular class of *inference to the best explanation*. The latter concept was formulated by the Princeton philosopher Gilbert Harman in his paper 'The Inference to the Best Explanation' (Harman, 1965). Arguably the idea goes back to Charles Sanders Peirce. "*Abduction*, or *inference to the best explanation*, is a form of inference that goes from data describing something to a hypothesis that best explains or accounts for the data. Thus abduction is a kind of theory-forming or interpretive inference" (Josephson & Josephson, 1994, p. 5). The name *abduction* in this sense was introduced by Peirce. One of the ways abduction has been described in artificial intelligence is as "modus ponens turned backwards". John Josephson (ibid., p. 5) prefers this pattern:

> D is a collection of data (facts, observations, givens).
> H explains D (would, if true, explain D).
> No other hypothesis can explain D as well as H does.
> Therefore, H is probably true.

Wilbert Spooren (2001), reviewing Luuk Lagerwerf's linguistics doctoral dissertation (1998), explains as follows Lagerwerf's approach, next to a "mini-summary" entitled "Abduction revalidates flawed causality":

> In abductive reasoning, causes are inferred from results. Logically this is invalid, as one can only validly infer a state of affairs Q from a state of affairs P if P is temporally prior to Q; nevertheless abductive reasoning is very common in everyday and scientific reasoning. Lagerwerf suggests that abductive causality is a case of epistemic causality (in which conclusions are inferred from arguments) that goes back to real world causality:
>
> > (5) (Q) Greta was ill, because (P) she stayed at home.
>
> Being ill is a real world cause for a real world consequence 'staying at home'. In (5) the cause is inferred from the consequence. This then is a case of flawed causality. But Q is also a conclusion and P an argument. Since arguments are logically (if not temporally) prior to conclusions, the causality is revalidated.

Then, even though this is "an elegant treatment of abductive links" (Spooren, 2001, p. 138), Spooren wonders about "the extent to which Lagerwerf wants to equate epistemic causality with epistemic reasoning" (ibid.), and agrees with a statement in Lagerwerf (1998, p. 48) to the effect that: "Without abduction, epistemic interpretation is still possible" (Spooren, 2001, p. 139).

Scholars have discussed various modes of inference and considered their respective suitability as inference to the best explanation. For example, Harman himself considered in that respect *enumerative induction* (Harman, 1968). Another philosopher, Peter Lipton (2007), published 'Alien Abduction: Inference to the Best Explanation and the Management of Testimony'. His concern was with

> how we decide whether to believe what we are told. Inference to the Best Explanation, a popular general account of non-demonstrative reasoning, is applied to this task. The core idea of this application is that we believe what we are told when the truth of what we are told would figure in the best explanation of the fact that we were told it. We believe the fact uttered when it is part of the best explanation of the fact of utterance. Having provided some articulation of this account of testimonial inference, the paper goes on to consider whether the account is informative and whether it is plausible.[33]

---

[33] Lipton (2007), from the abstract.

2.2 Reasoning About a Charge and Explanations: Seminal Tools

Peter Lipton also published the book *Inference to the Best Explanation* (Lipton, 2004: revised, augmented edition):

> How do we go about weighing evidence, testing hypotheses, and making inferences? The model of 'inference to the best explanation' (IBE) — that we infer the hypothesis that would, if correct, provide the best explanation of the available evidence — offers a compelling account of inferences both in science and in ordinary life. Widely cited by epistemologists and philosophers of science, IBE has nonetheless remained little more than a slogan.[34]

And yet, computational research such as that conducted by Thagard, or by the Josephsons, is surely more than a slogan. It is something quite useful for modelling reasoning. In her own paper 'The Inference to the Best Explanation', Yemima Ben-Menahem (1990), a philosopher, remarked:

> In a situation in which several explanations compete, is the one that is better qua explanation also the one we should regard as the more likely to be true? Realists usually answer in the affirmative. They then go on to argue that since realism provides the best explanation for the success of science, realism can be inferred to. Nonrealists, on the other hand, answer the above question in the negative, thereby renouncing the inference to realism.[35]

Her own approach in that paper was (ibid.) to

> separate the two issues. In the first section it is argued that a rationale can be provided for the inference to the best explanation; in the second, that this rationale cannot justify an inference to realism. The defence of the inference rests on the claim that our standards of explanatory power are subject to critical examination, which, in turn, should be informed by empirical considerations. By means of a comparison of the realist's explanation for the success of science with that of conventionalism and instrumentalism it is then shown that realism does not offer a superior explanation and should not, therefore, be inferred to.

2.2.1.7 The von Bülow Trials

Thagard (2004) compares two models of causal inference: explanatory coherence in the ECHO tradition (which he prefers), and Bayesian networks,[36] applying both of them to the von Bülow trials. Claus von Bülow was tried for the episode in

---

[34] Lipton (2004), from the publisher's blurb.

[35] Ben-Menahem (1990), from the abstract.

[36] A Bayesian network is a directed acyclic graph (i.e., a graph without loops, and with nodes and arrows rather than direction-less edges), such that the nodes represent propositions or variables, the arcs represent the existence of direct causal influences between the linked propositions, and the strengths of these influences are quantified by conditional probabilities. Whereas in an *inference network* the arrow is from a node standing for evidence to a node standing for a hypothesis, in a Bayesian network instead the arrow is from the hypothesis to the evidence. In an inference network, an arrow represents a relation of support. In a Bayesian network, an arrow represents a causal influence, and the arrow is from a cause to its effect. "Bayesian Networks (BNs) are an efficient and comprehensible means of describing the joint probability distribution over many variables over their respective domains. The variables are created and assigned a meaning by the compositional modeller, and their probability distributions are calculated from the combined response of the influences that affect them." (Keppens et al., 2005a, section 2.1). The classic book on Bayesian networks is by Judea Pearl (1988), the scholar who introduced and developed that formalism during the 1980s.

December 1980, when his wealthy wife, Martha von Bülow (nicknamed Sunny), lapsed into a coma. The husband was accused of having tried to kill her by injecting her with insulin, and her coma being a result of this. In a trial by jury in 1982, the husband was found guilty of two counts of assault with intent to murder, but when he was tried on appeal in 1985, he was acquitted on both counts.

Thagard (2004) provided a formal analysis of jury decision making as a kind of causal evidence, this being a case study of those two trials. "In general, legal reasoning in trials such as those of Claus von Bülow's can be characterized as inference to the best overall causal story" (ibid., p. 231).[37] For the account of the trials, Thagard relied on a book by one of the defence lawyers at both trials, Alan Dershowitz, who argued there (Dershowitz, 1986, p. 37, quoted in Thagard, 2004, p. 232) that the prosecution's case in the first trial "was based heavily on hard scientific evidence, eyewitness testimony and compelling motives".

The victim's maid testified at the first trial that she had found a bag of the husband containing insulin in the month before the wife went into a coma. The victim's son from a previous marriage testified that he found that bag in the husband's closet, after the inception of the coma, and that the bag contained three hypodermic needles, one of which was the needle that had been used when the victim went into a coma. Scientific tests found on that needle a residue of insulin, and moreover the victim's blood, taken and tested after she was taken from hospital, showed a high insulin level. As excess insulin can induce a coma or even death, the accusation was that the husband had injected the victim with excess insulin, his intent being murder. But nobody had seen the husband make that injection.

At the first trial, the husband's mistress testified that she had demanded that he divorce his wife, i.e., the victim. Moreover, the husband's banker testified that the accused stood to gain a large inheritance if his wife died, but would receive little if he divorced her. So there appeared to be both pecuniary and romantic motives to the accused perpetrating the crime for which he was standing trial. At the second trial, evidence was presented that the victim's maid and the victim's son may not be saying the truth. At the first trial, a witness for the defence claimed that she had frequently given the victim exercise instruction, and that the victim had told her that insulin injection was a good way to avoid gaining weight. To the defence, this supported a hypothesis that the victim had injected herself with insulin, and that her coma was caused by this self-injection. But the credibility of the alleged instructor suffered from records of the exercise studio showing that she had actually instructed the victim not as often as she had claimed, and that there were no records of her teaching the victim at all during the year when the victim supposedly told her about insulin use. Thereforte, indirect evidence (from trstimony) against the husband was strong, and indirect evidence that would exonerate him was weak. The jury found him guilty, which is not surprising, given that state of affairs.

At the second trial, the defence had been able to use access it had obtained, to the notes made by a private investigator hired by the victim's son. Based on those notes, the victim's maid was shown not to have mentioned finding insulin

---

[37] See Section 2.2.1.6 above.

2.2 Reasoning About a Charge and Explanations: Seminal Tools

in the husband's bag until after the victim's coma had been identified as insulin related. It was suggested at the trial that the maid's terstimony was motivated by her dislike of the accused. The victim's son's testimony, too, was weakened, because a detective who had been with him when he found the husband's bag had seen no needles in the bag. Scientific experts for the defence cast doubt about the coma being insulin-induced. As to the needle with a residue of insulin on it, it was claimed by expert testimony that the insulin found on it may not have been there because of an injection. (Therefore, the defence no longer argued that the wife had injected herself, which at the first trial it had.) The husband's banker was not allowed to testify at the second trial about how much the husband stood to inherit. The defence at the second trial claimed that the victim's coma was likely to have been caused by her many health problem, by her taking many drugs, and by her failure to avoid eating ice cream sundae notwithstanding her having blood sugar problems.

2.2.1.8 Thagard's Treatment of the von Bülow Trials: Using ECHO and a Coherence Network, vs. Producing a Bayesian Network with JavaBayes

Thagard (2004, pp. 245–246) encoded the input for ECHO simulation of the first trial in 11 evidence propositions, other 11 propositions representing prosecution hypotheses, 3 propositions being defence hypotheses, one statement of contradiction, 10 statements being prosecution explanations, 7 statements (also being *explains* functions) being motives, 5 statements being defence explanations, and one statement of data.

Thagard (2004, pp. 247–249) encoded the input for ECHO simulation of the second trial in 13 evidence propositions, other 9 propositions representing prosecution hypotheses, 7 propositions representing defence hypotheses, 10 statements being prosecution explanations, 6 statements (also being *explains* functions) being motives, 9 statements being defence explanations, 2 statements of contradiction that also were part of the defence explanations, and one statement of data.

Thagard remarked (2004, p. 237):

> Note how ECHO naturally encodes the two competing causal stories about why Sunny went into a coma. The theory of explanatory coherence and the computational model of ECHO are highly compatible with the predominant psychological theory of jury decisions, according to which jurors choose between competing stories of what happens (Pennington & Hastie, 1992, 1993; see also Byrne, 1995).

Concerning the results of the simulation for both trials, Thagard stated the following (2004, p. 238):

> For the first trial, ECHO ends up accepting the hypothesis that Claus injected Sunny with insulin, but for the second trial ECHO ends up rejecting it. This result occurs regardless of whether the neural network or greedy algorithms are used to maximize constraint satisfaction. To simulate decision making in the first trial, the connectionist[38] algorithm

---

[38] "Artificial neural networks are often referred to as connectionist networks, and the paradigm of neural networks is often referred to as 'connectionism'. Some scientists are interested in

requires 188 cycles of updating activations before the network has settled, and the greedy algorithm requires around 16 flips to reach the same partition of propositions into accepted and rejected. The connectionist algorithms can easily handle much larger networks.

Thagard (2004, p. 239) raised the issue of subjectivity of the numerical values, which could be a criticism of his approach, and felt able to reject such criticism:

> How subjective is the analysis of two trials presented in the appendices [of his paper]? It may seem that ECHO simulations require many numerical values such as excitation, inhibition, and decay that depend on arbitrary decisions by the programmer. In fact, however, I use the same numerical values (e.g., .04 for excitation, −.06 for inhibition) in all ECHO runs, and sensitivity analyses have shown that the actual values do not much matter as long as excitation is greater than inhibition. More problematic is the specification of the "explains" relations which requires the programmer to understand the causal structure of the case. But the same understanding is required for simulations using Bayesian networks [which Thagard also discussed in the same paper]. Marking a proposition as "data" is not arbitrary: In the legal context, the data are the utterances made by witnesses that are observed by everyone in the room.

Thagard (2004) contrasted his ECHO simulation of the von Bülow trials, to a Bayesian network analysis of only the first trial, produced using a graphic software tool from Carnegie Mellon University, JavaBayes (Cozman, 2001). In the graph being a Bayesian network and produced on the screen, arrows indicate relations of probabilistic dependence, i.e., of conditional probability, and darker nodes are the ones observed to be true propositions. If there is an arrow from A to B, this represents the dependence of the probability of B on the probability of A.

This is also interpreted as a causal relation: the arrow from A to B indicates that A causally influences B. It is this interpretation of the arrows as causal relations that is used in the analysis of trials as Bayesian networks. Analysing the inferences in trials as Bayesian networks is typical of David Schum's work, such as in Kadane and Schum (1996). The connections in the Bayesian network are unidirectional, whereas the connections are bidirectional instead in the coherence network of propositions associated with Thagard's ECHO simulations.

Thagard (2004, pp. 240–241) criticised Bayesian network representations of trials, because of the need to estimate probabilities, for example: the need to give as input the estimated probability that what a given witness says is true, given that this witness says it. "Even more problematic was coming up with conditional probabilities in cases where there are two arrows coming into a node" (ibid., p. 240). Nevertheless, the Bayesian network simulating the jury at the first von Bülow trial found him guilty, like in the actual trial.

Thagard expressed his doubt about the Bayesian explanation juror reasoning at such trials as follows (ibid., p. 242):

> These doubts derive from what I shall call the *interpretation problem* and the *implementation problem*. The interpretation problem is that there is no plausible meaning for the probabilities used in the Bayesian simulation. The network [he showed] is unproblematic if

---

artificial neural networks as a tool in helping to understand the neural networks in our own brain. 'Connectionist' is sometimes used to emphasize that neural nets are being used for the purpose of computing with no concern for biological realism" (Callan, 1999, p. 223).

2.2 Reasoning About a Charge and Explanations: Seminal Tools

the arrows are interpreted as causal relations. [...] But Bayesian networks require also that the arrows have a probabilistic interpretation so that conditional probabilities can be specified [but Thagard] argue[d] that there is no satisfactory interpretation of the probabilities that would be needed for legal applications.

Of the two kinds of interpretations of probability, namely, frequency-type and belief-type, the former is not appropriate at all for judging a unique event about which the court is called to pass judgement. Proponents of Bayesian networks for analysing trials endorse belief-type probabilities. Thagard, like other critics of the probabilistic approach, found it to be problematic as a representation of how juries reason, because people's degrees of belief (abundant psychological evidence shows) do not conform to the calculus of probability. Therefore, Bayesian simulations of juries are not realistic.

One counterargument is that this is a defect of human adjudicators, and that it would be more rational if fact-finders (or human decision-making in everyday life) were educated enough to conform to the calculus of probabilities. That is to say, a *prescription* for fact-giving is given by supporters of probabilistic reasoning about legal narratives, whereas Thagard is rather interested in a *descriptive* simulation of human reasoning.

2.2.2 ALIBI, a Planner for Exoneration

2.2.2.1 1989: An *Annus Mirabilis*?

As mentioned earlier, Thagard published his first paper on ECHO in 1989. The year 1989 also saw the very first publication on the ALIBI project, led by Ephraim Nissan (Kuflik, Nissan, & Puni, 1989). Interestingly, and quite independently, that same year 1989 also saw the publication of Lutomski (1989), on reasoning with statistical evidence, for assisting an attorney. Lutomski's paper appeared in the *Proceedings of the Second International Conference of Artificial Intelligence and Law*, thus, in a forum specifically devoted to AI & Law, unlike Thagard's first paper on simulating jury decision-making by using ECHO, and unlike Nissan's first paper on ALIBI. It cannot be said that Lutomski had at the time a following within AI & Law, either.

Intriguingly, 1989 was also the year of the earliest report about the *MarshalPlan* project (Schum & Tillers, 1989), about which, see in Section 4.1.1 below. Moreover, Robert W. Goldsmith, who had been publishing already before about probabilistic models of legal evidence, and who in 1989 was affiliated with the Department of Applied Psychology of the University of Lund in Sweden, on that year outlined a rather preliminary sketch of the "overall plan of a computer program under development". In practice, Goldsmith's contribution was a procedure, which could be applied manually or with the assistance of a computer. We are going to say something about that design, based on Goldsmith (1989), in Section 4.1.2. That will be in the context of our discussion *procedural-support systems* (Section 4.1). Before turning to such tools, we are going to discuss argumentation in Chapter 3, and at various places in this book we are going also to discuss the controversy about probabilistic models.

2.2.2.2 Workings and Structure of ALIBI

In the rest of the present Section 2.2.2, we are going to focus on ALIBI. Apart from the paper on ALIBI that first appeared in press in 1989, my publications on ALIBI also included Fakher-Eldeen et al. (1993), Nissan and Rousseau (1997), Nissan and Dragoni (2000), Nissan and Martino (2004b, pp. 200–206). ALIBI is an AI planner which impersonates a person who is being accused. ALIBI receives as input a simple accusation, which includes some ascertained facts and interprets them as, say, burglary or robbery.

ALIBI decomposes the actions involved hierarchically, and separates the actions themselves from *deontic* (i.e., moral or legal) connotations: this way, e.g., stealing is interpreted as taking in given circumstances (somebody else's property, while the agent is unseen). See Fig. 2.2.2.2.1. Reasoning on effects is also carried out. An alternative plan is composed hierarchically, which claims exoneration or, in a version called ALIBI 3, pleads to a lesser computed liability.

"Processing has the program recursively decompose the actions in the input, into a tree[39] of actions, down to elementary, atomic actions. Moreover, actions are stripped of their deontic connotation. For example, 'stealing' is stripped down to 'taking', and it's up to the system to concoct such a plan where that act of taking fits in a way that is legitimate for the defendant. Generating the justification corresponds to a reconstitution of actions into a different tree. Then the terminal actions in the decomposition tree are differently reconstituted into alternative explanations that eliminate or minimize liability" (Nissan, 2000a).

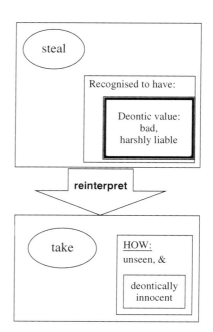

Fig. 2.2.2.2.1 *Steal* vs *take* in ALIBI

---

[39] A *tree* is such a graph, that any two nodes are connected by exactly one path.

2.2 Reasoning About a Charge and Explanations: Seminal Tools

Figure 2.2.2.2.2 shows the architecture of ALIBI, and how its modules invoke each other. Also see Fig. 2.2.2.2.3 for further detail. Figure 2.2.2.2.4 shows the basic conceptual progression of the control. Figure 2.2.2.2.5 shows the hierarchical decomposition of situated actions included in the accusation, their separation from deontic values, and then their recomposition into a different narrative, such that the

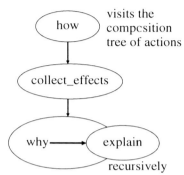

Fig. 2.2.2.2.2 ALIBI's architecture and control flow

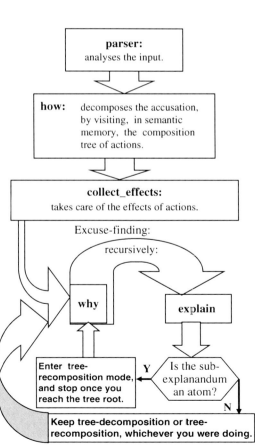

Fig. 2.2.2.2.3 The architecture and the control of ALIBI, in further detail

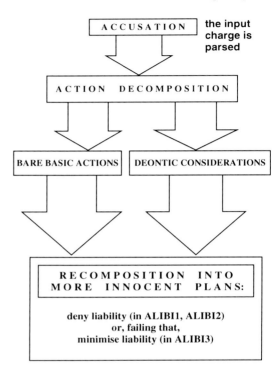

Fig. 2.2.2.2.4 Stages in how ALIBI operates: the process of justification

Fig. 2.2.2.2.5 *Actus reus* and *mens rea* separation in ALIBI. Hierarchical decomposition of imputed behaviour in a given episode, into constituent actions separate from deontic values; followed by recomposition into an alternative plan, i.e., a narrative that is claimed by the suspect to be the one fitting his intentions

2.2 Reasoning About a Charge and Explanations: Seminal Tools

actus reus is still there, or at any rate, the behaviour observed, per se is not challenged, and yet *mens rea* as imputed to the suspect in the input accusation is denied.

2.2.2.3 Examples of ALIBI's Output

"[I]n some instances the explanation or excuse the [suspect] caught red-handed would make is hilariously meagre in probatory terms. The latter, however, happened because the given situation was desperate, and ALIBI, while impersonating the suspect, was trying [so hard,] too hard to explain out the ascertained narrative elements by denying 'mens rea',[40] that the emplotment, however sensibly contrived, is unconvincing" (Nissan, 2000a).

For example, in one session the input accusation states that the accused broke the glass of a jeweller's display window, got inside, shot and wounded the jeweller, and then ran away carrying valuables with him. ALIBI states that "he" broke the glass accidentally, and that "he" got inside in order to leave a note with his coordinates. (If the accusation states that the accused opened, e.g., a drawer where money was held, or even the cash-register, then a possible pretext could be that he was looking for a pencil and paper, so he could leave his name and address.)

He was carrying a weapon in legitimate circumstances. He shot the jeweller accidentally. Or then, he may play the hero, and claim that he heard voices from which he reckoned that the jeweller was in danger, and then he got inside in order to help. Once the jeweller was wounded, the accused ran away in order to seek medical help, as he could not provide it himself. He took away the valuables in order to return them, because the wounded jeweller could not guard his own property (in fact, incapacitation is an effect of being wounded); the accused, while going out to seek medical help, would guard the goods in the meanwhile, on the owner's behalf.

While the first version of ALIBI used to take, as input, for example:

```
done(rob,diamonds_pack,jeweller-s_shop).
done(injure,sub-machine_gun,jeweller).
done(break,body,display_window).
done(sneak,display_window,jeweller-s_shop).
done(take,diamonds_pack,jeweller-s_shop).
```

the subsequent version, ALIBI2, accepts the equivalent English-like statement:

```
the defendant robbed the diamonds_pack from a
jewellers_shop.
he wounded the jeweller by a sub_machine_gun.
he broke the display_window with his body.
he sneaked into the jewellers_shop through
the display_window.
he took_away the diamonds_pack from the
jewellers_shop.
```

---

[40] *Mens rea* in relation to computerising criminal law was discussed by Bennun (1996).

The defendant is charged with having robbed a jeweller's shop, and carried away a pack of diamonds. He broke the display window, by throwing himself against it (a variant could be that he threw a stone at it). Then, he sneaked inside the shop through the broken glass. On seeing the jeweller, the defendant fired with a sub-machine gun and wounded the jeweller, and then took away the pack of diamonds.

Excuses are necessary for several details of this accusation. Let us start by the way the defendant entered the shop. First, he has the choice of claiming that

- either he broke the window intentionally,
- or it was an accident.

If he claims it was an accident, as he was pushed, so he fell, then it is sensible, perhaps, to have got in, in order to leave a note with one's address. That is, the defendant plays the righteous and law-abiding member of the public.

Otherwise, he may admit he broke the window on purpose, because inspired by heroic sentiments: he heard strange voices inside, so somebody needed help, or a crime had to be prevented, and the defendant got in as a saviour. See Fig. 2.2.2.3.1.

Now, an excuse is needed for the worst offence: the shooting of the jeweller. If accident there was, then the defendant may have shot on falling. Another possibility could have been if the defendant entered the shop in the dark: if he claims he got in to help, then he may have mistaken the jeweller for an evil-intentioned person unduly there.

Next, let us explain why the defendant took the jewels and run away. The wounded jeweller was helpless. He could not guard his property by himself, and he needed medical care. The defendant took the jewels in order to guard them, with the intention of giving them back. Medical care is a special kind of help that can be

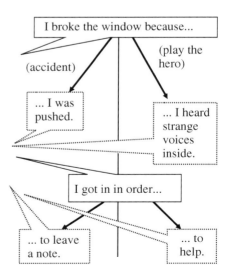

Fig. 2.2.2.3.1 Possible self-exoneration structure (part a)

2.2 Reasoning About a Charge and Explanations: Seminal Tools 59

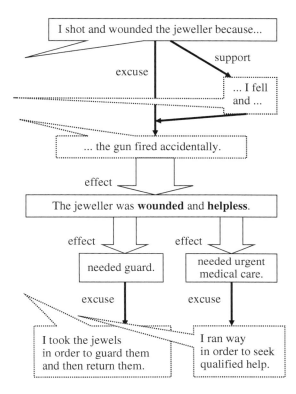

Fig. 2.2.2.3.2 Possible self-exoneration structure (part b)

given by qualified personnel: the defendant ran away to seek professional medical care. See Fig. 2.2.2.3.2.

Here is another accusation, which also was an input as early as the first version of ALIBI. In a session with ALIBI, involving armed threat at a bank teller, the accused claims forgetting about the weapon he was carrying (for some legitimate purpose unrelated to going to the bank) when entering the bank and facing the employee at the teller.

The defendant robbed a bank. He threatened the employee with a rifle (or with a knife instead), and snatched the money. An excuse is needed for the very fact of going around armed. ALIBI tries with this compound excuse: "I did not aim at the employee with the rifle." (Or, respectively: "with the knife.") And then, for the rifle: "I had the rifle because I went hunting." Or: "because I was on vacation from the army." (However, the police could easily check the latter.)[41] For a knife,

---

[41] Colwell et al. (2006) claimed: "In general, truth-tellers provide more detailed accounts than deceivers. They are also more likely to include the time and location, unique or unusual facts (e.g., the perpetrator limped), portions of the conversation that took place (e.g., I yelled "HELP"), and interactions between the perpetrator and themselves. Deceivers, on the other hand, may offer fewer details to reduce the chance of contradicting themselves when asked to repeat the story. They might also lack the knowledge or are unable to imagine/create plausible, complex descriptions. Deceivers

ALIBI proposes the following excuse: "I held the knife because I was carrying it to a grinder to have it sharpened."[42] And then: "The employee panicked and gave me the money."

ALIBI resorts to common-sense knowledge on the workings and the effects of threatening. See Fig. 2.2.2.3.3. Armed threat involves holding a weapon. It is even more flagrant if the victim is aimed at with that arm. The effect is having the victim understand he or she is in a dilemma: to prevent being harmed, the victim is expected to comply. A major effect of *threat* is *fear*, which can motivate an employee at the teller to hand out cash without further ascertaining the intentions of the defendant.

Several excuses are needed for armed threat and the acceptance of its effects, unless the defendant chooses to admit that he intended to threat the victim. The defendant did not try to dispel the fear of the employee, but he can claim he did not notice this emotional state in the victim (playing the absent-minded one, on this point, is in agreement with having forgotten about the arm he was carrying).[43] If the defendant had asked for a loan, then being offered money by the employee is not surprising.

---

rely on thoughts and logic to account for their actions within fabrications [...]. Since interrogators can investigate the fact's credibility, deceivers refrain from disclosing certain details that would reveal their lies. As mentioned earlier, truth-tellers customarily make spontaneous corrections to assure the accuracy of their story, while deceivers tend to give their accounts in chronological order, making their statements easier to detect."

ALIBI does not take into account the need for checking, e.g., such relevant temporal information as pertaining to the hunting season, or to having been inducted into the armed forces reserve. In 1991 in mid January, on the eve of the deadline of the Allied strike against Iraq and thus of Saddam's threat to attack Israeli cities with missiles possibly carrying nonconventional weapons, in Israeli cities people were in a hurry, sealing rooms and even baby cots against chemicals, so the sight of armed uniformed personnel queuing at a bank teller was clearly projected against the global situational backdrop – e.g., its being the eve of the first expected Scud missile strikes – as it was being interpreted by observers also queuing at the bank. I saw such a scene myself, at a bank in Beer-Sheva, and everybody was gloomy and as the impending attack that the civilian population would suffer was quite focal on people's mind (on the bus, a young mother was staring in a kind of disbelief or stupor at her toddler, as though this was to be the end of their lives), there were no suspicions that the uniformed, conspicuously armed personnel queuing at the bank would try to rob the bank. Which in fact they did not.

[42] Bear in mind that in New York City, it did happen that policemen shot dead a man carrying a knife in the street. They misunderstood his motives for carrying the knife. He was a Jewish slaughterer, and therefore had precise rules to follow about the standards of his knife, and actually a slaughterer needs to have the knife regularly checked by a rabbi, who would verify compliance. There also was an episode in Britain, when a man who was carrying the leg of a piece of furniture was shot dead by the police, who miinterpreted his intentions.

[43] Why did the person accused accept cash from the employee? An excuse for that could be that the accused misunderstood, and believed that he was entitled to receiving the money. Or then he may have been sort of a "distract professor", who for the very same reason did not realise that the employee was feeling under threat. But the circumstances are such, that we would find it hard to believe this. By contrast, there was no reason to conjecture ulterior motives, when I myself (then an undergraduate, in the late 1970s) and other students were leaving the classroom with our professor, and in the corridor he asked: "Where am I going?", and one of us students replied: "To your office".

2.2 Reasoning About a Charge and Explanations: Seminal Tools 61

Fig. 2.2.2.3.3 Common sense considerations about excuses for armed threat at the bank teller[44]

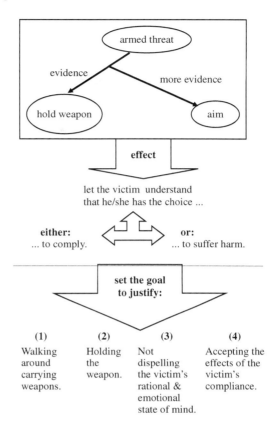

2.2.2.4 Knowledge Representation in ALIBI

The ALIBI1 version of ALIBI was developed in 1987–1988. It is a Prolog planner, synthesising alibis. The algorithm was already there in full: ALIBI1's input format was rudimentary, in Prolog propositions, but ALIBI1 analysed the actions involved, taking off their connotations (e.g., 'stealing' is reduced to 'taking' as in given circumstances); then, alternative explanations of the charged behaviour are put together and displayed. In the database of the system, semantic knowledge is stated about connotations (in terms of legality), component actions, and effects. Action verbs are decomposed into constitutive actions, hierarchically. As at run-time, compound actions are involved in the generation of an alibi, the planner core is recursively applied to semantic knowledge, and relates effects to actions, after having related

---

[44] Bear in mind that whereas in ALIBI we didn't develop a model of the emotions, in artificial intelligence the emotions are not infrequently being modelled, in systems from the 1990s and 2000s. Nissan (2009c) is a survey of such approaches. Cf. Nissan (2009d); Nissan, Cassinis, and Morelli (2008); and Cassinis, Morelli, and Nissan (2007).

actions to "atomic" constitutive actions. ALIBI1 was implemented by two of my *Expert Systems* and *Prolog* students, namely, Tsvi Kuflik and Gilad Puni.

In the ALIBI2 version of ALIBI, developed in 1989, semantics was reorganised, in a format inspired by Fillmore's *case-grammars* (Fillmore, 1968). A simple English parser was added, which analysed the sentences of a small textual file given as input. ALIBI2 was implemented by two students of my *Computational Linguistics* course, Roni Salfati and Yuval Shaul, by reusing code from ALIBI1.

The ALIBI3 version of ALIBI, developed in 1990, was implemented in Lisp as an undergraduate project under my supervision by Auni Spanioli. The most important thing about ALIBI3 is that instead of just excluding incriminating excuses, a mechanism was included that explicitly computes a score of liability for plans, or parts thereof, being generated.

Moreover, in 1990, SKILL was implemented in Prolog as an undergraduate project by Fadel Fakher-Eldeen under my supervision. In SKILL, justification was extended to areas other than for criminal behaviour. Skills in performing at some task were judged by SKILL according to common-sense knowledge about the task, about classes of performers (e.g., age-groups), and about the environment. An important aspect of SKILL is that it represents some socially widespread prejudices about skills explicitly; for example, there is a widespread expectation than women (but not men) should be able to cook.

In the ALIBI2 version of ALIBI, the following simple generative grammar was used for parsing; it could have been refined in a subsequent version, by allowing, for example, recursion in sentences (and, thus, compound sentences):

sentence	→	noun_phrase + verb_phrase
noun_phrase	→	preposition + noun_phrase
noun_phrase	→	determiner + mod_noun
noun_phrase	→	mod_noun
verb_phrase	→	verb + noun_phrase
verb_phrase	→	verb + adverb + noun_phrase
verb_phrase	→	verb + noun_phrase + adverb
mod_noun	→	noun
mod_noun	→	noun + noun_phrase
mod_noun	→	mod_adjective + mod_noun
mod_adjective	→	adjective
mod_adjective	→	adverb + mod_adjective

The preliminary syntactical analysis yields predicates that are used during the following phase, which, in turn, is meant to produce a formal description of actions, to be used by the process of action decomposition. The second phase of parsing involves semantics, and a representation based, more or less, on *deep case grammars* (Fillmore, 1968; cf. e.g. Harris, 1985).

We were aware of the fact that separating syntax and semantics in cascaded phases is not the best choice. Not only that: semantic analysis should be enabled to exploit common-sense knowledge stored in the knowledge-base that ALIBI already

2.2 Reasoning About a Charge and Explanations: Seminal Tools 63

exploits when looking for excuses. Knowledge – other than linguistic semantic knowledge – is episodic memory, and knowledge of usual (or likely) patterns of episodic knowledge.

In the ALIBI2 prototype, we dealt with syntax separately, as we had been trying to modularise as much as possible in the first instance, so we could spot more clearly elements needed in the architecture at the technically specific level: heuristics of justification. (By *heuristics*, we mean *rules of thumb*.) In due process, it should have been possible, we reckoned, to better realise which modules should be closely integrated.

We allow specific attributes that are particular kinds of deep cases; that way, for example, *target* is a particular case of *location*. For the action of throwing a stone on the glass, as stated in the input accusation, analysis yielded the following, as an element in episodic memory:

```
action:   throw
actor:    defendant
object:   stone
source:   defendant (by default, it's the defendant's hand)
target:   glass
```

The structure of the representation, for this given instance, is a nested list:

```
[ [ throw,        action ],
  [ defendant,    actor  ],
  [ object,       stone  ],
  [ target,       glass ] ]
```

As to the source of the motion of the stone thrown, this is, plausibly, the actor, and there is no need to include this as data in episodic memory, as it belongs in semantic memory on the act of throwing.

Bear in mind that in subtle ways, common sense tends to confuse facts and indictment. In human memory, incoming information may pollute the memories previously held. Also in natural-language processing, in Dyer's BORIS multi-paragraph story automated understander (Dyer, 1983a) – it is discussed in Section 5.2.9 below – there was a rather similar effect by which by querying BORIS and in so doing stating that given facts had taken place, BORIS could be tricked into incorporating them in its episodic memory, thus tacitly accepting that they took place.[45]

---

[45] The subjectiveness of perception in eyewitness reports has been dealt with, for example, by Cesare Musatti (1931) in Italy. Elizabeth Loftus (already in Loftus, 1975, 1979) has observed that leading questions cause eyewitnesses to unwittingly complete their recollections by reconstruction; in Boris, a question-answering program for the analysis of narratives, a phenomenon was noticed that its developer, Dyer, first considered to be a bug, but then recognised that it is valuable, as it

For the same action of stone throwing just discussed in relation to ALIBI, it would have been possible to derive the following representation, according to knowledge on the usual pragmatics of throwing: focus is on the presumed target (it is already a conjecture), while the stone would be considered as merely an instrument, instead of the object, as the case is literally, at the surface level of verbal description:

```
[ [ PROPEL,      action ],
  [ defendant,   actor  ],
  [ objective,   glass  ],
  [ instrument,  stone  ] ]
```

We recognised that ALIBI should avoid being tricked into such a representation, as it embeds a hidden assumption that is detrimental to the interests of the suspects: it predefines the suspect's intentions.

Values of attributes should not be restricted to names or nominal compounds: they may be internally defined symbols, which point to instances individuated (stone0 is the first instance of stone met), or to the internal representation of phrases or sentences. This is necessary in order to account for semantic compositionality. For example, in order to indicate the relative temporal order between actions, the temporal case could have as value a pointer to another elementary episode.

The semantic knowledge stored in ALIBI includes a representation of the structure of objects. Let us consider, for example, an accusation we have already seen earlier, and which has the defendant hitting the glass with a stone, thus causing the display window to be broken, which in turn allowed the defendant to get in.

ALIBI "knows" that in a display window, there is a glass, and it relates the two concepts, when they occur in the accusation. The defendant may have been stated to have hit a part (the glass), and ALIBI would understand that the whole (the display window) was broken, and vice versa.

The following predicate employs *PROPEL*, one of the primitive acts of Roger Schank's *conceptual dependency theory*,[46] as a general concept, and, according to the specific action imputed or claimed, select a suitable verb, and construct appropriate phrases – with *deep-case* arguments inserted – to accompany it (the coding here is like in the Prolog logic programming language):

select_PROPEL_act(hit, What) :- done(hit, _ , What).
select_PROPEL_act(threw, Upon_what) :- done(throw, _ ,Upon_what).

---

simulates the Loftus effect on recollections: episodic memory modifications occur during question answering (Dyer, 1983a, in subsections 1.5, 5.5, 12.1, 12.2).

[46] See Sections 5.2.8 and 5.2.9 in this book, and see e.g. Schank (1972), Schank & Riesbeck (1981), Dyer (1983a).

2.2 Reasoning About a Charge and Explanations: Seminal Tools

that is to say: "Select the verb *hit* or *threw* according to the accusation stressing one action or the other." Moreover:

```
select_PROPEL_act(threw, Target_of_PROPEL) :-
    done(throw, _ , Upon_what),
    ( is_part_of(Upon_what, Target_of_PROPEL) ;
      is_part_of(Target_of_PROPEL, Upon_what)   ).
```

that is "A broader or a narrower concept may have been stated as being the target of the PROPEL act: a part of the whole may be hit implying that the whole was hit, or, vice versa, the whole may have been stated as being the target, whereas it is a particular component that was actually hit."

ALIBI "understands" as well the chain of enablements: removing an obstacle that guarded property, enables access to the property. Both the de/composition of actions, and the set of effects of actions, constitute an AND/OR tree, in our representation. An AND/OR tree is a simple data structure from computer science (and graph theory), such that in the various generations (i.e., levels) of the hierarchy (this is what *tree* means), a node requires subsets of its children nodes to co-occur (the graph edges reaching for them are united then by an arc, which imposes the AND condition), otherwise they can be alternative to each other (this is the OR condition). Figure 2.2.2.4.1 shows an example of AND/OR tree.

Let us go back to ALIBI. Predicates that, in semantic memory, state the constitution of compound actions, invoke effects as well. An example follows, drawn from Kuflik et al. (1989, section 4), of a rule coded in Prolog, and which describes the compound action of *threatening by means of a gun*:

```
compound_action(threaten, [aim, hold])  :-
    done(threaten,X,Threatened_Victim),
    is_a(X,gun),
    asserta(has_as_effect(frightened)),
```

and so forth. It is rendered, in English, by the statement[47]:

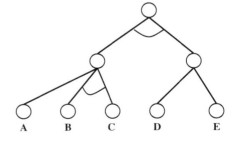

Fig. 2.2.2.4.1 An example of AND/OR tree. It identifies the sets {A, D}, {A, E}, {B, C, D}, {B, C, E}. This is because B and C must co-occur, and so do both first-generation branches

A   B   C   D   E

---

[47] Within studies of the *pragmatics of communication*, Nicoloff (1989) has discussed *threats*. By contrast, Joel D. Hamkins and Benedikt Löwe (2008) have introduced a *modal logic of forcing*. In a study in psychology, Kassin and McNall (1991) discussed promises and threats in police interrogations, by pragmatic implication.

"*threaten* is a compound action that has to be assumed as constituted by the sequence of actions *aim* and *hold*, **if** the accusation ascribes to the defendant, the defendant's having threatened the victim by using a gun as an instrument. **If** this is the case indeed, **then** define, as being an **effect**, a predicate

> has_as_effect(frightened).

where frightened is assumed to refer to the victim. (And so forth.)"

Then, the predicate has_as_effect will appear among the conditions belonging to the antecedent of at least one rule whose left part is the predicate explain with a suitable value as argument.

For example, stemming from an ascertained or claimed situation where threatening led to the victim being frightened, one possible heuristic for devising excuses in such a situation is expressed by:

> asserta(goal(gave_in_panic, _ , Threatened_Victim)).

which means "Define, as a goal to be currently pursued, the generation of an excuse claiming that the victim, in panic, gave the defendant property he is accused of having obtained unlawfully (robbed, as the situation requires the presence of the possessor)."

It is invoked in the antecedent of a rule, after the condition

> has_as_effect(frightened).

which is itself included in the same antecedent. Note that in Prolog, an underline character _ stands for an unspecified argument.

Besides, an effect predicate states the effects:

- help_needed (for the victim), and
- guard_needed (for property)

which follow the effect frightened:

```
effect(frightened, [help_needed,
                    guard_needed] ).
```

The antecedent of explain predicates especially includes predicates of three kinds:

- done (a condition requiring that a certain kind of action be included in the accusation),
- has_an_effect (which selects one of the effects of such an action), and
- goal (which invokes the generation of an excuse according to a given heuristic that is suited for the particular situation).

2.2 Reasoning About a Charge and Explanations: Seminal Tools   67

For example, the following invokes, for the predicate `explain(aim)`, the generation of two alternative excuses, claiming that the defendant aimed at the victim accidentally, because he had fallen through the way of access (say, a broken display-window), or denying that the defendant ever aimed at the victim:

```
explain(aim) :- done(threaten,X,Y),
                has_as_effect(fall_through),
                goal(accidentally_aim,X,Y).

explain(aim) :- done(threaten,X,Y),
                goal(not_aim,X,Y).
```

In case shooting, not just aiming, is part of the accusation, then a modified heuristic is invoked for the predicate `explain(shoot)`.

Explanations are developed separately for the various actions imputed, but, if this is relevant, with knowledge of other actions having occurred, or having to be assumed. From the viewpoint of the discipline of *systems & control*, we could say that objective testimony belongs to the space of *observability*, and constitutes the basis of both the imputation and of possible excuses, which all exploit degrees of freedom in state estimation.

Whereas ALIBI provides alternative interpretations for the ascertained facts underlying the charge, ALIBI did not tackle the subjectiveness of perception or imperfect recollection on the part of witnesses.

Complications such as *complicity* were not accounted for, in the versions of ALIBI that were implemented, but then Nissan and Rousseau (1997) discussed how to combine the capabilities of a tool like ALIBI, with capabilities of a virtual theatre of characters, a system whose agents are characters in a story. See Section 2.2.2.7 below.

Moreover, bear in mind that the parties in a trial may explain differently not only the narrative upon which a charge of an offence revolves, i.e., alleged and charged behaviour of the defendant at a criminal case, but they may differ on any relevant detail militating towards their different legal narratives. For example, consider the following explanation, given by a man, Warder Cresson, whose wife and son had him declared a lunatic in court in Philadelphia,[48] but then this was overturned

---

[48] Incidentally, the evolution of commitment law in the nineteenth century has been discussed by Appelbaum and Kemp (1982). "The generally accepted interpretation of the evolution of commitment law in the nineteenth century is challenged by means of an historical investigation of the law's development in a single state – Pennsylvania." (ibid., from the abstract). That is precisely the U.S. state relevant for Cresson. The abstract of Appelbaum and Kemp (1982) points out: "Rather than an abrupt switch from relaxed commitment procedures to a system of stringent safeguards, which most historical accounts of the period describe, examination reveals that Pennsylvania law underwent a slow accretion of procedural protections, with the essential discretionary role of families, friends, and physicians left undisturbed. The implications for current policy of this challenge to the traditional account are discussed".

on appeal in May 1851. The trial revolved upon his religious conversion, but his opponents had also sought to undermine his appearance of sanity with an anecdote, according to which he once drove his sleight on bare ground, there being no snow[49]:

> To show how far persons can be influenced by every ridiculous and unjust means, in such cases of pretended Lunacy, to carry out their point, I will here mention one. It was asserted by my family "That I brought half a barrel of water in the bottom of my sleigh, all the way from the State of New York, upon bare ground." Now, is this possible to be true? for the very jumping of the sleigh would dash it all out, and all over me, before I drove three hours,

---

[49] In his 1852 book *The Key of David* (which is now available online), Cresson pointed out in an appendix this argument to show his lunacy that the prosecution made in the case brought by his wife. In Appendix F (now accessible at http://www.jewish-history.com/cresson/cresson42.html) Cresson also pointed out that his son's testimony against him, concerning his joining the Shakers, was about events that took place when the son was only a few weeks old. "What a most remarkable *Precocious* Boy this, in his *malignity* to, and *persecution* of his *own father.*"

In Nissan (2010e), I discussed the phenomenon of cultural traits or ethnic or religious identities being sometimes medicalised, i.e., considered in medical terms. This was not infrequent in the 19th and early 20th century (cf. Nissan & Shemesh, 2010). But some disliked religion was only one context for mental flaws to be ascribed (Mark Twain summed it up nicely: "If the man doesn't believe in what we do, we say he is a crank, and that settles it. I mean, it does nowadays, because now we can't burn him"). Another context involved supposedly inferior races or cultures. For example, in the second half of the 19th century, just as both women and Jews were seeking emancipation, pseudo-scientific claims would be made about both groups's inferiority and predisposition for madness: "Jews, like women, possessed a basic biological predisposition to specific forms of mental illness. Thus, like women, who were also making specific political demands on the privileged group at the same moment in history, Jews could be dismissed as unworthy of becoming part of the privileged group because of their aberration." (Gilman, 1984, p. 157). "Jews, like women, possessed a basic biological predisposition to specific forms of mental illness. Thus, like women, who were also making specific political demands on the privileged group at the same moment in history, Jews could be dismissed as unworthy of becoming part of the privileged group because of their aberration" (ibid.). It was also claimed that Black people either freed or seeking freedom, while not ones accepting slavery, were mad (ibid.).

In one section of Nissan (2010e), I considered a trial for lunacy from Philadelphia. Warder Cresson (1798–1860) was born to a Quaker family, and grew up to become a farmer and preacher in the area of his native Philadelphia, where he eventually married and had six children (see on him Fox, 1971). While a young man, he experimented with millenarist groups. From the late 1820s, he published religious tracts. In 1844, he published a visionary tract about Jerusalem, and on that same year, he went there on pilgrimage. While in Jerusalem, his views changed, and he converted to Judaism. Bear in mind that by the mid 19th century, Jerusalem already had a clear Jewish majority, and this population was religious and economically sustainable because of alms from abroad. The standard discourse of Jerusalemite Judaism, by which Cresson let himself be convinced, was complex and cogent by its inner logic. This was something not visible in Cresson's original social environment in Philadelphia.

It is understandable that to a religious Protestant family in 1848, seeing a husband and father come back a Jew, it seemed to be a good explanation that he had lost his reason – apart from their goals of controlling his assets. To his family, he forfeited the salvation of his soul, by adopting an identity that was utterly unappealing – and ostensibly that of a defeated, despised creed and nation. At the same time, there was widespread religious effervescence among Protestant denominations in the Early Republic, and it clearly was a sign of civil maturity for the United States of America that a court of law (albeit not the lower court) resisted the proposition that choosing Judaism of all denominational options was proof of lunacy.

2.2 Reasoning About a Charge and Explanations: Seminal Tools

even if I had not taken the trouble just to take hold of the side-stays of the sleigh and turn it all out in a few seconds.

The truth is, in the winter of 1831, having made up my mind to come on from New Lebanon, State of New York, to my family near Philadelphia, and the snow being very deep, and the North River having been frozen all the way up for weeks and weeks; having two excellent match-horses and a sleigh, and finding, by reading the papers, that the sleighing was very good all the way on the Philadelphia, I concluded, as I could not come in my carriage, I would come in my sleigh, a distance of about 350 miles, which I completed in five and a half days; but the last day, when reaching as far as Trenton, it began to thaw, and, by the time I reached Philadelphia, the snow was partly gone in the middle of the turnpike, (as is generally the case,) although it was good on the sideroads. I reached my family, residing in Byberry, about half after ten o'clock upon the night of the sixth day, and, as is common, the thaw was succeeded by a rain during the night, which left two or three quarts of water in the bottom of my sleigh. So much for the "half a barrel of water from the State of New York that I brought in the bottom of my sleigh upon bare ground," just like the **snow-bank** tale in the Morgan Hinchman case, to try to make him out **Insane**.

This was part of a *cause célèbre* in antebellum America.[50]

2.2.2.5 An Illustration of the Conceptual Factors Involved in Common Sense About the Jeweller's Example

Figures 2.2.2.5.1 and 2.2.2.5.2 illustrate factors involved when a person hits the display window of a jeweller's, if the reason given is, say, killing a fly. That same person (like anybody else) is supposed to know that glass is fragile, that it is costly, and that it protects property, and as in comparison killing a fly is a trivial goal, that reason is not credible.

Let us discuss the rather complex Fig. 2.2.2.5.2, part by part. First of all, consider Fig. 2.2.2.5.3, which includes such items of common sense as a display window being part of a shop (within knowledge about shops), glass being part of a display window, glass being fragile, the likelihood being high that if something fragile is hit, then it would be broken.

---

[50] When Cresson returned to Philadelphia, in order to settle his matters before going back to Jerusalem, he was involved in local Jewish life, regularly attended service at the Mikve Israel synagogue, and continued (as he was already doing from Jerusalem as early as 1844) to write for Isaac Leeser's magazine *The Occident*. His wife, Elizabeth Townsend, and his son Jacob applied to the court and obtained a commission in lunacy. This decision of the lower court was reversed in a trial that became a *cause célèbre*, with eminent counsel retained by both parties, and much attention from the press. The hearing extended over six days in May, 1851, and nearly one hundred witnesses were called. Upon his return to Jerusalem, Cresson married a Sephardic Jewish woman, Rachel Moleano, he used to dress as a Jerusalemite Sephardic Jew, and the community he joined honoured him so much that his funeral in 1860 was with honors befitting a prominent rabbi. It must be said that prior to his conversion, Cresson was very close to two prominent rabbis in Jerusalem, but when he converted in 1848, this took place once opposition was overcome, from the *beth din* (rabbinic court) and the chief rabbi, Abraham Chai Gagin. This was because of a general reluctance to proselitise was (and is) accompanied by wariness lest, if a request to be converted is fulfilled, the convert would not be up to his or her new duties.

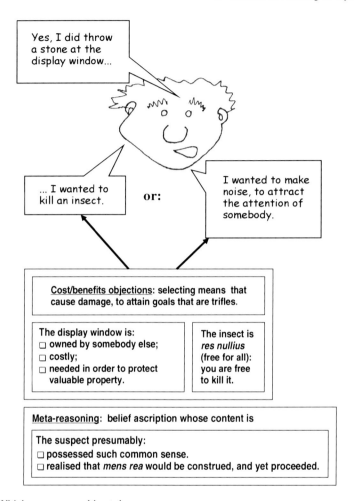

Fig. 2.2.2.5.1 Which excuses would not do

Moreover, there is rudimentary knowledge about shops, in that a shop requires security: a shop requires monitored access to merchandise stored in the shop. It is a requirement for the shop's security that neither doors, nor the display window be broken. This, too, is shown in Fig. 2.2.2.5.3. A more formal representation of the same is found in Fig. 2.2.2.5.4.

As shown in Fig. 2.2.2.5.5, adult persons who are "normal" (and we assume by default that the suspect is such a person) are socially competent enough, to possess such items (which we call α in the figure) of common sense about glass, display windows, shops, and shop security. Items of common sense about glass, display windows, shops, and shop security. Besides, Fig. 2.2.2.5.5 also shows that "normal" adults, including the suspect, also possess item β of common sense, namely:

2.2 Reasoning About a Charge and Explanations: Seminal Tools 71

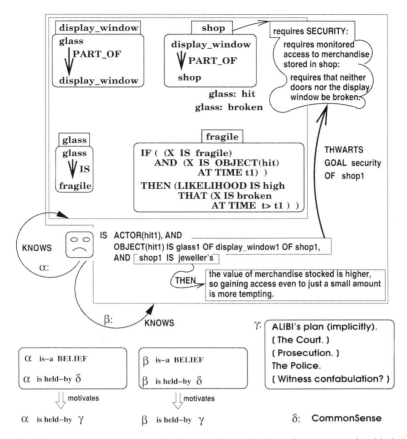

Fig. 2.2.2.5.2 Common sense involved in interpreting a situation where a person has hit the glass of a jeweller's display window. A set of figures equivalent to the present one is given in Figs. 2.2.2.5.3 to 2.2.2.5.6, where the sense intended unfolds step by step. The bottom of this figure corresponds to Fig. 2.2.2.5.6

- that he or she, the suspect, is the `actor` of hitting episode `hit1`,
- that the object being hit was the glass of the given display window of the given shop, and
- that this particular shop is a jeweller's, and that therefore the value of the merchandise stored is higher than at your average shop, so gaining access to even just a small amount is more tempting.

Figure 2.2.2.5.6 contains further details from Fig. 2.2.2.5.2, namely:

- α and β are beliefs,
- α and β are held by δ (i.e., by common sense),
- the previous two items motivate α and β being held by γ

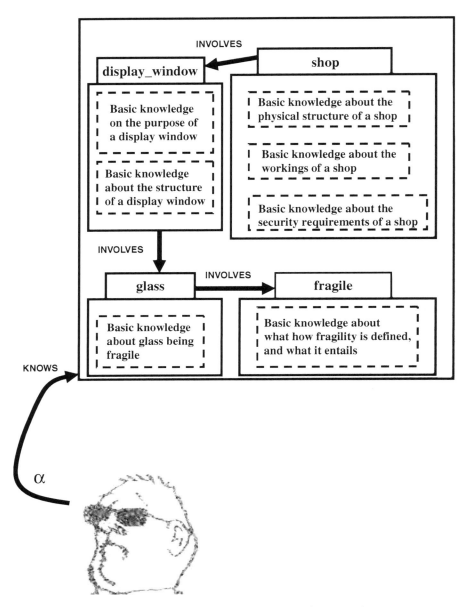

Fig. 2.2.2.5.3 Any competent person, including the suspect, can be expected to possess common sense about the concept *shop*, and in particular about how a shop works, how it is physically made, and the security requirements of a shop; about the concept *display window*, and its containing glass; about the concept *glass*, and its being fragile; and about the concept *fragile* (without the philosophical intricacies that empiricist philosophers recognise to the *disposition* of being fragile)

2.2 Reasoning About a Charge and Explanations: Seminal Tools

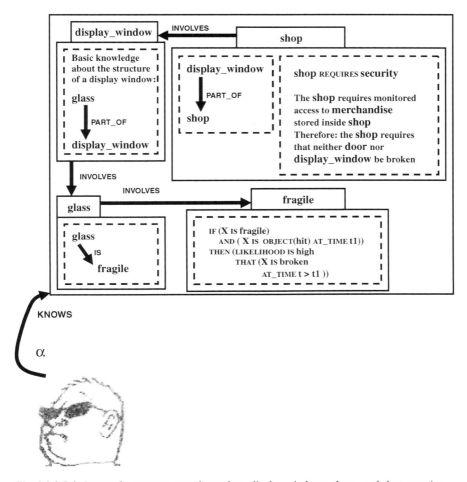

Fig. 2.2.2.5.4 Items of common sense about glass, display windows, shops, and shop security

- γ comprises ALIBI's plan, the police, and if this applies, also the court and the prosecution, as well as the witnesses (which in turn may involve witness confabulation, something undesirable for the veracity of testimony).[51]

---

[51] *Confabulation* in depositions occur when a witness is inferring, rather than merely reporting. This may be an effect of witnesses having discussed their recollections, which has modified what they later think they remember. Witnesses must report what they perceived, not what they inferred. In particular, if it was two eyewitnesses who saw the same event and discussed it, this may influence what they later claim to remember; this is sometimes referred to as *memory conformity*. Concerning the latter, see, e.g., Memon and Wright (1999), Gabbert, Memon, and Allan (2003), Gabbert, Memon, Allan, and Wright (2004), Luus and Wells (1994), Meade and Roediger (2002), Meudell, Hitch, and Boyle (1995), Principe and Ceci (2002), Skagerberg (2007).

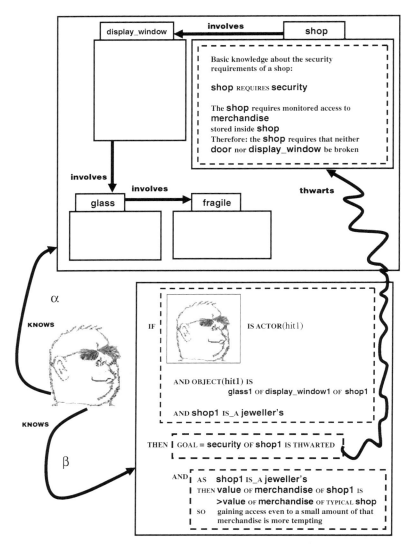

Fig. 2.2.2.5.5 The suspect presumably possesses common sense about display windows and shop security. In particular, the suspect is expected to know that if he hits the glass of the display window of a shop, this will thwart the security goal of that shop, and moreover, that if the shop is a jeweller's, then gaining access to even a small amount of the merchandise is tempting more than with other kinds of shops, because the value of the merchandise at a jeweller's is higher

2.2 Reasoning About a Charge and Explanations: Seminal Tools 75

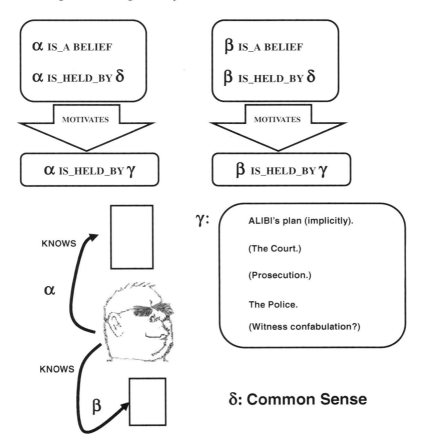

Fig. 2.2.2.5.6 Who holds which beliefs which are themselves items of commonsense?

2.2.2.6 An Afterlife of Some ALIBI Sessions

It is not only common sense that ALIBI relies upon. Prototypical behaviour is also affected, when people reason about it, by tropes. This may partly explain why ALIBI's sessions had an afterlife, so to speak. Especially ones that share something with folklore. Let us see how.

Interestingly, during several years following public lectures (including to non-specialists) the present author gave about ALIBI, single-panel gag cartoons appeared in an Italian weekly, that either independently developed, or otherwise echoed the notion of a computer program that invents excuses; or, then, such cartoons in which either a suspect criminal or his lawyer makes excuses that are not very credible because of the damning circumstances.

If the evidence is damning, the accused's trying hard to explain it out by taking it apart into its constituent components may be funny, because of the evident effort invested in producing an explanation that falls short of being convincing. On occasion, this happens with the output of ALIBI. The following passage is quoted here from Nissan (1996):

> This [quotation] is concerned with the mutants of items from the output of ALIBI [...] In folklore studies, it is being realized that assuming an ubiquitous progression from oral storytelling to written narrative is oversimplistic. As it turns out, some narratives have switched instead from literacy to oralcy. The following bears witness to a recession presumably from oral deliveries about ALIBI, through oralcy, into popular written/graphic media. The trigger may have been a talk I gave in Urbino, in May 1993, to a heterogeneous Italian audience. [Unless it was a talk given in 1990 at the Milan Technical University.] The sample set of inputs and outputs I had devised for ALIBI, has seemingly receded to oral jokes, reappearing in written form, as jokes or cartoons (and no mention of computing), in Italy's leading crosswords and trivia magazine. I had sporadic access to issues of Milan's *La Settimana Enigmistica*, from late 1994 and early 1995. Certain items in a few of them are relevant. [...] The Urbino lecture is the likeliest channel for the reappearance of at least two of the examples — respectively as a cartoon, and as a textual joke with a variant (also from the lecture) transposed into a cartoon. [...] The story is unmistakable:
>
>> "In court, the defendant – an ex-con – explains to the judge: 'It's quite false, that on the night of February 18 I plundered that shop! I just unwittingly knocked against the shop-window. the door opened, and I got inside to leave my name and address. If I was surprised by a cop with my hands inside the counter, it's just because I was looking for paper and pen, to write down my data'." [... §46162 in "Spigolature", *La Settimana Enigmistica*, year 64, no. 3276(1) (Milan, 7 Jan. 1995): p. 12.] This version from the magazine exhibits a few added or slightly modified details, with respect to the relevant example from ALIBI. [...]

Variants drawn out of the same pretext generated by ALIBI – to the effect that the defendant claims he fell on the jeweller's window because he was pushed – appeared in a one-panel gag cartoon in *La Settimana Enigmistica*, year 63, no. 3266 (29 Oct. 1994), p. 10. The moon shines in the dark. A grim-faced policeman, holding a cudgel, stands in front of two stereotyped underworld characters. These stand sheepishly, one in front and one on the side of a jeweller's broken window glass. The second offender fingers his companion, and says (as common sense has us ascribe to him the caption): "It's his fault: he pushed me." (Nissan, 1996).[52] See Fig. 2.2.2.6.1.

The cartoon in Fig. 2.2.2.6.2, instead, corresponds to no example from ALIBI, but it may have originated as a novel item in the same family of jokes. This one was published towards the end of October 1994 (*La Settimana Enigmistica*, year 63, no. 3266, 29 Oct. 1994, p. 10), 2 weeks before the issue in which the cartoon shown

---

[52] A distinction is to be made between jokes about self-exoneration from crime that do resemble indeed some output from ALIBI, in that they try to explain out some ascertained facts from the charge either innocently, or in not as damning a manner, and jokes that invoke extenuating circumstances. A well-known joke of the latter kind is that of the son who kills his parents, and then expects mercy in court because he is an orphan. Another such joke, from the United States (Shebelsky, 1991), is about a defence lawyer who points out to the judge that his client was characterised as an incorrigible bank robber, without a single socially redeeming feature. The lawyer claims that he intends to disprove that. The judge asks how. The lawyer replies that it's by proving beyond a shadow of doubt that the note his client handed the teller was on recycled paper. What stands out in the latter joke is that the defendant is apparently pleading guilty, but is seeking extenuating circumstances. At any rate, the defendant admits he handed the teller a threatening note.

2.2 Reasoning About a Charge and Explanations: Seminal Tools 77

Fig. 2.2.2.6.1 "It's his fault: he pushed me."

— E' colpa sua: mi ha dato una spinta.

Fig. 2.2.2.6.2 "I was unable to read the price of that watch, through the glass: it was steamed up."

— Non riuscivo a leggerlo, il prezzo di quell'orologio, attraverso il vetro appannato!

in Fig. 2.2.2.6.1 appeared. The following is an English translation of the caption in Fig. 2.2.2.6.2: "I was unable to read the price of that watch, through the glass: it was steamed up."

And then again, a different output from ALIBI reappeared as a cartoon in *La Settimana Enigmistica* (year 64, no. 3286, 18 March 1995, p. 8); it shows a lawyer, smiling sheepishly to the judge, and pleading the case of the ultimate ex-con cartoon character standing by, bald and unshaven. A halo on his head, the ex-con's eyes stare upwards, cunningly. The caption goes: "It's all a mistake, Your Honor! My client had no intention to rob the bank: he just wanted to get a loan, and showed his submachine gun in order to pawn it..." (Nissan, 1996). See Fig. 2.2.2.6.3.

Fig. 2.2.2.6.3 "It's all a mistake, Your Honor! My client had no intention to rob the bank: he just wanted to get a loan, and showed his submachine gun in order to pawn it..."

— C'è stato un malinteso, signor giudice! Il mio cliente non intendeva affatto rapinare la banca: voleva semplicemente un prestito e mostrava il mitra come pegno...

Fig. 2.2.2.6.4 "I am preparing on the computer a program of various excuses, so I could use them when you'll be mad at me". Was this cartoon inspired by rumours about ALIBI's existence? (The Italian caption was: "Sto preparando al computer un programma di scuse varie da usare nel momento in cui sarai arrabbiata con me.")

At the long last, in the issue of the weekly dated 23 August 1997 (year 66, no. 3413, p. 42), a cartoon appeared that arguably depicts the very notion that a computer program such as ALIBI exists. Refer to Fig. 2.2.2.6.4. In the caption, the man tells his wife: "I am preparing on the computer a program of various excuses, so I could use them when you'll be mad at me".

2.2 Reasoning About a Charge and Explanations: Seminal Tools

Apparently, however, this resulted from a simplification of the idea embodied in ALIBI, as the program in the cartoon may just be a trivial list of ready-made excuses, to be selected according to some rather simple input conditions. (It's a little bit like the supposedly smart politician who, asked by a broadcaster why an ongoing military operation was named "Grapes of Wrath", blurted out: "I don't know. The computer made it up".)

It must be said that some time later on, the same weekly published a cartoon – by the same cartoonist and with the same characters – showing a husband telling his wife he is developing a *database* of excuses; i.e., just a collection of ready-made pretexts. This much diminishes the task which, in contrast, ALIBI carried out. Perhaps this is how somebody, about to make use of the idea of such a program, made sense of it, whether or not he or she believed that such software actually existed.

If one explains out something inconvenient by providing a narrative account that happens to occur in jokes about making excuses, then one can expect to have a hard time sounding convincing. It may be that pretexts made up by ALIBI were successful as jokes, because they appear to be variants of the international tale type 1624, described as follows by the folktale scholar Hans-Jörg Uther (2004, Vol. 2, p. 335):

> *Thief's Excuse: The Big Wind.* A man ([or in particular a] Gypsy) is caught stealing vegetables from a garden. He claims that the wind carried him over the fence and also uprooted the vegetables. When he is asked how the vegetables got into his sack, the thief says he was wondering about that himself.

In his classification of international tale types from folklore, Uther (ibid.) lists Latvian, Spanish, Flemish, German, Swiss, Hungarian, Serbian, Rumanian, Bulgarian, Greek, Byelorussian, Jewish, Gypsy, Kurdish, Armenian, and Iranian variants.

2.2.2.7 Extension with the *Dramatis Personae* Approach

Complicitous agency is a particular kind of collaborative plans. It can possibly be dealt with in terms of the economic concept of *incentive contracting*, that has received attention in AI (Kraus, 1996).[53] Delegating in a society of agents is discussed in Castelfranchi and Falcone (1998; cf. 2010, a book whose focus is on trust, including and especially in a computational modelling framework).

---

[53] *Subcontracting* in a *multiagent system* is the subject of Grant, Kraus, and Perlis (2005). "We present a formalism for representing the formation of intentions by agents engaged in cooperative activity. We use a syntactic approach presenting a formal logical calculus that can be regarded as a meta-logic that describes the reasoning and activities of the agents. Our central focus is on the evolving intentions of agents over time, and the conditions under which an agent can adopt and maintain an intention. In particular, the reasoning time and the time taken to subcontract are modeled explicitly in the logic" (ibid., p. 163).

It can be said that a *multiagent system* architecture[54] is conceivably suitable for a society of characters who carry out their respective behaviour within a narrative framework, with a character corresponding to an agent in the architecture; it is so, because "the encounters that occur among computing elements in a multi-agent system are *economic* encounters, in the sense that they are encounters between *self-interested* entities" (Wooldridge, 2002, p. 9). In fact (ibid.):

> the issues studied in the multiagent systems community have a rather different flavour to those studied in the distributed/concurrent systems community. We are concerned with issues such as how agents can reach agreement through negotiation on matters of common interest, and how agents can dynamically coordinate their activities with agents whose goals and motives are unknown.

Mutual beliefs are modelled in part of artificial intelligence's models of teamwork. We quote from an overview of multi-agent research within artificial intelligence, by Katia Sycara (1998, pp. 84–85):

> [A particular] direction of research in cooperative multiagent planning has been focused on modeling teamwork explicitly. Explicit modeling of teamwork is particularly helpful in dynamic environments where team members might fail or be presented with new opportunities. In such situations, it is necessary that teams monitor their performance and reorganize based on the situation.
> The *joint-intentions framework* (Cohen and Levesque, 1990) focuses on characterizing a team's mental state, called a *joint intention*. A team jointly intends a team action if the team members are jointly committed to completing the team action while mutually believing they were doing it. A *joint commitment* is defined as a joint persistent goal. To enter into a joint commitment, all team members must establish appropriate mutual beliefs and commitments, which is done through an exchange of request and confirm speech acts[55] (Cohen and Levesque, 1990). The commitment protocol synchronizes the team in that all members simultaneously enter into a joint commitment toward a team task. In addition, all team members must consent, using confirmation, to the establishment of a joint commitment goal. If a team member refuses, negotiation could be used; however, how it is done remains an open issue.

Nissan and Rousseau (1997) discussed how to combine the capabilities of a tool like ALIBI, with capabilities of a virtual theatre of characters, a system whose agents are characters in a story. Whereas ALIBI does not incorporate a mechanism specifically intended for handling complicitous action in a scenario where characters cooperate, Nissan and Rousseau (1997) discussed how to provide such an extension of ALIBI, and argued that management of the narrative's cast of characters could benefit from a multi-agent scenario (Rousseau, 1996), along with explicit modelling of the dialectic of actors' mental states and linguistic exchanges – in line with Rousseau's PSICO (Rousseau, 1995; Rousseau, Moulin, & Lapalme, 1996; Moulin & Rousseau, 1994).

With just ALIBI, even though the program itself does not have a strong model of episodes, to humans faced with ALIBI's input and output the reasoning has typically appeared to be definitely concerned with a coherent episode. The optimisation side of ALIBI (i.e., trying to minimise liability, instead of just trying to deny it) more

---

[54] *Multiagent systems* are the subject of Section 6.1.6 below.
[55] *Speech acts* are the subject of Searle (1969), the classic about this subject.

2.2 Reasoning About a Charge and Explanations: Seminal Tools

clearly entered the picture with the version named ALIBI3. This is because there was a subjective, built-in quantification of the deontic value of atomic actions in the knowledge representation, and such numeric values were just added up. The overall plan reconstituted and proposed as output had to exhibit as low a total liability as possible.

Like ALIBI1 and ALIBI2 (the latter enhanced with a simple natural-language processing interface), ALIBI3 proposes several alternative accounts of the actions appearing in the charge, with an effort being made to exclude from the explanation such admissions that involve liability. Moreover, ALIBI3 is also able, short of finding a totally innocent explanation, to propose such exonerating explanations that admit to some lesser offence than as emerging from the input rudimentary "police report".

In ALIBI's knowledge-base, information is stored in logic form about standard actions, effects, and situations. Distinguish between *typical* situations in the cognitive sense (cf. Nissan, 1995a), and *clear* cases in the legal sense. The court has to determine whether the extremes of certain sets of conditions apply to the case at hand. There is a debate, in jurisprudence, as to whether a demarcation can be found between *clear cases*, i.e., cases for which agreement between competent lawyers can be expected, and *hard cases*, which lead to expert disagreement. In the 1980s, Anne von der Lieth Gardner developed a celebrated program (Gardner, 1987) that tries to distinguish easy from hard cases.

ALIBI, instead, is not really concerned with a legal setting. Explanations are at the lay commonsense, not technically legal level. In ALIBI, excuse-finding exploits degrees of freedom within the non-observable part of the process whose ascertained part is interpreted in the given accusation: as an early phase of performing its task, ALIBI identifies mischievous elements ascribed in this accusation. Classificatory reasoning concerning this phase was the issue in a system developed by Jeffrey Meldman (1975) – cf. Gardner (1987, Section 4.4.1) – which tries to identify, in an input set of facts, intentional torts in cases of assault and battery; examples match exactly, or by replacement in an abstraction hierarchy of objects or kinds of events. ALIBI does not try to figure out whether there is going to be disagreement in court on *judicial* grounds. Instead, in a rudimentary and commonsensical manner, it tries to deny the broader, non-observed context implied by accusers, and it is that way that offences are denied or diminished, and at any rate, *mens rea* is denied.

Moreover, ALIBI is weak on the story coherence side. In handling the stories, I still feel it is important to be able to combine the lessons learnt from the conceptual-dependency school of narrative processing (e.g., Dyer, 1983a) – see on it Section 5.2.9 below – and such constraints as, in a sense, the undeniable elements in the charge which is the input to ALIBI.

Unlike Rousseau's PSICO (see below), ALIBI does not have an actual capability for dialogue. Moreover, to the extent that the narrative to be reasoned about embeds linguistic expression, ALIBI cannot handle it. Therefore, assessing verbal threats (as opposed to armed threat) is outside ALIBI's capabilities. Computational approaches to intentionality and ascription based on the analysis of natural-language utterances were discussed as early as Allen (1983a). In psychology, the ascription of intentions is just a facet of *attribution*, i.e., "the ways in which ordinary people, acting as 'intuitive scientists', explain human actions and events to themselves" (Edwards & Potter, 1995, p. 87).

Distinguish between a situation in which a person is requested to provide an explanation about specific, circumscribed facts – as in a defence situation seeking exoneration – and, in general, a narration about the Self. In the latter kind, an account is conceptualised and proposed possibly of long spans out of one's biography. Like in testimony about oneself when seeking exoneration, such a task also requires coherent reorganisation of events and mental states (cf. Linde, 1993).

Even when no liability is involved, there is no way self-narration may fit a rigid schema ("emptying the sack", as though, where discrete, fixed objects are supposedly to be found). On top of the task of *re-storying one's experiences*, there is also the aspect of *story-connecting*, which introduces sharing experiences or agency with other agents; connecting to each other's stories occurs, e.g., when individual stories of spouses continue as a couple's story (Parry, 1991).

To augment a model such as ALIBI's with the ability to handle mental states and dialogue, consider Rousseau's PSICO. The latter (Rousseau, 1995; Rousseau et al., 1996; Moulin & Rousseau, 1994) is a prototype that simulates interactions between software agents which interpret, plan, and perform communicative acts as well as to reason on mental states such as goals and beliefs. The approach used in PSICO takes into account phenomena one encounters in human conversations, such as turn-taking, stereotyped sequences (openings, closings, and so forth), as well as interconnected speech acts.

It is a *desideratum*, for ALIBI, to enable reasoning about a story with a cast of characters, instead of just one individual, the accused as in ALIBI. The discussion in Nissan and Rousseau (1997) drew upon Barbara Hayes-Roth's *CyberCafe*, a Stanford project in which Daniel Rousseau had taken part (Rousseau, 1996). *CyberCafe* is an application of the *Virtual Theater* project (Hayes-Roth & van Gent, 1997). In a *Virtual Theater* application, synthetic actors (portraying characters) – either autonomous and fully improvising, or "avatars" directed in the main by users and only partly improvising – can interact with each other and with users to create interactive stories resorting to text, animation and possibly speech.

CyberCafe used to feature an autonomous actor playing the role of a waiter, and an avatar portraying a customer. The user-interface contains two windows: one presenting the actions that a user can select for his or her avatar, and one textually describing how the story unfolds in the current context. A user can direct his or her avatar by selecting buttons corresponding to actions that can be performed by the customer in the current context. Actions performed by any actor are displayed by a text animator in a window containing the description of the interaction.

Cybercafe is based on local improvisation, which means that all characters decide their behavior relying on the current state of the world and the actions that they can perform. Reasoning on mental states is quite simplified in the system. Possible states of the world, that can be considered as potential goals, and transitions between those states are modeled using state machines. Actions that an actor can perform to enact the (possibly multi-agent) transitions correspond to its abilities.

2.2 Reasoning About a Charge and Explanations: Seminal Tools

A synthetic actor knows a list of irrelevant actions for each potential state (e.g., a character who is seated can neither sit down, nor walk). The focus of the *CyberCafe* project was the expression of character personality, but characters enacted a (flexible) scenario. An abstract scenario is enacted by the characters, with freedom allowed up to some (variable) degree.

Other relevant capabilities are related to those of Anthony Jameson's IMP (Jameson, 1983; we mentioned it at the end of Section 2.1.4). IMP is a dialogue system (impersonating a real estate agent) that may try to mislead on purpose, without actually lying. It would not volunteer damaging information, unless a direct, specific relevant question is made. IMP has a goal of maintaining a neutral image of itself and an impression of completeness for its own answers. It was even reported to simulate insulted surprise if an intervening question by the customer seems to imply (by detailed questioning) that IMP is concealing information.

Nissan and Rousseau (1997) strove to propose a unified vision of how to formalise actions in a setting involving several agents, and the mental states that could be associated with them[56]: "Augmenting an ALIBI remake with such a (possibly syncretistic) formalism would enable the artificial defendant (or, possibly, any character from the investigative or legal narrative) to reason on the mental states and the actions to discover self-alibis that could be used to exculpate or incriminate someone accused of a crime".

The approach of Nissan and Rousseau (1997) distinguished between action schemas and action instantiations, as in planning systems like STRIPS (Fikes & Nilsson, 1971) and PSICO (Rousseau, 1995). An action schema is a generic definition of an action, commonly composed of parameters, preconditions, sub-actions, effects, and other useful characteristics. An action schema specifies the types of its parameters.

Most of these parameters take values once the schema is instantiated. Actions are simple or compound. A high-level action is composed of sub-actions, and is commonly called a *stereotyped plan* or *recipe*. Those sub-actions may have to be performed in a certain order, but not necessarily. An atomic action is not composed of sub-actions, and can be performed directly.

Let us consider the propositional content of an action first. An action's propositional content is what the action is about, its conceptual description. In order to describe the propositional content of an action, in Nissan and Rousseau (1997) we proposed to use a formalism based on *conceptual graphs* (Sowa, 1984), in linear form, i.e., by representing the graph by means of formulae.

Such graphs express the semantics of the parameters that are associated with the action. These express the action parameters semantics. They are an extension

---

[56] A rather rudimentary, and application-specific device for representing formally concerted action between agents in a juridic setting was described in Nissan (1995b). The formal framework was SEPPHORIS, which combined a representation of events, stipulations, and legal prescriptions, with a kind of *graph-rewriting grammars* (i.e, a device for transforming parts of graphs, step by step). It actually was a *hypergraph-grammar*. A *hypergraph* can be conceived of as a set of sets. A much more flexible formalism I developed for representing narratives is *episodic formulae*, to which we shall come back elsewhere in this book. See Section 5.3.

of first-order logic predicates, because they draw on modal and upper-order logics. Also, they are very convenient for generating and understanding natural language sentences (Moulin, 1992).

For each parameter of a conceptual graph, we distinguish the conceptual relation and the concept. For instance, for the action prototype 'to steal' we get this graph (here represented in linear form):

Steal(AGT(v-agent), OBJ(v-object), PAT(v-agent2))

AGT, OBJ, and *PAT* are conceptual relations; *v-agent, v-object, and v-agent2* are variables corresponding to concepts once they are instantiated. *AGT* indicates that *v-agent* performs the action of stealing. *OBJ* specifies that *v-object* is what is stolen. *PAT* shows that *v-agent2* is the victim of the stealing. For example, "John steals Mary's wallet" could be modelled as:

A1:   *Steal(AGT(John), OBJ(wallet), PAT(Mary))*

The conceptual relations we use are based on Sowa's set of relations he proposed (Sowa, 1984), but are not necessarily the same. This is especially true for the relations regarding time. In the previous example, no relation about time is necessary, because the instantiation is at the present tense by default. But we can specify the time an action is performed when it is necessary by using special relations. For instance, "John stole Mary's wallet" could be represented by:

A2:   *Steal(AGT(John), OBJ(wallet), PAT(Mary), TENSE(Past))*

"John stole Mary's wallet yesterday" could be represented by:

A3:   *Steal(AGT(John), OBJ(wallet), PAT(Mary), TIME(yesterday))*

However, weighty considerations from linguistics militate against coalescing the notions of time and of tense. We did not delve into problems of temporal representation, but these, especially in connection with the legal domain and legal narratives in particular, have been dealt with elsewhere.[57]

---

[57] E.g., Poulin, Mackaay [sic], Bratley, and Frémont (1992), Vila and Yoshino (2005), Knight, Ma, and Nissan (1998), Zarri (1998), Farook and Nissan (1998), Valette and Pradin-Chézalviel (1998). Nissan (2011a) applies Petri nets to textual interpretation, other than in law. Spatial reasoning, which in particular may be in the legal domain (Nissan, 1997a, 1997b) – is amenable to commonsense modeling (Asher & Sablayrolles, 1995), possibly exhibiting similarities with modeling temporal relations (Cohn, Gotts, Cui, Randell, & Bennett, 1994; Bennett, 1994; Randell & Cohn, 1992).

Adderley and Musgrove (2003a), who applied neural networks to the *modus operandi* modelling of group offending (in particular, to burglaries carried out by gangs) remarked about temporal analysis: "Certain offenders have a propensity to offend within certain hours of the day and on particular days of the week. The detected crimes were compared against the crimes attributed to the

2.2 Reasoning About a Charge and Explanations: Seminal Tools

More simply in the present treatment, consider that here, *A1*, *A2* and *A3* are labels we associate with action instantiations in order to be able to refer to them easily; it is especially useful when we want to specify a temporal order between actions. For instance, that action *A5* was performed before action *A6* would be represented by: *BEFORE(A5, A6)*.

A concept can be composed of several objects. For instance, "John and George stole Mary's wallet" could be represented by:

A4: Steal(AGT(John,George), OBJ(wallet), PAT(Mary), TENSE(Past))

We model an action schema using a formalism that adds to the usual characteristics of planning operators such information that could be useful to incriminate or exculpate someone. As an example, here is a possible action schema for stealing:

```
ACTION-SCHEMA:    Steal(AGT(v-agent),
                        OBJ(v-object),
                        PAT(v-agent2))
PRECONDITIONS:    Own(AGT(v-agent2),OBJ(v-object))
                  ~Int.to(v-agent2,Give(AGT(v-agent2),
                        RCPT(v-agent),OBJ(v-object)))
EFFECTS:          + Own(AGT(v-agent),OBJ(v-object))
                  - Own(AGT(v-agent2),OBJ(v-object))
                  + ~Int.to(v-agent, Give(AGT(v-agent),
                                          RCPT(v-agent2),
                                          OBJ(v-object)))
CONSTRAINT:       NON-EQUAL(v-agent,v-agent2)
ALTERNATIVES:     Take(AGT(v-agent),OBJ(v-object))
                  Borrow(AGT(v-agent),
                  OBJ(v-object),
                  FROM(v-agent2))
TRAIT: Honesty(-5)
```

The PRECONDITIONS specify the conditions that must be present before the action is applied. They can be physical or mental states. *Int.To* is an example of modal operator for a mental state like intention. It is based on Grosz and Kraus (1996), except in that we just use the first two parameters in an action schema, without considering time. *Int.To(x,y)* means that *x* has the intention to perform the action *y*. Negation is represented by the ~ operator used as a prefix.

The EFFECTS specify the new states after the performance of the action (preceded by a + sign) and the states that are no longer effective at that stage (preceded

---

Primary Network to ascertain whether there were similarities or differences between times and days. Temporal analysis presents problems within the field of crime-pattern analysis due to the difficulty of ascertaining the exact time at which the offense occurred. There are generally two times that are relevant: the time that the building was secured and the time that the burglary was discovered, the from time/date and the to time/date. [...]" (ibid., p. 187).

by a – sign). Constraints apply to the parameters of the action description. An alternative can be used to exculpate the agent performing the action by attenuating his or her action.

The set of preconditions and effects is slightly different for those alternatives to be less incriminating for the agent performing the action. In the example, stealing could be considered as a kind of taking if the agent did not know that the object belonged to somebody else.[58] It could be considered as a kind of borrowing if the agent had the intention to give back the object to its owner later.[59]

TRAITS specify how the action is evaluated with respect to some personality traits. For this purpose, use is made of a numeric scale going from –10 to 10. Provisionally, let us assume this kind of representation of traits is acceptable for the domain of application we have been envisioning. In the example considered, –5 would correspond to the dishonesty (or legal unacceptability) of the act of stealing, the negative value standing for it being an offence.

Clearly, in a legal context it may be questionable that a judgement that belongs in court be already attached to a core description of action, and moreover, that a quantification of severity be stated beforehand. The scoring in ALIBI3 is somewhat more sophisticated – in respect to the action (characters' TRAITS are ignored) – but the same remark applies to it as well. The representation of the scores of honesty, as shown here, is very simple; it is akin to the way the scoring of characters' traits works in *CyberCafe* (Rousseau et al., 1996).

More generally, considerations must be made concerning the rationale and the, so to speak, mechanics behind such a rating.[60] Personality traits can be very complex; they are in some relation to experienced and displayed emotions and attitudes toward others. For instance, a character can be very friendly in general (say, a value of 8), except when he or she is most angry at someone (value of –8). In the quite simple universe of *CyberCafe*, a character with such a personality would act violently only if he or she is angry, which restricts opportunities for violent behaviour.[61]

---

[58] *Moral luck* is a broader issue. It is your moral luck in that you were not in a given kind of situation, and therefore did not have the opportunity to perpetrate something reprehensible that would fit that kind of situation.

[59] Agents' beliefs about their own or others' obligations were discussed, for example, in Nissan and Shimony (1997).

[60] Some probability or other likelihood factor could perhaps be associated with the PRECONDITIONS or EFFECTS. Such factors could be used to interpret events when some facts are missing, to understand clearly what happened.

[61] In the early 1970s, the late Maria Nowakowska developed a *motivational calculus* (Nowakowska, 1973b, 1984, Vol. 1, chapter 6), and a *formal theory of actions* (Nowakowska, 1973a, 1973b, 1976a, 1978; cf. Nowakowski [sic] 1980), whose definitive treatment was in Nowakowska (1984, Vol. 2, chapter 9). She also developed a *formal theory of dialogues* (Nowakowska, 1976b, 1984, Vol. 2, chapter 7), and a *theory of multimedia units* for verbal and nonverbal communication (Nowakowska, 1986, chapter 3). In 'Theories of Dialogues', chapter 7 in her *Theories of Research*, Nowakowska (1984) devoted chapter 5 to a mathematical model of the "Emotional dynamics of a dialogue", and Section 5.3 to a formalization of a "Provocation threshold". This is relevant, and potentially useful for present-day conversational models involving

emotions, in the design of computer interfaces, or of software supporting the interaction among a group of human users.

In natural-language processing (NLP), Kenneth Mark Colby's PARRY program (Colby, 1975, 1981) embodies in its response mechanism a model of symptoms of paranoia. PARRY used to run in conversational mode, taking as input sentences from a human interviewer. The program embodies in its response mechanism a model of symptoms of paranoia. PARRY impersonates a person experiencing negative emotions or emotional states, the latter being represented by numerical variables for 'anger', 'fear', and 'mistrust'. Colby (1981) "describes a computer simulation model embodying a theory that attempts to explain the paranoid mode of behavior in terms of strategies for minimizing and forestalling shame induced distress. The model consists of two parts, a parsing module and an interpretation-action module. To bring the model into contact with the conditions of a psychiatric diagnostic interview, the parsing module attempts to understand the interview input of clinicians communicating in unrestricted natural language. The meaning of the input is passed to an interpretation-action module made up of data structures and production rules that size up the current state of the interview and decide which (linguistic) actions to perform in order to fulfill the model's intentions. This module consists of an object system which deals with interview situations and a metasystem which evaluates how well the object system is performing to attain its ends" (ibid., from the abstract).

A psychiatrist from Harvard Medical School, Theo Manschreck (1983) – while conceding that "Colby's approach represents an ambitious undertaking, and in some respects it has been successful" (ibid., p. 340) – proposed a narrower interpretation of the results claimed by Colby for PARRY. For example: "Colby's theory sheds virtually no light on the pathogenesis of delusions, the reasons delusions remain fixed and unarguable, the rarity of some delusions and commonness of others, the transient nature of some delusions, the reasons delusions arise suddenly before associated features are present, or at times only when associated features have been persistently present, and so forth. Most clinicians and research psychopathologists would insist that these questions are central to the problem of paranoid behavior and even to the mode of paranoid thinking" (Manschreck, 1983, p. 341).

Colby retorted (1983). He remarked: "The theory presented in the target article proposes that the paranoid system described approximates an instance of a theoretical purposive-cognitive-affective algorithmic system physically realized in the model. Both in the target article and in my Response to the first round of commentaries, I stressed that *the theory proposed does not account for the initial origin of the paranoid mode*. It is limited to explaining in part how the empirical system *works now*. It is not an ontogenetic explanation of what factors in the patient's history resulted in the acquisition of his paranoid mode of processing information. It formulates proximate, not ultimate causes" (ibid., p. 342). It is important to realise that just as Manschreck was a psychiatrist, Colby, too, was affiliated with psychiatry: he was with the Neuropsychiatric Institute at the School of Medicine of the University of California, Los Angeles. The focus of Colby's interests, too, was in psychiatry.

A much more sophisticated NLP program than PARRY in respect of artificial intelligence (rather than of psychological claims), namely, BORIS, was developed by Michael Dyer (1983a), an author who afterwards made significant contributions to connectionist NLP, as well as to the emerging paradigm of "artificial life". BORIS, that by now must be put into a historical context, but still offers important insights, detects or conjectures characters' affect on processing narrative textual accounts. Reasoning is carried out according to this kind of information. For example, a character is likely to be upset because of a plan failure (which to BORIS heightens arousal: possibly anger, though not specifically frustration). Characters' plan failures within a plot are the central concept employed by BORIS for understanding the narrative. Such NLP processing requirements were the only criterion when designing the representation and treatment of affects in BORIS (Dyer, 1983a, p. 130). "BORIS is designed only to understand the conceptual significance of affective reactions on the part of narrative characters. To do so BORIS employs a representational system which

Rating an action in terms of personality traits is just an indication about whether such an action would be likely to be selected by a character, based on his or her personality. It must said right away that whereas one may choose to incorporate such representations in an automated storytelling environment, such a choice is fraught with insurmountable difficulties if the model is intended for making sense of a legal narrative, or even as a predictor of behaviour or a descriptor of behaviour patterns of given individuals from real life.

First and foremost, people make moral choices, and the bottom line is that they are endowed with free will. The rationality of an individual's decision-making, in terms of normative models and expected utility, may vary subjectively or ideologically (cf. Baron, 1994). Moreover, there are cultural norms which are learned quite early while personality develops in a social context.

Emotional *displays* are not universal among cultures, in that differences have been pointed out in culture and emotion research about culture-bound social norms about acceptability, as well about patterns shaping emotion in ways that to some researchers can be conceptualised as being script-like. Cross-cultural psychology is a thriving area of research.[62] One direction of research is into how different cultures

---

shares AFFECTs to one another through decomposition and shared inferences" (ibid.). For example, somebody who has just been fired may go home and kick his dog; the former event explains the latter (ibid., p. 131). Admittedly, there was no intent to model emotions or emotional states as such. Also see Dyer (1983b, 1987) on affect in narratives, or on computer models of emotions.

Apart from BORIS, the treatment of emotion in OSCAR deserves mention. This program, described by John Pollock in his book *How to Build a Person* (1989), embodies a partial model of human cognitive states and emotions. Besides, William S. Faught (1978) described "a model based on conversational action patterns to describe and predict speech acts in natural language dialogs and to specify appropriate actions to satisfy the system's goals" (ibid., p. 383). Faught credits Izard's (1971) *differential emotion theory* (cf. Izard, 1977, 1982) and his own (Faught, 1975) "extension of it into affect as motivation for other thought processing" (Faught, 1978, p. 387).

A model of artificial emotions was proposed by Camurri and Ferrentino (1999). They argued for its inclusion in multimedial systems with multimodal adaptive user-interaction. Their applications are to dance and music. In its simplest form, to Camurri and Ferrentino, an artificial agent's "emotional state is a point in space, which moves in accordance with the stimuli (carrots and sticks) from the inside and the outside of the agent" (ibid., p. 35). The agent is robotic, and movements (for choreography) are detected. The stimuli change the agent's affective "character", which is a point in a space of two dimensions (ibid., p. 38).

> The two axes represent the degree of affection of the agent towards itself and towards others, respectively. We call these two axes "Ego" and "Nos", from the Latin words [for] "I" and "We". A point placed in the positive x (Ego)-axis represents and agent whose character has in a good disposition towards itself. A point towards the left (negative) Ego would mean an agent fairly discouraged about itself. The emotion space is usually partitioned into regions [...] labeled by the kind of character the agent simulates.

[62] In their textbook, Shiraev and Levy remarked (2007, pp. 22–23): "One of the assumptions in contemporary cross-cultural psychology is that it is not possible to fully understand the psychology of the people in a particular ethnic or any other social group without a complete understanding of the social, historic, political, ideological, and religious premises that have shaped people of this group. Indigenous theories, including indigenous psychology, are characterized by the use of

2.2 Reasoning About a Charge and Explanations: Seminal Tools

shape the expression of emotion (e.g., Kitayama & Markus, 1994; Nissan, 1997c). It must be said that the pendulum has been swinging between the cultural relativism – "revived in the 1980s" (Griffiths, 2003, p. 300) – of the social constructionists, in emotions research, and the universalists. But eventually, the two camps have become less incompatible (ibid.).[63]

Paul Griffiths also remarks: "It is true that [the universalist] Ekman has argued that the 'display rules' that modulate emotional behaviors according to social context are acquired, culturally specific, and do not interfere with the actual internal working of the automatic appraisal mechanism and the affect programs" (ibid., p. 299).[64]

Peter Stearns, himself the author of histories of specific emotions in U.S. history[65] (Stearns, 1989, 1994; Stearns & Haggerty, 1991; Stearns & Stearns, 1985, 1986, 1988), has elsewhere (Stearns, 1995) provided a clear description of the controversy about "nature or nurture" in emotions.[66] Constructionists argue, in contrast, that emotions are culture-specific: "Constructionism is the great new theoretical

---

conceptions and methodologies associated exclusively with the cultural group under investigation (Ho, 1998). [...] Maybe because of disappointing beliefs that contemporary psychologists cannot really comprehend all other cultures, a growing interest in indigenous psychologies has emerged."

[63] So Griffiths (2003, pp. 300–301): "One influential argument starts from the widely accepted idea that an emotion involves a cognitive evaluation of the stimulus. In that case, it is argued, cultural differences in how stimuli are represented will lead to cultural differences in emotion. If two cultures think differently about danger, then, since fear involves an evaluation of a stimulus as dangerous, fear in these two cultures will be a different emotion. Adherents of Ekman's [universalist] basic emotions theory are unimpressed by this argument since they define emotions by their behavioral and physiological characteristics and allow that there is a great deal of variation in what triggers the same emotion in different cultures. Social constructionists also define the domain of emotion in a way that makes basic emotions research less relevant. The six of seven basic emotions seem to require minimal cognitive evaluation of the stimulus. Social constructionists often refuse to regard these physiological responses as emotions in themselves, reserving that term for the broader cognitive state of a person involved in a social situation in which they might be described as, for example, angry or jealous."

[64] Discussing transactional theories of emotions, Griffiths (2003, p. 299) remarked: "To behave angrily *because* of the social effects of that behavior is to be angry insincerely. This, however, is precisely what transactional theories of emotion propose: emotions are 'nonverbal strategies of identity realignment and relationship reconfiguration' (Parkinson, 1995, p. 295). While this sounds superficially like the better-known idea that emotions are 'social constructions' (learnt social roles), the evolutionary rationale for emotions view, and the existence of audience effects in non-human animals, warn against any facile identification of the view that emotions are social transactions with the view that they are learnt of highly variable across cultures. Indeed, the transactional view may seem less paradoxical to many people once the idea that emotions are strategic, social behaviors is separated from the idea that they are learnt behaviors or that they are intentional actions."

[65] Jan Plamper, who interviewed three leading practitioners in the history of the emotions, has pointed out: "The history of emotions is a burgeoning field – so much so, that some are invoking an 'emotional turn' " (Plamper, 2010, p. 237).

[66] Stearns (1995, pp. 38–39): "The most belligerent camps in the emotions field involve naturalists or universalists on the one hand, and constructionists on the other. [...] [M]any scholars reject compromise [...]. Naturalists, often building from Darwinian beliefs about emotions' role in human survival, tend to argue for a series of innate emotions, essentially uniform (at least from one group of people to the other) and often, as with anger or fear, biologically grounded (Kemper [etc.]). [...]

paradigm of the late twentieth century in emotions research [...]. Naturalists focus on the functions that emotions offer individuals, though they may assume some societal response to uniform signals. Constructionists focus more clearly on connections between social needs that cause a particular kind of emotional display, and the social results that same display generates." (Stearns, 1995, p. 39). Another practitioner of the history of emotions, William Reddy, published an article entitled 'Against Constructionism' (Reddy, 1997). Also see his book Reddy (2001).

For actions in crime stories as per our *dramatis personae* approach, a higher-level plan would include a decomposition indicating the sub-actions that are components of the action schema. For instance, robbing a bank would include the following actions: entering the bank, getting the money, and leaving. Those actions should be executed in order to get the expected effects. We can use temporal relations between actions to specify their order (e.g., as in Knight, Ma, & Nissan, 1998).[67]

Mental states such as beliefs, mutual beliefs, intentions, commitments, and abilities are very important to determine the responsibility of an agent in any legally significant situations possibly involving being an accessory to crime.

In relation to agents' abilities, *incentive contracting* is possibly involved in complicitous action. In incentive contracting (Kraus, 1996; Sappington, 1984), an agent may contract out to another agent (that does not necessarily share the same goals) a task that the former cannot perform (either at all, or as effectively). Sarit Kraus noted (1996, p. 298):

> There are two main ways to convince another self-motivated agent to perform a task that is not among its own tasks: by threatening to interfere with the agent carrying out its own tasks, or by promising rewards[68] [...]. This paper concentrates on subcontracting by rewards which may be accomplished in two forms: The first approach is a bartering system, where one agent may promise to help the other with future tasks in return for current help. However, as has long been recognized in economics, bartering is not an efficient basis for cooperation, particularly in a multi-agent environment. An agent wishing to subcontract a task to another agent may not have the ability to help it in the future, or one agent that can help in fulfilling another agent's task may not need help in carrying out its own tasks. The second approach is a monetary system which is developed for the provision of rewards, and which can later be utilized for other purposes.
>
> In this paper we present a model of automated agents where incentive contracting is beneficial, We propose to use a monetary system in a multi-agent environment that allows for side payments and rewards between the agents, and where profits may be given to the

---

Other approaches to naturalism are possible that move away from fixed emotion lists while preserving the importance of an innate, physiological component. Psychoanalyst Daniel Stern (1985), utilizing studies of infants, has posited a set of 'vitality affects', defined as very general surges of emotional energy in infants that are then shaped by contacts with adult care-givers into discrete emotions. Possibly some combination approach will turn out to work well, with a few basic emotions (like fear) combined with the more general vitalities that can be moulded into a more variable array including such possibilites as jealousy (found in many cultures but not all, and probably involving a blend of several distinct emotions including grief, anger and fear) or guilt."

[67] In Section 8.4.2.3 we are going to briefly deal with formal models of time.

[68] Incidentally, in a study in the psychology of interrogations, Kassin and McNall (1991) discussed promises and threats in police interrogation, by pragmatic implication.

2.2 Reasoning About a Charge and Explanations: Seminal Tools

owners of the automated agents. The agents will be built to maximize expected utilities that increase with the monetary values, as will be explained below. Assuming that each agent has its own personal goals, contracting would allow the agents to fulfill their goals more efficiently as opposed to working on their own.

Nissan and Rousseau (1997) proposed to use a formalism based on Grosz and Kraus (1996) in order to model the modalities necessary to reason on mental states with respect to the action schemas. Namely, the following, as introduced by Grosz and Kraus, would be resorted to:

Bel(G,p,T_p,C_p): agent G believes that the proposition p is true at time T_p in the context C_p (a proposition may be a state or any of the modalities described here);

MB(G_1,G_2,p,T_p,C_p): agents G_1 and G_2 mutually believe that the proposition p is true at time T_p in context C_p;

Int.To(G,a,T_i,T_a,C_a): agent G has the intention, at time T_i, of performing action a at time T_a in context C_a;

Int.Th(G,p,T_i,T_p,C_p): agent G has the intention, at time T_i, that proposition p be true at time T_p in context C_p;

Pot.Int.To(G,a,T_i,T_a,C_a): at time T_i, agent G considers the possibility of performing action a at time T_a in context C;

Pot.Int.Th(G,p,T_i,T_p,C_p): at time T_i, agent G considers the possibility of wanting that proposition p be true at time T_p in context C_p;

Exec(G,a,T_a,C_T): agent G has the ability to perform action a at time T_a under the constraints C_T;

Commit(G,a,T_a,T_i,C_a): agent G commits him/her/itself at time T_i regarding the performance of action a at time T_a in context C_a;

Do(G,a,T_a,C_T): agent G performs action a at time T_a under constraints C_T.

Actions and propositions are described using conceptual graphs, as we do in action schemas. We can use those modalities in several ways with respect to the action schemas. Consider the following example:

> John and George wanted money. They went to a bank. John pointed a revolver to a cashier and asked for money. George pointed a revolver to other people over there. After John got the money from the cashier, they ran away.

John and George clearly obtained the money from the bank by means of armed robbery. We can likely establish their responsibility because of the following mental states:

- John and George both believed that the cashier, representing the bank, had money;
- John and George shared the belief that they could get the money by force;
- John showed his intentions of robbery, by pointing a gun on the cashier;
- George showed his intention to unlawfully obtain the money by aiming a revolver at people who were at the bank while John was with the cashier;

- Once they had the money, they ran away, and there is no reason to believe[69] that they went into that trouble harbouring any intention to bring it back (an intention they didn't state, and of which they made no display).

Contrast the latter to another situation, in which somebody sharing your place (possibly a relative) takes a banknote from the table and rushes away before the post office closes down. You see, there is a bill to pay, and the person also blurted out something about the bill, the timetable, or the post office. You have no reason to entertain the hypothesis the the given person is about to elope (moreover leaving in place far more valuable property).

We could eventually have different possible types of mental states associated with an action. For instance, aiming with a revolver at someone for joke,[70] or, instead, to

---

[69] On the dynamics of epistemic states, cf. e.g. Gärdenfors (1988). We don't concern ourselves with the philosophical debate on whether true belief amounts indeed to knowledge (Sartwell, 1992), on epistemic luck (Engel, 1992), and so forth. Trenton Merricks (1995) takes issue with Alvin Plantinga's (1993a, 1993b) concept of *warrant*, i.e. – as quoted from Plantinga (1993a) by Merricks (1995, p. 841) with a correction – "that, whatever precisely it is, which makes the difference between knowledge and mere true belief". "A *warranted belief*, for our [i.e., Merricks'] purposes, is one that, given its content and context, has enough by way of warrant to be knowledge" (Merricks, 1995, p. 841, fn. 2), which is focal to a debate in the philosophy of knowledge, but is arguably a moot point for jurisprudence. On justified belief within the theory of justification in philosophy, cf Alston (1989), Goldman (1986), Sosa (1991), and Clay and Lehrer (1989). From the literature of AI, see, e.g., Maida (1991) and Ballim and Wilks (1991).

[70] Luciano Re Cecconi, born in 1948, was a well-known football player in Italy (his club was Lazio). He was shot dead in Rome in the evening 18 January 1977 by a jeweller, Bruno Tabocchini, when Re Cecconi carried out a prank by posturing as though he was threatening him in order to rob him. Re Cecconi did so in the mistaken belief that he, being a celebrity, would be promptly recognised and the jeweller would realise he was just joking. Re Cecconi was accompanied by another well-known football player, Pietro Ghedin, and of Giorgio Fraticcioli, the owner of a perfumery. The purpose of the visit to the jeweller's was so that Fraticcioli could consign two perfume bottles he was ordered. On the spot, it occurred to Re Cecconi, with a raised collar, to simulate that his right hand inside a pocket of his coat was a pistol. He exclaimed: "Datemi tutto, questa è una rapina!" ("Give me everything, this is a robbery!"). The jeweller wasn't a football fan, and didn't recognise Re Cecconi, all the more so as he hadn't been looking at his visitors: Re Cecconi had shouted behind the back of the jeweller, so the latter turned and shot in the chest Re Cecconi, who died half an hour later. On falling, Re Cecconi whispered: "Era uno scherzo, era solo uno scherzo"("It was a prank, just a prank"). Ghedin had raised his own hands, identified himself, turned towards Re Cecconi and told him to stand up as the prank was over, but then noticed that his companion was bleeding.

The jeweller had been recently robbed twice, so he had a pistol hidden under the till, and he had already had the opportunity to use it in order to defend himself from a robbery (he had shot and wounded two robbers). Tabocchini was arrested, and tried 18 days later for unintentional excessive legitimate defence ("eccesso colposo di legittima difesa"). He was acquitted, as he had shot for putative legitimate defence ("legittima difesa putativa"). Comments about the tragedy pointed out that re Cecconi was one of the few players of Lazio who didn't own a firearm.

That episode is retold at: http://it.wikipedia.org/wiki/Luciano_Re_Cecconi and http://www.laziowiki.org/wiki/La_tragedia_della_morte_di_Re_Cecconi (a site of Lazio football club) The journalist Enzo Fiorenza published an instant book about that tragedy (Fiorenza, 1977), paradoxically with a publisher called "Centro dell'Umorismo Italia".

get something from that person or another person (or a group of persons including the one threatened: who on the other hand, could even be an accomplice), or, then, to kill that particular person.

Arguably, a model of complicitous action would benefit not only from extant formalism of collaborative action as well as incentive contracting, but also from Antonio Martino's *logic for politics*, originally introduced in an Italian-language article (Martino, 1997), but whose English-language version is now accessible online.[71]

Martino (1997) introduced two modal operators for political action: operator P stands for seeking authority or rights, whereas operator C stands for performing conformity as a form of support or obeisance, this being the price which those seeking rights (pressure groups, or citizens) pay those political individuals or bodies from which they hope to obtain them.

Moreover, Martino (ibid.) suggested that an operator or a relation may stand for each of various political functions (protection, arbitrage, jurisdiction, regulation, allocation). Other modal operators, according to Martino's proposal, would take care of possibility and necessity, which is in order to distinguish between actual and desirable states of affairs.

Yet other operators or types of operators would handle those preferences that sort out the political actors in order to (a) elect the candidates, and (b) elect policies, the preferences having to be defined by taking into account considerations on relations in general, and on hierarchical relations in particular. Martino avers that generally speaking, those who seek rights pay for these rights with their political support. But who it is who gives such support is often not interchangeable (as he stated while giving a talk in Pisa in 1997, the prime minister would be much more relieved, were it the boss of Fiat who rings him up and voices support, rather that Prof. So-and-So who is sitting here). One person, one vote, Martino noted, is fine for the elections, but in everyday actions, social actors are situated (*posizionati*), and their support depends not only (and not as much) on its quantity, but, as well, on its position with respect to violent or symbolic resources.

We only briefly quote here some introductory concepts from the English version of Martino (1997):

let us create an operator "P" as "political action".

A political action: $A1\ldots An \vdash B$
    $PA1\ldots PAn \vdash PB$

What is implied by political action as a whole is a political action. $A1\ldots An$ is any kind of whole (it can even be empty) and B is a statement or sequence that can also be empty but cannot be a sequence with more than one statement. Since B is a statement, it can be denied and in general all the operations can be done with it that are possible with statements.

Because it is a unitary operator P the formal characteristics very close to negation.

---

[71] http://www.antonioanselmomartino.it/index.php?option=com_content&task=view&id=26&Itemid=64

We can even go further: "political action" is clear but generic. Positive political action is the search for guaranteed conformity, whereas passive political action is the giving of support or consensus. Thus we could limit operator P to the first kind of political action: search for guaranteed conformity and search for authority, whereas we can represent the giving of support or consensus with the operator C. C is not an independent operator but one that can be defined based on P as a complementary operator. For this we have to use the notions of complement in the class logic. Given a class of any a, its complement 'a' is the class of all the object that do not belong to a. This presupposes a universe where either one belongs to a or to its complement. From class logic it is very easy to pass to quantificational logic, given that, after all, classes are none other than the expression of classical categorical propositions.

A complement can also be a term and not a class [...] For example the complement of the term "voting" we write "non-voting" but the complement of the latter we would write "voting" instead of "non non-voting". Conversion, or the converse in categorical propositions could not be validly deduced for A; for example all dogs are animals, the converse "all animals are dogs" is not valid. Medieval logicians managed to solve the problem with the so-called conversion by limitation. The converse of a given proposition contains exactly the same terms as this (with the order inverted) and has the same quality. [...]

Our operator C, on the one hand is the "obverse" of P, in the sense that those that struggle for power have P with reference to all the others, B, C, D...N, whereas these are found in relation C with the A's. Moreover, not only is it the inverse but also the converse, given that changing the terms of the predicate subject and keeping its quality, P and C as operators can be interdefined.

A has P with reference to B, C, ...N, and B, C, ... N have C
with reference to A.

Given that the meaning of logic signs is shown in a context of deduction using their usage and function, it is possible, once the context is specified, to give the criteria for introduction and elimination in such a context. A logic for politics consists in this. Then it is necessary to go to verify in pragmatic contexts what the rules are that best adapt themselves to this existing practice.

Of course, when it comes to evidence, that co-defendants were an accessory to the crime of which the other one is accused is something to be proven. For example, consider the following casenote, which I owe to Jeb McLeish of Edinburgh (pers. comm., 2010), and that comes from the Proceedings of the Old Bailey in London, which are now accessible online:

**Sarah Gideon, Anne Wood,
Grand Larceny, 10th of December 1712**

Sarah Gideon and Anne Wood of the Parish of St. Mary Woolchurch, were indicted for stealing Eight Shillings and Six Pence from James Marriot on the 27th of November last, Mr. Marriot depos'd, that the Prisoners came into his Shop to buy Two Half-pounds of Rice; and while Wood was buying; Gideon fish'd the Money out of the Till with a piece of Whalebone and Birdlime; which he perceiving something of seiz'd her in the Fact the Money and Whalebone Being found upon her, and both clammy with the Birdlime. She had nothing to say in her Defence, but deny'd she knew Wood, as Wood did also that she knew her, and said she only went to buy the Rice; whereupon she was acquitted, and Gideon found Guilty of Felony.

This is a case in which either the co-defendants had not been complicitous and had only been believed to have been so when Sarah Gideon was caught red-handed, or

2.2 Reasoning About a Charge and Explanations: Seminal Tools 95

then Anne Wood had been an accessory and had deliberately facilitated the crime of Sarah Gideon, but then the latter sought to exonerate her, and to protect her from conviction.

2.2.2.8 Wells and Olson's Taxonomy of Alibis

Two forensic psychologists, Gary Wells and Elizabeth Olson, from Iowa State University, began their article (Wells & Olson, 2001)[72] by claiming: "We are interested in the psychology of alibis. Nevertheless, there is little if any empirical literature on alibis". Olson and Wells (2002, pp. 3–4) identified some relevant items from the scholarly literature:

> Although an empirical literature on alibis has not yet been developed, there are a few empirical studies that have used alibis to test hypotheses about other issues, principally eyewitness identification issues. Leippe (1985) for example, used alibi testimony to examine mock juror judgments of various forms of eyewitness identification and non-identification evidence, but the alibi information was held constant, not manipulated. McAllister and Bregman (1989) manipulated whether an alibi witness positively identified the defendant (thereby corroborating the alibi) or not and, as expected, failure of the alibi witness to corroborate the defendant's alibi led to more guilty verdicts from mock jurors. Lindsay, Lim, Marando, and Cully (1986) manipulated whether or not an alibi witness was a relative of the defendant and found that only the nonrelative alibi witness was able to reduce convictions when there was an eyewitness who had identified the defendant as the culprit. Although all three of these studies used alibi witnesses, the studies were focused primarily on issues of eyewitness identification, not alibis. Alibis were used merely as tools to find out how people think about eyewitness identification issues. The only empirical study that we have been able to find that was devoted to alibis per se was one conducted by Culhane and Hosch (2002).[73] In their study, the alibi witness was either a neighbour or a girlfriend and the witness was either certain or not certain in making either an identification or non-identification of the defendant as being at his home during the time of the crime. Their results, like those of Lindsay et al., showed that mock jurors were persuaded by the alibi only if the alibi corroborator had no relationship with the defendant.
>
> Clearly, the relationship between the defendant and the alibi corroborator affects the believability of the alibi. But this represents a small start to what seems to us to be a potentially rich literature. [...]

---

[72] This, like a more extensive report, Olson and Wells (2002), also published at the website of Gary Wells (and accessed by myself in 2011), was based on Olson's master's thesis. Portions of the data in Olson and Wells (2002) were presented at the 2001 Biennial Meeting of the Society for Applied Research in Memory and Cognition. Olson and Wells (2002) included the description of the results of experimentation. "Participants were 252 students from a large Midwestern university recruited for an experiment titled 'Police Detective Reasoning Skills'" (ibid., p. 11).

[73] Cf. Culhane and Hosch (2004). Incidentally, it is worthwhile to note that Culhane et al. (2004) researched possible bias on the part of crime victims serving as jurors, whereas Culhane and Hosch (2005) researched whether there is bias against the defendant on the part of law enforcement officers serving as jurors. Scott Culhane is affiliated with the Department of Criminal Justice at the University of Wyoming. He earned a Ph.D. in legal psychology at the University of Texas at El Paso in 2005.

Literally, an *alibi* is a plea that the suspect or defendant one wasn't at the scene of the crime, so that being removed therefrom, one cannot be the guilty party.[74] First of all, Wells and Olson (2001) distinguished between true and untrue alibis. Untrue alibis are either fabricated alibis, or mistaken alibis. In the latter, the person providing the alibi claims to have been at some given place by believing that claim to be true, because of an honest memory error. They mentioned the case of Ronald Cotton, who had claimed an untrue alibi, and this was a factor in his being found guilty and sent to prison, even though he was innocent.

> So we know what an alibi *is*, but we don't know what makes an alibi *good*. In our opinion a strong, believable alibi is one that keeps the person providing the alibi OUT of hot water: either by keeping him or her out of prison or out of the suspect pool altogether.

To establish an alibi, that is to say, to make an alibi credible, some evidence has to be provided: "some type of evidence that solves a time/space problem: the evidence MUST speak to both the space one was in and the time that one occupied that space." In order "to help codify what is a strong, believable alibi", Wells and Olson (2001) proposed a taxonomy. Writing in 2001 their informal article (it is posted at the website of Gary Wells, itself a helpful resource for eyewitness research), they acknowledged that they kept refining that taxonomy, and that before using it, one would better find out with them what their current thinking is. (I accessed their posted paper in 2011.)

---

[74] In some circumstances, it may even not be obvious to a perpetrator that he needs an alibi. But then an innocent person may also not have a provable alibi. Don Vito Cascio Ferro (1862–1943) had been an anarchist agitator in Sicily in 1892; he afterwards became a mafia boss, and moved to the United States, where, welcomed by the Mano Nera criminal organisation, allegedly he was the one who introduced the practice of protection money (or *racket*, in Sicilian *u pizzu*, i.e., their own "beak" that blackmailers want to wet). Having moved back to Sicily in 1904, he became well connected with persons in the institutions. When the New York City police detective Lieutenant Joe Petrosino came to Italy to investigate him, Cascio Ferro had him stalked all the way. In the evening of 12 March 1909, Petrosino was killed in Piazza Marina in Palermo. (Eventually, New York city hall dismissed the police chief, who was considered responsible for the secret of Petrosino's trip not being kept.) Baldassare Ceola, a Northerner who was questor (police chief of the province) in Palermo and had been questor in Milan earlier on, had Cascio Ferro arrested. Cascio Ferro appeared surprised, and did not even have an alibi. But the case was taken away from Ceola, who was moved elsewhere with the rank of prefect (governor of a province). The inquiry ended with Cascio Ferro not being prosecuted, because the evidence against him was considered insufficient. It was only in 1930 that Cascio Ferro got a life sentence for *correità morale* (as a moral accessory) in two other murders. While in prison, Cascio Ferro stated that he was the one who carried out Petrosino's murder, and that this was the only time he had personally killed somebody. He claimed that on the given evening, he was hosted at dinner by a member of Parliament, that he left for a while in order to kill Petrosino, and that then he returned to the dinner. That statement was published in the *New York Times* on 6 July 1942. Arrigo Petacco, in his biography of Petrosino (1972), disbelieved Cascio Ferro's claim, remarking that at the time of the murder, Cascio Ferro was a guest for dinner of a member of Parliament indeed, but that the place was Burgio, not Palermo, so Petrosino would not have had the time to also be in Palermo and kill Petrosino, then return to that dinner. It is usually conceded that Cascio Ferro had some role in the murder (Pallotta, 1977, pp. 24–28, 106–107). It is interesting that being a guest for dinner could be an alibi, unless a "momentary" absence is noticed. But when arrested for Petrosino's murder, Cascio Ferro did not have an alibi.

Our taxonomy follows the approximate order with which we think alibis will be evaluated in terms of their credibility in the eyes of most people (including police, judges, lawyers, and jurors). Our taxonomy of alibis factorially combines multiple levels of two types of variables, namely physical evidence (such as receipts or video) and person evidence (someone who can vouch for your whereabouts).

Wells and Olson (2001) claimed that the *alibi process* operates in two general psychological domains: the *generation domain*, and the *believability domain*. "The *generation domain* includes within it issues of memory – the autobiographical memory of the alibi provider[75] as well as the memories of the people who are asked to corroborate an alibi". Wells and Olson (2001) identified two phases, within the generation domain, namely: the *Story Phase*, at which the alibi provider makes the memory statement, and the *Validation Phase*, at which "the evidence offered in support of the alibi is researched. This can be undertaken by many people, including the alibi provider and police investigators".

From the validation phase of the generation domain, the alibi process moves, according to Wells and Olson (2001), into the *believability domain*, which also has two phases. The first phase is the *Evaluation Phase*, "undertaken by anyone who experiences the alibi – police, newspaper consumers, lawyers. People decide for themselves the strength of the alibi". And finally, there is the fourth phase of the entire alibi process, that is, the second phase of the believability domain. This is the *Ultimate Evaluation Phase*, one that not all alibis reach. Some alibis do not reach this phase. This is when the (legal) truth of the alibi is decided in court. Having been presented in court, the fact-finder (either trained judges at a bench trial, or otherwise a jury) decides which account of the events to accept. "Other evidence surrounding the case will influence this phase".

Before turning to the taxonomy, Wells and Olson (2001) offered some propedeutic "Taxonomy Notes". They remarked that alibi generation is a time/space problem, so "all evidence you gather to support your alibi must speak to BOTH the space you occupied and the time you occupied it". They distinguished between *Physical Evidence* (which may be any of the following: nonexistent, easy to fabricate, or difficult to fabricate), and *Person Evidence*. The latter depends on how credible persons are, based on their respective expertise and trustworthiness.

Wells and Olson (2001) then proposed the roles of the Motivated Other, the Non-Motivated Stranger, and the Non-Motivated Familiar Other. A motivated other is concerned with the outcome, and whereas this person can rule out the possibility of mistake (that person's expertise is high), that same person's trustworthiness is low, because he or she is very likely to be motivated to lie. The non-motivated stranger, by contrast, is unconcerned with the outcome. This is a person who by definition only saw the accused once. Therefore, the trustworthiness is high, but expertise is low. Wells and Olson (2001) averred about the non-motivated stranger: "May be

---

[75] Olson and Wells (2002, p. 27) supplied this definition: "The term *alibi provider* refers to the suspect or defendant who is being questioned regarding his or her whereabouts at the time of the crime. We call a person whose statements are put forward to support the alibi an *alibi corroborator*. Although an alibi corroborator is 'providing an alibi' for the suspect in the colloquial sense, we reserve the term *alibi provider* for the suspect him or herself."

mistaken (like an eyewitness) but people not likely to consider this. Scientists may be a little leery about this category but most people would not likely distinguish too much between these". The third role is that of the non-motivated familiar other. While unconcerned with the outcome, such a person "could be acquaintance or someone who sees you on a regular basis (bus driver) but does not know you (trustworthiness high, expertise moderate/high)". For the non-motivated roles, motivation to lie is unlikely, but some hidden motivation may affect the non-motivated familiar other.

Wells and Olson proposed a "Factorial Taxonomy" of the strength of the alibi, as well as a "Full-Page Taxonomy". In the factorial taxonomy (Table 2.2.2.8.1), the rows correspond to the categories of physical evidence, whereas the columns correspond to the categories of person evidence.

As to Wells and Olson's (2001) "Full-Page Taxonomy", its rows are degrees of alibi strength, whereas the columns are: "Alibi Strength", "Properties" (comprising two columns: "Person Evidence", and "Physical Evidence"), and "Examples". For alibi strength 1 ("No Alibi"), the value for both Person Evidence and Physical Evidence is "None", and examples include: "I don't even remember", and "I was home alone in bed". For alibi degree 2 ("Weak"), there are two rows. Of these, the first row has "None" for the person evidence, and "Easily Fabricated" for the physical evidence. Wells and Olson's (2001) examples are: "Computer file showing creation time", and "Store receipt for cash purchase". Also for alibi strength 2 ("Weak"), there also is this other row: the person evidence is "Motivated Other", and the physical evidence is "None". The example include: "I was home with Mom", and "My best friend and I were playing video games".

Also for alibi strength 3 ("Moderately Weak") there are two rows. The first of these has as person evidence "Stranger", and as physical evidence, "Easily Fabricated". The examples include: "Subway security officer", and "Elderly couple at the next campsite". The other row for alibi strength 3 ("Moderately Weak") has as person evidence "Familiar Other Non Motivated", and as physical evidence "None". The example is: "Bus driver on your usual route".

For alibi strength 4 ("Moderately Strong"), again Wells and Olson (2001) have two rows. The first of these has as person evidence "Stranger", and as physical evidence, "Easily Fabricated". The example is: "Person in tour group corroborates and you have a dated/timed ticket stub". The other row for alibi strength 4 ("Moderately Strong") has as person evidence "Familiar Other Non Motivated", and as physical evidence "Easily Fabricated". The example is: "Signed, dated receipts from shopping and your usual bus driver remembers".

Table 2.2.2.8.1 Wells and Olson's (2001) factorial taxonomy for alibi strength

Physical evidence		Person evidence			
	None	1	2	3	3
	Easy to fabricate	2	3	4	4
	Difficult to fabricate	5	5	5	5

For alibi strength 5 ("Strong"), Wells and Olson have four rows. All four rows have "Difficult to Fabricate" as physical evidence. Of these four rows for strong alibis, the first row has "None" as person evidence, and examples include: "Plane ticket stub", and "Security camera video at another location". The second row has "Motivated Other" as person evidence, and the example it this ascribed utterance: "I was flying to Vegas with my wife". The third row has "Stranger" as person evidence, and the example is: "Plane ticket and the flight attendant". The fourth and last row has "Familiar Other Non Motivated" as person evidence, and the example is: "On camera with retinal scan while checking through security at a defense contractor company". Retinal scan is a *biometric* method employed in *personal authentication systems*, and based on an individual person's body or sometimes behavioural features. Biometric methods are resorted to also in e-banking, e-commerce, smart cards, and access to sensitive databases, as well as (such as in the example) for access into premises with security requirements.

It appears from this that how easy it would be to fabricate the physical evidence was deemed to be stronger than ther person evidence. Olson and Wells claimed (2002, pp. 9–10):

> Based on the ease-of-fabrication construct, we created multiple levels of person and physical evidence for the taxonomy. However, we felt that the ease-of-fabrication construct did not capture all of what needed to be captured for the person evidence dimension. A person who corroborates an alibi might be either lying or mistaken. A complete stranger runs the risk of misidentifying the alibi provider, but has no motive to lie. A person with a close relationship to the suspect (e.g., spouse), on the other hand, is unlikely to misidentify the alibi provider, but has a potential to lie for the suspect in order to protect him or her. Attribution theories show strong support for the principle of discounting in which the presence of one explanation leads observers to discount another explanation (Gilbert & Malone, 1995). Hence, attribution theory might predict that the focal explanation for the alibi corroborator's claim (i.e., the corroborator actually saw the suspect at the critical time) would be discounted by the possibility of mistaken identification in the stranger case and by lying in the close relationship case. Perhaps the most believable corroborator is one who is familiar with the alibi provider but not motivated to protect or lie for the alibi provider — a non-motivated familiar other. Hence, we thought it would be important for the taxonomy to distinguish between three kinds of alibi corroborators: a motivated familiar other (who is not likely to be mistaken but might lie), a complete stranger (who is not motivated to lie but might be mistaken), and a non-motivated familiar other (who also is not motivated to lie for the person and also is not likely to have mistakenly identified the person).

2.3 A Quick Survey of Some Bayesian and Naive Bayesian Approaches in Law

Andrew Stranieri and John Zeleznikow

2.3.1 Underlying Concepts

The present Section 2.3 is based on section 28.1 in chapter 6 of our book *Knowledge Discovery from Legal Databases* (Stranieri & Zeleznikow, 2005a). Bayesian methods provide formalism for reasoning about partial beliefs under conditions of uncertainty. In this formalism, propositions are given numerical values, signifying the degree of belief accorded to them. Bayesian classifiers are statistical classifiers that can predict class membership probabilities – such as the probability that a given sample belongs to a particular class. Han and Kamber (2001) claim that studies comparing classification algorithms have found that the *naïve Bayesian classifier* is comparable in performance with classifiers[76] based on either *decision trees*,[77] or *neural networks*.[78]

Naive Bayesian classifiers assume the effect of an attribute value on a given class is independent of the other attributes. This assumption is made to simplify computations – hence the use of the word *naive*. Bayesian belief networks are graphical models, which unlike naive Bayesian classifiers allow the representation of dependencies among subsets of attributes. Bayesian belief networks can also be used for classification. They depend upon Bayes' Theorem, which we now discuss.

Suppose we are considering two events A and B. Bayes Theorem states that there is a relationship between the "after the fact" or posterior probability of A occurring given that B has occurred, denoted as $Pr(A|B)$ and:

(a) the probability that B occurred, and
(b) the probability that A occurred, and
(c) the probability that B occurs given that A occurred

Bayes theorem states that:

$$Pr(A|B) = Pr(A \& B) / Pr(B)$$
$$= Pr(B|A) * Pr(A) / Pr(B)$$

where

$Pr(A \& B)$ is the probability that A and B occur simultaneously and
$Pr(B)$ is the probability that B occurred.

An example outside law is illustrative. Suppose we have a hypothesis that asserts that copper will be discovered at a location:

H1 We will find copper at location X
E The rocks at location X are batholithic.

The probability of finding copper given that the rocks are batholithic, denoted as $Pr(H1|E)$, is difficult to estimate directly. However, using Bayes theorem the problem is transformed to one of finding batholithic rocks given there is copper $Pr(E|H_1)$

---

[76] Classifiers will be discussed in Chapter 6, which is about *data mining*.
[77] Lior Rokach and Oded Maimon's (2008) is the first book entirely dedicated to *decision trees* in *data mining*.
[78] Neural networks are the subject of Section 6.1.14 in the present book.

2.3 A Quick Survey of Some Bayesian and Naive Bayesian Approaches in Law

and the probability of finding batholithic rocks Pr(E) and copper in isolation $P(H_1)$. These probabilities are typically easier to estimate in the real world. We need only to examine past sites where copper was discovered to estimate the probability of finding batholithic rocks given copper Pr(E|H1). The prevalence of copper and of batholithic rocks overall is also relatively easily estimated.

The next example illustrates a Bayesian approach to law. Let us take for example a hypothesis H, that a man killed his wife and the evidence (each piece of which is independent) consists of the following events:

E_1 the man will receive \$1,000,000 from his wife's insurance policy in the case of her death;
E_2 the wife was killed by the same make of gun, as one owned by the husband;
E_3 the husband had the wife's blood on his clothes;
E_4 an eyewitness saw the husband leave the marital home, five minutes after he heard a shot fired.

The total evidence is the union of events

$$E = E_1 \cup E_2 \cup E_3 \cup E_4$$

and the probability of the hypothesis given the evidence is

$$Pr(H|E) = Pr(H\&E)/Pr(E) = Pr(E|H)^* Pr(H)/Pr(E)$$

Again, it is difficult to estimate the probability that the husband killed the wife given the direct evidence. So now, rather than working out the probability of the husband killing the wife given the evidence, we are focusing on the probability that the evidence is true given the husband killed the wife. We can achieve this by noting how many murders of a wife by her husband in the past involved the evidence in the current case.

Again, it is difficult to estimate the probability that the husband killed the wife given the direct evidence. So now, rather than working out the probability of the husband killing the wife given the evidence, we are focusing on the probability that the evidence is true given the husband killed the wife. We can achieve this by noting how many murders of a wife by her husband in the past involved the evidence in the current case.

There are two main problems associated with the use of Bayes theorem in practice:

(a) The probability of each element of evidence and the hypothesis must be known, or accurately estimated in advance. This is often difficult to quantify. For example, how would one estimate the probability that a husband has his wife's blood on his clothes?

(b) Bayes theorem assumes that A is defined to be independent of B if

$$\Pr(A\&B) = \Pr(A)^* \Pr(B).$$

In this case

$$\Pr(A|B) = \Pr(A)$$

as would be expected. This is often too strong an assumption to make in practice.

Let us turn to *Naive Bayes*: for a given sample we search for a class c_i that maximises the posterior probability

$$P(c_i|x;\ \theta')$$

by applying Bayes rule. Then x can be classified by computing

$$c_l = \arg\max_{c_i \in C} P(c_i|\theta') P(x|c_i;\theta')$$

Bayesian Belief Networks developed by Pearl (1988) are graphs that, by making convenient assumptions about Bayes theorem, enable inferences to be drawn in the presence of uncertainty. There are many excellent books on the use of probabilistic reasoning for the construction of intelligent systems. Schum (1994) is one such text.

Figure 2.3.1.1 illustrates a Bayesian belief network example adapted from Heckerman (1997) and is related to credit card fraud. The nodes in the network represent relevant factors.

Building a network involves identifying relevant nodes, assigning a probability to the occurrence of each value on a node and establishing links between nodes that influence each other. The node *Fraud* in Fig. 2.3.1.1 has a probability of occurrence of 0.00001 that represents the prevalence of fraud. The probability that jewellery is the object of a fraud is dependent upon the age and sex of the purchaser and the prevalence of fraud. Age and sex are not factors that influence the probability of petrol fraud.

Bayesian belief networks provide a graphical model of causal relationships on which learning can be performed. *Bayesian belief networks* are also known as *belief networks*, *Bayesian networks* and *probabilistic networks*.

A Bayesian belief network is defined by two components:

(a) A directed acyclic graph where each node represents a random variable and each arc represents a probabilistic dependence. Each variable is conditionally dependent of its non-descendents in the graph, given its parents. The variables may be discrete or continuous.

2.3 A Quick Survey of Some Bayesian and Naive Bayesian Approaches in Law

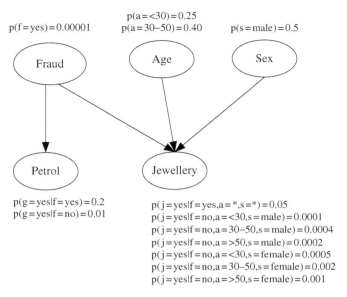

Fig. 2.3.1.1 A Bayesian belief network related to credit card fraud

(b) A *conditional probability table* (*CPT*) for each variable,

$$\Pr(X|\text{parents}(X))$$

The network structure may be given in advance or inferred from the data. The network variables may be observable or hidden in all or some of the training samples. If the network structure is known and the variables are observable, then training the network consists of computing the CPT entries; similar to the case of computing the probabilities involved in naive Bayesian classification.

When the network structure is given and some of the variables are hidden, then a method of gradient descent can be used to train the Bayesian belief network. The object is to learn the values for the CPT entries. See Han and Kamber (2001) for details.

Dempster-Shafer theory (Shafer, 1976) has been developed to handle partially specified domains. It distinguishes between uncertainty and ignorance by creating belief functions. Belief functions allow the user to bound the assignment of probabilities to certain events, rather than give events specific probabilities. Belief functions satisfy axioms that are weaker than those for probability theory. When the probabilistic values of the beliefs that a certain event occurred are exact, then the belief value is exactly the probability that the event occurred. In this case, Dempster-Shafer theory and probability theory provide the same conclusions.

2.3.2 Some Applications in Law

Bayesian theory requires the specification of a complete probabilistic model before reasoning can commence (Pearl, 1988). This is not generally possible in the legal domain. However, as applications of Bayesian classification by Pearl (1988), Davis and Pei (2003), and Halliwell, Keppens, and Shen (2003) illustrate, the probabilities required for a Bayesian Belief network can be derived from expert heuristics, physics models or innovative applications of *fuzzy sets*.[79] As large datasets in law become prevalent, the probabilities required can conceivably be generated directly from real data.

Although the application of Bayesian approaches to modelling reasoning in the legal domain is relatively new, a number of innovative applications illustrate substantial potential. Two approaches will be reviewed here. Davis and Pei (2003) applied a Bayesian model to reconstruct the most plausible account of a traffic accident and Halliwell et al. (2003) applied Bayesian classification in forensics.

The reconstruction of a traffic accident involves the combination of evidence from a number of sources including eye-witnesses, skid marks, speed estimates, and weather conditions. Davis and Pei (2003) note that *counterfactual statements* are important for traffic accident reconstruction. These are statements of the form: "If the vehicle had not been speeding the collision would not have occurred" and are contrasted with statements that assert a fact such as "the vehicle was speeding". They identify three steps that are typically deployed in an accident reconstruction (a) the vehicle's initial speed is estimated, (b) a counterfactual value for the vehicle's initial speed is suggested, and (c) the initial speed estimate and the counterfactual

---

[79] Fuzzy set theory uses the standard logical operators $\wedge$ (and), $\vee$ (or), $\sim$ (not). Thus given truth values (or membership values) $\mu(p)$ for p and $\mu(q)$ for q, we can develop truth values (or membership values) for $p \wedge q$, $p \vee q$ and $\sim p$. These values are determined by

(a) $\mu(\sim p) = 1 - \mu(p)$,

(b) $\mu(p \wedge q) = \min\{\mu(p), \mu(q)\}$,

(c) $\mu(p \vee q) = \max\{\mu(p), \mu(q)\}$

Fuzzy logic is the subject of Section 6.1.15 in this book. Fuzzy logic is a many-valued propositional logic where each proposition P rather than taking the value T or F has a probability attached (thus between 0 and 1) of being true. It would take the value 0 if it were false and 1 if it were true. Logical operators and probability theory are then combined to model reasoning with uncertainty. Fuzzy rules capture something of the uncertainty inherent in the way in which language is used to construct rules. Fuzzy logic and statistical techniques can be used in dealing with uncertain reasoning.

Philipps and Sartor (1999) applied fuzzy reasoning as well as neural networks in an AI & Law context. Stranieri and Zeleznikow (2005a) remarked: "[Philipps & Sartor, 1999] argue that fuzzy logic is an ideal tool for modelling indeterminancy. But what is indeterminancy? Indeterminancy is not uncertainty. To quote the Roman maxim – *Mater semper certa est, pater semper incertus* – one can never be certain that a man was the real father of a child, even if he was the mother's husband. But the concept of a father is certainly determinate."

2.3 A Quick Survey of Some Bayesian and Naive Bayesian Approaches in Law

estimate are used to infer the likelihood that the vehicle could have stopped to avoid the collision.

In the study by Davis and Pei (2003), twin Bayesian Belief networks are built using forensic knowledge and models of mass and movement that derive from physics. The twin networks represent a possible world depicted by a counterfactual statement such as "If the vehicle had not been speeding the collision would not have occurred". By comparing the probabilities of key nodes in the belief network with those in the possible world network, an assessment of the plausibility of the alternate world can be made. The study was evaluated using four case studies. The evaluation results were promising.

Let us turn now to an example of Bayesian networks being used for forensic statistics. To attempt to avoid miscarriages of justice forensic statistics has emerged as an increasingly important discipline, by providing techniques, such as the likelihood ratio (Balding & Donelly, 1995), to evaluate evidence in term of its relative support of claims made by the prosecution vs. claims made by the defence. Halliwell et al. (2003) claim that these methods provide a statistical characterisation of expert testimony. For example, that there is strong support for the defence or prosecution position. Due to the lack of experimental data, inferred probabilities often rely on subjective probabilities provided by experts. Because these are based on informed guesses, it is very difficult to express them accurately with precise numbers. Yet, conventional Bayesian Networks can only employ probabilities expressed as real numbers.

A central component of their work is the use of Bayesian Networks to compute the probability $Pr(E|C)$ of obtaining certain pieces of evidence E given a claim C. An example of $Pr(E|C)$ is the probability of finding a certain number of glass fragments in the clothes of a person assuming that that person has smashed a window. This is not a trivial task because many factors influence the production of evidence. In this example, the number of glass fragments retrieved in the laboratory from clothes worn by the suspect depends on the way the window was smashed, the movements of the perpetrator after the crime (which may cause some glass fragments to fall from the garment) and the laboratory techniques employed. Bayesian Networks provide an effective way of organising this knowledge. Additionally, they enable the use of efficient algorithms to compute the probability of interest.

A common criticism of the Bayesian approach is that it requires too much information in the form of prior and conditional probability tables, and that this information is often difficult or impossible to obtain. In principle, most values could be obtained through experimentation. Following the scenario above, for example, the probability of glass fragments being transferred to the suspect's garment, might be determined by smashing a representative population of glass panels of the same make as the shop window with a piece of fabric similar to that of the garment in question. But such experiments are obviously difficult to design and conduct correctly and are both time-consuming and expensive. In practice, therefore, it is often necessary to rely on subjective probability estimates provided by experts.

The difficulty of obtaining point estimates of (e.g. prior) probabilities in general has been widely reported. Moreover it has been reported (Zimmer, 1984) that verbal expressions of probabilistic uncertainty were more accurate than numerical values in estimating the frequency of multiple attributes through experimental studies. In addition subjective probability assessments are not generally precise and it has been claimed that it is misleading to seek to represent them precisely. Various studies (e.g., Budescu & Wallsten, 1985), have concluded that point estimates of probability terms are highly variable between subjects and exhibit great overlap between terms. All this suggests that it would be useful to involve probabilistic terms directly in probabilistic models.

Halliwell et al. (2003) presented a novel approach to the representation of subjective probability assessments known as *linguistic probabilities*. Fuzzy sets have been widely used to represent the inherent *vagueness* in linguistic descriptions.[80] They have sometimes found application in AI & Law.[81] Furthermore, a number of psychometric studies have evaluated the claim that fuzzy sets may be used to model qualitative probabilities with generally positive conclusions. So, for example, Wallsten, Budescu, Rapoport, Zwick, & Forsyth (1986) have considered various methodological issues in detail, and established that experimentally obtained fuzzy sets do indeed seem to provide a model for everyday probabilistic assessments. The approach of Halliwell et al. (2003) approach allows for the expression of subjective probabilities as fuzzy numbers, which more faithfully respect expert opinion. By means of a practical example, they show that the accurate representation of this lack of precision in reasoning with subjective probabilities has important implications for the overall result.

Shortliffe and Buchanan (1975) developed the use of certainty factors as part of the MYCIN expert system for medical diagnosis.[82] They argued that a rigorous application of conditional probability and Bayes theorem is unwise. Instead, they used a belief measure that indicates an expert's confidence in her advice. Whilst Grady and Patil (1987) illustrate an early use of certainty factors in the legal expert system in pension planning (developed to assist screening by the Internal Revenue Service), certainty factor approaches to uncertainty are not prevalent. A brief overview of certainty factors is provided because data mining approaches can conceivably be applied to discover certainty factors if data-sets were sufficiently large. They introduced measures of belief, M_B and disbelief, M_D for a hypothesis H given evidence E. A new piece of evidence E changes the measures of belief and disbelief thus:

If $\Pr(H) = 1$ then $M_B(H|E) = 1$

---

[80] Concerning vagueness, see in Sections 4.6.2.2 and 6.1.13.12 below. Fuzzy logic is discussed in Section 6.1.15.

[81] Xu, Kaoru, and Yoshino (1999) constructed a case-based reasoner to provide advice about contracts under the United Nations Convention on Contracts for the International Sale of Goods (CISG). They adopted a fuzzy approach to case-based representation and inference in CISG. Philipps and Sartor (1999) applied fuzzy reasoning as well as neural networks in an AI & Law context.

[82] Shortliffe (1976) is a book about MYCIN.

otherwise $M_B(H|E) = \{\max[Pr(H|E), Pr(H)] - Pr(H)\}/(1-Pr(H))$

If $Pr(H) = 0$ then $M_D(H|E) = 1$
otherwise $M_D(H|E) = \{Pr(H) - \min[Pr(H|E), Pr(H)]\}/(Pr(H))$

The certainty factor $CF(H|E)$ is defined by

$$CF(H|E) = MB(H|E) - MD(H|E)$$

The certainty factor varies from -1 to $+1$. A positive certainty factor indicates that the new evidence supports the original hypothesis H, a negative certainty factor indicates it opposes the hypothesis.

Suppose we have an example where the original evidence E is that a wife killed her husband with a knife whilst he was asleep. She pleads not guilty by way of battered wife syndrome. New evidence becomes available suggesting that the husband had a history of beating his wife. Suppose that in general, the wife's probability of being acquitted is $Pr(H) = 0.3$. However her probability of being acquitted, given that her husband had a history of wife abuse, is $Pr(H|E) = 0.8$. Then

$$\begin{aligned}M_B(H|E) &= \{\max[Pr(H|E), Pr(H)] - Pr(H)\}/(1-Pr(H))\\ &= \{\max(0.8, 0.3) - 0.3\}/0.7\\ &= 0.5/0.7\\ &= 0.71\end{aligned}$$

$$\begin{aligned}M_D(H|E) &= \{Pr(H) - \min[Pr(H|E), Pr(H)]\}/(Pr(H))\\ &= \{0.3 - \min[0.8, 0.3]\}/0.3\\ &= 0\end{aligned}$$

Thus

$$CF(H|E) = 0.71$$

Hence the new evidence that the husband had a history of abusing his wife increases our belief that the wife will be acquitted of murder. There is no theoretical basis underlying certainty factors. Nor do the certainty factors associated with a MYCIN hypothesis correspond to the Bayesian probability model. However, certainty factors have proven to be effective in numerous fields outside law.

2.4 The Controversy Concerning the Probabilistic Account of Juridical Proof

Ronald Allen is a consistently articulate critic of the application of probability theory to juridical proof. Among the other things, Allen and Pardo (2007a, p. 109) find that scholarship pursuing that line of inquiry suffers from a deep conceptual problem that makes ambiguous the lessons that can be drawn from it – the problem of reference classes. The implications of this problem are considerable. To illustrate the problem, consider the famous blue bus hypothetical. Suppose a witness saw a bus strike a car but cannot recall the color of the bus; assume further that the Blue Company owns 75% of the buses in the town and the Red Company owns the remaining 25%. The most prevalent view in the legal literature of the probative value of the witness's report is that it would be determined by the ratio of the Blue Company buses to Red Company buses, whether this is thought of as or plays the role of a likelihood ratio or determines information gain (including an assessment of a prior probability) [...] But suppose the Red Company owns 75% (and Blue the other 25%) of the buses in the county. Now the ratio reverses. And it would do so again if Blue owned 75% in the state. Or in the opposite direction: it would reverse if Red owned 75% running in the street where the accident occurred (or on that side of the street) and so on. Or maybe the proper reference class has to do with safety standards and protocols for reporting accidents. Each of the reference classes leads to a different inference about which company is more likely liable, and nothing determines the correct class, save one: the very event under discussion, which has a likelihood of one and which we are trying to discover.[83]

"The blue bus hypothetical with which we began this paper exemplifies the general implications of reference classes, and those implications would hold for practically any attempt to quantify a priori the probative value of evidence" (ibid., p. 113). "The reference-class problem [...] is an epistemological limitation on attempts to establish the probative value of particular items of legal evidence" (ibid., p. 115, citing Pardo, 2005, pp. 374–383). This is so "because different classes may point in opposite directions and nothing, other than the event itself, necessarily privileges one over another" (ibid., p. 115).

Allen and Pardo (2007a) claimed their paper was making three contributions: "it is a further demonstration of the problematic relationship between algorithmic tools and aspects of legal decision making" (ibid., p. 110); "it points out serious pitfalls to be avoided for analytical or empirical studies of juridical proof", and "it indicates when algorithmic tools may be more or less useful in the evidentiary process" (ibid.).

They enumerated and exemplified "limitations on attempts to mathematically model the value of legal evidence" (ibid., p. 115). Namely (ibid., pp. 115–116):

First, and most important, the probative value of legal evidence cannot be equated with the probabilities flowing from any given reference class for which base-rate data are available. Related to this point, probative value likewise cannot be equated with the difference between prior and posterior probabilities on the basis of such data, nor is it sensible simply to translate directly an available statistic into a prior probability. Second, the above problem regarding establishing probative value cannot be solved by merely specifying the relevant classes with more detailed, complex, or "realistic" characteristics. Third, while

---

[83] "How to specify the appropriate reference class for determining hypothesis confirmation has been a prominent issue in the philosophy of science. Hans Reichenbach (1949, p. 374) suggested we choose the smallest class for which reliable statistics were available; Wesley Salmon, by contrast, advocated that for single cases we ought to select the broadest homogeneous class. For a discussion of these positions see Salmon (1967, pp. 91, 124)" (Allen & Pardo, 2007a, p. 112, fn. 9). In legal theory, within the Bayesianist camp Tillers (2005) discussed reference classes.

2.4 The Controversy Concerning the Probabilistic Account of Juridical Proof

switching from objective to subjective probability assessments better accommodates unstable probative values of evidence, it nevertheless still illustrates the pervasiveness of the reference-class problem because of its presence even when evaluating such subjective assessments. Finally, the reference-calss problem is so pervasive that it arises whenever one assesses the probative value of evidence, even when one is not trying to fix a specific numeric value to particular items of evidence – for example, when assessing whether evidence satisfies a standard of proof. [...] The limitations that are discussed, we contend, undermine the strong conclusions that are drawn from such models.

A referee committed to Bayesianism, commenting in 2006 on an article of mine – about computer tools for legal evidence and how to further develop the field – proposed this "future trend: more computer power. In view of which, an anti-Bayesian stance is somewhat like built-in obsolescence". Will the skeptics agree? This is not likely at all, and their arguments are weighty. There is a lot of cogency about them. Moreover, suppose the Bayesianists are right, and those who believe it to be somewhat in the same category as astrology are wrong. Society derives a sense of justice being made from there being a modicum of consensus about how verdicts are reached. Should verdicts in future increasingly rely on calculations of probabilities (through the intervention of expert witnesses making use of these), and should an important segment of legal scholars continue to view these calculations as utterly lacking credibility, the societal benefit from there being courts of law in operation would diminish.

The problems with Bayesian approaches go way beyond computational complexity. This is laid out, for example, in a paper by Ron Allen (1997) from a journal special issue (Allen & Redmayne, 1997) devoted to the controversy. There are deep incompatibilities between the structure of juridical proof and any probabilistic approaches. A more recent demonstration of this was provided e.g. by the already cited Allen and Pardo (2007a).[84] Nevertheless, the availability of more computer power undoubtedly spurs more work in a Bayesian or at least probabilistic framework.[85] Artificial intelligence practitioners should not be oblivious to the contentiousness of some approaches.

Arguably the real potential of artificial intelligence to make a significant contribution is in harnessing explanation-generation techniques, while also applying criteria of comparison among explanations that are offensive to neither camp in the Bayesianism controversy. That is to say, except in well-delimited domains such as DNA evidence, in which statistical methods are fairly cogent, applications of artificial intelligence would better not just plump for Bayesianism because it is there,

---

[84] See Allen (1997, 2001b, 2003), Allen and Lively (2003 [2004]), and Allen and Pardo (2007a, 2008).

[85] That same Bayesianist referee also claimed: "The Bayesian side of things is clearly in the ascendant, which the article might wish to note. And the largest reason for that, which the article might also wish to note [...] due to the availability of greater computational capacity, leading to success for Bayesian net technology in modeling, and Markov Chain Monte Carlo simulation methods in optimization and learning".

but instead, ambitiously, go the *explanationism* way,[86] which is something at which artificial intelligence harbours the potential of doing rather well, within tasks that should be explicitly circumscribed.

Even from the Bayesianist camp, there have been on occasion calls for caution, including in an informal forum. Consider the following cautionary comment made by Peter Tillers[87] about a paper by Martin Neil and Norman Fenton (Fenton & Neil, 2000) which supported the claim (against using knowledge of prior convictions against suspects) that there exists a so-called *Jury Observation Fallacy*; in so doing, Neil and Fenton made use of Bayesian networks to present probabilistic legal arguments, with the calculations carried out by a tool, HUGIN, which belongs in the category of Bayes/Belief Net software: "I think the paper's authors assume a bit too readily that evidence and inference problems in the courtroom are computationally tractable". Bear in mind that, even though here he was calling for caution, Tillers is prominent within the camp, among legal scholars, who support Bayesianism in law.[88] The skeptics' camp maintains that the conceptual limits of Bayesianism go way beyond computational power. The arguments are weighty. Sometimes one gets the feelings that they are not listened to as carefully as they deserve, as this is

---

[86] See Allen's paper (2008a) "Explanationism All the Way Down"; cf. Allen and Pardo (2008). Allen claims (2008a, p. 325):

> A more promising approach to understanding juridical proof is that it is a form of inference to the best explanation. Conceiving of cases as involving the relative plausibility of the parties' claims (normally provided in story or narrative form) substantially resolves all the paradoxes and difficulties [...]

[87] In an e-list posting from 2 July 2001 (at bayesian-evidence@vuw.ac.nz), Peter Tillers, a legal scholar who is a prominent supporter of Bayesianism in the Bayesianism debate.

[88] Here is a fuller quotation from Tillers' posting (the brackets are Tillers' own):

> I think the paper's authors assume a bit too readily that evidence and inference problems in the courtroom are computationally tractable. Even with HUGIN, some real-world cases – many real-world cases – will be computationally intractable (even with the use of very powerful computers) unless the cases – the problems of evidence – are simplified. And the question of how complex inference problems should be simplified to make them computationally-tractable while assuring that the resulting probability computations are still informative and not misleading is not an easy one. (If the simplification cannot be done "mechanically" or "objectively," there is little to be said for the proposition that "experts" should decide how otherwise computationally-intractable complex [courtroom] cases and problems should be simplified.)

My quoting offhand comments from an email, or rather from an informal posting from a scholars' e-list, or then from a confidential referee report, itself calls for comment. Readers will have noticed that this book has a huge bibliography. When what is to be covered is such a wide range, it is very difficult to fully satisfy all criteria that are clearer or even obvious to specialists of given domains. Even with measures taken to be as precise as possible, a rather mundane problem that may occur sometimes, and that I freely acknowledge, is that citations are exemplificative, without following the historical development of debate within the given specialism. For example, it does happen sometimes that I cite rather derivative work, while not some seminal work. It should be clear that this is not to deny credit to the latter. This book is already long the way it is, and we cannot aim at tracing the history of all disciplines involved.

unfeasible in given institutional and biographical contexts, or rather because the mathematics looks so powerful and enticing, whether it is problematic or not. But should we look for a lost key under a lamppost, only because under a lamppost we can see better? My own feeling is that much remains to be done for developing acceptable models of plausibility that would not incur the kind of criticism that reliance on Bayesianism attracts.

Allen (1997) discussed what "those of us who have been branded Bayesian skeptics" (ibid., p. 256) consider to be at issue and what is not at issue. He formulated questions, and answered them. He was not contesting the formal validity of Bayes' theorem, or probability theory more generally, but rather contesting interpretation, application, and their implications (ibid.). Bayes' theorem is only normative if its necessary conditions are satisfied, but this is a tautology: "The question is whether the juridical context does, can or should generate the conditions necessary for the operation of Bayes' theorem", which is problematic (ibid., p. 257). Moreover (ibid., pp. 257–258):

> Surely if juridical fact finding is typically like predicting the outcome of events like coin flipping, or if a person wishes to form and think about the relationship between subjective probabilities (and wants to form the immense number of numerical values such thinking requires, and has the computational capacity to compute them all [...]), then Bayes' theorem will surely be frequently useful, as it is in many statistical settings. But this again bears no obvious relationship to the inquiry into the nature of juridical fact finding. The Bayesian enthusiasts must show that juridical fact finding is generally like flipping coins or the formation of subjective belief states in a fashion amenable to the use of Bayes' theorem before they can demonstrate that the use of the theorem has any general utility at trial. The Bayesian skeptic has the opposite task.[89] [...]

2.5 A Quick Sampling of Some Probabilistic Applications

2.5.1 Poole's Independent Choice Logic and Reasoning About Accounts of a Crime

Tillers and Schum (1998) presented a theory of preliminary fact investigation. Jøsang and Bondi (2000) apply a subjective logic, using probability theory, to legal evidence. Dragoni and Animali (2003) developed a formal approach, based on belief

---

[89] Answering his own question 4, namely, "Whether there are any juridical fact-finding contexts in which Bayes' theorem might be useful", Ron Allen answers it this way: "The Bayesian skeptic is not this skeptical. There may very well be situations involving virtually purely statistical evidential bases in which Bayes' theorem would be a useful analytical tool. It is even possible that Bayes' theorem might prove useful in some extremely impoverished nonstatistical evidential settings. The skeptical claim, by contrast, doubts that Bayes' theorem is very useful for real human decision making in the typical juridical context involving a rich, highly complex set of interdependent pieces of evidence" (ibid., p. 258).

revision and the Dempster-Shafer statistical approach (Shafer, 1976),[90] for representing inconsistencies among and inside witness assertions. Shyu, Fu, Cheng, and Lee (1989) described an evidential reasoning method based on Dempster-Shafer, but even though their paper appeared in the proceedings of a conference on legal computing, they didn't explicitly indicate how to apply their results in the judicial domain.

David Poole (2002) sketched and applied a formalism, he called *Independent Choice Logic (ICL)*, to legal argumentation about evidence. Poole's formalism can be viewed as a "first-grade representation of Bayesian belief networks with conditional probability tables represented as first-order rules, or as a [sic] abductive/argument-based logic with probabilities over assumables" (ibid., p. 385). On the one hand: "It is a way to add Bayesian probability to the predicate logic" (ibid., p. 387). On the other hand: "It is a way to lift belief networks into first-order language. The belief network can be seen as a deterministic system with noise input. The deterministic system is modeled as a logic program", by "writing the conditional probability tables in rule form" (ibid.). Moreover: "It is a sound way to have probabilities over assumptions. Explaining observations means that we use abduction; we find the explanations (sets of hypotheses) that imply the observations, and from these we make predictions", by probabilistic inference (ibid., p. 388). Poole developed collections of clauses in order to represent a sample story proposed by Peter Tillers at the beginning of the same volume. The collection of observations as stated by Poole (ibid., p. 389) was:

> Peter says that he went to the Happy Valley Store.
> Peter says that harry was a clerk at the Happy valley Store.
> Peter says that harry is a vicious SOB.
> Peter says that he observed a blinding flash.
> Peter said that the doctor said that he was shot.
> Peter said that the newspaper said harry disappeared.

For those propositions, Poole wrote quite simple logical clauses (ibid., p. 389), without any attempt to formally represent the temporal relations:

```
says(peter,wentto(peter,hvstore))
says(peter,clerk_at(harry,hvstore))
says(peter,vicious_sob(harry))
says(peter,observed(peter,blinding_flash))
```

---

[90] "Dempster-Shafer theory [Shafer, 1976] has been developed to handle partially specified domains. It distinguishes between uncertainty and ignorance by creating belief functions. Belief functions allow the user to bound the assignment of probabilities to certain events, rather than give events specific probabilities. Belief functions satisfy axioms that are weaker than those for probability theory. When the probabilistic values of the beliefs that a certain event occurred are exact, then the belief value is exactly the probability that the event occurred. In this case, Dempster-Shafer theory and probability theory provide the same conclusions." (Stranieri & Zeleznikow, 2005a).

2.5 A Quick Sampling of Some Probabilistic Applications

says(peter,says(doctor,shot(peter)))
says(peter,says(newspaper,disappeared(harry)))

Poole (ibid., pp. 389–390) wrote clauses about witness honesty, stating that honest people rarely state deliberate lies, and that people assumed to be honest are more likely not to be honest once they have said a few lies. The clauses are as follows, the upper case letters standing for universally quantified variables, whereas truthful_h(P,F) specifies the probability that person P, who is honest, would say something F by thinking it to be true and relevant, and by contrast, untruthful_d(P,F) specifies the probability that person P, who is dishonest, would say something F by thinking it to be untrue:

says(P,F) ← thinks_true(P,F) &
relevant(P,F) &
honest(P) &
truthful_h(P,F).
says(P,F) ← thinks_true(P,F) &
relevant(P,F) &
dishonest(P) &
truthful_h(P,F).
says(P,F) ← honest(P) &
untruthful_h(P,F).
says(P,F) ← dishonest(P) &
untruthful_d(P,F).

Poole provided examples specifying the alternatives and their respective probabilities:

random([relevant(P,F):0.05;irrelevant(P,F):0.95]).
random([honest(P):0.999,dishonest(P):0.001]).
random([truthful_h(P,F):0.9999;untruthful_h(P,F):0.0001]).
random([truthful_d(P,F):0.998,untruthful_d(P,F):0.002]).

Poole went on writing clauses representing commonsense rules, and sometimes (but not always) associating probabilities in the same format as given above. Some such commonsense rules were about someone thinking something is true while being or not being mistaken, or about having the means and opportunity to shoot someone if they are both at the same place, or about bad character as being a motive to shoot some people, or about likely explanations for a blinding flash (a picture being taken, vs. the person being shot).

Poole (ibid., pp. 394–395) formulated as follows the two most likely explanations for the observations. Here is the most likely explanation:

[Truthful_h(peter,says(newspaper,disappeared(harry))),
relevant(peter,says(newspaper,disappeared(harry))),

notmistaken_t(peter,says(newspaper,disappeared(harry))),
truthful_h(newspaper,disappeared(harry)), honest(newspaper),
relevant(newspaper,disappeared(harry)),
notmistaken_t(newspaper,disappeared(harry)),
disappeared_when_criminal(harry),
truthful_h(peter,says(doctor,shot(peter))),
relevant(peter,says(doctor,shot(peter))),
notmistaken_t(peter,says(doctor,shot(peter))),
truthful_h(doctor,shot(peter)), honest(doctor),
relevant(doctor,shot(peter)), notmistaken_t(doctor,shot(peter)),
truthful_h(peter,observed(peter,blinding_flash)),
relevant(peter,observed(peter,blinding_flash)),
notmistaken_t(peter,observed(peter,blinding_flash)),
actually_shot(harry,peter), vicious_sob_shot(harry,peter),
truthful_h(peter,vicious_sob(harry)),
relevant(peter,vicious_sob(harry)),
notmistaken_t(peter,vicious_sob(harry)),
just_true(vicious_sob(harry)),
truthful_h(peter,clerk_at(harry,hvstore)),
relevant(peter,clerk_at(harry,hvstore)),
notmistaken_t(peter,clerk_at(harry,hvstore)),
just_true(clerk_at(harry,hvstore)),
truthful_h(peter,wentto(peter,hvstore)), honest(peter),
relevant(peter,wentto(peter,hvstore)),
notmistaken(peter,wentto(peter,hvstore)),
just_true(wentto(peter,hvstore))].

Poole (ibid., p. 395) claimed for this a prior probability of 2.6485e-019. He wrote (ibid.) the second most likely explanation as follows, and stated that its prior probability is 1.15225e-019:

[untruthful_d(peter,says(newspaper,disappeared(harry))),
untruthful_d((peter,says(doctor,shot(peter))),
truthful_h(peter,observed(peter,blinding_flash)),
relevant(peter,observed(peter,blinding_flash)),
picture_taken(peter), untruthful_d(peter,vicious_sob(harry)),
untruthful_d(peter,clerk_at(harry,hvstore)),
truthful_h(peter,wentto(peter,hvstore), dishonest(peter),
relevant(peter,wentto(peter,hvstore),
notmistaken_t(peter,wentto(pedter,hvstore)),
just_true(wentto(peter,hvstore))].

This is a relatively simple example of applications among others that could have been presented here. Personally I feel uneasy with the ascription of probabilities, as it is unclear by reference to what they are determined. Poole averred (ibid., p. 395):

2.5 A Quick Sampling of Some Probabilistic Applications

My goal is to allow people to determine whether the axioms are appropriate, whether they are true, whether they cover all of the cases, and whether the probabilities are appropriate. (Of course, my axioms for Tillers' example fail on all of these counts.)

Arguably the problem is that with increased sophistication, some fundamental problems might not just end under the carpet. For sure, there have been (including in the very same volume where that paper appeared) impressive applications, but when one is impressed, it is the right time to beware about the foundations. Still, there is something arrestingly elegant about a method, sophisticated and given a cultured motivation, in Snow and Belis (2002), in the same volume as Poole (2002). See Section 2.5.2.

2.5.2 Dynamic Uncertain Inference Concerning Criminal Cases, and Snow and Belis's Recursive Multidimensional Scoring

"Dynamic uncertain inference is the formation of opinions based upon evidence or argument whose availability is neither disclosed to the analyst in advance nor disclosed all at once" (Snow & Belis, 2002, p. 397). We have already considered in Section 2.1.2 a model by Dragoni and myself for dealing with that kind of situation. Another formal model is briefly discussed in the present Section 2.5.2.

Paul Snow and Marianne Belis (2002) analysed "a celebrated French murder investigation" (ibid., p. 397). Snow and Belis (2002) "apply ideas about credibility judgments structured by graphs to the problem of dynamic uncertain inference. By *dynamic*, we mean that assessments of credibility change over time without foreknowledge as to the types of evidence that might be seen or the arguments that the [crime] analyst might entertain over time" (ibid., p. 397), in contrast with such "kind of belief change that occurs" when the possible outcomes of experiments "are typically known before one learns the actual outcomes" (ibid., pp. 397–398).

Snow and Belis (2002) contributed to how to model the emergence of hypotheses, a crux of this entire field of scholarly inquiry. The same murder case of which Omar Raddad was convicted (in Nice, France, in 1994) and then pardoned, is analysed in Snow and Belis (2002), and, in the same volume (MacCrimmon & Tillers, 2002), in the article by Tod Levitt and Kathryn Laskey. Levitt and Laskey (2002) apply Bayesian inference networks as being combined with knowledge representations from artificial intelligence, and, both elegantly and usefully (for those who do not have qualms about Bayesianism in law), develop the discussion in detail, with several diagrams corresponding to processing by an actual software tool.

Snow and Belis (2002) were conspicuously aware of the history of the ideas behind their own approach. For example (ibid., p. 399):

> Probability was introduced into game theory by von Neumann in order to establish that all games of a certain class enjoyed a particular kind of equilibrium solution. As originally proposed, this was envisioned as an objective probability in the sense of being the output of a physical randomizing device. The gist of von Neumann's theorem was that a strategic problem could be transformed into a lottery and in that form would have the solution claimed, a solution based on the expected payoff of the plays. The expected utility of desirability

was added later, in reponse to criticism of the earlier result that average outcomes failed to describe people's preferences among lotteries.

The path was short from game theoretic expediency to promotion as the exclusive paradigm of rational deliberation. Bayesians had no difficulty substituting judgmental probability for the objective original. In that stroke, the domain of application became global.

Moreover (ibid., p. 403), "there is no sharp line between assessing desirability and assessing credibility."[91] Snow and Belis pointed out (ibid., p. 404): "There seems to be little interest among decision practitioners in applying multidimensional scaling techniques to questions of credibility. Elaboration of alternatives more directly exploits the Bayesian theory, which is, after all, a story about how the beliefs in some propositions determine the belief in others. The concept that credibility might be multidimensional in character is also contrary to the historical teachings." Nevertheless, Marianne Belis herself developed "a method for the assessment of probabilities that relies upon recognition of multiple dimensions of causal considerations" (ibid.), and "suggested a directed acyclic graph data structure to organize these calculations" (ibid.),[92] one advantage being in that such a "structure is also convenient for supporting automated explanations of the assessments made" (ibid.), and another advantage being in that "Belis's technique for probability is easily implemented on a spreadsheet. The ubiquitous computerized spreadsheet program is just a directed acyclic graph manager with a tabular interface" (ibid.).

Such methods are static, and Snow and Belis (2002) adopted a dynamic approach instead, because of the need to account for unexpected evidence. "Unexpected evidence poses the additional practical challenge of keeping track of what is going on and what relates to what, subject to revision at any time without notice. We hope to show that the recursive[93] application of scaling ideas expressed in a directed acyclic graph can provide structure to dynamic deliberation" (ibid., p. 404). Once dimensions along which things can be scaled are identified, those scales are projected onto a single-dimensional ordering, and this basic operation is applied repeatedly. In particular (ibid., p. 405):

> If we have some hypotheses, then we identify dimensions along which they can be scored. To do a projection, we must have weights for those dimensions. Sometimes we can provide those weights easily. Where recursion comes in is that other times we cannot easily provide the weights, and so we approach that weighting task as an instance of the original problem type. We find other dimensions along which the first set of dimensions can be scaled to illuminate their relative importance to the original problem. If we cannot intuitively weight those dimensions, then we look for dimensions along which they can be scaled and try to weight the new dimensions. The process ends when we do have some intuitive notion about how to weight the dimensions that arise in some derived problem. That information can then be sued to scale the dimensions in the derived problem's "children", which in turn scale their

---

[91] The relations between causality, propension, and probability which take up the first part of Snow and Belis (2002), were also discussed by Marianne Belis, in French, in Belis (1995).

[92] See Belis (1973), and Belis and Snow (1998).

[93] *Recursion* is a mode of processing by which a procedure carries out some operations and then invokes itself, until a given condition is satisfied.

own children's dimensions, and so on, eventually determining the projection required in the original problem.

New evidence is evaluated for whether it suggests a dimension along which any known objects can be scaled, and is also evaluated for what weight might be given to its scaling. The accommodation to new evidence may also direct our attention to areas where our previous analysis was incomplete.

2.6 Kappa Calculus in the Service of Legal Evidence

Solomon Eyal Shimony and Ephraim Nissan

2.6.1 Preliminary Considerations

The present Section 2.6 is based on our article Shimony and Nissan (2001).[94] It concerns the use of *kappa calculus* in order to express evidentiary strength. The *kappa value* of a *possible world* is the "degree of surprise" in encountering that possible world, a degree measured in non-negative integer numbers. We applied that approach to a representation proposed in his paper 'Towards a Logical Theory of Legal Evidence' by Lennart Åqvist (1992), who had proposed a logical theory of legal evidence, based on the Bolding-Ekelöf degrees of evidential strength: see, e.g., Bolding (1960), Ekelöf (1964). Shimony and Nissan (2001) restated Åqvist's approach in terms of the probabilistic version of Spohn's introduction (Spohn, 1988) of kappa calculus as developed in artificial intelligence research. Nevertheless, we readily concede that proving the acceptability of the kappa-calculus based model in the legal context was beyond the scope of our argument in Shimony and Nissan (2001), albeit the epistemological debate about Bayesian Law clearly is an important caveat. It is a matter of how you are going to use it. If it is inside a tool for the prosecutor to decide whether to prosecute, to offer a plea bargain, or to renounce prosecuting, there is no real harm in using even Bayes theorem, as it's rather an evaluation in terms of costs/benefits. It would be quite different if one was to decide about guilt by means of statistics, and from this we demur.

Åqvist (1992) provides a grading mechanism on worlds, and then defines the degrees of evidential strength on the basis of the grading mechanism. The idea of using a probability measure as a grading mechanism is then explored in that paper. Åqvist's model draws its notion of degrees of evidential strength from two authors that are likewise Swedish legal scientists: as mentioned, Bolding (e.g., 1960) and Ekelöf (e.g., 1964). In this short section, instead, we would like to draw the reader's attention to a grading mechanism, the so-called *kappa calculus*, which bears several

---

[94] In his formative period in the 1990s, Eyal Shimony's disciplinary affiliation within AI research was closely associated with belief networks and uncertainty as well as with abductive reasoning (e.g., Charniak & Shimony, 1990, 1994; Shimony & Charniak, 1990; Shimony, 1993; Santos & Shimony, 1994). These are subjects he is still pursuing in his current research (e.g., Shimony & Domshlak, 2003; Domshlak & Shimony, 2004).

similarities to Åqvist's scheme of degrees of evidence. The kappa calculus was originally developed by Spohn (1988), but then adapted for probabilistic reasoning in artificial intelligence, particularly for diagnostic reasoning and a qualitative decision theory for actions (Pearl, 1993; Henrion, Provan, Del Favero, & Sanders, 1994). In the present section, a semantic comparison between the schemes is made, followed by a discussion of each mechanism's advantages and deficiencies as relating to degrees of evidence in evidentiary reasoning. We then suggest ideas for overcoming deficiencies existing in both schemes. More generally, we offer cautionary comments relating to legal evidence.

Consider causal relations. Around 2000, entries from a debate at an e-list pondered, or rather wondered, about whether and how (if at all) AI approaches grounded in Judea Pearl's probabilistic belief networks dovetails with the goals of Bayes Law (whereas they clearly do not satisfy the skeptics in the controversy about Bayesianism in law). Whether or not this is appropriate for juridical proof, from the viewpoint of AI it can be observed that mutual amenability of Bayes and Pearl is not inconceivable, in terms of representational syntax. Even if ancillary evidence in the legal context was to require special treatment, then nevertheless (short of unnaturally making explicit such causal relations that still defy precise pinpointing) one could figure out some filter within an architecture, enabling such evidentiary contribution to be parametrically attuned; or then, perhaps, one could well envisage adopting, say, Igal Kvart's (1994) theory of *overall positive causal impact* (or *opci*). Kvart's theory is concerned with token causal relations (i.e., such that hold between particular actual event tokens), instead of type (i.e., generic) causal relations; and, most importantly, *opci* implies causal relevance, but is a weaker notion than causing or being a cause; furthermore, Kvart distinguishes *opci* from both "purely positive causal impact", and *spci*, i.e., "some positive causal impact" (in the rest of this book, we are not going to return to Kvart's approach).

Admittedly, representational sophistication by itself does not clear the way of epistemological concerns with whether, in principle, such a probabilistic approach would be true to its purpose of capturing likelihood in as complex a domain as legal evidence. Answering that question is beyond our present scope in this section. What we think all camps would eventually agree about, is that *probability* (in the Bayesian Law sense), or even *plausibility* (in Ron Allen's sense) is anyway part of a much broader picture: the commonsense of narrative conceptualisation, for example, is an enticing, perhaps exciting challenge for AI & Law, a challenge to which the research community will hopefully respond across traditional disciplinary compartments. In this sense, when we approached the task of rethinking Åqvist's paper, we were fully aware that it is merely concerned with the tip of an iceberg. How to calculate the threshold of persuasion, in a legal burdens of proof perspective, arguably is not as interesting as the entire process of conceptualising and handling whatever turns out in argumentation about evidence. Pinpointing truth values in a legal probative context would not be the right ambition, for AI modelling of legal evidence (even if we were to correctly distinguish between legal truth and factual truth; on truth

2.6 Kappa Calculus in the Service of Legal Evidence

and verdicts, see, e.g., Jackson, 1998a, 1998b, 1998c). Supporting, by otherwise empowering, human judgment at such tasks arguably is the proper practical one, in the set of appropriate goals that the evidentiary subdiscipline within AI & Law should adopt.

2.6.2 A Review of Åqvist's Scheme

Several mechanisms were suggested in Åqvist's paper (1992), but rather than start with his 4-level scheme and proceed to the general mechanism, we begin with his generalised notion of a grading mechanism, in the interest of concision. The scheme uses a set W of disjoint, internally consistent, "possible worlds", consisting of all possible courses of events. Every fact X (a propositional logical formula) can be either true or false in each of the possible worlds. A formula thus corresponds to the set of worlds in which X is true. A grading mechanism is defined over the possible worlds. We begin with the formal definition of the grading mechanism, paraphrased from Åqvist's paper, and correcting a number of typos found there in the relevant passages.

A k-level grading mechanism on a set of possible worlds is a structure

$$G = (W, \geq, \{C_1, C_2, \ldots, C_k\})$$

where:

- W is a non-empty, finite set of possible worlds.
- $\geq$ is a weak ordering, i.e. a transitive and total binary relation on W. For any worlds $w, w' \in W$, the relation $w \geq w'$ means that w is at least as probable as w'.
- The set $\{C_1, C_2, \ldots, C_k\}$ is a partition of W, such that, if $w \in C_i$ and $w' \in C_j$, then $w \geq w'$ if and only if $i \geq j$.

Relative to the grading mechanism, Åqvist defines a notion of evidential strength, in support of any formula X, with P_i denoting positive evidence:

$$P_i X \quad \text{iff} \quad X \text{ is true in all the worlds in } \cup_{j \geq i} C_j$$

with $P_1 X$ denoting strongest possible evidence for X, and R_i denoting negative evidence:

$$R_i X \quad \text{iff} \quad X \text{ is false in all the worlds in } \cup_{>k-i} C_j$$

this time with $R_k X$ denoting *strongest* possible evidence *against* X.

Åqvist shows that $P_i X$ if and only if $R_{k-i+1} \sim X$ (where $\sim X$ is the negation of X, which we could have as well notated as ¬X, which is also a widespread notation), that $P_i X$ is inconsistent with $R_j X$ for any i, j, and that $P_i X$ implies $P_{i+1} X$ for positive integer $i < k$. Åqvist proceeds to define a "non-vacuous" version of the above definition, where C_k must be non-empty.

In Åqvist's paper the initial definitions are in terms of $k = 4$, where the C_i are identified with legal evidential grades, as follows. C_1 is identified with the set of "non approved" (*non approbatur*) members of W, C_2 with "just approved" (*approbatur*), C_3 with "approved, not without distinction" (*non sine laude approbatur*), and C_4 with "approved with distinction" (*cum laude approbatur*).

The P_i X in this case are named "obvious" for $i = 1$, "certain" for $i = 2$, "probable" for $i = 3$, and "presumable" for $i = 4$.

A probability measure p is then imposed on the set W, consistent with the axioms of probability theory, and with the grading mechanism, such that $w \geq w'$ if and only if $p(w) \geq p(w')$. The standard definitions of conditioning are introduced. In order to avoid the collapse of all the grading structure, the *principle of preponderance* is introduced, which requires that for any X, if P_i X then $p(X) > \frac{1}{2}$.

2.6.3 A Review of Kappa Calculus

As in Section 2.6.2, we have a set of disjoint possible worlds W and formulas can be true or false in each possible world. Again, a propositional formula φ is identified with the set of possible worlds in which it is true. Instead of a grading mechanism, each possible world is given a *kappa value*, where *kappa* is a function from worlds to non-negative integers:

$$\kappa : W \to \mathcal{N} \cup \{0\},$$

such that $\kappa(w) = 0$ for at least one $w \in W$. The kappa value of a possible world is the degree of surprise in encountering that possible world. Intuitively, the lower the kappa, the higher the probability, and worlds with $\kappa = 0$ are considered serious possibilities. The definition of κ is extended to sets of possible worlds (propositions and propositional formulas) via Spohn's calculus, as the minimum for all such w that belong to φ, of all $\kappa(w)$, that is to say, as expressed by *Spohn's minimum formula*:

$$\varphi = \min_{w \in \varphi} \kappa(w)$$

where if φ is false in all possible worlds, $\kappa(\varphi)$ is defined to be infinity, ∞, and moreover the definition of κ is also extended to conditioning, as expressed by *Spohn's conditioning formula*:

$$\kappa(\varphi|\psi) = \kappa(\varphi \wedge \psi) - \kappa(\psi)$$

The kappa assignment is frequently (Pearl, 1993) seen as an order-of-magnitude approximation of a probability function $p(w)$ defined over W, as follows: write $p(w)$ as a polynomial in some small quantity ε, and take the power of the most significant term of that polynomial to be the kappa, that is to say, as expressed by this

2.6 Kappa Calculus in the Service of Legal Evidence

approximation formula:

$$p(w) \approx C\varepsilon^{\kappa(w)}$$

for some constant C. Treating ε as infinitesimally small, Spohn's calculus is consistent (and follows from) the axioms of probability theory. Note that seemingly the only way to state that a proposition φ is certain, or even very likely, is to state that the degree of surprise in encountering the negation of φ, that is to say, $\sim\varphi$, is high, i.e. stating that $\kappa(\sim\varphi) > 0$. Also, if $\varepsilon < \frac{1}{2}$ then clearly $\kappa(\varphi) > 0$ implies $\kappa(\sim\varphi) = 0$, but not vice versa (that is to say, it is certainly possible that $\kappa(\varphi) = \kappa(\sim\varphi) = 0$).

2.6.4 A Comparison of the Schemes

We begin by comparing kappa-calculus to Åqvist's grading mechanisms without considering probabilities. Later on we introduce the probability distribution and continue the comparison.

2.6.4.1 Equivalence of Kappa-Calculus to Grading Mechanisms

Ignoring for the moment the probability measure on the set of possible worlds, or the value of ε for kappa calculus as an order-of-magnitude probability approximation, we begin defining a natural mapping between the schemata. Given a k-level grading mechanism G over the set of possible worlds W, we define a function from worlds to positive integers

$$G: W \to \mathcal{N},$$

being the *grade of a world*, such that $G(w) = i$ just when $w \in C_i$ in the grading mechanism G. We now define a level-to-kappa mapping function, from positive integers to non-negative integers,

$$F_k: \mathcal{N} \to \mathcal{N} \cup \{0\}$$

as:

$$F_k(i) = k - i$$

The mapping from a grading mechanism to kappa calculus is simply defining

$$\kappa(w) = F_k(G(w))$$

for each $w \in W$, and extending the definition to sets of possible worlds as for the earlier definition of κ in Spohn's minimum equation with the special case $\kappa(\emptyset) = \infty$ (that is to say, κ of the empty set is infinity). It is clear (by construction) that the grading mechanism G is non-vacuous (that is, C_k is non-empty) if and only if there exists a world $w \in W$ for which $\kappa(w) = 0$.

Likewise, define a kappa-to-k-level mapping function from non-negative integers to positive integers

$$F'_k : \mathcal{N} \cup \{0\} \to N,$$

as follows:

$$F'_k(i) = \max(1, k - i).$$

Now, given a set of possible worlds W, and a kappa ranking, we define the k-level grading mechanism over W as the partition uniquely determined by:

$$w \in C_i \quad \text{if and only if} \quad F'_k(\kappa(w)).$$

The following theorem follows from the definitions:

Theorem 1 *F'_k is the left-inverse of F_k (that is, $F'_k(F_k(i)) = i$ for any $k, i \in \mathcal{N}$), and the k-level grading mechanism is equivalent to κ-calculus where the κ values are limited to the range $\{0, \ldots, k{-}1, \infty\}$.*

Obviously, since the mapping is semi-invertible, kappa-calculus subsumes Åqvist's grading mechanisms (and if we allowed grading mechanisms to have an infinite number of partitions, they would be equivalent). Åqvist could have just used kappa-calculus directly in his paper, instead of having to invent grading mechanisms.

The degrees of evidential strength in Åqvist's paper have no immediate counterpart in kappa-calculus, but we could define them as follows:

$$P_i\,X \text{ if and only if } \kappa(\sim X) \geq k - i + 1, \text{ and } R_i\,X \text{ if and only if } \kappa(X) \geq i.$$

This definition is far more concise than the one given by Åqvist, yet it is essentially equivalent:

Theorem 2 *$P_i\,X$ in a k-level grading mechanism G, if and only if $P_i\,X$ in the respective kappa-calculus representation (and likewise for $R_i\,X$).*

Proof ($\to$) Suppose $P_i\,X$ in a k-level grading mechanism. Then for every $j \geq i$, we have

$$w \in C_j \to w \in X,$$

and thus

$$G(w) \geq i \to w \in X,$$

or alternately, using the k-level to kappa mapping, $F_k(i) = k - i$, we have

$$\kappa(w) \leq k - i \to w \in X.$$

2.6 Kappa Calculus in the Service of Legal Evidence

Thus, since possible worlds are internally consistent, the is no $w \in \sim X$ such that $\kappa(w) \leq k - i$, and since the kappa value of a set of possible worlds is the minimum kappa of the set, we have $\kappa(\sim X) \geq k - i + 1$, proving the implication.

($\leftarrow$) Suppose $P_i X$ in the kappa-calculus representation; that is, where

$$\kappa(w) = F_k(G(w)).$$

Then $\kappa(\sim X) \geq k - i + 1$, and thus

$$w \in \sim X \rightarrow \kappa(w) \geq k - i + 1 \rightarrow F'_k(\kappa(w)) \leq i - 1.$$

Therefore,

$$w \in \sim X \rightarrow G(w) \leq i - 1$$

(since F'_k is the left-inverse of F_k), and thus $C_j X$ for all $j \geq i$. ■

Proof of the theorem for $R_i X$ is similar, but also follows immediately from the proof for $P_i X$ and the following theorem.

Theorem 3 *The degrees of evidential strength defined above for kappa-calculus have the same properties as for grading mechanisms, i.e.*

- $P_i X$ if and only if $R_{k-i+1} \sim X$
- $P_i X$ is inconsistent with $R_j X$ for any i, j
- $P_i X$ implies $P_{i+1} X$ for positive integer $i < k$

Proof immediate from the definitions, as follows (item for item):

- By the already seen definition

$$P_i X \text{ if and only if } \kappa(\sim X) \geq k - i + 1,$$
$$\text{and } R_i X \text{ if and only if } \kappa(X) \geq i.$$

$P_i X$ if and only if $\kappa(\sim X) \geq k - i + 1$, and $R_{k-i+1} \sim X$ if and only if $\kappa(\sim X) \geq k - i + 1$, which is exactly the same term as for $P_i X$.

- If $P_i X$ for some $1 \leq i \leq k$ then $\kappa(\sim X) \geq k - i + 1 > 0$. Suppose that $R_j X$ for some $1 \leq j \leq k$. Then by same definition

$$P_i X \text{ if and only if } \kappa(\sim X) \geq k - i + 1,$$
$$\text{and } R_i X \text{ if and only if } \kappa(X) \geq i.$$

this formula will be verified: $\kappa(X) \geq j > 0$. However, every possible world $w \in W$ must satisfy either X or $\sim X$ (using the same "excluded middle" assumption made by Åqvist), and there exists $w \in W$ such that $\kappa(w) = 0$. If this possible world w

is in X, then by Spohn's minimum equation, it will be $\kappa(X) = 0$, a contradiction. Likewise if $w \in \sim X$.
- By the definition

$$P_i \, X \text{ if and only if } \kappa(\sim X) \geq k - i + 1,$$
$$\text{and } R_i \, X \text{ if and only if } \kappa(X) \geq i.$$

$P_i \, X$ implies $\kappa(\sim X) \geq k - i + 1 \geq k - i$, and $\kappa(\sim X) \geq k - i + 1 \geq k - i$ implies $P_{i+1} X$. ∎

It is also possible to prove the theorem by applying Theorem 2.

2.6.4.2 Reintroducing the Probabilities

Now that we have a mapping between grading mechanisms and kappa-calculus (which was just shown to be a variant, or slight extension, of grading mechanisms), we can introduce the probability distribution over possible worlds. Note that the common trend of using kappa-calculus as an approximation of order-of-magnitude probabilities, implies that the "principle of preponderance" is obeyed.

We must point out, however, that kappa-calculus is strictly consistent with the axioms of probability only if we use an infinitesimal ε. Thus, probabilities of possible worlds in different sets of the partition in the grading mechanism should also be stratified by "an order-of-magnitude" probability ratio. It is not clear that this is indeed the case in the definitions in legal reasoning. Nevertheless, perhaps the mere institution of these grades in legal reasoning is an indication that at least *subjectively* (i.e., probabilities subjectively assigned to such possible worlds by a human) this is the case.

The main problem in combining probabilities with a grading-system was typified by the example given in Åqvist's paper (for $k = 4$): a violation of the "principle of preponderance". That is, we get a case where a proposition is "presumable", yet is less likely than its negation. The suggestion (made by Åqvist) that we insist on $p(C_4) > \frac{1}{2}$ is an obvious, albeit somewhat ad-hoc solution.

A more general statement of the problem is that, if probabilities in different sets (i.e., different C_i) in the grading mechanism are not "orders of magnitude" apart, then in fact the disjunction of several propositions can "graduate" to a higher grade, if we only make such a disjunction into a primitive proposition (thereby modifying the set of possible worlds, W). It is thus the case that the grading mechanism is very sensitive to the syntax of the propositional formulas, and to the set of possible worlds which we allow to participate in the grading mechanism.

Forcing $p(C_k) > \frac{1}{2}$ may prevent unlikely facts from being accepted as "probable" or "presumable" or "certain", but would not prevent us from passing merely "probable" facts as "certain" without really changing the probability distribution, but just the syntax of the propositional formulas. This is certainly an undesirable property of the grading scheme.

2.6 Kappa Calculus in the Service of Legal Evidence

For example, paraphrasing Åqvist's "cause of death" example (Åqvist, 1992), with possible worlds: w_1 = poisoned by wife, w_2 = accidental liquid poisoning, w_3 = taking poison deliberately (suicide), w_4 = murdered by someone else (not wife), w_5 = accidental gas poisoning, w_0 = other cause of death. Suppose now (modifying the original example) that the evidence is such that (with a 4-level grading mechanism), we have $C_4 = \{w_1\}$, $C_3 = \{w_4\}$, $C_2 = \{\}$, and $C_1 = \{w_0, w_2, w_3, w_5\}$. Suppose the following probability distribution is assigned: $p(w_1) = 0.7$ (thus obeying the "principle of preponderance"), $p(w_4) = 0.1$, and $p(w_0) = p(w_2) = p(w_3) = p(w_5) = 0.05$. Total probability is 1 as required.

Now, suppose we want to decide a case where the deceased's brother is a beneficiary of a life-insurance policy taken out on the deceased. The beneficiary is claiming for double-indemnity, to be awarded in case of murder. In this example, the proposition "death by murder", entitling claimant to double indemnity payments, is "certain" (since all possible worlds in C_4, C_3, C_2 entail "death by murder"). In this case, the claimant would win his double-indemnity case if the required degree of evidence for such a claim were "certain", "probable" or "presumable".

However, one could claim that this is incorrect, and state: all accidental deaths are equivalent here, and thus we should *not* have both w_2 and w_5, but instead some w_6 = accidental poisoning, with a probability 0.1 (which is the same distribution, just changing the syntax and creating a predicate that stands for a disjunction). Intuitively, this should change nothing in the certainty of "death by murder", but this is not the case in this model. We have $C_3 = \{w_4, w_6\}$ and since w_6 not in "death by murder", then "death by murder" is only "presumable". Now, if the requirement for the evidence level is "certain" or "probable", the claimant would now lose his double-indemnity case, where he would have otherwise won it!

2.6.5 Suggested Solution

Observe that the above undesirable effect could not occur if we used kappa-calculus with infinitesimal epsilon (or the equivalent probabilities in the grading mechanism). Nevertheless, this would require that we consider facts "approved not without distinction" as having infinitesimal probabilities, which is somewhat counterintuitive.

To avoid this problem, it is sufficient if we required the following constraint, in addition to $C_k \neq \emptyset$ (i.e., being other than the empty set), for all $w \in W$:

$$w \in C_i \rightarrow p(w) > \Sigma_{j<i} \Sigma_{w' \in C_j} p(w')$$

This constraint implies that the principle of preponderance, and subsumes Åqvist's requirement that $p(C_k) > \frac{1}{2}$. Observe that the example in the previous section, while obeying the principle of preponderance, violates our constraint, since

$$p(w_4) = p(w_2) + p(w_5)$$

while $w_4 \in C_3$ and $w_2, w_5 \in C_1$.

2.6.6 Contextual Assessment of the Method

However mathematically sound the restatement of the Åqvist model may be, its usefulness entirely depends on compatibility with the context that has to provide the qualitative grading of the elements of evidence, that in turn the Åqvist model uses as input. What makes the Åqvist model (and, perhaps all the more so, our probabilistic reformulation of it) problematic in the broad perspective of juridical proof, is that it is what lays upstream of it that perhaps defies modelling, and anyway is not addressed at all by either Åqvist's model, or our restatement of the method. The input is a subjective grading of the elements of evidence, and is supposed to be provided by human experts. In elaborating the input they are to provide, this is to be the end product of complex mental processing (not merely cognitive: consider colouring by emotion). Such mental processing involves both perception and "higher" (cognitive or noncognitive) functions which invoke each other recursively, or, anyway, are pervasively interwoven (even the cultural vs. bio- or physiological extremes are not uncontroversially demarcated; cf. Nissan, 1997c). Among the other things, a rather obvious aspect of this is that by reasoning, new goals for perception are set, in both the investigation, and, say, cross-examination. However, at the end of the day, the sad, inescapable fact remains that if anybody is to provide subjective estimates as input to an automated or otherwise formal component embodying the Åqvist model, then the diminutiveness of this component within the broad picture of legal evidence and proof is an inescapable fact.

Our contribution in the present Section 2.6 has been to show that the formalism proposed by Åqvist is entirely amenable to, and thus is fully compatible with, the statement in terms of probabilistic reasoning of the kappa calculus. Probabilistic reasoning is a well-researched, powerful tool outside as well as within artificial intelligence. It can contribute to Bayesian Law, or to its critique, or, perhaps more usefully if possible, to overcoming the divide (see Section 2.6.7). For the latter purpose, however, it is other facets of the extant panoply of AI & Law or just AI techniques that could most usefully contribute: such themes as argumentation, agents' epistemic states, narrative coherence, and so forth, are all facets that deserve development. (For example, culture-laden literary concepts of narrative improbability sometimes impinge on lay perceptions of a crime narrative as reported by the media: see Section 5.2.20.3 in this book, concerning the Jama narrative.)

2.6.7 An Application to Relative Plausibility? Considerations About a Role for the Formalism

One thing that can be expected to have been noticed by such readers who are already generally conversant with the subject to which Chapter 2 in this book is devoted, is that our proposal of a kappa-calculus based formalism is predicated upon the assumption that somebody or something upstream in the conceptual architecture will be providing quantified probative values, and that the architectural module

2.6 Kappa Calculus in the Service of Legal Evidence

described here in Section 2.6 accepts this "no questions asked", because it is not its task to ask questions about what it is fed.

Arguably, leaving things noncommittal that way would not be entirely responsible, once one consider the state of the art. Such readers who would accept as obvious either conventional Bayesianism, or resorting to the integration into it of causality by means of Bayesian networks, the formalism introduced by Judea Pearl (see Pearl, 1988) – as scholar admittedly "only a half-Bayesian"[95] (Pearl, 2001) – may assume, *ex silentio*, that kappa calculus the way we employed it may be yet another frill of the same broad paradigm.

This however dodges the question of usefulness. Hopefully our formalism could be put to use in more innovative attempts to capture formally a framework of *relative plausibility*,[96] based on coherence and other facets of narrative accounts proposed to adjudicators in a judicial setting (or perhaps as well in tools for prosecutors pondering whether to prosecute).

---

[95] Judea Pearl began his paper (2001) by claiming (ibid., p. 19, his brackets):

> I turned Bayesian in 1971, as soon as I began reading Savage's monograph *The Foundations of Statistical Inference* [Savage, 1962]. The arguments were unassailable: (i) It is plain silly to ignore what we know, (ii) It is natural and useful to cast what we know in the language of probabilities, and (iii) If our subjective probabilities are erroneous, their impact will get washed out in due time, as the number of observations increases.
>
> Thirty years later, I am still a devout Bayesian in the sense of (i), but I now doubt the wisdom of (ii) and I know that, in general, (iii) is false. Like most Bayesians, I believe that the knowledge we carry in our skulls, be its origin experience, schooling or hearsay, is an invaluable resource in all human activity, and that combining this knowledge with empirical data is the key to scientific enquiry and intelligent behavior. Thus, in this broad sense, I am still a Bayesian. However, in order to be combined with data, our knowledge must first be cast in some formal language, and what I have come to realize in the past ten years is that the language of probability is not suitable for the task; the bulk of human knowledge is organized around causal, not probabilistic relationships, and the grammar of probability calculus is insufficient for capturing those relationships. Specifically, the building blocks of our scientific and everyday knowledge are elementary facts such as "mud does not cause rain" and "symptoms do not cause disease" and those facts, strangely enough, cannot be expressed in the vocabulary of probability calculus. It is for this reason that I consider myself only a half-Bayesian.

[96] See in Section 5.1.2 below. "The distinction between the structure of proof and a theory of evidence is simple. The structure of proof determines what must be proven. In the conventional [probabilistic] theory [which Allen attacks] this is elements to a predetermined probability, and in the relative plausibility theory [which Ron Allen approves of] that one story or set of stories is more plausible than its competitors (and in criminal cases that there is no plausible competitor). A theory of evidence indicates how this is done, what counts as evidence and perhaps how it is processed" (Allen, 1994, p. 606). The central thesis of Allen (1991) was summarised in Allen's paper 'Explanationism All the Way Down' (2008a, p. 325) as: "A more promising approach to understanding juridical proof is that it is a form of inference to the best explanation. Conceiving of cases as involving the relative plausibility of the parties' claims (normally provided in story or narrative form) substantially resolves all the paradoxes and difficulties [...]". In Allen (2008b), the relationship between juridical proof and *inference to the best explanation* (*IBE*) was thoroughly examined.

The challenge is to compare (in civil cases) the (non-Bayesian) plausibility of two competing narratives, or (in criminal cases) to find out whether the account of the prosecution has no *plausible* narrative competing with it at all. The latter is so, because the standard of proof in criminal cases must be "beyond reasonable doubt". It is not easy to figure out, for the time being, how to produce a computational comparator of plausibility, without falling back into Bayesianism, but this is worth trying. One may devise either a set of binary criteria of assessment for various aspects of a narrative or subnarrative, or instead some multi-valued formalism that is not binary, and therefore would have to quantify. The real challenge is to avoid the *reference-class problem* we mentioned in Section 2.4. In Chapter 5, those conceptual tools that artificial intelligence research has already produced and offers for processing narratives will be surveyed. Ideally this should be combined with argumentation tools like those discussed in Chapter 3.

Chapter 3
Argumentation

3.1 Types of Arguments

In court, lawyers seek to *persuade* the adjudicator. By contrast, their attitude towards the other party is conflictual, *eristic*, and they do not expect to persuade the other party while in court. If however a settlement out of court is sought, then a solution for the conflict of interests is sought by *negotiation*. Walton and Krabbe (1995, p. 66) proposed a classification of dialogues through which argumentation unfold. See Table 3.1.1. Figure 3.1.1 shows how to determine the type of dialogue (Walton & Krabbe, 1995, p. 81).

MacCormick (1995, pp. 467–468) defined argumentation as follows:

> Argumentation is the activity of putting arguments for or against something. This can be done in speculative or in practical contexts. In purely speculative matters, one adduces arguments for or against believing something about what is the case. In practical contexts, one adduces arguments which are either reasons for or against doing something, or reasons for or against holding an opinion about what ought to be or may be or can be done.

"A reason given for acting or not acting in a certain way may be on account of what so acting or not acting will bring about. Such is teleological reasoning. All teleological reasoning presupposes some evaluation" (p. 468). "Deontological reasoning appeals to principles of right or wrong, principles about what ought or ought not to be or be done, where these principles are themselves taken to be ultimate, not derived from some form of teleological reasoning" (p. 468).

"Robert Summers [(1978)] has proposed the term 'reasons of substance' or 'substantive reasons' as a name for those reasons that have practical weight independently of authority" (MacCormick, p. 468). MacCormick discusses "institutional argumentation applying 'authority reasons' as grounds for legal decision" (p. 467), and "explores the three main categories of interpretative argument", namely, linguistic arguments, systemic arguments, and teleological and deontological arguments (p. 467).

Systemic arguments are kinds of "arguments which work towards an acceptable understanding of a legal text seen particularly in its context as part of a legal system" (p. 473), e.g., the argument from precedent, the argument from analogy, and so forth.

Table 3.1.1 Typology of argumentation. (based on Walton & Krabbe, 1995, p. 66; cf. Wooldridge, 2002, p. 155)

Type	Initial situation	Main goal	Participants aim
Persuasion	Conflict of opinions	Resolve the issue	Persuade the other
Negotiation	Conflict of interests	Make a deal	Get the best for oneself
Inquiry	General ignorance	Growth of knowledge	Find a "proof"
Deliberation	Need for action	Reach a decision	Influence outcome
Information seeking	Personal ignorance	Spread knowledge	Gain or pass on personal knowledge
Eristics	Conflict/antagonism	Reaching an accommodation	Strike the other party
Mixed	Various	Various	Various

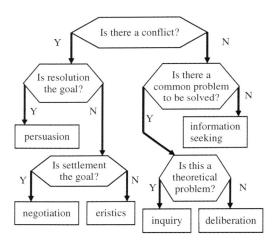

Fig. 3.1.1 Determining the type of a dialogue (based on Walton & Krabbe, 1995, p. 81; cf. Wooldridge, 2002, p. 156)

3.2 Wigmore Charts vs. Toulmin Structure for Representing Relations Among Arguments

3.2.1 Preliminaries

John Henry Wigmore (1863–1943) was a very prominent exponent of legal evidence theory (and of comparative law) in the United States. A particular tool for structuring argumentation graphically, called Wigmore Charts and first proposed by Wigmore in the *Illinois Law Review* (Wigmore, 1913), thus has been in existence for the best part of the twentieth century, yet was basically ignored (notwithstanding Wigmore's acknowledged prominence in other respects, among legal scholars) until it was resurrected in the 1980s.

Wigmore Charts are a handy tool for organising a legal argument, or, for that matter, any argument. They are especially suited for organising an argument based on

3.2 Wigmore Charts vs. Toulmin Structure for Representing Relations...

a narrative. Among legal scholars, Wigmore Charts had been "revived" by Terence Anderson and William Twining (1991); already in 1984, a preliminary circulation draft of that book was in existence; it includes (to say it with the subtitle of the draft) "text, materials and exercises based upon Wigmore's *Science of Judicial Proof*" (Wigmore, 1937). Anderson (1999a) discusses an example, making use of a reduced set of symbols from his modified version of Wigmore's original chart method.

David Schum (2001) made use of Wigmore Charts while introducing his and Peter Tillers' computer tool prototype for preparing a legal case, *MarshalPlan*, a hypertext tool whose design had already been described in 1991, and of which a prototype was being demonstrated in the late 1990s, and currently making use of *Revolution* development software. Also see Schum (1993), on how to use probability theory with Wigmore Charts.

In computer science, in order to represent an argument, it is far more common to find in use Toulmin's argument structure (Toulmin, 1958), possibly charted. See Figs. 3.2.1.1, 3.2.1.2, and 3.2.1.3.

Two or more arguments may be related to each other, in a Toulmin chart, because of the overlapping of one of the elements of Toulmin's structure. Basically, the use of Wigmore Charts and Toulmin's structure is equivalent, but Schum argues strongly in favour of the former. Some AI & Law scholars such as John Zeleznikow use Toulmin, whereas Henry Prakken when working on evidence uses Wigmore Charts.

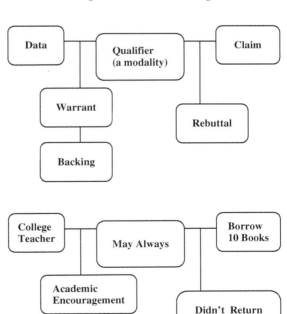

Fig. 3.2.1.1 Toulmin's structure of argument: the abstract schema

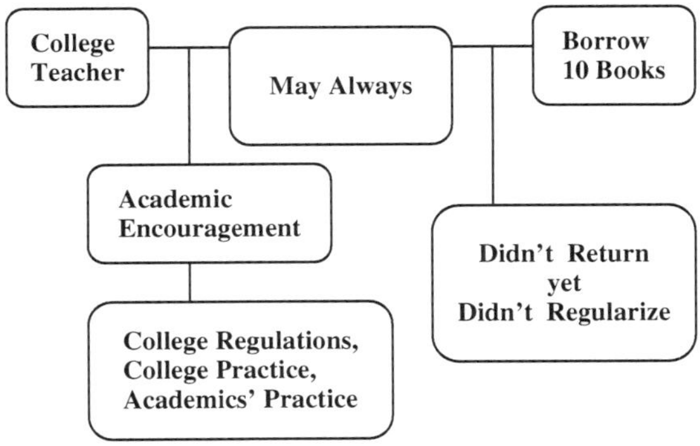

Fig. 3.2.1.2 Toulmin's structure of argument. An example drawn (with modifications) from a talk given by Uri Schild in Glasgow in 2002

Fig. 3.2.1.3 Toulmin's structure of argument. An example drawn (with modifications) from a talk given by Uri Schild in Glasgow in 2002

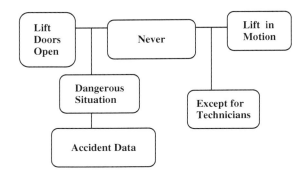

3.2.2 The Notation of Wigmore Charts

Consider, in Toulmin's structure from Fig. 3.2.1.1, how a rebuttal to a claim is notated. Anderson's modified Wigmore Charts resort to an "open angle" to identify an argument that provides an alternative explanation for an inference proposed by the other part to a case. An empty circle (which can be labelled with a number) stands for circumstantial evidence or an inferred proposition, whereas an empty square stands for a testimonial assertion. For example, proposition 2 being a rebuttal of proposition 1 is notated as shown in Fig. 3.2.2.1.

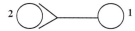

Fig. 3.2.2.1 Argument 2 attacks argument 1 in Wigmore Chart notation

Had the open angle been closed, i.e., a triangle, it would have stood for an argument corroborating the inference. In order to indicate what an inference is based upon, using the triangle is not the most usual practice. Rather, then in order to indicate the relation between a *factum probans* (supporting argument) and a *factum probandum* (what it is intended to prove), that relation is notated as a line with a directed arrow from the former to the latter. See the upper row in Table 3.2.2.1, whose remainder shows how to notate other kinds of relation between arguments.

An infinity symbol ∞ notated near something indicates that this is sensory evidence (testimonial assertions being heard, of real evidence that will be perceived in court with other senses). A paragraph symbol ¶ notated near a circle, stands for "facts the tribunal will judicially notice or otherwise accept without evidential support" (Anderson, 1999a, p. 57), whereas **G** near a circle stands for a commonsensical background generalisation "that is likely to play a significant role in an argument in a case, but that is not a proposition that will be supported by evidence or that the tribunal will be formally asked to notice judicially" (ibid., p. 57).

3.2 Wigmore Charts vs. Toulmin Structure for Representing Relations...

Table 3.2.2.1 Various relations in Wigmore Chart notation

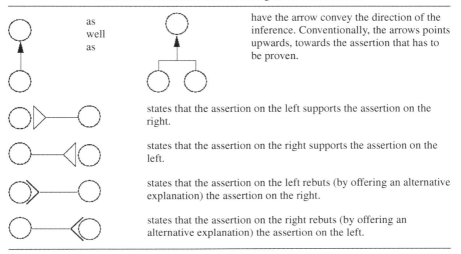

as well as	have the arrow convey the direction of the inference. Conventionally, the arrows points upwards, towards the assertion that has to be proven.
	states that the assertion on the left supports the assertion on the right.
	states that the assertion on the right supports the assertion on the left.
	states that the assertion on the left rebuts (by offering an alternative explanation) the assertion on the right.
	states that the assertion on the right rebuts (by offering an alternative explanation) the assertion on the left.

3.2.3 A Wigmorean Analysis of an Example

3.2.3.1 The Case, the Propositions, and the Wigmore Chart

In this subsection, a Wigmorean analysis is given, for an example of reasoning about the evidence supporting or disconfirming an accusation. It is not from the judiciary. A boy is accused of having taken and eaten sweets without his mother's permission. On the face of it, one would think that it is a trivial matter. Yet, the argumentation is articulate, and deserves a Wigmore Chart.

Let us develop a Wigmorean analysis for an invented case. What is special about this case, is that the context is informal: a boy, Bill, is charged with having disobeyed his mother, by eating sweets without her permission. The envelopes of the sweets have been found strewn on the floor of Bill's room. Bill tries to shift the blame to his sister, Molly. The mother acts as both prosecutor, and factfinder: it is going to be she who will give a verdict. Dad is helping in the investigation, and his evidence, which may be invalid, appears to exonerate Bill. This is based on testimony which Dad elicited from Grandma (Dad's mother), who is asked to confirm or disconfirm an account of the events given by Bill, and which involves Grandma giving him permission to eat the sweets and share them with Molly.

Grandma's evidence is problematic: Dad's approach to questioning her was confirmationist. Grandma has received from Dad a description of the situation. She may be eager to spare Bill punishment. Perhaps this is why she is confirming his account. Yet, for Mum to make a suggestion to the effect that the truthfulness of her mother-in-law's testimony is questionable, is politically hazardous, and potentially explosive.

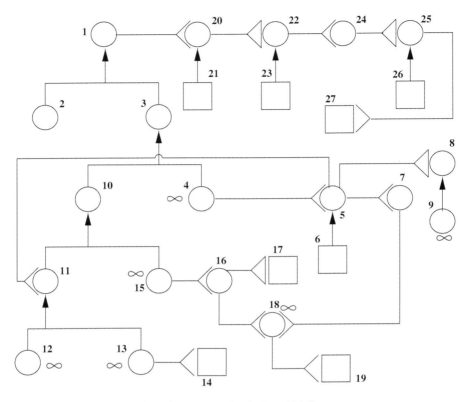

Fig. 3.2.3.1.1 A Wigmore Chart for the example of Bill and Molly

Key list of Fig. 3.2.3.1.1: Circles are claims or inferred propositions. Squares are testimony. An infinity symbol associated with a circle signals the availability of evidence whose sensory perception (which may be replicated in court) is other than listening to testimony. An arrow reaches the *factum probandum* (which is to be demonstrated) from the *factum probans* (evidence or argument) in support of it, or possibly from a set of items in support (in which case the arrow has one target, but two or more sources). A triangle is adjacent to the argument in support for the item reached by the line from the triangle. An open angle identifies a counterargument, instead.

A Wigmore Chart is given in Fig. 3.2.3.1.1, showing the argumentational relations between the propositions listed below.

1. Bill disobeyed Mum.
2. Mum had instructed her children, Bill and Molly, not to eat sweets, unless they are given permission. In practice, when the children are given permission, it is Mum who is granting it.

3.2 Wigmore Charts vs. Toulmin Structure for Representing Relations...

3. Bill ate the sweets.
4. Many envelopes of sweets are strewn on the floor of Bill's room.
5. It was Molly, not Bill, who ate the sweets whose envelopes were found in Bill's room.
6. Bill says it was Molly who ate the sweets and placed the envelopes in his room, in order to frame him.
7. Molly is very well-behaved.
8. Bill would not have left around such damning evidence, implicating him as being the culprit.
9. The envelopes were very conspicuously strewn on the floor of Bill's room.
10. Medical evidence suggests that Bill ate the sweets.
11. Bill's teeth are aching, the reason being that he ate the sweets.
12. Bill has bad teeth.
13. Bill's teeth are aching at the time the charge against him is being made.
14. Bill says that his teeth were already aching on the previous two days.
15. Mum is a nurse, and she immediately performed a blood test on Bill, and found an unusually high level of sugar in his bloodstream.
16. If there was a mix–up, then Molly is the culprit, not Bill.
17. Bill rang up Dad and claimed that Bill insisted with Mum to test also Molly's blood, not only Bill's blood, and that Mum did so, but must have mixed up the results of the two tests.
18. Mum tested both Bill and Molly for sugar in their bloodstream, and both of them tested positive.
19. Molly says she only ate sweets because Bill was doing so and convinced her to do likewise.
20. Bill was justified in eating the sweets.
21. Bill rang up Dad, related to him his version of the situation, and claimed to him that Grandma had come on visit, and while having some sweets herself, instructed Bill to the effect that both Bill and Molly should also have some sweets, and Bill merely complied.
22. Dad's evidence confirms that Bill had Grandma's permission.
23. Dad rang up Grandma, and she confirmed that she gave Bill the permission to take and eat the sweets.
24. Dad's evidence is not valid, because Dad told Grandma about Bill's predicament, and Grandma wanted to save Bill from punishment.
25. What Dad admitted, confirms that his way of questioning Grandma may have affected whether she was being sincere.
26. Dad confirms that he told Grandma about Bill's predicament, and didn't just ask her whether she had come on visit first, and next, whether sweets were being had.
27. Dad: "How dare you question Grandma's sincerity?!".

3.2.3.2 Considerations About the Situation at Hand

Proposing that exceeding benevolence and leniency for one's grandchildren is typical behaviour for grandmothers, is an example of background generalisation. This could have been one more proposition in the list. "Children are fond of sweets" and "Children are less likely to resist temptation for something they crave" are other generalisations. "Molly is very well-behaved" is an example of character evidence, and is related to a background generalisation, "A person who on record is very well-behaved, is unlikely to be a perpetrator (if a suspect), or to be an offender again (if guilt is proven, but extenuating circumstances are invoked)".

In turn, a counterargument against this generalisation is yet another generalisation, conveyed by the English proverb "Who has once the fame to be an early riser, may sleep till noon" and equivalent proverbs from other languages (Arthaber, 1929, §476), or the more explicit Latin proverb *Saepe habet malus famam boni viri* ("Oftentimes, one who is wicked has a reputation of being an honest man"; cf. in the Italian dialect of Bergamo, also quoted in Augusto Arthaber's comparative anthology: *Se 'n balos l'è stimat bu, / Che 'l fassa mal, no i cred nissu* – "If a despicable fellow is deemed good, / Even if he does evil, nobody would believe it"). Proverbs belong in folklore, yet they encapsulate generalisations or, like in the latter case, a caveat. Also consider the English proverb: "The best horse will sometimes stumble", which is more charitable for Molly. Generalisations are dangerous in a judiciary context, if they are implicit and assumed uncritically.

Note that Molly is not necessarily lying, even in case Grandma actually gave Bill permission for both Bill and Molly, not in Molly's presence. Molly may simply have been suspicious of Bill's sincerity. It may be that she topped this up by littering his room with sweets envelopes, in order to have him ensconced as being the one responsible. Or then, Bill may have littered his room unthinkingly.

Some inconsistency in Bill's reports is not necessarily fatal for his case. Bill's insisting on Mum's testing also Molly's blood may be out of his desire for equal treatment as being a suspect, or then out of vindictiveness and spite (children hate being pricked with a needle, and less stoic than adults in this respect, so being pricked is already penalising Bill, and he would want the inconvenience shared by Molly, too, even in case she is innocent).

Importantly, Mum's having tested both Bill's and Molly's blood enables Bill to claim that there was a mix-up; yet, in case he is guilty, this trick only makes sense if he didn't expect also Molly to have a high sugar level, and whereas they both testing positive in as much as they both have a high sugar level suggests that both Bill and Molly ate sweets, perhaps Bill was under the impression that Molly was reluctant to partake. She may even have succumbed to the temptation for sweets at a later stage (not when she was witnessing, or perhaps approached by, Bill about the sweets), of which Bill is unaware.

"How dare you question Grandma's sincerity?!" is an example of a political consideration about the evidence. In the American law of evidence, rules of extrinsic policy (in Wigmore's terminology) are a category of exclusionary rules (i.e., rules excluding or restricting the use of admitted evidence), such that they give priority

3.2 Wigmore Charts vs. Toulmin Structure for Representing Relations... 137

to other values over rectitude of decision. These are rules which are not so much directed at ascertaining the truth, but rather which serve the protection of personal rights and secrets. For a discussion of evidential rules and the judicial role in criminal trials, see Stein (2000).

Nissan (forthcoming b) is a very extensive analysis, in ca. 800 propositions and 100 Wigmore Charts, of the argumentation of the closing speech to the bench (by a barrister who is also among Italy's most prominent forensic psychologists) on February 2006 in a trial on recovered memories. The treatment is so detailed because it was done a posteriori, on the transcription of a long speech with features typical of oralcy. Incorporating in the Wigmore Charts not only the logical structure, but also the rhetorical tactics, is novel. It must be said that such an extensive analysis is warranted by rhetorical studies, whereas work on practical Wigmore Charts as intended for preparing a case in court can be expected to be much more contained.

3.2.4 Another Example: An Embarrassing Situation in Court

3.2.4.1 An Episode During a Trial

We are going to analyse the situation described in the following report from the free newspaper *Metro London* of Friday, January 21, 2000, p. 3, col. 5 (punctuation is reproduced without modification):

> **Lawyer: My dog ate the evidence**
> AS mitigation goes, barrister Stephen Rich knew it was going to sound pretty lame.
> When the defence counsel arrived at Newcastle Crown Court without vital video evidence for a criminal trial he told the judge: 'The dog ate it, m'lud'.
> The schoolboy excuse received the same cool response from judge David Hodson as it has from generations of teachers and the case was adjourned.
> Mr Rich, 58, whose bull mastiff, Nalla, devoured the tape after he left a box of evidence unattended, said: 'It was very embarrassing and the judge didn't seem too impressed.'
> Fortunately, for Mr Rich, the video came from closed-circuit TV and he was able to get another copy.

This story is amenable to interesting analysis, because of the role that background generalisations play in it. Namely, the explanation the defence lawyer gave for the missing evidence was suspiciously all too similar to the classical schoolboy's excuse that his dog ate his homework. I have devoted a book, *All the Appearance of a Pretext* (Nissan, forthcoming a), to that archetype; as well as 'The Dog Ate It', in The American Journal of Semiotics (Nissan 2011f). In the situation at hand, there is mapping (Fig. 3.2.4.1.1) between patterns (the awkward real-life episode from the courtroom in Newcastle, and the cultural expectation of the classroom situation of a pupil making excuses), a mapping which was activated by the claim made by the defence barrister, an event which unwittingly evoked the archetypal situation of a pupil making excuses about his or her homework having been eaten by a pet dog belonging to the pupil (see Fig. 3.2.4.1.2, cf. Fig. 3.2.4.1.3).

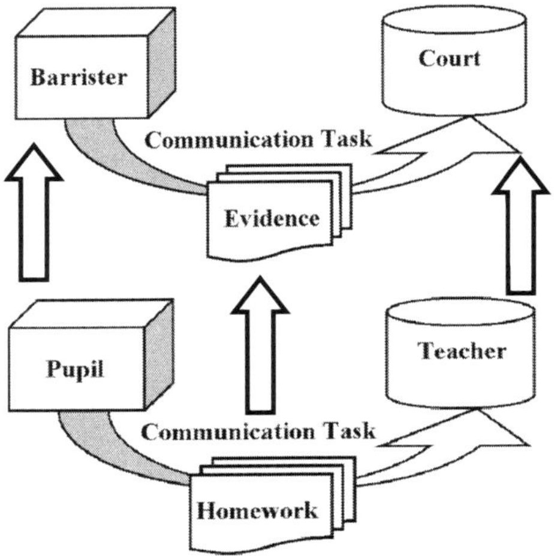

Fig. 3.2.4.1.1 The episode in the courtroom in Newcastle was unwittingly evocative of the archetypal situation of a pupil blaming his dog for his missing homework

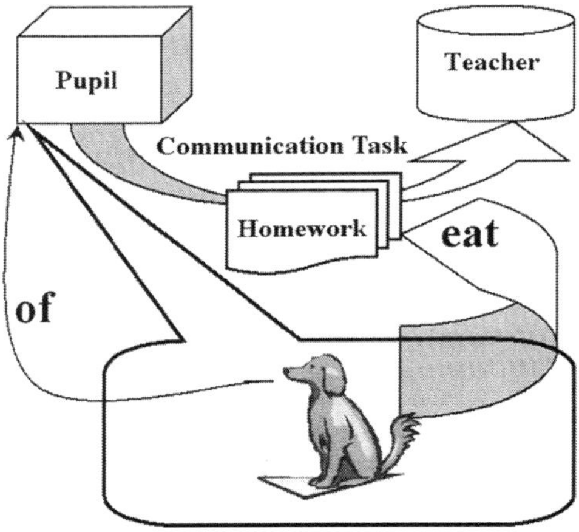

Fig. 3.2.4.1.2 The archetypal situation of which the explanation given by the barrister in Newcastle was unwittingly evocative

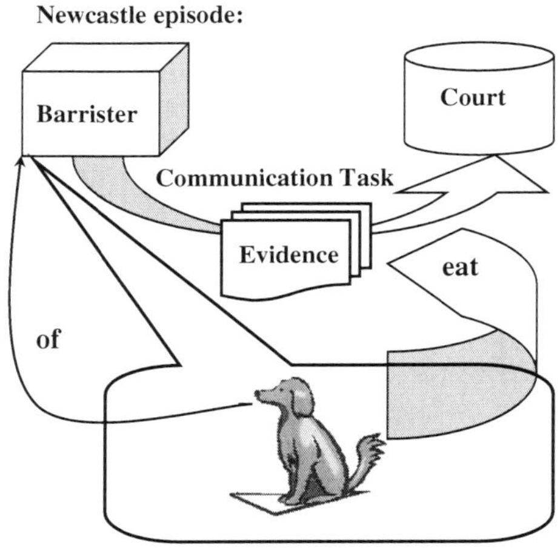

Fig. 3.2.4.1.3 The explanation given by the defence barrister in Newcastle concerning the missing evidence

3.2 Wigmore Charts vs. Toulmin Structure for Representing Relations... 139

3.2.4.2 The Propositions and Their Wigmore Charts

In this subsection, we are listing the propositions representing the arguments involved in the episode from the courtroom in Newcastle, and we also provide Wigmore Charts that capture the relations between those propositions.

1. Rich left a box of evidence unattended at home.
2. The tape was inside the box.
3. Nalla ate the tape.
4. The tape was destroyed.
5. The tape is no longer available.
6. Nalla did access the box.
7. Nalla could access the box.
8. Being able to access the box, while the tape was inside, would enable to access the tape, if the box is not safely closed.
9. Nalla is a dog.
10. Nalla is Rich's dog.
11. Nalla lives at Rich's home.
12. Pet dogs typically live at their owner's home.
13. A tape is not edible for dogs.
14. Dogs sometimes chew inedible things.
15. The dog could not conceivably swallow the box.
16. The box is too large.
17. It is unnecessary for the dog to swallow the box, for it to destroy the tape.
18. The box was not safely closed.
19. Did Nalla digest the tape? (a possible objection).
20. It is unnecessary for the dog to have fully digested the tape.
21. It is enough for the tape to be destroyed, that the dog would chew and damage it beyond repair.
22. Did Rich try to repair the tape? (a possible objection).
23. It is unnecessary for Rich to have actually tried to repair the tape.
24. Rich would be able to assess at sight the unrecoverability of the tape's functionality.
25. Rich is a barrister.
26. Rich was the defence counsel of a criminal suspect.
27. The box contained evidence for the defence at the given trial.
28. Evidence is necessary for a party to a trial to seek a favourable factfinding.
29. The unavailability of defence evidence which previously existed, weakens the prospects of the defence.
30. The destroyed tape is no longer available for the defence.
31. The tape contained video evidence which was vital for the defence.
32. The defence case was harmed, if the video evidence could not be presented.
33. Rich had to justify in court why evidence announced was now unavailable.
34. Rich explained that his dog had eaten that piece of evidence.
35. Rich told the judge: "The dog ate it, m'lud".

Fig. 3.2.4.2.1 A preliminary argument-structure for assertions 1–5

Fig. 3.2.4.2.2 A refinement of the argument-structure, for assertions 1–12

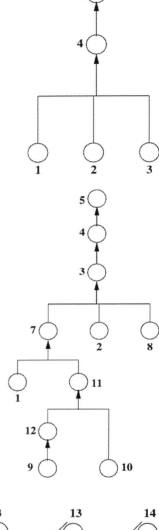

Fig. 3.2.4.2.3 A possible objection, and its refutation

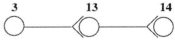

The propositions given thus far are organised in Figs. 3.2.4.2.1, 3.2.4.2.2, 3.2.4.2.3, 3.2.4.2.4, 3.2.4.2.5, 3.2.4.2.6, 3.2.4.2.7, and 3.2.4.2.8. Figure 3.2.4.2.2 is a refinement with respect to Fig. 3.2.4.2.1, and can replace it. Whereas Fig. 3.2.4.2.1 only considers the assertions 1–5, in Fig. 3.2.4.2.2 the assertions involved are 1–12. Figure 3.2.4.2.3 shows a possible objection (assertion 13, objecting to assertion 3), and an objection to the objection: assertion 14 retorts to assertion 13, and thus corroborates assertion 3. Note that Fig. 3.2.4.2.3 is contained in Fig. 3.2.4.2.5.

3.2 Wigmore Charts vs. Toulmin Structure for Representing Relations... 141

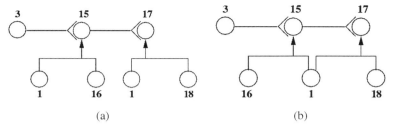

Fig. 3.2.4.2.4 (a) One more possible objection, and its refutation. (b) An enhanced Wigmore Chart, replacing (a)

Fig. 3.2.4.2.5 A refinement of the reasoning of Fig. 3.2.4.2.3

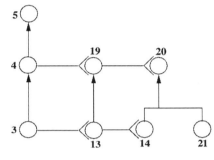

Fig. 3.2.4.2.6 How could Rich be sure that the tape had become useless?

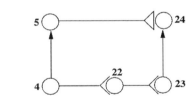

Fig. 3.2.4.2.7 Effect of the video evidence being unavailable

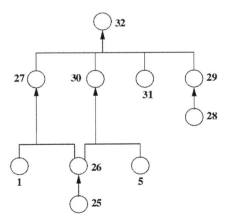

Fig. 3.2.4.2.8 What the barrister did in court

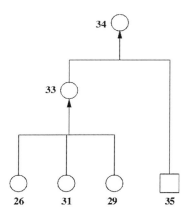

The Wigmore Chart of Fig. 3.2.4.1.4 is given here in two variants: Fig. 3.2.4.2.4 (a), and (b). The latter enables to avoid repeating the same node of the graph twice. In fact, the node labeled 1 (because it stands for assertion 1) has been put in the middle between node 16 and node 18, so that two-pronged arrow whose sources are node 16 and 1, as well as the two-pronged arrow whose sources are node 1 and node 18, can share node 1 graphically. This also illustrates the convention that the order of the nodes from left to right, in a two-pronged or multi-pronged arrow, does not matter. It does matter, instead, that arrows go upwards, and never downwards, so that one can see at a glimpse what the direction of the inference is.

Let us continue listing the propositions concerning the episode in Newcastle:

36. When people don't manage to get it their way, they may be prone to resort to pretexts.
37. "The dog ate it" is a famous pretext.
38. "The dog ate it" is a pretext typically associated with pupils who didn't do their homework.
39. "The dog ate it" is a suspicious excuse, for a pupil to use.
40. "The dog ate it is a very poor excuse for grown-ups to use, if their aim is to be believed.
41. The judge took a dim view of the barrister claiming that his dog had eaten that important piece of evidence.

Figure 3.2.4.2.9 shows a Wigmore Chart with the argument structure of propositions 36–41.

We could further represent (which we are not going to do here) the argument that the loss of the tape was due to *force majeure*, thus beyond the control of the barrister, as well as one more factor: the barrister is expected to be careful with the evidence in his or her care. Therefore, for a dim view to emerge subsequently to the claim being made that the dog ate the evidence, the contributions include this being a culturally canonical typification of a poor excuse, as well as a consideration

3.2 Wigmore Charts vs. Toulmin Structure for Representing Relations...   143

Fig. 3.2.4.2.9 The effect of the claim about the missing evidence

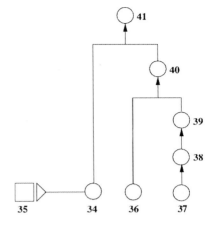

about professionalism. Fortunately for Mr. Rich, the loss was not irretrievable. Let us continue listing the propositions:

42. Later on Rich was able, within the timescale of the proceedings, to produce another copy of the video evidence.
43. The tape that was destroyed was only one copy of that given video sequence.
44. Another copy of the video evidence was in existence.
45. Being able to produce the video evidence "saved the day" for the defence, i.e., the effect was as though the evidence had been there with no delay.
46. There was no lasting negative impact of Rich making the suspicious claim about why the evidence was unavailable.
47. As the evidence was there after all, there is little reason to believe that Rich had made up the story of his dog having eaten the evidence.

Propositions 41–47 are structured in the Wigmore Chart of Fig. 3.2.4.2.10.

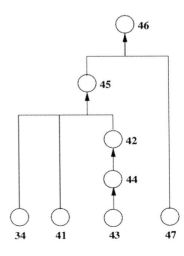

Fig. 3.2.4.2.10 Saving the day

Let us go on listing the propositions:

48. That Rich would claim that his dog had eaten the missing evidence had been very suspicious.
49. It was at least as likely as not that such evidence had never existed, or that a tape existed with evidence much less helpful than claimed.
50. Suppose that there was no such vital evidence in the first place.
51. The defence would have referred to it as though it had been in existence, as this would have hopefully been useful for its case.
52. Once unable to produce it, defence could still hope for some benevolence on the part of the factfinder.
53. The judiciary may resist the hypothesis that a barrister would allow himself such misconduct as deliberately telling an outright lie.
54. A barrister is likely to be aware of such reluctance.
55. After all, at modern trials, factfinding depends on what factfinders come to believe.
56. There no longer is a rigid dependence on being able to assess and measure the evidence when coming to a verdict.[1]

Propositions 48–56 are structured in the Wigmore Chart of Fig. 3.2.4.2.11. Figure 3.2.4.2.12 shows a unified chart replacing Figs. 3.2.4.2.1, 3.2.4.2.2, 3.2.4.2.3, 3.2.4.2.4, 3.2.4.2.5, and 3.2.4.2.6.

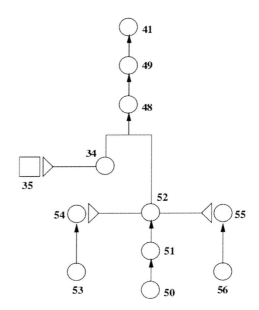

Fig. 3.4.2.11 The adverse argument about the missing evidence

---

[1] Unlike in the age of torture.

3.2 Wigmore Charts vs. Toulmin Structure for Representing Relations... 145

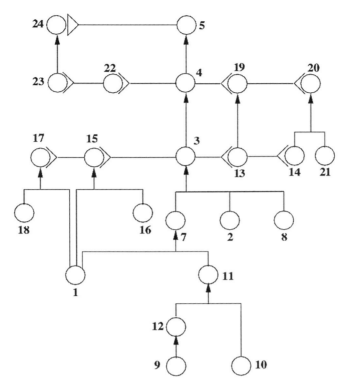

Fig. 3.4.2.12 A unified chart replacing Figs. 3.2.4.2.1, 3.2.4.2.2, 3.2.4.2.3, 3.2.4.2.4, 3.2.4.2.5, and 3.2.4.2.6

In fact, that the barrister was able, during the same hearing albeit on a different day, to produce a valid copy of the evidence that had been lost (eaten by his dog) is no longer evocative of the archetype of the pupil making excuses to his teacher, but rather of a different kind of situation that is also socio-culturally known (see Fig. 3.2.4.2.13).

Fig. 3.2.4.2.13 Thought to be lost, yet recovered

3.3 Pollock's Inference Graphs and Degrees of Justification

Much of current research into argumentation resorts to graphs. Whereas Wigmore Charts are intended to be of practical use while preparing or analysing a legal case, graphs used by argumentation scholars are sometimes more formally defined. Nevertheless, the various graphical approaches tend to resemble each other.

John L. Pollock of the Department of Philosophy of the University of Arizona, Tucson, developed OSCAR, a cognitive architecture for intelligent (artificial) agents, and this agent architecture is based on defeasible reasoning,[2] this in turn being represented as a network of arguments, called an *inference-graph*. We quote from an article of 2009 that appeared posthumously (Pollock, 2010, p. 7):

> The current state of a defeasible reasoner can be represented by an *inference-graph*. This is a directed graph, where the nodes represent the conclusions of arguments (or premises, which can be regarded as a special kind of conclusion). There are two kinds of links between the nodes. *Support-links* represent inferences, diagramming how a conclusion is supported via a single inference-scheme applied to conclusions contained in the inference-graph. *Defeat-links* diagram defeat relations between defeaters and what they defeat. [...]
>
> Inferences proceed via inference-schemes, which license inferences. We can take an inference scheme to be a datastructure one slot of which consists of a set of premises (written as open formulas), a second slot of which consists of the conclusion (written as an open formula), and a third slot lists the scheme variables, which are the variables occurring in the premises and conclusion. Inference schemes license new inferences, which is to say that they license the addition of nodes and inference-links to a pre-existing inference-graph. Equivalently, they correspond to clauses in the recursive definition of "inference-graph". The inference-graph representing the current state of the cognizer's reasoning "grows" by repeated application of inference-schemes to conclusions already present in the inference-graph and adding the conclusion of the new inference to the inference-graph. When a conclusion is added to an inference-graph, this may also result in the addition of new defeat-links to the inference-graph. A new link may either record the fact that the new conclusion is a defeater of some previously recorded inference in the inference-graph, or the fact that some previously recorded conclusion is a defeater for the new inference.

Pollock recognised "that arguments can differ in strength and conclusions can differ in their degree of justification" (ibid., p. 8). He measured degrees of justification "by either real numbers, or more generally by the extended reals (the reals with the addition of 1 and –1)" (ibid.). As a matter of convenience, Pollock represented by the value 0 being equally justified in believing a proposition and its opposite (but if convenient, Pollock would assume for this a value different from zero). Moreover (ibid.):

> Justification simpliciter requires the degree of justification to pass a threshold, but the threshold is contextually determined and not fixed by logic alone. When we ignore degrees of justification, a semantics for defeasible reasoning just computes a value of "defeated" or "undefeated" for a conclusion, but when we take account of degrees of justification, we

---

[2] "Nonmonotonic reasoning, because conclusions must sometimes be reconsidered, is called *defeasible*; that is, new information may sometimes invalidate previous results. Representation and search procedures that keep track of the reasoning steps of a logic system are called *truth maintenance systems* or TMS. In defeasible reasoning, the TMS preserves the consistency of the knowledge base, keeping track of conclusions that might later need be questioned" (Luger & Stubblefield, 1998, p. 270).

3.3 Pollock's Inference Graphs and Degrees of Justification

can view the semantics more generally as computing the degrees of justification for conclusions. Being defeated simpliciter will consist of having a degree of justification lower than some threshold.

There are two sources of variation of degrees of justification (ibid., p. 9):

> [C]hanging the degrees of justification for the premises of an argument can result in different degrees of justification for the conclusion. But there is a second source of variation. New conclusions are added to the inference-graph by applying inference-schemes[3] to previously inferred conclusions. Some inference-schemes provide more justification than others for their conclusions even when they are applied to premises having the same degrees of justification.

If there are no arcs in the graph that reach a given node (that is to say, its *node-basis* is empty), then that node is initial. In particular, it gets no *node-defeaters*. Initial nodes are undefeated. "A non-initial node is undefeated iff all the members of its node-basis are undefeated and all node-defeaters are defeated" (ibid., p. 10). "Let us define an inference/defeat-descendant of a node to be any node that can be reached from the first node by following support-links and defeat-links (in the direction of the arrows)." (ibid.).

Pollock discussed *inference/defeat loops* (ibid.):

> The general problem is that a node Q can have an inference/defeat-descendant that is a defeater of Q. I will say that a node is Q-dependent iff it is an inference/defeat-descendant of a node Q. So the recursion is blocked in inference-graph [...] by there being Q-dependent defeaters of Q and ~Q-dependent defeaters of ~Q.

where Q is a proposition, and ~Q is "not Q". "Iff" stands for "if and only if". "Most of the different theories of defeasible reasoning differ in their assignments of degrees of justification only in how to handle inference/defeat-loops while making the assumption that all degrees of justification are either 0 or 1" (ibid.), but this assumption is too restrictive.

Pollock discussed "the ways in which allowing conclusions to have intermediate degrees of justification can affect the computation of degrees of justification and hence can affect the semantics for defeasible reasoning, focusing initially on loop-free inference-graphs." (ibid., p. 11). Pollock discussed three ways, starting with *diminishers*, exemplified through two different persons, Smith and Jones, whose reliability may be regarded to be different, who predict whether it is going to rain (ibid., p. 12). Jones is a professional weatherman, with a track record of successful predictions (ibid.).

> Suppose his predictions are correct 90% of the time. On the other hand, Smith predicts the weather on the basis of whether his bunion hurts, and although his predictions are surprisingly reliable, they are still only correct 80% of the time. Given just one of these predictions, we would be at least weakly justified in believing it. But given the pair of predictions, it seems clear that an inference on the basis of Jones' prediction would be defeated outright. What about the inference from Smith's prediction. Because Jones is significantly more reliable than Smith, we might still regard ourselves as weakly justified in believing that it is going to rain, but the degree of justification we would have for that conclusion seems significantly less than the degree of justification we would have in the absence of

---

[3] An example of an inference scheme is the statistical syllogism (ibid.).

Smith's contrary prediction, even if Smith's predictions are only somewhat reliable. On the other hand, if Smith were almost as reliable as Jones, e.g., if Smith were right 89% of the time, then it does not seems that we would be even weakly justified in accepting Jones' prediction. The upshot is that in cases of rebutting defeat, if the argument for the defeater is almost as strong as the argument for the defeatee, then the defeatee should be regarded as defeated. This is not to say that its degree of justification should be 0, but it should be low enough that it could never been justified simpliciter. On the other hand, if the strength of the argument for the defeater is significantly less than that for the defeatee, then the degree of justification of the defeatee should be lowered significantly, even if it is not rendered 0. In other others, the weakly justified defeaters acts as *diminishers*.

Moreover, consider reasoning from multiple premises to a conclusion. "[M]any philosophers have found it convincing that reasoning from multiple premises can produce conclusions with degrees of justification lower than the degrees of justification of the premises." (ibid.). This is the second way, of the three preannounced. The third way, is with multiple arguments supporting the same conclusion: "A widely shared intuition is that if we have two independent arguments for a conclusion, that renders the conclusion more strongly justified than if we just had only one of the arguments. If so, a theory of defeasible reasoning must tell us how to compute the degree of justification obtained by combining multiple independent arguments." (ibid., p. 13). This is the principle of *accrual of arguments* (ibid., p. 18). Pollock discussed whether this principle is true (ibid., pp. 19–20):

> When we know the probability of a conclusion given each of two sets of evidence, the probability given the combined evidence is the joint probability. The preceding observation is that we often know that the joint probability is higher than either constituent probability, and this gives us a stronger reason for the conclusion, and we get this result without adopting an independent principle of the accrual of reasons. To further confirm that this is the correct diagnosis of what is going on, note that occasionally we will have evidence to the effect that the joint probability is lower than either of the constituent probabilities. For instance, suppose we know that Bill and Stew are jokesters. Each by himself tends to be reliable, but when both, in the presence of the other, tell us something surprising, it is likely that they are collaboratively trying to fool us. Knowing this, if each tells us that it is raining in Tucson in June, our wisest response is to doubt their joint testimony, although if either gave us that testimony in the absence of the other, it would justify us in believing it is raining in Tucson in June. So this is a case in which we do not get the effect of an apparent accrual of reasons, and it is explained by the fact that the instance of the statistical syllogism taking account of the combined testimony makes the conclusion less probable rather than more probable.

Pollock also considered other kinds of situations as well, and then proposed: "Having multiple arguments for a conclusion gives us only the degree of justification that the best of the arguments would give us." (ibid., p. 21). Pollock acknowledged: "Thus far, I have been unable to find a case in which taking account of degrees of justification has a significant impact on reasoning. All cases I have discussed can be handled by appealing to simple principles for computing the degrees of justifications, the most notable being the weakest link principle. Most importantly, there is no way to make the accrual of reasons work. However, there is one final case to be discussed in which I believe that a correct account of defeasible reasoning requires us to appeal more seriously to degrees of justification." (ibid.). That case is that of diminishers. "Perhaps the most compelling argument for diminishers is that if the degree of justification of a defeater is only marginally less than the strength of the argument it attacks, surely that should not leave the argument unscathed." (ibid.). "The upshot is that the only cases of defeasible reasoning in which we need something more serious than the weakest link principle to handle and implement defeasible reasoning are cases involving diminishers. To handle those cases correctly, we need a principle governing how diminishers lower degrees of justification." (ibid.).

3.4 Beliefs

3.4.1 Beliefs, in Some Artificial Intelligence Systems

In communication, agents reason about the beliefs of their interlocutor. *Nested beliefs* have been used in various computational systems modelling dialogic argumentation, such as Sycara's PERSUADER (Sycara, 1989a, 1989b, 1990, 1992; Lewis & Sycara, 1993) – see below in Section 3.5 – or NAG of Zukerman, McConachy, and Korb (1998), or then DAPHNE of Grasso, Cawsey, and Jones (2000). Whereas in *cooperative dialogues,* i.e., such dialogues that none of the participants is committed to any form of deception, three levels of nesting of beliefs are sufficient, this is not enough when it comes to modelling some situations involving deception, and deeply-nested belief levels are required, as argued by Jasper Taylor (1994a, 1994b).[4]

---

[4] Modelling *suspicion* in such a society of agents that deception may occur in it (de Rosis, Castelfranchi, & Carofiglio, 2000; Carofiglio & de Rosis, 2001a). Sergot (2005) was concerned with modelling unreliable and untrustworthy agent behaviour. Lying and deception from the viewpoint of forensic psychology (see fn. 9 in Chapter 1) are the theme of Vrij (2000 [revised 2008]), 2001, 2005), of Vrij, Akehurst, Soukara, and Bull (2004), Vrij, Mann, Fisher, Leal, and Milne (2008), of Granhag and Strömwall (2004), and of de Cataldo Neuburger and Gulotta (1996); cf. Castelfranchi and Poggi (1998), whose perspective on lying is that of cognitive science. Also see Leach, Talwar, Lee, Bala, and Lindsay (2004), DePaulo, Lindsay, Malone, Muhlenbruck, and Charlton (2003), Vrij and Semin (1996), Strömwall and Granhag (2003a, 2003b, 2007), Strömwall, Hartwig, and Granhag (2006), Hartwig, Granhag, Strömwall, and Vrij (2005), Hartwig, Granhag, Strömwall, and Doering (2010), Mann, Vrij, and Bull (2004), Porter, Woodworth, Earle, Drugge, and Boaer (2003), Zuckerman and Driver (1985), Zuckerman, DePaulo, and Rosenthal (1981), and Burgoon and Buller (1994). Earlier work by Bella DePaulo – the originator of the Emotional/Motivational approaches to deception – includes, e.g., DePaulo and Kashy (1998), DePaulo and Pfeifer (1986), DePaulo, Lanier, and Davis (1983), DePaulo, Stone, and Lassiter (1984), DePaulo, Kirkendol, Tang, and O'Brien (1988), DePaulo, LeMay, and Epstein (1991).

"In contrast to guilty suspects, innocent suspects approach the interview less concerned with strategic information management and instead seem to focus on providing a complete and unedited account as a way to prove their innocence" (Hartwig et al., 2010, p. 11). Hartwig et al. (2010) "mapp[ed] the reasoning of guilty and innocent mock suspects who deny a transgression. Based on previous research, we proposed that suspects will engage in two major forms of regulation: impression management, which requires the purposeful control of nonverbal and demeanor cues; and information management which involves the regulation and manipulation of speech content to provide a statement of denial. We predicted that truth tellers and liars would both be engaged in impression management, but that that they would differ in the extent to which they will engage in information management. The results supported this prediction" (ibid., from the abstract).

Eve Sweetser (1987) is concerned with the definition and the semantic prototype of "lie". Also Raskin (1987, 1993) is concerned with the semantics of lying. One may be influenced into sincerely

Take two of the propositions, one encapsulating a background generalisation, from our Wigmorean analysis of the Newcastle episode (see Section 3.2.4):

Proposition 53: The judiciary may resist the hypothesis that a barrister would allow himself such misconduct as deliberately telling an outright lie.
Proposition 54: A barrister is likely to be aware of such reluctance.

---

recollecting something untrue. McCornack et al. (1992) applied *information manipulation theory* to find out when the alteration of information is viewed as deception. A team of psychologists, Gabbert, Memon, and Wright (2006), discussed the effects of socially encountered misinformation, which may be because of memory conformity: witnesses influenced each other by discussing what they recollected (the main title of their paper was "Say it to my face").

Several works by Ekman (1985, 1996, 1997a, 1997b) are psychological studies of lying; cf., e.g., Ekman and O'Sullivan (2006). Several of Ekman's papers can be downloaded from his website, at http://www.paulekman.com/downloadablearticles.html Tsiamyrtzis, Dowdall, Shastri, Pavlidis, and Frank (2005) discussed the imaging of facial physiology for the detection of deceit. Memon, Vrij, and Bull (1998, revised 2003) is a very important book about methods for ascertaining the truth and detecting lies in police investigations, and about the flaws of such methods. Also see Frank and Ekman's (2003) *Nonverbal Detection of Deception in Forensic Contexts*. Trankell (1972) is concerned with methods for analysing and assessing how reliable witness statements are. How liars attempt to convince is the subject of Colwell, et al. (2006), who researched strategies of impression management among deceivers and truth tellers. Colwell, Hiscock-Anisman, Memon, Rachel, and Colwell (2007) discussed vividness and spontaneity of statement detail characteristics as predictors of witness credibility.

One area of detecting deception, in psychology, is the assessment of *feigned cognitive impairment* (Boone, 2007), a kind of deception which is also known by the names *malingered neurocognitive dysfunction*, or *noncredible cognitive performance*. There are kinds of behaviour that are ascribed to *malingering actors* and *probable malingerers* (ibid.). In particular, *malingering* has to be assessed by forensic psychiatrists in *criminal forensic neuropsychological settings:* a criminal offender may simulate *insanity* or, at any rate, *mental incompetence* in the specific context of a given episode, in order to exonerate him- or herself from a charge. Such simulation involves *symptom fabrication*. The assessment of the mental state at the time of the offence is the task of forensic psychiatrists (Denney & Sullivan, 2008). Another area for assessment is *noncredible competence* on the part of witnesses who claim a role as forensic experts (Morgan, 2008); dubious experts may actually believe they are experts.

In France, Guy Durandin has researched lies and untruthful communication from a psychological viewpoint. His main work on the subject is the book Durandin (1972a). A slimmer volume, Durandin (1977), discusses why people find it difficult to tell lies. Yet another book, Durandin (1982), is concerned with lies in propaganda and advertisement. Advertisement he considers ideology, in Durandin (1972b). Durandin (1978) is an article on the manipulation of opinion. Durandin (1993) is a book on information and disinformation. Psychological warfare is the subject of the books by Daugherty and Janowitz (1958), Mégret (1956), and Louis (1987).

For the computer modelling of *trust and deception* in a society of agents, see, e.g., Castelfranchi and Tan (2002). Argumentation in deceptive communication is treated in Carofiglio, de Rosis, and Grassano (2001), Carofiglio and de Rosis (2001b). Floriana Grasso (2002a) discusses fairness and deception in rhetorical dialogues; Grasso (2002b) is more generally concerned with computational rhetoric. Concerning the modelling and evaluating trust in a public key infrastructure, within the area of computers and security, see Basden, Ball, and Chadwick (2001), Chadwick and Basden (2001), Ball, Chadwick, and Basden (2003), Chadwick, Basden, Evans, and Young (1998). Betrayal within a narrative context was treated computationally (in the BRUTUS story-generating program) by Bringsjord and Ferrucci (2000). A logic representation for a character betraying another one was incorporated in the AURANGZEB model (Nissan, 2007b).

3.4 Beliefs

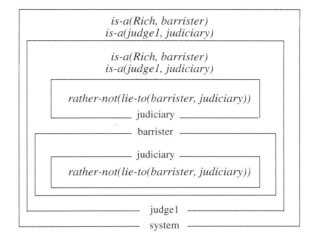

Fig. 3.4.1.1 Nested beliefs for propositions 53 and 54 from the Newcastle episode

This is part of the reasoning we may ascribe to the judge or to anybody else, on hearing the barrister make the suspicious claim about his dog having eaten the evidence.

In Fig. 3.4.1.1, we propose the nesting of beliefs involved in the reasoning about those two propositions in the context of the Newcastle episode which we have been discussing in Section 3.2.4. The notation is as follows:

- A box with a label below stands for the set of beliefs of the agent identified by that label.
- A box with a label above stands for a belief or a set of beliefs about the object identified by that label (in particular, this may be another agent).
- An outer box with a label below (an agent's box) includes logical predicates, or then one or more other boxes, and the contents of the agent's box are what that agent believes.

This notation is taken from Ballim, Wilks, and Barnden (1990).

Figure 3.4.1.1 means the following:

- The overall system believes that Rich is a barrister, and that *judge1* is a member of the judiciary.
- The overall system believes that *judge1* believes that Rich is a barrister, and that *judge1* is a member of the judiciary.
- The overall system believes that *judge1* believes that the judiciary believes that a barrister would rather not tell a lie to the judiciary.
- The overall system believes that *judge1* believes that a barrister believes that the judiciary believes that a barrister would rather not tell a lie to the judiciary.

Mutual beliefs are modelled in part of artificial intelligence's models of teamwork (e.g., Sycara, 1998). What psychologists call *attribution* and in artificial intelligence is termed *agent beliefs* – i.e., how people (and computational cognitive models) reason about their own beliefs and the ones they ascribe to others – was applied to legal evidence in two papers that adopt different approaches: Ballim, By, Wilks, and Liske (2001), and Barnden (2001). Previously Ballim and Wilks (1991) proposed an AI formalism for nested beliefs, which in Ballim et al. (2001) they applied to legal narratives.[5] Barnden (2001) describes an application of agents' simulative reasoning by agents on each other, by means of the *ATT-Meta* system, which deals with agents' beliefs in respect of a formal approach to uncertain reasoning about them. The application is to reasoning about legal evidence. It is valuable, yet may be vulnerable to a Bayesio-skeptic critique: "by adopting a bold stance about how to mathematically treat uncertainty in a legal context, one is threading on the hornet's nest that the debate about forensic statistics is, among legal theorists. Some will applaud, some would not, and causing this by itself is beyond reproach" (Nissan & Martino, 2004b).

It is important to point out that it has not been necessarily the case that computer tools that envisaged guessing (mindreading) the intentions of some player, have done so by explicitly incorporating a representation of agents' nested beliefs. In particular, when just one level of ascription is involved, some other schema of representation may also be useful in practice. The following exemplifies this. BASKETBALL is an expert system that was developed in an *ad hoc* fashion (rather than according to some neat theory) by two students of mine under my direction. BASKETBALL is an expert system that gives advice to a basketball team on the opening five and the playing strategy, for a given upcoming match. It does, by analysing the present assets of the two teams, and based also on the likely course of action of the adversary team, even though the information about the present state of the adversary team is likely to be only partial; some general information about the league or the place is also relevant (Simhon, Nissan, & Zigdon, 1992). This is relevant, in our present context, because the reasoning in BASKETBALL is partly based on *reading the minds* of the other team, by considering how they are likely to plan how they should play, according to their assets. Yet, no further levels of nesting are involved: BASKETBALL does not consider the possibility that the other team, too, may be trying to guess how our own team is going to plan its own strategy, based on our own assets.

3.4.2 Dispositional Beliefs vs. Dispositions to Believe

A philosophical (epistemological) controversy on knowledge and belief is the one between Vendler (1975a, 1975b) and Aune (1975). Our propositions 53 and 54 for the Newcastle episode are such that it is relevant to consider the difference between *dispositional beliefs* and *dispositions to believe*. Robert Audi (1994) questioned the explanatory validity of *antecedent belief*:

---

[5] On agents' beliefs, also see Maida (1991). Maida (1995) is a review of Ballim and Wilks (1991).

3.4 Beliefs

Do you believe that this sentence has more than two words? [...] It would be natural to answer affirmatively. And surely, for most readers considering these questions, that would be answering truly. Moreover, in affirmatively answering them, we seem to express antecedent beliefs: after all, we are aware of several words in the first sentence by the time we are asked if it has more than two [...]. Antecedent belief of the propositions in question – believing them before being asked whether we do – is also the readiest explanation of why we answer the questions affirmatively without having to think about them. These considerations incline many people to attribute to us far more beliefs than, in my judgment, we have. [...] I contend that, here, what may seem to be antecedently held but as yet unarticulated dispositional beliefs are really something quite different: dispositions to believe. [...] The terms 'tacit belief' and 'implicit belief' have been used for both dispositional beliefs and dispositions to believe [...] (ibid., p. 419).

3.4.3 Common Knowledge, and Consequentialism

In the nested boxes of Fig. 3.4.1.1 about propositions 53 and 54 from the Newcastle episode, we see that there is some common belief which is assumed to be shared at the very least between members of category *barrister* (thus, including Rich, the defence barrister from the trial in Newcastle whose dog ate the evidence) and members of category *judiciary* (thus, including *judge1*). The notion of common knowledge plays a significant role both in artificial intelligence models of agents' beliefs, and in game theory. Mokherjee and Sopher (1994) is a paper on real players' belief learning behaviour in economic games (ibid., pp. 62–63):

The assumption of Nash equilibrium plays a central role in modern noncooperative game theory. This theory is usually based on the notion that players have "common knowledge" regarding the payoffs and behavior modes of each other (see Aumann (1987) and Brandenburger and Dekel (1987)). It is commonly acknowledged that the assumption of common knowledge is a demanding one, and that a satisfactory theory should also describe the process by which players arrive at their beliefs (see, e.g., Binmore (1985)). Moreover, it is unlikely that most real players rely entirely on a cognitive process of thinking in order to arrive at their beliefs, rather than past experience at playing the same or related games.

In the nested beliefs related to propositions 53 and 54 from the Newcastle episode, the approach may be too "neat", too idealised, in that it appears to assume that players are *consequentialist* in how they behave. Baron (1994) investigates nonsequentialist decisions, from a psychological viewpoint, with examples about convenience and examples in ethics:

According to a simple form of consequentialism, we should base decisions on our judgements about their consequences for achieving our goals. [...] Yet some people knowingly follow decision rules that violate consequentialism. For example, they prefer harmful omissions to less harmful acts, they favor the status quo over alternatives they would otherwise judge to be better, they provide third-party compensation on the basis of the cause of an injury rather than the benefit from the compensation, [...]. I suggest than nonconsequentialist principles arise from overgeneralizing rules that are consistent with consequentialism in a limited set of cases. Commitment to such rules is detached from their original purposes (ibid., p. 1).

Pietroski (1994) criticises Baron: "Because the many senses of 'should' are (somehow) related, it is easy to vacillate between different normative claims. I think Baron has done this, leaving his model without any clear function". The sense of the 'should' in a given normative claim may be instrumental, i.e. to fulfil a (possibly implicit) desire of the agent, but desires may conflict. To Pietroski, a "pragmatic" sense of 'should' is that "agents should make those decisions that, all things considered, they think will satisfy their desires on the whole. Agents typically do what they should in this sense". The attractions of Baron's "model may result from the slogan, 'Decisions should maximize the good'. However, what about moral readings?". Baron's model as a moral thesis is amenable to utilitarianism.[6] Pietroski claims "there is a 'should' of idealization."

An example is the ideal gas law, valid if one chooses to ignore certain facts. A reading of Baron is possible in view of this, Pietroski maintains, and proceeds to criticise it. "Finally, it is of practical importance that some decisions should be made in the idealization, but not pragmatic sense (or vice versa). But the only other sense of 'should' relevant to public policy that I can think of is *moral*. And again, we do not want Baron's consequentialism for our moral theory".

3.4.4 Commitment vs. Belief: Walton's Approach

3.4.4.1 The Problem of Recognising Belief, Based on Commitment

Writing for the benefit of legal scholars in the journal *International Commentary on Evidence*, Douglas Walton and Fabrizio Macagno (2005) claimed that

> tools of argument analysis currently being developed in artificial intelligence can be applied to legal judgments about evidence based on common knowledge. Chains of reasoning containing generalizations and implicit premises that express common knowledge are modeled using argument diagrams and argumentation schemes.

Moreover, they argued for what they conceded is a controversial thesis (ibid.): "It is the thesis that such premises can best be seen as commitments accepted by parties to a dispute, and thus tentatively accepted, subject to default should new evidence come in that would overturn them". According to that approach, also common knowledge

---

[6] Cf. in criminology: "The rational choice perspective (Clarke & Felson, 1993) states that committing a crime is a conscious process by the offender to fulfil his or her commonplace needs, such as money, sex, and excitement", in the words of Adderley and Musgrove (2003a, p. 184), who applied "data mining techniques, principally the multi-layer perceptron, radial basis function, and self-organising map, to the recognition of burglary offenses committed by a network of offenders" (ibid., p. 179). Moreover: "Routine activity theory (Cohen & Felson, 1979; Felson, 1992; Clarke & Felson, 1993) requires that there be a minimum of three elements for a crime to occur: a likely offender, a suitable target, and the absence of a suitable guardian. Offenders do not offend twenty-four hours a day committing crime. They have recognizable lives and activities, for example, go to work, support a football team, and regularly drink in a public house. They have an awareness space in which they feel comfortable, which revolves around where they live, work, socialize and the travel infrastructure that connects those places" (Adderley & Musgrove, 2003a, p. 183).

3.4 Beliefs

is commitment, rather than knowledge: "Common knowledge, on this view, is not knowledge, strictly speaking, but a kind of provisional acceptance of a proposition based on its not being disputed, and its being generally accepted as true, but subject to exceptions" (ibid.).

Walton (2010) saw the need to overcome a problem in artificial intelligence concerning beliefs, and proposed a model such that (ibid., p. 23):

> a belief is defined as a proposition held by an agent that (1) is not easily changed (stable), (2) is a matter of degree (held more or less weakly or strongly), (3) guides the goals and actions of the agent, and (4) is habitually or tenaciously held in a manner that indicates a strong commitment to defend it. It is argued that the new model overcomes the pervasive conflict in artificial intelligence between the belief-desire-intention model of reasoning and the commitment model.

Walton's model "uses argumentation schemes for practical reasoning and abductive reasoning. A belief is characterised as a stable proposition that is derived abductively by one agent in a dialogue from the commitment set (including commitments derived from actions and goals) of another agent" (ibid.). Walton's "paper offers a definition of the notion of belief and a method for determining whether a proposition is a belief of an agent or not, based on evidence. The method is based on a formal dialogue system for argumentation that enables inferences to be drawn from commitments to beliefs using argumentation schemes" (ibid.). Walton claimed (ibid.):

> The approach offers a middle ground between the two leading artificial intelligence models that have been developed for programming intelligent agents. According to the commitment model, a commitment is a proposition that an agent has gone on record as accepting (Hamblin, 1970, 1971). In the belief-desire-intention (BDI) model (Bratman, 1987), intention and desire are viewed as the pro-attitudes that drive goal-directed reasoning forward to a proposal to take action. The BDI model is based on the concept of an agent that carries out practical reasoning based on goals that represent its intentions and incoming perceptions that update its set of beliefs as it moves along (Wooldridge, 2002).

Walton explained why distinguishing between commitment and belief is important, by making the example of lying in court (ibid., p. 31):

> The third reason [why do we need a notion of belief, as opposed to commitment] has to do with negative concepts like insincerity, self-deception and lying, all of which appear to require some notion of belief. For example, the speech act of telling a lie could be defined as putting forward a statement as true when one believes (or even knows) that it is false. These concepts are fundamentally important not only in ethics, but also important in law in the process of examination in trials (including cross-examination), as well as in witness testimony and the crime of perjury. It is one thing to commit yourself in a dialogue to a proposition that you are not really committed to, as judged by your prior commitments in the dialogue. There might be many reasons to explain such an inconsistency of commitments. Perhaps you just forgot, or you can somehow explain the inconsistency. Maybe you just changed your mind, as some new evidence came into the dialogue. But lying is a different thing. To lie, you have to really believe that the statement you made is false. In short, negative notions of a significant kind, like lying, self-deception, and so forth, cannot be fully understood only through applying the notion of commitment, but also require reference to belief. Lying is also closely related to notions like lying by omission, equivocation,

deception, and using ambiguity in argumentation, and these notions are in turn related to the study of informal fallacies.

Walton remarked (ibid., p. 29):

> Commitments, on Hamblin's view [(Hamblin, 1970)], are public and social. If you make an assertion of a statement A in a way that indicates you are committed to it, and there is a public record of your speech act of asserting A in this manner, then that is evidence you are committed to A. For example, if you confess to a murder under police questioning, and the interview was videotaped, then the videotape provides evidence that you are committed to the statement that you murdered the victim. In law, the videotape itself is called evidence, and when it is shown in court, it provides evidence for the accusation that you are guilty of the crime as alleged. Thus, once you have committed yourself to a statement, say by asserting it in public so that your assertion can be recorded or be put 'on record', then that is evidence of your commitment to it. Thus, commitment is inherently a social notion that has to do with public dialogues in which two parties or more engage in public conversations. Commitment is basically public. Your commitments are inferred from what you have gone on record as saying in some context of dialogue.
>
> Belief, although it can sometimes be public, as when we talk about commonly held beliefs, is a more private matter. If belief is an internal psychological matter of what an individual really thinks is true or false, the privacy of belief makes it more difficult to judge what an individual believes. People often lie or conceal their real beliefs. And there is good reason to think that people often do not know what their own beliefs are. If Freud was right, we also have unconscious beliefs that may be quite different from what we profess to be our beliefs. Belief is deeply internal and psychological, and public commitment to a proposition is not necessarily an indication of belief. But perhaps there is a way to infer belief from commitment.

3.4.4.2 Walton's Argument Schemes and Critical Questions for Argument from Commitment

In their book *Argument Schemes*, Walton, Reed, and Macagno (2008, p. 335) presented two types of an argument scheme called *argument from commitment*. The simpler type is as follows:

> *Commitment evidence premise*: In this case, it was shown that a is committed to proposition A, according to the evidence of what he said or did.
>
> *Linkage of commitments premise*: Generally when an arguer is committed to A, it can be inferred that he is also committed to B.
>
> *Conclusion*: In this case, a is committed to B.

This first version of the argument-from-commitment scheme is associated with the following critical question:

> CQ_1: What evidence in the case supports the claim that a is committed to A, and does it include contrary evidence, indicating that a might not be committed to A?

The second type of the argument scheme is in the context of a dialogue:

> *Major premise*: If arguer a has committed herself to proposition A, at some point in a dialogue, then it may be inferred that she is also committed to proposition B, should the question of whether B is true become an issue later in the dialogue.

3.4 Beliefs

Minor premise: Arguer a has committed herself to proposition A at some point in a dialogue.

Conclusion: At some later point in the dialogue, where the issue of B arises, arguer a may be said to be committed to proposition B.

This second type of the argument-from-commitment scheme is associated with this other critical question:

CQ_2: Is there room for questioning whether there is an exception in this case to the general rule that commitment to A implies commitment to B?

3.4.4.3 Walton's Argument Scheme and Critical Questions for Telling Out Belief Based on Commitment

Walton conceded (2010, p. 30):

> The problem is how the bridge between commitment and belief can be crossed. That is, how can one draw a rational inference from a person's commitment to a statement to the conclusion that he believes this statement is true? The inference is surely a hazardous one in many instances. A participant in a discussion will often make or incur commitment to some proposition for the sake of argument without really believing that proposition, or even being in a position to know for sure whether it is true or not. However, an argument from commitment is a defeasible argumentation scheme, and this aspect of it might be quite favourable for using it to argue from commitment to belief.

Questioning is a manner to find about about belief from commitment (ibid., p. 37):

> Suppose that you believe a particular proposition A, and A is not in your commitment set, nor is there any subset of propositions within your commitment set that logically implies A. Still, it may be the case that you believe that proposition A is true. What then is the link between your commitment set and your belief that proposition A is true? The link is that I can engage in an examination dialogue with you about proposition A, and about other factual propositions related to A, and judge from the commitments I can extract from you in this dialogue whether you believe proposition A or not. I can even ask you directly whether you believe A or not. Even if you claim not to believe A, I can ask you whether other propositions you have shown yourself to be committed to in the dialogue imply belief in A. So we can say that although there is no link of deductive logical implication between belief and explicit commitment, there can be defeasible links between sets of one's commitments, both implicit and explicit.

Walton added, concerning examination dialogues (ibid., pp. 39–40):

> Examination dialogue is a type of dialogue that has two goals (Walton, 2006[a]). One is to extract information to provide a body of data that can be used for argumentation in an embedded dialogue, like a persuasion dialogue for example. Examination dialogue can be classified as a species of information-seeking dialogue, and the primary goal is the extraction of information. However, there is also a secondary goal of testing the reliability of the information. Both goals are carried out by asking the respondent questions and then testing the reliability of the answers extracted from him. The formal analysis of the structure of the examination dialogue by Dunne et al. (2005) models this testing function of the examination dialogue. In their model, the proponent wins if she justifies her claim that she has found an inconsistency in the previous replies of the respondent. Otherwise the respondent wins. To implement this testing function, the information initially elicited is compared with other statements or commitments of the respondent, other known facts of the case, and known

past actions of the respondent. This process of testing sometimes takes the form of attempts by the questioner to trap the respondent in an inconsistency, or even in using such a contradiction to attack the respondent's ethical character. Such a character attack used in the cross-examination of a respondent can often be used as an ad hominem argument,[7] where for example, the testimony of a witness is impeached by arguing that he has lied in the past, and that therefore what he says now is not reliable as evidence.

Concluding his paper, Walton (2010, p. 43) proposed this "basic defeasible argumentation scheme for an argument from commitment to belief in":

> *Premise 1*: a is committed to A in a dialogue D based on an explanation of a's commitments in D in the dialogue.
> *Premise 2*: a's commitment to A is not easily retracted under critical questioning in D.
> *Premise 3*: a's commitment to A is used as a premise in a's practical reasoning and argumentation in D.
> *Conclusion*: Therefore a believes A (more strongly or weakly).

where included in a's commitments are a's goals, actions and professed beliefs. Walton conceded (ibid.) that:

> This scheme is built on the assumption that there is some way of ordering the comparative weakness or strength of the propositions in an agent's set of beliefs, representing how firmly the agent is committed to that belief. Such firmness is indicated by how easily the proposition is given up under critical questioning by the other party in the dialogue, and by how prominently it is used as a premise in a's argumentation.

Walton (ibid.) associated the scheme we have quoted above, with the following critical questions:

> CQ_1: What evidence can a give that supports his belief that A is true?
>
> CQ_2: Is A consistent with a's other commitments in the dialogue?
>
> CQ_3: How easily is a's commitment to A retracted under critical questioning?
>
> CQ_4: Can a give evidence to support A when asked for it?
>
> CQ_5: Is there some alternative explanation of a's commitments?

Moreover, Walton (ibid.) also proposed this "comparative scheme for argument from commitment to belief with the conclusion that a believes A more strongly than B":

> *Premise 1*: a is committed to A more strongly than B in a dialogue D based on a's explicit or implicit commitments in D in the sequence of dialogue.
> *Premise 2*: a's commitment to A is less easily retracted under critical questioning in D than a's commitment to B.
> *Premise 3*: a's commitment to A is used as a premise in a's practical reasoning and argumentation in D more often and centrally than a's commitment to B.
> *Conclusion*: Therefore a believes A more strongly than B.

This scheme in turn was associated with the following critical questions (ibid., p. 44):

---

[7] *Ad hominem* arguments, i.e., such arguments that attack the person claiming the truth of a proposition in order to attack that proposition, are the subject of Walton (1998b).

3.4 Beliefs 159

CQ_1: How stable is a's commitment to A over B during the course of D?

CQ_2: Is there evidence from the alternative explanations available so far in D suggesting that a does not believe A more strongly than B?

CQ_3: How easily is a's tenacity of commitment to A rather than to B retracted under critical questioning?

CQ_4: Can a give stronger evidence to support A when asked for it, rather than to the evidence he gives to support B when asked for it?

Examinations may involve evasiveness. By pretending to cooperate, a person being interrogated may hide evasive action, something that has been researched in scholarship about argumentation (Galasinski, 1996). "A speaker resorting to covert evasion can be seen as trying to make her/his interlocutor believe that her/his utterance is cooperative and does answer the question posed. Covert evasion therefore is necessarily deceptive on a metadiscursive level. Thus it is a violation of what has been called by Grice [in Grice (1975, 1981)] a Cooperative Principle in general and its maxim of relation in particular" (Galasinski, 1996, p. 376). The design of the protocol of interrogation needs be skillful enough to reflect the examiner's taking notice of, say, covert evasiveness on the part of the person interrogated.

3.4.4.4 Another Approach to Critical Questions

Bex, Bench-Capon, and Atkinson's paper (2009) 'Did he jump or was he pushed? Abductive practical reasoning' adopts (ibid., p. 83) Atkinson and Bench-Capon's (2007) formal model underlying the generation of arguments and critical questions, a model itself based upon Wooldridge and van der Hoek's (2005) *Action-based Alternating Transition System* (*AATS*). As explained in Bex, Bench-Capon, and Atkinson. (2009, p. 83):

> Essentially, an AATS consists of a set of states and transitions between them, with the transitions labelled with *joint actions*, that is, actions comprising an action of each of the agents concerned. To represent the fact that the outcome of actions is sometimes uncertain, in the scenario we use in this paper we will add a third "gent" which will determine whether the actions had the desired or the undesired effect. The transitions will be labeled with motivations, corresponding to the values of Bench-Capon (2003b), encouraging or discouraging movement from one state to the next. [...] We use a transition system which is a simplified version of the AATS used in Atkinson and Bench-Capon (2007) to ground the practical reasoning argumentation scheme, but this will still allow us to hypothesise the reasoning concerning the events that may have taken place.

A *story* is a chain of arcs inside the graph (Bex et al., 2009, p. 83):

> Given an AATS and a number of arguments generated from the AATS, a story (a sequence of events) is a path through the AATS. An argument explains why that path was followed, and so gives coherence and hence plausibility to the story. For example, 'John wrote a paper, John went to Florence' is a story, but it has more coherence expressed as 'John went to Florence because he had to present the paper he had written.'

The story Bex et al. (2009) used throughout their paper is as follows (ibid., p. 83):

> Picture two people on a bridge. The bridge is not a safe place: the footpath is narrow, the safety barriers are low, there is a long drop into a river, and a tramline with frequent traffic

passing quite close to the footpath. One of the persons, call him Ishmael, is standing still, whereas the other, Ahab, is running. As Ahab reaches Ishmael, Ishmael falls into the river. Did he jump or was he pushed? To answer this we will need a story explaining either why Ahab chose to push Ishmael, or why Ishmael chose to jump to his doom. If Ahab is on trial, the story we believe will be crucial: if Ahab intended Ishmael's death it will be murder, if there is a less damning explanation for the push it may be manslaughter, and if Ishmael jumped, Ahab is completely innocent. We illustrate the critical questions by reference to this example scenario.

Given that here "'explanation' stands for 'the performance of joint action A in previous circumstances R'" (ibid., p. 84), by which "we mean physical explanation, how performing an action in R caused the new state of affairs S, as opposed to a mental explanation, what motivated an agent to do a particular action", *critical questions for choice of explanation* that Bex et al. (2009) enumerate are the following (ibid., p. 84):

CQ1 "Are there alternative ways of explaining the current circumstances S?", subdivided into (a) "Could the preceding state R have been different?", and (b) "Could the action B have been different?"

CQ2 "Assuming the explanation, is there something which takes away the motivation?"

CQ3 "Assuming the explanation, is there another motivation which is a deterrent for doing the action?"

CQ4 "Can the current explanation be induced by some other motivation?"

CQ5 "Assuming the previous circumstances R, was one of the participants in the joint action trying to reach a different state?"

For example, the answer they provide (ibid.) for CQ5 is as follows:

Answer: in R, even though one agent performed his part of A with motivation M, the joint action was actually A' which led to S', where $A' \neq A$ and $S' \neq S$
'Ahab wanted to push Ishmael out of the way of the tram to get him out of danger, but nature did not cooperate (and Ishmael fell off the bridge)'

Next, Bex et al. (2009) enumerated (ibid., p. 85) *critical questions for problem formulation,* for example: "Assuming the previous circumstances, would the action have any consequences?" The argument scheme and all those critical questions were then expressed formally, by adopting a notation in terms of an AATS (ibid., section 3.2). A state transition diagram was drawn (ibid., p. 90) for the scenario explaining the circumstances of the Ahab and Ishmael narrative. Then, by adopting Bench-Capon's (2003) *Value-based Argumentation Framework* (*VAF*), a diagram was drawn (Bex et al., 2009, p. 92) showing arguments, objections and rebuttals. Different orderings of values result in a number of competing explanations. The most preferred value is important for providing an ordering of the motivations of Ahab and Ishmael. Alternatives for Ahab's motivation are: murder, arguable manslaughter, he did not push, or mercy killing. Alternatives for Ishmael's motivation are: suicide, sacrifice to let Ahab pass, or he did not jump (ibid., pp. 92–93). Bex et al. (2009, p. 94) acknowledged that the most relevant related work is Walton and Schafer (2006).

3.5 Arguments in PERSUADER

Negotiation involves discretionary decision making. PERSUADER has been a classical example of a computer tool supporting human negotiation. Some tools for negotiation belong in AI & Law, and have proven useful for avoiding litigation in court: this is the case of *Split Up*, a tool developed in Australia in order to help divorcing couples; it makes use of an argument-based knowledge-representation in order to meet the expectations of both spouses, so that they be spared the expenses of litigation (Zeleznikow & Stranieri, 1998).

Some of the research into computational models of argumentation has been concerned with persuasion arguments, i.e., such arguments that the parties put forth in an attempt to convince each other. Prakken (2006) provided an overview of formal systems for persuasion dialogue. Gilbert, Grasso, Groarke, Gurr, and Gerlofs (2003) described a *Persuasion Machine*. Persuasive political argument is modelled in Atkinson, Bench-Capon, and McBurney (2005c). For a treatment of AI modelling of persuasion in court, see Bench-Capon (2003a, 2003b). Also see Bench-Capon (2002) and Greenwood, Bench-Capon, and McBurney (2003).

One possibility – in the words of Bex et al. (2009, p. 92) – is to

> form the arguments into a Value-based Argumentation Framework (VAF), introduced in Bench-Capon (2003b). A VAF is an extension of the argumentation frameworks (AFs) of Dung (1995). In an AF an argument is admissible with respect to a set of arguments S if all of its attackers are attacked by some argument in S, and no argument in S attacks an argument in S.

In contrast (ibid.):

> In a VAF an argument succeeds in defeating an argument it attacks only if its value is ranked as high as, or higher than, the value of the argument attacked. In VAFs audiences are characterised by their ordering of the values.[8] Arguments in a VAF are admissible[9] with respect to an audience A and a set of arguments S if they are admissible with respect to S in the AF which results from removing all the attacks which do not succeed with respect to the ordering on values associated with audience A. A maximal admissible set of a VAF is known as a Preferred Extension (PE).

Katia Sycara's PERSUADER is a computer system for argumentation-based negotiation (Sycara, 1989a, 1989b, 1990, 1992; Lewis & Sycara, 1993). Its application is to labour negotiation. As being a multi-agent system, it involved three agents: a trade union negotiating on behalf of its workers, a company, and a mediator. These try to reach an agreement. There is an iterated cycle of exchanging proposals and counter-proposals. The issues of the negotiation in the PERSUADER project were various, including wages, pensions, seniority, and subcontracting.

For each agent, its beliefs were represented in PERSUADER, and these beliefs were about that agent's goals, and the interrelationships among those goals. For a

---

[8] For *audiences* in *argumentation frameworks*, see Bench-Capon, Doutre, and Dunne (2007).
[9] The *acceptability* of arguments is the subject of Dung (1995), the paper that introduced *argumentation frameworks*.

particular position, generally PERSUADER could generate more than one possible argument. The weaker type of argument was presented first, and then arguments were presented by increasing strength (Sycara, 1989b, p. 131), in the following order:

1. appeal to universal principle;
2. appeal to a theme;
3. appeal to authority;
4. appeal to "status quo",
5. appeal to "minor standards";
6. appeal to "prevailing practice";
7. appeal to precedents as counter-examples,
8. threaten.

Given goals of an agent were ranked by means of an integer value quantifying their respective strengths. For example,

> Importance of wage-goal1 is 6 for union1

Starting from this statement, PERSUADER would, in order to generate arguments, search the goal-graph of the opposing agent (the company), and (according to Sycara, 1989b, p. 131) find out that:

> Increase in wage-goal1 by company1 will result in
>   increase in economic-concessions,
>   labour-cost1,
>   production-cost1
> Increase in wage-goal1 by company1 will result in
>   decrease in profits1
> To compensate, company1 can
>   decrease fringe-benefits1,
>   decrease employment1,
>   increase plant-efficiency1,
>   increase sales1

How does such a remedy on the part of the company conflict with the union's goals? PERSUADER would detect right away, based on the union's goal-graph, that:

Only   decrease fringe-benefits1,
       decrease employment1
   violate goals of union1
Importance of fringe-benefits1 is 4 for union1
Importance of employment1 is 8 for union1
Since importance of employment1 > importance of wage-goal1
One possible argument found

3.5 Arguments in PERSUADER

The argument generated (Sycara, 1989b), made to the trade union after this has refused a proposed wage increase, is that:

If the company is forced to grant higher wage increases, then it will decrease employment.

In fact, the company could remedy by reducing employment, because it has the option to resort to subcontracting, or to increase automation. The graph shown in Fig. 3.5.1 represents the beliefs of a company, whose overarching goal is to maximise its profits. In order to increase profits, the company believes that it should decrease production costs or increase sales. In order to increase sales, the company should set for itself the subgoals of increasing quality or decreasing prices. In order to decrease production cost, the company should set for itself the subgoals of increasing plant efficiency, decreasing materials cost, or decreasing labour cost. In order to achieve a decrease in labour cost, the company could decrease employment

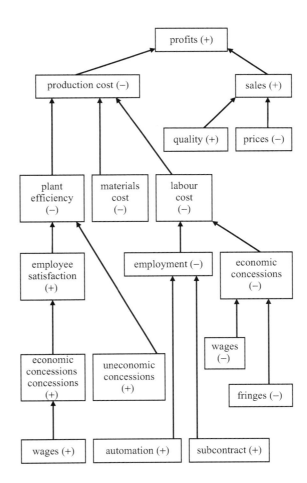

Fig. 3.5.1 The hierarchy (tree) of beliefs of a company concerning what its goals are, and how they relate to each other

(by increasing automation or subcontracting), or then it should obtain economic concessions from their workforce, by decreasing wages or by decreasing fringe benefits. An increase in employee satisfaction would be beneficial for increasing plant efficiency. Employee satisfaction would increase if uneconomic concessions are made, or then if economic concessions are made by increasing wages.

A possible criticism that could be levelled at such workings of PERSUADER is that it makes the respective positions of the parties too rigid. Human negotiators often possess more knowledge of the specifics or of contingencies than in a general goal-hierarchy,[10] as well as knowledge that either parties or both may be reluctant to make explicit, except when it is convenient. This is why human negotiators may find some leeway when requesting or making concessions.

A logical representation was adopted by Kraus, Sycara, and Evenchik (1998), in order to model ideas about negotiation that were present in PERSUADER. My former colleague Sarit Kraus authored a related book (2001), *Strategic Negotiation in Multiagent Environments*.

3.6 Representing Arguments in *Carneades*

3.6.1 *Carneades vs. Toulmin*

In Toulmin's model, as seen in Fig. 3.2.1.1, an argument consists of a single premise ("Datum" or "Data"), of the Claim (which is the conclusion), of a Qualifier which states the probative value of the inference (e.g., *necessarily,* or *presumably*), of the Warrant – which is a kind of rule which supports the inference from the premise to the conclusion of the argument – and of the Backing (an additional piece of data, which provides support for the warrant), as well as of a Rebuttal (which is an exception).

---

[10] The goal-trees (goal hierarchies) of both parties in PERSUADER are somewhat reminiscent of the goal-trees in Jaime Carbonell's POLITICS. Realising the hierarchy of goals, or their relative importance, is essential, as shown by Jaime Carbonell (1978, 1979, 1981) in his POLITICS system. Carbonell related about a bug which earlier on in his project had caused the programme – when reasoning about the perception of the imminent threat of the Soviet Union invading Czechoslovakia (in 1968) requiring the American president to intervene at a time when the relations between the U.S. and the Soviet Union had recently soured (because of allegations about spying) so that the influence of the President on Brezhnev could be expected to be less effective concerning the Czechoslovak crisis – to wrongly infer that the President of the United States should congratulate Brezhnev, as this is what people are supposed to do when they need to improve their relations. The achievement of a lesser goal was being suggested, with a plan that would harm a more important goal. This problem was fixed. Other AI tools known from the research literature have been reasoning about international politics. ABDUL/ILANA was an AI programme that used to simulate the generation of adversary arguments on an international conflict (Flowers, McGuire, & Birnbaum 1982); such arguments are intended to persuade a third party, but not one's opponents.

3.6 Representing Arguments in *Carneades*

Gordon and Walton (2006)[11] described a formal model, implemented in *Carneades,* using a functional programming language and Semantic Web technologies. In the model underlying this tool, instead of Toulmin's single datum there generally is a set of premises. A Rebuttal is modelled using a contrary argument. The Qualifier, which in Toulmin's approach indicates the probative weight of the argument, in *Carneades* is handled by means of a degree, out of a set of proof standards (see below). *Carneades* treats Warrant and Backing differently from Toulmin. In fact, *Carneades* does not directly allow arguments about other arguments, and the conclusion of an argument must be a statement. Therefore, with *Carneades* the equivalent of Toulmin's Warrant is to add a presumption for the warrant to the premises of an argument. "Backing, in turn, can be modelled as a premise of an argument supporting the warrant" (ibid.).

3.6.2 Proof Standards in Carneades

Let us consider in particular the standards of proof[12] as represented in *Carneades*. Gordon and Walton (2006) define four proof standards,[13] for *Carneades*. "If a statement satisfies a proof standard, it will also satisfy all weaker proof standards".

1. The weakest is SE (scintilla of evidence): "A statement meets this standard iff it is supported by at least one defensible pro argument".
2. The second weakest is PE (preponderance of the evidence): "A statement meets this standard iff its strongest defensible pro argument outweighs its strongest defensible con argument".
3. A stronger standard is DV: "A statement meets this standard iff it is supported by at least one defensible pro argument and none of its con arguments is defensible".
4. The strongest is BRD (beyond reasonable doubt: not necessarily in its legal meaning): "A statement meets this standard iff it is supported by at least one defensible pro argument, all of its pro arguments are defensible and none of its con arguments are defensible".

3.6.3 The Notation of Carneades

In Gordon and Walton's (2006) notation for argument graphs, a circle node is an argument, a box is a statement. The labels for the argument or the statement are inside the circle node or the box node. Arguments have boxes on both sides in the

---

[11] The *Carneades* model is also the subject is the subject of both Gordon and Walton (2006), and Gordon, Prakken, and Walton (2007).
[12] Cf. Bex and Walton's (2006) 'Burdens and Standards of Proof for Inference to the Best Explanation'. Also see Atkinson and Bench-Capon (2007).
[13] Cf. Freeman (1994), and see Section 3.11.4.2 below in this book.

path: boxes and circles alternate in the path. Edges in the graph are labelled as follows.

If there is a black filled circle (which means *presumption*) at the end of an edge —• which touches an argument node, this indicates that the statement in the source node (a box) is a presumption, and as such it is a premise of that argument.

If the circle is hollow, instead, then this edge —∘ stands for an exception, and the exception statement is a premise for the argument. Had the edge an arrow head, then the statement in its source would have been an ordinary premise.

In the formulae which accompany the argument graph within the same approach, each formula is labelled with an argument identifier, and each formula has a left-hand side (the set of premises), a right-hand side (a statement identifier, this being the conclusion), and an arrow from the left-hand side to the right-hand side.

The arrow indicates this is a pro argument, but if its head is not an arrow head but rather a hollow circle, then this is a con (contrary) argument.

The left-hand side of the rule is a list of premises, separated by commas. The premises may be statement identifiers with no circle prefix (then this is an ordinary premise), or a statement identifier prefixated with a black circle (then this is a presumption), or a statement prefixated with a hollow circle (then this is an exception).

Examples of formulae are shown in Table 3.6.3.1.

Table 3.6.3.1 Examples of notation in *Carneades*

a1.	b, ∘c	—>	a
a2.	d, •e	—∘	a

These are two out of five formulae which in Gordon and Walton (2006) accompany their Fig. 1, a reduced version of which (representing only the two formulae given above) appears here as Fig. 3.6.3.1.

Fig. 3.6.3.1 A tree-like representation of formulae

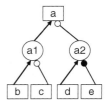

3.7 Some Computer Tools that Handle Argumentation

Not all computer tools handle argumentation in the same perspective, or with the same theoretical foundations, or with a similar interface structure or protocol. Take *Convince Me* (Schank & Ranney, 1995), one of the argumentation visualisation tools reviewed in van den Braak, van Oostendorp, Prakken, and Vreeswijk (2006). It is

3.7 Some Computer Tools that Handle Argumentation

based on Thagard's Theory of Explanatory Coherence (e.g., Thagard, 1989, 2000a, 2000b, 2004), and the arguments consist of causal networks of nodes (which can display either evidence or hypotheses), and the conclusion which users draw from them. *Convince Me* predicts the user's evaluations of the hypotheses based on the arguments produced, and gives a feedback about the plausibility of the inferences which the users draw.

Some tools envisage collaboration among users. *Reason!Able*, developed by Tim van Gelder (2002),[14] a philosopher from the University of Melbourne, is not designed for collaboration: the intended primary usage is by one user per session. *Reason!Able* guides the user step-by-step through the process of constructing an argument tree,[15] containing claims, reasons, and objections, the latter two kinds being complex objects which can be unfolded to see the premises. *Reason!Able* is intended for single-user instruction and learning of argumentation techniques, for which it is well suited.

Collaborative problem identification and solving is the purpose of IBIS, an Issue-Based Information System. Problems are decomposed into issues. *QuestMap* (Carr, 2003) is based on IBIS, mediates discussions, supports collaborative argumentation, and creates information maps, in the context of legal education.

The convenience of displaying the structure of arguments visually has prompted the development of tools with that task[16]; e.g., Carr (2003) described the use of the already mentioned computer tool, *QuestMap* (Conklin & Begeman, 1988) for visualising arguments, for use in teaching legal argumentation; the paper was published in a volume itself devoted to software tools for visualising argumentation. Reed and Rowe (2001), at the University of Dundee in Scotland, described an argument visualisation system called *Araucaria*.[17] Arguments analysed using this tool can be saved in a format called *AML* (for *Argument Markup Language*), which is an XML language (concerning XML, see Section 6.1.7.2 in the present book). According to Walton et al. (2008, p. 24),

> Araucaria is similar to a software tool called Reason!Able [... see above], which has been well tested and is very simple and easy to use. Where Araucaria is aimed at argument analysis, for researchers and undergraduate teaching, Reason!Able is aimed at argument construction, for more introductory teaching earlier in the curriculum. The two thus complement each other.

Araucaria is not only a software tool for argument analysis; it makes it possible to found the analysis on argumentation schemes. This was discussed by Walton et al. (2008, pp. 367–415), who showed "how, with an understanding of defeasibility in schemes, various techniques can be used to formally describe argumentation

---

[14] Cf. van Gelder and Rizzo (2001).

[15] A *tree* is such a graph, that any two nodes are connected by exactly one path.

[16] In 2007, the journal *Law, Probability and Risk* published a special issue (Tillers, 2007) whose title is *Graphic and Visual Representations of Evidence and Inference in Legal Settings*.

[17] *Araucaria* is available for free at http://www.computing.dundee.ac.uk/staff/creed/araucaria

schemes" (ibid., p. 392). Prakken, Reed, and Walton (2003), a paper on using argumentation schemes for reasoning on legal evidence, is mainly an exploration of applying *Araucaria* to an analysis in the style of Wigmore Charts. That article discussed appropriate argument structures for reasoning about evidence in relation to hypothesising crime scenarios. Bart Verheij (1999, 2003) described the *ArguMed* computer tool for visualising arguments, whereas Loui et al. (1997) proposed a tool called *Room 5*. *ArguMed* was discussed from a comparative perspective in Walton et al. (2008, pp. 397–399). In particular, they remarked about a peculiar trait (ibid., p. 398):

> In ArguMed, undercutting moves, like asking a critical question, are modelled by a concept called entanglement. The question, or other rebuttal, attacks the inferential link between the premises and conclusion of the original argument, and thereby requires the retraction of the original conclusion. On a diagram, entanglement is represented as a line that meets another line at a junction marked by an X.

In his book *Virtual Arguments*, Verheij (2005) discussed the design of software tools being "argument assistants" for lawyers and other arguers. Several tools or approaches to argument visualisation were reported about in a paper collection edited by Kirschner, Buckingham Shum, and Carr (2003).

3.8 Four Layers of Legal Arguments

Lodder (2004) proposed a procedural model of legal argumentation. Prakken and Sartor (2002) usefully "propose that models of legal argument can be described in terms of four layers.

1. The first, *logical* layer defines what arguments are, i.e., how pieces of information can be combined to provide basic support for a claim.
2. The second, *dialectical* layer focuses on conflicting arguments: it introduces such notions as 'counterargument', 'attack', 'rebuttal' and 'defeat', and it defines, given a set of arguments and evaluation criteria, which arguments prevail.
3. The third, *procedural* layer regulates how an actual dispute can be conducted, i.e., how parties can introduce or challenge new information and state new arguments. In other words, this level defines the possible speech acts, and the discourse rules governing them. Thus the procedural layer differs from the first two in one crucial respect. While those layers assume a fixed set of premises, at the procedural layer the set of premises is constructed dynamically, during a debate.
4. This also holds for the final layer, the *strategic* or *heuristic* one, which provides rational ways of conducting a dispute within the procedural bounds of the third layer" (Prakken & Sartor, 2002, section 1.2).

3.9 A Survey of the Literature on Computational Models of Argumentation

3.9.1 Within AI & Law

Within AI & Law, models of argumentation are thriving. In the compass of this book we can cite relevant work, but the extent to which we actually delve into their content is limited. Let us start by citing the literature. We shall turn to a short discussion next. A good survey from which to start, is Prakken and Sartor (2002), which discusses the role of logic in computational models of legal argument. "Argumentation is one of the central topics of current research in Artificial Intelligence and Law. It has attracted the attention of both logically inclined and design-oriented researchers. Two common themes prevail. The first is that legal reasoning is defeasible, i.e., an argument that is acceptable in itself can be overturned by counterarguments. The second is that legal reasoning is usually performed in a context of debate and disagreement. Accordingly, such notions are studied as argument moves, attack, dialogue, and burden of proof" (ibid., p. 342).

"The main focus" of major projects in the "design" strand "is defining persuasive argument moves, moves which would be made by 'good' human lawyers. By contrast, much logic-based research on legal argument has focused on defeasible *inference*, inspired by AI research on nonmonotonic reasoning[18] and defeasible argumentation" (ibid., p. 343).

One should not mistakenly believe that models of argument are just either logicist, or pragmatic *ad hoc* treatments which are not probabilistic. There also is an important category, probabilistic models of argument, with which we are not concerned in this chapter. We deal with probabilistic models elsewhere, in this book.

In the literature on computational models of argumentation within AI & Law, the HYPO system, CABARET, and CATO (in chronological order) were prominent during the 1990s.[19] Other important research was conducted by Bench-Capon's team

---

[18] "Traditional mathematical logic is *monotonic*: It begins with a set of axioms, assumed to be true, and infers their consequences. If we add new information to this system, it may cause the set of true statements to increase. Adding knowledge will never make the set of true statements decrease. This monotonic property leads to problems when we attempt to model reasoning based on beliefs and assumptions. In reasoning with uncertainty, humans draw conclusions based on their current set of beliefs and assumptions. In reasoning with uncertainty, humans draw conclusions based on their current set of beliefs; however, unlike mathematical axioms, these beliefs, along with their consequences, may change as more information becomes available. *Nonmonotonic reasoning* addresses the problem of changing belief. A nonmonotonic reasoning system handles uncertainty by making the most reasonable assumptions in light of uncertain information. It then proceeds with its reasoning as if these assumptions were true. At a later time, a belief may change, necessitating a reexamination of any conclusions derived from that belief" (Luger & Stubblefield, 1998, p. 269). See, e.g., Antoniou (1997).

[19] See Ashley (1991) on the HYPO system (which modelled adversarial reasoning with legal precedents), which was continued in the CABARET project (Rissland & Skalak, 1991), and the CATO project (Aleven & Ashley, 1997).

in Liverpool, and by Prakken and his collaborators. Books include Prakken (1997), Ashley (1991).[20] There also are several paper-collections, stemming from conferences, which are devoted to computational models of argumentation, and of legal argument in particular.[21] The literature is vast.[22]

For a treatment of the generation of intentions through argumentation, see Atkinson, Bench-Capon, and McBurney (2005a); cf. Atkinson, Bench-Capon, and McBurney (2005b). Kowalski and Toni (1996) discuss a logical model of abstract argumentation, in an AI & Law forum. Bondarenko, Dung, Kowalski, and Toni (1997), also stemming from Kowalski's team at Imperial College, London, approached default reasoning by means of an abstract argumentation-theoretic framework. Toni and Kowalski (1996) apply an argumentation-theoretic approach to the transformation of logic programs. The starting point of Cayrol and Lagasquie-Schiex (2006) is bipolar argumentation frameworks, i.e., such frameworks that the interaction between arguments can be not only attack, but also, explicitly support; they go on to propose a framework "where conflicts occur between sets of arguments, characterised as coalitions of supporting arguments".

In logic-based research, "the focus was first on reasoning with rules and exceptions and with conflicting rules. After a while, some turned their attention to logical accounts of case-based reasoning [...]. Another shift in focus occurred after it was realised that legal reasoning is bound not only by the rules of logic but also by those of fair and effective procedure. Accordingly, logical models of legal argument have been augmented with a dynamic component, capturing that the information with which a case is decided is not somehow 'there' to be applied, but is constructed dynamically, in the course of a legal procedure" (Prakken & Sartor, 2002, p. 343).[23]

---

[20] See now the book by Besnard and Hunter (2008), as well as several books by Walton (1996a, 1996b, 1998a, 2002, 2004), Walton, Reed, and Macagno (2008).

[21] Paper collections include, e.g., Dunne and Bench-Capon (2005), Reed and Norman (2003), Prakken and Sartor (1996b), Grasso, Reed, and Carenini (2004), Carenini, Grasso, and Reed (2002).

[22] See as well, e.g., Dix, Parsons, Prakken, and Simari (2009), Prakken (2008a, 2008b, 2005, 2004, 2000), Bex and Prakken (2004), Bex, Prakken, Reed, and Walton (2003), Bex, et al. (2007), Bex, van Koppen, and Prakken (2010), Prakken, Reed, and Walton (2004), Bench-Capon (1997), Bench-Capon, Coenen, and Leng (2000), Vreeswijk and Prakken (2000), Amgoud, Caminada, Cayrol, Doutre, and Lagasquie-Schiex et al. (2004), McBurney and Prakken (2004), Caminada, Doutre, Modgil, Prakken, and Vreeswijk (2004), Bench-Capon, Freeman, Hohmann, and Prakken (2003), as well as Allen, Bench-Capon, and Staniford (2000), Loui and Norman (1995), Sartor (1994), Prakken and Sartor (1995a, 1995b, 1996a, 1998), Freeman and Farley (1996), Rissland, Skalak, and Friedman (1996), Skalak and Rissland (1992), Zeleznikow and Stranieri (1998), Stranieri and Zeleznikow (2001b), Hunter, Tyree, and Zeleznikow (1993), Zeleznikow (2002a), Prakken (2002), Prakken and Vreeswijk (2002).

[23] For studies of argumentation, also see Verheij (2000, 2002). In particular, refer to Alexy's (1989) *A Theory of Legal Argumentation*. The approach of Walton (1996a, 1996b, 1998a) eventually evolved into Gordon and Walton (2006), which describes a formal model implemented in *Carneades*. By Douglas Walton, also see e.g. his books *Legal Argumentation and Evidence* (Walton, 2002), and *Abductive Reasoning* (Walton, 2004). Bourcier (1995) adopts a semantic approach to argumentation. Van-Eemeren, Grootendorst, and Kruiger (1987) approach

Of course, legal argument is not necessarily about the evidence. Dung, Thang, and Hung (2010), a team based in Thailand, presented an application of AI & Law to the interpretation of contracts. As Grasso, Rahwan, Reed, and Simari (2010, p. 4) summarise Dung et al. (2010):

> Interaction between parties needed to interpret a contract can be abstractly perceived as the exchange of arguments in support or against a given interpretation of the contract. Following this view, the main contribution of the work is an argument-based formalism that handles contract dispute resolution where the court will play the role of resolving the ongoing contract dispute by enforcing an interpretation of the contract that could be considered as representing the mutual intention of the involved parties in a fair manner. The formalism is based on modular argumentation, a recently proposed extension of assumption-based argumentation for modelling contract dispute resolution, and the appropriateness of this formalism is demonstrated by applying it to common laws. An example is developed using the system called MoDiSo (MOdular Argumentation for DIspute ReSOlution) that consists of three doctrines here modelled.

3.9.2 Within Other Research Communities

Computational modelling has concerned itself with arguments also outside the research community of either AI & Law, or communication in multi-agent systems or the work of scholars who contributed to those domain anyway. This is the case of a philosopher, Ghita Holmström-Hintikka (2001), who has applied to legal investigation, and in particular to *expert witnesses* giving testimony and being interrogated in court, the Interrogative Model for Truth-seeking that had been developed by Jaakko Hintikka for use in the philosophy of science; a previous paper of hers (Holmström-Hintikka, 1995), about expert witnesses, appeared in the journal *Argumentation*.[24] In 2010, Taylor and Francis launched their journal *Argument & Computation*.

This followed several conferences, and well as thematic issues in various journals. Journal special issues about computational models of argumentation include ones published in the journals *Artificial Intelligence* (Bench-Capon & Dunne, 2007); *IEEE Intelligent Systems* (Rahwan & McBurney, 2007); *International Journal of Intelligent Systems* (Reed & Grasso, 2007); *Argumentation*, this one on current use of Toulmin (Hitchcock & Verheij, 2005); *Journal of Autonomous Agents and Multi-Agent Systems*, on argumentation in multi-agent systems (Rahwan, 2005); *Artificial Intelligence and Law* (Bench-Capon & Dunne, 2005); *Journal of Logic*

---

argumentation theory from the viewpoint of pragmatics and discourse analysis. The interface of argumentation with pragmatics is relevant also for the handbook entry Van Eemeren, and Grootendorst (1995). Also see Van Eemeren, Grootendorst, and Snoek Henkemans (1996).

[24] Distinguish between the examination or cross-examination in court of witnesses, including expert witnesses if any, and the interrogation of suspects on the part of the police. Seidmann and Stein (2000) developed a game-theoretic analysis which appears to show that a suspect's right to silence helps the innocent.

and Computation (Brewka, Prakken, & Vreeswijk, 2003); *Informal Logic Journal* (Gilbert, 2002); *Computational Intelligence* (Chaib-Draa & Dignum, 2002).

In the introduction to the inaugural issue of *Argument & Computation*, Grasso et al. (2010, p. 1) remarked:

> Over the past decade or so, a new interdisciplinary field has emerged in the ground between, on the one hand, computer science – and artificial intelligence in particular – and, on the other, the area of philosophy concentrating on the language and structure of argument.
>
> There are now hundreds of researchers worldwide who would consider themselves a part of this nascent community. Various terms have been proposed for the area, including "Computational Dialectics," "Argumentation Technology" and "Argument-based Computing," but the term that has stuck is simply *Argument & Computation*. It encompasses several specific strands of research, such as:
>
> - the use of theories of argument, and of dialectic in particular, in the design and implementation of protocols for multi-agent action and communication;
> - the application of theories of argument and rhetoric in natural language processing and affective computing;
> - the use of argument-based structures for autonomous reasoning in artificial intelligence, and in particular, for defeasible reasoning;
> - computer supported collaborative argumentation – the implementation of software tools for enabling online argument in domains such as education and e-government.
>
> These strands come together to form the core of a research field that covers parts of artificial intelligence (AI), philosophy, linguistics and cognitive science, but, increasingly, is building an identity of its own.

Models for generating arguments automatically have been developed by computational linguists whose research is mainly concerned with tutorial dialogues (Carenini & Moore, 1999, 2001). ABDUL/ILANA was a tool from the early 1980s, also developed by computational linguists. It was an AI program that used to simulate the generation of adversary arguments on an international conflict (Flowers et al., 1982). In a disputation with adversary arguments, the players do not actually expect to convince each other, and their persuasion goals target observers. Persuasion arguments, instead, have the aim of persuading one's interlocutor, too.[25]

---

[25] Of course, there has been much research, in computational models of argumentation (the subject of the present Chapter 3), into adversary argumentation: litigants in the courtroom try to persuade not each other, but the adjudicator. Moreover, they may *prevaricate*, in order to avoid an undesirable outcome. Dunne's (2003) 'Prevarication in Dispute Protocols' resorted to Dung's (1995) *argumentation frameworks* – in which an argument is admissible with respect to a set of arguments S if all of its attackers are attacked by some argument in S, and no argument in S attacks an argument in S – in order to "present various settings in which the use of 'legitimate delay' can be rigorously modeled, formulate some natural decision questions respecting the existence and utility of 'prevaricatory tactics', and, finally, illustrate within a greatly simplified schema, how carefully-chosen devices may greatly increase the length of an apparently 'straightforward' dispute" (Dunne, 2003, p. 12). Lengthening the dispute avoiding it reaching a conclusion is a kind of tactics in noncooperative argumentation. Dunne (2003) was concerned "one aspect of legal argument that appears to

3.9 A Survey of the Literature on Computational Models of Argumentation

Gilbert et al. (2003) described a *Persuasion Machine*. Persuasive political argument is modelled in Atkinson et al. (2005c). For a treatment of AI modelling of persuasion in court, see e.g. Bench-Capon (2003a, 2003b). Also see Bench-Capon (2002) and Greenwood et al. (2003).[26]

Arguments are also used by a rational agent on his own, when revising his beliefs: see on this Paglieri and Castelfranchi (2005), Harman (1986). Work on argumentation by computer scientists may even have been as simple as a mark-up language for structuring and tagging natural language text according to the line of argumentation it propounds: in 1999, Delannoy (1999) tentatively proposed that his own argumentation mark-up was unprecedented, but he was unaware of a previous proposal which in 1996 was published by Nissan and Shimony in a journal (Nissan & Shimony, 1996) and demonstrated by tagging an article in biology.

Parsons and McBurney (2003) have been concerned with argumentation-based communication between agents in multiagent systems.[27] This is also the context of Paglieri and Castelfranchi (2005), even though the latter is rather concerned with an agent revising his beliefs through contact with the environment. Kibble (2004) uses Brandom's inferential semantics and Habermas' theory of communicative action (which are oriented to social constructs rather than mentalistic notions), "in order to develop a more fine-grained conceptualisation of notions like *commitment* and *challenge* in the context of computational modelling of argumentative dialogue".[28] Commitments are intersubjectively observable (Singh, 1999), whereas "agent design in terms of notions such as *belief* and *intention* faces the software engineering problem that it is not generally possible to identify data structures corresponding to beliefs and intentions in heterogeneous agents [(Wooldridge, 2000)], let alone a 'theory of mind' enabling agents to reason about agents' beliefs" (Kibble, 2004).

---

have been largely neglected in existing work concerning agent discourse protocols – particularly so in the arenas of persuasion and dispute resolution – the use of legitimate procedural devices to defer 'undesirable' conclusions being finalised and the deployment of such techniques in seeking to have a decision over-ruled. Motivating our study is the contention that individual agents within an 'agent society' could (be programmed to) act in a 'non-cooperative' manner: thus, contesting policies/decisions accepted by other agents in the 'society' in order to improve some national 'individual' utility." (ibid.).

[26] Atkinson and Greenwood are the same person.
[27] Multiagent systems are the subject of Section 6.1.6 in this book.
[28] It is not merely an argumentative dialogue, in the courtroom: lawyers are not trying to persuade the other party, or the witness they are cross-examining. Rather, they are trying to persuade the adjudicator. Also consider the notion of *ideal audience* in legal argument, which is the subject of a book by George Christie (2000).

3.10 Computational Models of Legal Argumentation About Evidence

3.10.1 Some Early and Ongoing Research

David Schum (1993, p. 175) makes the following considerations:

> I have often wondered how many of the subtleties in evidence presented at trial are actually recognized by factfinders [i.e., jurors or the judge] and then incorporated in their conclusions. William Twining (1984) goes even farther in wondering how skilful are advocates themselves in recognizing evidentiary subtleties and then in explaining their significance to factfinders. One thing certain is that skilful advocates do not usually offer evidence haphazardly at trial but according to some design or strategy, the objective in such strategies being the presentation of what advocates judge to be the best possible argument on behalf of their clients. [...] That different arguments are possible from the same evidence is one reason why there is to be a trial in the first place.

David Schum is the scholar who first combined computing, evidence, and argumentation. A scholar who is prominent in applying to legal evidence computational, logic-based, theoretically neat models of argumentation is Henry Prakken, who has done so with different co-authors. Prakken has done so at a time when, as well as shortly after, a body of published research started to emerge, of AI techniques for dealing with legal evidence (mainly in connection with mostly separate organisational efforts by Nissan, Tillers, and Zeleznikow). Until Prakken's efforts,[29] the only ones who applied argumentation to computer modelling of legal evidence were Schum (in several publications), and Gulotta and Zappalà (2001): the latter explored two criminal cases by resorting to an extant tool for argumentation, DART, of Freeman and Farley (1996), as well as other tools.

Prakken and Renooij (2001) explored different methods for causal reasoning: section 5 in that paper is about argument-based reconstruction of a given case involving a car accident. The main purpose of Prakken (2004) "is to advocate logical approaches as a worthwhile alternative to approaches rooted in probability theory" (Prakken, 2004), discussing in particular logics for defeasible argumentation. "What about conflicting arguments? When an argument is deductive, the only possible attack is on its premises. However, a defeasible argument can be attacked even if all its premises are accepted": "One way to attack it is to *rebut* it, i.e., to state an argument with an incompatible conclusion. [...] A second way to attack the argument is to *undercut* it, i.e., to argue that in this case the premises do not support its conclusion" (Prakken, 2004, section 3.2).

---

[29] Prakken's relevant papers include: Prakken (2001), Prakken and Renooij (2001), Prakken et al. (2003), Bex et al. (2003), and so forth. His publications are accessible online at www.cs.uu.nl/people/henry/publications.html from which site they can be downloaded.

3.10 Computational Models of Legal Argumentation About Evidence

Prakken (2001) "investigates the modelling of reasoning about evidence in legal procedure. To this end, a dialogue game model of the relevant parts of Dutch civil procedure is developed with three players: two adversaries and a judge" (ibid., p. 119). "[I]n the current models the judge's role, if modelled at all, is limited to the simple activity of determining the truth of the parties' claims. Yet in actual legal procedures judges have a much more elaborate role. For instance, in Dutch civil procedure judges allocate the burden of proof, determine whether grounds sufficiently support a claim, complete the parties' arguments with legal and common knowledge, decide about admissibility of evidence, and assess the evidence" (ibid., p. 119).

Limitations of the dialogue game in Prakken (2001) listed there include the following (ibid., p. 128):

> Firstly, the requirement that each move replies to a preceding move excludes some useful moves, such as lines of questioning in cross-examination of witnesses, with the goal of revealing an inconsistency in witness testimony. Typically, such lines of questioning do not want to reveal what they are aiming at. Secondly, at several points, the present ways to model legal-procedural acts have no clear one-to-one correspondence with the language of legal decisions. For instance, judges often merge their decisions on internal and dialectical strength of an argument: usually they regard the presence of a defeating counterargument as evidence that the argument is not internally valid.

Prakken et al. (2003) developed an analysis of evidence in the style of Wigmore Charts, using the *Araucaria* software of the University of Dundee in Scotland (Reed & Rowe, 2001, 2004), and argued for the use of argumentation schemes, which capture recurrent patterns of argumentation. Examples of recurrent patterns are to be found, that paper pointed out, in "inferences from witness or expert testimonies, causal arguments, or temporal projections". The criminal case used in Prakken et al. (2003) and Bex, Prakken, Reed, and Walton (2003) by way of an example, is *Commonwealth v. Umilian* (1901, Supreme Judicial Court of Massachusetts, 177 Mass. 582), and is taken from Wigmore's *Principles* (1931, pp. 62–66). It is a case that also David Schum uses on occasion for illustrating his own methods. Umilian, a farm labourer along with Jedrusik, was accused of murdering the latter, after discovering that Jedrusik was the author of a letter in which he falsely advised a priest that Umilian had a wife and children in the old country, so that Umilian's marriage to a local maid at the farm would not take place. Umilian's wedding was eventually celebrated, but he threatened to take revenge on Jedrusik, who disappeared and whose body was then found. For the period around the murder, Umilian and Jedrusik had been isolated in the area of the barn where the body was eventually found. It is an interesting case, its argumentation being displayed in Wigmore Charts.

Selmer Brigsjord with Shilliday, Taylor, Clark and Khemlani (2006) described *Slate*, a computer tool for supporting reasoning by argumentation, which produces explanations in simplified English. Part of the exemplification is about reasoning about hypotheses in criminal investigation.[30] It is unclear to me whether *Slate* can be usefully applied to serious crime analysis and intelligence analysis in real-world situations, as the exemplification seen in the given paper was rather like a whodunit puzzle,[31] but reportedly Brigsjord has been working on real case studies in intelligence analysis for the United States' ARDA.[32]

3.10.2 Stevie

Susan van den Braak and Gerard Vreeswijk, computer scientists from the University of Utrecht, and Prakken's colleagues, have developed *Stevie* (van den Braak & Vreeswijk, 2006). *Stevie* is a knowledge representation architecture, "based on known argument ontologies and argumentation logics", "to be used as a support tool to analyse criminal cases" "by allowing case analysts to visualize evidence in order to construct coherent stories. It allows them to maintain overview over all information during an investigation, so that different scenarios can be compared. Moreover, they are able to express the reasons why certain evidence supports the scenarios". "*Stevie* is able to represent multiple cases and to support multiple users". Permanent links to external source documents can be set. Other links, to external databases, enable "to retrieve simple factual information such as quotes from witness testimonies and other original source documents".

In the *Stevie* approach, stories are "hypothetical reconstructions of what might have happened". "*Stevie* uses defeasible reasoning [...] to distill stories out of large quantities of information", where "a story is a conflict-free and self-defending collection of claims (I-nodes). A *story* is conflict-free if (and only) if it does not contain a conflicting pair of I-nodes". Moreover, "a story is self-defending if (and only if) every argument (made of of I-nodes and S-nodes) against an element of that story can be countered with an argument made up of I-nodes that belong to that story". Besides, "a third constraint on stories" is "that they must be temporally consistent".

An *I-node* is "an elementary piece of information that is used in modeling cases", and is either a quotation node, or an interpretation node. An *S-node* is a *scheme instance*, where *schemes* are "predefined patterns of reasoning. A single scheme describes an inference, the necessary prerequisties for that inference, and possible critical questions that might undercut the inference".

---

[30] Criminal investigation is the subject of, e.g., Newburn, Williamson, and Wright (2007), Sanders (1977), and Ericson (1981).

[31] What is more, when reading that paper I was worried about stereotyping of perpetrators.

[32] A document about that particular case study can be found on the Web at http://kryten.mm.rpi.edu/SB-LOGGER_CASESTUDY.tar.gz whereas a demo of Slate as applied to the Philadelphia bombing can be found at this other address: http://www.cogsci.rpi.edu/research/rair/slate/visitors/PhiladelphiaBombing.wmv at the website of Rensselaer Polytechnic Institute in Troy, NY.

3.11 Argumentation for Dialectical Situations, vs. for Structuring Knowledge Non-dialectically, and an Integration of the Two

Andrew Stranieri, John Zeleznikow, and John Yearwood

3.11.1 Three Categories of Concepts Grouping Concepts of Argumentation

The present Section 3.11 is based on an article by the same authors, Stranieri, Zeleznikow, and Yearwood (2001). Let us begin by saying something about conceptualisations of argumentation. According to James Freeman (1991), argumentation involves a family of concepts that can be broadly grouped into three categories:

- concepts related to the process of engaging in an argument,
- procedures or rules adopted to regulate the argument process, and
- argument as a product or artefact of an argument process.

The first two categories, process and procedures, are intimately linked to a dialectical situation within a community of social agents. Freeman (1991, p. 20) defines a dialectical situation as

> one that involves some opposition among participants to a discourse over some claim, that it involves interactive questioning for critically testing this claim and this process proceeds in a regimented, rule governed manner.

A dialectical situation need not occur between two independent human agents in that monologues can be represented dialectically. For instance, a mathematician engaged in a solo demonstration that a proposition follows from axioms does not overtly engage in a discourse. Nevertheless the reasoning can be seen as a linguistic reconstruction of an imaginary discursive exchange within a community of mathematicians. Argumentation as a product or artefact of an argument process involves viewing the linguistic reconstruction of what the argumentation process and procedure have generated. It involves laying out the premises, claims and layout of claims. For Freeman (1991), the distinction between the three views of argumentation – process, procedure and product – is largely illusory and unnecessarily confusing, particularly for his objective of identifying diagramming techniques for the clear articulation of arguments.

Argumentation concepts have been applied from the 1990s in a variety of knowledge engineering applications, typically without a clear delineation of argumentation as process, procedure or product, according to Freeman's (1991) classification. The central claim advanced in this Section 3.11 (and in Stranieri et al., 2001) is that benefits inherent in the use of argumentation frameworks for information system knowledge engineering can be substantially enhanced if key features of the distinction between argumentation as *process, procedure* and *product* are maintained.

3.11.2 From the Toulmin Argument Structure, to the Generic Actual Argument Model

The rise of argumentation research within artificial intelligence, as early as the 1990s, has taken various forms. A variety of logics have been developed to represent argumentation in the context of a dialectical situation such as a dialogue. In contrast to the dialectical approach, argumentation has also been used non-dialectically, in order to provide structure for knowledge. As already seen in this book, the Toulmin Argument Structure (Toulmin, 1958) – see Fig. 3.11.2.1 – has been popular among those computer scientists who have devoted some attention to argumentation: the Toulmin structure has often been adopted to structure knowledge non-dialectically Nevertheless, most studies that apply the Toulmin structure do not use the original structure, but vary one or more components. Variations to the Toulmin structure can be understood as different ways to integrate a *dialectical perspective into one which is essentially non-dialectical.*

In this Section 3.11, the label *dialectical argumentation* is used to describe the modelling of discourse. This is contrasted with non-dialectical argumentation. Drawing the dialectical/non-dialectical distinction enables the specification of a framework, called the *Generic Actual Argument Model (GAAM)*, that is expressly

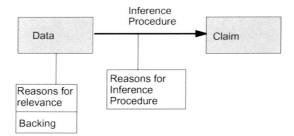

Fig. 3.11.2.1 Our version of the Toulmin Argument Structure[33]

---

[33] Figure 3.11.2.1 represents the basic template for the knowledge representation we call a generic argument. A generic argument is an instantiation of the template that models a group of arguments. The generic argument includes: (a) a variable-value representation of the claim with a certainty slot; (b) a variable-value representation of the data items (with certainty slots) as the grounds on which such claims are made; (c) reasons for relevance of the data items; (d) inference procedures that may be used to infer a claim value from data values; (e) reasons for the appropriateness of the inference procedure.

The idea is that the generic argument sets up a template for arguments that allows the representation of the claim and the grounds for the claim. The claim of a generic argument is a predicate with an unspecified value (which can be chosen from a set when an actual argument is being made). Each data item is also a predicate with an unspecified value which can be taken from a specified set of values. The connection between the data variables and the claim variable is called an inference procedure. An inference procedure is a relation between the data space and the claim space.

non-dialectical.[34] The framework enables the development of knowledge-based systems that integrate a variety of inference procedures, combine information retrieval with reasoning and facilitate automated document drafting. Furthermore, the non-dialectical framework provides the foundation for simple dialectical models. Systems based on our approach have been developed in family law, refugee law, determining eligibility for government legal aid, copyright law, and eTourism.

The central theme of the present Section 3.11 is that a distinction between argument as process and procedure, called here *dialectical*, and argument as product, called *non-dialectical*, serves useful purposes for knowledge engineering in that it has motivated the development of a knowledge representation framework that clearly separates the two perspectives. A framework for knowledge engineering that supports the non-dialectical perspective expressively is described. The non-dialectical framework called the *Generic Actual Argument Model* (*GAAM*) directly facilitates the development of hybrid systems, intelligent document drafting, data mining and intelligent information retrieval. Furthermore, the non-dialectical framework provides a knowledge representation base that is the foundation for dialectical models.

The *Generic Actual Argument Model* (*GAAM*) is a variant of the layout of arguments advanced by Toulmin (1958). Arguments for non-dialectical purposes are represented at two levels of abstraction; the generic and the actual level. The generic level is sufficiently general so as to represent claims made by all members of a discursive community. All participants use the same generic arguments to construct, by instantiation, their own actual arguments. The generic arguments represent a detailed layout of arguments acceptable to all participants whereas the actual arguments capture a participant's position with respect to each argument. The actual arguments that one participant advances are more easily compared with those advanced by another, in a dialectical exercise because, in both cases, the actual arguments have been derived from a generic template that all participants share.

3.11.3 Dialectical vs. Non-Dialectical Argumentation

Recall that we agreed that in this Section 3.11, the label *dialectical argumentation* is used to describe the modelling of discourse. This is contrasted with *non-dialectical argumentation*. Argumentation as *dialectic* (process and procedure) is used in order to model situations that involve discourse within a community of agents. The agents need not be independent human agents engaged in group discussion but may even be a single software agent that has internal processes that involve dialectical exchange. In contrast, non-dialectical argumentation describes the use of argumentation to order, organise or structure knowledge without directly modelling a dialectical exchange.

Until recent decades, argumentation theories have been advanced for philosophical pursuits and not specifically to enhance knowledge engineering. As a

---

[34] The latest treatment this topic received from us is in Yearwood and Stranieri (2006, 2009).

consequence, the distinction between dialectical and non-dialectical use of argumentation concepts is rarely prominent.

For example, Aristotle presented three types of arguments; demonstrations, dialectical deductions and contentious deductions (*Topics*, Book 1, 100a, 27–30). Although each of Aristotle's three types of argument can be seen as arising out of discursive exchanges, there is an implicit emphasis on the dialectical perspective for dialectical deductions because these arguments are made on the basis of premises that are debatable. They typically concern opinions that are adhered to with variable intensity by community members whereas demonstrations are assumed to have more of a ring of universal acceptance. Demonstrations are arguments whose claims are made from premises that are true and primary known, in more modern terminology, as analytic proofs. Contentious deductions are arguments that appear acceptable at first sight but, upon closer inspection, are not.

The analysis of argument advanced by Toulmin (1958) does not distinguish dialectical from non-dialectical argumentation. By illustrating that logic could be seen as a kind of generalised jurisprudence rather than as a science, Toulmin (1958) advanced a structure of argument that captures the layout of arguments. Jurisprudence focuses attention on procedures by which legal claims are advanced and attacked and, in a similar way, Toulmin sought to identify procedures by which any claim, in general, is advanced. He identified a layout of arguments that was constant regardless of the content of the argument.

As already seen earlier in Section 3.2 in this book, Toulmin (1958) concluded that most arguments, regardless of the domain, have a structure which consists of six basic invariants:

- *claim,*
- *data,*
- *modality,*
- *rebuttal,*
- *warrant*, and
- *backing.*

Every argument makes a claim based on some data. Let us consider an example. The argument in Fig. 3.11.3.1 is drawn from reasoning regarding refugee status according to the 1951 United Nations Convention relating to the Status of Refugees (as amended by the 1967 United Nations Protocol relating to the Status of Refugees), and relevant High Court of Australia rulings. The claim of the argument in Fig. 3.11.3.1 is the statement that Reff has a well founded fear of persecution. This claim is made on the basis of two data items, that Reff has a real chance of persecution and that relocation within Reff's country of origin is not appropriate. A mechanism is required to act as a justification for why the claim follows from data. This justification is known as the warrant which is, in Fig. 3.11.3.1, the statement that "The test for well founded fear is real chance of persecution unless relocation affords protection". The backing provides authority for the warrant and in a legal argument is typically a reference to a statute or a precedent case. The rebuttal component specifies an exception or condition that obviates the claim. Reff may well

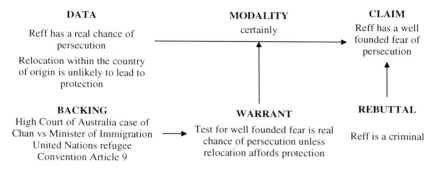

Fig. 3.11.3.1 Toulmin argument for well founded fear

have a real chance of persecution and relocation within the country of origin is unlikely to lead to protection; however the claim that his fear is well founded does not hold if Reff's persecution is due to criminal activities.

The validity of the dialectical/non-dialectical distinction for knowledge engineering is demonstrated by noting that many applications of the Toulmin structure to knowledge modelling during the 1990s have varied the structure in one way or another. However *ad hoc* the variations seem at first sight, they can be understood if seen as attempts to emphasise the dialectical as opposed to the non-dialectical perspective, to different extents.

In Section 3.11.4, diverse applications of the Toulmin argument structure are compared and contrasted in order to demonstrate that the variations are best understood as attempts to integrate dialectical argumentation with non-dialectical argumentation. In Section 3.11.5, the GAAM is presented. By specifically attempting to develop a non-dialectical model at a level that is generic to a discursive community, a variation of the Toulmin structure is derived that does not itself model dialectical exchanges. Rather, it enables dialectical exchanges to be readily modelled once communal knowledge is organised using the non-dialectical model. Applications developed with the use of the GAAM are discussed in Section 3.11.6 together with some insights regarding the dialectical model that is to be developed on the basis of the non-dialectical frame.

3.11.4 Variations of Toulmin's Structure

Argumentation has been used in knowledge engineering in two distinct ways; with a focus on the use of argumentation to structure knowledge (i.e. non-dialectical emphasis) or with a focus on the use of argumentation to model discourse (i.e. dialectical emphasis). Dialectical approaches typically automate the construction of an argument and counterarguments normally with the use of a nonmonotonic logic where operators are defined to implement discursive primitives such as *attack*, *rebut*, or *accept*. Carbogim, Robertson and Lee (2000) presented a comprehensive survey of defeasible argumentation.

Dialectical models have been advanced by Cohen (1985), Fox (1986), Vreeswijk (1993), Dung (1995), Prakken (1993a, 1993b), Prakken and Sartor (1996a), Gordon (1995), Fox and Parsons (1998) and many others. In general these approaches include a concept of conflict between arguments and the notion that some arguments defeat others. Most applications that follow a dialectical approach represent knowledge as first order predicate clauses, though they engage a nonmonotonic logic to allow contradictory clauses. Mechanisms are typically required to identify implausible arguments and to evaluate the better argument of two or more plausible ones. For example, Fox and Parsons (1998) analyse and extend the non standard logic LA of Krause, Ambler, Elvang-Goransson, and Fox (1995). In that formalisation, an argument is a tuple with three components:

(Sentence : Grounds : Sign).

The *sentence* is the Toulmin claim though this may be a simple claim or a rule. The *sign* is a number or symbol that indicates the confidence warranted in the claim. The *grounds* are the sentences involved in asserting the claim and can be seen as the reasoning steps used to ultimately reach the conclusion.

The preference for one argument over others has been modelled in a variety of ways. Prakken (1993a, 1993b) extends the framework proposed by Poole (1988) by using a concept of specificity. The claim that a penguin flies because it is a bird and all birds fly is less specific that the claim that a penguin does not fly. Preference relations between rules are elicited from experts and explicitly specified in the defeasible reasoning logic described by Antoniou (1997).

In applications of argumentation to model dialectical reasoning, argumentation is used specifically to model discourse and only indirectly used to structure knowledge. Concepts of conflict and of argument preferences map directly onto a discursive situation where participants are engaged in dispute. In contrast, many uses of argumentation for knowledge engineering application do not model discourse. This corresponds more closely to a non-dialectical perspective.

A non-dialectical representation facilitated the organisation of complex legal knowledge for information retrieval by Dick (1987, 1991). She illustrates how relevant cases for an information retrieval query can be retrieved despite sharing no surface features if the arguments used in case judgements are represented as Toulmin argument structures. Marshall (1989), Ball (1994) and Loui, et al. (1997) have built hypertext based computer implementations that draw on knowledge organised as Toulmin arguments. Hypertext links connect an argument's assertions with the warrants, backing and data of the same argument and also link the data of one argument with the assertion of other arguments. Complex reasoning can be represented succinctly enabling convenient search and retrieval of relevant information.

Clark (1991) represented the opinions of individual geologists as Toulmin argument structures so that his group decision support system could identify points of disagreement between experts. Matthijssen (1999) provides a further example of benefits that arise from the use of the original Toulmin structure. He represented user tasks as Toulmin arguments and associated a list of keywords to the structure. These keywords were used as information retrieval queries into a range of databases.

3.11 Argumentation for Dialectical Situations, vs. for Structuring Knowledge...   183

Results indicate considerable advantages in precision and recall of documents as a result of this approach compared with approaches that require the user to invent queries.

Johnson, Zualkernan, and Tukey (1993) identified different types of expertise using this structure and Bench-Capon, Lowes, and McEnery (1991) used the Toulmin argument structure to explain logic programming conclusions. Branting (1994) expands the Toulmin argument structure warrants as a model of the legal concept of *ratio decidendi*, that is to say, the rationale of a decision. In the *Split Up* project, Zeleznikow and Stranieri (1995), and Stranieri, Zeleznikow, Gawler, and Lewis (1999) used the Toulmin argument structure to represent family law knowledge in a manner that facilitated rule/neural hybrid development.

Toulmin (1958) proposed his views on argumentation informally and never claimed to have advanced a theory of argumentation. He does not rigorously define key terms such as warrant and backing. He only loosely specifies how arguments relate to other arguments and provides no guidance as to how to evaluate the best argument or identify implausible ones. Nevertheless, the structure was found to be useful as a tool for organising knowledge.

According to James Freeman (1991), the Toulmin layout does not explicitly model discourse. Operators to question, attack or qualify opposition assertions are not explicit. Nor is there the facility to represent an agent's beliefs as they differ from another agent's. Not surprisingly, many knowledge engineering applications of the Toulmin framework have not modelled discursive exchanges at all, but have applied the framework to structure knowledge.

Despite the immediate appeal of the Toulmin argument structure as a convenient frame for structuring knowledge, most researchers that use the Toulmin layout vary the original structure. Each variation can be seen to be an attempt to integrate some aspects of dialectical reasoning into a structure that, for knowledge engineering purposes, is largely non-dialectical. In the following section three variations are presented. These can be understood as attempts to integrate a dialectical approach into a non-dialectical one.

3.11.4.1 Johnson's Variation of the Toulmin Layout

Johnson, Zualkernan, et al. (1993) claimed that any argument's backing can be classified into one of five distinct types of backing which they label *Type 1* to *Type 5*. Each type of backing corresponds to a distinct type of expertise and also to a particular philosophical paradigm of reasoning as follows:

- *Type 1 arguments* reflect axiomatic reasoning. Data and claim for these arguments are analytic truths. The supporting evidence derives from a system of axioms such as Peano's axioms of arithmetic. Examples of what Aristotle called demonstrations would be captured as Type 1 arguments.
- *Type 2 arguments* assert a particular medical diagnosis on the basis of empirical judgements from a number of patients who have presented with similar symptoms in the past.

- *Type 3 arguments* are characterised by backings which reflect alternate representations of a problem. A medical diagnosis based on a model of the heart as a pump analyses symptoms to be consistent with that model. An alternate presentation that has the heart as a muscle provides other evidence.
- *Type 4 arguments* differ from Type 3 arguments in that the alternate representations are conflicting. In this case the argument involves supporting evidence that is conflicting. An assertion is made by creating a composite representation from conflicting ones.
- *Type 5 backings* refer to paradigms that reflect a process of inquiry.

The Type 1 and 2 backings that Johnson, Zualkernan, et al. (1993) identifies are markedly different from Types 3, 4 and 5. In the latter group, a claim is ultimately backed by recourse to alternate representations of a problem.

The resolution of conflicting representations is akin to a dialectical process. A common solution is sought from the exchange that is stimulated from conflicting representations. In Type 1 (axiomatic) or Type 2 (empirical) arguments, the backing is made from one perspective. There are no alternate representations and no common solutions. This is an example of a non-dialectical perspective.

The variation as per Johnson, Zualkernan, et al. (1993) does not introduce or eliminate components of the original Toulmin layout. However, by discerning non-dialectical backings from dialectical ones, it imposes a typology of backing that can be seen as an attempt to extend the structure toward somewhat of a dialectical application. The approach is limited by the unclear nature of the Toulmin warrant.

Broadly speaking, Toulmin formulates the warrant as an inference procedure. It is a procedure for inferring a claim given data. For example, the statement that "Most Italians are a Catholic" can be used as an inference rule to infer the claim that Mario is (probably) a Catholic given data that he is a Catholic. However, the statement that "Most Italians are a Catholic" can also be interpreted as a reason for the relevance of the data item "Mario is a Catholic" in the argument.

The distinction between a warrant as an inference rule and a warrant as a reason for relevance can be seen in the refugee argument of Fig. 3.11.3.1. The warrant statement that reflects that the High Court case of Chan introduced a "real chance of persecution" as the test for well founded fear is readily seen as a reason for the relevance of the real chance data item. It is less obviously viewed as an inference rule that can be applied to infer the claim.

Below, issues related to what James Freeman (1991) calls the *problematic notion of warrant* are discussed. However, it is important to note the Johnson typology applies to backings for warrants that are inference procedures but may not apply in the same way to warrants that are statements indicating a reason for the relevance of a data item.

3.11.4.2 The Freeman and Farley Variation on Toulmin Warrants

Arthur Farley and Kathleen Freeman (1995) recognised the need to extend the warrant component in order to develop a model of dialectical reasoning more formal than that proposed by Toulmin. Their main objective was to develop a system that could model the burden of proof concept in legal reasoning. The concept of burden of proof is often used to refer to the onus a discourse participant has, to supply evidence. So, as Prakken (2001) notes in modelling this form of burden of proof using a dialogue game model, a judge directs the pleadings phase of proceedings by requiring one litigant or another to supply evidence to support their claims. However, the form of burden of proof that was the focus of attention for Farley and Freeman (1995) involves the extent to which evidence is required in order to draw a conclusion. This varies with the severity of the misdemeanour. Except as otherwise provided by the law, the burden of proof requires *proof by a preponderance of the evidence*. In a criminal case, the state must prove all elements of the crime to a beyond reasonable doubt level. In cases of tax fraud, the burden of proof in a tax case is generally on the taxpayer (Black, 1990)

In an earlier paper than Farley and Freeman (1995), Kathleen Freeman (1994) described two types of warrants she called wtype1 and wtype2. The first warrant type, wtype1, classifies the relationship between assertion and data with category labels she calls *explanatory* or *sign*. Causal links are examples of explanatory warrants because they explain an assertion given data. Fire causes smoke. The consequent is explained by recourse to a cause/effect link. Other types of *explanatory warrants* include *definitional relationships* or *property/attribute relationships*. A *sign relationship* represents a *correlational link* between data and assertion.

The second warrant type, wtype2, represents the *strength* with which the assertion can be drawn from data. Examples of this type of warrant proposed by Kathleen Freeman represent the strength with which the consequent can be drawn from the antecedent. *Default type warrants* represent default relationships such as birds fly. *Evidential warrants* are less certain. *Sufficient warrants* are certain and typically stem from definitions.

Kathleen Freeman explicitly represents reasoning methods in addition to the two types of warrant. The reasoning types reside outside the Toulmin argument structure but interact with warrants in order to produce credible outcomes. Her model incorporates four reasoning mechanisms, *modus ponens, modus tollens, abduction* and *contra positive abduction*. For example, some reasoning mechanisms are stronger than others according to heuristics she devised. *Modus ponens* and *modus tollens* are assigned a strong link qualification if used with sufficient warrants, whereas the same reasoning types are assigned a "credible" qualification if used with evidential warrants.

Reasoning types interact with warrant types to control the generation of arguments according to reasoning heuristics. For example, *modus ponens/abduction* combinations are not permitted for two explanatory warrants unless both are evidential. Kathleen Freeman (1994) demonstrates a capacity her model has for dialectical reasoning. An assertion is initially argued for with the use of heuristics she defined. Then, an alternate argument is compared with the initial argument constructed and support for it is ascertained. The comparisons require the notion of *level of proof* which include *beyond reasonable doubt, scintilla of evidence* and *preponderance of evidence*. (Cf. in Section 3.6.2 in this book.)

Kathleen Freeman's model is a sophisticated extension to the Toulmin argument structures that displays impressive dialectical reasoning results. She advances types of relationships between consequents and antecedents (wtpye1) and assigns the link a strength (wtype2). The discernment of two types of warrant is essential for her because her model of burden of proof relies on it. By specifying reasoning types and heuristics for their interaction with warrants, Farley and Freeman (1995) can be seen to provide a way to extend the Toulmin structure so that it can be applied to model dialogue. The ambiguity in the original Toulmin warrant is dealt with by reserving one type of warrant for the inference rule and the other to indicate the strength of the rule. This adds a representation of uncertainty to some extent, but as we shall describe below, the strength of the data items and strength of claims is not represented. Furthermore, there is no attempt to incorporate information regarding the broader context of the argument.

In contrast, the issue of context is paramount for Bench-Capon (1998), who is not intent on modelling the burden of proof in legal reasoning but on implementing a dialogue game that engages players in constructing arguments for and against assertions initially made by one party.

3.11.4.3 Bench-Capon's Variation of the Toulmin Layout

Bench-Capon (1998) does not distinguish types of backing as Johnson, Zualkernan, et al. (1993) do, or types of warrant following Farley and Freeman (1995). Instead, he introduces an additional component to the *Toulmin argument structure.* The presupposition component of the Toulmin argument structure represents assumptions made that are necessary for the argument but are not the object of dispute, so they remain outside the core of the argument. A presupposition for the refugee argument illustrated in Fig. 3.11.3.1 would indicate that the country in which the argument is raised is a signatory to the United Nations Convention. As Australia is a signatory to the Convention, the data items and warrant that relate to the UN Convention are entirely appropriate. If Australia were not a signatory then those data items may not be as appropriate. This is illustrated in Fig. 3.11.4.3.1.

Making explicit presuppositions in the argument structure is important for the use Bench-Capon (1998) makes of the Toulmin argument structure. A program that plays the part of one or both players in a dialogue game is often exposed to utterances in discourse that represent presuppositions and are not central to the discussion at hand.

The presuppositions can become critical if parties to a game do not share them. Bench-Capon (1998) interprets the warrant as an inference procedure much as Toulmin originally did. The dialogue game does not directly add dialectical operators such as rebut, attack or accept into the structure but these are instead encoded into the control mechanism that represent the rules of the dialogue game. The inherent ambiguity in the Toulmin warrant is not addressed; however, the context of the argument is modelled by the addition of a presupposition component.

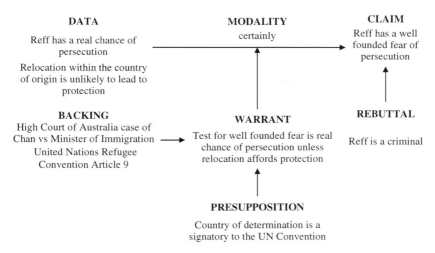

Fig. 3.11.4.3.1 Toulmin Argument Structure with presupposition component

3.11.4.4 Considerations Concerning Toulmin Variations

The three variations to the Toulmin argument structure presented thus far in Section 3.11.4 can be seen to be attempts at clarifying how the structure can be used within a dialogue. This objective motivated Johnson, Zualkernan, et al. (1993) to add types of backings. Each new backing type derives from the use of arguments by a discursive community. Farley and Freeman (1995) were more direct and developed specific reasoning heuristics so that an argument and counterargument are constructed as it would be within a discursive community. Bench-Capon (1998) defined a dialogue game that regulated the dialogue between two players who each encode their utterances as Toulmin components.

In the next section, Section 3.11.5, a variation of the Toulmin argument structure is proposed that specifically aims to model the structure of arguments in a non-dialectical manner. This is done in a manner that is at a sufficiently high level of abstraction so as to represent shared understanding between participants to a discourse which ultimately simplifies the specification of a dialectical model. However, even without extension into a dialectical model, the non-dialectical frame facilitates hybrid system development, document drafting and intelligent information retrieval.

3.11.5 A Generic Non-dialectical Model of Argumentation: The Generic Actual Argument Model (GAAM)

3.11.5.1 The Argument Template

Figure 3.11.5.1.1 represents a template for knowledge representation that varies the Toulmin argument structure. The template differs from the Toulmin structure in that it includes:

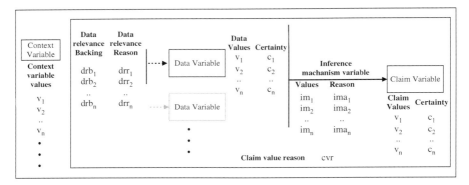

Fig. 3.11.5.1.1 Non-dialectical argument template

- a variable-value representation of claim and data items,
- a certainty variable associated with each variable-value rather than a modality or force associated with the entire argument,
- reasons for the relevance of the data items in place of the warrant,
- a list of inference procedures that can be used to infer a claim value from data values in place of the warrant,
- reasons for the appropriateness of each inference procedure,
- context variables,
- the absence of the rebuttal component present in the original formulation,
- the inclusion of a claim value reason component.

The argument template represents knowledge at a very high level of abstraction. There are two levels of instantiation made in applying the template to model arguments within a domain; the generic level and the actual level. A generic argument is an instantiation of the template where the following components are set:

- claim, data and context variables are specified but not assigned values,
- relevance reason statements and backing statements are specified,
- inference procedures are listed but a commitment to any one procedure is avoided,
- inference procedure reasons are specified for each procedure
- claim and data variables are not assigned certainty values

The generic argument is sufficiently general so as to capture the variety of perspectives displayed by members of a discursive community.

Figure 3.11.5.1.2 illustrates the refugee argument above, as a generic argument. The claim variable has been labelled *Well founded fear* and acceptable values specified. There are three inference procedures known to be appropriate in this example; the first is a rule set that derives from heuristics an immigration expert uses, the

3.11 Argumentation for Dialectical Situations, vs. for Structuring Knowledge...

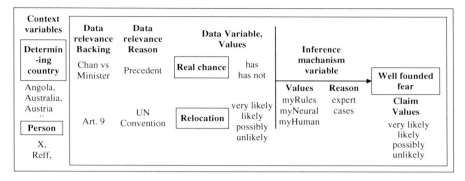

Fig. 3.11.5.1.2 Generic argument for well founded fear

second is a neural network[35] trained from past cases and the third is a human inference. This latter inference indicates that a human is empowered with sufficient discretion to infer a claim value from data item values in any way he or she likes.

In the *Generic Actual Argument Model* (*GAAM*), the Toulmin warrant has been replaced with two components; an inference procedure and a reason for relevance. This relates to two different roles a warrant can play in an argument from a non-dialectical perspective. As described above, the warrant indicates a reason for the relevance of a data item and on the other hand the warrant can be interpreted as a rule which, when applied to the data items, leads to a claim inference.

An inference procedure is an algorithm or method used to infer a claim value from data item values. Under this interpretation, an inference procedure is a relation between data variable values and claim variable values. It is any procedure that will perform a mapping from data items to claim items. A mathematical function, an algorithm, a rule set, a neural network, or procedures yet to be discovered are examples of inference procedures.

Actual arguments made are instances of a generic argument where each data slot has a value (*data item value*), an inference procedure is chosen and executed to deliver a value for the claim slot (*claim value*). Each generic argument has a claim, data items, reasons for why each data item is relevant, the names of the associated inference procedures and reasons for their appropriateness. Figure 3.11.5.1.3 shows a generic argument in detail. It consists of: a conjunction of data items or slots each with a reason for its relevance and the backing for this; a choice of inference procedures and the reasons for each one of these mechanisms and of course, the claim slot. All data slots act as input to the inference procedures. Each inference mechanism in the inference procedure slot provides a means of reaching a claim value from the input data values. Inference mechanisms may include rule sets, trained neural networks, case-based reasoners or human reasoning. The choice of a particular inference mechanism (other than human inferencing) and the reasons for that

---

[35] Neural networks are the subject of Section 6.1.14 in this book.

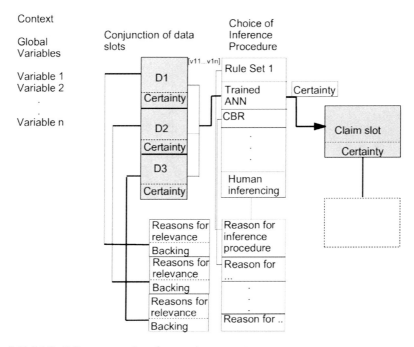

Fig. 3.11.5.1.3 Full representation of a generic argument

inference procedure provide a reason for arriving at a particular claim value. In the case of human inferencing there will still be a need to provide a justification for the claim. At the generic argument level this explanation cannot be given.

Figure 3.11.5.1.3 also includes *certainty* slots for each data item, claim and inference procedure. These recognise that there is uncertainty in the processes of developing actual arguments. The certainty values are assigned when values are assigned in the process of constructing an actual argument. A generic argument is an agreed approximation to a world but still may only be partial knowledge. We do not explicitly put a certainty or confidence value on a generic argument although we permit generic arguments to change over time. The structure of generic arguments that describe a domain will not be static. As knowledge within the domain evolves new versions of the generic argument structure will be required. New factors emerge as being relevant to some arguments and new inference procedures may be needed as new legal rules emerge or new cases become precedents. Most actual arguments in a domain are then underpinned by a particular version of the generic argument structure. Figure 3.11.5.1.3 also depicts variables that are required to capture the context of the generic argument. Context variables are conceptualised as factors that are critical for the appropriate instantiation of actual arguments from the generic template. However, context variables do not directly take part in the reasoning within an argument. For example, the reasoning used to infer claims about tours does not include the geographical region as a data item because the reasoning applies regardless of region.

3.11.5.2 Discussion

Many inference procedures can be implemented in software. Thus, they can be automated in computer based systems. However, this need not be necessarily the case for a knowledge engineering framework. Claims can sometimes be inferred from data items by human agents without the explicit specification of an inference procedure. This occurs frequently in discretionary fields of law where, as Christie (1986) notes, decision makers weight and combine relevant factors in their own way without articulating precisely how claims were inferred. This situation is accommodated within the Generic Actual Argument framework with the specification of an inference type labelled, simply, human.

The original Toulmin warrant can also be seen to be a reason for relevance or an inference procedure. Past contributions to a marriage are relevant in Australian family law. Past contributions appears as a data item in a generic argument regarding property distribution following divorce because a statute dictates that contributions are relevant. The wealth level of a marriage in Australia is made relevant by past cases and not by statute. The hair colour of the wife is considered irrelevant because there is no statutory or precedent basis for its relevance. Further, domain experts can think of no reason that would make this feature *relevant*.

The concept of *relevance* is in itself difficult to define generally. See Section 4.6 in this book. van Dijk (1989) describes the concept of relevance as it applies to a class of modal logics broadly called *relevance logics* as a concept grounded firmly in the pragmatics, and not the semantics or syntax of language. Within a discursive community, the data items in a generic argument must be relevant to the claim to the satisfaction of members of the community.

A generic argument in the field of family law property division may include hair colour as a relevant data item for inferring property division if a reason for its relevance that is acceptable, even if not held, by many in the community, is advanced. Perhaps the utterance

Blonde women will remarry more readily.

as a reason for the relevance of hair colour as a data item may not be held by all participants to a discourse but reflects a belief that is understood as plausible by many.

The argumentation framework advanced here not only departs from the Toulmin formulation by distinguishing inference procedure from reason for relevance but it also represents context explicitly. Figure 3.11.5.1.2 illustrates two context variables; the *Determining country* and the *Person* about which the argument is being made. The respective values are a list of world nations for the *Determining Country* and Reff or the more universal X for the *Person*.

Context variables represent something of the background knowledge that impacts on the generic argument. For example, the context variable *Determining country* in Fig. 3.11.5.1.2 represents a scope constraint on the argument. This indicates that an actual argument can be made based on the generic argument however the determining country sets a context for the argument. The context variable is an articulation of the presuppositions that underpin the generic argument.

The context variable can also represent the scope of variables used in the generic argument. For example, the *Person* context variable will be assigned the value X for a discourse participant intent on making the more universal argument that relates to well founded fear of anyone. The participant that restricts the argument to Reff does so be setting the context variable to Reff. In general, context is a difficult concept to define. In the framework defined here, context is defined as presupposition and variable scope. However, other definitions can also be accommodated as long as they can be captured as variable-value tuples.

There is no rebuttal component in the generic argument. The rebuttal is more clearly regarded to be a dialectical component and is therefore omitted from this essentially non-dialectical frame. For instance, discursive participants may create actual arguments as instances of the same generic argument in ways that are quite different from others. Participant A may assert a different claim value than B, yet have perfect agreement on all data item values because a different inference procedure was selected. Any discussion regarding this difference, including exchanges that make the point that the difference constitutes an attack, or exchanges that seek to defend A or B's assertion, or exchanges that seek to identify the stronger argument involve dialectical exchange and are omitted from the non-dialectical frame.

3.11.5.3 Representing Actual Arguments

Figure 3.11.5.3.1 represents an *actual argument*. This is the second level instantiation of the argument template in Fig. 3.11.5.1.1. An *actual argument* corresponds to a position held by a participant in a discourse. It is an instantiation of a generic argument. The context variable *person* in the generic argument is instantiated to "Reff" indicating that the claim only applies to him and not to others.

The data item value in Fig. 3.11.5.3.1 represents the situation that "Reff is likely to have a well founded fear". The inference procedure for the actual argument is the ruleset called myRules. As a consequence of applying that ruleset, the claim value is instantiated to represent that Reff is likely to have well founded fear.

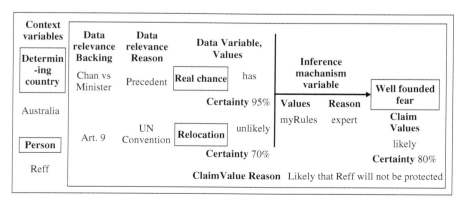

Fig. 3.11.5.3.1 Actual argument for Reff has well founded fear

The *claim value reason* for this actual argument provides a reason for the specific claim value inferred rather than other claim values. The claim value reason in Fig. 3.11.5.3.1 expresses a reason for why well founded fear is likely, given the data items and inference procedure selected. The *claim value reason* is not a reason for the inference rule. First of all the inference procedure need not be a rule. If it is a mathematical function or has mechanisms that are not visible, such as a neural network, then the articulation of a reason for the inference procedure is impossible. Conceptually, it is more correct to say it is a reason for a particular value that has arisen as a result of the application of an inference procedure.

Certainty values are assigned when a participant creates an actual argument. The certainty value represents the degree of certainty the participant has that the claim (or data) variable value selected is the true value. A certainty value may be set directly by the participant or calculated by the inference procedure, if the variable value is set by an inference procedure. The certainty value of 80% associated with the data item value, "likely", for the well founded fear variable in Fig. 3.11.5.3.1, is read as a high (80%) degree of certainty that well founded fear of persecution is likely. This is calculated by the inference procedure selected, myRules. However, if the inference procedure selected does not calculate certainty values (e.g., human inferences) then the participant must set a certainty value. The way in which the data item certainty values are combined is a feature of the mapping performed by the particular inference procedure selected so is not made explicit in the GAAM.

Linguistic variables values such as *very elderly, elderly, middle aged, young* and *very young* seem to represent certainty in themselves so as to make the specification of a certainty value redundant. However, the inclusion of a certainty value slot in the GAAM enables the specification of membership function values if fuzzy reasoning[36] was selected as the inference procedure, conditional probability if a Bayesian inference was selected or certainty factors if MYCIN-like rule inferences (i.e., rules of the kind made popular in expert system following the MYCIN expert system for medical diagnosis)[37] were used as the inference procedure.

Generic and actual argument structures correspond to a non-dialectical perspective. They do not directly model an exchange of views between discursive participants but rather describe assertions made from premises and the way in which multiple claims are organised. Claim variables are inferred using an inference procedure, which may not necessarily be automated, from data item values. The reasoning occurs within a context and the extent to which the data items correspond to true values, according to the proponent of the argument, is captured by certainty values.

The generic argument provides a level of abstraction that accommodates most points of view within a discursive community and anticipates the creation of actual arguments, by participants, as instantiations of a generic argument. However, it is conceivable that, given the open textured nature of reasoning, that a participant

---

[36] Fuzzy logic is the subject of Section 6.1.15 in this book.
[37] MYCIN is the subject of Shortliffe (1976); Shortliffe and Buchanan (1975).

will seek to advance an actual argument that is a departure from the generic argument. This is a manifestation of discretion and can be realised with the introduction of a new variable (data, claim or context) value, with the use of a new inference procedure, or with a new claim value reason.

A non-dialectical argumentation model must model discretion and open texture. The concept of open texture was introduced by Waismann (1951) to assert that empirical concepts are necessarily indeterminate. A definition for open textured terms cannot be advanced with absolute certainty unless terms are defined axiomatically, as they are, for example in mathematics. Gold may be defined as that substance which has spectral emission lines, X, and is coloured deep yellow. However, because the possibility that a substance with the same spectral emission as gold, but without the colour of gold will appear in the future, cannot be ruled out, the concept for gold is open textured.

The concept of open texture is significant in the legal domain because new uses for terms, and new situations constantly arise in legal cases. Prakken (1993a) discerns three sources of open texture; reasoning which involves defeasible rules; vague terms; or classification ambiguities. Judicial discretion is conceptualised by Christie (1986) and Bayles (1990) as the flexibility decision-makers have in weighing relevant factors when exercising discretion, although articulating an assignment of weights is typically difficult. This view of discretion does not derive from defeasible rules, vague terms or classification ambiguities, so is regarded as a fourth type of situation that contributes to the open textured nature of law.

The link between the GAAM and discretion is described in detail by Stranieri, Yearwood, and Meikl (2000). Broadly, discretion manifests itself as the flexibility for a participant to construct an actual argument from a generic argument by:

- Adding data item factors into the actual argument that are not in the generic tree.
- Removing a data item factors from the actual argument that is in the generic tree.
- Selecting a data, claim, or context variable value from those specified in the generic tree.
- Selecting a data, claim, or context variable value that has not been specified in the generic tree.
- Selecting an inference procedure from the list specified in the generic tree
- Selecting an inference procedure not specified in the generic tree.
- Leaving data items, reasons for relevance, inference procedure, and reasons for the appropriateness of inference procedures implicit.
- Introducing a claim value reason statement.
- Selecting certainty values.

This framework including the generic/actual distinction, the clear separation of inference procedure from other components and the inclusion of reasons for relevance and context introduces a non-dialectical structure that represents knowledge applicable to a discursive community, but does not include elements that are clearly needed to model dialectical exchanges. In the next Section 3.11.6, the way in which a the specification of a comprehensive non-dialectical structure facilitates

3.11 Argumentation for Dialectical Situations, vs. for Structuring Knowledge... 195

hybrid reasoning, document drafting and information retrieval is described before illustrating steps toward a dialectical model based on the GAAM non-dialectical frame.

3.11.6 Applications of the Generic/Actual Argument Model

The use of the GAAM for facilitating hybrid reasoning is illustrated with the knowledge based system called *Split Up*, that predicts marital property distribution decisions following divorce made by judges of the Family Court of Australia. This research is reported by Stranieri, Zeleznikow, Gawler, and Lewis (1999); cf. Stranieri (1999).

3.11.6.1 The *Split Up* System for Negotiating a Divorce

The *Split Up* project (Stranieri et al., 1999) collected data from cases heard in the Family Court of Australia dealing with property distribution following divorce. The objective was to predict the percentage split of assets that a judge in the Family Court of Australia would be likely to award both parties of a failed marriage. Australian Family Law is generally regarded as highly discretionary. The statute presents a "shopping list" of factors to be taken into account in arriving at a property order. The relative importance of each factor remains unspecified and many crucial terms are not defined. The age, state of health and financial resources of the litigants are explicitly mentioned in the statute as relevant factors, yet their relative weightings are unspecified. The Act clearly allows the decision-maker a great deal of discretion in interpreting and weighing factors.

In the *Split Up* system, the relevant variables were structured as data and claim items following the generic argument outlined above into 35 interlocking arguments. The ultimate claim, representing the percentage split of assets a judge would be likely to award the husband and wife, was the root of an *argument tree*. Unlike in dialogical argumentation, using an argument tree in non-dialogical argumentation, namely, in order to structure knowledge, aims at securing the following benefit: the argument tree is a hierarchy of relevant factors, and enables to decompose one large data mining exercise into many smaller ones.

Nodes in the argument tree of *Split Up*, illustrated as Fig. 3.11.6.1.1, are claim/data items. Variable values, inference procedures, reason for relevance and context are omitted from this diagram. The arguments interlock in that the claim of one argument is a data item for another, higher up a tree such as the one depicted in Fig. 3.11.6.1.1. For example, the variable *Contributions of the husband relative to the wife* is a data item for the ultimate claim and also the claim for an argument that has four data items.

In the *Split Up* system all claim variable values were inferred using automated inference procedures from the data item values. In 15 of the 35 arguments, claim values were inferred from data items with an inference procedure that involved the use of small rule-sets that represent expert heuristics whereas neural networks,

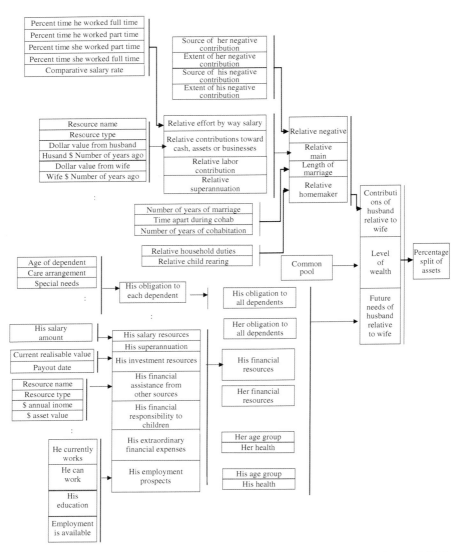

Fig. 3.11.6.1.1 The argument tree in the *Split Up* system (details are shown in Figs. 3.11.6.1.2, 3.11.6.1.3, and 3.11.6.1.4)

trained on data from past Court cases, were used to infer claim values in the remaining 20 arguments.

The *Split Up* application illustrated that the generic/actual argument model captures knowledge in way that leads to readily maintainable knowledge bases, a requirement that is particularly important in law. The tree of arguments underpinning *Split Up* was first elicited with the assistance of domain experts in 1994. Since then, property division in family law has changed in that domestic violence is now

3.11 Argumentation for Dialectical Situations, vs. for Structuring Knowledge... 197

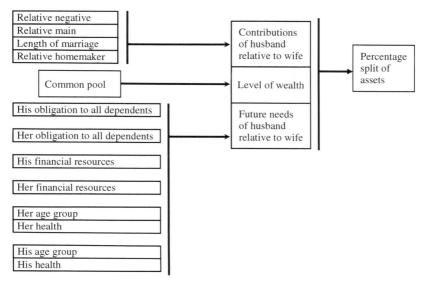

Fig. 3.11.6.1.2 The downstream part of the argument tree in the *Split Up* system

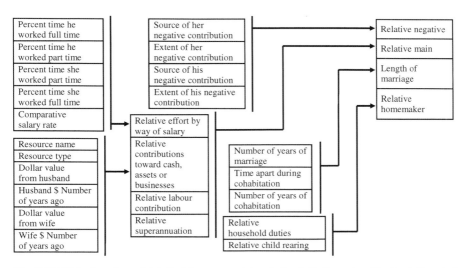

Fig. 3.11.6.1.3 An enlarged detail of the argument tree in the *Split Up* system (the top left part of Fig. 3.11.6.1.1)

recognised as a relevant consideration in property proceedings following a divorce. The framework localises this change to a single argument that does not impact on any other argument. Furthermore, an examination of the process that led to the introduction of domestic violence illustrated that the generic argument framework can clarify judicial reasoning.

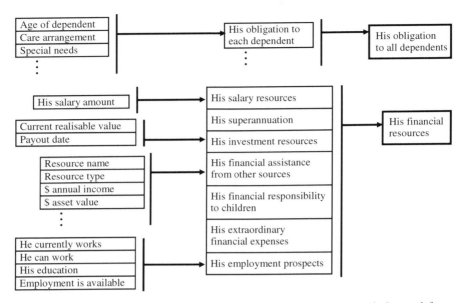

Fig. 3.11.6.1.4 An enlarged detail of the argument tree in the *Split Up* system (the bottom left part of Fig. 3.11.6.1.1)

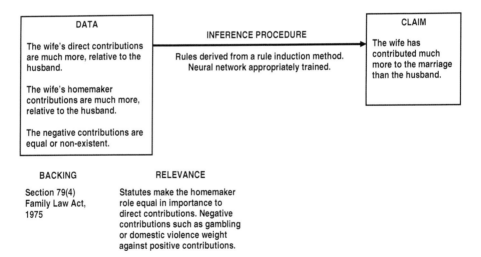

Fig. 3.11.6.1.5 Why the wife deserves more, in a given case (data to claim)

Behind the argument tree, there is an argument which in represented by means of the Toulmin argument structure, in Figs. 3.11.6.1.5, 3.11.6.1.6, and 3.11.6.1.7.

In her thesis about family law in Australia, Renata Alexander (2000) noted that during the 1990s, numerous unsuccessful attempts were made to persuade judges

3.11 Argumentation for Dialectical Situations, vs. for Structuring Knowledge... 199

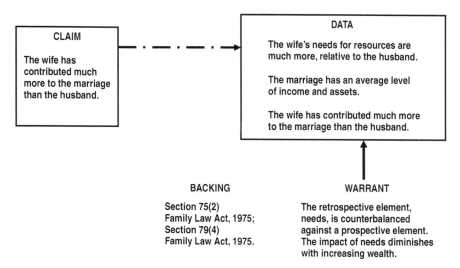

Fig. 3.11.6.1.6 Why the wife deserves more, in a given case (claim to data)

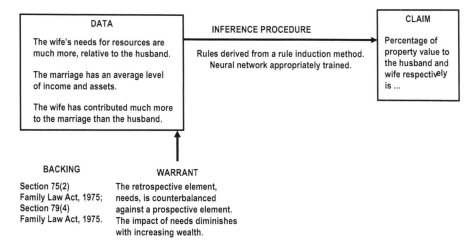

Fig. 3.11.6.1.7 Why the wife deserves more, in a given case (with another claim)

to award a more generous property settlement to victims of domestic violence. This corresponds to the situation where an argument is advanced that departs from existing generic arguments by the introduction of a new data item. In recent years, a small number of Family Court judges began to accept the domestic violence argument. Many of the early cases were appealed and precedents set by higher Courts so that domestic violence is now undeniably a relevant consideration in property division. However, as Alexander (2000) notes, there is still some ambiguity in practice in that some judges have attributed domestic violence as a past contribution factor whereas others have recognised it as a factor that increases the victim's future needs. The ambiguity corresponds to a situation where a new factor has currently been inserted in two places in the argument tree. The discursive community, judges, lawyers and analysts of Australian family law await the resolution of this apparent conflict.

The *Split Up* application also demonstrates that the generic/actual model provides a convenient frame for task decomposition that is particularly useful for data mining. Data mining is restricted to an exercise in discovering the inference procedure within each argument. Although the total number of relevant variables is large (103 in the *Split Up* system) most arguments have a small number of data items. Mining for an inference procedure involving a small number of variables is far more readily tractable than a large set. Furthermore, a flat list of all variables requires huge numbers of cases and often includes missing values. For example, values associated with children are empty for childless marriages and appear in a flat list as null values. Null values severely hamper data-mining attempts. However, if the variables are organised into a generic tree, each argument has a small number of variables (data items). This means that relatively small numbers of cases can be used to discover inference procedures that are accurate.

Accurate inference procedures are particularly important in the *Split Up* system because users (typically, a couple) are non-experts and need the system to prompt them for all relevant facts in order to infer all claims leading up to the culminating claim. This is in contrast to the *Embrace* system, which is configured to make no automated inferences at all, yet illustrates the document drafting and information retrieval benefits of the GAAM.

3.11.6.2 The *Embrace* System for Assessing Refugee Status

Yearwood, Stranieri, and Anjaria (1999) report the application of the generic actual model to supporting reasoning regarding the assessment of refugee status in Australia. Refugee law is highly discretionary and extremely difficult to model. The main statute, the United Nations Convention, lists factors to be taken into account in reaching a determination on the refugee status of an applicant, but does not specify the weighting factors should have.

Ensuring that the decision making is as consistent as possible in this complex and discretionary domain is critical for just outcomes. Yearwood et al. (1999) have modelled reasoning in this field using over 200 generic arguments derived from members of the body established to hear appeals from unsuccessful applicants, the Refugee Review Tribunal. Inference procedures have not been specified for any generic argument in order to ensure that the information system facilitates decision making but does not directly infer outcomes which are left entirely to Tribunal members. Nevertheless, the argument structures have proven to be useful in modelling refugee decisions and in generating XML documents that are plausible first draft determinations.

3.11 Argumentation for Dialectical Situations, vs. for Structuring Knowledge...

Refugee Review Tribunal determinations are documents that express the reasoning steps a member of the Tribunal followed in order to infer conclusions regarding the status of an applicant. Although, it is reasonable to expect that a mapping between the reasoning steps used by judges and the structure of the judgement produced would clearly be apparent, Branting, Callaway, Mott, and Lester (1999) note that such a mapping is by no means obvious. They make some progress beyond boilerplate templates with the sophisticated use of discourse analysis using speech act and rhetorical structure theory.

Yearwood and Stranieri (1999) have identified a simple heuristic for traversing a tree of actual arguments that leads to a plausible document structure. This is achieved without the use of discourse analysis methods, largely because the generic/actual framework is a succinct, yet expressive frame for capturing reasoning.

The document generation facility has been implemented as a module of an argument shell, called *ArgumentDeveloper*. Yearwood and Stranieri (2000) describe the program that has been written to facilitate the development of knowledge based systems that use the generic actual argument model. This module traverses the actual argument tree for a user in the order specified by the algorithm and generates an XML document with an appropriate document type definition file. When this is paired with a style sheet customised for refugee law, a determination is automatically generated that expresses the flow of reasoning in a manner that is quite plausible despite using no discourse analysis techniques.

Yearwood and Stranieri (2000) developed and implemented their "Argument Developer Agent" shell which allows the building and storage of versions of the generic argument framework within a domain and an interface for the development of actual arguments. The argument shell consists of the following components:

- A generic argument editor that enables a knowledge engineer to enter a tree of generic arguments within a domain.
- An actual argument editor that enables a user to enter actual arguments made by users. This identifies the appropriate argument in the generic structure based on the text used by the user in a notepad interface. It was then replaced by a dialogue interface to interact with the TOURIST agent, in an application to tourism which we briefly discuss in Section 3.11.6.4 below.
- An inference engine that can infer a value for a claim from data item values by invoking the procedure embedded in an argument.
- A dialogue generator that models the relationships between arguments such as A supports B, A rebuts C and D, A extends G; This is important for modelling the way in which two or more parties apply arguments in a dialogue.

A knowledge engineer using the argumentation shell first maps out all the generic arguments. The claim of each generic argument except for the culminating one, is a data item for another argument so a tree of arguments is constructed.

In addition to the need to generate draft determinations rapidly, the *Embrace* project provided the vehicle for demonstrating that the generic actual model improves information retrieval. This is implemented with the development of the information retrieval module into the *ArgumentDeveloper* shell. This module automatically generates a search engine query by assembling all terms used in an argument with a list of keywords associated with the argument. Matthijssen (1999) demonstrated improved precision and recall figures using keyword lists attached to the original Toulmin argument structure. The information retrieval query takes all variable names and values in addition to a list of terms associated with each generic argument in order to generate a query.

3.11.6.3 The *GetAid* System for Legal Aid Eligibility

The *GetAid* system operates in the field of legal aid eligibility where rapid prototyping of a web based application is more important. The generic actual framework has been applied to acquire knowledge regarding decisions made by officers of Victoria Legal Aid, a government funded provider of legal services for disadvantaged clients, in assessing whether an applicant should receive legal aid. Applicants for legal aid must pass a merits test which involves a prediction about the likely outcome of the case in Court. This assessment involves considerable discretion and is performed by grants officers who have extensive experience in the practices of Victorian Courts.

A web-based knowledge based system called *GetAid* was rapidly developed using the shell, WebShell, reported by Stranieri and Zeleznikow (2001a). Knowledge was modelled using two distinct techniques: decision trees for procedural-type tasks and generic argument trees for tasks that are more complex, ambiguous or uncertain.

The *GetAid* development demonstrated that the generic actual argument model (GAAM) is a useful representation for rapid knowledge acquisition. In order to construct a generic argument tree, the expert is initially prompted to articulate factors (data item variables) that may be relevant in determining the ultimate claim without any concern about how the factors may combine to actually infer a claim value. For every factor (data item variable) articulated, a reason for the items relevance must be able to be articulated. The possible values for each data item are then identified. The next step in the knowledge acquisition exercise involves viewing each data item as a claim and eliciting the data items that are used to infer its value.

Once the tree is developed as far back as the expert regards appropriate for the task at hand, attention can be then by focussed on identifying one or more inference procedures that may be used to infer a claim value from data item values. This proved difficult for the *GetAid* experts to articulate as rules because the way in which the factors combine is rarely made explicit but forms part of the expertise gathered over many cases. Although it is feasible to attempt to derive heuristics, the approach we used was to present a panel of experts with an exhaustive list of all combinations of data items as hypothetical cases and prompt for a likely decision. The decisions from a panel of experts were merged to form a dataset of records that were used to train a neural network for each generic argument.

The construction of the systems, *GetAid*, *Split Up* and *Embrace* illustrate the benefits in the use of the non-dialectical framework. These include hybrid reasoning, task decomposition, information retrieval, document generation and knowledge acquisition. These benefits can be seen to derive from the effectiveness of the generic actual model to structure reasoning. In the e-Tourism application, first steps have been made toward the development of a dialectical model that is based on the non-dialectical model.

3.11.6.4 An Application Outside Law: *eTourism*

In the *eTourism* system, developed by Avery, Yearwood, and Stranieri (2001), dialogue occurs between three types of software agents: tourists, tour advisors and tour operators. The human tourist invokes an instance of a tourist agent on commencing a consultation session. The tour advisor has no human counterpart. The dialogue between the tourist and advisor agents is aimed at realising the community goal of recommending tours the tourist will enjoy. The tour operator invokes an operator agent in order to inform the advisor of tours it operates. A key feature of the approach presented here is that all agents share the same generic argument tree but can instantiate their own actual arguments. In this way, each agent's beliefs are represented by actual arguments, but because these are instances drawn from a common generic argument tree, negotiation can be simplified.

Jennings, Parsons, Sierra, and Faratin (2000) noted that negotiation underpins any attempt at coordinating multiple agents (human or software). For instance, the architecture for the eTourism application is based on an agent-oriented approach where each software agent represents world knowledge as arguments and interacts with other agents according to dialogue rules. An agent based framework that places emphasis on *negotiation* must include three main components:

- a negotiation protocol,
- a negotiation object, and
- an agent's decision-making model.

Generic arguments are used in the *eTourism* project as a means of representing the shared knowledge that an agent community has. In this approach each agent's beliefs are represented by actual arguments. Because these instances are drawn from a common generic argument tree, negotiation between agents can be simplified. The mapping between the negotiation protocol, the negotiation object and the agent's decision making model has been discussed and lays the groundwork for developing applications based on multiple agents negotiating outcomes because knowledge represented as generic/actual arguments helps to: constrain the negotiation protocol; constrain the negotiation objects; constrain the agent's decision making model.

The generic argument[38] constrains negotiation protocols in a convenient manner for agent-oriented architectures (this kind of software is discussed below in Section 6.1.6). The actual arguments of multiple agents can be readily compared and contrasted because each actual argument is an instantiation of the same generic argument. Operators that appear in dialectical argumentation such as *attack* and *accept* are readily implemented. An argument, A, attacks another argument, B, if A has a different claim value than B for the same claim variable. The source of the attack can be readily isolated. It may be due to different data item values, certainties, or different inference procedures. An argument, C accepts another argument, D if it has the same claim variable and value. *Identical acceptance* is operationalised as the same claim, data and inference procedures, whereas *similar acceptance* occurs if the claims are the same but data or inferences are not. Research was conducted in order to develop the dialectical model based on the generic/actual split.

Figure 3.11.6.4.1 illustrates an actual argument with data values set and a particular inference mechanism selected. It is an instantiated generic argument from

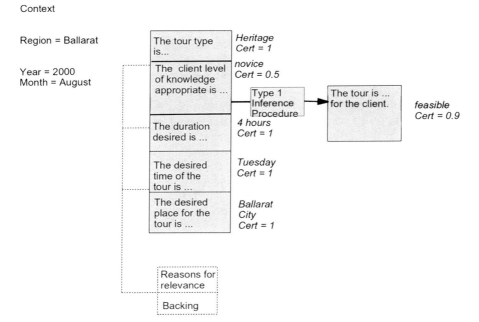

Fig. 3.11.6.4.1 An actual argument in the Tourism domain to support customised delivery of Tourism Information

---

[38] In the project for assisting prospective tourists, the generic argument structure forms the basis for both the TOURIST agent and the TOUR advisor agent. The TOURIST agent currently interacts with a human tourist agent via text in a notepad interface which is parsed. This was developed into a dialogue interface. The shell permits the construction of both agents and the simple trusted negotiation mechanism is being implemented. More complex interactions were also studied.

Tourism where the claim is "The tour is *feasible* for the client", based on the data items and values given in the diagram. The inference procedure may simply be a query against a data base of information on tours. The justification can be given as one of the answers that satisfies the query and the appropriate information.

Stranieri and Zeleznikow (2001b) proposed an agent-based knowledge based approach to help regulate copyright. Five knowledge-based systems were described that are sufficiently flexible to protect authors rights without denying the public access to works for fair use purposes. The owner of a work and users who wish to copy a portion of the work are participants in the discursive community and share the same generic arguments. In order to copy the work, users construct their own actual arguments. The agent representing the owner determines whether to release the work or not by constructing its own actual argument. The generic/actual framework simplifies the negotiation protocol and assists in the deployment of an agent-oriented approach.

3.11.7 Envoi

Argumentation can be seen to have been applied to knowledge engineering in the 1990s and 2000s in two ways; with an emphasis on the dialectical nature of argumentation or with an emphasis on the structure of reasoning from a non-dialectical perspective. From the dialectical perspective, the way in which two or more participants in a discourse propose arguments that attack, rebut, defeat, subsume or accept others is paramount. From a non-dialectical perspective the way in which claims are laid out and inferred from premises is the object of attention. The argument structure proposed by Toulmin (1958) does not clearly delineate a dialectical perspective from a non-dialectical. Many applications of the Toulmin layout of arguments for knowledge engineering purposes vary the structure.

The variations made by and Kathleen Freeman (1994), Trevor Bench-Capon (1998), Johnson, Zualkernan, et al. (1993), and others can be understood as the result of different emphases on the dialectical or non-dialectical perspective, though in many cases the distinction is still blurred. A variation to the Toulmin structure called the Generic Actual Argument Model has been advanced in the present Section 3.11, where the distinction between dialectical and non-dialectical argumentation concepts is clearly defined. The GAAM is a non-dialectical model that facilitates hybrid reasoning, information retrieval, document drafting, knowledge acquisition and data mining. The non-dialectical GAAM has been applied for the construction of systems in refugee law, family law, eligibility for legal aid, copyright law. A dialectical model that is based on the GAAM is under investigation though early results with the automated provision of e-Tourism advice using an agent architecture indicate that a dialogue model is more readily realised simplified if built on the non-dialectical base.

Chapter 4
Computer Assistance for, or Insights into, Organisational Aspects

4.1 Computer Help for Organising

4.1.1 Procedural-Support Systems for Organising the Evidence: CaseNote, MarshalPlan, Daedalus

E-justice, within *e-government*, is the use of information technology within judiciary systems. Applications of *e-justice* are a means to manage court proceedings, legal bars, as well as (e.g. in Argentina) reform at the legislative level.[1] For example, Politis, Donos, Christou, Giannakopoulos, and Papapanagiotou-Leza (2008) is a case study of three countries in the Balkans. Their experiences are analysed as an illustration of the experiences and problems in applying e-justice on a national scale.

> The development of software for such a court of justice ranges from customized applications and in-house support for small scale computerization schemes that keep track of the judge's calendar and court records, up to large scale, cross-court internetworked pieces of software monitoring all aspects of court computerization like evidence book, decision delivery date book, summons, petitions, entries of court hearing outcomes, filling of appeals, etc. to all types of decisions issued by a lower or an appellate court.

It must be said that most often, the kind of technology resorted to in e-justice is not part of artificial intelligence. Moreover, it is only seldom that anything sophisticated used to be done concerning legal evidence within e-justice, as opposed to computer techniques used by forensic scientists in order to process the evidence in their respective forensic discipline. Nevertheless, there exist some projects that

---

[1] The information technology aspects of the preparation of the *Digesto Jurídico Argentino* were supervised by Antonio Martino, a well-known scholar in AI & Law. A consortium carried out two tasks, namely, the reduction of a Legislative Technical Manual (this was coordinated by Martino, and was completed in 2001), and the revision of every normative texts emanated since the 1853 Constitution (this was directed by Atilio Alterini). At www.sp.unipi.it/dsp/didattica/Digesto/manual.html (hosted by the website of the University of Pisa in Italy) it is possible to access a virtual reading room of all the laws, as well as an exemplificative method of law writing assisted by the computer.

deserve notice, and that are within e-justice rather than on its periphery. These are *procedural-support systems* for organising the evidence.

Substantive, as opposed to *procedural*, pertains to the rules of right administered by a court, rather than to how to administer it. For example, the order in which the parties and their witnesses testify belongs in procedure. Such terminology turns up in references to kinds of computer tools for assisting humans in handling court cases. The starting point of Prakken and Renooij (2001) is: "When procedural-support systems are to be useful in practice, they should provide support for causal reasoning about evidence", where: "Procedural-support systems are AI & Law programs that lack domain knowledge and thus cannot solve problems, but that instead help the participants in a dispute to structure their reasoning and discussion, thereby promoting orderly and effective disputes".

An important commercial tool for lawyers to organise the evidence for a trial (in a U.S. context), is *CaseMap*. What does already exist and is available to legal practitioners, to assist them with evidence? Products of CaseSoft, an American firm[2] – itself a division of DecisionQuest, the U.S. leading provider of trial consulting services – include the *CaseMap* case analysis software, *TimeMap* chronology-graphing software, and the *NoteMap* outliner (the latter, upstream of a document-processor or of the generation of a slide-show presentation).

With no relation to CaseSoft, there is a competitor of *CaseMap*, namely, *MarshalPlan*, which has long been a prototype developed in U.S. academia by David Schum and Peter Tillers (respectively, of George Mason University in Arlington, Virginia, and of the Cardozo Law School in New York). *MarshalPlan* was described in Schum (2001). The early prototype was developed in *HyperCard*. Since the mid-2000s, *MarshalPlan* has been making use of *Revolution* development software (of Runtime Revolution Ltd. in Edinburgh, Scotland). By 2009, the version advertised on the Web was *MarshalPlan 3.0*.[3] Version 4.0 was accessible online, in 2011.[4]

Early reports about the project which led to *MarshalPlan* are Schum and Tillers (1989, 1990a, 1990b, 1991). The initial research that ended up generating *MarshalPlan* was funded by the U.S. National Science Foundation. David Schum was the grantee, and Peter Tillers was the principal consultant (the identification numbers of the grants being SES-8704377 and SES-9007693). The NSF support lasted for a total of seven years, and ended in the early 1990s (with no application for more NSF support). Tillers and Schum continued to study the use of software to marshal evidence. Tillers conducted those post-NSF studies largely by experimenting with the software concept which eventually came to be called *MarshalPlan*.

---

[2] www.casesoft.com

[3] http://tillerstillers.blogspot.com/2009/07/release-of-marshalplan-30.html (accessed in 2011). At another webpage, http://tillerstillers.blogspot.com/2009/09/theoretical-underpinnings-and-purposes_22.html one can access theoretical notes on *MarshalPlan*.

[4] http://tillers.net/MarshalPlan.4.0/Web/MarshalPlan.html "Evidence marshaling software on the web: MarshalPlan 4.0 (for the time being use Firefox 3.x; Chrome and Internet Explorer won't work for some reason)".

4.1 Computer Help for Organising

MarshalPlan is a tool for marshalling the evidence and structuring the chronologies and the arguments by means of a formalism, based on Wigmore Charts, at pre-trial and trial within the American system of legal procedure (not only for criminal cases, but in civil cases as well). The formalism is organised as an algebra. Statistical processing can be added. *MarshalPlan* is intended to provide:

(a) An environment allowing the development of a case-specific database of evidence and evidentiary details;
(b) Support for the development of lines of fact investigation;
(c) Support and documentation of investigation protocols;
(d) Organisation of evidence relevant to given proposed hypotheses or scenarios;
(e) Visual representation of the chronological relationships between facts according to hypothesised scenarios;
(f) Visual representation of chronologies involved in the narrative and proceedings;
(g) Visualisation of argument structures;
(h) Support and protocols for checking, testing, and evaluating evidence;
(i) Temporal consistency checking;
(j) A bridge to forensic disciplines such as forensic statistics.

Daedalus is a tool for the Italian *sostituto procuratore* (examining magistrate during investigation, and prosecutor at trial). In the late 1990s, it was adopted by magistrates in the offices of the judiciary throughout Italy. The Ministry of Justice had come to support it because of how magistrates had expressed their preference for it. It was developed single-handedly by Carmelo Àsaro (now a judge in Rome), and used by him in his daily routine as a *sostituto procuratore* in Lucca, Tuscany.

The great advantage of *Daedalus*, a tool whose conception is especially suited for countries whose criminal justice was shaped by the Napoleonic code (France, Italy, and the Netherlands are among them), is that it validates the procedure (the user is not allowed to take the wrong step), and provides a record of this having been the case (Asaro et al., 2001). In Section 4.1.3, we are going to provide details of *Daedalus*.

A sequel project of *Daedalus* is *Itaca* (initially called *Daedalus-Cassazione*), whose development for the Court of Cassation in Rome was contracted to Siemens, but whose original design is Asaro's. The needs to which *Itaca* responds were stated by the Criminal Sections (*Sezioni Penali*) of the Court of Cassation. These needs comprise the calculation of when preventative detention and generally preventative measures are going to expire; when prescription (i.e., bar of the statute of limitations) is going to apply to the offences concerned; and in general, data processing concerning offences. Both the data and juridical rules are coded. Of course, the jurisdiction in Italy is significantly different from that of Anglo-Saxon countries, and even within the United Kingdom, there are difference between Scottish procedural and substantive law with respect to England and Wales. It is nevertheless important to also get a feel of tools for a jurisdiction from the Continent.

Elsewhere in this book, we are going to discuss link analysis (Chapter 6) and then (Chapter 7) Richard Leary's FLINTS project, whose earlier phases had been within the police, and then in academia (as a doctoral project), before further development within corporate business. In the late 1990s, a Detective Inspector at the West Midlands Police, with headquarters in Birmingham, Leary was playing host to well-received talks on formal approaches to evidence; e.g., in 1998 David Schum gave there, in front of about 70 police officers, a "talk on computer applications to discovery and fact investigation", and he "focused of course on *MarshalPlan*" (from a posting by Schum at an e-list), by which time he had already spent about seven years about the project together with Peter Tillers.

Nevertheless, *MarshalPlan* is not only for fact investigation. It is a tool that finds application in litigation, not only in criminal cases, but also in civil cases. Potential users of *MarshalPlan* include:

(a) Police officers engaged in the investigation in criminal cases;
(b) Prosecutors and defence counsel engaged in informal and pretrial fact investigation;
(c) Litigation paralegals (legally-trained assistants to lawyers), at legal practices which specialise or engage in civil litigation, for the purposes of fact investigation in connection with civil cases;
(d) Expert witnesses with respect to questions of fact;
(e) Investigating (examining) magistrates, in countries where this role applies; and elsewhere (such as in the U.S.A.): judges when required to pass on the adequacy of investigations conducted either by public prosecutors or private counsel;
(f) Where this is allowed (the U.K. and some Commonwealth countries): judges, for the purposes of summation of the evidence by the judge for the benefit of a jury;
(g) Law teachers involved in trial practice programs and clinical education in litigation.

4.1.2 The Lund Procedure

Robert Goldsmith (1989), working at the University of Lund in Sweden, outlined a plan for a piece of software, to be implemented using logic programming, and "consist[ing] of three basic levels: a database level, an information management level, and a user interface level" (ibid., p. 322). The user was to be given an online tutorial about how to use the so-called *evidentiary value model*, and then the program would be used for "analyzing a specific case after the user has gained access to the evidence in its entirety" (ibid.).

The user would provide assessments about how the case was to be structured, and the program would provide some guidance. First, the user would provide "some general designation of the case together with some basic facts about it" (ibid., p. 323), and the next stage would have the user input *scenarios*: "one or more brief accounts of the events which the evidence suggests may have occurred" (ibid.).

4.1 Computer Help for Organising

Next, "the user decides what evidentiary themes should be considered and inputs a brief description of each", being able to refer to the scenarios (ibid.). Thus, a *structured list of themes* would be created. Next, the user would produce an *evidentiary list*, by subdividing the body of evidence. Next, at the user's discretion, "information of various types which can be of help in evaluating the evidence" would be fed in by the user; e.g., "comments by the user; general information external to the case but of possible relevance to it; arguments by the prosecutor, the defense attorney, or the counsels to the litigants; and conclusions and arguments of a statistical nature" (ibid., p. 324).

Next, the user would access "both the evidentiary list and the structured list of themes", in order to produce a preliminary *list of evidentiary facts*, and being "a list of separate portions of the evidence which appear to possibly be related in a causal or logical implicative way with one or more of the themes, or with the negation of these (as counterevidence)" (ibid.).

The next stage concerns *evidentiary relationships*: "The user is to indicate for each theme separately, which of the evidentiary facts appear linked with it in terms of a possible evidentiary relationship. If two or more themes are viewed as belonging to a chain of evidence, they are dealt with partly as a unit" (ibid.). For each evidentiary relationship, the user was also expected at this stage to state "whether it can be seen as supporting the theme or supporting the negation of the theme" (ibid.), and "whether it appears to involve the theme being a cause of the evidence, the evidence being a cause of the theme, or the evidence logically implying the theme" (ibid., p. 325). A preliminary *list of evidentiary relationships* would have thus been produced by the user.

During the next stage, the user would have been shown that list, and required to apply to each item in it "the quality of evidence criteria (for adequacy of investigation, and for specificity and coherence" (ibid.). In case those criteria were, in the user's opinion, not met, then an evidentiary relationship would be removed (and possibly an evidentiary fact would be removed, but it may be involved in more than one relationship). Any item thus removed was to be placed on the evidentiary list, where it would be "marked as having failed to meet the respective criteria" (ibid.).

It is at the next stage, *Evidentiary Value* (Goldsmith's ninth step), that the computer would have played any role other than in structuring the editing. It is also at this stage, that Goldsmith's procedure became quite committed to quantification either in line of the Scandinavian school of legal "science", in terms of strength of evidence (Ekelöf, 1964), or of outright probabilistic models. "The user's task is to assess, either directly or with varying degrees of computational help from the computer, the combined evidentiary value of the evidentiary facts in question in supporting the theme. (If only one evidentiary fact is seen as pertaining to a given theme, the user simply assesses its evidentiary value directly.)" (ibid.).

The computer would be fed intuitive assessments from the user, and would apply to them prescriptive rules. "The user is also given the choice, whether receiving computational help or not, of conceptualizing evidentiary value in strictly probabilistic terms or in terms of strength of evidence" (ibid., p. 326). The output of this stage is the *structured list of themes and evidentiary values*.

Goldsmith's tenth step was *Subordinate Decisions*: "the user may decide here to make various subordinate decisions applying either to individual themes, or to sets of themes that are logically related. Each such decision concerns whether or not the theme or set of themes in question should be accepted, that is, seen as adequately supported by the evidence" (ibid.). The final stage was for the user "to reach an overall decision" (ibid., p. 327). Goldsmiths envisaged that the program could be used for training, or "for facilitating research on use of the model and on the evaluation of judicial evidence generally" (ibid.), or for assisting a person working on the judicial evidence of a specific case.

Goldsmith conceded that the third kind of use, i.e., for practical purposes "in a manner which could directly affect the outcome of a case" (ibid.), would have necessitated further study that would involve "careful evaluation of the program's limitations and weaknesses" (ibid.), and to include features "aimed at counteracting insofar as possible whatever tendency the user might have to place undue reliance on the program" (ibid., pp. 327–328). In fact, because of the use made of quantification, especially if a probabilistic model is adopted, stage nine was threading on controversial ground, especially if the program was intended for use while working on a case on which the court was yet to find.

Therefore, Goldsmith's (1989) project fits among procedural-support systems, and its main contribution is the procedure itself. The description was quite vague about argumentation, yet relationships clearly had to capture argument structure. Goldsmith (1989) intended the user to use the so-called *evidentiary value model* – but he also described an alternative model, being the *theme probability model*, about which he had already written in Goldsmith (1986), and which applies to judicial decision-making "an approach to probability assessment which is a widely accepted one within the natural and social sciences, whereas the evidentiary value model represents a more unconventional approach to probability assessment, one which has been examined mainly within the judicial decision making area, where the model itself is still not particularly well known. Neither model can be said to contradict the other, however, in probability theoretical terms" (ibid., p. 321). The difference between the two models consists "in the event to which probability assessments apply, this being for the theme probability model the truth of the theme, for the evidentiary value model the existence of a causal or logical link between the evidence and the theme" (ibid.).

4.1.3 Daedalus, a Procedural-Support Tool for the Italian Examining Magistrate and Prosecutor

Carmelo Asaro, Ephraim Nissan, and Antonio A. Martino

4.1.3.1 Background of the Project, and Its Users

Daedalus is a computer tool, developed by an Italian magistrate – Carmelo Àsaro (now a judge) – and integrated in his own daily routine as an examining magistrate conducting inquiries, then as a prosecutor if and when the case investigated goes to court. This is a role that in Italy goes by the name *sostituto procuratore*.

Around the year 2000, *Daedalus* was adopted by magistrates in judiciary offices throughout Italy, spawning moreover other related projects. Interestingly, whereas the tool was initially used by Asaro himself in his judiciary office in the Tuscan town of Lucca, it was eventually offered to other *sostituti procuratori* to try, and their positive response provided a strong incentive for Italy's Ministry of Justice to have *Daedalus* adopted in the offices of all *sostituti procuratori*. In practice, the ministry was complying with the requests of the intended users.

Unlike in the Anglo-American system, in Italy inquiries are directed by an examining magistrate, and if the decision is eventually reached to take the suspects to court, that is, to prosecute, then the examining magistrate may well become the prosecutor (in Italian, *pubblico ministero*, or *P.M.* for short). The now Rome-based Judge Asaro, who used to carry out these roles while a *Sostituto Procuratore della Repubblica* in Lucca, in the late 1990s put to good effect his computing programming skills and developed *Daedalus* single-handedly.

This resulted in the tool being especially appealing to his Italian colleagues, as the ergonomics was tailored exactly to fit their day-to-day routine, validating every step they may take. At first, the use of this computer tool became integrated in Asaro's daily routine, both while investigating cases, and while prosecuting.

Subsequently, the tool was distributed and experimented with by *sostituti procuratori* throughout Italy, and their overwhelming support of the tool encouraged steps of official endorsement of *Daedalus* being taken on the part of the Italian Ministry of Justice, which distributed it to all judiciary offices in the country. For a while, Asaro was seconded to a public body entrusted with the computerisation of public administration and the judiciary.

In this chapter, we have already mentioned *Daedalus* in Section 4.1.1. In the main, the present Section 4.1.3 is based on Asaro et al. (2001). The illustrations are based on screens of *Daedalus*, but the text appears here in English instead of in Italian, which is the language of *Daedalus*.

4.1.3.2 General Remarks About Italian Procedural Law

In the 1990s and around the year 2000, procedural law was being reformed in various countries in Continental Europe, including Italy (as well as various countries in Eastern Europe). The general trend was towards moving away, at least to some extent, from the *inquisitorial* system that has been traditional in those countries, towards an *adversarial* system inspired by the Anglo-American system, usually without going all the way, but by just incorporating major aspects of the adversarial system. The Italian legal system used to be of the inquisitorial type, being part of Continental Law, and based on the Napoleonic code, like French law and Dutch law.

In 1989, Italy's new *Codice di Procedura Penale* (code of criminal procedure) was introduced, which adopted the adversarial system. Until 2010, the import of this reform was rather enfeebled (bringing back elements of the old system) by about eighty legislative interventions, introducing exceptions to the reform, and that have made the input of the evidence into a trial more complex.

Quite importantly – notwithstanding there also being lay judges (*giudici popolari*, i.e., jurors) – professional judges who preside over criminal trials in Italy are much more important for the adjudication, than in trials by a jury the United States or the United Kingdom.

In the Anglo-American system, the jury provides a verdict, but does not give a motivation for their decision. It has been said that in a sense, this aspect of the jury still retains a principle of the older trials by ordeal. The jury does not have to rationalise their conviction, in the way that trained judges on the Continent need to do while providing a written motivation for their verdict.

By contrast, in the Anglo-American system there is *evidence law*, and in particular, *exclusionary rules* about the admissibility of the evidence. In Italy (like also in France), so stern a regulation about the admissibility of the evidence is not to be found, and this absence is obviated by there being the possibility to bring the matter to a *Corte d'Assise* (Court of Assizes, but the sense is not identical with those in, say, Scotland or the United States).[5]

At any rate, in Italy a verdict comes with a judicial motivation. In Italy, the judge is required, while writing down the motivation, to take into account also counter-evidence to the decision taken, the final speeches to the bench given by the lawyers of both parties, and what emerged from cross-examination.

Even so, with a judicial motivation, there is no way to observe or to probe into the "internal forum" (*foro interno*) of the judge, i.e., into what actually went on in the judge's cognition. In the United States in the second half of the 19th century, the prominent jurist O. W. Holmes, Jr., suggested that how an adjudicators actually makes decision may even depend on his digestion. The psychology of judicial sentencing is the subject of Fitzmaurice and Pease (1986) and of Pennington and Lloyd-Bostock (1987).

---

[5] Up to 2000, Italy had the following kinds of judges and courts: *Giudice di pace* (Justice of Peace), without criminal jurisdiction; *Pretura* (Magistrate's Court), which has been abolished since, and used to be a court of first instance, with a civil and criminal jurisdiction; *Tribunale*, being a court of first instance for more serious civil and criminal cases (moreover, it used to hear appeals from the *pretura*); *Giudice di sorveglianza*, responsible for the enforcement of sentences; *Tribunale per i minorenni* (Juvenile Court); *Corte di appello* (Court of Appeal); *Corte di cassazione* (Court of Cassation: the highest court of appeal). Special courts included: the *Corte di assise* (Court of Assizes, only for criminal prosecutions); the *Commissario per la liquidazione degli usi civici* (Commissioner for easements and rights of use), and the *Tribunale superiore delle acque* (High Court of Waters).

In June 1999, a reform of the system started to be implemented, intended to gradually modify the tasks and functions of the judicial offices firstly in the civil and then (from January 2000) in the criminal sector. Through the institution of a *giudice unico di primo grado* (single-judge court of first instance), aimed at making trials more rapid and procedures easier, the jurisdictions of the *preture* (magistrates' courts) and *tribunali* (courts) have been merged and the *pretore* office (i.e., the judge sitting in the *pretura*) abolished.

4.1 Computer Help for Organising

When it is more than one professional judge who adjudicate at a trial, and the verdict is reached by a majority, in Italy there is no possibility of the judge in the minority writing down a *minority opinion* (*motivazione dissenziente*).

There is a paradox, in Italy, in that whereas judges have to provide a written motivation for their finding in a case, nevertheless in such trials that a procedural shortcut (*giudizio abbreviato*) was adopted, the judge releasing the motivation may even be different from the judge who gave the verdict. Some jurists in Italy find this surprising, as this exception severs the dependency of the judicial motivation upon the proceedings that took place in court.

Italian law does not envisage such a situation that a judgement be invalidated because the judicial motivation is insufficient. But nevertheless, mistrial can be declared because of a defect of the judicial motivation. For example, in a particular case, a handwritten motivation has been invalidated because unreadable. The Giuffrida Committee decided that this was a "general annulment" (*nullità generale*), so the case was returned to the first-degree court. Had it been "relative annulment" (*nullità relativa*) instead, the case would go to a court of appeal.

4.1.3.3 The Phases of an Inquiry in Italy

In the Italian legal system, procedure for a criminal case basically consists of three phases:

(1) The preliminary inquiry (carried out by an examining magistrate). In the old inquisitorial system, this would be conceived of as an objectively conducted stage (just as the judge, in the trial which follows, is above the opposed parties). However, the 1989 reform has redefined the inquiry as being the activity of one of the parties, in a quasi-adversarial perspective (a very limited form of Americanisation);
(2) The debate in court (in Italian: *il dibattimento*);
(3) Appeal (in Italian: *il giudizio di impugnazione* or *appello*).

Subsequently to the 1989 reform, *trial* (Italian: *processo*) is a name that only competes to the second and third phase, as the accusation, put forth by the prosecutor (*pubblico ministero*), is submitted to the judgement of an impartial third party, namely, the judge.

This is a bench trial, judged by a trained judge (unlike the involvement of lay factfinders, i.e., jurors, in the Anglo-American system: the reform in Italy introduced the *giudici popolari* for some trials, but these are under the firm control of the judge, who is the actual judicial decision-maker).

Since the 1989 reform, proof is construed during the debate in court, out of the dialectic between the prosecution and defence. A consequence of this is that the inquiry of the examining magistrate, turned prosecutor, can no longer be used (or even, for that matter, known) by the judge. Said otherwise, the state is represented by the prosecutor and is represented by the judge, but these two functions are now neatly separated.

The examining magistrate conducts an inquiry not out of a preconceived notion that the accusation will be proven, but rather in order to identify sources of evidence that will eventually be submitted to the judge during the trial (by which time, the examining magistrate will have become the public prosecutor in the case at hand). This is clearly a legacy of the inquisitorial system, and it is bound to be there for the very reason that the chief investigator and the prosecutor are both magistrates, and for that matter, they usually are the very same person.

Nevertheless, the rule stated above – the one by which the preliminary inquiry as conducted by the examining magistrate cannot be used (or even known) by the judge – does not always apply. There are given categories of cases, explicitly stated in the Italian criminal procedure code, in which the activities carried out by the investigating magistrate can be both known and used as evidence by the judge. These are situations in which those activities could not be usefully "replicated" at trial by the prosecutor because of reasons which are either inherent *ab origine* (such as when the evidence pertains to a requisition or perquisition which took place during the inquiry), or *intervenient* (such as when a person who made a deposition during the inquiry, died meanwhile, and therefore cannot testify in person at trial; contrast this to how hearsay is treated in Anglo-American law).[6]

The stage at which the inquiry takes place is the one with which *Daedalus* is principally concerned. It starts once the examining magistrate receives the notification of the crime (called in Italian a *notizia di reato*). This act may take various forms: either the Polizia Giudiziaria (which is the usual case), or a private person communicates to the Procura (where a substitute procurator will take care of the case *qua* examining magistrate) a notification (*atto*) which may be a *denuncia* (accusation), or an *esposto* (petition), or a *querela* (suit), and in which one or more persons are indicated as being the perpetrator of one or more offences.

The examining magistrate checks the *notizia di reato*. In case he or she does not need discard it (as in the case of an anonymous denunciation), s/he takes the step of having the *persona indagata* (i.e., the person subjected to the inquiry: the suspect) inscribed in the *registro degli indagati*, with a mention of the offences ascribed to the given person.

This step is crucial. It has important effects:

- firstly, it demarcates the *subjective boundaries* permissible for the inquiry (that is to say, it is forbidden to investigate persons who are different from the ones who were so inscribed in the *registro degli indagati*);

---

[6] Hearsay testimony especially in the context of the Italian jurisdiction was discussed in a book by Balsamo and Lo Piparo (2004). An interesting different subject is the status of the testimony given by somebody at a related trial or a trial for a related crime; this was discussed in a book by Bargis (1994), in the Italian context. This is also treated in Ferrua (2010, section 15). The relevant act is Italy's art. 192 c.p.p. (according to the new *Codice di Procedura Penale*), paragraphs 3 and 4. The law makes such testimony admissible, on a par with the testimony of a co-defendant at the same trial. Such testimony can be evaluated, but more caution is need than with other witnesses: it can only become proof if there is independent corroboration.

4.1 Computer Help for Organising 217

- secondly, it demarcates the *objective boundaries* of the inquiry (as only those offences which were recorded in the given entry of the *registro degli indagati* can be permissibly investigated);
- and thirdly, it sets the beginning of the *indagini preliminari* (i.e., the preliminary inquiry), whose duration is to be no longer than six months, unless some limited prorogation is obtained.

This phase, concerning the *registro degli indagati*, is of course subserved by *Daedalus*.

Once the *notizia di reato* is so recorded in the *registro degli indagati*, the examining magistrate starts the inquiry, which s/he could then either carry out in person, or delegate to the Polizia Giudiziaria. If there is such a delegation indeed, it may be concerning individual actions within the inquiry, or then of the inquiry as a whole.

If it is only individual actions within the inquiry which are being delegated to the Polizia Giudiziaria, the latter is only one authorised to carry out those specific actions as well as such actions which are their direct consequence, but such being the case, the Polizia Giudiziaria is not authorised to carry out the inquiry itself.

In contrast, if the examining magistrate delegated the inquiry as a whole to the Polizia Giudiziaria, then both the strategic choices and the responsibility remains in the hands of the Polizia Giudiziaria, except the taking of such measures which by law it's only the examining magistrate who may take.

The examining magistrate carries out the inquiry by taking actions out of a set of categories (*attraverso l'emissione di atti tipici*), whose kinds are defined by the criminal code. Such actions include: a perquisition (*la perquisizione*), a requisition (*il sequestro*), the order to show something (*l'ordine di esibizione*), inspecting somebody or something (*l'ispezione di persone o cose*), eavesdropping to (*l'intercettazione di*) communications or conversations, taking information (*l'assunzione di informazioni*), or, then, carrying out an interrogation of a person subjected to the inquiry.

If so delegated, the Polizia Giudiziaria can nevertheless only take actions falling in a few of those categories – and then only if some conditions are verified (e.g., the Polizia Giudiziaria is allowed to take the initiative of carrying out a perquisition or a requisition only if an offender is caught redhanded, i.e., *solo nella flagranza del reato*, but otherwise must seek and obtain an authorisation from the examining magistrate beforehand) – whereas in contrast the investigating magistrate is allowed to take any of those actions.

Moreover, among the actions which can be taken there are such measures that restrict the personal freedom of a person subjected to the inquiry; this is only permissible when severe offences are concerned. Such measures include various kinds: incarceration as a precaution (*la custodia cautelare in carcere*), house arrest (*gli arresti domiciliari*), the obligation to only reside in a given place (*l'obbligo di dimora*), the obligation to sign (*l'obbligo di firma*).

However, the examining magistrate (the *pubblico ministero*, or *P.M.* for short) cannot currently, according to the present code of criminal procedure in Italy, on his or her own initiative restrict the personal freedom of a person; such a measure can only be taken by a different magistrate: the so-called "judge for the preliminary inquiry", i.e., in Italian, the *giudice per le investigazioni preliminari* (whose acronym is *G.I.P.*). This role was introduced by law in order to check and validate the lawfulness of what the *pubblico ministero* does during the inquiry. The G.I.P. examines the evidence presented by the police and decides whether it is sufficient to send the accused for trial. This is much like the Crown Prosecution Service in England and Wales.[7]

The G.I.P. intervenes in the following few situations:

- Whenever the personal freedom of a person is involved;
- When the inquiry is concluded, which occurs when the P.M. decides to either dismiss the case or enact the *rinvio a giudizio*, i.e., take the case to court.
  - If the P.M. wants to go to court indeed, then the G.I.P. checks that there is enough evidence indeed to support the accusation. In case the G.I.P. finds that this is not the case, then the G.I.P. may either give order that a new inquiry be undertaken, or decide the *archiviazione del procedimento*, that is, that the case be dismissed.
  - If, when the inquiry is concluded, the P.M. wants the case dismissed and requests the *archiviazione del procedimento*, then the G.I.P. may either agree or disagree; if the latter, the G.I.P., deeming that there is enough evidence for pursuing the suspect in court, gives to order to prosecute.

4.1.3.4 The Criteria of an Inquiry

The actions taken by the P.M. during the preliminary inquiry are each expressly categorised by law (*atti tipici*). For the purposes of their being lawful, it is necessary that all conditions required for each action be verified; namely:

- that the action concerns a person subjected to the inquiry;
- that the given person has been inscribed indeed in the *registro degli indagati*;
- that the given action subserves the ascertainment of an offence;
- that the given kind of action be permissible for the given kind of offence the ascertainment of which it is intended to subserve.

---

[7] The kinds of prosecutions in Italy around 2000 (at a time when magistrate's courts, the *preture*, hadn't been abolished as yet) included the following. Prosecutions were carried out by: the *Procuratore della Repubblica presso la Pretura* (Public Prosecutor attached to the Magistrate's Court); the *Procuratore della Repubblica presso il Tribunale* (Public Prosecutor attached to the County or Assizes courts); the *Procuratore della Repubblica presso il Tribunale per i minorenni* (Public Prosecutor attached to the Juvenile Court); the *Procuratore generale della Repubblica presso la Corte di appello* (State Prosecutor General attached to the Court of Appeal); the *Procuratore generale della Repubblica presso la Corte di cassazione* (State Prosecutor General attached to the Court of Cassation). There also are special public prosecutors: the *Procuratore nazionale antimafia* (State Anti-Mafia Prosecutor), and the *Procuratore distrettuale antimafia* (District Anti-Mafia Prosecutor).

4.1 Computer Help for Organising   219

The latter point is especially important. *Daedalus* punctiliously applies this criterion, by setting (so to speak) "roadblocks" along the control sequence of a session, so that actions be not taken that are unlawful. For example, consider eavesdropping on telephone communications. According to the Italian law, such a measure cannot be taken in order to ascertain any kind of offence. It is only permitted for some very severe offences (such as *ricettazione*, i.e., receiving stolen goods), which are expressly indicated in the code of criminal procedure, and this because eavesdropping impinges on the constitutional right of free communication.

Therefore, if the P.M. wants that a telephone conversation be subjected to eavesdropping, the authorisation to do so must be previously obtained from the G.I.P., and such an authorisation can only be given when the crime being investigated is as severe as to warrant eavesdropping. This situation had therefore to be reflected in *Daedalus*, at the time when the software came into being.[8]

Now, consider how the evidence is marshalled. As the inquiry unfolds, the P.M. tries to discover and elucidate the events, by gathering new elements of evidence. These are not "proof" (*prove*), but rather "sources for proof" (items of evidence, in Italian: *fonti di prova*). These in turn can be either "personal" or "real". "Real sources" (*fonti reali*) are such things or documents from which informations can be obtained that are useful to support the accusation. "Personal sources" (*fonti personali*) are such persons who have knowledge concerning the events, as well as, to some extent, the *indagati*, that is, the suspects, those very persons who are being subjected to the inquiry.

By law, the suspect, the *indagato*, is recognised the right not to answer questions that the P.M. is making during an interrogation. That the suspect actually opts to avail him- or herself of the right to silence[9] is, by law, considered not as evidence (*fonte di prova*), but rather as a means of defence.

Yet, those statements that were actually made to the P.M. by the informed person (who eventually at trial may called as *teste*, i.e., witness) or by the person investigated (who eventually at trial may have become a defendant, in Italian: *imputato*), can be used at trial as evidence, if the witness or the defendant are making at trial such statements that are in contradiction with something the same person had stated during the inquiry. If such a situation eventuates indeed, then the P.M., in his or her role as prosecutor at the trial, can signal the contradiction and have the court proceedings (*gli atti del Giudice*) incorporate those statements which had been made during the inquiry.

---

[8] Wiretapping has been much debated in Italy in 2010, and is likely to undergo changes: this is not because of use by law enforcement, but because of widespread use on the part of journalists, and these sometimes publish confidential documents of the judiciary. One supporter of change has claimed that six million persons (out of a population of sixty million) have been wiretapped in just one year.

[9] The right to silence and alternative self-protective choices for a person who is a suspect (*indagato*) in an inquiry, in an Italian context, are the subject of a book by Marafioti (2000).

Let us turn now to how the inquiry is closed. When the P.M. deems that the case has been adequately investigated,[10] the P.M. concludes the inquiry, in either way:

- If the P.M. deems the hypothesis that the suspect is not guilty of the offence ascribed (*nell'ipotesi di* opinio delicti *negativa*), then the P.M. requests that the case be dismissed (*archiviato*).
- If the P.M. sees merit instead to the accusation based on the evidence gathered during the inquiry, then the P.M. releases one of the *atti tipici* which the code of criminal procedure envisages, namely:
  □ the request, made to the G.I.P., to
    ➢ either prosecute (*citazione a giudizio*), or
    ➢ prosecute directly (*citazione diretta a giudizio*), which is appropriate for lesser offences;
  □ the request to condemn by decree (*richiesta di decreto penale di condanna*);
  □ expressing an opinion concerning whether to agree the investigated person's demand that s/he be subjected to a lesser penalty (*parere sulla domanda di oblazione formulata dall'indagato*);
  □ expressing an agreement concerning the investigated person's request of a shorter judicial path (*consenso alla richiesta di giudizio abbreviato formulata dall'indagato*). Actually, the path can be shortened to different degrees: there may be a *giudizio abbreviato*, or then a *giudizio direttissimo*, or even a *giudizio immediato*.

Let us consider these options in turn, leaving the discussion of the *citazione a giudizio* to the next subsection.

Condemnation by decree (*il decreto penale di condanna*): the P.M. asks the G.I.P. for a *decreto penale* if the P.M. deems that the appropriate penalty consists only of a fine (and not of restricting personal freedom of the person investigated). This also applies if detention is appropriate, but it is permissible and proper that detention be converted into a fine. The *conversione* procedure applies in given kinds of situations, and allows to forego detention at the rate of one day of detention corresponding to a fine of Lit. 75,000 (which was the case in 2001).

Such a procedure is not allowed if the offence can be pursued on the initiative of the plaintiff (i.e., if the offence is *perseguibile a querela della persona offesa*).

If the G.I.P. agrees the request made by the P.M., the G.I.P. releases a decree by which the person investigated – which by now is an *imputato*, i.e., a defendant – is condemned to pay the fine of the amount required. If within a given deadline the defendant does not appeal the decree, then this *decreto penale* (or *D.P.* for short) becomes operational (the Italian adjective for this is *esecutivo*).

---

[10] The case being investigated is being *istruito*: this Italian participle for 'investigated' (only applied to the case, not to a person) is derived like the noun *istruttoria* and the nominal compound *fase istruttoria*, which also refer to the *indagini [preliminari]*, i.e., the inquiry.

4.1 Computer Help for Organising

If the defendant appeals the decree instead, then the D.P. is no longer valid, and the G.I.P. has the defendant prosecuted in court (*rinviato a giudizio*), so that the defendant's liability be determined with those legal guarantees which a trial ensures.

Reduced fine (*l'oblazione*): by law, the person investigated can extinguish the offence by paying a fine whose amount is (according to the situation) one third or one half of the maximal *pena pecuniaria* (i.e., "fine") which is envisaged by law.[11] The *oblazione* procedure is only allowed for such offences which are punished either only with a fine, or with a *pena alternativa* ("alternative penalty"), i.e., detention convertible into a fine.

If the person investigated requests an *oblazione*, then the P.M. expresses his or her opinion, which he or she does by checking the case at hand: the P.M. may deem it to be the case that the request should not be granted, if there is a repeated offence (i.e., in case of recidivism), or if there are otherwise aggravating circumstances. If the P.M. deems that the suspect's request of an *oblazione* be granted, the P.M. transmits the P.M.'s favourable opinion to the G.I.P., so that the inquiry be closed.

Plea bargaining (*il patteggiamento*): the 1989 Italian code of criminal procedure has introduced this notion, which is commonplace in Anglo-American law,[12] but used to be unknown to the Italian procedural tradition. This notion has two formal names in the Italian legal lexicon, one with a higher formality, *applicazione della pena su richiesta*, and the other one, *patteggiamento*, being more usual and of a lesser degree of formality.[13]

In the new Italian code of criminal procedure, the two parties, i.e., the P.M. (the prosecution) and the *indagato* who faces becoming a defendant (*imputato*), have the option of reaching an agreement concerning which penalty is to be applied to the concrete case at hand. In order to make such an agreement easier to reach, the code allows a reduction of the penalty to be applied, namely, a deduction of up to one third of the penalty which could be expected to be obtained in court if there was no plea bargain. If the plea bargain consists of a penalty which envisages up to three months of detention, then it can be converted into a fine.

Daedalus can handle plea bargaining as well, with special buttons for increasing or decreasing the penalty; when during a session such a penalty eventually results that is lesser than three months of detention, then automatically a conversion grid to a fine is displayed by *Daedalus*. If, however, during the negotiation to reach a bargain the penalty increases back to three months of detention or more, then the conversion grid disappears from the screen.

4.1.3.5 Once the Decision to Prosecute is Taken

As announced in the previous subsection, let us discuss now the *citazione a giudizio*, i.e., when the decision is taken to prosecute a person investigated, who then becomes

---

[11] In Italian, a fine is also called *ammenda* or, informally, *multa*.
[12] Arno Lodder and John Zeleznikow provided an overview of computer-assisted dispute resolution (as being an alternative to litigation) in a book (Lodder & Zeleznikow, 2010). Plea bargaining is the subject of section 5.9 in that book.
[13] Already an Italian book by Gambini (1985) discussed plea bargaining.

a defendant in court. Like any other action concluding an inquiry (*atto conclusivo dell'indagine*), the step being taken to prosecute (*la citazione a giudizio*), too, requires that the accusation be written down (*la previa redazione dell'imputazione*).

How is the *imputazione* (charge) edited? At the start of the inquiry, when the P.M. had been notified of the offence and had inscribed the name(s) of the person or persons to be investigated in the *registro degli indagati*, along with the charges ascribed, the P.M. had formulated sort of an accusation. This, however, was only to be a provisional charge, a hypothesis that the inquiry was to either confirm or discard.

When concluding the inquiry, the P.M. who is preparing the prosecution case is transforming the mere mention of the name (the *nomen juris*) of the given offence(s) into a discourse which explicates the temporal, spatial, and personal identity circumstances, in which the event took place in which the offence concretely took place.

It is no longer a category of offence which is being applied to the person investigated, but, rather, a concrete instance, with a constellation of contextual details. The charge, in the case of the prosecution, must be concrete enough for the defendant(s) to be enabled to try and defend him- or her- or themselves, and if the P.M. fails to make the accusation adequately concrete, it must be nullified because of its overly general statement.

The case of the prosecution delimits both objectively and subjectively the proof whose construal is sought in court. *Daedalus* contains an environment, called *Laboratorio*, in which the items of the *imputazione* can be edited into the prosecution report.

The next stage is the *citazione a giudizio*, and the case goes to court (i.e., the *vocatio in jus* takes place). The P.M. convokes the defendant to court, to be tried by the judge and so that the defendant could defend him- or herself from the accusation. The defendant has a right to "his day in court", as the English idiom has it.

For severe offences, there is an intermediate stage (which is sort of a filter) before going to court: there is a preliminary hearing (*l'udienza preliminare*) in front of the G.I.P., whose task is to decide whether there is enough evidence to warrant starting a trial. If the G.I.P. deems that this is not the case, then the G.I.P. can dismiss the case by giving an exonerating verdict (*una sentenza di proscioglimento*, acquittal). This is quite a delicate stage. Therefore, *Daedalus* activates a battery of validation checks, so that the completeness and the sufficiency of the inquiry be verified.

4.1.3.6 A Sample Session: The Bindi Extortion Case

We are going to describe the workings of *Daedalus* on a particular inquiry, based on one of the sections in Asaro et al. (2001). The inquiry considered is "Procedure no. 1250/2000 against Calogero Lo Dico, with the complicity of unknown persons". The initial image (Fig. 4.1.3.6.1) provides the start menu for the *Daedalus P.M. Assistant* program. The magistrate is registering the notification of offence against Calogero Lo Dico, accused of attempted extortion and damage resulting from fire.

The facts: during the morning of 3 Feb 2000, unknown criminals set fire to the warehouse belonging to Massimo Bindi, manager of a wholesale business trading in cereals, which had lately increased its activity. During the afternoon a man called

4.1 Computer Help for Organising

Fig. 4.1.3.6.1 The start menu of *Daedalus*

Calogero Lo Dico, a decorator, comes into Massimo Bindi's office and ascribes the fire to very dangerous "brainless riffraff" which it would be much better to pacify with an adequate sum of money. He proposes the sum of Lit. 50,000,000 ("Lit." are Italian Liras). Massimo's son, Luigi, who is observing at a distance, recognises Lo Dico as an habitual poker player at the "I Nuovi Dei" bar in Florence, which he himself frequents since he is sentimentally attached to Eleonora Ricci, the publican's daughter, who is the cashier there.

The Carabinieri immediately arrive, gather information from all those present and draw up the notification of offence which the magistrate is about to register. The magistrate clicks on the "New Registration" button Then he (it was Asaro) selects the item "Known – 1" (i.e., a given suspected person) from the list of known suspects (Fig. 4.1.3.6.2).

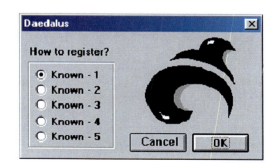

Fig. 4.1.3.6.2 A list of known suspects

Fig. 4.1.3.6.3 The initial record of a given suspect. In Italy, 'free' stands for any of 'unmarried', 'divorced', and 'widowed', on identity cards

Suspect:

Surname	Lo Dico
Name	Calogero
Marital status	free
Sex	M
Offences	☒☒☐☐☐

Fig. 4.1.3.6.4 One of the subtables in the Crime Table of *Daedalus*

No	TABLE NAME
1	Crimes against the person, honour, family, domicile
2	Crimes against patrimony
3	Crimes regarding water pollution
4	Crimes regarding waste materials
5	Crimes regarding atmosferic pollution
6	Crimes regarding acoustic pollution

A registration grid opens up into which the fundamental elements (surname, name, offences for which proceedings are being brought forward) are inserted. The magistrate individuates two offences (damage resulting from fire – art. 424 Penal Code; attempted extortion – arts. 56–629 Penal Code). Refer to Fig. 4.1.3.6.3.

The offences have not been typed in directly, but they have been taken from the Crime Table (see Fig. 4.1.3.6.4), one of the environments upon which *Daedalus'* structure is based. The Crime Table comprises a set of tables; they each cluster together homogeneous offences. The data on the single offences, which *Daedalus* gathers with the user's input, are at the basis of all the following operations: calculation of the sentence in procedures by decree; calculation of plea bargaining (see Fig. 4.1.3.6.5); validation procedure; sufficiency checks; analysis of the effectiveness of rules of law, and so forth. A layout (i.e., pattern), which enables the unloading of information on offences from external databases or from the Web, is provided for.

After inserting the offences, the magistrate examines those tables which require additional information. This information is optional since, by default, *Daedalus* proposes as competent, the magistrate's office; as source of notification, a charge made by the Polizia Giudiziaria; as state of inquiry, the heading "to be examined". In this case, the magistrate still has to make his (or her) ideas clear. Therefore, he (or she) leaves the default options unchanged (see Fig. 4.1.3.6.6). Then he (or she) clicks on the "Continue" button, that is to say, on the >> button.

4.1 Computer Help for Organising

📄 Plea Bargaining

Components	Arrestation (year, month, day)	Ammenda (Fine) In the case at hand	Detention (years, months, days)	Multa (Fine) as envisaged by the law
Basic punishment	Y M D		Y 5 M 0 D 0	L. 1.000.000
1 Aggravating	Y M D		Y M D	
2 Aggravating	Y M D		Y M D	
1 Extenuating	Y M D		Y 3 M 4 D 0	L. 670.000
2 Extenuating	Y M D		Y 2 M 2 D 20	L. 450.000
Continuation	Y M D		Y M D	
Final punishment	Y M D		Y 1 M 5 D 25	L. 300.000

V° By approval
of the Public Prosecutor
Dr Augusto Rossetti

Fig. 4.1.3.6.5   The plea bargaining table in *Daedalus*

Other data:

Source of notification	Police office
Kind of notification	Charge made by Police
Notice of closed inquiry	No
State of the inquiry	to be examined
Police reference	Fin. Marco Orselli

Acts and notes:

To close now	No
To delegate to the Police	No
Competent office	Procura presso Tribunale
Office location	Florence
Memo	No
To the secretary:	Nothing

Fig. 4.1.3.6.6   Supplementary data

Daedalus carries out a fairly complex activity of organisation and elaboration of the data and creates a file. This is the linking and propulsion centre of the judicial inquiry. On the one hand, it gathers and organises information; on the other hand, it bears all knowledge relative to the inquiry construction/validation routine. The file has various modules which correspond to distinct inquiry acts. These are organised in sets of information regarding the operation which must be carried out and, by means of set courses or action messages, they avoid deviation from the legal paradigm or from what was laid out by the user.

Daedalus doesn't confine itself to this. It also checks how many times, when and how the user makes use of its modules, as well as checking the results of the enforcement of the measures drawn up with the help of the modules themselves. This produces progress in the inquiry as the activities related to the investigation unfold, and it also brings about an increase in the knowledge of the facts regarding

Field	Data
registration date	3/2/00
inquiry's deadline	18/9/00
special register number	108/00-INT
number of known suspects	1
number of offenses	2
source of notification	Police office
kind of notification	Charge made by Police
inquiry's extension request	
position of the dossier	T1
notice of closed inquiry	no
state of the inquiry	to be examined
police reference	Fin. Marco Orselli
closed inquiry	no

Fig. 4.1.3.6.7 General data table in *Daedalus*. "Fin." (i.e., *guardia di Finanza*) indicates that police constable Marco Orselli belongs to the branch of the police which investigates money-related offences. In the last row, "no" stands for "not closed"

the inquiry, something we may term a "metainquiry" aimed at further development and at addressing the validation procedures.

Let us get back to our sample case: the Bindi inquiry. *Daedalus* has already calculated the deadline for the preliminary inquiry (six months, which are suspended during the attorneys' holidays period, i.e., from August the 1st to September the 15th), and has organised the general data (see Fig. 4.1.3.6.7). It has, furthermore, created an individual file for the suspect (see Fig. 4.1.3.6.8). The magistrate reads the notice of offence again. There are some people whom it would be advisable to hear, namely: apart from the victim, i.e., Massimo Bindi, also his son Luigi Bindi, as well as Eleonora Pecci, the cashier at the "I Nuovi Dei" bar. The name of the victim is recorded automatically. The other two names must be inserted with the Add button (see Fig. 4.1.3.6.8).

Figure 4.1.3.6.8 shows the Subjects Window. This window applies to those involved in the procedure the same functions that the Crime Table carries out in regard to the offences. In fact, it puts the people's names in order, it classifies them according to their role, it gives information and performs operations that are important in a judicial context. For example, if Luigi Bindi is selected, then the Contact button will open the window shown in Fig. 4.1.3.6.9.

4.1 Computer Help for Organising

Suspect n. 1

1. Personal data

surname	Lo Dico
name	Calogero
sex	M
marital status	free
birth place	
birth date	
town of residence	
home address	None

Fig. 4.1.3.6.8 The record of the suspect in the Bindi case, as being an example of a record of one of the members of the public who are involved in the inquiry

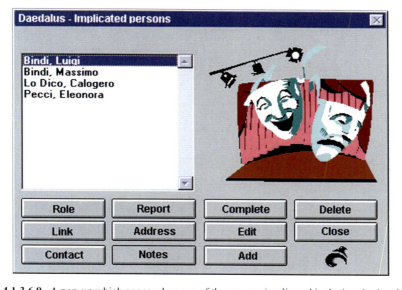

Fig. 4.1.3.6.9 A pop-up which opens when one of the persons implicated in the inquiry is selected

Fig. 4.1.3.6.10 Luigi Bindi, a witness who is the son of the victim, is given notice to appear

The window shown in Fig. 4.1.3.6.10 presupposes the knowledge that the magistrate is able to make contact with a person who is not a suspect, such as Luigi Bindi, in order to gather information, not only to charge with an offence which is the case of an interrogation of the suspect. Luigi Bindi, a witness who is the son of the victim, is given notice to appear.

On the contrary, if it is the name of Calogero Lo Dico, who is a suspect, is selected before activating the Contact, then *Daedalus* will open the window shown in Fig. 4.1.3.6.11, and which proposes interrogation as being the typical kind of contact between a suspect and the examining magistrate.

Calogero Lo Dico is accused of two offences: damage resulting from arson, and attempted extortion. These charges must be made clear. To record an individual it is sufficient to give information on his or her personal data, type of offence, and place where the fact took place. But in order to develop the inquiry and, in particular, draw up the act of accusation, something more is necessary. Alleging that Calogero Lo Dico has perpetrated an attempted extortion will not be enough. It is also necessary to enter what it consisted of, and in which manner and by which means it was carried out, in which circumstances of time and place, and whom is was perpetrated against.

The *Laboratory* helps in doing this. It is a typical *Daedalus* environment for the creation of acts of accusation or charges. It is a tool assisting with document drafting. *Daedalus* has two distinct environments which are also connected: the

Fig. 4.1.3.6.11 Contact with the suspect, Calogero Lo Dico

4.1 Computer Help for Organising

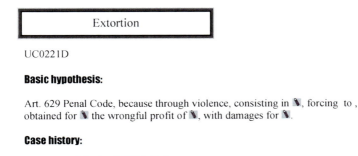

Fig. 4.1.3.6.12 The *Workshop* general pattern for extortion, within *Daedalus*

Workshop, structured as a charge layout editor; and the *Laboratory*, structured as an editor of charges. In the *Workshop* we can create a general pattern which is valid for any case. In the *Laboratory* instead we apply the general pattern to the particular case which is the object of the judicial inquiry.

Figure 4.1.3.6.12 shows the *Workshop* pattern for extortion. The *Basic Hypothesis* states: Art. 629 of the Penal Code, because [the perpetrator: known to the system] by violence, consisting in (enter data here), forcing [the victim: known to the system] to [something known to the system] obtained for the perpetrator the wrongful profit (enter data here), with damages for (enter data here). There also is an entry for the *Case History*.

The magistrate notices that the pattern (or layout) presents a case of extortion with violence while not that of extortion with threats. The magistrate decides to insert the latter hypothesis. In order to do this, the magistrate must implement the case history giving way to the procedure with the New Case button on the toolbar, as shown in Fig. 4.1.3.6.13. The magistrate inserts the new case, by formatting the text with the layout editor buttons: see Fig. 4.1.3.6.14.

Now the layout is ready to be used in the *Laboratory*. The magistrate closes the Crime Table and goes back to using the file. He clicks on the *Laboratory* button, that is to say, a button showing the icon of a robot. As an effect of this, *Daedalus* opens the pop-up window shown in Fig. 4.1.3.6.15.

Two function modes are provided: one in *self-composition*, when an accusation layout already exists, created by the *Workshop*; and one in *assembly*, when it is

Fig. 4.1.3.6.13 As the examining magistrate intends to insert a charge of "extortion with threats", further to the already entered charge of "extortion with violence", on the toolbar the magistrate clicks on the button for a new case

art. 629 Penal Code, because, by means of threats, consisting in ✏, forcing [] to [], the defendant obtained for ✏ the wrongful profit of ✏, with damages for ✏.

Fig. 4.1.3.6.14 The magistrate enters a charge for extortion with threats. Distinguish between the red crayon, where it is the user who has to insert data, and the empty space which we represent here as [], and which is some data (e.g., the name of the victim, and what the victim was forced to) that *Daedalus* is expected to insert automatically, because it already knows about it in the particular case at hand

Fig. 4.1.3.6.15 The *Laboratory* pop-up of *Daedalus*

necessary to create the layout from scratch. The magistrate selects *Self-composition* and then, one by one, the two offences included in the charge: see Fig. 4.1.3.6.16. A relevant article of the *Codice [di Procedura] Penale* is selected.

Daedalus shows the *Workshop* layouts (i.e., patterns) for elaborating charges. Let us see how a charge for extortion is processed. First of all the *Workshop* layout is shown, to which, as we have seen, the case of extortion with threats has been added: see Fig. 4.1.3.6.17.

The red crayons with which the text is interspersed have two functions: they are the place cards for the data necessary to complete the layout, but they are also a

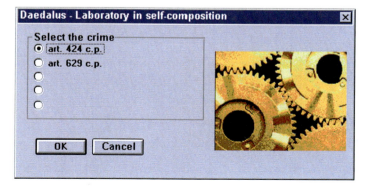

Fig. 4.1.3.6.16 The *Laboratory self-composition* pop-up of *Daedalus*

4.1 Computer Help for Organising

UC0221D

Basic hypothesis:

Art. 629 Penal Code, because through violence, consisting in ◼, forcing to [], obtained for ◼ the wrongful profit of ◼, with damages for ◼.

Case history:

	A	Basic hypothesis
	B	Extortion with threats

Fig. 4.1.3.6.17 The *Workshop* general pattern for extortion, once the charge for extortion with threats has been entered

Fig. 4.1.3.6.18 An example of advice provided by *Daedalus* about how to fill in information requested by a *red* crayon (a place-holder)

source of information on the type of data required. If the user asks *Daedalus* for help with selecting this mode for data insertion, the user will receive precise suggestions; e.g., in Fig. 4.1.3.6.18 the advice is that unlawful profit was sought by the defendant.

This capability of *Daedalus*, of providing help upon request when it comes to filling in data into a pattern, is especially useful when collaborators of the prosecutor are entrusted with preparing the bill of indictment. Asaro claimed that in such situations, *Daedalus* acts as a "cultural prosthesis" (*protesi culturale*), enabling the human collaborator of the prosecutor to be up to the task.

In processing the charge, *Daedalus* uses its juridic and linguistic knowledge and logic, it matches them to the information obtained from the user, and generates a linguistically correct document made up of descriptive proposals for the charge, which is legally suitable for being the bill of indictment (*atto d'accusa*). Once the latter is done, it is then transferred into an environment called *Storehouse*, from which it will be taken for all subsequent uses. See Fig. 4.1.3.6.19, which shows the *Storehouse* containing, in the *Management* data, the items: Origin of the last charge: Alpha; Procedure number: 1250/00; Number of charges: 1; Relapse Check: no. The *Charges* section states, under the name "LO DICO Calogero", one entry, namely, (a), whose text states:

> Offence p. and p. from art. 56-110-629 Penal Code, because, together with other people not yet identified, after having set fire to the warehouse belonging to the business whose manager is Massimo Bindi, dealer in cereals, by means of threats, consisting in implicitly pointing out that further serious damage would be incurred by his possessions and person, suitable action was taken to force Massimo Bindi to pay him and his partners the wrongful profit of Lit. 50,000,000, to Massimo Bindi's prejudice.

Management data:

* Origin of the last charge: `alpha`
* Procedure number: `1250/00`
* Number of charges: `1`
* Relapse check: `no`

Charges:

Lo Dico Calogero:

a) Offence p. and p. from art. 56-110-629 Penal Code, because, together with other people not yet identified, after having set fire to the warehouse belonging to the business whose manager is Massimo Bindi, dealer in cereals, by means of threats, consisting in <u>implicitly pointing out that further serious damage would be incurred by his possessions and person</u>, suitable action was taken to force Massimo Bindi to pay <u>him and his partners</u> the wrongful profit of Lit. <u>50,000,000,</u> to <u>Massimo Bindi's</u> prejudice.

Verified in Florence 3 Feb. 2000

Fig. 4.1.3.6.19 The *Storehouse* environment in the Bindi case

The next line states: "Verified in Florence, 3 Feb. 2000".

Now that the record for the charge is ready, the magistrate seeks a contact with competent people to verify it. The magistrate activates the *Person* window, and selects Massimo Bindi. A form is given for the draft of an *Examination* record. At this point, *Daedalus* provides assistance by supplying the following three procedures: (a) check of the charge; (b) study of the case; (c) processing of the questions.

With the first of these three procedures, *Daedalus* provides the magistrate with information concerning the main points of the prosecution, in order to direct the magistrate in the examination of the competent person. See Fig. 4.1.3.6.20. With the other two procedures, *Daedalus* respectively studies the case and processes the questions to be asked (see Fig. 4.1.3.6.21).

Daedalus is not equipped with a repertoire of ready-made questions, but it resorts to modules which pertain to given judicial situations, and which have morphological and syntactical cues for their assembly, and logical structures for coordination. The magistrate completes the examination by asking for additional information. In this specific case important circumstantial evidence makes it advisable that Lo Dico, the person accused of having committed the offence, be taken into custody. The magistrate clicks on the file's *Acts* button. *Daedalus* invites the magistrate, by means of a dialogue window (see Fig. 4.1.3.6.22), to choose specifically whether he or she wishes to develop, or just operate, or if he or she wants to end the current investigation instead.

Bindi Massimo's examination
Check of the charge's element -a)

↓ **Charge's text:**
a) *Offence p. and p. from art. 56-110-629 Penal Code, because, together with other people not yet identified, after having set fire to the warehouse belonging to the business whose manager is Massimo Bindi, dealer in cereals, by means of threats, consisting in <u>implicitly pointing out that further serious damage would be incurred by his possessions and person</u>, suitable action was taken to force Massimo Bindi to pay <u>him and his partners</u> the wrongful profit of Lit. <u>50,000,000</u>, to <u>Massimo Bindi's</u> prejudice.*

Verified in Florence 3 Feb. 2000.

↓ **Accused persons:**
   Lo Dico Calogero

↓ **Elements to be proven:**
The violent action carried out: **in implicitly pointing out that further serious damage would be incurred by his possessions and person**
Advantaged Person: **him and his partners**
wrongful profit obtained: **Lit. 50.000.000**
Disadvantaged Person: Bindi Massimo

Fig. 4.1.3.6.20 Check of the charge, in the presence of the victim

In this specific case, the magistrate chooses to develop. *Daedalus* invites the magistrate to select the suspect and the offence. In proceedings against more than one person this is a fundamental junction since *Daedalus* uses the dialogue window, for the act that we wish to perform, in order to:

- Check that the act is justified for the offence for which we are proceeding; e.g., imprisonment would not be permitted where a simple fine is appropriate.[14]
- Check that the offence, for which we are proceeding, has previously been ascribed to the suspect, to avoid that the action about to be taken, be wrongly

---

[14] Incidentally, measuring how serious an offence is, is a subject that has been researched in criminology (Parton, Hansel, & Stratton, 1991; Pease, Ireson, Billingham, & Thorpe, 1977).

taken concerning suspect A, whereas the offence is intended to be ascribed to suspect B.
- Check that the data are complete and that the guarantees for the defence have been fulfilled.
- Check that the prescriptive and factual requirements for the bill of indictment have been fully complied with.

Mr. Bindi, this Office is proceeding for a case of extortion, a crime committed in Florence the 3/2/2000. Are you aware of facts?

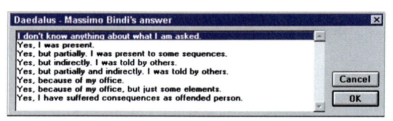

Fig. 4.1.3.6.21 The examining magistrate questions the victim

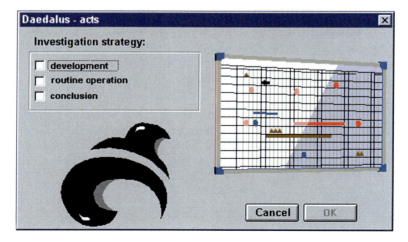

Fig. 4.1.3.6.22 The *Acts* pop-up of Daedalus: what to do with the inquiry?

4.1 Computer Help for Organising 235

Fig. 4.1.3.6.23 *Daedalus* signals an error concerning the charge

Fig. 4.1.3.6.24 *Daedalus* prevents the magistrate from wrongly requesting incarceration

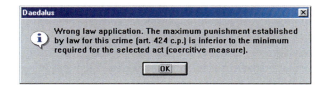

The magistrate tries to ask for custody in prison only for the damage to the warehouse. *Daedalus* checks the data and notes that the charge formulated in the *Laboratory* is for extortion and not damage resulting from fire, which is only quoted. It therefore blocks the magistrate with the reaction shown in Fig. 4.1.3.6.23.

Nevertheless, even if this charge is set up, the magistrate would not succeed in trying to ask for custody in prison for such an offence. *Daedalus* observes that such a criminal hypothesis does not consent custody in prison and blocks the magistrate by displaying a message, as shown in Fig. 4.1.3.6.24.

However, going ahead with the more serious offence of attempted extortion, *Daedalus* opens a dialogue window so that the magistrate may specify the measure requested and the precautionary requirements: see Fig. 4.1.3.6.25.

Take note that until at least one precautionary requirement is selected, the OK button remains disabled. This is a typical way in which *Daedalus* enforces compliance with important juridical precepts. This is an important function of *Daedalus*: every stem is validated.

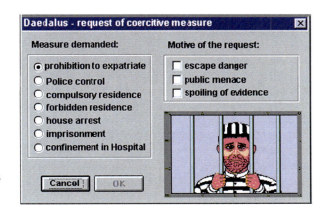

Fig. 4.1.3.6.25 *Daedalus'* menu concerning limitations of a suspect's personal freedom

4.1.3.7 Effects of the Jurisdiction: Why Is *Daedalus'* Emphasis on Step-by-Step Validation So Important in Italy? And Why Is the Statute of Limitations So Important in *Itaca*?

A sequel project of *Daedalus* is *Itaca* (initially called *Daedalus-Cassazione*), whose development for the Court of Cassation in Rome was contracted to Siemens, but whose original design is Asaro's. The needs to which *Itaca* responds were stated by the Criminal Sections (*Sezioni Penali*) of the Court of Cassation. These needs comprise the calculation of when preventative detention and generally preventative measures are going to expire; when prescription is going to apply to the offences concerned; and in general, data processing concerning offences. Both the data and juridic rules are coded.

In Italy, the statute of limitations (*prescrizione*) for offences is a major problem, as it is calculated starting when the offence was perpetrated, rather than starting when it was uncovered, and such time limitations are not stopped when a trial begins, but also apply to when the matter must be tried by, by the last court entrusted with the case, be it even the Court of Cassation. It is therefore more likely that the statute of limitations would run out before the deadline, i.e., in Italy, before the final verdict be given (this peculiarity of the statute of limitations in Italy is noted as surprising, in the 2009 Report on Italy of the Council of Europe).

Moreover, in Italy regulations make it easier for a trial to be nullified as mistrial. What may be of little consequence in jurisdictions other than Italy, in Italy may be fatal for the case of the prosecution (this shows why the emphasis on automatically validating each step of the user, in *Daedalus*, is paramount). Or then, a defect of form may invalidate a trial at which the defendant was acquitted, and this may result in a conviction later on. (This happened at the *cause célèbre* of Adriano Sofri and his co-defendants, who later had to serve a life sentence.)

It is a recognised problem that in Italy, it is more likely that offences would go unpunished because of the statute of limitations having run out, than elsewhere in Western Europe. The so called Legge ex Cirielli shortened the statute of limitations, instead of lengthening it. Besides, 12% of all hearings at criminal trials in Italy are adjourned, because people who had to appear in court did not; such delays militate towards lengthier trials, and therefore, towards the expiry of the deadlines set by the statute of limitations (Biondani, 2010).

According to the 2008 CEPEJ Report of the Council of Europe, the Italian judiciary completes more criminal trials per year than any other member state (1,150,000 in Italy, vs. 864,000 in Germany, 655,000 in France, 437,000 in Russia, and 388,000 in Spain), but in Italy 465 crime victims per day get no justice, in that the perpetrators remain unpunished, because because of the statute of limitations having run out.

An important aspect of the matter is that in Italy if at the first trial, a conviction is obtained by the prosecution, the sentence may be delayed until after the appeal, or even until the Court of Cassation has heard the case. But in Italy's prisons, over half the inmates are awaiting trial. Unfortunately, those in custody awaiting trial tend to be from the socio-economically weaker segments of society, whereas suspects from the better classes can successfully avoid detention until the verdict is given at the last trial, and this not only because they can afford to instruct lawyers whom they would pay themselves, but also because they have better access to a defence lawyer appointed by the state. While a petty criminal is likely to have one appointed, that defence lawyer may even just devote a few minutes to the case, and not appeal the conviction. (Of course, the problem of justice for the rich vs. justice for the poor is prevalent under a variety of national jurisdictions.)

4.1.3.8 Further Considerations About *Daedalus*, and About Select Aspects of the Human Process It Subserves

Upon close scrutiny, the design of *Daedalus* features no flamboyant, hallmark AI technique that has not become commonplace by the 1990s. It could even be said that the technology is straightforward and simple. Still, *Daedalus* is a successful tool, because of how closely this tool suits the judiciary task in its ergonomical, practical context.

Daedalus checks for the integrity of the procedure and data, and advises the user about how to proceed; it even "becomes upset" upon noticing that action was taken by the magistrate or the police without *Daedalus* itself being informed and kept abreast. And for good reason for that matter, especially if one is to consider the effects of the Napoleonic wars on Continental law. Tracing the impact of the French *Code d'Instruction Criminelle* on Dutch courtroom practice, Nijboer and Sennef (1999, pp. 14–15) point out that

> the dossier was the central file to which "internal" control of higher authorities was applied. Law enforcement officials performed their checks using the dossier as the exclusive source of information about what happened in a case. In the dossier they could check whether all necessary, formal controls had been met and whether or not all relevant formalities had been carried out. The importance of the dossier is reflected in the Latin [maxim]: *Quod non est in actis, non est in mundo* (what cannot be found recorded in the dossier, does not exist in reality).

Especially in the Anglo-American tradition, practitioners and scholars would beg to differ from that maxim. Nevertheless, even in such jurisdictions there arguably are lessons to be learnt from *Daedalus*. In democratic societies, law enforcement agencies and the judiciary, e.g., the police when arresting somebody or when carrying out interrogations, are under pressure to show that the rights of suspects were rigorously observed. *Daedalus* is an example of how, in Italy, in the 2000s such concerns have been taken on board, by means of a tool that not only documents all steps taken by the authorities during an inquiry, but also carries out validity checks on those steps at the time they are taken.

Waegel (1981) has discussed how investigators build pools of suspects for future crime-solving. Interrogating criminal suspects in an inquiry in countries like Italy is directed by the examining magistrate; the situation is different in countries such as the United Kingdom and the United States. Marcus (2000) has discussed the process of interrogating criminal suspects in the U.S.

Interrogations involve emotional labour for the one examined, as well as for the examiner; Stenross and Kleinman (1989) discussed the emotional labour of investigative detectives in the United States. "The detectives we studied disliked their encounters with victims, but enjoyed their encounters with criminals. The detectives discounted criminals' emotional displays as inauthentic" (ibid., p. 435).

There are kinds of inconsistency that *Daedalus* may detect. One may think of probative weights, too, in relation to *Daedalus*, but such a path has been avoided. By November 1999, a version of *Daedalus* was developed which envisaged weights of evidentiary value and of credibility; this wasn't developed into an integral part of the workings of *Daedalus*, to avoid threading on contentious ground.

It is interesting to consider how, around 2000, Italy's Minister of Justice described *Daedalus*, as it pointed out what especially stands out with respect to software available until then for assisting the legal professions:

> [...] The *Daedalus* project is about applied software whose ideation and coding were carried out by the aforementioned Dr. Asaro. It is intended for assisting a prosecutor during the inquiry up to the indictment of a defendant. The piece of software as implemented does not confine itself to making a form available to the magistrate for editing documents, or for selecting the charges, but rather offers an expert system for integrated assistance; the core idea of *Daedalus* is that the computer program, while providing an environment for editing the texts of measures to be taken, also records them and makes such knowledge available for validating the continuation of the inquiry. Remarkably, there is a check of lawfulness — i.e., the program responds with appropriate messages, every time the user is about to take an impermissible measure — and a sufficiency check, applied to the items of evidence that have been gathered. [...].[15]

An advantage of *Daedalus* is "Documentation and system transparency", to say it with the title of section 12 in Schartum's (1994) discussion of case-processing systems in the context of Norwegian administrative procedure, and of "investigations of legal contents of case-processing systems in public administration, as well as investigations in the development of such system" (ibid., p. 329). The obvious difference is that *Daedalus* pertains to criminal procedure; it is therefore capable of impinging more dramatically on some citizens' lives.

What is remarkably original, in *Daedalus*, is that every step fits in an embedded validation mechanism, for constraining the measures taken as they are adopted and unfold, as well as for future reference – to show that the examining magistrate and

---

[15] "[...] Il progetto Daedalus riguarda un applicativo ideato e scritto dal suddetto dr. Asaro, concepito per l'assistenza al Pubblico Ministero nel corso delle indagini preliminari e sino alla citazione a giudizio dell'imputato. Il software realizzato non si limita a mettere a disposizione del magistrato un formulario per la redazione di atti o la selezione di capi di imputazione, ma fornisce un sistema esperto di assistenza integrata; l'idea centrale di Daedalus è che il programma informatico nello stesso momento in cui mette a disposizione un ambiente per la redazione dei provvedimenti, li registra e fornisce tale conoscenza per validare il successivo corso dell'indagine. Particolarmente interessanti sono il controllo di legalità — reazione del programma con specifici messaggi tutte le volte che si intenda adottare un provvedimento non consentito — ed il controllo di sufficienza, con specifico riferimento alle fonti di prova raccolte. [...]".

prosecutor (typically, the same person at different stages) acted in formal fairness, as far as this can be ascertained from the syntax of what they did, rather than from the recondite semantics and its pragmatic uses, which will perforce elude a computer tool.

Distinguish between computerised procedural support for prosecutors, as provided by *Daedalus*, and the use of computer tools in order to analyse how prosecutors reason and go about their business. Given aspects of strategic communication and of the argumentation structure of criminal cases from Italy have been discussed, in relation to experimentation with computer tools, by Gulotta and Zappalà (2001): "Our present goal is to understand and illustrate what the public prosecutor does in order to achieve the prosecution's objective" (ibid., p. 91).

4.2 On Some Criminal Justice Information Systems or Other Tools

4.2.1 Tools for Decision Support, vs. Tools for Applying a Procedure

Giancarlo Taddei Elmi (1992, subsection 3.2) provided a discussion, in an Italian context, of the "meta-documentary" level of automation in the legal sphere; at that level, he included both tools for decision support and tools for legislation. Having identified four phases in the decision-making process – namely, (a) recognizing what the current law is, (b) interpretation, (c) logical integration, and (d) the selection of the solution among those logically correct – he indicated in phase (c), the one that "is, with no doubt, the most fertile terrain for computing" (ibid., p. 122, my translation). "Attempting to computerise juridical decision-making invariably produces the remarkable result of forcing us to rigorously reconsider the manners in which reasoning is carried out" (ibid., p. 123).

Philosopher of law Fernando Galindo, of the University of Zaragoza (Spain) – in a paper (Galindo, 1996) introducing a conference session devoted to such systems whose aim is to assist with juridical decision-making – was asking, in the very title of his article, whether such systems are possible at all.

In the second paragraph, he provided a positive answer: "Respondo afirmativamente" (ibid., p. 631). He then proceeded to list five arguments, or rather one argumentation line consisting of five propositions. The fourth of these was that such tools have been constructed, and that they work indeed. We could rephrase this by saying that the proof is in the pudding. In practice, those projects Galindo was mentioning represented a broader scope than judicial decision-making.

Immediately preceding Galindo's paper (1996) in the same volume, another article, this one by Zulueta Cebrián (1996), pointed out that in Spain, it was procurators who had come earlier to recognise the necessity of mastering new technologies for the administration of justice.

Daedalus, a tool originating with and intended for the Italian judiciary, does not belong to the narrowly intended category of tools that are specifically devised for the judge, who is the factfinder, the adjudicator. Especially in Italy's reformed legal system, the inquiry, though led by an examining magistrate, is identified with one of the two parties in a trial: the prosecution.

Daedalus assists the examining magistrate in conducting the inquiry, and next it assists in the preparation of the prosecution case for the proceedings in court. Its assistance permeates the process, organises it, validates it step by step, and documents its phases for future reference (including in order to prove that the rights of members of the public, and in particular the suspects', were properly safeguarded).

To readers used to the Anglo-American legal system, a tool such as *Daedalus* is likely to appear to be a mix of what looks like a police information system, and a tool for the legal operators at pre-trial and trial. In the United States, such tools or prototypes as *MarshalPlan* (a concept developed by Schum and Tillers) and *CaseMap* (the first dedicated piece of software offered on the American market) have emerged in the 2000s, for supporting the construction of the evidence upstream of as well as in court, under the Common Law system. See Section 4.1.1 above.

4.2.2 Risks of Too High Data Concentration

In the late 2000s, several breaches of security concerning confidential databases of the British public administration and containing data of many private persons have come to the attention of the media. Not only that. The authorities did not appear to be responsive to computer scientists' concerns lest putting in place huge databases would lend itself to confidential data being inferred by resorting to *data mining* techniques. A concern better known to the broad public is computer security, in the sense of information systems being vulnerable to unallowed or (in particular) malicious access. When it comes to police information systems, sometimes in the form of cross-border criminal databases, concerns for safeguarding privacy have arisen, something already discussed by Tupman (1995).

Around 2000, a website of the Programme in Comparative Media Law & Policy (PCMLP) of the Centre for Socio-Legal Studies, at Wolfson College of the University of Oxford was stating (PCMLP, n.d.):

> Privacy International was formed in 1990 as a watchdog on surveillance by governments and corporations. With members in more than 40 countries, it has created an international movement that has helped to counter abuses of privacy by way of information technology. Privacy International has conducted campaigns in Europe, Asia and North America to raise awareness about the dangers of ID card systems, military surveillance, data matching, police information systems, and credit reporting. It is based in London, UK, and is administered by the Electronic Privacy Information Center (EPIC) in Washington, D.C. Privacy International publishes a quarterly newsletter (the International Privacy Bulletin) and organizes conferences each year on privacy and technology.

4.2.3 Support from User Communities, vs. Tools Bestowed from Above

How do countries cope with the adoption of computer tools devised for home affairs (in particular, the police), and the judiciary? In Italy, support for *Daedalus* among the magistrates has encouraged the state to take a more active role in promoting the tool. It also quickened the recognition, on the part of the Ministry of Justice, of recognising the need to take on board the transition from tools supported by mainframe computers, to personal computing.

Eventually, a project, *Itaca*, also ideated by Judge Asaro and porting ideas from *Daedalus* to subserving the needs of the Court of Cassation, was contracted by the state to a big multinational corporation, in striking contrast to *Daedalus*, whose ergonomics being tailored for the intended user was subserved by the software having been not only specified, but also designed and implemented single-handedly by Asaro himself, at the time a *sostituto procuratore*.

It is important to realise that *Daedalus* being adopted by the Ministry of Justice on the wave of support already obtained in the users' community is not the typical situation. Arguably, it is far more typical that large state organisations decide by themselves about which systems to develop, sometimes with consultations whose outcome is often perceived to have foregone conclusions, and at any rate the information technology policy is bestowed upon the intended users, especially if these are numerous.

Consider now the information technology strategy of the police in Scotland. Excerpts follow, from the chapter devoted to Her Majesty's Chief Inspector of Constabulary for Scotland Report for 1998/1999 (Her Majesty's... 1998/1999). The first quotation is from the section entitled 'Thematic Inspection':

> 1. The thematic inspection (Getting IT Right) on the specification and deployment of information technology systems in the Scottish police service was published during the year, making use of the internet as a medium of circulation, and made a number of recommendations. The report covered not only the 8 Scottish forces but also the central service establishments of the Scottish Crime Squad, SCRO and the Scottish Police College. [...]

The following is from a subsequent section, entitled "Scottish Police Information Systems/Information Technology (IS/IT) Strategy (SPIS)":

> 4. In recent years the forces have responded to technological change by agreeing a more unified approach to IS/IT issues. Since 1993 SPIS has been developed and agreed by all chief constables as the standard approach to the development of new IT systems in Scotland. In the last year a committee structure to manage the implementation of the strategy has been established [...]
>
> 6. The IS/IT Co-ordinating Committee continues to work towards identifying priorities. The following individual systems are being developed:
>
> - Criminal intelligence;
> - Personnel;
> - Custody recording;
> - Incident recording; and
> - Firearms licensing.

Further down in the same document, one reads, in a section entitled "Integration of Scottish Criminal Justice Information Systems (ISCJIS)":

> 12. Co-operation between different agencies involved in the Scottish criminal justice system is hugely important in pursuing efficiency and effectiveness. The Scottish Executive led project, ISCJIS, applies particularly to the advantages to be gained by working towards an integrated IS/IT strategy. Pilot sites are due to begin in the latter part of 1999.
>
> 13. "Getting IT Right" recognised the importance of the Scottish police service undertaking a study to determine the common standards which need to be defined to facilitate the inter change of information between the police and other stakeholders. [...] As part of the developing ISCJIS programme, pilot work on a groundbreaking Legal Information Network for Scotland (LINETS) is underway and to go live within selected sites in early 2000. It will contain legal information from the Statute Law Database (maintained by the Statutory Publications Office) and several agencies within the Scottish criminal justice community, with each providing relevant national information to the benefit of all involved and accessible from a single source. [...]

In Hutton, Tata, and Wilson (1994), the design was described of a prototype of a Sentencing Information System for the High Court of Justiciary in Scotland, a system whose eventual adoption, it was claimed, "will arguably be the first major reform of sentencing to take place in Scotland", a country with a "strong tradition of judicial independence" (ibid., p. 255). Section 3 in that paper surveyed a number of *sentencing information systems* from jurisdictions in Canada and Australia. Doob and Park's system (Doob & Park, 1987–1988; Doob, 1990) had been in operation for several years in the 1980s in four Canadian provinces, but by 1990 only Saskatchewan had retained it, and explanations offered by the designer and reported in Hutton et al. (1994, p. 259, citing Doob, 1990), were to the effect that:

> First, judges in Canada had little interest in information about current court practice. They are not accustomed to using information in this numerical form nor does their legal tradition give any weight to current sentencing practice. Second, such authority as exists in sentencing comes from the Court of Appeal. The Sentencing Information System carried no institutional authority.[16]

British Columbia, which until 1987 had used the Doob and Park system, from 1987 to 1992 operated a different system, described by John Hogarth (1988), but it, too, was discontinued, which was ascribed to "insufficient judicial consultation and involvement" and high costs (Hutton et al., 1994, p. 260). *Daedalus* clearly avoided the first of the latter pitfalls (as it was devised by a member of the intended user community), and a useful tool was made available for free to the Italian state by Asaro and distributed by the Italian Ministry of Justice to the judiciary offices in the country; also maintenance was relatively inexpensive, given the nature of the tool.

---

[16] Social psychologist Anthony N. Doob has also researched Canadian jurors (Doob, 1978), as well as Canadian justices of the peace (Doob, Baranek, & Addario, 1991); thus his are not just *ad hoc* explanations as may be provided by an information technologist. The psychology of judicial sentencing is the subject of Fitzmaurice and Pease (1986).

4.2 On Some Criminal Justice Information Systems or Other Tools   243

As to the Scottish project, it "was based on the New South Wales model" from Australia (Hutton et al., 1994, p. 260). In turn, the computerised sentencing system for New South Wales Courts was described by Chan (1991) and Spears (1993). Several pages in Hutton et al. (ibid., pp. 269–280) are devoted to illustrating by means of computer screens and of schemata, a session concerning a case of aggravated robbery. That kind of presentation is rather similar to our present style adopted for describing a session with *Daedalus*.

4.2.4 Past Cases, New Cases, and Using the Former for the Latter

The Scottish, Australian, and Canadian projects mentioned above are functionally different from *Daedalus*: unlike *Daedalus*, those systems are mainly about documenting past cases, rather than managing the minutiae of new ones. To say it with quite an important article on judicial software, Tata, Wilson, and Hutton (1996):

> Formally, a Sentencing Information System is descriptive rather than prescriptive. That is, it contains no guidance as to how a sentencer might use this information to help in making the sentencing decision in a particular case. A Sentencing Information System (SIS) can display the range of sentences for the particular combination of offence and offender characteristics selected. The sentencer will have no guidance as to what extent and in what direction the appropriate sentence for the case at hand should vary from the average. This decision is a matter for the discretionary judgement of the sentencer. However, the frequency distribution indicates the highest and lowest sentences previously passed for the type of case at hand. In a well trodden area it might be assumed that a sentencer would have to have good reasons for straying outside the upper and lower limits, although there are no formal reasons why a sentencer should not choose to do so nor does the SIS restrict the sentencer's choice in any way.

Moreover (ibid.):

> A hybrid approach involving both rule based and case based systems has been developed by Bain (1989a). The programme begins with an empty case-library and a handful of heuristics for deciding sentences when no cases can be applied to a new situation. After only a few cases, however, it begins to retrieve 'remindings' of its own cases from memory and to modify the strategies associated with those cases to form new sentences.
>
> The idea of a case based reasoning system unsupported by heuristics has also been used as a basis for modelling the sentencing process. Murbach and Nonn (1991) report progress on a project to develop a sentencing support system for fraud cases in Canada. Their system provides information about penalties but also includes information on case factors not included in the categories of offence used in the penal code but agreed by judges to be relevant to sentencing. There is thus an attempt to include information which reflects judicial perceptions of seriousness in order to make the system more sensitive and thus more useful to sentencers. Computer technology has been used to assist these reforms and to encourage greater consistency in sentencing. ASSYST (Applied Sentencing systems) has been developed by the US Federal Court system so that criminal justice personnel could easily compute, record, archive and examine the implications of the US Sentencing Commission Guidelines (Simon and Gaes, 1989; Simon, Gaes, and Rhodes, 1991).

At this point, Tata et al. (ibid.) mentioned what was to become *The Judge's Apprentice*, before turning to Bainbridge's (1991) system:

A part- simple retrieval system, part- expert system approach to sentencing support has been reported by Bainbridge (1991). The system focuses on sentencing practice in magistrate courts in England and Wales and contains components covering sentencing law and penalty statistics. The sentencing law component is intended to assist the magistrate by checking that the chosen sentence complies with relevant sentencing law. This part of the system is arguably more like an expert-system than a simple retrieval system, although it only answers the question, 'Is this sentence legally competent?' rather than, 'What is the appropriate sentence for this case?'. When a judge has selected a legally competent sentence, it is then possible to consult the penalty information section of the system. This shows the distribution of penalties for the offence in the form of probability calculations. Information is only available for two statutory offences of theft and burglary and for only 600 cases from four magistrate courts.

Uri Schild (1995) had reported about what still was work in progress, "to develop a case-based advisory system for sentencing. The domain knowledge was elicited from a senior judge, and the system uses 'hierarchical discrimination trees' in order to retrieve relevant information" (Tata et al., ibid.). Schild noted: "It is obvious that the area of sentencing is associated with an enormous amount of both common-sense and domain knowledge". However, a model which would include this knowledge was considered impracticable and it was therefore decided to use only the domain knowledge without any additional "common-sense knowledge" (Schild, 1995, p. 232). This was to become *The Judge's Apprentice*, Yaakov HaCohen-Kerner's doctoral project.[17]

The Judge's Apprentice is an expert system concerned with given categories of offences, and its aim is to assist in enhancing uniform sentencing at Israeli courts; these are akin to courts in the Anglo-American system, but there only are *bench trials* (i.e., such trials that the decision making is by professional judges), as there are no juries. In the English abstract of his thesis, Yaakov HaCohen-Kerner (1997) pointed out that of the few previously described programs "which actually assist in sentencing" and "deal each in its own way with the problem of a lack of uniformity in sentencing", none is case-based. He also noted that on the other hand, such case-based systems (other than for law)[18] which require common-sense knowledge to be represented and used,

---

[17] Schild and Kerner (1994), HaCohen-Kerner and Schild (1999, 2000, 2001), HaCohen-Kerner, Schild, and Zeleznikow (1999), and HaCohen-Kerner (1997).

[18] Note that in social science, Michael A. Redmond and Cynthia Blackburn (2003) described an application of *case-based reasoning* (*CBR*) and other methods for predicting repeat criminal victimisation. Theirs was an empirical analysis. Also see Janet L. Lauritsen's (2010) 'Advances and Challenges in Empirical Studies of Victimization'. Cf. Lauritsen (2005), Ybarra and Lohr (2002), and Planty and Strom (2007). Redmond and Blackburn (2003) explained: "some criminologists are interested in studying crime victims who are victims of multiple crime incidents. However, research progress has been slow, in part due to limitations in the statistical methods generally used in the field. We show that CBR provides a useful alternative, allowing better prediction than via other methods, and generating hypotheses as to what features are important predictors of repeat victimization. This paper details a systematic sequence of experiments with variations on CBR and comparisons to other related, competing methods. The research uses data from the United States' National Crime Victimization Survey. CBR, with advance filtering of variables, was the best predictor in comparison to other machine learning methods" (ibid., from the abstract).

can only be the prototype for a model whose practical application in industry is highly improbable or impossible. In contrast, our model has been applied to a system intended for use in real life. Our system deals with a limited domain and the necessary information is well defined and bounded. This information includes: a database of fifty precedent cases, the legal knowledge relevant to sentencing, and a hierarchical tree that contains over three hundred legal concepts relevant to sentencing at various levels of abstraction.

Bain's JUDGE system (Bain, 1986, 1989a, 1989b) is, among the other things, a tool whose AI mechanism is *case-based reasoning*. It adopts a hybrid approach involving both rule-based and case-based systems. JUDGE is a cognitive model of judges' decision-making when sentencing (and indeed it was based on interviews with judges); yet, it didn't have the aim of suggesting a sentence in a real judicial context; this is a major functional difference with respect to HaCohen-Kerner's *Judge's Apprentice* (HaCohen-Kerner, 1997, p. 49).

Bain's research, according to Bain (1989a, p. 93),

> has been directed at modeling by computer the behavior of judges who sentence criminals. Our [i.e., Bain's] effort has been not to examine sentencing as a representative example of legal reasoning. Instead, we have viewed it as a more generic reasoning task in which people learn empirically from having to produce relative assessments of input situations with respect to several different concerns.

Bain's JUDGE used 55 represented legal precedents, mostly invented ones, the domain being violent confrontations resulting in manslaughter or murder. In contrast, *The Judge's Apprentice* is specialised in cases of sexual assault or robbery. In Bain's system, precedents are retrieved and processed based on "indexes" capturing situations; in addition, HaCohen-Kerner and Schild's tool also resorts to empirical "conceptual indexes" which resulted from interviews with judges (HaCohen-Kerner, 1997, p. 53).

Moreover, *The Judge's Apprentice* seeks to preserve uniform sentencing by reference to a "base-sentence", not just to retrieved precedents – which is how Bain's system works: JUDGE works in a black-box fashion, whereas HaCohen-Kerner's tool provides comparisons to precedents and justifications for the sentence it suggests (HaCohen-Kerner, 1997, pp. 53–54, 84–85).

Trying to achieve consistent sentencing the subject of Donald Pennington and Sally Lloyd-Bostock's edited volume (1987) *The Psychology of Sentencing: Approaches to Consistency and Disparity*. The psychology of judicial sentencing is also the subject of Fitzmaurice and Pease (1986).

A team from Portugal (Costa, Sousa, & Neves, 1999) reported about an application to legal precedents of case retrieval nets (with similarity arcs and relevance arcs), within the case-based reasoning class of methods. In Florence, Paolo Guidotti (1994) used *Reflective Prolog* to show how "the similarity between the concrete fact situation and the abstract fact situation of a norm may be translated into a similarity relation between predicates". He also proposed a meta-interpreter to enable the processing, based on analogy, of precedents constituted by previous court decisions.

Penalty statistics within a system for sentencing support has been mentioned before, in relation to Bainbridge's project (Bainbridge, 1991). Actually, for several decades now "find[ing] a relationship between certain factors and circumstances in a court case and the decision reached by a judge" (Combrink-Kuiters,

De Mulder, & van Noortwijk, 2000, p. 109) has been the aim of *jurimetrics*. Fact-pattern analysis in judicial decision-making was carried out in a North American context in the 1960s (e.g., Nagel, 1962; Ulmer, 1969). Jurimetrical methods are still quantitative, and include linear regression, Bayesian statistics,[19] and neural networks (Combrink-Kuiters et al., 2000).

Indexing for case-based reasoning for the purposes of enhancing uniform sentencing is arguably in some relation (problems of scale apart) to "the applicability of data mining techniques to legal databases" in areas where many thousands of cases are decided", and the discovery of association rules[20] is sought: "We would generally wish to assume that some rule is being followed so that like cases are decided in a like manner. Is there a way of deciding what the rule being followed is from an automated consideration of the data?", in the words of Bench-Capon, Coenen and Leng (2000, p. 1056). The latter article, from Liverpool, reporting about a project with such concerns, found potential in the outcome of experimentation. "If the aim is to confirm particular hypotheses about the data, the information necessary to provide this structure is available".

The Liverpool project was descriptive, and admittedly high-sky research, whereas HaCohen-Kerner and Schild's project was prescriptive and intended for use by judges. In both projects there was however a shared concern with uniformity in factfinding when cases are similar. At any rate, it must be said, concerning *The Judge's Apprentice*, that even though judges consulted were appreciative and supportive, they had not been envisaging using the system themselves in practice.

4.2.5 Prosecutorial Discretion and Judicial Discretion

Discretionary is opposed to *mandatory*. In particular, as applied to judicial decision-making, discretionary is what is up to the judge to decide, unfettered by mandatory rules. Likewise, when plea-bargaining is involved, or to the extent that a prosecutor is free not to prosecute, then the prosecutor is exercising his or her *discretionality*.

---

[19] This kind of application of statistics has nothing to do with, and is definitely not as controversial as, probative weight and the use of probabilities to determine whether to convict in a given case, for which, see e.g. Allen and Redmayne (1997).

[20] "Association rules represent relationships between items in very large databases. [...] An example would be 'given a marker database, it was found that 80% of customers who bought the book 'XML for beginners' and 'internet programming' also bought a book on 'Java programming'.' If X and Y are two sets of disjoint terms, then an association rule can be expressed as conditional implication $X \Rightarrow Y$ i.e. the occurrence of the set of items X in the market basket implies that the set of items Y will occur in this market basket. Two important aspects of an association rule are confidence and support [...]. The confidence of an association rule r: $X \Rightarrow Y$ is the conditional probability that a transaction contains Y given that it contains X, i.e. confidence$(X \Rightarrow Y) = P(X, Y)/P(X)$. The support of an association rule is the percentage of transactions in the database that contains both X and Y, i.e., Support$(X \Rightarrow Y) = P(X, Y)$. The problem of mining association rules can be stated simply as follows: Given predefined values for minimum support and minimum confidence, find all association rules which hold with more than minimum support and minimum confidence." (Chan, Lee, Dillon, & Chang, 2001, p. 278, citing Agrawal & Srikant, 1994 for the definition of confidence and support).

4.2 On Some Criminal Justice Information Systems or Other Tools

The goal of, say, uniformity in sentencing as supported by computer tools (e.g., *The Judge's Apprentice*) should not be to the detriment of *judicial discretion*, and the latter, in turn, is distinct from *prosecutorial discretion*. Legal discretion is a subject discussed, e.g., by Hawkins (1992).

The following quotation is from a book review (Nissan, 2001e) of a paper collection in law, and this quoted text is in turn quoting from a section of four papers – a section on *plea bargaining*, which pertains to *prosecutorial discretion* indeed:

> "In the past it was accepted that the question of whether a person committed a crime (and particularly a serious one), or what sentence should be imposed on the person convicted of that crime, should be answered only after the hearing of the evidence. Criminal courts were not asked to give effect to compromises at which the prosecution and accused had arrived regarding the nature of the conviction or regarding the sentence" — Harnon points out (p. 246) — but "in common law systems, the recognition that this does not reflect the reality has been growing this [i.e., the 20th] century. There has been an ever-increasing awareness, that in many criminal cases, no evidence is submitted to the court, since the accused plead guilty, following a plea-bargain" (246). In the same section, Goldstein deals with how, to cope with system overload, national legal systems are borrowing institutions and practices from each other, with a trend of "abandoning the principle of obligatory prosecution, so common in Continental Europe, and turning instead to the exercise of prosecutorial discretion" (169). "In Italy, where guilty pleas had never existed and plea bargaining was anathema, the adversarial trial has been introduced and with it the guilty plea and the explicit grant of sentencing concessions for such pleas. Even more dramatically" (169), European countries formerly within the Soviet orbit are turning away from inquisitorial systems; yet, for American Law reform, insights are being sought in a comparative criminal justice perspective, "looking in the direction of the European continent for guidance on how to reconcile discretion and plea bargaining with principles of legality" (170). [...]

In the American system, but since the 1990s also in some European jurisdictions that previously did not allow it, plea bargaining is commonplace, and economic factors (in terms of costs/benefits whether a case goes to court) affect the prosecutor's decision whether to prosecute; potentially, this is fertile ground for decision support systems. Let us turn now to discretion in general, in a legal context.

Bodard, Hella, Poullet, and Stenne (1986), from Belgium, outlined the functions of the ADP prototype for assisting, in two manners, with "judicial decision making: the first is assistance in documentary search from elements of reasoning pertaining to a judgment and the second is assistance in assessing a judgment's coherence" (ibid., p. 187). A representation in propositional logic was adopted. Tests envisaged for *checking internal coherence* included a so-called *polarization test*, attached weights were examined, there was an *intercomposition check*, as well as a *check of external coherence* of a judgment in relation to external reference elements (ibid., p. 197).

As already seen above in Section 4.1.2 in the present book, Goldsmith (1986) – building upon Scandinavian legal thinking – presented an *evidentiary value prescriptive model*, and contrasted it to a so-called *theme probability model*, which Goldsmith challenged as far as criminal cases are concerned. Goldsmith also considered results he had obtained empirically "concerning the evaluation of evidence by Swedish judges and prosecutors, and involving a comparison of the apparent use of the one model versus the other" (ibid., p. 229). In an appendix, Goldsmith listed rules for integrating evidence according to the model he was proposing: rules for compatible evidence, rules for conflicting evidence, and rules for chains of evidence (ibid., pp. 244–245). His treatment was probabilistic, and this is something quite contentious in the legal theory debate on formalisms for evidence. Probabilistic treatment is not as contentious if the explicit purpose is to evaluate the costs vs. the benefits of going to court vs. plea bargaining.

Discretionary decision-making by decision-support systems for judicial sentencing was discussed by Tata et al. (1996). Meikle and Yearwood (2000) are concerned with the provision of support for the exercise of discretion, and how the need to avoid the risk of adversely affecting it when using a computer tool, inspired the structural design of *EMBRACE*, a decision support system for Australia's Refugee Review Tribunal on which see Sec. 3.11.6.2 above.

Leithe (1998) has warned about the limitations of the potential of AI to fully do justice to legal knowledge for practical purposes, when it comes to modelling the actors, these being the legal decision makers. In particular, the concern is that judicial discretion be restricted, if computer tools come to be involved in the judicial decision-making process. See also Taruffo (1998).

Daedalus is restricted to merely supporting the inquiry and then the prosecution. It does not impinges on prosecutorial discretion, and only places a necessary obstacle whenever an impermissible step is going to be taken. Such a "lack of ambition" is arguably *Daedalus'* blessing in disguise. Moreover, *Daedalus* is in line with Leith's (1998) and Meikle and Yearwood's (2000) shift of emphasis, in computer tools, from expert systems to decision-support systems.

Meikle and Yearwood (2000, p. 101) classify legal decision-making in four quadrants, according to two operational dimensions:

> One dimension is the extent to which a system should either be an 'outcome predictor' (a highly convergent aim) or should give access to diverse resources about the issues of interest (a highly divergent aim). This is the *predictive–descriptive* dimension. The other is the extent to which a system either needs to support discretion (by permitting complete autonomy, perhaps because the domain has no constraints) or needs to support weak discretion (by permitting only that allowable within prescribed constraints). This is the *strong–weak discretion* dimension.

It was proposed that *EMBRACE*, as well as Bench-Capon's PLAID (Bench-Capon & Staniford, 1995), may be placed in the quadrant characterised by strong discretion and descriptiveness (instead of predicted outcome, which when there is strong discretion lets the user override the prediction either partly or altogether).

A prosecutor's decision to offer a suspect a plea bargain, or then a prosecutor's decision not to prosecute because based on the evidence available, it is unlikely that a prosecution of a suspect would succeed in securing a conviction in court, involve a *prediction* as to the outcome. Prosecutorial discretion exploits such an evaluation. But no case is foregone, because judges or juries have their own discretion (short of blatant mistrial).

Take Italy. Following the reform of 1989 which introduced the new Italian criminal procedure code, the Italian prosecutor has been enabled to offer a plea bargain.

But the prosecutor (along with the role of the examining magistrate, upstream of prosecution) is now, in Italy, one of the parties in the trial, not *above* them which is what the judge is. Investigations must be fair, and the prosecution, carried out by magistrates who like the judge, are after all in the employment of the Ministry of Justice, cannot afford "outcome prediction" *vis-à-vis* the suspects other than by way of formulating falsifiable hypotheses, then checking them.

Needless to say, the factfinders (the adjudicators) themselves (which the public prosecution is definitely not) deontically (i.e., by normative or moral obligation) cannot be *predictive* in the sense of being biased. They *ontologically* can, *deontically* cannot[21]: there may exist some judge or juror who is biased in a given situation, but then that is a deplored situation of an adjudicator contravening on the duties of the role. In an article entitled 'The witch hunt as a structure of argumentation', Walton stated (1996c, p. 401):

> One important characteristic of a fair trial is the requirement that the judge or jury, who decides the outcome, must not have made up its mind on that outcome before all the evidence has been presented. That is, the judge or jury must be sufficiently unbiased, at the beginning stage, that they can be swung one way or the other by evidence produced during the argumentation stage of the trial. Otherwise the trial is pointless, from a normative perspective of judging the case on the balance of all the relevant evidence presented. The opposite quality is characteristic of the witch hunt.

Also as far as fair prosecution is concerned, the kind of argumentation required is that of a critical discussion, and prosecution, *qua* participant in that debate, must be ready to admit that an argument made does not hold, and ultimately to admit defeat in court, just as it must be willing to discard hypotheses out of fairness while preparing a case. "This willingness to admit defeat is an important characteristic that distinguishes the critical discussion from the quarrel, or eristic type of dialogue" – Walton states on the same page (1996c, p. 401), citing Walton (1989, p. 4) – yet partisan arguments, or advocacy, are not ruled out altogether from a critical discussion.

4.3 Evaluating Costs and Benefits

4.3.1 Evaluating Costs and Benefits While Preparing a Case

4.3.1.1 Ways Economics and Evidence Meet: The Rules of Evidence in Terms of Economic Rationality

Will the spread, among practitioners, of the kinds of software tools described in this book empower the citizenry, or rather further empower corporations against the individual, and institutions when the other party in litigation is a private person?

---

[21] One also speaks of *normative ability*. See, e.g., Wooldridge and van der Hoek (2005).

Will such tools reduce, or deepen the divide between justice as affordable to the rich, and unaffordable or perfunctory justice for the impecunious? In my opinion, both outcomes are possible.

There are other ways of looking at the economics. One of the ways economics and evidence meet, concerns the *rules of evidence*, i.e., the regulation of which evidence is admissible. There exist, in legal scholarship, theoretical approaches that explain the way the law of evidence is, in terms of *economic rationality*: see, e.g., Posner (1999). Discussing the principles underlying evidence law in the Anglo-American legal systems, Alex Stein states (2005, p. 2):

> A non-utilitiarian risk-allocating scheme may well crystallize. Under the utilitarian approach, allocation of the risk of error is always instrumental to the trade-off that reduces the aggregate sum of error costs and error-avoidance expenses (the total sum of substantive and procedural costs). The rights-based legal systems overturn this relationship of means and ends. Under these systems, fact-finding expenditures are instrumental to the right apportionment of the risk of error, rather than vice versa. These systems rely on a non-utilitarian political morality that transforms into individual rights. These rights do not merely escape from utilitarian calculus. They actually trump utility. Consequently, rights that litigants have with respect to risk-allocation are not measured against the substantive and procedural costs that they incur. Because the prevalent political morality favours these rights, it deems the costs that these rights incur money well-spent.

4.3.1.2 Alvin Goldman's Concept of Epistemic Paternalism

In an article in epistemology (the philosophy of knowledge) whose title is "Epistemic paternalism", Alvin Goldman (1991) began with the *requirement of total evidence* (*RTE*), a popular principle (cf. Good, 1983 and Chapter 6 in Horwich, 1982) in epistemology and the philosophy of science. Its weak and strong versions are:

> (W-RTE) A cognitive agent X should always fix his beliefs or subjective probabilities in accordance with the total evidence in his possession at the time.
> (S-RTE) A cognitive agent X should collect and use all available evidence that can be collected and used (at negligible cost).

Then Goldman, whose concern is with moral and legal aspects, concedes that the strong principle is best understood in purely epistemic terms. By contrast, invasion of privacy or harmful experimentation on human subjects would be objectionable. Then Goldman remarks (1991, p. 114):

> A plausible-seeming corollary, or extension, of S-RTE is a principle governing the practices of a second agent, Y, who is in a position to control the evidence made available to X. This interpersonal principle would say that Y should make available to X all evidence that is subject to his (Y's) control. Of course, like S-RTE itself, the envisaged extension or corollary of S-RTE must be restricted to epistemic contexts or concerns. Thus, we might formulate the "control" version of RTE roughly as follows:

4.3 Evaluating Costs and Benefits

(C-RTE) If agent X is going to make a doxastic decision[22] concerning question Q, and agent Y has control over the evidence that is provided to X, then, from a purely epistemic point of view, Y should make available to X all of the evidence relevant to Q which is (at negligible cost) within Y's control.

The restriction to the epistemic viewpoint is again important. In legal settings, for example, there are many nonepistemic reasons for refusing to provide relevant evidence to jurors. Available evidence may have been illegally obtained. Relevant evidence may be obtainable from the defendant, but the Fifth Amendment forbids his being compelled to testify against himself. Or the defendant may have testified elsewhere under a grant of limited immunity, providing that his testimony would not subsequently be used against him. In these cases, the judge (Y) is obliged not to provide the jurors (X) with all available evidence logically relevant to the question of guilt. These constraints, though, are not of an epistemic nature.

Goldman argues that C-RTE is unacceptable. At any rate, "existing provisions and practices, both in the law and elsewhere in society, contravene C-RTE" (ibid.). Goldman endorses such limitations on the quest for evidence: "Although I shall not defend each provision and practice in detail, many of them seem to be quite reasonable. This raises some interesting questions for a branch of epistemology that I have elsewhere called *social epistemics*" (1991, p. 114, citing Goldman, 1986, pp. 1, 5–9, 136–138; and 1987a, 1987b).

Framers of the rules of evidence, Goldman claims (1991, p. 118), "and judges themselves, often wish to *protect* jurors in their search for truth. If, in the framers' opinion, jurors are likely to be misled by a certain category of evidence, they are sometimes prepared to require or allow such evidence to be kept from the jurors. This is an example of what I shall call *epistemic paternalism*". Goldman concedes that it is primarily the parties to the litigation who are the prime objects of such protection, rather than jurors. "The indicated parties are protected, however, by getting

---

[22] In philosophy and in logic, the adjective *doxastic* means "of or relating to belief". *Doxastic logic* is the branch of modal logic that studies the concept of belief. More broadly, *doxastic* may refer not only to something pertaining to belief, but alternatively also to something pertaining to states sufficiently like beliefs, namely: thoughts, judgments, opinions, desires, wishes, or fears. But usually, in a *doxastic attitude* what one holds is a belief. In epistemology (the philosophy of knowledge), *evidentialism* is generally applied to justified beliefs distinct from unjustified beliefs one may hold in a doxastic attitude. *Evidentialism* in epistemology is defined by the following thesis about epistemic justification:

(EVI) Person S is justified in believing proposition p at time t if and only if S's evidence for p at time t supports believing p.

Daniel Mittag (2004) explains:

As evidentialism is a thesis about epistemic justification, it is a thesis about what it takes for one to believe justifiably, or reasonably, in the sense thought to be necessary for knowledge. Particular versions of evidentialism can diverge in virtue of their providing different claims about what sorts of things count as evidence, what it is for one to have evidence, and what it is for one's evidence to support believing a proposition. Thus, while (EVI) is often referred to as the theory of epistemic justification known as evidentialism, it is more accurately conceived as a kind of epistemic theory. In this light, (EVI) can be seen as the central, guiding thesis of evidentialism. All evidentialist theories conform to (EVI), but various divergent theories of evidentialism can be formulated.

jurors to make accurate judgments. Protection of the jurors' epistemic ends therefore assumes derivative importance" (Goldman, 1991, p. 119).[23]

4.3.1.3 The Litigation Risk Analysis Method

For computer tools assisting with the evidence, there is an important application that deserves mention. Prosecutors do not prosecute all cases that have merit. Economical considerations matter, and if it appears to be the case that the odds of winning the trial are not too good and the financial loss would be too great for the kind of offence involved, then the prosecutor may choose to offer a plea bargain (in such countries where plea bargaining is admitted).

A useful application is the development of such decision-support systems that would assist the prosecutor in evaluating a case at hand, so that he or she could more confidently decide whether to prosecute. Considerations in terms of cost/benefits analysis are important for the parties involved in litigation, in both criminal and civil cases. It may be important to be able to evaluate a case for settlement at an early stage of a suit or claim, both because of the cost of litigation, and the risks of the outcomes of a trial; alternative dispute resolution may be convenient to consider, and moreover, foreseeing legal costs, alternative fee arrangements with the attorneys may be entered. Arno Lodder and John Zeleznikow provided an overview of computer-assisted dispute resolution (as being an alternative to litigation) in a book (Lodder & Zeleznikow, 2010, cf. 2005).

Peter Tillers (personal communication, March 2006) kindly identified, for the present author, as Marc B. Victor (http://www.litigationrisk.com/) the developer, whom he had mentioned years before, of a decision-theoretic tool, which assumes the chances of proving this or that. Victor's Litigation Risk Analysis^{TM}, Inc., based in Kenwood, CA, provides consulting, training, and software. Here is some information based on that firm's own promotion.

The Litigation Risk Analysis method (developed and taught by Victor from the early 1980s on) can be applied by performing the analysis by hand; alternatively it can be performed by a user who understand that method, using a decision tree software called *TreeAge Pro* (formerly known as *DATA*), produced by TreeAge

---

[23] In view of this, it is somewhat ironic that in an article on computerised sentencing information for judges, Doob and Park (1987–1988) began by stating: "There are few, these days, who would not argue that those making important judgments should have access to relevant information. The difficulty usually is not only having the information, but having it reasonably accessible and produced in a usable form". In their case, they were seeking "to provide judges with some of the information that is relevant to the passing of sentences". Clearly, the context was very different of that of exclusionary rules of evidence. Rather, Anthony Doob and Norman Park had assumed that judges would be very interested in learning about current sentencing. Developing their computerised system intended to aid judges in sentencing required that those developing the computer system would figure out beforehand what kind of information would be useful: "The history of this project illustrates the difficulties in knowing *a priori* what information will be most useful and illustrates the necessity of working closely with the eventual information user" (ibid., p. 54). See Section 4.2.3 above.

4.3 Evaluating Costs and Benefits

Software, Inc., to be installed on Windows^{TM}. The tool makes use of pull-down menus, and graphics. Trees are constructed by adding nodes and branches, and typing the names and probabilities.

The users targetted are ones who need evaluate litigation risk – corporations, or their lawyers – who when litigating may undervalue a case, pass up a chance to settle and then lose the trial, or vice versa, may overvalue a case, settle and pay too much. Such clients include corporate law departments, as well as the claim units at insurance companies. In the analysis, the evidence and the arguments are taken into account, yet the probabilities are assumed.

According to his website, Victor's clients are offered libraries of decision trees for various types of claims (for example, there are ready-made sets of models for personal injury & products liability claims, and for medical malpractice claims). Such availability reduces, according to the promotion, the time needed to construct correct trees. Victor's firm also offers to develop tailored models. As a consultant for the attorneys of a client, Victor elicits from them quantified input concerning the legal and factual uncertainties involved in a case, and concerning both liability issues and damage issues, he probes the relationships between the uncertainties, explores consequences from each possible combination of rulings and findings, and assesses with the attorneys the likelihood of good versus bad results.[24]

According to his method, the expected value of litigating is the probability-weighted average of all possible outcomes (and how changes in various probabilities would affect the expected value is quantified by means of sensitivity analyses). This is useful when the client can afford to "play the averages", whereas in some cases, the probability of extreme consequences militates against "playing the averages" in the given case: the range and likelihood of possible outcomes is shown in a probability distribution chart.

4.3.1.4 Bargaining, and Game Theory

Julia Barragán (1989) provided a short discussion of bargaining, but not plea-bargaining (at any rate, not explicitly), even though the forum in which the paper appeared was in computing for law. Rather, she sketched (not very convincingly) an application to software design. At the beginning, her paper stated it "will consider the bargaining process as rational behaviour, and bargaining models as a part of a General Theory of Rational Behaviour" (ibid., p. 49). The approach she overviewed is from *game theory*. "Bargaining models are related to Game Theory, since the bargaining problems domain is concerned with decision making in a social setting, in the very particular context of uncertainty known as a game" (ibid., p. 51). In a game, "three elements enter: (1) alternation of moves, which can be either personal or random (chance) moves, (2) a possible lack of knowledge, and (3) a payoff function" (Owen, 1995, p. 2). In *graph theory* (which is itself part of *topology*), a *tree* is such a graph, that any two *nodes* (also called *vertices*) are connected by exactly one *path*,

---

[24] http://www.litigationrisk.com/m-con-mbv.htm

itself made of one or two consecutive *edges*. A formal *game* can be represented as a *game tree* (also called a *topological tree*), with a distinguished node which is taken to be the starting node of the tree, i.e., the starting point of the game. A game with n players must have:

1. a *starting point* (a distinguished node in the game tree);
2. a *payoff function*, which associates n values with each terminal node of the tree (terminal nodes are such nodes that no path from the starting node can continue any further);
3. a partition of nonterminal nodes of the tree game into $n+1$ sets, called the *player sets*: these are the chance move, S_0, and the moves of all players, i.e., $S_1, \cdots S_n$.
4. "a randomization scheme at each chance move" (Owen, ibid.): "a probability distribution, defined at each vertex of S_0, among the immediate followers of this vertex" (ibid.);
5. a division "of a player's moves into 'information sets': he knows which information set he is in, but not which vertex of the information set" (ibid.): each *player set* S_i is partitioned "into subsets S_i^j, called *information sets*, such that two vertices in the same information set have the same number of immediate followers and no vertex can follow another vertex in the same information set" (ibid.);
6. an index set associated with each information set, along with a one-to-one mapping of that index set onto the set of immediate followers of each vertex of that particular information set.

Clearly, game theory is appropriate for modelling bargaining problems in general; this potentially applies to plea-bargaining, too. It is arguably not by chance, that perhaps the best known formal game of all (actually a case of *noncooperative bimatrix game*, a *two-person general-sum game*) is the *Prisoner's Dilemma*: two prisoners are in two cells, cannot communicate with each other, and are each offered a deal. If he pleads guilty and implicates the other prisoner, he himself will get a reduced sentence, and the other prisoner will get the lowest payoff, i.e., the stiffest sentence. Should neither of the two prisoners agree to the deal, neither would confess, and they would both get off with a light sentence, or would even avoid having to serve time in prison after the trial. Should both of them agree to the deal, plead guilty and implicate the other prisoner, this would be the only *equilibrium* pair, and both of them would get a very low payoff, i.e., they would both get rather stiff sentences. But if none of them would agree to the deal, they would be rather better off, and would both get a mild sentence. But the best payoff for a prisoner in this game is if he double-crosses the other. This is represented in the *payoff matrix* of Table 4.3.1.4.1, which is based on the example in Owen (1995, p. 164).

By contrast, in *two-person cooperative games*, "cooperation between the two players is allowed. This means that binding contracts can be made, that correlated mixed strategies are allowed, and that utility can be transferred from one player to the other (though not always linearly)" (Owen, 1995, p. 190). "A serious objection can be raised to Nash's bargaining scheme, and it is that it does not take threats into

4.3 Evaluating Costs and Benefits   255

Table 4.3.1.4.1 The payoff matrix in the Prisoner's Dilemma. The parentheses inside each cell are the payoff vectors of the terminal nodes in the game

	Prisoner P2:	
Prisoner P1:	Confesses:	Does not confess:
Confesses:	(1, 1)	(10, 0)
Does not confess:	(0, 10)	(5, 5)

account" (ibid., p. 198). Theorem IX.2.2 in Owen (1995) states: "Any bimatrix game has at least one equilibrium pair of threat strategies (x, y)" (ibid., p. 200). Guillermo Owen then goes on to discuss how to formalise bargaining with threats, and next, how to deal with time-restricted bargaining (where, for example, it may be much better to accept deal now, than later on, like in an industrial dispute with a strike).

4.3.2 Evaluating the Effects of Obtaining or Renouncing a Piece of Evidence

Levitt and Laskey (2002) combined Bayesian inference networks with knowledge representation from AI, in order to structure and carry out an analysis of evidential argumentation about an infamous murder case. In their Section 1.5, they enumerated desiderata concerning current and future tools for supporting judicial proof: such tool should allow to represent hypotheses and supporting or denying evidence (ibid., Section 1.5.1), to compare beliefs between alternative hypotheses (ibid., Section 1.5.2), to update belief based on incrementally accrued evidence (ibid., Section 1.5.3), and to examine variations of the same hypothetical–evidential scenario (ibid., Section 1.5.4).

In their Section 1.5.4, they wrote (ibid., pp. 381–382): "A unique application of sensitivity analysis" (the sensitivity analyses reported in their article, in Section 1.4.4., being performed by Keung-Chi Ng) "has been provided for" Bayesian networks (BNs) "that provides a quantitatively powerful, scientifically meaningful, and qualitatively intuitive measure of the relevance and importance of evidence to the truth or falsity of a target hypothesis or BN query".

Gathering evidence may be costly and time-consuming. Does what is to be proven really require a given piece of evidence to be obtained?

> Before evidence is observed, we can assess the impact of observing any possible state of an evidence variable, as well as the impact, if relevant, of failing to learn anything about the evidence available. We can examine the degree to which the probabilities in which we are most interested would be affected by observing the evidence. We can rank the different evidence-gathering strategies by impact on the conclusion and prioritize evidence gathering accordingly. When there are monetary or other costs to evidence gathering, these techniques provide tools for balancing the information gain of evidence gathering against the cost. [...] (Levitt & Laskey, ibid., p. 382).

An important consideration we can make is that if the purpose is to assess beforehand whether to incur the costs of obtaining this or that evidence, then this is not as vulnerable to a Bayesio-skeptic critique in the controversy about Bayesianism's application to judicial decision-making, as actually trying to model the strength of the evidence for conviction in the actual trial, and proposing such statistics as evidence, would be. In fact, making use of Bayesianism for a costs/benefits analysis so that a decision is made, during fact investigation or the preparation of a trial, to either obtain or renounce some evidence, belongs in the economics of one party in the trial preparing its case. A private party turning to the courts, or called to respond, are within their rights to adopt a flawed method, or consult an astrologer, if they so wish, as well as to mismanage their case, and therefore have no case to answer if charged with methodologically unwarranted assumptions by the Bayesio-skeptics.[25]

When it comes to the prosecution preparing its cases, they are more vulnerable to critique, if they demonstrably grossly mismanaged a case. Nevertheless, especially in the adversarial system of procedure from Anglo-American jurisdictions (unlike, until recently, in many countries of the European Continent), in criminal cases the prosecution has the discretion whether to prosecute at all. Therefore, Bayesian methods being used in a costs/benefits analysis of whether to obtain some evidence, or then of whether to prosecute or offer a plea bargain instead, are practically immune from Bayesio-skeptic attacks.

4.3.3 Benefits, Costs, and Dangers of Argumentation

Negotiators hope to benefit from negotiating successfully, and more in general, people who engage in exchanging arguments also expect some benefit from such an activity. And yet, the very choice of engaging in such activities incurs costs and is fraught with dangers. If there is a category of a potential arguers who are acutely aware of this, this is people who are considering whether to turn to the courts. You

---

[25] The debate about Bayesianism in judicial context is complex. In a sense, concrete misgivings, apart from mathematical niceties and whether they do model the world reliably, boil down to this: that the problems of Bayesianism cannot be solved by mere computational powers, and that all it takes, to cause the calculations go wrong, is for some supposedly expert and honest witness (e.g., some physician specialised in serving insurance companies) to say whatever suits those instructing them, and then Bayesianism could not possibly put that right. The real danger is overly relying on a formalism, when it is the adjudicator's common sense (however flawed) that should stay alert, in acute awareness that there is no safety net. Reliance on formalisms may give raise to a delusion that things are being taken care for, whereas they actually are not.

Allen and Pardo stated (2007b, p. 308): "[W]e are not uncompromising sceptics, and we even concede that the formal models may be useful in evaluating evidence and that it may not be unreasonable for parties to argue, or fact-finders to evaluate evidence, along the lines suggested by such models. To say that such models may be useful is not, however, to accept them as the sole or even a particularly reliable method of discovering the truth. Our objection is to scholarship arguing just that such models establish the correct or accurate probative value of evidence, and thus implying that any deviations from such models lead to inaccurate or irrational outcomes".

4.3 Evaluating Costs and Benefits

may lose, have to pay your lawyers, and also have to pay the costs of the other party. Or then, this may be an area of litigation in which even if you win, the law usually does not envisage recovery *inter partes*, and what you spent in order to have your day in court may loom too large an amount for you to derive a financial benefit from having turned to the courts. The emotional strain, too, comes at a cost.

In negotiation, arguing comes at a cost (Karunatillake & Jennings, 2004, p. 235)[26]:

> Although argumentation-based negotiation can be effective at resolving conflicts, there are a number of overheads associated with its use. It takes time to persuade and convince an opponent to change its stance and yield to a less favourable agreement. It takes computational effort for both parties of the conflict to carry out the reasoning required to generate and select a set of convincing arguments, and to evaluate the incoming arguments and reason whether to accept or reject them. However, not all conflicts need to be resolved. Thus, for example, when faced with a conflict, an agent could find an alternative means to work around the situation; thereby evading the conflict rather than attempting to resolve it. [...] Given the overheads of argumentation, and the alternative methods available for overcoming conflicts (evade and re-plan), we believe it is important for agents to be able to weigh up the relative advantages and disadvantages of arguing, before attempting to resolve conflicts through argumentation.

A modicum of caution is also required when one is faced with the choice whether to argue, also in dialogical domains different from negotiation. In an article entitled 'Why argue? Towards a cost–benefit analysis of argumentation', Paglieri and Castelfranchi (2010) extend the discussion indeed, and consider not only the costs of arguing, but also the dangers, which they separate from the costs. Paglieri and Castelfranchi (2010) develop a neglected topic from the study of argumentation. An agent's decision whether to argue or not is governed by strategic considerations, that they set to highlight. They "propose a tripartite taxonomy and detailed description of the strategic reasons considered by arguers in their decision-making: benefits, costs, and dangers" (ibid., p. 71), and "contextualise such notions within the general framework of expected utility theory" (ibid., p. 73). They "insist that the implications of acknowledging the strategic dimension of arguing are far-reaching, including promising insights on how to develop better argumentation technologies".

People are often reluctant to argue, e.g., with one's boss, or with one's partner in a romantic relationship. The very fact of arguing may damage the relationship. Such "reluctance to argue is not a form of lamentable timidity, but rather the expression of strategic concerns: we do not engage in argument when doing so is likely to have an overall negative outcome" (ibid., p. 71).

Disagreement may escalate, so arguing could be ruinous (Paglieri, 2009; Paglieri & Castelfranchi, 2010). *The emotional well-being* of the arguers is affected (ibid., p. 82), and there are other factors militating to make escalation in disagreement an utterly undesirable outcome. And this is just one kind of danger. There also is a danger to the *reputation* of the arguer (ibid., p. 83). "A further danger of arguing concerns drawing unwanted attention from the counterpart on topics that it would

---

[26] Karunatillake (2006), a doctoral dissertation, provides further details.

be in the arguer's best interest to keep hidden or out of focus" (ibid., p. 82). Yet another danger (ibid., p. 81) is that

> an argument may 'backfire', to use Cohen's (2005) apt terminology, in the sense of *undermining the credibility of the conclusion it aimed to prove*. When an argument fails to prove its conclusions, this should not be taken to indicate that the audience is left with the same views on the matter they had before being exposed to the argument. Quite often, what happens is that a failed argument is taken as *evidence to the contrary*: the very fact that an argument for *p* failed is easily interpreted as an argument for [its negation,] which is clearly a highly unsatisfactory result for the arguer. Even more dramatically, once argumentative failure has occurred, the more effort the arguer put into the original argument, the more likely it is that the audience will consider this failure as good proof of the falsity of the intended claim. After all, if a determined and competent arguer, after putting so much effort into arguing for *p*, still failed to prove it, the most likely reason for that failure is that *p* is false, since there is no question as to the competence and motivation of the arguer. Like in a nightmarish subversion of all standard values, backfiring arguments may happen to retort against the arguer his very best efforts. This also implies that the dangers of arguing, in terms of negative effects on the credibility of the conclusion, increases as a function of duration, efforts, and quality of the argumentative process.

Strategic considerations about whether it is worthwhile to argue do matter not only for human arguers or prospective arguers, but also for computational tools applied to argumentation: "argument-based technologies for open systems are likely to be more effective if they are not 'doomed to argue', but rather allowed to opt for different interactive modalities in different contexts, arguing only when it is expedient doing so" (Paglieri & Castelfranchi, 2010, p. 71).

In an endnote, Paglieri and Castelfranchi suggest that the neglect, in computational models of argument, of taking into account whether it would be a benefit rather than a disbenefit to argue in the first place, is related to the relative neglect of dialogical or procedural aspects of argument: "strategic consideration of costs[27] and benefits still remains ahead of much of the field, since the issue becomes relevant only after acknowledging argumentation as an essentially dialogical process, involving communication between multiple agents" (ibid., p. 87, n. 1).

Another reason for the neglect of cost–benefit analysis in argumentation research, and in particular in computational models of argument, is that relatively few scholars

---

[27] This is not to say that algorithmic and complexity issues relating to computational models of argument have not been researched. Quite on the contrary, there is such a flourishing direction of research (e.g., Ben-Capon & Dunne, 2007). "However, in this case, the preoccupation is with the tractability of a given argumentation framework, whereas our concerns here are on a completely different scale: even assuming that a given argumentation framework is tractable, the individual agent still has to make a strategic decision on whether arguing is rational or not, given current goals, available resources and relevant context. Obviously, the tractability of the underlying argumentation framework impacts on the strategic considerations of the agent. If the framework makes argumentation intractable or typically very costly for the agent, the likelihood of considering such practice worthwhile is either non-existent or comparatively low. But the crucial point is that, even when argumentation is tractable and its costs are in principle affordable, it does not immediately follow that arguing is the best option for the agent. It is this crucial decision problem that so far has been largely overlooked in argumentation theories, both within and outside AI: our aim now is to move some preliminary steps to explore the issue" (Paglieri & Castelfranchi, 2010, p. 73).

4.3 Evaluating Costs and Benefits

have considered computation to be resource-bounded. But when modelling agents, it stands to reason to bear in mind that realistically, agents are resource-bounded, and that in particular, they have bounded rationality, too. For the latter, refer to Rubinstein's book (1998) *Modelling Bounded Rationality*. Also see Gigerenzer and Selten (2001). Gabbay and Woods (2003) are aware of the importance of studying argumentation under assumptions of bounded rationality.

Paglieri and Castelfranchi (ibid., p. 87, n. 2) quote Amgoud and Maudet (2002, p. 406) as recognising that "Ideal agents compute [...] for free. But computation takes resources, and for instance spending too much time trying to determine the acceptability of an argument may be a poor strategy. What if the agent cannot conclude within the bound of the resources? [...] The role of strategy is even more crucial when taking into account the resource-bounded nature of agents". But such considerations are certainly instead on the mind of people who resort to the services of lawyers, or balk at doing so. Litigation is costly.

"[D]ialogical goals are rarely terminal, i.e. they tend not to be ends in themselves" (Paglieri & Castelfranchi, ibid., p. 74). "Dialogical goals are often instrumental to extra-dialogical goals: the car dealer wants to persuade you of the superiority of a given model in order to sell you that model, not just for the sake of discussion" (ibid.). Arguing is instrumental, and is a plan you may adopt or not adopt when pursuing extra-dialogical goals (ibid., pp. 74–75):

> This implies a form of *argumentative instrumentalism*: both the overall decision to argue and more fine-grained choices of specific moves are ultimately affected by the extra-dialogical goals of the arguer. Argumentative instrumentalism has three facets: first, dialogical sub-goals are instrumental to some dialogical end (e.g. lauding the design of a given car is instrumental to persuade you of its superiority as a purchasing option), which in turn is instrumental to some extra-dialogical goal (e.g. selling you the car); second, the extra-dialogical goal has *priority* over the dialogical one, so if a given move is likely to foster the former but not the latter, the arguer should choose that move (e.g. observing that only few chosen people can afford to buy that model may be instrumental to selling you the car by appeasing your vanity, even if this point has no bearing on the alleged superiority of that particular model over others); third, a given move or set of moves may be instrumental to some other extra-dialogical goal of the arguer, different from the one which motivated to argue in the first place (e.g. the seller may try to impress an attractive female client with his elocution not as an effective mean to sell her the car, but rather hoping to get a date with the client).

Bear in mind that in a courtroom situation, the arguing parties, as well as the judge, are not merely concerned with persuasion in the case at hand. Bernard Jackson (2010) points out:

> If we find a "a variety of different voices interlaced in the judge's discourse" ([Azuelos-Atias, 2007], p. 99), thus fulfilling his role of impartiality (p. 93), this represents the judge's personal goal of presenting himself to his colleagues according to the accepted image of good judicial behaviour. Even more so, in the case of the lawyers. Their audience is not confined to the parties to the particular case, or some notional reasonable reader; their discourse is directed to their professional peers and particularly those in whose hands lie decisions as to their professional advancement. From the very fact that some lawyers are known within the profession as mavericks, willing to fight for their clients (within the law and legal procedures) with little display of respect for institutional players such as the police, we become

aware of the fact that those who do "play the game" are in fact playing their own game as well as that of their clients. Nor should we exclude the presence here of a purely internal discourse: the communication by the lawyer of messages *to himself* (the same *acteur* playing different actantial roles, both sender and receiver), in constituting or fortifying a particular sense of personal identity.

4.3.4 Costs and Benefits of Digital Forensic Investigations

Richard Overill and Jantje Silomon devoted a paper (2010) to what they term *digital metaforensics*, i.e., "quantifying the investigation" into digital crime cases. Overill et al. pointed out (2009, from the abstract):

> From the perspective of a digital investigation, it is the duty of digital investigators or forensic examiners to retrieve digital traces so as to prove or to refute the alleged computer acts. Given the resource constraints of most organizations and the limited time-frame available for the examination, it is not always feasible or indeed necessary for forensic examiners to retrieve all the related digital traces and to conduct a thorough digital forensic analysis.

Overill et al. (2009) and Cohen (2009) tried to develop metrics of cost-effectiveness, for the purposes of a costs/benefits analysis of forensic investigations into digital crime. Overill and Silomon (2010) provided a survey. In the summer of 2010, a software application, *Digital Forensic Advisor*, was being developed jointly at King's College London (by Overill's team), and Hong Kong University, with funds from Innovation China UK.

Overill and Silomon remarked (2010, section 2.2):

> With law enforcement resources (principally manpower, money and time) already overstretched in relation to the number of digital forensic investigations requested, it becomes important to develop methods of determining whether or not any particular investigation is worthwhile undertaking. This leads naturally to the concepts of forensic triage and prioritisation. A preliminary filtering or pre-screening phase will enable evidentially hopeless investigations to be abandoned quickly, and the remainder to be ranked in probable order of evidential strength. A number of criteria have been proposed for making the initial assessment, including cost-efficiency [(Overill et al., 2009)] and return-on-investment (ROI) [(Cohen, 2009)].

Of those two measures, *cost-efficiency* "ranks the recovered evidence against the expected evidence for a known type of crime. A forensic technician is guided through the assessment by a software application" such as *Digital Forensic Advisor*, "in a pre-determined sequence which seeks out the most evidentially significant traces first, and, among traces of equal evidential weight, the lowest cost traces first" (Overill & Silomon, section 2.2). The advantage is that "an evidentially hopeless assessment can be detected early on and abandoned, while only those assessments which exceed a pre-determined evidential threshold [...] are passed on to an experienced forensic examiner for full processing" (ibid.).

By contrast, *return-on-investment* (ROI), a measure used by Cohen (2009) and inversely related to the *cost-benefit ratio* (CBR), is calculated as follows. Let i be a given trace, and w_i be its evidential weight, and c_i be its cost. Then:

4.3 Evaluating Costs and Benefits

$$\text{ROI}(i) = w_i/c_i$$
$$\text{CBR}(i) = c_i/w_i$$

Overill and Silomon (section 2.2), citing Cohen (2009), point out:

> The evidential traces for a known type of crime can be ranked in order of descending ROI (or of ascending CBR) and then assessed in that order. Refinement of this scheme is possible: for example, where a particular trace i contributes to $n_i > 1$ evidentiary chains then its effective weight is given by $w'_i = n_i \times w_i$ and the effective ROI is then $(n_i \times w_i)/c_i$

Nevertheless, Cohen (2009) also proposed different metrics, namely,

$$n_i + (c_i/10)$$

and

$$n_i/c_i$$

Which metric (which ranking) to choose, for a digital forensic laboratory, "will depend on its individual priorities (for example, throughput *versus* resources) as well as on the nature of the suspected digital crime (for example, civil *versus* criminal, or large scale *versus* small scale)" (Overill & Silomon, section 2.2).

Overill et al. (2009) were concerned with digital traces T_i of a digital crime, that can be detected on a hard disk. Let there be m such traces. The team wanted to be able to find the relative cost ranking of those traces. They notated this as:

$$T_1 \leq T_2 \leq \cdots \leq T_{m-1} \leq T_m$$

Overill et al. claimed (2009, section 2):

> As a direct consequence of this ranking, the minimum cost path for the overall investigation is immediately uniquely defined. It is worth to denote here that different organizations can adopt different relative costs to similar traces in order to meet with the organizational goals.

As an example, they drew a *path diagram* with four traces. There are different paths by which one may reach the permutation $T_1T_2T_3T_4$. Four arcs depart from the initial node, Ø, of the graph. Those arcs respectively reach nodes $[T_1]$, $[T_2]$, $[T_3]$, and $[T_4]$. The next level of nodes includes $[T_1T_2]$ (which is reached from $[T_1]$ and from $[T_2]$), $[T_1T_3]$ (which is reached from $[T_1]$ and from $[T_3]$), $[T_1T_4]$, $[T_2T_4]$, and $[T_3T_4]$. The next level of nodes comprises $[T_1T_2T_3]$ (reached by arcs from respectively $[T_1T_2]$ and $[T_1T_3]$), $[T_1T_2T_4]$, $[T_1T_3T_4]$, and $[T_2T_3T_4]$ (the latter by arcs from respectively $[T_2T_3]$ and $[T_2T_4]$). And finally, arcs reach the last node, $[T_1T_2T_3T_4]$, in the path graph. $[T_1T_2T_3T_4]$ is the *minimum cost path*.

In Overill et al. (2009), the evidential weight associated with the investigation is

$$\mathbf{W} = \sum_{i=1}^{m} w_i$$

where the relative fractional importance w_i of each trace T_i is either assigned by moderated independent expert peer review, or by default is set equal to $1 = m$. We note in passing that this process only needs to be undertaken once as a pre-processing step for each distinct digital crime template. The estimate **W** should be compared with unity. If **W** is sufficiently close to unity, this signifies that the *prima facie* of the case can probably be established; otherwise, it is unlikely that the available digital traces are sufficient to support the case. In other words, the differential gap between **W** and unity can formulate a "cut-off" condition that can avoid identifying all traces exhaustively in a forensics investigation.

Section 3 in Overill et al. (2009) is about missing traces, when "there is no way that an examiner can fully ascertain the trace evidence of the case." If trace T_j is not found, then all paths involving T_j must be deleted, and it must also be deleted from the minimum cost path. Then the associated weight associated with the investigation is

$$\mathbf{W} = \sum_{i \neq j}^{m} w_i$$

If the missing traces are T_j and T_k, then all paths involving either must be deleted, the minimum cost path will of course not include either trace, and the associated weight associated with the investigation is

$$\mathbf{W} = \sum_{i \neq j,k}^{m} w_i$$

Next, Overill et al. (2009, section 4) proposed a two-phase schema for performing a digital forensic examination at minimal cost. The first phase is one of preprocessing, and its task is to detect the traces:

1. Enumerate the set of traces that are expected to be present in the seized computer based on the type of computer crime that is suspected of having been committed.
2. Assign relative investigation costs to each of the expected traces.
3. Rank the expected traces in order of increasing relative investigation costs.
4. Assign relative importance weights w_i to each of the ranked traces.
5. Rank the expected traces within each cost band in order of decreasing relative importance weight.
6. Set **W**, the cumulative evidential weight estimate, equal to zero.
7. Set W_{rem}, the remaining total of available weights, to 1.
8. For each expected trace, taken in ranked order:
    8.1 Search for the expected trace.
    8.2 Subtract the relative importance weight w_i of the expected trace from W_{rem}.
    8.3 If the expected trace is present add its relative importance weight w_i to **W**.
    8.4 If **W** is suffciently close to 1 then proceed immediately to *Phase 2*.
    8.5 If $(\mathbf{W} + W_{rem})$ is insufficiently close to 1 then abandon the forensics investigation.

4.4 ADVOKATE, and Assessing Eyewitness Suitability and Reliability

As to *Phase 2* in Overill et al. (2009, section 4), its task is to analyse the traces, and it resorts to a *Bayesian network*[28]: "Set up a full Bayesian Network model for the hypothesis of the digital crime and run and analyze the Bayesian Network model for the hypothesis of the digital crime as described previously in" Kwan, Chow, Law, and Lai (2008), which is an earlier paper from the same team.

We are going to come back to digital forensics in Section 6.2.1.5, and at the end of Section 8.3.2. The context of the latter is the debate about the role of statistics in the forensic sciences. As there was nothing specific to the technical aspects of investigating digital crime in our present discussion, we were able to treat models of such investigations' costs and benefits within the same compass as other kinds of costs/benefits analysis we have been considering in Section 4.3.

4.4 ADVOKATE, and Assessing Eyewitness Suitability and Reliability

4.4.1 The Turnbull Rules

Identification by eyewitness is far from safe. This is why in some jurisdictions with a jury, jurors receive judicial directions concerning this.[29] Bromby, MacMillan, and McKellar (2007) pointed out (ibid., p. 306):

> Miscarriages of justice due to inaccurate eyewitness identifications are not new. In England and Wales, the inquiries into the trial of Mr Adolf Beck in 1904 and the arrest of Major R. O. Sheppard in 1925 acknowledged the erroneous identifications in those cases, but failed to recognize the inherent weakness associated with all eyewitness evidence. The Beck case led to the establishment of the Court of Appeal in England and Wales. In *R v Williams*, counsel for the defence asked the court to give a general direction that where the only evidence against an accused person was identification by one witness, the jury should be

---

[28] A Bayesian network is a directed acyclic graph (i.e., a graph without loops, and with nodes and arrows rather than direction-less edges), such that the nodes represent propositions or variables, the arcs represent the existence of direct causal influences between the linked propositions, and the strengths of these influences are quantified by conditional probabilities. Whereas in an *inference network* the arrow is from a node standing for evidence to a node standing for a hypothesis, in a Bayesian network instead the arrow is from the hypothesis to the evidence. In an inference network, an arrow represents a relation of support. In a Bayesian network, an arrow represents a causal influence, and the arrow is from a cause to its effect.

[29] Bromby et al. (2007, p. 303) discussed, in relation to eyewitness identification in Commonwealth jurisdictions, criminal jury directions, i.e., such judicial directions to the jury that are intended "to guard against wrongful convictions based upon erroneous eyewitness identification evidence. Factors known as the Turnbull Rules, derived from the English case R v. Turnbull, are of significance within many common law jurisdictions when considering the accuracy of eyewitness identifications and the practice of jury directions or mandatory warnings. The influence of these rules, together with variations in the approach taken by Commonwealth jurisdictions, illustrates that while the factors identified in Turnbull are to be found in the approaches adopted across the various jurisdictions studied, there is diversity in terms of whether or not such directions are mandatory and also as to their form and scope."

warned that it would be dangerous to convict without corroboration. The Lord Chief Justice, Lord Goddard, in quashing the conviction due to mistaken eyewitness identification, held that the Court of Criminal Appeal would lay down no hypothetical directions for a jury, as suggested by counsel. By contrast, in 1962 in the Republic of Ireland, the Supreme Court held that a general warning should be given, as juries in general might not be fully aware of the dangers involved in visual identification: [...]

Bromby et al. (2007, p. 308) also remarked about jurisprudence from England and Wales:

In 1976, following several high profile cases of mistaken identity and poorly conducted line-ups in England and Wales, the Devlin Report [(Devlin, 1976)] provided a thorough analysis of identification evidence in criminal proceedings. The report had been commissioned by the Home Secretary to review all aspects of the law and procedure relating to evidence of identification in criminal cases and to make recommendations. [...] It was recommended that the trial judge should be required by statute '... to direct the jury that it is not safe to convict upon eyewitness evidence unless the circumstances of the identification are exceptional or the eyewitness evidence is supported by substantial evidence of another sort'. Such a statutory direction was never enacted. Although the committee did not wish to define the exceptional circumstances in which a conviction could be secured on the basis of eyewitness evidence, it did summarize the chief points, which in the normal course of events, a summing-up might be expected to cover: [...]

A list was based on input that the Devlin committee received from the Magistrates' Association, which does not imply that the factors listed were in common use to guide the judiciary in their summing-up (Bromby et al., 2007, p. 309):

(i) *The witness himself.* Whether he appeared in examination and crossexamination as careful and conscientious or as obstinate or as irresponsible. Whether the experience, for example, in the case of violent crime, might have affected an identification.
(ii) *Conditions at the scene.* How good the lighting levels were and whether the vantage point afforded an uninterrupted view. How much of the criminal was seen and whether there has been a single period or multiple periods of observation.
(iii) *Lapse of time.* The duration between the observation and the subsequent identification.[30]

---

[30] Delay has an effect upon the accuracy of identification by eyewitness, but also age has an impact. For example, cf. Memon, Bartlett, Rose, and Gray (2003) "The aging eyewitness: The effects of face-age and delay upon younger and older observers", whereas Memon and Gabbert (2003b) tried to find up such arrangements at lineups that would affect the identification accuracy of old witnesses. Dysart, Lindsay, MacDonald, and Wicke (2002) considered the effects of alcohol on eyewitness accuracy. Caputo and Dunning (2006) discussed post factum indicators of eyewitness accuracy, so that accurate identifications could be distinguished from erroneous ones. Horry and Wright (2008) found that viewing *other-race faces* may an impairing effect on context memory, in the sense that the eyewitness may recall having seen that face, but not be quite accurate or sure about where he or she saw that face of that person from a race other than one's own. This may be

(iv) *Description*. What does a comparison show? The judge and jury should bear in mind that the ability to identify correctly and the ability to describe correctly are distinct.
(v) *Identification parade*. Whether there are any criticisms of the line-up conditions. Did any witnesses, for example, make no identification or pick out someone other than the suspect?
(vi) *Identified person*. Whether the suspect is easy to recognise (distinctive) or unremarkable in comparison to others (nondescript).
(vii) *No circumstantial evidence*. Whether other statements might have been expected or identifiable objects retrieved that relate to the eyewitness's evidence.

"Following the Devlin Report, the first case to give serious consideration to eyewitness identification was *R v Turnbull*" (ibid.). Lord Chief Justice Widgery followed the Devlin Report as to jury directions, and acknowledged that occasionally eyewitness identification may be fallible. Nevertheless, as Bromby et al. point out (2007, pp. 309–310):

> He made a distinction between cases with good quality identification evidence and those with evidence of a poorer quality. Differing sharply from the Devlin Report, the *Turnbull* judgment stated that prosecutions based solely upon a single eyewitness identification of 'good quality' should not fail automatically. This implies that good eyewitness identification on its own should be sufficient to secure a conviction without the requirement for further corroborative evidence. Although 'good identification evidence' and 'poor identification evidence' may be easy to define at extremes of the spectrum, cases which fall between the two cannot be classified so easily. The majority of cases where identification is disputed will present evidence either in between the two extremes or scattered along the entire spectrum of quality.

The following eight factors are known as Turnbull Rules, and as summarised here they are taken from Bromby, MacMillan, and McKellar (2003, p. 101):

(1) the visibility and lighting conditions at the time of the offence
(2) the distance of the eyewitness from the perpetrator
(3) the duration of observation of the crime by the eyewitness
(4) whether the observation of the crime was impeded
(5) whether the perpetrator was known to the eyewitness

---

because of which faces one is more used to see, under the assumption that people are more used to see faces of people from one's own race. Arguably (as a research hypothesis we suggest here) experimenting with eyewitness who have been other-race adopted children and were raised in an environment where almost everybody is from the same race as their adoptive parents could show that their context memory is more accurate when having to identify individuals (and the time of viewing) such that their faces are racially akin to those of the environment in which they were raised, rather than their own. Cf. Chance and Goldstein (1995); whereas Meissner and Brigham (2001) are concerned with the *own-race bias in memory for faces*.

(6) the duration between the sighting of the offence and the reporting of the incident
(7) the reasons the eyewitness recalls that the perpetrator was at the scene of the crime
(8) the differences between the description of the perpetrator and the actual appearance of a suspect.

4.4.2 The ADVOKATE Project

Working at the Joseph Bell Centre for Forensic Statistics and Legal Reasoning of the University of Edinburgh, Bromby et al. (2003) set for themselves the task of developing knowledge-based software for evaluating eyewitness evidence. For that purpose, they adopted a *CommonKADS* approach, based on a framework developed by Schreiber, et al. (1999).

"The CommonKADS analysis identifies gaps where more information should be obtained and how the accumulated knowledge could be represented in a useful and accessible format" (Bromby et al., 2003, p. 101). As they explained (Bromby et al., 2003, p. 100):

> This paper discusses the modelling of a legal knowledge-based system that will alert a user on the reliability of eyewitness testimony. There is a large field of research and opinion on the performance and ability of humans to perceive, encode, store and retrieve facial images. By combining existing knowledge from different domains of expertise, such a system can draw attention to the dangers of allowing a jury to accept flawed eyewitness testimony.
>
> The model includes information such as the distance between the witness and the perpetrator; the duration of the observation; and the visibility or lighting conditions. These elements, along with several other event factors are commonly referred to as the 'Turnbull Rules' derived from the case *R v Turnbull*. The application of these factors has now become a requirement in England and Wales when considering the admissibility of eyewitness testimony in court. The Turnbull Rules have been applied by other common law jurisdictions, notably Ireland, Canada and Australia.
>
> This paper presents a CommonKADS approach to designing a small-scale system to evaluate eyewitness evidence. CommonKADS is a Knowledge Acquisition Design System using computer-generated models to represent how tasks are performed, which agents are involved, their expertise and the communication involved in the process of evaluating eyewitness evidence. The knowledge modelled for the application has been drawn from sources such as: the police, the prosecution service, lawyers and psychologists.

The team analysed the current protocol for the inclusion of eyewitness evidence, and this produced "a multi-dimensional representation of knowledge, procedure and methodology. These three elements are central to any criminal investigation. Using the CommonKADS methodology, three models were constructed to identify and describe the complex process involved in analysing eyewitness evidence" (Bromby et al., 2003, pp. 101–102). The three models are the *organisation model*, the *agent model*, and the *task model*.

The organisation model represents how the investigation or case progresses through the legal system, and captures the rules of evidence. It deals with the issues

4.4 ADVOKATE, and Assessing Eyewitness Suitability and Reliability

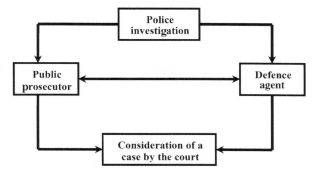

Fig. 4.4.2.1 The *top layer* of the organisation model. Redrawn from Bromby et al. (2003, p. 102). By accessing one of the boxes, it is possible to obtain further details from a sub-layer, e.g. the box on the court has information associated about which kind of court should hear a case about a given kind of crime.

of admissibility and sufficiency of eyewitness evidence so that a case in court would be established. Figure 4.4.2.1 shows the top layer of the organisation model for a criminal case, and is redrawn from Bromby et al. (2003, p. 102). The boxes in the figure have more detailed information associated at a sub-layer.

The agent model represents relationships among individual agents (such as the police, the judge, the jury, the accused, the defence, and the prosecution, or then inanimate props). The agents are connected by actions. Figure 4.4.2.2 shows the most significant agents in the agent model, as far as eyewitnesses (possibly including the victim) are concerned. This figure is redrawn from Bromby et al. (2003, p. 103). "Other" may even be an inanimate object, such as a car. The boxes in this figure each contain either an agent or a concept. Ellipses contain relationships.

The task model in Bromby et al. (2003) identifies the main lines of inquiry so that eyewitness evidence could be gathered and evaluated. There is a sequence of three

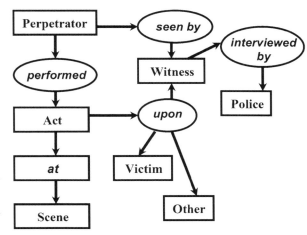

Fig. 4.4.2.2 Agents and relationships most relevant for eyewitness evidence, from the agent model of Bromby et al. (2003). This figure is redrawn from that same paper (ibid., p. 103).

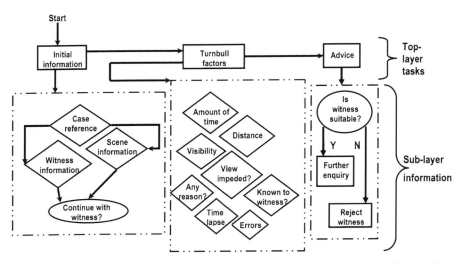

Fig. 4.4.2.3 The task model from Bromby et al. (2003). This figure is redrawn from (ibid., p. 104).

top-level tasks, and they are each exploded into a sub-layer of further information. This is shown in Fig. 4.4.2.3, which is redrawn from Bromby et al. (2003, p. 104). In this figure, each box contains a plan. A lozenge contains an enquiry. An ellipse contains a decision.

The project concerned is in the same domain as ADVOKATE,[31] a software tool developed by Michael Bromby in Glasgow and Maria Jean Hall at La Trobe University in Australia, was reported about in Bromby and Hall (2002) and Bromby et al. (2003). ADVOKATE is about the evaluation of the credibility of eyewitness evidence. "Directed graph techniques are used to model rule based knowledge", whereas "discretionary decisions and argumentation are modelled a technique derived from Toulmin argumentation" (Bromby & Hall, 2002, p. 143). Various factors, such as competency, compellability, and practicality, apply to witness suitability (which is applicable to all witnesses, and is primarily a legal test). Besides, there is witness reliability. A factor involved is mental capacity.[32]

---

[31] The ADVOKATE software was made available at http://advokate.bromby.vze.com/ This browser-accessible application was developed by using an expert system shell, WebShell.

[32] Michael Bromby first graduated in molecular and cell biology, and then earned a LLM, specialising in medical jurisprudence, intellectual property and artificial intelligence & legal reasoning. He also holds a diploma in forensic medical sciences. He co-developed ADVOKATE while a research fellow with the Joseph Bell Centre for Forensic Statistics and Legal Reasoning of the University of Edinburgh. He was for a while a technical consultant for a company specialising in police software solutions and facial composite systems, and then took up an academic position at the Law Department at Glasgow Caledonian University. According to his website at Glasgow Caledonian, "Michael's main research areas lie in facial recognition; his LLM dissertation examined the reliability and accuracy of automatic facial recognition systems as a tool for identification via CCTV

4.4 ADVOKATE, and Assessing Eyewitness Suitability and Reliability

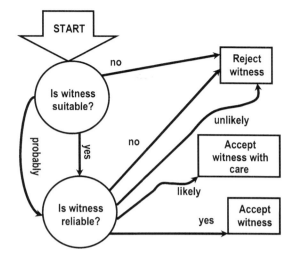

Fig. 4.4.2.4 The rule-based part of the architecture of ADVOKATE: a preliminary assessment of suitability is followed by the analysis of reliability. Redrawn from Bromby and Hall (2002, p. 144)

It is in the rule-based part of the architecture of ADVOKATE, that rules are represented as directed graphs. Nodes stand for concepts, whereas the possible values each concept in ADVOKATE can take as shown are arcs coming out of the node for the given concept. Figure 4.4.2.4 shows the rule-based part of the architecture of ADVOKATE, and is redrawn from Bromby and Hall (2002, p. 144). The rule-based part of the ADVOKATE model is followed by a part representing knowledge with discretionary inferencing. In fact, whether a witness is suitable and reliable is not determined by rule-based inferences. It is up to the discretionary decisions of the court.

Besides, also witness competency is assessed, based on age and mental comprehension. Does the witness understand the difference between truth and falsehood? Does the witness understand the duty to tell the truth? Is the witness able to give coherent testimony? (Bromby & Hall, 2002, p. 146). If the witness does not meet any of those three requirements, then the witness is not competent, and therefore this witness is not suitable.

"The *compellability* of a witness is determined by looking at two factors: the *connection* between the witness and the accused; and any *immunity* the witness may have" (ibid.). For example, by precedent in the law of Scotland, "communication between spouses during marriage is privileged and a spouse cannot be compelled to give such evidence" (ibid.). Figure 4.4.2.5 shows the test for witness compellability in ADVOKATE; it is redrawn from Bromby and Hall (2002, p. 146).

---

cameras, and his DipFMS dissertation concentrated on Expert Evidence in the UK. As a biochemist, he also carries an interest in DNA profiling, blood typing and other biological and forensic methods of identification for both civil and criminal systems." Identification via *closed-circuit TV cameras* (*CCTV*) is the subject of Bromby (2002, 2003).

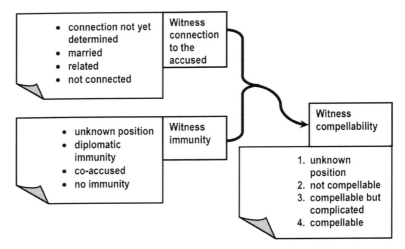

Fig. 4.4.2.5 The test for witness compellability in ADVOKATE. Redrawn from Bromby and Hall (2002, p. 146)

4.4.3 More on Taxonomies of Factors

It is important to realise that the taxonomy of factors in ADVOKATE is *ad hoc*, and is not necessarily uniform in eyewitness research.[33] For example, a basic distinction one comes across in the literature is between *estimator variables* and *system variables* affecting eyewitness testimony. In the lecture handouts of a course she has been teaching, Amina Memon pointed out:

> Evidence in criminal trials is often based upon eyewitness testimonies. A large part of what we know about eyewitness identification comes from empirical research on the factors influencing eyewitness performance. Research in this area can help us understand under what conditions witness evidence may be reliable.
>
> Estimator variables are factors over which the criminal justice system exerts little or no control. [Gary] Wells called these factors estimator variables because, although these variables may be varied in research, they cannot be controlled in the actual criminal situation and their influence on identification accuracy can at best only be estimated post hoc. We will focus on a number of estimator variables, in particular own race bias.

See Wells (2000), Wells and Olson (2003), Wells, Olson, and Charman (2003) Wells, Memon, and Penrod (2006).[34] By contrast, Memon pointed out:

---

[33] Various categories of persons hold beliefs about factors affecting the reliability of eyewitness testimony: Magnussen, Melinder, Stridbeck, and Raja (2010) has drawn a comparison, in that respect, of judges, jurors and the general public. Brigham (1981) discussed how lawyers see the accuracy of eyewitness evidence.

[34] Also see the website of Gary Wells: http://www.psychology.iastate.edu/~glwells/

4.4 ADVOKATE, and Assessing Eyewitness Suitability and Reliability

System variables are factors that can, in principle, be directly controlled by the criminal justice system to increase the accuracy of eyewitness evidence. Knowledge about these factors can lead to changes in practice to improve the quality of evidence obtained from eyewitnesses and reduce the likelihood of error.

Clearly, it is on some system variables that ADVOKATE can intervene. A useful two-page compendium of factors that make eyewitness evidence less reliable was published by Sheriff Marcus Stone, who is both a barrister (formed in Glasgow) and a psychology graduate, in the British periodical *Criminal Law & Justice Weekly* (Stone, 2009). Even though – or rather for the very reason – that was a popularisation paper intended for lawyers, the classification of *situational factors* that can contribute to errors of observation or reporting on the part of an eyewitness as presented by Stone comes handy. This classification is separate from *forgetting* and various *corruptions of memory*.

Situational factors can be subdivided into (1) features of *the nature of the event*, (2) the *conditions of observation*, and (3) the *condition of the witness*. The latter can be subdivided into (3a) *physical hindrances to observation*, and (3b) *mental factors affecting observation*. The latter concern what was the *focus* of the observation, as a person cannot attend to every visible thing simultaneously. What gains priority is what the observer considers important or urgent. If there is an assault in the street, the witness is likely to attend to that, but by the same token, the witness may not notice something else in the environment.

"A cross-examiner should always probe what a witness was actually looking at when the incident happened. Motivation may impair observation in other ways" (ibid., p. 533). *Emotion* intervenes. "Often eyewitnesses of crimes become agitated and partial even if they are unconnected with them. They often respond to events by becoming excited, angry, frightened or sympathetic which may develop into taking sides. This creates a risk that their hostility and thirst for justice might bend their perception of the facts" (ibid.). *Expectations* are another intervening factor. "A witness's mindset, namely, his expectations, may cause him to think that he sees what he expects where facts are uncertain or ambiguous. This could apply to hidden police looking out for attempted car thefts in an unlit carpark" (ibid.).

Physical hindrances to observation may include (ibid.):

- Limitations of eyesight: "Witnesses may have permanent limitations such like poor overall sight, weakness for short or long distances, colour blindness or variable sensitivity to poor light" (ibid.).
- Whether remedial measures for poor eyesight were taken: "Whether spectacles were worn at the time may be important" (ibid.).
- Whether the witness was wounded: "Victims' injuries may impair their ability to see things properly. They may be dazed or distracted by pain or bleeding" (ibid.).
- Health conditions: "Witnesses' awareness of a situation may also be diminished by illness" (ibid.).
- The effects of pharmaceuticals or narcotics: "Either prescribed or prohibited drugs may have incalculable effects on witnesses' appreciation of what happened" (ibid.). A particular case is alcohol: "However alcohol is the most

common physical source of interference with the efficiency of observation" (ibid.). The amount of alcohol intake has an effect: "Depending on the amount which witnesses have drunk and complex physiological process their state of consciousness may range from mild euphoria to complete confusion or coma" (ibid.).

Something that Stone did not include among "Physical hindrances to observation" were environmental obstacles. One thinks of false witnesses in judicial history, claiming to have seen from where they were things they could not possibly see, such as through a keyhole, or the case decried and derided by Voltaire, when members of the public came forth to accuse Jean Calas (the Huguenot executed in France for allegedly killing his own son because he intended to convert to Catholicism): some individuals claimed to have seen things happening in another part of town, or in enclosed space, which they could not possibly have watched.

Rather, in Stone's classification, that is a kind of phenomena that pertains to Stone's category 2, namely, "The Conditions of Observation". Factors include: *lighting, distance, weather*, and *obstructions*. For example, "If a witness was too far away for a clear view he might have filled in gaps in his evidence by discussion with others, inference or imagination" (ibid., p. 533), apart from the fact that "[e]stimates of distances by different witnesses often vary" (ibid.). There are subdivisions. Weather-related factors comprise meteorological phenomena ("Snow, rain, mist or fog reduce visibility"), sunshine ("Bright sunshine may dazzle observers"), how the observer was compelled to walk or stand ("Icy pavements or high windscan distact witnesses"), or then the conditions of transparent partitions ("Wet windows, windscreens or spectacles limit vision"). Obstructions may be fixed, or temporary: "Trees, bushes, hedges, walls, railings, people or vehicles blocking one's view may limit observation of something totally or partly", and this has an undesirable effect on the quality of the testimony: "This [limit on observability] may create a risk that testimony is completed by speculation or information from other persons" (ibid.). Stone remarked (ibid.):

> Criticism of these conditions [of observation] usually emerge in cross-examination. A prudent advocate should foresee this and fortify evidence against it in examination-in-chief.[35] This has the merit of preparing the witness for the challenge. Frequently witnesses who testified firmly in examination-in-chief will resist suggestions that they could not see what they claim.

Factors relating to the nature of event (this was Stone's category 1: I am adding labels to the subcategories) include: (1a) *duration of exposure*, (1b) *movement*, (1c) *watching several separate persons* – it may confuse witnesses, especially if those observed persons move in different directions, – (1d) *violence*, as the observer may become distraught, and focused on getting away, (1e) *ambiguous facts*, because that

---

[35] *Examination-in-chief* is when a lawyer asks questions of his own witness, as opposed to *cross-examination* by the lawyer of the other party, to the lawyer asking more questions of his own party's witness following the cross-examination, and to questions being asked by the judge.

is fertile ground for mistakes or doubts arising from impression, (1f) *salient facts*: if you were focused on a weapon being aimed at you, other things may be inaccessible to memory, even if registered subliminally, (1 g) *abstract qualities* (descriptions of *intangible facts* tend to be subjective), such as: (1gA) vehicle speeds, (1gB) distances, (1gC) dates, times, or intervals, (1gD) the sequence of events, (1gE) relationships between things, (1gF) dimensions, weights, and quantities (ibid.).

One may wonder how useful can a psychologist as an expert witness prove, when commenting about eyewitness testimony. Flowe, Finklea, and Ebbesen (2009) discussed the limitations of expert psychology testimony on eyewitness identification. This was in Cutler's (2009) *Expert Testimony on the Psychology of Eyewitness Identification*.

4.5 Policing: Organisational Aspects of Intelligence, and the Handling of Suspects

4.5.1 Organisational Problems of Police Intelligence Systems

Information theory was applied to the organisation of policing in *Crime and Information Theory*, a classic by Willmer (1970). That was the age of *unit beat policing*. Police officers on the beat would observe the territory they were policing, and a lot of *information* would come to their attention. Sheptycki points out (2004, p. 310) that Willmer observed (1970, pp. 24–34) "that, as the territory being policed becomes more densely populated, or the geographical remit more widely spread, it becomes increasingly difficult to translate [the information collected] into *intelligence*" (Sheptycki, 2004, p. 310). Already Willmer referred to still experimental computer applications.

The 1990s saw *re-tooling* at governmental institutions, including the policing sector, through the adoption of new information and communication technologies. New information and communication technology within the police (e.g., Chan, Brereton, Legosz, & Doran, 2001) is an application of the "information revolution" that is sometimes referred to as *e-policing*. This required reconfiguring of the ways work used to be done within organisations, so there was considerable organisational flux, inside law enforcement agencies just as this was happening also within other governmental institutions.

Criminologist and sociologist of law James Sheptycki was formed in the United Kingdom, and is based in Toronto, Canada. Both national realities are reflected in his work. Sheptycki (2004) is concerned with organisational pathologies in *police intelligence systems*. Concomitantly with the emergence of *e-policing* in the 1990s, another phenomenon came into being: policing put emphasis (as an aspiration if not in practice) on *intelligence-led policing*, in order to better deal with serious and organised crime. Data have to be collected and analysed, so that the resulting picture of the organised crime situation could assist law enforcement authorities in their fight against organised crime.

Prevention is as important indeed as investigation of crimes already perpetrated. The task of intelligence analysts is distinct from that of detectives, even though detectives have often tended to consider intelligence analysts as being subservient to the routine and needs of detectives. By contrast to the focus on formal models of intelligence systems as found in much of the literature about intelligent-led policing against serious and organised crime, Sheptycki (2004) drew upon his own empirical research (Sheptycki, 2003), and provided a lexicon of eleven organisational pathologies, organisational problems that bedevil how police information systems are organised.

Of Willmer (1970), Sheptycki (2004, p. 310) remarks: "As he described it, the intelligence function essentially consists in the acquisition of knowledge and the processing of that knowledge into meaningful and digestible packages that lead to action". Already at the time of *unit beat policing*, which was Willmer's, there already was a back-office professional role concerned with police intelligence: "He focused on the role of the 'collator' (a precursor to today's crime analysts) in helping to interpret information and smooth the processes of communication internal to the police organization" (Sheptycki, 2004, p. 310).

Link analysis techniques (see Section 6.1.2.2 below), which in their present form utterly depend upon computing, and are one of the forms of *data mining* technology (see Chapter 6 below), had been in existence since the First World War (Gilbreth & Gilbreth, 1917), being applied at the time to how to best design the layout of a machine shop based upon distances traveled during assembly operations. Harper and Harris (1975) described how to use tables and diagrams in order to apply link analysis to the analysis of organised crime. But link analysis by means of a computer was already reported about, albeit for a different kind of application, by Haygood, Teel, and Greening (1964).

Some of the computer applications to police work that were being pioneered in several countries at the time when Willmer (1970) was writing were "to criminal records, *modus operandi* searches, personal description searches and vehicle registration searches, as well as routine administrative tasks, but [Willmer claimed] that 'Great Britain appears to be alone in considering the application of computers to intelligence information' ([Willmer] 1970: 33)" (Sheptycki, 2004, pp. 310–311). The state of the art of *intelligence-led crime control* by the 1990s was discussed in Maguire (2000) and Maguire and John (1995), and both the professional roles (e.g., undercover officers, and tasked criminal informants) and the techniques (many of them computer-based) had become remarkably sophisticated (Sheptycki, 2004, p. 311). Visual surveillance devices and closed circuit television (CCTV) were becoming widespread.

In the United Kingdom, the National Intelligence Model (NIM) was imposed, whereas other European countries adopted their own approaches. "The dominant nomenclature in the UK context has been set down within the terms of the NIM, which stipulates a cycle in five phases (Sheptycki, 2004, p. 311). The first phase is "*direction* (when the 'customer's intelligence needs' are established)" (ibid.). The second phase is "*collection* (during which information is amassed)". The third phase is "*processing* (when the information is analysed and turned into 'intelligence

4.5 Policing: Organisational Aspects of Intelligence, and the Handling of Suspects

packages')". The fourth phase is "*dissemination* (when 'packages' are given to customers')". The fifth and last phase of the cycle is "*formal review* (when customers and providers jointly assess what has been accomplished and decide on the direction to take in the next round)" (ibid.).

The NIM cycle also has three levels. They correspond to increasing expanses of terrain, and were defined by the National Criminal Intelligence Service (2000, p. 8, cited by Sheptycki, 2004, pp. 311–312). Level 1 is *local issues*: "usually the crimes, criminals and other problems affecting a basic command unit or small force area". The scope of the crimes is defined as follows: "The scope of the crimes will be wide-ranging from low-value thefts to great seriousness such as murder. The handling of volume crime will be a particular issue at this level" (ibid.). Level 1 is at the level of one basic command unit. Level 2 is for regional tasking and coordinating groups. Level 2 is about *cross-border issues*: "usually the actions of a criminal or other specific problems affecting more than one basic command unit". Handling this will be the task of a group of basic communal police units, neighbouring forces of group of forces, and they may resort to other resources as well: Issues will be capable of resolution by Forces, perhaps with support from the National Crime Squad, HM [i.e., Her Majesty's] Customs and Excise, the National Criminal Intelligence Service, or other national resources". Key issues for those law-enforcement players involved "will be the identification of common problems, the exchange of appropriate data and the provision of resources for the common good" (ibid.). As to Level 3, it is about *serious organised crime*, and intelligence operations contemplated would be "usually operating on a national and international scale, requiring identification by proactive means and response primarily through targeting operations by dedicated units and a preventative response on a national basis" (ibid.).

There are differences in the criminological literature in how criminal markets and organised crime are described,[36] but Sheptycki (2004, p. 312) remarks: "What cannot be contested is that intelligence systems models are based on hierarchies of information flow. [...] A complicating factor is that the police sector is not a unified whole, but is itself a variegated institutional field", and moreover a host of other governmental agencies, such as Inland Revenue or benefits authorities, "also contribute to and draw on information circulating in the intelligence 'system'" (ibid.).

Sheptycki (2004, p. 313) identified eleven organisational pathologies affecting the sharing of criminal intelligence in a multi-agency setting. "These are: digital divide; linkage blindness; noise; intelligence overload; non-reporting; intelligence gaps; duplication; institutional friction; intelligence-hoarding and information silos; defensive data concentration; and the differences of occupational subculture" (ibid.).

The *digital divide* concerns both the difference of *information storage systems* (often because of *legacy systems*: data were historically stored at different times and using different coding structure), and the *communications divide*: Sheptycki (2004, p. 314) exemplified it by mentioning an incident when two little boys went missing

---

[36] Sheptycki (2004, p. 312) cites, concerning this, Block (1994), Gregory (1998), Hobbs (1998) – who responded to Gregor (1998), Levi (1998), and Williams and Savona (1995).

in 2001 in the Staffordshire constabulary area, and the search for them went on even as the boys had been found and taken to a police station in the neighbouring Cheshire constabulary area within an hour of being reported missing. "One implication of the digital divide is that intelligence analysis based on timely (ideally real-time) data is impossible" (ibid.).

In *crime series analysis*, Egger's book *Serial Murder* (1990) introduced the concept of *linkage blindness*. It describes the problem when, because of lack of adequate data, analysts fail to spot right away linkages in crime series. Sheptycki remarked (2004, p. 315): "When a crime series transgresses territorial boundaries, and the horizontal connections for sharing relevant intelligence are inadequate or non-existent, linkage blindness occurs. This is not the same issue as the digital divide, although it is related". To Sheptycki, the digital divide is a technical problem, whereas linkage blindness is a system problem. It typically is about personnel failing to adhere to standard practice as set down, for information sharing: "field observations indicated that, even where there is a rule-based framework for doing so, horizontal flow in information hierarchies is often poor because most effort is directed at ensuring vertical flow" (ibid.).

All information is subject to interpretation, but the flow of processed information circulating in the intelligence system is subjected to *noise*: much less useful information keeps arriving: "intelligence outputs are in fact a distorted form of the input, which itself may be of dubious value" (Sheptycki, 2004, p. 315). Sometimes, intelligence packages are described as *over-sanitised*; the processing of information into police intelligence being at a remove from origination is the reason for noise being produced (ibid., p. 316):

> The volume of noise in an information system seems to be related to the distance between the reporting, recording and interpretation of data. The greater the gaps between information-reporting, intelligence analysis and dissemination, the greater the capacity for generating noise. This is because police personnel who turn information into intelligence often know little about recording decisions. Analysts who operate at a degree removed from such decisions are less able to qualify their interpretation of specific intelligence properly.

In turn, noise is the cause of *intelligence overload*, which however "is also more than that. Across the policing sector there is a pronounced lack of analytical capacity and associated administrative support" (ibid.). On the one hand, analysts as being a resource are sometimes squandered, being put in charge of data input, and also of culling information considered to be no longer useful, or to be out of date. Out-of-date information often clutters up the information environment. On the other hand, as there often is a shortage of investigative personnel, analysts are frequently given tasks that pertain to investigation rather than analysis (ibid.). Therefore, there is less analytical manpower available than supposed to be in place, and this, coupled with voluminous intelligence-reporting, results in intelligence overload, and this in turn "can very quickly paralyse an intelligence system". What is more: "Undercapacity in relation to the volume of information throughput, because capacity is taken up in data input, periodic record-screening of investigative analysis, may further contribute to the undue production of noise" (ibid.).

4.5 Policing: Organisational Aspects of Intelligence, and the Handling of Suspects

Sheptycki (2004, p. 316) also identified a factor, *compulsive data demand*, which exacerbates intelligence overload. As surveillance is widespread, there is a tendency for demanding more data rather than better data, or better data analysis. "Observing the volume of data coming from the financial system, one intelligence officer likened the task of intelligence analysis to 'drinking from a fire-hose'" (ibid., p. 317). It has to be said that *data mining* capabilities, which we discuss in Chapter 6 below, are important for making better use of massive volumes of data from the financial system.

Another organisational pathology which Sheptycki identified (2004, pp. 317–318) is *non-reporting and non-recording relevant intelligence*. But recording in standardised formats is time-consuming, and it must be recognised that the requirements for resorting to *data mining* do nothing to alleviate this problem, quite to the contrary. It makes the *burden of paperwork* which afflicts the police even worse. But in terms of organisational pathologies affecting intelligence: "Intelligence-reporting rarely contributes to successful prosecution outcomes; therefore effort is put into making records associated directly with law enforcement 'case building' at the expense of intelligence-reporting" (ibid., p. 318). Lack of compatibility between databases results in the information not being integrated. Quite not by chance, Sheptycki mentions this while discussing non-reporting (ibid.). The latter is the cause of *intelligence gaps* that could have been prevented, and another outcome may be linkage blindness indeed.

Intelligence gaps, Sheptycki (ibid.) points out, may result from any of the pathologies listed earlier, and may also be "the product of the hierarchical nature of the intelligence system". The *nominals* of Level 1 of criminality in the NIM cycle explained earlier "are criminals whose ambit of activity is geographically narrowly circumscribed. Many of these are teenage boys and young men who are considered to be prolific offenders" (ibid.). In the *pyramid of criminality*, Sheptycki identified a significant intelligence gap between Levels 2 and 3, considering that Level 2 "nominals" are criminals of regional scope, and offenders with such territorial ambit include e.g. teams of burglars or armed robbers, when their "activities range across divisional and force boundaries. Level 3 'nominals' are understood to be serious criminals of national importance" (ibid.). Sheptycki quoted one police officer as saying: "The real problem is between the level twos and threes. You get what you might call a level two-and-a-half. These are criminals whose activities are beyond us. They may be drug dealers who travel to Manchester from here and we don't have the resources to take that on", whereas the National Crime Squad would consider such a suspect to be light-weight, and therefore a low priority, because that dealer is only turning over half a kilo narcotics per week (ibid., pp. 318–319).

An aspect of intelligence gaps is that as surveillance resources are scarce, it is difficult to focus them on a large population of suspects. Sheptycki also explained indeed that the nature of the targets themselves also contributes to the gap: because Level 1 nominals (i.e., local-level offenders) are perceived to be primarily opportunistic, and because surveillance of such individuals is perceived to be time-consuming, so it is crime hot spots that are preferably subjected to surveillance, whereas conventional mobile surveillance and telephone intercepts are considered by police officers to be suitable for "[n]ominals spanning the range at the 'top level' of Level 1 and into Level 2" (ibid., p. 319).

Duplication of efforts is another pathology identified by Sheptycki (ibid.). Another pathology is *institutional friction* (ibid., p. 320). It not only occurs when different agencies have to share intelligence collaboratively: "Particularly in large multi-functional organizations such as police departments, there is variability of definitions of 'the job', so that institutional friction can occur within an ostensibly unified command structure" (ibid.). Sheptycki notes that because of this kind of pathology, "intelligence products are but fricative emanations" (ibid.). "Institutional friction may result in a specific set of pathologies relating to the intelligence function: 'information-hoarding' and, what is but a structural expression of the same thing, 'information silos'" (ibid.). As taking credit for a "good pinch" is good for one's career prospects, one would try to monopolise some kinds of information. But, Sheptycki remarks, this is rather symptomatic of "the enforcement-based subcultures common in the police sector" (ibid., p. 320), whereas *intelligence-led policing* needs to obey a different logic, for it to work (ibid., p. 321). "Intelligence-hoarding is corrosive of the principles of intelligence-led policing. Hoarding need not be deliberate; it may be a *post hoc* rationalization for not communicating relevant information that stems, in the first instance, from institutional friction" (ibid.). Or then it may "be an expression of non-reporting or non-recording — such information, in effect, being 'hoarded' inside the head of the individual officer who finds the task of double-keying information too time consuming" (ibid.).

The difference with respect of *information silos* is that the latter "are the structural expression of hierarchical information systems" (ibid.). Intelligence is expected to flow upwards, in the intelligence system, but what is lost is "an emphasis on horizontal linkages between crime types. It may be more useful for linkages between intelligence relating to different 'sectors of criminality' ([such as] vehicle [theft] and drug crime) to be made at the local level, than for this information to flow to the top of their respective information silos" (ibid.), and only then either be disseminated back down the silo, or "be released out into the wider information environment from the top" (ibid.).

Yet another pathology identified by Sheptycki is *defensive data concentration*. As, owing to the very existence of the pathologies listed earlier, there is pressure to do something and achieve the goals that were set for players in the intelligence environment, "one obvious short-term solution is to take steps to gather relevant data for a given problem" (ibid.). As it is difficult to get data or to get an accurate strategic picture, extra efforts may go into the creation of a task-specific database (ibid., p. 322). This increases the demand on others (who are already over-stretched) in the police sector, for reporting for the purpose of building that task-specific database. But this reinforces the "focus on themes that are already enforcement priorities" (ibid.), so "strategic analysts may be systematically robbed of the chance to develop information about lesser-known problems that are not already systemically reported" (ibid.). More problems result from such defensive data concentration. One of those problems is that duplication is exacerbated (ibid.).

4.5 Policing: Organisational Aspects of Intelligence, and the Handling of Suspects 279

And finally, Sheptycki (2004, pp. 322–327) discusses the organisation pathology associated with *occupational subcultures*, first intra-agency, and then inter-agency. "The rivalry between detectives and uniformed patrol officers is standard fare in the policing literature (Reiner, 2000). Less is known about these sorts of rivalry in other parts of the police sector" (ibid., p. 323). Sheptycki examined how well the new job profile and type of expertise, namely, *crime [intelligence] analysis*, was "being introduced into an already established division of labour" (ibid.). One woman analyst, three years in her post, for the first two years had just been made to type memos, and it was only in the third year that she had worked with actual crime intelligence, which is what because of her training she was supposed to do in the first place (ibid.). Sheptycki then stated (ibid., pp. 323–324):

> It was not uncommon for young female staff trained as analysts to report being given 'inappropriate' tasks. Long-serving personnel may have difficulties in adapting their ways of thinking to accommodate the new intelligence-based approach. Detectives involved in policing at divisional level have built their role around crime investigation and arrest leading to successful prosecution. To detectives, information equates with evidence and so, in the words of one senior analyst, intelligence can be 'subverted into detections by another name'. In certain circumstances, the long-entrenched subcultural expectations of detective work may reduce the intelligence process to evidence gathering and evaluation. In contrast to detectives, analysts are trained to loom at information more broadly. They are not merely interested in the evidence in a criminal case, although they can be involved in that too. Rather, intelligence analysts provides tools for the discovery of trends and patterns and tries to explain why these occur (Dintino and Martens, 1983). Since the detective role is more long-standing and is a relatively high-status role within the police agencies (and key performance indicators reflect this), there is an observable tendency to co-opt crime analysis for the purposes of crime investigation. Some analysts clearly identify with the detective worldview. [...]

Sheptycki found such problems at various kinds of agencies. Because of chronic shortage of personnel, training or retraining of existing staff for them to carry out intelligence work may be perfunctory, or at any rate inadequate. This, however, he expected would solve itself "as younger cohorts come of age under the intelligence-led paradigm and move into positions of responsibility" (ibid., p. 324). Another aspect of the problem is that it is often the case that intelligence analysts are civilians working with the police, and therefore their career prospects are very limited. Moreover, their analytical skills are in demand elsewhere, especially in the financial sector, and therefore, having gained experience and training, analysts leave their jobs in police organisations and sell their skills for much higher rewards (ibid.). There also a problem with whether credit is properly given: "Intelligence officers frequently report that they do not receive the same acknowledgment for their role that detectives have traditionally claimed. The 'good pinch' looms large in this occupational milieu: crimes detected are granted higher status than crimes prevented" (ibid.). According to Sheptycki (ibid., p. 324), both such *intra-agency* subcultures divide problems, and problems with *inter-agency occupational subcultures* are variants of *institutional friction*. Inter-agency differences of terminology are also contributing factors, they "indicate contrasts in subcultural style" (ibid., p. 326), and when agencies are required to collaborate, "this may result in suboptimal working practices" (ibid.).

The literature of criminal intelligence analysis in the national context of the United States is covered in such texts as Carter (2004), IACP (2002), Loyka, Faggiani, and Karchmer (2005), Peterson (2005). Also see Ratcliffe (2008). Ratcliffe (2007), in a report concerning intelligence and crime analysis in the United States, pointed out (ibid., p. 14):

> Crime analysis is a term used to describe a broad range of activities and ideas. Of potentially greater value is the term problem analysis. Problem analysis stems from Herman Goldstein's concept of problem-oriented policing (1990) and has come to signify a form of crime analysis that is "conducted within the police agency [and] in which formal criminal justice theory, research methods, and comprehensive data collection and analysis procedures are used in a systematic way to conduct in-depth examination of, develop informed responses to, and evaluate crime and disorder problems" (Boba, 2003, 2). It is closely allied with the framework of problem-oriented policing, a process that not only concentrates on the identification and remedy of crime problems but also is a more comprehensive framework for the improvement of the police response to all aspects of their work (Scott, 2000). Problem solving is the thought process by which officers and analysts achieve their goals, and is often articulated through the SARA (Scanning, Analysis, Response, and Assessment)[37] process (Eck and Spelman, 1987). For our purposes here, we can consider crime analysis to be the overarching generic term that can collectively represent these more specific activities.

The introduction of information technology has speeded up the growth of crime analysis (Ratcliffe, 2007, pp. 14–15):

> Unlike criminal intelligence, crime analysis is a relatively new discipline within law enforcement. While criminal intelligence may have remained in the "murky backwaters of policing" for over one hundred years (Christopher, 2004, 179), it does at least have name recognition both internally and externally to law enforcement. By comparison, crime analysis is a young upstart whose growth has occurred largely as a result of the digitalization of the policing world. Only since the 1980s have significant numbers of police departments discovered that they were able to use data originally recorded for statistical purposes for more than just annual summaries of crime frequencies. Even with this discovery, the lack of suitable computer hardware and software applications inevitably hampered the growth of the crime analysis field. Only in the last decade or so have we seen the creation of off-the-shelf, commercial crime analysis products to replace programs that were previously created by programmers hired by police departments or on contract from universities. This growth has generated the professional field of crime analysis. Goldstein argues that "in a police agency in which individual officers may not know what has occurred outside the areas in which they work or during periods when they are not on duty, crime analysis has been the primary means for pooling information that may help solve crimes" (1990, 37).

Ratcliffe proceeded to dispel some misconceptions (2007, p. 15): "As there are misconceptions with criminal intelligence, so there are misconceptions with crime analysis." A variety of skills are required of the crime analyst: "Given the aim of exploring both crime events and broader trends in crime patterns, good crime analysts have to understand a wide range of technical and theoretical areas" (ibid.). Software is involved in the activities of the crime analyst: "an experienced crime

---

[37] See http://www.popcenter.org/about-SARA.htm concerning the SARA model.

analyst might have an understanding of quantitative research skills using a variety of software packages, probably uses a geographical information system to analyse spatio-temporal crime activity,[38] creates analysis products and conducts officer briefings, and has a knowledge of the basics of environmental criminology" (ibid.). It is a common misconception to mistake the output to be expected of a crime analyst, for management statistics: "the perception sometimes is that crime analysts just provide management with charts and breakdowns of overtime and sick leave or simple counts of the numbers of different crime types that have happened in the last week. These tasks are not crime analysis but are simply the provision of management statistics" (ibid.). This misuse of skills is demotivating for crime analysts: "Such requests for help in areas unrelated to crime can often be a considerable drain on the enthusiasm of some analysts, and police executives should be wary of allowing their analysts to engage in work that is far removed from the central aims of crime reduction and prevention" (ibid.). The skills of a crime analysts are covered in Clarke and Eck's (2005) *Crime Analysis for Problem Solvers in 60 Small Steps*.

4.5.2 Handling the Suspects: Equipment, Techniques, and Crucial Problems

4.5.2.1 Polygraph Tests: A Deeply Controversial Tool

In a paper from the controversy about probabilities in a judicial context, Allen and Pardo stated (2007b, p. 307)[39]:

> The inferences drawn from legal evidence may be understood in both probabilistic and explanatory terms. Consider evidence that a criminal defendant confessed while in police custody. To evaluate the strength of this evidence in supporting the conclusion that the defendant is guilty, one could try to assess the probability that guilty and innocent persons confess while in police custody.[40] Or one could make the same assessment based on any

---

[38] For example, Boba (2005) is concerned with crime mapping for the purposes of crime analysis.

[39] Cf. Allen and Pardo (2007b, p. 308): "[W]e are not uncompromising sceptics, and we even concede that the formal models may be useful in evaluating evidence and that it may not be unreasonable for parties to argue, or fact-finders to evaluate evidence, along the lines suggested by such models. To say that such models may be useful is not, however, to accept them as the sole or even a particularly reliable method of discovering the truth. Our objection is to scholarship arguing just that such models establish the correct or accurate probative value of evidence, and thus implying that any deviations from such models lead to inaccurate or irrational outcomes".

[40] False confessions are the subject of Gudjonsson (2001, 2006), Gudjonsson, Sigurdsson, Asgeirsdottir, and Sigfusdottir (2006) Gudjonsson, Sigurdsson, Asgeirsdottir, and Sigfusdottir (2007), Steingrimsdottir, Hreinsdottir, Gudjonsson, Sigurdsson, and Nielsen (2007), Sigurdsson and Gudjonsson (1996, 2001), Gudjonsson and Sigurdsson (1994), Gudjonsson and MacKeith (1982). Gisli Gudjonsson's team conducted that kind of research on, e.g., adolescents in places like Iceland or Denmark. Also see Levine, Kim, and Blair (2010), Blair (2005). Important research on false confessions was carried out in the U.S. by psychologist Saul Kassin and his team. See Kassin (2004, 2005), Kassin, Meissner, and Norwick (2005), Russano, Meissner, Narchet, and Kassin (2005), Kassin and Kiechel (1996). False confessions are also the subject of Redlich and

number of other characteristics shared by the defendant or the context of the confession. The problem of reference classes arise quite readily because each of these different classes would likely yield different results, some of which will take one closer to, and some further away from, the correct conclusion of whether this defendant in fact is guilty. Alternatively, one could evaluate how well the conclusion that the defendant is guilty explains the evidence of the confession. [fn. 1: Both approaches involve inductive inferences; the probability approach employs enumerative inferences and the explanation approach employs abductive inferences.] How well the defendant's guilt explains the evidence will depend on the strength of alternative explanations such as whether a false confession was coerced, or the defendant was trying to protect another person from conviction, or the police are lying about whether a confession was ever given, etc.

A witness may be inadvertently inaccurate. This is quite distinct from lying.[41] There exists a very vast literature about assessing the accuracy of eyewitness

---

Goodman (2003). Other works on false confessions include Leo, Drizin, Neufeld, Hall, and Vatner (2006), Leo and Ofshe (1998), Ofshe and Leo (1997a, 1997b), Santtila, Alkiora, Ekholm, and Niemi (1999) and Horsenlenberg, Merckelbach, and Josephs (2003). The concern of White (1997) is primarily with law, rather than psychology, concerning false confessions. Bem (1966) was concerned with inducing belief in false confessions.

Kassin and Norwick (2004) considered the relation between being innocent, and reasons why individuals sometimes waive their statutory right to remain silent during interrogation. In *Miranda v Arizona* [384 U.S. 436 (1966)], the United States Supreme Court ruled (384 U.S. 436 (1966)) that prior to any custodial interrogation the accused must be warned: (1) That he has a right to remain silent; (2) That any statement he does make may be used in evidence against him; (3) That he has the right to the presence of an attorney; (4) That if he cannot afford an attorney, one will be appointed for him prior to any questioning if he so desires. According to that ruling, unless and until these warnings or a waiver of these rights are demonstrated at the trial, no evidence obtained in the interrogation may be used against the accused.

[41] Memon, et al. (1998) are concerned with assessing the truthfulness of testimony, including of statements made by suspects during investigation. Also see Gisli Gudjonsson's (1992, revised 2003) *The Psychology of Interrogations, Confessions and Testimony*, as well as Aldert Vrij's (2000) *Detecting Lies and Deceit: The Psychology of Lying and Implications for Professional Practice*; cf. Vrij (1998b). Memon and Bull (1999) is a *Handbook of the Psychology of Interviewing*. Gudjonsson and Clark (1986) proposed a social psychological model of suggestibility in police interrogation. Police interrogations is the subject of Kassin (2006), Kassin et al. (2007), Kassin and Fong (1999), and Kassin and McNall (1991). Investigative interviewing is also the subject of Milne and Bull (1999) and of Gudjonsson (2007). White (1989) was concerned, from a legal viewpoint, with police trickery in inducing confessions. Police interrogations and confessions are the subject of Inbau, Reid, Buckley, and Jayne (2001). Daniel Lassiter edited the volume (2004) *Interrogations, Confessions and Entrapment*. Concerning *entrapment*, the term denotes such circumstances of obtainment of evidence that the perpetrator was deceived, by being allowed or even enabled or incited to commit an offence, with law enforcement personnel present or even participating. Osborne (1997, p. 298) remarked that in England, some cases

> clearly established that, even when policemen acting in plain clothes and participating in a crime go too far and incite criminals to commit offences which would otherwise not have been committed, the law of evidence will not be used to discipline the police. There is no defence of 'entrapment' known to English law and the law of evidence could not be used to create such a defence by the device of excluding otherwise admissible evidence. Where police had gone too far, the question of their misconduct will be dealt with in police disciplinary proceedings; but insofar the accused was concerned, entrapment would only be relevant to mitigate the sentence imposed, not to the question of admissibility.

identifications.[42] Especially the research of Elizabeth Loftus and her collaborators has cast heavy doubts on the reliability of eyewitness identifications[43] and of witnesses in general.

In his critique of Bayesian probabilistic accounts of judicial proof, Ron Allen has touched upon physiological symptoms being subjectively taken to be indicators of lying or otherwise. Allen did so, while pointing out problems with subjective Bayesianism, and in particular when discussing claims made by the philosopher Alvin Goldman (Allen, 2008a, p. 325):

> Alvin Goldman has tried to bring some order to all of this through an interesting theorem that demonstrates that under certain assumptions there is a positive probability of evidence increasing the probability of a truthful verdict, but in fact his theorem highlights the incompatibility of juridical proof and Bayesianism (Goldman, 1992, 245–52). Similar to the convergence to truth theorems, Goldman's proof requires objectively true likelihood ratios, but, outside of the rare occurrence of something like indisputable DNA, that condition never obtains at trial. The likelihood ratios that fact finders would create are just as subjective as their initial priors, and there is no means of adjudicating their differences. One juror might think sweating means lying and another that it is a sign of a witness striving to remember the truth, and so on.

Assumptions concerning the physiological symptoms of a person being interrogated, taken to be indicators of lying, underlie *polygraph tests*. Polygraph tests –

Concerning police interrogations, also see Leo's book (2008) *Police Interrogation and American Justice*. Out-of-court witness statements are the subject of Heaton-Armstrong, Wolchover, and Maxwell-Scott (2006). The psychology of confession evidence is the subject of Williamson (2007), Kassin and Gudjonsson (2004), Kassin and Wrightsman (1985), Kassin (1997), Kassin and Neumann (1997), Kassin and McNall (1991), Gudjonsson (1992). Confirmationism, which tends to confirm expectations of guilt, is the subject of Kassin, Goldstein, and Savitsky (2003). See Home Office (2003) for the codes of practice for the police in England and Wales.

[42] Suffice it to cite here Lindsay, Ross, Read, and Toglia (2006), Cutler and Penrod (1995), or Levine and Tapp (1982), Wells (2000), Wells, Memon, and Penrod (2006), Behrman and Davey (2001), Behrman and Richards (2005). Elsewhere in this book we have cited more specific literature from eyewitness research. By Gary Wells, see e.g. Wells (1978, 1984, 1985, 1988, 2000, 2006), Wells and Bradfield (1998, 1999), Wells and Charman (2005), Wells and Hryciw (1984), Wells and Leippe (1981), Wells and Loftus (1991), Wells and Murray (1983), Wells and Quinlivan (2009), Bradfield and Wells (2000), Bradfield, Wells, and Olson (2002), Clark and Wells (2007), Lindsay and Wells (1980), Luus and Wells (1994), Hasel and Wells (2006), Wells, Leippe, and Ostrom (1979a), and Wells, Lindsay, and Ferugson (1979b), Wells, Ferguson, and Lindsay (1981), Wells, Rydell, and Seelau (1993), Wells et al. (1998), Wells, et al. (2000), Wells, Olson, and Charman (2003), Wells, Memon, and Penrod (2006).

Bull (1979) was concerned with the effect of stereotypes on person identification, whereas Chance and Goldstein (1995) discussed, to say it with the title of their article, "The Other-Race Effect and Eyewitness Identification". Cf. Horry and Wright (2008), also on memory and *other-race faces*. Meissner and Brigham (2001) are concerned with concerned with the *own-race bias in memory for faces*.

Various categories of persons hold beliefs about factors affecting the reliability of eyewitness testimony: Magnussen, Melinder, Stridbeck, and Raja (2010) drew a comparison, in that respect, of judges, jurors and the general public.

[43] Loftus (1979, 1981a, 1981b, 1993b, 1998, 2003a, 2005), Loftus and Zanni (1975), Penrod, Loftus, and Winkler (1982), and Loftus and Greene (1980).

the subject of Vrij's (1998a) – albeit commonly performed in countries including the U.S., are frowned upon in European countries including the U.K. Nevertheless, AI research applied to polygraph testing has actually been carried out at Manchester Metropolitan University, in England. Clearly any results would not be applicable to law enforcement in Britain, as the British police does not use polygraph tests.

"The use of the polygraph is widespread in the USA. In the 1980s, it was believed that over one million tests were given every year" (ibid., p. 78), "includ[ing] tests as part of job selection, state security selection, and criminal investigation" (ibid., p. 78). "The number of cases since the introduction of the *Polygraph Protection Act* in 1988, which banned most tests for personnel selection purposes", resulted in a quantitatively dramatic decline in the global use of the polygraph in the United States, with the figures down to a 40,000 estimate (ibid., p. 78). "Other countries which are known to use polygraph tests to detect deception are for instance Israel, Japan, South Korea and Turkey", while "polygraph tests are not used in West European countries" (ibid., p. 78).

The two leading and probably most distinguished scientific polygraph researchers, David Raskin and David Lykken,[44] have engaged in prolonged controversy over the reliability and validity of various polygraph tests" (Vrij, 1998a, p. 79). "Several different polygraph tests exist. One of the first tests widely used was the relevant/irrelevant technique" (ibid., p. 79). "The control question test [CQT] is the polygraph test most widely used in the USA in criminal investigations" (ibid., p. 80). Higher arousal in the examinee in response to control questions than to relevant is considered by examiners to be an indicator of innocence. Yet, a flaw of this method is that the examinee must believe in the infallibility of the test and in the infallibility and fairness of the examiners, and often this would not be the way the examinees think. Innocent suspects may think that "if police methods are fallible enough to make them falsely suspicious, their polygraph test also may be fallible" (ibid., p. 86). They may "fear that the polygraph examiner will misjudge them" (ibid.); "may distrust the polygraph" and be aware of how controversial it is; may be generally fearful persons who "might respond more to the relevant questions than to the control questions"; and "even though innocent, ha[ve] an emotional reaction to the events involved in the crime" (Vrij, ibid.): these criticisms are based on Ekman (1985).

Moreover, there is the risk that guilty suspects would successfully resort to physical or mental countermeasures:

> Physical countermeasures include physical activities such as tongue biting and foot tensing (by pressing the toes against the floor). This can for instance be done when answering the control questions, resulting in a stronger physical response concerning these questions (Vrij, ibid., p. 94),

and that would thwart expectations for the profile of physiological responses from a guilty suspect, or may be misinterpreted by the polygraph examiner as though the examinee was innocent (if the examiner could reach conclusions at all).

---

[44] By Lykken, see his book (1998) *A Tremor in the Blood: Uses and Abuses of the Lie Detector.*

An apparently rather better method than the CQT, yet one that is overlooked in the U.S. (while being more often used in Japan and Israel than the CQT) is the *guilty knowledge test* (GKT), with questions being asked in a multiple choice format, and based on the assumption that knowledge known only by the actual perpetrator and by the police (including the examiner) would trigger higher arousal when mentioned among the optional answers; yet the GKT has limited applicability (Vrij, ibid., pp. 87–89).

Also for this technique, there is the risk that a guilty suspect would successfully resort to countermeasures (Vrij, ibid., p. 94):

> Examples of mental countermeasure techniques are counting sheep or counting backward. The result of this technique will be that the examinee does not process the questions (control question test) or the alternatives (guilty knowledge test). As a result, a similar physical response to each question or each question alternative is likely, which will lead to an inconclusive test outcome.

Whereas some researchers found countermeasures ineffective, the manner the experiment was conducted may have been flawed (ibid.), and actually "[s]everal studies showed that training in countermeasures can be very effective in defeating polygraph tests" (ibid.).[45] In Britain, the introduction of polygraph tests was considered, but the 1986 final report of the British Psychological Society rejected the validity of the tool. Not only is the literature divided between opponents and supporters; there also are disagreements within the polygraph community. Notwithstanding the fact that psychologists in Britain have long considered polygraph tests anathema, and in fact the fallibility of the technology makes the argument all the more weak for introducing it in such countries where it is not used, there have been developments in the United Kingdom that have been most unwelcome to psychologists in the country who have looked into the domain.

In 2008, a weaker technology than even polygraphs proper, namely, voice-based lie detectors which analyse how even minimally tremulous the voice is, of an interlocutor over the phone, were introduced by the Department of Work and Pensions for testing people who claim benefits. The matter found its way into a late evening news broadcast on BBC Radio 4, on 7 May 2008. The head of a professional association of psychologists sharply criticised this move, and pointed out that studies found voice-based lie detection to be no better than chance.

The only concession he made was that at best, the technique could be used in order to deter, rather than to detect. (Tested claimants are told.) The minister of Work and Pensions was then interviewed, and was apparently not even realising

---

[45] Apart from the already mentioned Ekman (1985), other works by Ekman about the detection of deception include Ekman and O'Sullivan (1989, 1991a, 1991b, 2006), Tsiamyrtzis et al. (2005), Bugental, Shennum, Frank, and Ekman (2000), Ecoff, Ekman, Mage, and Frank (2000), Ekman, Friesen, and O'Sullivan (1988), Ekman, O'Sullivan, Friesen, and Scherer (1991), Ekman, O'Sullivan, and Frank (1999), Ekman (1981, 1988a, 1988b, 1989, 1996, 1997a, 1997b), Frank and Ekman (1997), Ekman and Frank (1993), O'Sullivan, Ekman, and Friesen (1988), and Ekman and Friesen (1969, 1974). Also see the book by Frank and Ekman (2003). In particular, Feinbert, Blascovich, Cacioppo, Davidson, and Ekman (2002) is a report about polygraph tests.

how damning the psychologist's opinion was (even though not to sound jarring, it was diplomatically somewhat understated), and in particular, what the implication is, if a technique is no better than chance. Undeterred, the minister insisted that it would help to detect fraud, and that the potential was considerable. It wouldn't be the only criterion, he conceded, for deciding whether a benefit claimant is genuine.

Even the psychologist's concession that this ineffectual technique may be useful at most as a deterrent, is up to a point humiliating for a claimant, as it may be taken to imply that a claimant would typically come from the less educated strata of society, and as he or she would gullibly believe that lie detection over the phone is genuine, he or she would be deterred from making a false claim. This does no justice to the claimant who, educated enough to believe that this is a quack technology, could only be expected to respond with a stressed voice. As pointed out by the psychologist interviewed, a person's voice may be under stress for various reasons. Insincerity is just one.

In the autumn of 2010, Britain's new coalition government – flatly though implicitly – disregarded the country's traditional aversion to lie detectors. On 20 September, Andrew Porter and Rosa Prince (2010) reported on the front page of *The Daily Telegraph*:

> [Deputy prime minister] Nick Clegg has singled out the middle class for being targeted for lie detector tests as part of greater scrutiny of their tax affairs. [...] Middle-class professionals could be subjected to lie detector tests under plans for private debt collection agencies to take on responsibility from Her Majesty's Revenue and Custom. [...]

One wonders whether such plan-making paid any attention to the country's native understandings concerning lie detectors. It should have been a matter of concern as well whether privatising tax collection on a national scale – it was already in force in some places at the municipal level – would have been a safe practice anyway, in face of anecdotal indications that private tax collectors at least on occasion disregard taxpayers' entitlements because the conflict of interests is apparently resolved to the benefit of greater profits to the firm. Perhaps against such a backdrop, whether lie detectors can truly be depended upon was not the actual overriding criterion.

The news had come along with other news about private companies from over the ocean going to be permitted to offer academic degrees in Britain, thus competing with a crowded local academic market that had already taken on lowbrow features in the last two decades. But perhaps whether this further commercialisation would benefit academic quality is a moot question. Arguably what matters is that some private capital would see a return on its investments in areas that were previously off limits. This raises the question whether the "expertise" for collecting taxes privately (i.e., for *taxfarming*) was going to be imported as well, from where lie detectors *are* admitted as evidence. This in turn calls for a reflection, whether an argument *ad veritatem*, and scientific truth, have any role to play when the political will exists anyway to enact this or that policy. At any rate, it can hardly be the case that if Britain is going to adopt lie detectors indeed, this would be evidence that a scholarly consensus in their favour is forming on both sides of the ocean.

4.5.2.2 A Caution Against Unquestioned Assumptions: A Digression on Juridic Cultures and the Evidentiary Value of Self-Incriminating Confessions

It is important to realise that the role of confession is not fixed in the history of ideas, but is a variable parameter of the legal system of a given society and culture. It is crucial for this point to be made, in an interdisciplinary book like this one, catering to audiences in a number of disciplines, such as computer scientists; audiences who therefore, in part will not be familiar with legal history. Not only are we forced to skip across jurisdictional contexts, here discussing a tool from Italy intended for local procedure, there discussing topics especially relevant for the United States, or the context of the United Kingdom (thus, the law of England and Wales, or the law of Scotland; also note that by the 2000s, in the aftermath of devolution, in some domains Wales has begun to introduce laws autonomously).

The unavoidable risks of mix-up also affect something more basic, which is the history of human cultures. It would be an error to hold the unquestioned belief that the testimony of the defendant has always and everywhere had a role in judicial proceedings, and in particular, that confessions carry value in all jurisdictions of criminal law. And yet, the medieval and early modern practice of torture during interrogation in Continental Europe entirely depended upon the value ascribed to confession.

From a present-day perspective, wrongful convictions of factually innocent defendants are discussed, e.g., by Rattner (1988). Regardless of polygraph tests, it has been claimed that policy could modify the incentives for guilty suspects to lie. Consider the suspects' *right to remain silent* (i.e., the right not to answer questions during police interrogations: it is a privilege against self-incrimination). South African legal scholar Pamela J. Schwikkard (2008) "looks at the status and application of the right to remain silent in a number of common law jurisdictions." (Her paper was in journal from Berkeley, California.) Her paper "explores the multiple rationales said to underlie the right to remain silent and concludes that there is only one that withstands scrutiny, namely, that the right to remain silent assists in preventing the abuse of public power." She argued that the right to remain silent is therefore *instrumental* in nature. This has implications for how to assess (against that stated rationale) infringements of the right to remain silent.[46] She then presents an argument and a counterargument (ibid.):

---

[46] Concerning differences among jurisdiction in regard to the right to remain silent, Schwikkard (2008) pointed out: "At the pre-trial stage the right to remain silent gives the accused immunity for his or her refusal to answer questions. And if he or she does make any admission or confession the prosecution must establish that such a statement was made voluntarily before it will be admitted into evidence — or phrased negatively without compulsion. These general principles are shared by most common-law countries with functioning democracies. The right to remain silent at trial grants the accused immunity from testifying. This too is a common feature of the Anglo-American jurisdictions surveyed. But nowhere is it an absolute right and depending on the circumstances there may be consequences for remaining silent. However, most of the jurisdictions surveyed do not tolerate imprisonment being imposed for the exercise of the right to silence. Although this cannot

Accordingly, if appropriate safeguards are in place minor encroachments such as the drawing of adverse inferences from silence should not create undue concern. However, given both the normative and instrumental value of the right to remain silent, it would be foolish to undermine the right in the absence of clear utilitarian gains for doing so and infringements should never be viewed as justified in the absence of appropriate safeguards against the abuse of public power.

According to a game-theoretic analysis by Seidmann and Stein (2000), this *right to silence* for suspects ultimately helps the innocent by reducing the likelihood that they would be convicted:

> A guilty suspect's self-interested response to questioning can impose externalities, in the form of wrongful conviction, on innocent suspects and defendants who tell the truth but cannot corroborate their stories. Absent the right to silence, guilty suspects and defendants would make false exculpatory statements if they believed that their lies were unlikely to be exposed. Aware of these incentives, triers of fact would rationally discount the probative value[47] of uncorroborated exculpatory statements at the expense of innocent defendants who could not corroborate their true exculpatory statements. Because the right to silence is available, innocent defendants tell the truth while guilty defendants rationally exercise the right when they fear that lying is exceedingly risky. [...]

In English law, "if the police are relying on a *confession* then by virtue of s. 76 of the 1984 Act the court needs to investigate the circumstances in which the confession was obtained to see whether it is admissible, that is whether it was obtained by *oppression* or whether there is anything in all the surrounding circumstances which might render it *unreliable*" (Osborne, 1997, p. 45). Moreover, "a confession may be excluded even if it is not *unreliable* if the circumstances in which it was obtained lead to the conclusion that the admission of the evidence could have an adverse effect on the fairness of the proceedings" (ibid.). Typically, the exclusion of confessions is in connection with police misconduct or omission.

Moreover, generally speaking: "Confessions are usually used as ground truth but are not 100 per cent reliable": so Vrij (1998a, p. 89), who discusses experiments with polygraph examinations. In fact, even "people considered as guilty by virtue of

---

be said to be true of all common law jurisdictions it would appear that in respect of those falling under the jurisdiction of the European Court of Human Rights that imprisonment as a sanction for silence will not be tolerated." Nevertheless (ibid., fn. 7): "Ireland for example has a number of legislative provisions authorising imprisonment consequent upon the withholding of information". There also is some variation in North America; for example: "In Canada the courts have held that drawing adverse inferences from silence at both the pre-trial and trial stages is unconstitutional. Nevertheless there are also exceptions to this prohibition, for example, an adverse inference may be drawn from the pre-trial failure to disclose an alibi defence." Importantly, in the United States the right to silence is not recognised to corporations: "The United States Supreme Court has also held that the Fifth Amendment does not apply to corporate entities."

[47] "Probative value is a relational concept that expresses the strength with which evidence supports an inference to a given conclusion. It is a crucial concept for determining admissibility (see Fed[eral] R[ules of] Evid[ence] 403, which instructs judges to exclude evidence when its probative value is substantially outweighted by its prejudicial, confusing, or duplicative effect) and for determining whether parties have satisfied their burdens of proof" (Allen & Pardo, 2007a, p. 108, fn. 2).

4.5 Policing: Organisational Aspects of Intelligence, and the Handling of Suspects

a confession may actually be innocent, as some innocent people do confess" (ibid.). "Criminal defense lawyers know how difficult it is to overcome a confession in a criminal trial, for juries find it hard to fathom why anyone would falsely implicate oneself" (Williams, 1996).

Bear in mind that the importance of a confession for convicting a defendant has not been a constant in legal history. Prior to the transition from the *rules of quantum and weight of proof* in Continental Europe to the *free judicial evaluation of the evidence* on the part of the fact-finder (the court), the prevalence of torture during the Middle Ages and the early modern period[48] depended on its being necessary to have a confession in order to convict. In Roman law, the confession of the accused was considered to be the best incriminating evidence, and it was this conception that determined the approach to confession in medieval Europe.

At the other extreme, there is rabbinic law, which deprives of evidentiary value the confession of one who is incriminating him- or herself, and this both in such criminal cases that could result in a capital sentence, and in such cases in which confession would result in oneself having to undergo divorce, or in one's alleged paramour having to divorce her husband, or in her child being considered illegitimate.[49]

A self-incriminating confession only has financial consequences, if any apply. Because of self-incriminating confessions having no value in capital criminal cases according to Jewish law, there was no incentive for torture as intended to obtain a confession: the law enforcers' motivation to extort a confession from a suspect perpetrator who could face the death penalty is absent ab initio. In such cases, conviction rests on two testimonies by eyewitnesses being in agreement and not having been disproven. For this rule of disallowing the court relying upon the defendant's confession, various explanations were historically offered by jurists within Jewish law:

- the testimony of a next of kin is not valid, and a person's is his own closest next of kin;
- its being unethical, indeed unlawful to commit suicide, including by self-incrimination;
- as well as (Maimonides' *Hilkhot Sanhedrin* 18:7) the risk that the confession not be truthful because of impaired mental capacity when giving it, or because a would-be suicide would falsely accuse himself in order to bring about his own death.

Criminal law in Israel is not according to rabbinic law, and in many respects (except the absence of the jury) resembles the Anglo-American system, but quite possibly there being a *right to silence* of the suspect during interrogation already by the

---

[48] See Nissan (2001b), Langbein (1977), Sbriccoli (1991), Fiorelli (1953–1954).

[49] Shereshevsky (1960/61), and cf. s.v. *hoda'at ba'al-din* in the *Encyclopaedia Talmudica*. Cf. Goldin (1952), Kirschenbaum (1970), Mendelsohn (1891, and edn. 1968).

mid-century owes no less to English law than to the influence of traditional Jewish law. (In England and Wales, the *right to silence* was gradually weakened during the 1990s. Note that in England, before 1898 a defendant in a trial was not allowed to testify at the same trial.)

Interestingly, the same confession that could not have effect in a capital criminal case under rabbinic law, *would*, under the same legal system, have effect in a civil case related to the same crime (e.g., the confessing adulteress loses the money to which, according to her nuptial contract, she would have entitled if divorced or a widow, regardless of her marriage surviving the confession in case her husband chooses not to believe her confession; and a confessing would-be adulterer who claims to be the father of the child of a woman married to somebody else becomes liable to pay for the child's maintenance, without the child's status being modified detrimentally because of the confession of his self-alleged father).

4.5.2.3 Computerised Identity Parades (Lineups)

In police practice, *identity parades* (also called *line-ups* or *lineups*) are means for identifying suspects. This is one of the ways in which facial identification evidence can be used by the police in order to identify suspects, by interviewing victims or eyewitnesses. The other way for using facial identification evidence during an investigation is to have victims or eyewitnesses view mugshots or, increasingly, *facial composites*: we devote Section 8.2.2 to the latter, within our chapter on the forensic sciences. Facial composites are appropriate when the police only have a verbal description of an offender. It is when the police already have some suspect that an identity parade can be resorted to.

In an identity parade, a victim or an eyewitness is required to recognise a suspect who is standing alongside others (known innocents, called *foils* or *look-alikes*). "On the other side of a screen, the victim studies them and picks out the one they think committed the crime. It is always stressed it is a one-sided mirror and the criminals [sic] cannot see the victims" (Backway, 2007). Identity parades are a domain of application for computing, and extant computerised alternatives to identity parades are relatively undemanding in terms of how sophisticated the computer techniques are.

In Britain, such a system was introduced in police practice around 2002. "The system is used across the country and [apart from the one described] there are around five other identification sites in London" (Backway, 2007). At the identification unit described, there are four police officers and three civilian staff. A video camera is used to record a video clip of the suspect, and other video clips of persons who look like the suspect are retrieved, and stored on an "ID parade disc". Hopefully there is nothing in the backdrop that would make the video clip with the suspect different from the other video clips on the disc. "There are around 25,000 images of volunteers stored on the database" (ibid.). "No images of suspects are stored on the system. The only copy is on the disc" (ibid.). "If no further action is taken, the disc and the image are destroyed" (ibid.). At the identification unit in South East London described by Helen Backway, around seven ID parade discs are created on a day.

4.5 Policing: Organisational Aspects of Intelligence, and the Handling of Suspects

Few forces use identity (ID) parades any more and things are a lot more sophisticated. At the territorial policing identification command, which deals with crimes in Bexley, Bromley, Lewisham and Greenwich [four boroughs in South East London], it is all done on video. In any crime where identity might be an issue, after a suspect is arrested they come into the ID suite at Lewisham police station in Lewisham High Street. They record a 15-second video clip and the image is fed into a computer, where eight similar images are chosen from the database. The suspect and their solicitor are given the option to change any of the similar images. Finally, the nine pictures are put onto a disc which is sealed and stored until the witness or witnesses come in. Rather than having to face the "criminal", the witness can be ushered into the room and watch the nine video clips as many times as they want to (Backway, 2007).

Arguably, such sequential viewing is not the same as watching a line up with physical presence, with several persons in view at a glance. Yet, there are advantages, too. "The beauty of the system being computerised is if a crime is committed away from where someone lives or if someone is housebound or in hospital, a laptop can be taken to them" (Backway, 2007). A sergeant, who pointed out that "witnesses identify the suspect in about half of all cases" (ibid.), remarked about the advantages of the video ID system: "We can get more done in a shorter period of time. This is better for witnesses and for suspects as it leads to early resolution of cases. It is also less intimidating for witnesses" (ibid.).

That same sergeant is quoted as saying: "We do not find eight people who look exactly the same. The law says we have to supply a parade which is a reasonable test of the ability of a witness to identify a person they have seen who was involved in an offence. They should resemble the person in image, height and general appearance" (ibid.). Isn't there a risk that witnesses would find it more difficult to evaluate the height of persons in the video clips? In general, it is known that witnesses tend to overestimate the stature of a person (and men, their own stature). Besides, Wells (1993) "warns against attempting to find foils that resemble the suspect as closely as possible" (Cutler & Penrod, 1995, p. 203). "The computer system is also used for more crimes than the previous ID parade process" (Backway, 2007). The inspector who heads the identification unit stated: "Years ago, we did ID parades only for serious cases. But the Crown Prosecution Service decided it should be done in any case when ID is an issue" (ibid.).

Amina Memon's eyewitness laboratory at the University of Aberdeen has carried out a project, funded by the Scottish Institute of Policing Research, to conduct experiments with VIPER, a video identity parade system adopted by Scotland police. Live parades have now been largely replaced by video parades; this has been made possible by development of the Video Identification Parade Electronic Recording (VIPER) system. "The procedure for administering VIPER is to show the entire lineup twice,[50] unless there is unequivocal identification and showing the witness the lineup again would cause distress to the witness" (Memon, 2008). At Memon's laboratory, Catriona Havard conducted work on child witnesses identification

---

[50] Hinz and Pezdek (2001) discussed the effect of exposure to multiple lineups on face identification accuracy.

abilities using VIPER. In a field evaluation, "Amina Memon, Catriona Havard, Brian Clifford and Fiona Gabbert analysed the responses of 1718 real witnesses who viewed video parades conducted in Scotland in 2008. The major variables of interest were; characteristics of the witness, characteristics of the suspect, offence type, delay since incident and aspects of the VIPER procedure" (ibid.). Among the findings: "In terms of identification outcome, the under 16 s (as compared to over 16 s) made more suspect identifications (81% vs. 67%) and fewer foil identifications (15% vs. 24%). Overall, children (there were 32 children under the age of 9 years) and young adults (Under 16 s and the 16-25 year-olds) made more suspect identifications and fewer foil identifications than adults aged 26–40; middle aged adults and adults over the age of 61." (ibid.).

There are quantitative models for assessing the diagnostic value of identity parades.[51] The following is quoted from Michon and Pakes (1995, pp. 521–522), who had previously discussed models for assessing evidential strength (e.g., Bayesian models and weighed average models, for which see in Chapter 2 above):

> Crucial to these models, irrespective of exactly how their belief revisions are computed, is how pieces of evidence are weighed. This evaluation determines the change in beliefs under the influence of new information. Wagenaar, Van Koppen and Crombag (1993) describe this as the assessment of the diagnostic value of pieces of evidence. What a piece of evidence tells you about the guilt of a suspect can be derived from a performance table. In Wagenaar and Veefkind (1992) the diagnostic value of line-ups for person identification is assessed. [...] Diagnostic value is the ratio of hits and false alarms which in this case is 75 per cent divided by 5 per cent equals 15. This means that if a suspect has been recognised in a line-up, she or he is 15 times more likely to be guilty than innocent. This value can be used in the computations concerning guilt or innocence.

---

[51] Besides, e.g. Valentine, Darling, and Memon (2007) researched whether strict rules and moving images increase the reliability of sequential identification procedures. In Darling, Valentine, and Memon (2008), those same authors discussed the selection of lineup foils in operational contexts. Valentine, Darling, and Memon (2006) were concerned with how to enhance the effectiveness of identification procedures. Memon and Gabbert (2003a) discussed the effects of a sequential lineup. Kneller, Memon, and Stevenage (2002) contrasted the decision processes of accurate and inaccurate witnesses, when viewing simultaneous vs. sequential lineups. Valentine, Pickering, and Darling (2003) tried to identify predictors of the outcome of real lineups. Garrioch and Brimacombe (2001) discussed the impact of lineup administrators' expectations on eyewitness confidence. The effects of post-identification feedback on eyewitnesses was also discussed in the literature (the risk is forced *confabulation*: witnesses will be influenced into remembering differently, by making inferences, and this may be an effect of their having been discussing their recollections). See, e.g., Wells and Bradfield (1998), Bradfield et al. (2002), Wright and Skagerberg (2007), Hafstad, Memon, and Logie (2004), and Hanba and Zaragoza (2007). Memon and Gabbert (2003b) tried to find up such arrangements at lineups that would enhance the identification accuracy of old witnesses.

Journals where papers at the interface of psychology, law and criminology are published include the *Journal of Applied Psychology*; the *Journal of Experimental Psychology: Applied*; the journal *Law and Human Behaviour*; the journal *Applied Cognitive Psychology*; the *Journal of Personality and Social Psychology*; the journal *Legal and Criminological Psychology*; the journal *Memory and Cognition*; as well as the *Psychonomic Bulletin & Review*; and the journals *Psychology, Public Policy and Law*; and *Memory*.

The empirical assessment of the diagnostic value of certain pieces of evidence does not imply that naive decision-makers will give a positive identification in a line-up the proper weight. In the cases they analysed Wagenaar, Van Koppen and Crombag (1993) claim that they found several instances in which judges under or over-valued certain pieces of evidence in spite of sound empirical findings concerning the value of that evidence.

Peter van Koppen (1995, p. 591) remarked: "Research on identification line-ups [...] has shown that the diagnostic value of a splendidly performed line-up is about 15 (Wagenaar & Veefkind, 1992), but what if not all the requirements are met to call it a very good line-up? And even then, some argue, the present tradition of laboratory research does not apply to forensic practice (Bekerian, 1993; Egeth, 1993; Wells, 1993; Yuille, 1993)". Cf. Penrod (2005).

Steven Clark and Gary Wells discussed the diagnosticity of lineups when there are more than one witness: "It is not uncommon for there to be multiple eyewitnesses to a crime, each of whom is later shown a lineup. How is the probative value, or diagnosticity, of such multiple-witness identifications to be evaluated?" (ibid., from the abstract). Their article

> calculates response diagnosticity for multiple witnesses and shows how diagnostic probabilities change across various combinations of consistent and inconsistent witness responses. Multiple-witness diagnosticity is examined across variation in the conditions of observation, lineup composition, and lineup presentation. In general, the diagnostic probabilities of guilt were shown to increase with the addition of suspect identifications and decrease with the addition of nonidentifications.

As a safeguard enforced (e.g., in the United States) against erroneous conviction resulting from mistaken identification, there is the presence of counsel (a defence lawyer) at post-indictment corporeal lineups. Nevertheless, this right of criminal defendants does not extend to photoarrays or any identifications tests conducted prior to indictment (Cutler & Penrod, 1995, pp. 205–208). It is based on the assumption "that attorneys recognise suggestive identification procedures when they encounter them" (ibid., p. 206). This is the *attorney sensitivity* assumption.

There also is a *judge sensitivity* assumption: "An attorney who believes that suggestive identification procedures rendered an identification equivocal will make this argument in a motion to suppress the identification evidence. This motion would contain a description of the procedures believed by the attorney to be suggestive" (ibid.), on the assumption that also judges, not only attorneys, "can accurately discriminate between procedures that differ in level of suggestiveness" (ibid.). *Jury sensitivity* is more problematic.

In Section 2.4 above, we considered the *reference-class problem*. Allen and Pardo remarked (2007a, pp. 113–114):

> The blue bus hypothetical with which we began this paper [and quoted in Sec. 2.4 above] exemplifies the general implications of reference classes, and those implications would hold for practically any attempt to quantify a priori the probative value of evidence. Consider another, and more realistic, example — that of an eyewitness identification made at a lineup. Any attempt to quantify the likelihood ratio of this evidence (the probability of picking the defendant given that he or she did it divided by the probability of picking him or her given that somebody else did it) quickly runs into the reference-class problem. Do we take the ratios of all identifications ever made? Those made (or not made, depending on the

circumstance) across racial differences? Those made by this witness? Those made by this witness under similar lighting conditions? Those made on the same day of the week, or month, or year, and so on? In each case, the reference class will likely change, and hence the quantified value will as well. But the evidence, the identification, has not changed. Thus it has no fixed, privileged, quantified value — save the event itself, which has a value of one or zero.

The demonstration above reveals several points. First, the value of evidence is not its likelihood ratio given a certain specified reference class. Evidence has countless likelihood ratios corresponding to its various reference classes. An explanation or justification for choosing any particular one must be provided, and there will invariably be reasonable alternatives. Second, for the same reason, the value of evidence is not, alternatively, its information gain in a given context, namely, the increase in probability of a hypothesis (for example, the defendant did it) from the prior probability without the evidence. This view still requires a likelihood-ratio calculation based on a chosen reference class; it just combines that likelihood with the prior probability. Third, instead of capturing the probative value of evidence, the various statistics or likelihood ratios flowing from various reference classes are just more evidence and, as such, must themselves be interpreted and explained.

There is a body of research on the effects of *lineup instruction bias*, and whereas in some experiments, subjects were aware that they were participating in an experiment, and the suggestibility effect resulted in a major increase in incorrect identifications, some other scholars reported experiments in which false identification rates did not differ significantly with biased instructions (Malpass & Devine, 1981; Cutler, Penrod, & Martens, 1987; Paley & Geiselman, 1989), and this was ascribed to the subjects being unaware that the perpetration event was not real but simulated (Maas & Köhnken, 1989), but the latter result is disputed in Cutler and Penrod (1995, p. 202).

Other kinds of bias are *foil bias* (ibid., pp. 202–203; Wells, 1993), *clothing bias* (Cutler & Penrod, 1995, pp. 203–204), and *presentation bias* (ibid., pp. 204–205), i.e., how the suspects and the *foils* (called *fillers* in the U.S.) are presented to eyewitnesses. Craig Osborne (1997, p. 307) points out a problem with the use of photographs:

> If the police already have a particular suspect in mind, or indeed have arrested anyone, there is no need for the use of photographs. Photographs should be used to enable the police to get some idea as to who might be a suspect where they have no immediate candidate. If there is a suspect then the police should go straight to the stage of identification parade because obviously there is less evidential value in such a parade where a witness has already recently identified a photograph.
>
> In a case where photographs have been used the defence are placed in a great dilemma. The defence would normally wish to cross-examine a witness searchingly about all matters relevant to his recollection and the circumstances of identification. The danger of course is that if they do this some reference to photographs will come out and the more alert members of the jury will inevitably infer that since the police had a photograph of the accused, the accused must have a criminal record.

"None of this should be confused with the situation where the police are trying to trace a *known* wanted person's whereabouts, e.g., by showing a photograph door-to-door or on television" (ibid., p. 308).

In Italy, an identity parade is called a *confronto all'americana*, i.e., literally: "a face-to-face confrontation the way they do it in America". A philologist, Stefano

Caruso, felt able to insert that name in the title of a scholarly article (Caruso, 2001), to describe a somewhat similar episode from medieval hagiography, namely, from the Greek-language *Life [and Miracles]* of St. Elias the Cave-Dweller from Reggio in Calabria, born in that city ca. 860, and who died in Melicuccà in 956.

In a Greek version (but not its Latin translation) of the tale of miraculous healing (by an apparition of the saint) of a paralysed and deaf-and-dumb youngster (who then joins a monastery), one finds: "In the morning, having brought the images of both the saint and other, they interrogated the youngster and asked him: 'Who is the one who this night appeared to you and healed you?'. He extended his arm and, fingering the image of the saint, replied: 'This one is the very same who appeared to me and healed me'" (my translation from Caruso's Italian translation from the Greek; ibid., p. 5).

Caruso (ibid., p. 3) deems it interesting, that "as a sequel of the taumaturgical event, one finds the only case of a precursor of a *confronto all'americana* one finds in Italo-Greek historical hagiography" (my trans.). Once the youngster was confronted with images, he supposedly recognised in one of them the saint whose apparition had healed him. If anything, that episode is similar to a witness (or victim) being shown several mugshots of suspects.[52] There is no identity parade to speak of, in the story. Moreover, Caruso does not problematise the recognisability of a given person, based on a portrait made according to the conventions of Byzantine art, thus, not realistically.

A crucial topic, for lineup or any eyewitness identification procedures, is that they should not be suggestive, so as to bias the testimony.[53] Psychologists Gary Wells and Deah Quinlivan (1999), writing in a U.S. perspective, dealt precisely with the problem of *suggestive eyewitness identification procedures.* Introducing the link to that paper at his website, Prof. Wells used these words: "Why the U.S. Supreme Court Needs to Revisit Manson v. Braithwaithe" (i.e., 432 U.S. 98, of 1977). Wells and Quinlivan explained (2009, p. 2):

> *Manson v. Braithwaite* was argued November 29, 1976 and the U.S. Supreme Court issued its decision on June 16, 1977. Braithwaite had been convicted of the possession and sale of heroin based solely on identification evidence by undercover agent Jimmy Glover. The agent-witness did not know the person he bought the heroin from but based on a description and the location of the apartment, a fellow officer, D'Onofrio, produced a single photo of Braithwaite. Using this single photo, Agent Glover reportedly made a positive identification of Braithwaite's photo as being a photo of the man from whom he bought the heroin.

Finding in that case, the Second Circuit, and then the Supreme Court, "concluded that the identification procedure was impermissibly suggestive, but then continued to the second inquiry (following *Neil v. Biggers* 1972) as to whether, under all the circumstances, that suggestive procedure gave rise to a substantial likelihood of

---

[52] Of course, psychologists have researched the effects of mugshot viewing on eyewitness accuracy (e.g., Memon, Hope, Bartlett, & Bull, 2002).
[53] For example, Lindsay and Malpass (1999) guest-edited a special issue of the journal *Applied Cognitive Psychology* about measuring lineup fairness.

irreparable mistaken identification." (ibid., p. 3). What is referred to as the second inquiry was the reliability test. It was "borrowed directly from *Neil v Biggers*. Having found that the identification procedure was unnecessarily suggestive, the Court asked whether the identification was reliable even though the procedure was suggestive." (ibid.). In *Manson v Braithwaithe*, the procedure wasn't even a lineup (Wells & Quinlivan, 2009, p. 7): "*Show-ups* are not lineups at all, but instead are procedures in which the eyewitness is shown only one person or a photo of one person without any fillers. Recall that *Manson v Braithwaite* was a show-up procedure and the Court found that it was unnecessarily suggestive but, based on the second prong (the reliability test), did not exclude it from evidence."

In 1977, the Supreme Court had introduced what then became known as "the *Manson* test" or "the *Manson* criteria" concerning suggestive procedures, arguably hoping that this would deter the police from using them: "The Manson criteria (view, attention, certainty, time, description) were meant to clarify the idea that the ultimate issue is the reliability of the identification, not suggestiveness per se" (Wells & Quinlivan, 2009, p. 16). Wells and Quinlivan explained (ibid., p. 3):

> Five criteria were articulated for the reliability test concerning (1) view, (2) attention, (3) description, (4) passage of time, and (5) certainty. The majority of the Court concluded that there was no substantial likelihood of irreparable mistaken identification and cited the witness' standing on the five factors outlined in *Biggers*:
>
> 1. *Opportunity to view*: Witness Glover was within two feet of the seller and the confrontation was at least "a couple of minutes." There was natural light from the window or skylight.
> 2. *Attention*: Glover was paying attention because, as a trained police officer, he realized he would have to find and arrest the dealer.
> 3. *Description*: He gave a detailed enough description that it enabled D'Onofrio to pick a single photo that was later shown to witness Glover.
> 4. *Time to identification*: Only 2 days passed between the crime and the photo identification.
> 5. *Certainty*: Glover had "no doubt" that Braithwaite was the person who had sold him heroin.
>
> Based on their analysis, the majority on the Court concluded that there was not a very substantial likelihood of irreparable misidentification. An even longer opinion, however, was written in dissent. [...]

Wells and Quinlivan (1999) argued that the *Manson* criteria were scientifically inadequate. Wells and Quinlivan (2009) pointed out the major progress made in the intervening thirty years since a previous ruling. Wells and Quinlivan stated (2009, p.1):

> Every day in the United States courts entertain arguments in pre-trial hearings that challenge eyewitness identification evidence based on suggestive eyewitness identification procedures. The arguments are familiar and the suggestive aspects common. They include using a show-up procedure (the suspect alone presented to the witness) when police could have conducted a lineup (embedding the suspect among fillers), conducting a lineup in which the

suspect stood out, failing to tell the eyewitness that the culprit might not be in the lineup, showing the witness a photo of the suspect before conducting a lineup, telling a potentially non-confident eyewitness that his or her choice was correct, or conducting a second lineup procedure in which the only person in common was the suspect. The defense argument for suppressing the identification in light of even the most highly suggestive procedures almost never prevails (Loftus and Doyle, 1997). Instead, courts end up ruling that the suggestiveness of the procedure is outweighed by the "reliability test" articulated by the U.S. Supreme Court in *Manson v. Braithwaite* (1977). *Manson v. Braithwaite* is, in effect, the law of the land on eyewitness identification. Although some state courts have tweaked the reliability test in *Manson*, the core idea remains largely as it was laid out in 1977.

Interestingly, it was around the time of *Manson* that psychological scientists began to conduct programmatic experiments on eyewitness identification with a strong emphasis on suggestive identification procedures (Wells, 1978). Since that time, hundreds of eyewitness experiments have been published in peer-reviewed journals, many of which bear on issues in *Manson*. Overall, the empirical data indicate that eyewitness identification evidence is not performing very well (Penrod, 2005). In addition, since the time of *Manson*, forensic DNA testing was developed and has been used to test claims of innocence. [...]

Wells and Quinlivan argued (2009, p. 19):

> Alternatives to *Manson* should have several characteristics that are absent in *Manson*. First, unlike *Manson*, they must provide an incentive to avoid suggestive procedures and never reward suggestive ones. This means that there has to be some real threat of suppression or some other cost to the government when unnecessarily suggestive procedures are used. Second, alternatives to *Manson* must recognize that suggestive procedures, whether unnecessary or not, confound the fact-finding process and require a much deeper analysis than the check-listing heuristic that characterizes *Manson*. Third, whatever the criteria for deciding to admit a suggestive identification, those criteria need to be independent of the suggestive procedure itself, which means that self-reports of the eyewitness are not likely to ever be good criteria unless it can be shown that they were assessed prior to the suggestive event.[54]

Andrew Roberts (2008) provided a critical analysis of procedural developments during the 2000s concerning *eyewitness identification evidence*. Of course, procedure concerning eyewitness identification evidence is not the same across different national jurisdictions.

---

[54] One of the points made by Wells and Quinlivan (2009) is as follows (ibid., p. 20): "The current approach in *Manson* is one in which the defense must request a hearing on the identification and attempt to show that the identification was not reliable. The burden clearly rests with the defense to show that the identification was not reliable and failure to do so results in admission of the identification evidence. But, it is unclear why the burden rests with the defense to show unreliability rather than with the prosecution to show reliability. It is unlikely that a shift in burden would matter much to the prosecution, of course, as long as the prosecution was able to continue to use the current *Manson* criteria in the context of trumping suggestive procedures. Under the shift-of-burden notion, the prosecution would have to make the case that the identification was reliable regardless of whether a suggestive procedure was necessary or unnecessary. The irrelevance of the 'necessity' aspect of suggestive procedures seems to us to comport better with the Court's own reasoning on these matters that 'reliability is the linchpin in determining the admissibility of identification testimony' along with our observation that the power of suggestive procedures is not moderated by whether the suggestiveness was necessary."

4.6 Relevance

4.6.1 Definitions

In a widespread textbook on legal evidence in England and Wales, *Cross on Evidence* (Cross & Tapper, 1985, 6th edn.), section 4 is 'Relevance, Admissibility and Weight of Evidence'. To begin with, it states: "The main general rule governing the entire subject is that all evidence which is sufficiently relevant to an issue before the court is admissible and all that is irrelevant, or insufficiently relevant, should be excluded" (ibid., p. 49). There is a subsection on the definition of *relevance* (ibid., pp. 50–51), and it begins by stating: "It is difficult to improve upon Stephen's[55] definition of relevance when", in *Digest of the Law of Evidence* (12th edn.), art. 1, "he said that the word 'relevant' means that:"

> any two facts to which it is applied are so related to each other that according to the common course of events one either taken by itself or in connection with other facts proves or renders probable the past, present, or future existence or non-existence of the other.

Cross on Evidence then mentions an attempt – made by Stephen in *General View of the Criminal Law* (1st edn., p. 236) – at logic formalisation of the definition of relevance (Cross & Tapper, 1985, p. 50):

> Elsewhere the same writer suggested as a test for determining whether one fact should be regarded as evidence of, or relevant to another, that the matter under discussion should be cast in the form of a syllogism of which the alleged evidentiary fact constitutes the minor premise; it is then only necessary to consider whether the major premise is a proposition the truth of which is likely to be accepted by the person who has to draw the conclusion – in the case of a lawsuit, a reasonable man.

An example was provided (Cross & Tapper, 1985, p. 50):

> For example, suppose that goods were found in the possession of the accused shortly after they were missed, and he was unable or unwilling to give an adequate explanation of the manner in which he came by them. These would be relevant facts on a charge of stealing because, if the matter was cast into the form of a syllogism, it could be stated in the following way: men found in possession of goods which have recently been missed are frequently guilty of stealing them if they do not give an adequate explanation of their possession of this

---

[55] This is Sir James Fitzjames Stephen (1829–1894). His *A General View of the Criminal Law in England* was published in London by McMillan (i.e., the present-day Macmillan) in 1863 (the first edition), and then in 1890 (the second edition). The second edition was reprinted in Littleton, Colorado, by F. B. Rothman in 1985. As to Stephen's *A Digest of the Law of Evidence*, the 12th edition is a revision by Sir Harry Lushington Stephen and Lewis Frederick Sturge. It was published in London by McMillan and Co. Ltd. in 1948. This was a reprint, with additions, of the 1936 edition. Clearly, Stephen's *Digest* was long-lived. *Analytical Tables of the Law of Evidence for Use with Stephen's Digest of the Law of Evidence*, by George Mifflin Dallas and Henry Wolf Bikle, was published in Philadelphia by T. & J. W. Johnson in 1903 (the notes referred to Stephen's *Digest*'s Second American Edition, itself based on the sixth English edition). *The Analytical Tables* were made available as an online resource accessible by licensing agreements, as a reproduction of an original copy from Harvard Law School Library, by Thomson Gale in Farmington Hills, Michigan, in 2004.

fact (major premise), the accused was found in possession of the goods in question shortly after they were missed, and he gave no adequate explanation of this fact (minor premise); therefore the accused may have been guilty of stealing the goods (conclusion). As the validity of the major premises on which the courts are invited to act can usually be taken for granted, the deductive method outlined above is seldom used in practice, but the test of the syllogism may be found useful whenever there is any doubt about the relevance of evidence.

According to the national jurisdiction, and the kind of court, there are criteria (sometimes set out explicitly as law of evidence) about whether to admit or exclude some items of information, even if they may be relevant. For example, take the U.S. law of evidence: *admissionary rules* are rules about which kinds of evidence can be admitted and heard in court. By contrast, *exclusionary rules* are rules concerning which kinds of evidence must be excluded and not heard in court.

Rules of extrinsic policy and *rules of auxiliary probative policy* are kinds of exclusionary rules. *Rules of extrinsic policy* are a category of rules excluding or restricting the use of admitted evidence. In interpretations of the American law of evidence, according to Wigmore's terminology,[56] *rules of extrinsic policy* are such exclusionary rules that give priority to other values over rectitude of decision. These are rules which are not so much directed at ascertaining the truth, but rather which serve the protection of personal rights and secrets.

Rules of auxiliary probative policy are a category of rules excluding or restricting the use of admitted evidence, as opposed to *rules of extrinsic policy*. In interpretations of the American law of evidence, according to Wigmore's terminology, *rules of auxiliary probative policy* are such exclusionary rules that are intended to promote rectitude of decision, avoiding unreliability or alleged prejudicial effect.

As seen, some kinds of evidence are excluded as a matter of policy. Sometimes, for reasons of policy, the law of some given jurisdiction may choose to disregard evidence that by common sense would prove adultery. By the law of England and Wales, until Parliament reformed family law in 1949, this was the case of evidence that could prove adultery because of lack of access of the husband, if a child was nevertheless born. Prior to 1949, such evidence was not admissible.

Sir Douglas Hogg, in his role as barrister in *Russell v. Russell* in 1924 (he had ceased to be Attorney-general earlier that year), had already tried to obtain admissibility for such evidence. "The question for the House of Lords was whether evidence of non-access might be given in divorce proceedings by one spouse with the result of bastardizing a child of the marriage. The answer was of great importance, not only to the parties to the suit, the sole evidence of the wife's adultery being the testimony of the husband that he did not have access to his wife at any time when the child could have been conceived, but also to all those who were interested in the proceedings in the Divorce Court, either as possible parties or as practitioners" (Heuston, 1964, p. 458).

The House of Lords deciding the case ruled such evidence inadmissible: it "held that on grounds of decency and public policy the law prohibited the introduction

---

[56] By the American jurist John Henry Wigmore (1863–1943).

of such evidence." (ibid.). Hogg had admitted that the evidence would be inadmissible in a legitimacy case, but "Hogg's argument was that the rule prohibiting the introduction of such evidence had never been applied to a case in which the object of the suit was to dissolve the bond of marriage on the ground of adultery, it only applied where there was a marriage in existence and the legitimacy of a child born in wedlock was in question" (ibid.). Hogg argued that "Where the issue is adultery the birth of a child is mere accident" (quoted ibid.). "This ingenious argument was rejected by the majority of the House, Lord Finlay saying: 'To what an extraordinary state would the admission of this evidence in the present case reduce the law of England! The infant may be illegitimate for the purpose of proving adultery; but legitimate for the purpose of succeeding to property or a title!'" (ibid.).

Social epistemics is how philosopher Alvin Goldman (1987a, 1987b) calls social aspects of the philosophy of knowledge. Because of such social aspects, the *requirement of total evidence* is an invalid principle, and an example of contravening on it is *exclusionary laws of evidence* in court: jurors are not given all the evidence, and Goldman (1991), who approves of this, calls this *epistemic paternalism*. See Section 4.3.2.2.

Curative admissibility is a concept that was so-called by Wigmore, and *Cross on Evidence* remarks (Cross & Tapper, 1985, p. 57):

> It is sometimes said that, if irrelevant evidence is adduced by one party, his opponent may seek to dispel its effect by calling irrelevant evidence himself. Whatever the position may be in certain American jurisdictions, this principle (which Wigmore described as one of 'curative admissibility') is not recognised by the English courts.

"The following four exceptions" to the general rule that all relevant evidence is admissible "are frequently stressed, but there are many others" (Cross & Tapper, 1985, p. 51): *hearsay* (when information is ascribed to somebody who is not called as witness); *opinion* ("Witnesses are generally not allowed to inform the court of the inferences they draw from facts perceived by them, but must confine their statements to an account of such facts", ibid.); *character* (the reputation of an accused person's), and *conduct on other occasions*. (The latter includes both *previous convictions*, and *uncharged behaviour*, as well as previous unproven charges that were actually made and possibly prosecuted but did not result in a conviction.) There is much discussion about which evidence should be admissible, and which evidence should be excluded even if relevant, as a matter of policy, and over the years, in given jurisdictions there has been a shift in such matters, usually in the direction of making more kinds of evidence admissible.

Cross on Evidence pointed out the risk of *manufactured evidence* (Cross & Tapper, 1985, p. 56):

> The courts rightly take the view that the degree to which an item of evidence is relevant to an issue diminishes in proportion to the likelihood of its having been manufactured, but it is open to question whether people are as prone to manufacture evidence as some judgments suggest, and the bogey has led to certain exclusionary rules, the mechanical application of which may lead to the rejection of evidence of real probative value. It has certainly played a large part in the development of the rule excluding hearsay, and especially the rule excluding evidence of previous consistent statements of a witness.

4.6 Relevance

In Section 2.6.1, we had already remarked:

> For example, for the purpose of explaining why, according to economic rationality, it makes sense that hearsay be not admitted as evidence in court — incidentally, an expert system dealing with the hearsay rule is the *Hearsay Rule Advisor* (Blackman, 1988, MacCrimmon, 1989) — legal scholars Shapira (2002) and Callen (2002) discuss what went wrong in the reasoning of Shakespeare's character of Othello, when believing rumours about Desdemona having supposedly betrayed him. Also see Stein (2001). Incidentally: the *hearsay rule* (in English and American law) "requires a court to exclude any written or oral statement not made in the course of the proceedings which is offered *as evidence of the correctness of the matter asserted*. A statement which is relevant independently of the real intention of the speaker [e.g., a contractually binding statement] or the truth of what is stated [e.g., an allegedly libellous statement] is not adduced for a testimonial purpose and is therefore outside the scope of the rule" (Pattenden, 1993, p. 138). This is not to say that in some jurisdictions hearsay is inadmissible; e.g., McNeal (2007) discusses hearsay at the Iraqi High Tribunal, in consideration of the legacy of international tribunals for war crimes or crimes against humanity. "The IHT allowed hearsay evidence and the reading of ex parte affidavits as evidence, two of the most criticized practices of the Nuremberg Tribunal. The IHT also allowed the admission of testimony by anonymous witnesses, a legacy of the Yugoslavia Tribunal which has since been rejected by that same court" (ibid., from the abstract).

4.6.2 Legal Formalism, Artificial Intelligence and the Indeterminacy of Relevance

Jonathan Yovel

4.6.2.1 Relevance, Within Law as Being a System for Processing Information

For lawyers, relevance is essentially a relation between information and the discursive space in which legal practices – such as litigation – take place. In an important sense, salient to the legitimacy of law as a rational practice, law (and adjudication in particular) can be seen as systems for processing information. Law's representational relation to "the outside world" – its need to relate to and reconstruct facts, events, narratives – lies at the basis of law's claims for legitimacy and rationality. Law's performance, its manipulation and use of power, require that law base itself on valid representational and reconstructive technologies. Law must credibly relate to a "real world" (rather than to fictitious ones) in the process of adjudication. In other words, its foremost challenge is epistemic, and information is thus a basic constituent of law no less than normativity. This Section 4.6.2 deals with the basic requirement for the introduction of any information into the court's practical space, that or *relevance*. It does not deal with ways in which law processes and otherwise manipulates information once it has been introduced into discourse.

The pivotal characteristic that governs any and all acts of admittance/barring of information by a court of law is that of relevance. Relevance, of course, is a criterion for sorting information in many other contexts, as well as in any conversational interaction (Grice, 1975). In law, In law, however, relevance is not only a criterion for valid treatment of information, but itself *an object of regulation*. This means that legal relevance, on top of being a second-order or meta-legal concept (as it would operate in other discourses such as science) is also first-order relation. It thus appears not just in legal theory, as a criterion for the attractiveness of technologies of legal epistemology, but in first-order legal norms, those identified by a legal system's *rule of recognition* (Hart, 1961a) or derived from its "basic norm" (Kelsen, 1967). In this chapter, I shall use as a paradigm for first-order regulation of relevance the applicable rule of the U.S. Federal Rules of Evidence, namely Rule 401.[57]

There is one discursive "division of labor" that I wish not to commit to in this chapter, indeed to regard as essentially misleading: thinking of relevance as "theoretical" and of the *legal admissibility* of information as "practical". Because in law, normative considerations apply in conjunction with epistemic ones (and sometimes compete with them), relevance is called on to operate on different levels and for different functions. Thus juristic "sorters" such as the notion of admissibility of evidence lay at the heart of the law of evidence and its independent normative functions (e.g., may we introduce information that was collected illegally, or that may create unfair bias for a party, even if it may have what lawyers call "probative value" – i.e., serve an epistemic function?). The law of evidence's criterion of admissibility expresses relevance concerns but is not identical with this, nor does it exhaust the complexities of legal relevance in general. This chapter discusses several problems of legal relevance beyond the standard treatment of the law of evidence (i.e. as a more general category constitutive of legal discourse) with special relation to AI and law.

4.6.2.2 Relevance: Why It Is Difficult for Formal Systems

Courts use complex modes of relevance judgments in regulating the introduction of information and construction of factual narratives. However, due to a plurality of values inherent to the legal process, relevance is not a strictly well-defined relation, or operator, in legal discourse. In fact, when lawyers claim that any information is either relevant or irrelevant (or sometimes, "minimally relevant")[58] in relation to a given legal process, they may mean something quite distinct from the meaning of relevance in other decision-making contexts or in communication in general. The present essay (Section 4.6.2 in the book), drawing on work in logic, linguistics and AI, attempts to clarify this ambivalence by offering several conceptualizations of relevance, centering on two paradigmatic meanings and discuss certain complications in the formal treatment of each. This in turn forms the basis for a theory of legal relevance, geared *inter alia* towards a critical examination of relevance operations.

---

[57] Available online at http://www.utd.uscourts.gov/forms/evid2009.pdf (May 2011).

[58] "Minimal relevance" echoes the Bayesian treatment of Hempel's so-called "Ravens paradox" (Good, 1960). Let E stand for some information, H for a narrative hypothesis, and O for all other information. E is "minimally relevant" to H if and only if the probability of H, given E and O, is different from the probability of H, given O alone (in Hempel's original, the proposition P "All ravens are black" is ostensibly strengthened by an observation O of a white dove (since P is logically equivalent to "anything that is not black is not a raven"), although no "meaning connection" exists between the two. The Bayesian approach is to acknowledge such minimal relevance yet consider the relation as typically weak and only marginally significant to decision-making processes. See Crump (1997).

4.6 Relevance

Relevance has proved difficult for formal systems because even in its most formal operation – that of a gatekeeper of information, a metaphor taken from law as much as from literature – it does more than simply signal information "in" or "out" of processes. Even in the case of *Daubert v. Merrell Dow Pharmaceuticals*, the leading 1993 U.S. case[59] on the legal admissibility of expert testimony on the grounds of relevance, the court could form no single, or even cohesive, set of parameters that would constitute a descriptive theory of relevance. Clearly, lack of relevance cannot mean *only* "waste," using information that a priori cannot influence the decision-making procedure, algorithm or heuristic process. That, I claim below, is one layer of relevance relations, which theories of information and theories of language mostly invoke. However, both communicative and normative critical insights – which legal discourse float time and again – show that relevance operates on a less well-defined level that, in law and general and in evidence law in particular, is its salient mode of operation. I shall offer to think of this in terms of "normative saturation." This constitutive characteristic means that relevance sometimes operates not as a semantic, causal or "topical" sorter of information that is "put to use" in the service of some practical (=normative) interest, but instead is infused with normativity to begin with. The challenge for AI, addressed in this essay but not resolved, is derived directly from AI's relative success in dealing with semantic or other topical relations as opposed to its difficulties in assisting, let alone simulating or replicating, decisional processes that are normatively saturated.

Normative saturation is not a common term, yet its view of the social sphere (in which law, language, and applied AI all operate) is easily recognizable from social and political theory. It is perhaps most indispensable in the work of Thomas Hobbes, still the most recognizable framework for liberal political discourse. Recall that in the pre-political stage in his *Leviathan*, persons are depicted as united by no shared normative framework (such as a social contract), and yet even in the total absence of positive normativity (let alone of law) they have the capacity to make, understand, and uphold promises: not due to an extensive metaphysics of natural law but as a direct result of being communicative agents.[60] The claim that for a practice, device, or operator – however one wishes to conceive of relevance – to be constituted by normativity should not then be seen as particularly objectionable. In our times, it is associated mainly with the work of Jürgen Habermas, briefly discussed below.

On the basis of normative saturation, I shall begin with exploring the incompleteness for legal relevance of three influential bodies of work: the conversational relevance of H. Paul Grice (1975), the cognitive approach of Sperber and Wilson (1986), and finally the work of Anderson and Belnap (1975) in what came to be known as *logic relevance*, extending to the critical work in pragmatics of van Dijk (1979, 1989). The main forms of incompleteness that I explore are expressed in

---

[59] *Daubert v. Merrell Dow Pharmaceuticals*, 509 U.S. 579 (1993). See on it, e.g., Cole (2009), responding to a thematic issue on the U.S. Supreme Court's very important expert evidence decision in *Daubert* – a Symposium Issue published by the *Tulsa Law Review*, vol. 43 (2007), as its Winter Issue, p. 229 ff.

[60] As seminally explored in Habermas (1981).

these models under different conditions. At the outset, however, it may be well to point to two major difficulties, both going to the conceptual core of relevance, as well as to enumerate the various types of *incompleteness* (or for some, *vagueness*) under these conditions.

1. The first is that relevance is not merely a relation between information and entailed or inferred statement, but a *disposition*: a relevance judgment pronounces the *potential* of information to effect a conclusion or a decision-making process, not its actuality or necessity. Tendencies or dispositions are notoriously difficult to work with empirically. For instance, what does it mean to say that glass has a tendency to shatter? Is this simply an ex-post statistical observation or can we maintain that the potential of glass to shatter justifies the statement independently of any evidence of glass ever actually shattering? That would require something quite distinct from statistical data – something we may call "a non-inductive theory of glass" that explains its disposition to shatter without recourse to such empirical events as glass actually shattering.[61] To return to relevance: in order to bar (or allow) a type of information from legal processes on the grounds of irrelevance, the first approach would require an empirical, statistical methodology, while the second would be confined to ex-ante considerations.
2. The second vagueness is more specific to legal relevance and is derived from law's own constitutive duality: *facticity* and *normativity*. The former means law's commitment to relate as validly as possible to occurrences and events outside itself (and which took place in the past), normally requiring various mechanisms of representation based on some sort of truth by correspondence. Yet where law is distinguished, it is in its being constituted by normativity, by normative interests other than truthful reconstruction of reality (lawyers preach the difference between "scientific" or "historical truth" and "legal truth"). Relevance is constitutive of both, and the vagueness of legal discourse owes to the fact that speakers do not differentiate between the operation of relevance in producing meaning (the realm of *facticity*) and that of a commitment to a normative order. In this Section 4.6.2 I argue that this is true even for jurists for whom all normativity is no more than shorthand for social conventionalism, i.e. legal positivists.[62]
3. The third vagueness owes to a topic rarely explored although recognized in practice, which is relevance as a rhetorical or persuasive device. Two senses must be distinguished here. One is the concern for abuses of relevance, the use of

---

[61] The example is taken of course from a widely-discussed problem for empiricists. See Chisholm (1965), Lewis (1973, 1997).

[62] Even when not empirical, legal positivism grounds normativity in facticity: N is a legal norm due to a set of social and historical facts that rendered it so (order of the sovereign, recognition by courts or their mere "habit", etc.). Neo-Kantian jurisprudence differs from empiricist jurisprudence precisely on the same grounds that Neo-Kantianism differs from empiricism generally: thus in Kelsen's "pure" theory of law the logical (rather than ontological) status of the *Grundnorm*, the basic norm that necessarily anchors any given legal system, is axiomatic, a "fiction" rather than a social fact. See Kelsen (1967).

4.6 Relevance

persuasive (or more generally, *perlocutionary*)[63] language – to a jury, a judge or other legal agent, in the context of bargaining or any other legal interaction. The point is to mask irrelevant input as relevant through rhetorical manipulation (e.g., focusing the argument on objectionable behavior of a perpetrator outside of any relevant causal link to the alleged crime, therefore creating a heuristic bias that builds on the general preference for perceived relevance).

4.6.2.3 Relevance and Legal Formalism

The several forms of incompleteness or vagueness explored above as to the nature of relevance put a dent, I believe, in any formalistic descriptive theory of legal relevance and thus, by extension, complicates AI treatments of it. Before attempting to justify this claim it would help to briefly clarify both what I mean by legal formalism and what I do not mean by it (Yovel, 2010).

At the basis of formalism stands what can be termed the "formalist fiction": that the process that produced the legal norms has exhausted normative and policy considerations, and thus law can be seen as a more or less "closed" normative system, and norms – typically, rules – are applicable to concrete cases without further recourse to external normative deliberation (such as principle, policy, and ethics).[64] Thus according to legal formalism, application is mainly a matter of logical inference and entailment. Under formalism, unless discretion or other "freedom levels" of decision-making are stipulated in the rule, legal deductions are, ideally, as unique and sustainable as the logical structures that underlie legal doctrine.[65] For example, in private law, such tight systems as the law of negotiable instruments[66] (governed

---

[63] Among speech acts, *perlocution* is when a person tells another, e.g., "It's so hot, in this room", and intends the effect that the recipient should open the window. This is a hint.

[64] A "classical" formulation frequently referred to as a model of formalist construction is Langdell (1880). See Grey (1983). My suspicion, that American pragmatism could not have wholly yielded to Langdellian formalism even during that era, is to an extent vindicated by Ernst (1998). Following Grey, Pildes (1999) identifies three characteristics of American legal formalism that to significant degrees do not overlap: 1. Formalism as *aconsequential morality in law* (i.e., a commitment to deontological ethics – of which Kantian ethics is the accepted paradigm – whereby the ethical evaluation of any rule is innate and does not stem from the consequences of its application in the world); 2. As *apurposive rule-following* (i.e., construction and application of rules that do not hinge upon their purposes – which in turn are seen as external to the rules themselves – such as literal or originalist construction); 3. As an overall efficiency-enhancing regulatory architecture (in contrast with (1) and possibly with (2)).

[65] For helpful discussions see, *inter alia*, Merrill and Smith (2000), Schwartz and Scott (2003), and Sebok (1998) (especially pp. 83–104); and Smith (2003). A useful general work offering a functionalist approach to formalism in terms of relative independence from context is Heylighen (1999).

[66] At http://www.referenceforbusiness.com/encyclopedia/Mor-Off/Negotiable-Instruments.html one can find, for *negotiable instruments*, the following definition from *The Encyclopedia of Business*, 2nd edition, in the entry for "Negotiable instruments" by David P. Bianco:

> Negotiable instruments are written orders or unconditional promises to pay a fixed sum of money on demand or at a certain time. Promissory notes, bills of exchange, checks,

in the United States by the Uniform Commercial Code Article 3 and a set of federal statutes and regulations) is frequently described as "formalistic" because decisions rest on a relatively closed set of logically organized rules,[67] while contract law tends to be more "relational" than formalistic as it deals with much wider sets of relations and cases.[68]

As a legal approach, classical formalism was largely discredited, in twentieth century jurisprudence, by legal realist critiques.[69] In the 1990s and 2000s, however, the label "new formalism" has emerged to denote a dominant and growing school of thought associated with the economic approach to law.[70] New formalism shares some traits with plain old formalism – mainly, a preference for autonomous modes of construction and relatively strict application of rules and restrictions. Yet the new differs from the old on some important levels, predominantly on the matter of justification. While old formalism regarded itself as a correct, even scientifically correct, descriptive theory of law, and jurisprudence as a "science for the sake of science"

---

drafts, and certificates of deposit are all examples of negotiable instruments. Negotiable instruments may be transferred from one person to another, who is known as a holder in due course. Upon transfer, also called negotiation of the instrument, the holder in due course obtains full legal title to the instrument. Negotiable instruments may be transferred by delivery or by endorsement and delivery. One type of negotiable instrument, called a promissory note, involves only two parties, the maker of the note and the payee, or the party to whom the note is payable. [...]

[67] This is of course a general typification lacking in nuance. For critical takes on the formalist structure of Article 3 see Yovel (2007), as well as the papers by Kurt Eggert (2002) and Grant Gilmore (1979).

[68] I owe this insight, like many others – including the intimate relation between law and sports – to Neil Cohen. Under the relational approach, contracts are not distinct legal instruments that exist independently of relations between the parties, but the aggregate of these relations, only some of which are articulated. While relational contract theorists supplied insights into understanding long-term and complex contractual relations, they also drew away from the view of contract as such being merely a mechanism for the rational allocation of risks. Reliance and future relations are important parameters of relational contracts. See Ian Macneil's book (1980) *The New Social Contract*.

[69] See Duncan Kennedy's (2001) encyclopedia entry on 'Legal Formalism'. Anthony Kronman (1988) offered a powerful and succinct critique. American jurisprudence has been almost obsessed with the question of formalism, especially in view of legal realist critiques. In its most offensive – for realists – manifestation, formalistic jurisprudence is a "science for the sake of science" absorbed exclusively with "the niceties of [law's] internal structure and the beauty of its logical processes", according to Roscoe Pound's (1908, p. 605) 'Mechanical Jurisprudence' (for which, see s.v. *Mechanical jurisprudence* in the Glossary of this book). But that kind of "old formalism" seems to have all but disappeared, as ("new") formalism today bases its legitimacy on functional grounds, mainly those of economic efficiency. A more lingering critique is that of Felix Cohen's (1935) 'Transcendental Nonsense and the Functional Approach', according to which formalism (or "conceptualism") supplies the philosophical basis for "objectifying" legal concepts or assuming that they stand for objects in the real world, namely normative entities, rather than artifacts or constructions, or ways of talk. For a rich reference, see Dagan (2007). See also Morton White's (1957) *Social Thought in America: The Revolt Against Formalism*.

[70] See the papers by Hanoch Dagan (2007) and Thomas Grey (1999).

4.6 Relevance

(as opposed to a substantive discourse involving various and competing normative types and concerns), new formalism justifies its approach on functionalist grounds. For instance, a formalist approach to the construction of contracts may justify a narrow, acontextual Parol (*sic*)[71] Evidence Rule as tending to create ex-ante incentives for efficient negotiating processes, in terms of utility and costs.[72] The process of shaping the rule exhausts the normative concerns (these will no longer direct the application directly, only through the interests entrenched in the rules; otherwise this would simply be a functionalist approach biased towards economic efficiency). New formalism resembles the older brand in another, ironic way: on the one hand, it is as committed – perhaps more than its predecessor – to a specific metaphysics and ideology of individualism. On the other hand, it attempts to shy away as much as possible from engaging in substantive ethical discourse, suspecting all ethical talk of relativism or at least lacking scientific rigor. The fact that a preference for economic efficiency is itself based on a substantive moral theory – utilitarianism – is acknowledged, of course, but mostly in the background of discourse where it is taken as a universal dogma.

Another approach to formalism may be termed "relational": taking its cue from so-called relational contract theory, it looks to formalism as a legal architecture that is justified not by general theoretical arguments – certainly not as a valid descriptive theory of law – but as an approach that emphasizes legal form over functionalist approach in those contexts where form is deemed important to protect the relevant legal relations. Relational formalism would urge courts not to follow formal requirements blindly or dogmatically, on the one hand, yet not to give up on legal forms within a purely functionalist approach, on the other hand. An example I explored elsewhere deals with the role of form in the law of negotiable instruments, long considered a paradigm for formalist jurisprudence; I show that several junctions and tensions expressed in the actual practices and court cases dealing with the law of negotiable instruments are best explained by relational formalism, rather than by either dogmatic formalism or functionalism.

Can relevance and AI be approached in a similar way? This preliminary essay cannot offer a worked-out account of how a relational approach to relevance would look like, but it can attempt to note what should be avoided as much as what should be sought. Thus, it is far too tempting to consider causal relevance more readily formalized than normative relevance, just as semantic relations are easier to formalize than pragmatic and contextual ones. This, I think, is a mistake; possibly, AI treatment of normative judgment in this context can be better executed and justified than causal relevance. Formalizing causal relevance requires predictions about cognitive processes – what would "tend" to make any fact "more probable or less

---

[71] This is no typo: *Parol Evidence Rule* is archaic spelling used by design, and it is found for example in the United States' Uniform Commercial Code, §2-202. See in the next note.

[72] In contract law, a Parol Evidence Rule restricts recourse to extra-textual sources (such as preliminary negotiations or the parties' behaviour) when a written contract governs the parties' relations. An example is the American Uniform Commercial Code (UCC), § 2-202.

probable" (FRE 401 again).[73] Formalizing normative relevance, on the other hand, would require a "gatekeeper" function (to invoke *Daubert*)[74] that should conceivably be easier to formulate in relation to any decision-making process (or institution) since it requires no prediction of causal relations within or of the outcomes of these processes. Thus, counterintuitively, normative relevance – the aspect that specifically characterizes legal relevance – seems more amenable to AI modeling and formal treatment than its causal counterpart.

4.6.2.4 Relevance, Evidence and Beyond: Three Theoretical Approaches

What does a court mean by declaring any given evidence "irrelevant" in such sentences as, e.g., "Verdict reached by a different jury (whether on the same or different evidence) in the earlier trial was irrelevant"? Surely, by "irrelevant" the court cannot mean that the information in question will necessarily prove *inconsequential*, in the sense that the decision-making process of the trial would be indifferent to it – that admitting it into the trial's discursive space is a sort of waste, since it would a priori play no part in the court's decision. On the contrary: it seems that in such cases as *Lam Chi-Ming v R*, a 1991 Hong Kong case[75] where information that proved correct and led to a conviction was on appeal ruled inadmissible due to its being extracted involuntarily from the defendants,[76] the court considered the evidence to carry considerable persuasive force: it *may* prove consequential, yet it *ought* not. Legal relevance, then, is normatively saturated from its very inception.

As I argued in a previous work (Yovel, 2003), courts and other legal agents rely on relevance to operate on two different levels: on one, it is expected to bar information that is useless for the process of legal decision-making, quite like relevance operates in other inferential frameworks, whether theoretical or practical.

---

[73] Short for "Federal Rules of Evidence, Rule 401". What appears in double quotes ("more probable or less probable") is the language of the Rule 401 of the U.S. Federal Rules of Evidence, that introduces the notion of relevance to this code of evidence law.

[74] This is the case of *Daubert v. Merrell Dow Pharmaceuticals*, the leading 1993 U.S. case on the legal admissibility of expert testimony on the grounds of relevance. *Daubert v. Merrell Dow Pharmaceuticals*, 509 U.S. 579 (1993).

[75] *Lam Chi-Ming v R* (1991), [1991] 2 App. Cas. 212 (P.C. 1991) (Hong Kong).

[76] The particulars are odd enough to merit a short description. The defendants were sentenced to death for the murder of a man who raped their sister. They used a knife that they subsequently disposed of in the sea. During the police investigation, the defendants confessed to the crime and reconstructed it on video, whereupon divers were successful in recovering the knife. At the trial, it was established that the confessions were extracted by police brutality and therefore were inadmissible. The question was how to deal with the video tapes and the knife. The trial judge found this original solution: he ruled that although all that was *said* by the defendants was inadmissible, the visual recordings of the re-enactments were not; and the video tapes were subsequently admitted *without sound*. The knife was considered material evidence, independent of its mode of discovery. The Court of Appeals was not amused, and disallowed the derivative evidence as well as the confession.

4.6 Relevance

As Sperber and Wilson show, relevance conceived this way is largely an economic device applied to cognitive processes:

> Human cognitive processes [...] are geared to achieving the greatest possible cognitive effect for the smallest possible processing effort [...] to communicate is to imply that the information communicated is relevant. (Sperber & Wilson, 1986, p. vii)

The qualifier "human" seems unnecessarily restrictive here, and it will perhaps be more correct to regard communication as involving *claims* of relevance, rather than implications ("imply" is too weak). While intuitively appealing, Sperber and Wilson's notion ignores that conditions of relevance are as much products of discourse, linguistic interaction and other practices as they are agents that shape them; and that, while economicity is generally advisable, it cannot be seen as an overarching goal of normative or practical processes. In other words, it is the case that legal relevance both does more than Sperber and Wilson claim (it expresses concerns other than economicity) and less (it does not always express economicity). A critically informed descriptive theory of legal discourse cannot disregard the plurality, non-reductionist and other non-parsimonious characteristics of the language used to express human experience – as well as normative ambiguities – that law requires. Any system that wishes to represent/replicate/reconstruct legal discourse would have to contend with such constitutive modes of description of the human experience; information is relevant due to its being *meaningful*, not necessarily linearly consequential. Far from being a stick in the wheels of AI and law, this only challenges legal AI to avoid collapsing into a simplistic set of syllogistic forms only to accommodate the economics of relevance.

Sperber and Wilson's second claim, that to make any contribution to discourse is to make an implied claim of its relevance is reflected in another influential work, H. Paul Grice's work on the "supermaxims of communication" (Grice, 1975). Grice discussed what he called "conversational relevance" and at one point I have taken this to be quite different from the "practical" relevance of legal discourse (the latter responds to concerns of decision-making theory, the former to those of intersubjective linguistic interaction), but the distinction now seems overstated. Grice's goal was to articulate, through a universal "ethnography" of conversational dynamics, a set of "supermaxims" that obey a standard "logic of conversation." One of those is the somewhat blunt "supermaxim of relation": "be relevant"; other maxims are effectively governed by notions of relevance, such as the "supermaxim of quantity": "make your contribution as informative as is required (for the current purpose of the exchange)", but although "questions [arise] about what different kinds and foci of relevance there may be",[77] the concept of relevance is treated by Grice, overall, as an inherently vague logical primitive.

Going beyond Grice's contribution entails thinking of relevance as a reasons-based and theory-dependent device of practical reasoning. In what sense then can relevance itself be in need of justification?

---

[77] Grice (1975, pp. 45–46).

It is a fact of logical discourse that relevance has not – perhaps not yet – found a canonical position in its seemingly natural habitat, modal logic (indeed relevance assisted in alienating another "logical" concept, entailment, from the calculus of possibility/impossibility). Recent studies suggest a reason for that. As Diaz (1981) convincingly argues, relevance thrives on the inability of standard modal conditionals to supply a satisfactory definition of "entailment". The emphasis here is on expectations of what the form of entailment must provide: "entailment" itself may be seen as well-defined in analytic terms, e.g. by the semantics of material implication, while neglecting the "meaning connection" that non-formal discourse ascribes to it. In formal-semantic terms, "→" is a representation of, and only of, the truth table TFTT.[78] It is only when we think of it as representing something else than semantic compatibility that we resent the fact that "a false proposition entails anything".

While this is not the place to elaborate on Lewis' (1973) modal treatment of entailment, a gloss is certainly required. Under the modal approach, impossible propositions "entail" – that is, are semantically compatible with – anything, and necessary propositions are "entailed" by anything. Thus "p entails q" is true if and only if it is impossible for p to be true and q false: $(p \Rightarrow q) \equiv \sim P(p \vee \sim q)$ (i.e., p entails q is modally equivalent to the impossibility of p being true and q being false, where $\Rightarrow$ stands for "strict implication" and P for Lewis' primitive modal predicate, "possible"). This formulation avoids the mislabeled "paradox of implication" where "a false proposition implies anything" (third and forth lines in the standard truth-table represented by p→q) and "a true proposition is implied by anything" (first and third lines). As → is, semantically, about compatibility of combinations (e.g. the compatibility of a false antecedent and true consequent), there is no paradox but instead a pragmatic difficulty. Critics such as Nuel Belnap express the need for an additional requirement from "entailment": that a condition of valid entailment be a "meaning connection" between antecedent and consequent. In other words, the additional "relevance requirement" is that for A to entail B the former must be "relevant" in respect to the latter. One way of looking at relevance, therefore, is as an (or perhaps *the*) intersection between modality and meaning. Meaning is cultural and logically contingent, which at least partially explains logic's traditional difficulty in dealing with relevance; but the *requirement* of a "meaning connection", whatever theory of meaning is subsequently employed, should not present such grave a problem.

Since the 1960s, logical approaches to relevance have emerged from various directions, mostly along two lines: modal inquiries and what came to be loosely termed *relevant logic* (*RL*) – see in Section 4.6.3 below – since a symposium bearing that designation took place in 1974. The latter project relies mainly on directions suggested by work by Anderson and Belnap to identify challenges, dilemmas and modes of approaching relevance, even when positions and conclusions are critical of it. Interestingly, Both Lewis' (1973) work in modal logic and Anderson and Belnap's (1975) and Anderson's (1960) work in RL stem, at least partially, from

---

[78] I.e.: true, false, true, true. The only position in which the material implication does not hold is when the antecedent is true and consequent is false.

4.6 Relevance 311

uneasiness with classical logic's handling of material implication relations. In a nutshell, two such problems were identified: one (the semantic inadequacy) finds fault with the question of the validity of material implication as divorced from any connection to consequent B being in any sense *dependent* on its antecedent A. In other words, the problem is that relevance is not essential to logically valid argumentation. Although the term "fallacy" is sometimes invoked in this context it better be avoided; Anderson and Belnap's critique is about the desirability and fruitfulness of classical implication in explaining and regulating both discourse and decision-making procedures, not about its internal coherence or completeness. The problem they identify is the lack, in deductive systems, of a serious requirement that a conclusion depend on its assumptions that a proof be *from* a hypothesis as opposed to being allowed by it.

For instance, in classical logic the following is an obviously valid argument form: (1) if A, then if B, then A (which we notate as: $A \to (B \to A)$). The relevance problem here is that the consequent/conclusion is not dependent, is not *derived* from the antecedents/assumptions A and B, respectively; there is no use for hypothesis B. Another example is that of validity on the force of contradiction, (2) if A, then if $\sim$A, then B (which we notate as: $A \to (\sim A \to B)$). In (2) the conclusion B is not derived from its assumptions; the formula is valid on what are basically semantic considerations: syntactically, an argument with an assumption that is a contradiction cannot be invalid because it can never be the case that the assumptions are true and the conclusion false. Semantically, a material implication whose antecedent is a contradiction is itself a tautology, because the second line of its standard truth-table TFTT, i.e. the only possibility for an implication sentence to be false, can never occur. In a telling sense, it is the very hyp procedure of natural deduction that is faulted here: if hypotheses can be added at will, in what sense is the conclusion entailed by them? Likewise consider Genzen's rule of introduction of the implication connective in "natural" deduction I$\to$, which allows introduction of the material implication connective between elements that just happen to occur in a hypothetical sequence. B's irrelevance is thus demonstrated in line j+k+1 in (1).

The point of this exercise is to show by a very simple manipulation of the standard Genzen rules of inference, how any hypothesis can be made to seem relevant though nothing is actually entailed by it. Here, a hypothesis is introduced from which the conclusion follows, yet the hypothesis is entirely superfluous. Such shortcomings of natural deduction in expressing relevance generated Anderson and Belnup's shift to a requirement of "use" as an interpretation of entailment in Relevance Logic: B is entailed by A not merely by virtue of following from A in natural deduction, but by A being *used* to infer B.

(1)   (1.1)

  i.   A
  j. | B   hyp   i. A
  j+k. |A   reit i   j. A   reit i
  j+k+1. B$\to$A   I$\to$ j, j+k
  1.   A   reit i

These very basic formulae show: (1) A is established. B is introduced as a hypothesis. A is reiterated. Thus A follows B. However, as seen in (1.1), B is not *used* in order to entail A. The point of this exercise is to show by a very simple manipulation of the standard Genzen rules of inference, how any hypothesis can be made to seem relevant though nothing is actually entailed by it. Here, a hypothesis is introduced from which the conclusion follows, yet the hypothesis is entirely superfluous. Such shortcomings of natural deduction in expressing relevance, generated Anderson and Belnup's shift to a semantic requirement of "use" as an interpretation of entailment in Relevance Logic: A is entailed by B not merely by virtue of following from B in natural deduction, but by B being *used* to infer A.

It was on the concept of *use* that Anderson's initial attempt to form a relevance requirement for deductibility rested. In simplified form, it allowed that B be relevantly deducible from a set of statements $\{A_1, \ldots, A_n\}$ if and only if there is a deduction from $\{A_1, \ldots, A_n\}$ in which each of the A_i are actually used. However, at least on the surface that criterion doesn't seem to work: the $A_i=B$ in (1) is, after a fashion, used – and its introduction definitely incurs a cost. What Anderson seems to suggest is a *sine qua non* condition: that in order to be relevant in P, each A_i must have actual significance in respect to P's outcome. This criterion means something quite different from actual use: it must mean something akin to *force*, the quality of potentially carrying an influence.[79] Note that B *has* an influence on (1): its introduction influences the number of stages and strategy of proving in (1). Perhaps then B is relevant in (1) if and only if it actually influences its conclusion: can that be the meaning of a conclusion being derived *from* an assumption, of an assumption *entailing* a conclusion?[80]

Indeed as (1.1) shows, B has no such significance in (1) because $A \rightarrow A$ whether B or $\sim$B; $(B \vee B) \rightarrow A$ (that is to say, that B or its negation entails A) is a tautology.[81] The *sine qua non* interpretation of relevance is, however, too strong a requirement: it defines relevance on terms of weight, it does not allow for overruling or outweighing a relevant factor. The solution must be dynamic rather than static: in order to be considered relevant, B must be held to have a particular force in respect to (1), which is the ability (but not the necessity) to make a difference in it in terms of outcome rather than process alone.

---

[79] I use "force" here mainly in deference to J. L. Austin's terminology in discussion illocutionary, locutionary and perlocutionary forces.

[80] K. F. Hauber offered to define as a "closed system" any n statements of the form $p \rightarrow q$ that satisfied the requirement that the antecedents exhaust all possible cases and the consequents exclude each other. The advantages of such a system for decision-making are clear: for every true assertion $p \rightarrow q$ it is also true that $\sim p \rightarrow \sim q$. (By $\sim$ the proposition is negated.) All necessary conditions are also sufficient ones and vice versa. Hauber's system marginalizes "implication paradoxes" but is not conducive toward forming a relevance requirement for entailment, as Anderson and Belnap demand.

[81] According to the law of excluded middle. Note that in this and other parts this study I neglect to examine intuitionistic treatments of relevance that do not accept this postulate.

4.6 Relevance

This approach differs from Anderson and Belnap's modification of the deductibility theorem, which distinguishes

$$(1) \quad A_1 \cdot A_2 \cdots A_n \to B$$

from

$$(2) \quad A_1 \to A_2 \to \ldots A_n \to B$$

on the basis of the requirement that in (2) each A_i be relevant to B, but not in (1) (Anderson & Belnap, 1975, p. 21). Diaz convincingly criticizes the distinction, which is consequently not followed here. This way or another, "used in" seems ambiguous enough to allow for the interpretation offered here. (1) Is an aggregate of conjunctives (A_1 and A_2 and ... A_n entail B) while (2) is a progressive sequence of entailment (if A_1 then A_2 then ... A_n entails B). (1) and (2) are semantically equivalent, although they differ on how the various elements are *used*.

This then is what I offer to term *causal relevance*. Establishing it does not require that the information in question actually tilt some metaphorical scales of decision making, only that it be identified by a theory of what is capable of influencing that particular process. That is why relevance is theory-dependent and theory-presupposing, and cannot be seen as a neutral, formal criterion for the attractiveness of theory. Why relevance can and must be conceptualized normatively also becomes apparent when we think of such cases as *Lam Chi-Ming* mentioned above: if a decision-making process is subject to a practical goal, relevance functions as a device for introducing and barring information that frustrate that goal, not because they (ontologically) cannot influence P's outcome (as B in (1)), but because they (permissibly) cannot, and should not.

The requirement of force substitutes for a requirement in terms of sufficient and necessary conditions. It would not do to determine relevance in terms of actual influence on a procedure P's outcome because, although it may be that element B possesses causal force in relation to P, other considerations may negate or neutralize that force. It may be that information be considered relevant (in the causal sense) in relation to P, yet eventually not allowed to influence its outcome on grounds (or *reasons*) that are external to the relation between B's causal force and P. A paradigmatic case, typical to the law of evidence, is when B, although maintaining causal relevance in relation to P, lacks *normative* relevance.

Normative relevance (NR) works on the grounds of subjecting legal discourse to normative considerations *always*, even when it seems that merely probative or epistemological concerns operate; this then is a product of the normative saturation of legal discourse. It becomes clearer how normative relevance acts within the set R1 pre-defined by practical causation, $R1 = \forall x(\text{rel } x(P))$. This, however, must not lead to an automatic conclusion that the set R2 produced by operators defined by normative relevance is necessarily a subset of R1. The reason for that, in a nutshell, is that practical causation is itself theory-dependent and that theory plays, in respect to dictating the behavior of relevance functions, a normative role. Normative relevance may be used to alter the theoretical considerations that define practical or causal relevance. R2 is not defined as logically subject to R1 and it is not the case that only when fulfilling R1 requirements, information becomes a candidate for R2 membership.

4.6.2.5 Considerations About Applying Relevance Logic

Seminal work in *relevance logic*[82] by van Dijk seems, at first look, especially applicable to practical and normative contexts, since unlike previous work by, e.g., Anderson and Belnap (1975), its focus is on pragmatics, communication, and text-context relations. His notion that "Relevance is a relative notion [...] relevance must always be construed with respect to a certain (con-)text: relevance for a certain speaker or hearer, relevance with respect to a certain problem, question, etc." (van Dijk, 1979, p. 113) is certainly a fruitful starting point for conceptualizing legal relevance.

While van Dijk's broad identification of relevance as signaling "some *degree of importance* to some property of the discourse" (ibid.) may be misleading in the context of legal relevance since – even when discounting the problem of "minimal relevance" discussed above, that identifies information as relevant even when consequentially unimportant to the discourse[83] – the definition is in fact broad enough to hold both senses of legal relevance, epistemic and normative. It is precisely the point that information may be normatively *irrelevant* even when "important" in an epistemological sense (to reiterate the initial point made above, legal relevance is itself an object of first-order legal regulation.) Van Dijk would simply shift the "importance" of the information from epistemic to some other value of the relevant discourse.

His framework, then, can easily absorb the approach of this chapter. Where it is perhaps less helpful is in attempting to base one primitive relation (i.e., relevance) on another (i.e., discursive importance). As shown above, this is a pragmatic mirroring of the same problem facing Anderson and Belnap. Additionally, not unlike Grice, van Dijk's emphasize is on what may be termed *conversational relevance*, whereby proposition A is "relevant" in relation to proposition B if their connection is considered "appropriate" (van Dijk, 1989) by a speaker in a specific pragmatic context. "Appropriateness" is supposed to be different from the "meaning connection" central to Anderson and Belnap (which they see as central to semantics) and certainly different from the syntactical requirements of well-formed propositions.

Where van Dijk floats a crucial point that Anderson and Belnap – as well as Grice – sometimes fail to emphasize, is that it is a condition for a valid determination of relevance (for instance, of a data item to a line of argument) that a pragmatic *reason* for the relevance can be both formed and defended according to the parameters of the given discourse. Reading "normative" – and in some instances that

---

[82] *Relevance logic* is briefly explained in Section 4.6.3 below.
[83] See above, text to note 58.

center on courts, "institutional" – as a subset of "pragmatic" underlines a similar approach to the examination of the different contexts of operation of legal relevance explored here.

4.6.2.6 A Refutation of the Argument from the Distinction Between Relevance and Admissibility

Before concluding, I wish to return to a point only cursorily made at the outset of the present Section 4.6.2. A common claim aims at neutralizing the basic argument made in this paper by invoking the distinction between relevance and admissibility. This distinction, so the claim goes, allocates all normative considerations and their ambiguities to the sphere of admissibility rules, while leaving relevance relatively – or entirely – causal or "topical". On this distinction, AI procedures meet different modes of operation; even when severely challenged in dealing with admissibility, the causal or topical links of "skeletal relevance" are much more given to potent information sorters that apply semantic, pragmatic, and other heuristic procedures.

There are two reasons why this distinction does nothing to solve any of the ambiguities discussed above.

1. In law as in any communicative medium, relevance permeates substantive as well as procedural or derivative discourse and procedures, not just the law of evidence. This means that forming claims in contract or criminal law, or in the law of civil procedure, requires as much relevance application as the law of evidence. In fact, it is a regretful mistake that most – not all – legal discourse of relevance is traditionally relegated to the theory of evidence. What may count as a binding contractual acceptance, for example, or what elements of happenstance may count towards a criminal defense, requires and in fact applies relevance criteria.
2. The argument from cultural cognition: in recent critical studies (Kahan & Braman, 2006), so-called cultural cognition studies have identified correlative links between cultural and ideological biases and perceptions of risk (e.g., a juror who is generally concerned about personal safety may be quicker to agree that a given individual suspect poses such risks than one guided by an opposite bias). My point here is not a direct application of cultural cognition to a critique of relevance, although it makes a similar basic point: that persons', and thereby institutions', relevance judgments are inter alia a product of unconscious specific (rather than merely general) epistemic biases. My point is neither to validate this point nor to refute it, but to acknowledge that as a practice (rather than a set of formal considerations), what may have a "tendency to make the existence of any fact that is of consequence to the determination of the action more probable or less probable"[84] is no less a matter of epistemic bias than are normative considerations. When Grice orders: "Be relevant!" he makes no claim as to what may, could, or would be considered a relevant contribution to the linguistic exchange.

---

[84] Federal Rules of Evidence, Rule 401.

The argument from cultural cognition points out that a general acceptance of the relevance requirement made by any rule or maxim – even on the most technical, strictly causal or epistemic interpretation – contributes nothing towards a consensus concerning what relevance entails, nor towards a unified application of its criteria.

Invoking admissibility, then, does not solve any of the problems that the indeterminacy of legal relevance gives rise to. Relevance operates and is crucial to forming legal claims where admissibility is not a recognized standard (if it would be, it would simply be another name for relevance); and relegating relevance to a much narrower set of questions (specifically, "causal" rather than normative) does little or nothing to mitigate indeterminacy, since causal inferences are given to the same kinds of bias-pluralism that normative ones are – if not, in fact, more so.

An added consideration stems from the role of relevance in legal and quasi-legal rhetoric. A classical example is supplied by the legal ethnographers who study the language of non-represented litigants, such as in small claims court. Thus Conely and O'Barr study (1990) of divergent approaches to relevance between the standard form of legal discourse and in particular, the formation of legal claims – the rule-oriented form of rule-breach-remedy – and more relational narrations of litigants who place probative value on information that doctrine entirely bars. Consider, e.g., a litigant in the context of an automobile accident who bases her claim largely on evidence of antagonistic or aggressive behavior of her antagonist immediately following the accident, which, for the court, is entirely irrelevant in adjudicating on the responsibility of the parties for the accident that allows only evidence of antecedent behavior: the court applies NR criteria that are simply different from the NR criteria assumed by the litigant. Legal formalists or proceduralists[85] would dismiss this critical insight on the grounds that the phenomenon it describes is simply a mistake, or an aberration, that requires no theoretical and certainly no practical consideration – the behavior and expectations need fixing, not the discursive framework. To those greatly concerned with serious gaps between the (bounded) rationality of legal practices and discourse and the (otherwise bounded) rationality of persons who approach it, such variations in understanding relevance is troubling indeed.

4.6.2.7 Conclusion of the Section About Relevance

The present Section 4.6.2 offers a set of critical insights rather than a central unified claim. It deals with a group of related problems that define legal theory's complex relation to the concept of relevance, with special emphasis on challenges for AI and law. Unlike some previous work, it extends beyond considerations typical of the theory of the law of evidence. Where it attempts to make a contribution, it is typifying

---

[85] Generally speaking, so-called "legal proceduralists" or (in this context) "formalists" emphasize the institutional and structural aspects of decision-making processes independently of context, outcome, or "substantive" normative considerations.

4.6 Relevance

tensions especially in the relations between approaches to relevance and several approaches to legal formalism, "old" syllogistic formalism, "new" functional formalism (associated mainly with the economic approach to law, Pildes (1999)) and finally a relational formalism that subjects legal forms to interests anchored in relations between parties without collapsing to functionalism (Yovel, 2010). One central argument of this analysis is that, counterintuitively, normative relevance should pose less problems for AI treatment than causal or epistemic relevance.

4.6.3 Relevance Logic

4.6.3.1 A Gentle Introduction to the Main Concepts

Jonathan Yovel's Section 4.6.2.5, 'Considerations about Applying Relevance Logic', are in a sense preamble to the explanation of *relevance logic* (a kind of non-classical logic) in the present Section 4.6.3. *Relevance logic*[86] (called by some[87] *relevant logic*) is a family of *modal logics*. relevance logic is typified by its requiring the antecedent and consequent of implications to be *relevantly* related. We quote from a nice and undemanding explanation[88]:

> Relevance logic aims to capture aspects of implication that are ignored by the *"material implication" operator*[89] in classical truth-functional logic, namely the notion of relevance

---

[86] See, e.g., an overview in Mares and Meyer (2001), in Mares (2006), and in Dunn and Restall (2002), the latter being a rewritten version of Dunn (1986). An in-depth treatment is provided in Anderson and Belnap (1975), in Anderson and Dunn (1992), as well as, e.g., in a book by Stephen Read (1988, revised 2010).

[87] Apparently more frequently so in Australian logicians, and also in Britain. The French name is *logique pertinente*. Practitioners of *relevant logic* have been referred to as *relevant logicians*. More often, one finds theme referred to as *Relevantists*, but usually in opposition to the Classicists, in the context of the controversy between advocates of relevance logic and advocates of classical logic.

[88] The quotation is from http://en.wikipedia.org/wiki/Relevance_logic Concerning the history of relevance logic (ibid.): "Relevance logic was proposed in 1928 by Soviet (Russian) philosopher Ivan E. Orlov (1886–circa 1936) in his strictly mathematical paper 'The Logic of Compatibility of Propositions' published in *Matematicheskii Sbornik*. The basic idea of relevant implication appears in medieval logic, and some pioneering work was done by [Wilhelm] Ackermann [(1956)], [Shaw-Kwei] Moh [(1950)], and [Alonzo] Church [(1951)] in the 1950s. Drawing on them, Nuel Belnap and Alan Ross Anderson (with others) wrote the *magnum opus* of the subject, *Entailment: The Logic of Relevance and Necessity* in the 1970s (the second volume being published in the nineties). They focused on both systems of entailment and systems of relevance, where implications of the former kinds are supposed to be both relevant and necessary."

The history as related by Stephen Read (1988, but in the revised edn., 2010, section 3.5, p. 44) is as follows: "In 1958, Anderson and Belnap took up ideas from Church and Ackermann, and started a research program into what in time became 'relevance (now often called, 'relevant') logic'. Their chosen name picked up an informal use before that time of the epithet 'relevant' to characterise a consequence relation, and an implication, which was not paradoxical in the way material and strict implication were [...]".

[89] See http://en.wikipedia.org/wiki/Material_implication

between antecedent and conditional[90] of a true implication. This idea is not new: C. I. Lewis was led to invent modal logic, and specifically *strict implication*, on the grounds that classical logic grants *paradoxes of material implication*[91] such as the principle that *a falsehood implies any proposition*. Hence "if I'm a donkey, then two and two is four" is true when translated as a material implication, yet it seems intuitively false since a true implication must tie the antecedent and consequent together by some notion of relevance. And whether or not I'm a donkey seems in no way relevant to whether two and two is four.

Thus far, however, we haven't seen the logical criterion for relevance. The same text continues as follows[92]:

> How does relevance logic formally capture a notion of relevance? In terms of a syntactical constraint for a *propositional calculus*, it is necessary, but not sufficient, that premises and conclusion share *atomic formulae* (formulae that do not contain any logical connectives). In a *predicate calculus*, relevance requires sharing of variables and constants between premises and conclusion. This can be ensured (along with stronger conditions) by, e.g., placing certain restrictions on the rules of a natural deduction system.[93] In particular, a Fitch-style *natural deduction* can be adapted to accommodate relevance by introducing tags at the end of each line of an application of an inference indicating the premises relevant to the conclusion of the inference. Gentzen-style *sequent calculi*[94] can be modified by removing the

---

[90] "The *material conditional*, also known as *material implication*, is a binary truth function $\rightarrow$ such that the compound sentence $p \rightarrow q$ (typically read 'if p then q' or 'p implies q') is logically equivalent to the negative compound: not(p and not q). A material conditional compound itself is often simply called a conditional. By definition of '$\rightarrow$', the compound $p \rightarrow q$ is *false* if and only if both p is true and q is false. That is to say that $p \rightarrow q$ is *true* if and only if either p is false or q is true (or both)" (http://en.wikipedia.org/wiki/Material_conditional).

[91] See http://en.wikipedia.org/wiki/Paradoxes_of_material_implication
Paradoxes of *material implication* include:

$$p \rightarrow (q \rightarrow p).$$
$$\neg p \rightarrow (p \rightarrow q).$$
$$(p \rightarrow q) \vee (q \rightarrow r).$$

where $\neg$ is negation, (like $\sim$ in Yovel's Sec. 4.6.2). Paradoxes of *strict implication* include:

$$(p \ \& \ \neg p) \rightarrow q.$$
$$p \rightarrow (q \rightarrow q).$$
$$p \rightarrow (q \vee \neg q).$$

[92] Also this quotation is from http://en.wikipedia.org/wiki/Relevance_logic

[93] "In logic and proof theory, *natural deduction* is a kind of proof calculus in which logical reasoning is expressed by inference rules closely related to the 'natural' way of reasoning. This contrasts with the axiomatic systems which instead use axioms as much as possible to express the logical laws of deductive reasoning" (http://en.wikipedia.org/wiki/Natural_deduction)

[94] "In proof theory, a *sequent* is a formalized statement of provability that is frequently used when specifying calculi for deduction. In the sequent calculus, the name *sequent* is used for the construct which can be regarded as a specific kind of judgment, characteristic to this deduction system" (http://en.wikipedia.org/wiki/Sequent). "In proof theory and mathematical logic, sequent calculus is a family of formal systems sharing a certain style of inference and certain formal properties. The first sequent calculi, systems LK and LJ, were introduced by Gerhard Gentzen in 1934 as

4.6 Relevance

weakening rules that allow for the introduction of arbitrary formulae on the right or left side of the *sequents*.

A notable feature of relevance logics is that they are *paraconsistent logics*: the existence of a contradiction will not cause *"explosion"*. This follows from the fact that a conditional with a contradictory antecedent that does not share any propositional or predicate letters with the consequent cannot be true (or derivable).

Edwin Mares (2006) explains:

> Relevant logicians point out that what is wrong with some of the paradoxes (and fallacies) is that is that the antecedents and consequents (or premises and conclusions) are on completely different topics. The notion of a topic, however, would seem not to be something that a logician should be interested in — it has to do with the content, not the form, of a sentence or inference. But there is a formal principle that relevant logicians apply to force theorems and inferences to "stay on topic". This is the *variable sharing principle*. The variable sharing principle says that no formula of the form A → B can be proven in a relevance logic if A and B do not have at least one propositional variable (sometimes called a proposition letter) in common and that no inference can be shown valid if the premises and conclusion do not share at least one propositional variable.
>
> At this point some confusion is natural about what relevant logicians have attempted to do. The variable sharing principle is only a necessary condition that a logic must have to count as a relevance logic. It is not sufficient. Moreover, this principle does not give us a criterion that eliminates all of the paradoxes and fallacies. Some remain paradoxical or fallacious even though they satisfy variable sharing. As we shall see, however, relevant logic does provide us with a relevant notion of proof in terms of the real use of premises [...], but it does not by itself tell us what counts as a true (and relevant) implication. It is only when the formal theory is put together with a philosophical interpretation that it can do this [...].

That is to say, when one deals with semantics. Concerning the semantics of *relevance logic*[95]:

> Relevance logic is, in syntactical terms, a substructural logic because it is obtained from classical logic by removing some of its structural rules (e.g. explicitly of some sequent calculus[96] or implicitly by "tagging" inferences of a natural deduction system). It is sometimes referred to as a modal logic because it can be characterized as a class of formulas valid over a class of *Kripke (relational) frames*.[97] In Kripke semantics for relevant logic, the implication operator is a binary modal operator, and negation is usually taken to be a unary modal operator. As such, the accessibility relation governing the operator is ternary rather than the usual binary ones that govern unary modal operators often read as "necessarily".
>
> A Kripke frame F for a propositional relevance language is a triple (W,R,*) where W is a set of indices (or points or worlds), R is a ternary accessibility relation between indices, and * is a unary function taking indices to indices. A model M for the language is an ordered pair (F,V) where F is a frame and V is a valuation function mapping sets of worlds (propositions)

---

a tool for studying natural deduction in first-order logic (in classical and intuitionistic versions, respectively)" (http://en.wikipedia.org/wiki/Sequent_calculus).

[95] Also this quotation is from http://en.wikipedia.org/wiki/Relevance_logic

[96] See note **94**.

[97] See http://en.wikipedia.org/wiki/Kripke_semantics

to propositional letters. Let M be a model and a,b,c indices from M. An implication is defined

$$M, a \models \phi \rightarrow \psi \iff \forall b, c((Rabc \land M, b \models \phi) \Rightarrow M, c \models \psi).$$

Negation (i.e., ¬) is defined

$$M, a \models \neg \phi \iff M, a^* \not\models \phi.$$

One obtains various relevance logics by placing appropriate restrictions on R and on $*$.

Bear in mind that the symbol ⊨ stands for *consequence*, whereas if the symbol is ⊭ (that is ⊨ with a slash overprinted on it) the sense is "not a logical consequence". The symbol ⇒ stands for "entails". The symbol ⇐ stands for "is entailed by"; both are combined in the symbol ⇔ The symbol → stands for "implies". The symbol ∧ stands for "and"; sometimes the symbol & is used equivalently. The symbol ∀ stands for "for all". The prefix ¬ (sometimes the symbol ∼ is found equivalently) negates the proposition whose symbol it precedes.

Edwin Mares (2006) explains, concerning the semantics of relevance logic:

> Like the semantics of modal logic, the semantics of relevance logic relativises truth of formulae to worlds. But Routley and Meyer[98] go modal logic one better and use a three-place relation on worlds. This allows there to be worlds at which $q \rightarrow q$ fails and that in turn allows worlds at which $p \rightarrow (q \rightarrow q)$ fails. Their truth condition for → on this semantics is the following:
>
>> $A \rightarrow B$ is true at a world a if and only if for all worlds b and c such that $Rabc$ (R is the accessibility relation) either A is false at b or B is true at c.
>
> For people new to the field it takes some time to get used to this truth condition. But with a little work it can be seen to be just a generalisation of Kripke's truth condition for strict implication (just set $b = c$).
>
> [...] One interpretation of the ternary relation [...] is suggested in Jon Barwise (1993) and developed in Restall (1996). On this view, worlds are taken to be information-theoretic "sites" and "channels". A site is a context in which information is received and a channel is a conduit through which information is transferred. Thus, for example, when the BBC news appears on the television in my living room, we can consider the living room to be a site and the wires, satellites, and so on, that connect my television to the studio in London to be a channel. Using channel theory to interpret the Routley-Meyer semantics, we take $Rabc$ to mean that a is an information-theoretic channel between sites b and c. Thus, we take $A \rightarrow B$ to be true at a if and only if, whenever a connects a site b at which A obtains to a site c, B obtains at c.

There are other interpretations as well. Mares himself proposed two interpretations, one in Mares (1997), and the other one in Mares (2004). He explains them informally in Mares (2006).

---

[98] See Routley, Meyer, Plumwood, and Brady (1983), whose second volume is Brady (2003).

4.6.3.2 Any Potential for Application in Automated Tools for Law?

Applications of relevance logic have been devised within mathematics, such as a Peano arithmetic developed by Meyer (Meyer & Friedman, 1992). Relevance logic is also at the basis of some *deontic logics* (i.e., logics of obligation and permissibility) developed by Anderson (1967), Mares (1992), and Goble (1999). Wansing (2002) developed and applied an *epistemic relevant logic*. *Epistemic logic* is about knowledge. Besides, in theoretical computer science there exists a variation on relevance logic called *linear logics*, introduced by Jean-Yves Girard, and being a logic of *computational resources*.

It may be that eventually, *relevance* as intended in jurisprudence could be modelled by means of relevance logic, but this would require a huge effort, and would not be understood other than by logicians. It may be however that this could form the basis of some software tool. The problem would then arise of convincing the legal scholars that neither the logical model, nor the software are faulty, and that quite important nuances are not merely hidden by the mathematics as embodied in the software. This in turn would call for the automated *generation of explanations* in the form of natural-language argumentation.

Separate generation of explanations is conceivable, and not unfeasible. Arguably, this is the way to go in future relevance-logic software for legal applications. With no relation to either legal relevance, or relevance logic, something rather similar was done in Andrew Stranieri and John Zeleznikow's *Split Up* knowledge-based system for assisting in negotiations concerning marital split of assets when spouses divorce. (Split Up will be used as an example again and again in Stranieri and Zeleznikow's subsections at the end of Section 6.1 in this book.) The inference in *Split Up* resorts to neural networks, but neural networks are notoriously opaque, rather than transparent, when it comes to onlookers trying to make sense of how they reach their conclusions. Therefore, within the *Split Up* architecture, a separate module generating explanations was provided, whose inference technique is not neural (see, e.g., Stranieri, Zeleznikow, Gawler, and Lewis, 1999).

It must be said however that arguably there is no really compelling reason to use relevance logic, rather than other kinds of logic, if one is to develop logic-based software concerned with legal relevance. For practical purposes of capturing some common-sense propositions or rules, the syntactic constraint on relevance, in relevance logic, is both excessive and therefore cumbersome, and inadequate. It is excessive and cumbersome, because it prevents straightforward expression of coincidences (possibly an expression upstream of formulating a hypothesis which would attempt to conceive of causality), or of correlation or even direct causality, if correlation[99] or a causal relation is kept implicit because people are supposed to be aware of it.

---

[99] If A causes B and A causes C, then B and C are *correlated*. By contrast, A and B are *related*, and A and C are *related*. See, e.g., Papineau's (1991) 'Correlations and Causes'.

In order to satisfy the syntactic constraint on there being shared, between the premises and the conclusion, atomic formulae if we are concerned with a propositional calculus, or variables or constants, if we are concerned with a predicate calculus, one can resort to tricks. Consider, for example, trying to express the concomitance of high tides and full moon, if we don't want to also make explicit the causal relation of the moon's force of gravity attracting the earth's vast expanses of water. One way to overcome the syntactic constraint would be to perfunctorily have observers appear in both the premises and the conclusion: if the place is such that there is some time when tides can be observed, then when one can observe (if view is unimpeded) a full moon, then one can also observe (if view is not obstacled) a higher tide with respect to the range of tide levels by which the given place is affected over time. At any rate, by syntax alone relevance logic can conceivably be fooled into accepting things that by common sense are not relevant. Moreover, as its criterion of relevance is syntactic, relevance logic may come across as too dumb for admitting as relevant some such things that we know to be relevant.[100]

One must say however that background information we don't want to provide in full every time, can be included among the premises, as simply a symbol for a proposition encompassing that information. Arguably future practical software systems using relevance logic, if they are to be achieved, would have to be able to access repositories of common sense, of encyclopedic knowledge, and of substantive and procedural law represented by means of some logical formalism. *Ontologies* are likely to play an important part. Sections 6.1.7.3, 6.1.7.4, and 6.1.7.5 in this book are concerned with ontologies.

---

[100] Hidden relevance is sometimes the key in a joke. For example, Richard Whitely (1993) tells a joke about a visitor passing in the countryside. The visitor stops and asks a farmer for the time. Crouching down beside a cow in the pasture, the farmer lifts her udder, and tells his interlocutor that it's ten to one. Astounded, the visitor asks him: "How can you tell time by feeling a cow's udder?" The farmer explains that by lifting up the udder, one can see the church clock across the valley. Clearly, here presentation matters, as the punchline (revealing that lifting the udder is relevant indeed) comes at the end of the narration. Lifting the cow's udder is relevant in the given context, because it was an obstacle to seeing the clock. The visitor is astonished because his expectation is violated, that it cannot possibly be relevant, for telling the time, that a person would feel a cow's udder. The general rule that if you feel a cow's udder, you become able to tell the time, is a false rule, because the premise and the conclusion are not relevant to each other. It is only in the given context – namely, that the cow's udder, as being an opaque object, cannot be looked through, and that behind it, in a straight line, the clock would be visible were it not for the obstacle – that lifting the udder is quite relevant for being able to tell the time.

Chapter 5
The Narrative Dimension

5.1 Legal Narratives

5.1.1 Overall Narrative Plausibility: Preliminaries

Adam Gearey's entry on 'Law and narrative' in a splendid encyclopedia of narrative theory (Gearey, 2005), following the entry introduction has sections entitled 'Narrative and adjudication', 'Law and literature', 'Narrative, philosophy and jurisprudence', and 'Law, narrative, and identity'. Section 'Narrative and adjudication' points out (Gearey, 2005, pp. 271–272):

> The work of Bernard Jackson (1988 [our 1988a]) provides a theoretically developed account of narrative in the area of adjudication. Jackson argues that narrative is an essential part of legal decision making, picking up and developing themes within schools of both positivist and realist jurisprudence. The theoretical suppositions underlying this work return to the structuralist semiotics of A.J. Greimas, which, in turn relies on the notion of a 'semio-narrative' level in the work of Vladimir Propp [... See Propp (1928)]. Narrative is understood as a sequence that moves from the setting of goals, the performance of those goals, and the reflection on success or failure [...]. Within this sequence there will be figures who aid or obstruct the subject [...].
>
> [...] Because analysis of the processes in a courtroom is complex, it is necessary to take an exemplary aspect: witness testimony. Testimony in court can be modelled in Greimasian terms. Imagine that the plaintiff has called a witness. The witness has a helper in the form of counsel for the plaintiff. The witness also has an opponent: counsel for the defence. [...] Jackson is drawing attention to basic positions that can be occupied by different actors as a narrative develops about the case in the courtroom [...].

"[L]awyers generally recognize the importance of stories in fact finding. Legal philosophers have argued that narrative coherence contributes to justification both of factual conclusions and choice and interpretation of legal rules" (MacCrimmon, 1989, p. 463), while she herself "focus[es] on the relationship between narrative coherence and factual conclusions. Two legal scholars who have addressed the problem and attempted to provide concrete examples are Karl Llewellyn[1] and Neil

---

[1] Karl N. Llewellyn (1893–1962) was professor at the University of Chicago Law School. His work focused mostly on the topic of legal realism. Llewellyn (1962, repr. 2008) is a compilation of his writings from the 1930s through the 1950s.

MacCormick [(MacCormick, 1980)]" (ibid.), and for this MacCrimmon also cites Jackson (1988a). Maley and Fahey (1991) discussed the construction of reality in court by means of the manner in which the evidence is presented. There is also a different disciplinary perspective: in the journal *Poetics,* Kurzon published 'How Lawyers Tell Their Tales' (Kurzon, 1985).

"Taking their inspiration from frame analysis in sociology, Bennett and Feldman [(1981)] sought to test a hypothesis derived from their observations of jury trials, combined with discussions with participants. Their hypothesis was that the construction of truth within the courtroom was primarily a matter of the *overall* narrative plausibility of the story told. They argued that it was not the weighing of individual elements in the story, each in terms of the evidence for that element, which rendered a case persuasive or not, but rather the plausibility of the story structure taken as a whole" (Jackson, 1996, p. 19). "In the end, it is the fit of the symbolised element into the larger structure, and not the pure documentation for the element itself, that dictates final judgment" (Bennett & Feldman, 1981, p. 113). They "presented an account of narrative structure in terms of settings, concerns, central action, and resolution", again in the words of Jackson (1996, p. 19), who also explained:

> The setting usually includes the time, the place, and some of the characters. The concern is an action that, given the setting, creates a climactic (eventful, ironical, suspenseful) situation. For example, if someone is rock-climbing [...] and slips and falls, slipping and falling are the concern. If the story ended at this point, the audience would be left wondering: what happened to the climber? Was he hurt or killed? A complete story will provide an answer to these questions. This stage is the resolution. The central action is the structural element that creates the central question the story must resolve. The resolution normally resolves both the predicament created by the problem and the questions the listeners might have had about the outcome

– e.g., that "the climber was taken to the hospital for treatment" (Bennett & Feldman, 1981, p. 20).

> However, plausibility to the jury is not merely a matter of intelligibility of the discourse as a (well-structured) story: it is a matter also of comparison with known substantive narrative typifications of behaviour. Every society [..] has its own stock of substantive narratives, which represent typical human behaviour patterns [...] (Jackson, 1996, p. 20).

Bernard Jackson, a legal semiologist, distinguishes between the semantics of the story, and its pragmatics. "Many trial lawyers would argue that plausibility turns not only on the content of that which is told, but also on the manner of telling it" (p. 20).

5.1.2 Approaches to Narratives from the "New Evidence Scholarship"

In the early 1980s, there was among scholars much interest in the nature of juridical proof. Bennett and Feldman (1981) brought stories/scripts *à la* Rumelhart (1980a, 1980b) to people's attention within legal scholarship, and Pennington and Hastie (1986, 1988, 1992, 1993) produced some empiricism as to how jurors reason consistent with the Rumelhart approach. However neither had a conceptualisation of not guilty or not liable. In addition, the dominant view was that some form of conventional probability underlay the structure.

In his scholarly output from that period, Ron Allen's answered the first question by demonstrating that it wasn't one but two stories that mattered. Secondly, he showed that the appraisal of those stories had to be ordinal, not cardinal (thus, in terms of *relative* plausibility). Implicit in this (see, e.g., the discussion of scripts, and so on) was the theory of evidence that a 1994 paper by Allen made explicit.

In the context of that debate, the *theory of anchored narratives* of Wagenaar, et al. (1993)[2] made its appearance. The anchored narratives approach (sometimes informally referred to as *AN* for short) built on the prior work mentioned earlier, but it has a conceptual limit: there is no rule of decision, nothing that says when a narrative is good enough for either a civil or criminal case. It has the same conceptual limit that Pennington and Hastie's approach[3] has, which is there is no operationalisation of 'not guilty' or 'not liable'.[4] For example, Ron Allen offered that critique, amid those legal scholars who offered a critical response to the theory of anchored narratives.

The central idea of the theory of anchored narratives is that juridical proof is organised around plausible narratives where "plausibility" is determined by the relationship between the story offered at trial and the background knowledge/common sense of the decision maker. In Allen's opinion, this conflates two separate issues: the macro structure of proof, and the micro analysis of evidence, but nonetheless it is more or less accurate. These two themes – the *macro structure of proof,* and the *micro analysis of evidence* – were precisely the themes of earlier work by Allen himself.

For example, in a paper entitled 'The nature of juridical proof', Allen had claimed (Allen, 1991): "The central question is often whether a richly textured human episode occurred at trial, and if so, its nature. Answering these questions requires finding an interpretation that best explains a complex set of interrelated data" (ibid., p. 393). "Indeed, often the 'facts' are indistinguishable from the interpretation" (Allen, 1991, p. 395). Allen (1991, p. 396), throughout a section that as per its title, deals with "the Tension Between the Official Epistemology and Juror Reasoning", discussed the earlier work by Bennett and Feldman (1981) and Pennington and Hastie (See note 3). Then in Allen (1991, p. 406), section 3, 'The Equally Well Specified Cases Proposal and its Criminal Counterpart', is essentially a generalisation of the theory that what occurs at trial is the comparison of the plausibility of the plaintiff's and defendant's cases, and in criminal cases a determination that there is a plausible story of guilt and no plausible story of innocence. Plausibility, in turn, is determined, as Allen (1991, section 2) argues, by references to the background knowledge/common sense of the decision maker. This approach by Allen

---

[2] See also Wagenaar (1996) and van Koppen (1995, pp. 593–604). The theory of anchored narratives of Wagenaar, et al. (1993) was discussed by Verheij (2000) in the context of a work on dialectical argumentation for courtroom decision-making.

[3] Pennington and Hastie (1986, 1988, 1992, 1993).

[4] 'Not guilty' belongs to criminal cases, whereas 'not liable' belongs to civil cases.

quite resembles (and anticipates) the anchored narratives approach, with one exception: AN has no operationalisation of 'not guilty', whereas Allen's theory does. Ron Allen's first article discussing this was Allen (1986).

Allen (1986) was an early effort to give a normative account of juridical proof that involved stories. It apparently was the paper, or one of the papers, that inspired the label "the new evidence scholarship". Allen (1991, 1994, 1997) announced a new research program in the nature of juridical proof that was exploring the limits of formal reasoning and proposed as a solution a version of a story model. This research program has stimulated a large literature especially in the United States.

The central thesis of Allen (1991) was summarised in Allen's paper 'Explanationism All the Way Down' (2008a, p. 325) as follows: "A more promising approach to understanding juridical proof is that it is a form of inference to the best explanation.[5] Conceiving of cases as involving the relative plausibility of the parties' claims (normally provided in story or narrative form) substantially resolves all the paradoxes and difficulties [...]". In Allen (2008b), the relationship between juridical proof and *inference to the best explanation* (*IBE*) was thoroughly examined.[6] Allen claimed (2008a, p. 325) that, if one accepts to conceive of cases as involving the *relative plausibility* of the parties' claims,

> the complexity problem is purely a function of the choices made by the parties. Indeed, this points out a subtle but important clarification of the role of the parties. They are sometimes thought of as ambiguity generators, but in reality they are ambiguity discarders. Rather than litigate on an infinite number of ways in which the universe might have been, they focus on a few and ask fact finders to decide which is the most plausible.

"In criminal cases, this amounts to determining whether there is a plausible story of guilt, and if so, in addition a plausible story of innocence" (Allen, 2008a, p. 328, note 3). Allen continued (2008a, pp. 325–326):

> To be sure, "plausible" may mean "more likely" but this does not mean comparative plausibility reduces to probability. Rather, what is "plausible" is a function of the explanation, its coherence, consistency, coverage, consilience, and how it fits into the background knowledge possessed by the fact finder.

This also affects the *relevance,* and therefore the admissibility of evidence in court. "Explanationism is not just the best explanation of the macro structure of proof; it is also the best explanation of such issues as relevance and weight of the evidence" (Allen, 2008a, p. 326).[7] In the explanationist account, relevance and the weight of evidence are conceived as follows (Allen, 2008a, p. 327):

---

[5] Concerning inference to the best explanation, see Section 2.2.1.6 above.

[6] Also see Allen (1994, 1997, 2003), and Allen and Pardo (2007a, 2007b).

[7] In his critique of Bayesianism for legal proof, Allen claims, concerning relevance and weight of the evidence, that (2008a, pp. 326–327) "it is difficult to see how to give a sensible probabilistic interpretation to such matters. A likelihood ratio explanation of both has superficial plausibility, but immediately runs aground of the universal lack of objective relative frequencies. The explanationist account is by contrast quite straightforward."

5.1 Legal Narratives

Evidence is relevant if it fits into an explanatory account, and its weight is a function of its significance for that explanatory account as compared to whatever other accounts may be under consideration. In one sense, the most critical limitation of the conventional probabilistic account of the evidentiary process is their modelling juridical proof as involving the probability of the hypothesis given the evidence. A more plausible account that is more consistent with the evidence I have discussed is that juridical proof involves the probability of the evidence given the hypotheses formulated by the parties, with the best, more or less, explanatory account winning out (Allen & Pardo, 2008).

There are some philosophical worries that emerge from this account. For example, it is fair that what I have described is not exactly what the philosophers refer to as inference to the best explanation, at least not in criminal cases, where the critical issue is whether there is a plausible story of innocence rather than whether it is the best. Fair enough, but the central point is the explanation-based nature of juridical proof. What is most plausible is another worry, for which I simply recur to common sense. This will not satisfy the philosophical worries (Lipton, 2004),[8] but another reminder that my aim is understanding, not conceptual purity, may be in order here. A similar comment is in order with regard to what an explanation is.

Against these worries are obvious advantages of the explanatory account. It explains how cases distribute uncertainty and ambiguity over the parties, supporting the system's norms. It has the fundamental virtue of being consistent with the way people actually reason rather than imposing an odd and alien form of thinking. Indeed, this is surely why it is quite consistent with the great bulk of evidentiary regulation (which is mostly nonregulation). And it captures the role of the parties, which is to determine the range of ambiguity and uncertainty over which to dispute.

In the theory of anchored narratives of Wagenaar et al. (1993), narrative (e.g., the prosecution's claim that John murdered his wife) is related to evidence (e.g., John's fingerprints on the murder weapon) by a connection that must be satisfactory for the narrative to hold once the evidence is accepted. To say it with Bex, et al. (2007, section 2.1), anchored narratives theory

> stresses that the only viable way in which crime investigation and judicial proof can proceed is by constructing alternative stories about what happened in a case, by comparing their quality as stories, and by comparing how well they are "anchored" in commonsense generalisations. A story can be anchored in two ways.1 The first is *internal anchoring*. Stories at least contain a sequence of events on a time line and stories become stronger if the connections between the events it contains are not just temporal but also causal (for example, shooting a gun causes a sound) or intentional (a man possessing a gun who is assaulted will shoot the attacker). The second type of anchoring is *external anchoring*: elements of a story can be anchored in the available evidence by sources of information, such as observation, memory or testimony. This also involves commonsense generalisations. For instance, a witness testimony supports a belief only by virtue of the common knowledge that witnesses usually tell the truth. Clearly, the general knowledge involved in anchoring stories can have exceptions and therefore anchors must be critically examined and refined when the facts indicate a possible exception. For instance, if two witnesses know each other, they may have influenced each other's testimonies: to discard this possibility a refined anchor may be needed, such as that if two witnesses agree but did not confer, they usually tell the truth.

Bex et al. (ibid.) pointed out that anchored narratives theory "does not give a detailed account of how stories can be connected to the available evidence", and proposed to do it better, by means of a logical model of argumentation (See Section 5.4). Bex,

---

[8] See Section 2.2.1.6 above.

Prakken, and Verheij (2006) adopted the anchored narratives approach. In contrast, Bernard Jackson is critical of anchored narratives. At any rate, Jackson states (1996, p. 10):

> [...] triers of fact [i.e., judges or, in some countries, the jury] reach their decisions on the basis of two judgments; first an assessment is made of the plausibility of the prosecution's account of what happened and why, and next it is considered whether this narrative account can be anchored by way of evidence to common-sense beliefs which are generally accepted as true most of the time.

For the story to be comprehensively anchored, each individual piece of evidence need be not merely plausible, but safely assumed to be certain, based on common-sense rules which are probably true. As Jackson[9] (1996 p. 25) in his critique of anchored narratives puts it:

> In short, the form of argument is an 'enthymeme', a rhetorical version of the logical syllogism where the major premise is a claim that something is *probably* true of (all) members of a class (see [...] Goodrich, 1986, pp. 189–191, [...]). [...] Not being a logically *conclusive* argument, the anchor is thus always capable of being contested.

5.1.3 Background Generalisations

Generalisations, or *background generalisations*, or *background knowledge*, or *empirical generalisations*, are common sense rules of thumb, which apply to a given instance of a belief held concerning a pattern, and are resorted to when interpreting the evidence and reconstructing a legal narrative for argumentation in court. Whereas generalisations are pervasive in how humans make sense of narratives (and also in how computers are made to make sense of them, in automated story-understanders), in the courtroom generalisations may be a pitfall in the reasoning, and one should be alert to generalisations creeping into the reasoning. They should be questioned. Making assumptions is often unwarranted.

For the reason why common sense is referred to as *background generalisations*, consider the end of this quotation from a paper by Ron Allen (2008a, p. 322):

> In finding facts, juridical fact finders are supposed to rely on the evidence produced at trial, but 'evidence' cannot be restricted to testimony, exhibits, and demeanor presented at trial. Exhibits and demeanor must be described by propositions to fit into deliberation, which is done by the fact finder. More deeply, the meaning of language, rules of logic, formations of likelihood ratios, or judgments of plausibility come from elsewhere than the 'evidence' presented at trial. The law reflects this in the explicit jury instructions[10] to rely on common sense, which means one's background, and to deliberate, which means share one's background.

---

[9] Bernard Jackson has discussed legal narratives in, e.g., Jackson (1988a, 1988b).

[10] *Jury instructions,* which jurors are given by the judge before they retire to deliberate, may have an important impact on the outcome, according to how they are formulated. For example, a team including the legal evidence scholar Craig Callen as well as Irwin Horowitz reported (Kerr, Boster, Callen, Braz, O'Brien and Horowitz 2008) about a jury simulation study. Previous research had shown "that evidence that was emotionally biasing for jurors (specifically, irrelevant information

5.1 Legal Narratives

Allen also pointed out the relation between making sense of a legal narrative and assessing plausibility, and jurors' own life experience, when they use common sense. Allen did so while referring to the instructions that juries receive from the judge (Allen, 2008a, p. 326): "Jury instructions further embed a comparative plausibility approach through instructions to rely on 'common sense'. This in essence means judge the stories you are hearing by comparison to what you have learned in your life."

Admitting that one's common sense comes from one's background is nevertheless fraught sometimes with controversy. Consider, in philosophy, Linda Martín Alcoff's defence of the U.S. Supreme Court new appointee Sonia Sotomayor (a woman of Puerto Rican background), in the aftermath of a national debate in June and July 2009 because of a speech, 'A Latina judge's voice', that Sotomayor had delivered in 2001 to the University of California Berkeley Law School (Sotomayor, 2002).

Alcoff (2010, p. 123) stated: "I would point out that the media and political controversy over Sotomayor's Berkeley speech was conducted through a repetition of just one sentence, that a 'wise Latina woman with the richness of her experiences would more often than not reach a better conclusion than a white male who hasn't lived that life.'"[11] By contrast, Alcoff continued, "The epistemological arguments she used to amplify, support, and qualify this claim – arguments that are widely held, even a kind of common sense – these arguments were not repeated or even aired at all, making her conclusion look more questionable and possibly based on a kind of identity essentialism. For these remarks, readers will no doubt recall, Sonia Sotomayor was vilified from coast to coast, [...]" (Alcoff, 2010, pp. 123–124). "She was also referred to, in the mainstream news outlets, as a schoolmarm, a broad, a hispanic chick lady, and a bully. Rush Limbaugh announced that he was going to send her a vacuum cleaner so she could clean up after the Supreme Court meetings. There was so much controversy that, in the actual confirmation hearings themselves, Sotomayor reneged on her Berkeley speech and repudiated her earlier views" (ibid., p. 124). Alcoff explained: "Sotomayor's claim that identity makes a difference to

---

about the character of a crime victim) exerted a stronger effect on juror judgment if those jurors had received instructions that explicitly endorsed jurors' ability to nullify rather than standard instructions – what one might call the 'amplification effect' of the nullification instructions." (Kerr et al., 2008, from the abstract). In their own study, Kerr et al. (2008) employed the same *nullification instructions* that had been used in the previous study, with one in addition: "one that explicitly cautioned mock jurors not to confuse the emotions aroused by the potential unfairness applying the law with similar emotions aroused by biasing information (the 'null plus' instructions). The null-plus instruction did not negate the amplification effect of the nullification instructions. Unexpectedly, mock jurors who received nullification or null plus instructions were more likely to convict the killer of an unsympathetic victim than of a sympathetic one, but those who received standard instructions were not sensitive to biasing victim information" (ibid., from the abstract).

[11] Biography and background do influence, in given context, a judge's leanings and performance. This is apparent from published biographies. Consider, e.g., Jacqueline McLeod's study (2011) of the life of Judge Jane Bolin, who on being appointed to New York City's domestic relations court in 1939 for the first of four ten-year terms, became the United States' first African American woman judge.

judgment is based on the idea that identity affects baseline knowledge as well as motivations, the direction of our attentiveness, and, most strongly, our ability in some cases to understand the experiences of others" (ibid., p. 127).[12]

---

[12] One may add that sometimes, dominant identity comes with innocent unawareness of complex patterns, or even historical facts that loom quite large in how a non-dominant group may feel, and explaining which may require exceptional articulacy of a litigant, or alternatively a considerably larger financial investment in one's counsel for the counsel to convey an articulate argument which ultimately may even not be considered relevant by the court. Whereas the court's decision concerning relevance is discretionary, it is also affected by the doxa that the judges have been fed since infancy, and whose inaccuracy, even with all good will, they may not figure out unless lectured about with the support of scholarly evidence. During the 2000s, an old Jewish lady in London won a case against a respondent that actually was the U.K. government, and specifically subordinates of the Secretary of Defence. She was born into a wealthy family of Iraqi extraction and with British citizenship in Hong Kong, and as an adolescent civilian captive under the Japanese occupation, she was turned into a sex slave by the enemy. It took that trial for her to be recognised an indemnification, which by policy, other things being equal, would have been given by the British authorities to British citizens of British stock, but not to people of Near Eastern stock in the Far East holding British citizenship.

In the media, it was pointed out that the judge was not a relative of the applicant, even though their family name was the same. It must be understood however that a British judge who is himself of Near Eastern family background (on the evidence of his family name) could not have been expected to be sympathetic to a grossly outdated governmental policy based on race, and still being held by the governmental respondent at that trial in the mid 2000s, so that a woman born a Briton but whose ancestry was not from the British Isles would be excluded from the rights of a British citizen. It is quite possible that at the ministry of Defence they had noticed that the appellant and the judge had the same family name, and that the judge's ethnic background was likely to make him unsympathetic to their line of defence, but they nevertheless went along with it, without daring however to request that that judge be excused from the case on the grounds of his own racial identity, *ex legitima suspicione*. The sum the old lady eventually won, which could have been the one year's salary of a poorly paid secretary, was presumably considerably less than the government spent in order to prepare the case and defend the indefensible.

There is much more that could be said. The horrid raise in hostility, and even offences, sometimes spectacular, whether reported or not, experienced by some Jews and especially Israelis in Britain during the 2000s – as well as, repeatedly, unsavoury episodes within the institutions – would be perceived, assessed, and interpreted differently if you assume that the U.K. wartime record was spotless, and that whatever anti-Semitism was around has been taken care of in the meantime, or if you know instead that in 1941 in Baghdad, in 1945 and 1948 in Libya, in 1947 in Aden, and in 1948 during the evacuation of civilians from the university and hospital from the besieged Mt. Scopus in Jerusalem, the British military, while present, were on orders not to intervene as Jewish civilians were being massacred massively. (It is a sad phenomenon, known all too well in the decolonised world, that things that would not occur in a colonial power's metropolis are let to occur in colonial space. But they amplify attitudes incubating in the metropolis.) If you are the child of a survivor of such a massacre (I am), you are likely to know, and even to think of it often, as do the survivors themselves. (The very final version of this book is submitted exactly seventy years after the massacre relevant to the family, and the sentiments that enabled it being watched on the spot and not prevented, let alone perpetrated, are still around, even sometimes in positions of responsibility.) If you come across attitudes, perhaps concerning a former colonial space that still retains a perhaps morbid attention among some in the metropolis, that dovetail with what you know did happen in living memory, you may make inferences that the unaware would not. *Unaware* does not mean *unaffected:* a zoologist may know something about an animal that the animal observed while carrying out a given behaviour perhaps has never thought about.

5.1 Legal Narratives

Factors involved in deliberation were appropriately invoked in Alcoff's discussion (2010, p. 127): "I want to introduce some epistemic concepts from market research and from research in social psychology that are highly relevant here. The

---

Nevertheless, as facts such as the crimes against humanity mentioned earlier are unknown to the public in the metropolis of the former colonial power, including the judiciary, it is as though those aware (and possibly still affected by survivor or survivor's children syndrome) and the unaware (including current promoters of intolerance, or the many more who tolerate this, usually to avoid antagonising the firebrands) live in different universes. With reference to the unapologetic persistence or resurgence and spread of such levels of hostility (now clad as a virtue) in the given society, once in the early 2000s (during a major upsurge of hostility) I told a retired British judge who happens to be Jewish that having or not having lost a world war can make all the difference to what is affordable in this society. He immediately looked behind him, visibly scared, even though nobody could overhear us. Let alone that this was inside a Jewish communal building. Arguably, this is not a kind of criticism he would have dared think is even conceivable in Britain. This in turn is sad, at the societal level, as the ability to be candid implies that there is trust between the parties, whereas unfeasibility disproves full integration. By contrast, in Italy, where I was raised, I and others could say things in the spirit of what I had said, and sometimes even be listened to (and even get very positive responses from some), precisely because a world war *was* lost, and because therefore knowledge of unsavoury facts from the nation's past is partly known to the local educated public, and unawareness of the rest is decreasingly withheld (cf. Nissan, 2008 [2010], 2011b, 2011c).

In the U.K., even though of course most people are good people (most people want to play by the rules), being as candid is simply not feasible, for historical allegations such as what I pointed out (but see below), even though part of them are buried inside scholarly literature for specialists published in the U.K. The unfeasibility of going public with that for the purposes of a public debate also concerning present attitudes depends on such things being so alien to the doxa: saying something so unlike what people are used to hear is shocking, coming out of the blue. You can tell individuals in private, and it is painful for both parties albeit well received once it is done but there can be no public or formal acknowledgement that there is something that should be owned up to at the societal level, and that it has explanatory power for some current phenomena, some of them resulting in the law of the land being honoured in the breach.

Interestingly, this is an observation which, I found, members of the visible minorities in London find easy to relate to, because of analogues from their own respective communal experiences, which produces a *blasé,* condescending, as well as emotionally deeply experienced attitudes towards wider local society, and especially and pointedly "formal" society. Actually such minority perspectives are potentially useful for a society bent on improving. Their being silent or silenced instead questions aspirational claims. This footnote is unlikely not to be resented, apart from its being awkward by conventions. This in turn is quite useful here, as it says something important in favour of Sotomayor's 2001 argument that because of experiences associated with her background, she but not her colleague is in some circumstances likely to spot something complex right away, of course with the duty to assess properly what suggested by intuitions that come under the rubric of background generalisations.

A bulky study by Anthony Julius (2010) on anti-Jewish prejudice in England from the Middle Ages to the present is invaluable, but too intellectual, and too focussed on textual analysis, therefore missing part of the phenomenon, the one that impinges most on people's lives. He also missed events in colonial space (an important exception being his tackling the heavily prejudiced subculture of the British administration in Palestine, which for example resulted in a British judge insulting a crowd in the courthouse, esplicitly because of their ethnoreligious identity.) All in all, Julius' book did not make an impact. In the information media, it was mentioned frivolously, in relation to the late Princess Diana (in the introduction, Julius, who had been her lawyer, related an anecdote). When (seldom) his book *was* discussed substantively, this was done superficially, and his claims were rejected out of hand (unsuprisingly, as in England the phenomenon studied tends

first concept is 'thin-slicing' – the idea of rapid judgments that short-circuit the normal time requirements of rational deliberation by filtering a small number of relevant factors from a large number of variables." Concerning snap judgement, Alcoff cited Gladwell (2005): "Malcolm Gladwell's book, *Blink*, provides numerous examples of accurate thin-slicing, from art dealers who correctly judge the authenticity or lack thereof of artworks; to marriage therapists who can judge the likely future of a marriage with 90% accuracy after simply watching a short video of the couple in conversation; to bird identification, medical diagnoses, and taste-testing" (Alcoff, 2010, p. 128). Alcoff pointed out that thin-slicing is, on the one hand, thoroughly involved in social and racial prejudices and stereotypes,[13] as well as, on the other hand, in judgments[14] that eventually turn out to have been accurate: "But we are inundated more than ever with a visual culture that confers associations between human 'types' and visible social categories. This renders the retraining of thin-slicing based on phenomenologies of appearance rather more difficult than

---

to be compartmentalised sectorially, and traditionally the chattering classes have been affected by prejudice more than other social sectors.)

It must be said that things do not remain static in a society, as well as in mutual collective perceptions, and societal change in attitudes is sometimes acknowledged in a solemn public statement on behalf of the state, whereas some other times a statement is aspirational, and aims at bringing about such change. Sometimes it is ineffectual, some other times it may be lip-service, but sometimes it is certainly sincere. Quite clearly, the Queen of England was touchingly sincere in the landmark speech she gave in Ireland on 18 May 2011. It will have given many, in both countries, a sense of closure and peace of mind. This is important for a better future. (It was a first, in being made to another nation or another ethnic group. On the previous year, an apology to the child migrants was given. On 24 February 2010, there was the prime minister Gordon Brown's apology to British child migrants to Australia, severed from families that were lied to: an apology made necessary in the U.K. because Australia was apologising to these adult, still traumatised people. At any rate, it did away with the notion that the polity never owns up.)

On the other hand, it is dubious that the perceived effect of the 18 May 2011 speech would have been so momentous, had the speech been given by an elected politician (the public tends to consider these cynically), other than somebody very revered, which in some countries is sometimes the case of a particular figurehead president with special qualities, either perceived or real. Moreover, going back to the Sotomayor controversy, it even happens sometimes that public acknowledgement is then used in order to deny that factors such as those mentioned by Sotomayor are still a reality. Some other times, a possibly little known document signed by a prime minister (such as the European Union's statement defining anti-semitism signed by Gordon Brown, though basically ornamental and only reported about in the communal rather than general information media), or released by a parliamentary committee (such as the bipartisan committee on anti-semitism at the British Parliament), can potentially be valuable as supporting evidence for an acknowledged state of affairs, in a courtroom context. This however contributes awareness of something general and possibly vague, not as situationally specific as what Sotomayor apparently meant.

[13] Concerning stereotypes, see e.g. the edited volume *Stereotypes and Stereotyping* (Macrae, Stangor, & Hewstone, 1996), and for stereotypes with a particular target, e.g. Ziv and Zajdman (1993), and much of the *ouevre* of Sander Gilman (e.g., Gilman, 1975, 1982a, 1982b, 1984, 1985, 1986a, 1986b, 1991, 1993a, 1993b, 1994a, 1994b, 1995, 1996a,1996b, 1996c, 1999, and 2006).

[14] In research in psychology, *stereotypical biases* in social decision making and memory are the subject of Bodenhausen (1988). *Illusory correlation* and stereotypes were discussed by Hamilton and Rose (1980). Hilton and Fein (1989) were concerned with the role of *diagnosticity* in stereotype-based judgments.

5.1 Legal Narratives

ever before" (Alcoff, 2010, p. 132). Undeniably, Limbaugh's vacuum cleaner jibe at Sotomayor is a case in point.

Concluding her paper, Alcoff (2010, p. 137) remarked: "If we conceptualize identities along the lines of hermeneutic horizons, this does not introduce a uniform set of interests, or point of view, or set of assumptions. We cannot assume from any candidate's or any nominee's identity that they understand that group's experience or share their politics, since horizons are neither uniform nor universally shared. Horizons are starting places, not endpoints." Next, Alcoff claimed that Sotomayor's critics misunderstood what identities are, "and how real knowing actually occurs. It seems likely that when Rush Limbaugh looked at Sonia Sotomayor, her packaging, for him, called up an image of a hotel maid. This is not a fringe phenomenon. Ignoring the effects of sensation tranference and thin-slicing on the process of our judgment will only keep locked the room in which much of our judgment takes place. If identities make an epistemic difference, then using identity as one criterion is a legitimate practice in choosing whom to vote for or how to assign a jury or a court or a committee. Of course, it is quite easy to use identities as covers for retrograde policies, for Republicans to appoint war-mongering women, or for Democrats to do so. But most people can see through that. In a snap" (Alcoff, 2010, pp. 137–138).

Anchoring by *empirical generalisations* translates, for artificial intelligence practitioners, into reliance on *common-sense beliefs*. In the literature on legal evidence, Twining (1999) is concerned with generalisations in legal narratives (see also Anderson, 1999b). Bex, et al. (2003, section 4.2) discussed such generalisations in the context of a formal computational approach to legal argumentation about a criminal case, as does Prakken (2004, section 4). The latter (ibid., section 4.2) lists four manners of attacking generalisations:

- "Attacking that they are from a valid source of generalisations",
- "Attacking the defeasible derivation from the source" (e.g., arguing that a given proposition is general knowledge indeed, but that "this particular piece of general knowledge is infected by folk belief"),
- "Attacking application of the generalisation in the given circumstances" ("This can be modelled as the application of applying more specific generalisations"), and
- "Attacking the generalisation itself".

Bear in mind that even statistics is interfaced to both argumentation, and narrative. Robert P. Abelson (well-known to cognitivists and to AI people) gave a textbook the title *Statistics as Principled Argument* (Abelson, 1995). Its publisher's blurb boldly proclaims:

> Many students [think] of statistical practice as a medical regimen. [...] However, a completely formulaic approach to statistics is wrong-headed. Statements of conclusions from statistical analysis importantly involve narrative and rhetoric. To communicate results, a coherent story is required and preparation is needed for the criticism of these interpretations with convincing counterarguments. There is an analogue between the claims of a statistical analyst and those of a lawyer [...].

True, in scientific inquiry resorting to statistics (as opposed to doctored statistics geared, say, to show the economic success of the Soviet regime) the goals and principles are different from those of a lawyer, who is intent to persuade and is anything but objective. Yet, both a lawyer and a statistician provide an interpretation purporting to be a plausible narrative. They do so by means of rhetoric.

5.1.4 The Impact of Modes of Communication

It would be too reductive to consider communication in court as though textual transcription alone would suffice. Nonverbal modes, too, affect responses. This is an aspect of legal narratives and the related court narratives to which Bernard Jackson has called attention (Jackson, 1994). He "argued elsewhere that the 'story in the trial' (e.g., the murder of which the defendant is accused) is mediated through the 'story of the trial' (that collection of narrative encounters manifest in the courtroom process itself)" (Jackson, 1998a, p. 263; citing Jackson, 1988a, pp. 8 ff, 33–36, and Jackson, 1995, p. 160 and chapter 10–12 *passim*). Jackson (2010) stated:

> The narrativisation of pragmatics, as developed in the semiotic tradition, prompts us to understand the speakers in the legal discourse as motivated to do more than merely persuade the audience(s) of their discourse of its correctness [(Espar & Mora, 1992)]. Each one is a subject of (communicative) action, with his own goals (personal and professional); each one, in his/her discourse(s) may perform multiple, and distinct (communicative) actions, which require separate analysis. I have suggested a distinction between the "story in the trial" and the the "story (properly: stories) of the trial" [(Jackson, 1988a)], the latter (through which alone the former is mediated) incorporating a multiplicity of exchanges, which may be directed to different audiences for different purposes.

Mertz and Yovel's (2005) is an encyclopedia entry about 'Courtroom narrative'. They begin by remarking:

> Research on courtroom narrative has shed light on the intricate relationship between social structure and power, on the one hand, and linguistic patterning and use, on the other. In addition, analysis of courtroom discourse has contributed to a deeper understanding of the complex facets of narrative, examining many discursive and sociolinguistic aspects together [...].
> Before reaching the courtroom, legal narratives typically undergo transformation from the less constrained format of speakers' spontaneous trouble-telling, through conversations in lawyers' offices and mediation settings, to formulation of court filings and discussions with court personnel, and finally to accounts rendered in courtrooms – ranging from more informal settings such as small claims courts through plea bargains and motions, to full-blown trials in more formal courtrooms (Conley and O'Barr 1998). The imposition of legal frames moves litigant narratives away from more emotional and relational stories toward accounts organised around theories of cause-and-effect and responsibility that respond to the requirements of legal rules [...].
> One obvious constraint on narratives in formal courtrooms in many countries is the frequent framing of accounts within question–answer sequences – with the notable exceptions of the less-constrained stories told by attorneys at the beginnings and ends of trials (Atkinson and Drew, 1979). [...]

5.1 Legal Narratives

In 1998, Kim Binsted[15] of Sony referred me to a robotic simulation; it was work going on at ETL: "I remember they had three talking heads, supposedly representing two lawyers and a judge, arguing a case. . ." (pers. comm.). ETL is the Electrotechnical Laboratory, in Tsukuba, of the Agency of Industrial Science and Technology (AIST) of Japan's Ministry of International Trade and Industry. Binsted's reference was to a paper published in 1997 by Katsumi Nitta, Osamu Hasegawa and Tomoyoshi Akiba in one of the satellite workshops of IJCAI, the leading AI conference worldwide (Nitta, Hasegawa, & Akiba, 1997). It is safe to say that three talking heads simulating a mock-trial do not ostensibly qualify as a model of the pragmatics of delivery in court, the way Jackson intended such pragmatics to be.

Forensic rhetoric is a discipline, and both verbal and other modes of communication have an impact, whether positive or adverse for a given party. It even happens that a lawyer advises his or her client beforehand to avoid exchanging stares with the judge while in the courtroom. That is prudent advice, but not because such silent communication would necessarily be harmful. You do tell a toddler not to touch a knife, but this is not because anybody using a knife would always be cutting him- or herself. It is toddlers who are more likely than the rest to cut themselves. Using facial expressions may have a beneficial or an adverse impact; if used at all, they should be used knowledgeably, and a lawyer may be more knowleadgeable at that than a client.

5.1.5 Pitfalls to Avoid: There Is No Shortcut for the Practically Minded, and No Alternative to Reading the Legal Literature on Evidence

Lack of familiarity with the more philosophical literature on the nature of juridical proof puts such artificial intelligence scholars who may wish to model legal evidence at risk of neglecting two of the crucial variables that motivated that literature, especially "the new evidence scholarship" (Allen, 1986 sqq., and so forth), and their problematic aspects, which were and are some of the key targets of the research program set forth in Allen (1986). Thinking of evidence at trial as either probabilistic or as involving narratives is nothing new. What was new were the limits of probabilistic reasoning, which this literature addresses (our present readers are urged to read, e.g., the papers collected in Allen & Redmayne, 1997), and the relationship between stories, juridical proof, and decision under uncertainty. The former should also be noted, but the latter is crucial.

One of the problems with both the Pennington and Hastie (1986, 1988, 1992, 1993) and the Bennett and Feldman (1981) story models is neither had a conceptualization of what 'not guilty' might mean. For that matter, neither had an explanation

---

[15] After earning her PhD in Edinburgh (supervised by Graeme Ritchie) with the project of an automated generator of punning verbal jokes, Kim Binsted moved to Japan, and in 1998 was organising a symposium on artificial intelligence models of humour. She later moved to the University of Hawaii.

for 'preponderance of the evidence'. The relative plausibility model that emerged from the "new evidence scholarship" research program explicitly handled that problem. Arguably, in the present large book on techniques we could not really do justice to the relative plausibility model from the legal literature, and were we to attempt to cover it, in a sense this would be a disservice to non-legal scholars who may then naïvely come to believe that they have read here everything that there is to know about the more "philosophical" things. This is definitely not the case. There is no serious substitute to accessing at least a few articles from the debate among legal scholars about matters that may make or break the seriousness and credibility of any artificial intelligence model for legal evidence.

For example, to say that proof is just something akin to inference to the best explanation[16] does not say when an explanation is good enough. To make a long story short, if the "best explanation" always wins at trial, then there is no difference between civil and criminal cases. But there must be, as the standards of proof[17] in criminal cases are far more demanding than they are in civil cases. Suppose now that the developer of an AI model would claim that his or her implemented or envisaged design could definitely handle telling out which explanation is the best, or at any rate telling out which explanation is better, out of a pair of explanations. And suppose that that same AI practitioner's solution would be to adopt any of the quantitative models available to an AI practitioner, e.g., some Bayesian model. This would elude a serious confrontation with epistemological problems which to legal scholars are of the utmost importance.

5.2 An Overview of Artificial Intelligence Approaches to Narratives

5.2.1 What Is in a Narrative?

Narratives[18] do not only belong in life events, or in literature, or, for that matter, in police investigations and then in the courtroom. Narrative is pervasive. Bear in mind that even the reasoning process unfolds in a narrative way. Peter Goodrich, in an encyclopedia entry entitled 'Narrative as Argument', has remarked: "At a formal level, narrative governs argument in that arrangement, the ordering or internal progression of a discourse, depends upon a narrative structure in which a premise is elaborated, developed, proved, or refuted. Narrative as arrangement is in this sense intrinsic to logic as well as to dialectic and rhetoric" (Goodrich, 2005, p. 348). The

---

[16] See Section 2.2.1.6 above.

[17] Cf. Bex and Walton's (2010) 'Burdens and Standards of Proof for Inference to the Best Explanation'.

[18] Nissan (2010d) is a different version of the present Section 5.2.

following quotation is from an encyclopedia entry by Marie-Laure Ryan (2005, p. 347):

> Here is [a] tentative definition of the cognitive construct that narratologists call 'story':
>
> 1. The mental representation of story involves the construction of the mental image of a world populated with individuated agents (characters) and objects. (Spatial dimension.)
> 2. This world must undergo not fully predictable changes of state that are caused by non-habitual physical events: either accidents ('happenings') or deliberate actions by intelligent agents. (Temporal dimension.)
> 3. In addition to being linked to physical states by causal relations, the physical events must be associated with mental states and events (goals, plans, emotions). This network of connections gives events coherence, motivation, closure, and intelligibility and turns them into a plot. (Logical, mental and formal dimension [...])

In some kinds of narrative forms, some condition is loosened. "The lifting of condition 1 describes the 'Grand Narratives' and their relatives. These constructs are not about individuated beings but about collective entities, and they display general laws rather than a concrete world to the imagination. But they retain a temporal dimension, and they provide global explanations of history" (Ryan, 2005, p. 348).

Computer scientists, when modelling the narratives of a society of embodied agents, such as a society of robots, may choose a threshold for the attribute 'non-habitual' in Condition 2. In the case of robots, reasoning about trajectories, collisions, and so forth, needs to consider also the rote scripts of habitual physical motion, but unless these interfere in what makes a given story peculiar, we can usefully disregard what is rote, and focus on what stands out as non-habitual. In virtual environments produced by information technology, what is habitual is captured by means of statements in some behaviour specification language. This makes is simpler to then feed the environment (or the cognitive agents associated with the individual characters) some specific story. In Nissan (2008b), I have actually advocated that computer scientists should be aware of the benefits of, and resort to, the results of scholarship into narratives, when developing virtual environments or even multi-robot environments. Arguably the criteria listed by Ryan (2005) are useful also when dealing with the cognitive dimension of the social actions of embodied agents as developed by computer scientists. This is true for animated characters in a virtual environment, where a variable story is enacted by interaction with the user (an interactive narrative), yet these criteria are also valid for a set of robots sharing the same spatial environment at the same time, and reasoning about each other, and acting accordingly.

5.2.2 A Fable Gone Awry: An Example of Story-Generation with TALE-SPIN

The fable about the fox that tricks a crow sitting on a branch into singing, and thus into releasing the cheese (or the piece of meat) it had been holding in its beak, is well-known.[19] In a Persian fable it is the bird, not the fox, that tries (unsuccessfully) to trick the fox into opening its mouth. The following is taken from a book of Persian proverbs (Haïm, 1956, pp. 384–385):

> [...] Why did you choose St. George [Jərjīs][20] from amongst all the prophets? (i.e. Of all possibilities you have chosen the least likely).
> {*From the following anecdote*}
> A fox once snatched a cock and run away, holding it firmly between its teeth. On the way the cock said, "O fox, since you have made up your mind to eat me, do so at least after mentioning the name of a prophet, or other holy person, so that it may become lawful for you to eat my flesh", intending thereby to obtain an escape in the event of the fox opening his mouth. But the cunning fox only squeezed the victim with greater force, and breathed out in a dragging manner the name "Jer-jee-s" (St. George). "Alas!" said the disappointed bird, "from amongst all the prophets you have chosen Jerjees!"
> *Note.* St. George, the patron saint of England, died as a martyr in the year 303 A. D. in the reign of Diocletian, and was looked upon as a (demi-)prophet by the Mohammedans.

The following story was made up automatically by TALE-SPIN, an artificial intelligence program developed at Yale University by James Meehan in the mid-1970s (Meehan, 1976). The quotation is from Meehan (1981a, p. 197; cf. 1981b):

> a program that writes simple stories. It is easily distinguished from any of the "mechanical" devices one can use for writing stories, such as filling in slots in a canned frame. The goal behind the writing of TALE-SPIN was to find out what kinds of knowledge were needed in story generation.

At one point in his presentation, Meehan states (1981a, p. 219):

> Here are some more rules. If you're hungry and you see some food, you'll want to eat it. If you're trying to get some food and you fail, you get sick. If you want some object, try bargaining with the object's owner. Innocuous, right?

Then Meehan quotes this sample output made up by his automated tool for story-generation (Meehan, 1981a, pp. 219–220; the brackets are Meehan's own):

> One day Henry Crow sat in his tree, holding a piece of cheese in his mouth, when up came Bill Fox. Bill saw the cheese and was hungry. [Bill has just been given the goal of satisfying hunger.] He said, "Henry, I like your singing very much. Won't you please sing for me?" Henry, flattered by this compliment, began to sing. The cheese fell to the ground. Bill Fox saw the cheese on the ground and was very hungry. [Satisfying hunger is about to be added to Bill's goals again.] He became ill. [Because satisfying hunger was already a goal of Bill's, it can't be added again. Hence, Bill fails to satisfy his hunger, so he gets sick.][21] Henry Crow saw the cheese on the ground, and he became hungry, but he knew that he owned the cheese.

---

[19] Aesop, *Fables*, clxv; Phaedrus, *Fables*, i.13; Apuleius, *De deo Socratis;* Jean de La Fontaine, *Fables*, i.2.

[20] The name *Jərjīs* (for 'George') belongs, e.g., to the onomasticon of Iraqi Nestorians.

[21] Instead of the hungry fox having his extant goal (the goal of seeking food) reinforced on seeing the cheese on the ground, an inadequate formulation of the set of rules (i.e., the ruleset) in TALE-SPIN caused the fox to become ill, with his goal unfulfilled, and being ill – which to TALE-SPIN was incapacitating for the ill character – knocked him out of action.

5.2 An Overview of Artificial Intelligence Approaches to Narratives

He felt pretty honest[22] with himself, so he decided not to trick himself into giving up the cheese. He wasn't trying to deceive himself, either, nor did he feel competitive with himself, but he remembered that he was also in a position of dominance over himself, so he refused to give himself the cheese. He couldn't think of a good reason why he should give himself the cheese [if he did that, he'd lose the cheese], so he offered to bring himself a worm if he'd give himself the cheese. That sounded okay, but he didn't know where any worms were. So he said to himself, "Henry, do you know where any worms are?" But of course, he didn't so he ... [And so on.]

Meehan explains how he fixed the problem with the program, that had caused it to be embroiled in such developments for the given output story: "The program eventually ran aground for other reasons. I was surprised it got as far as it did. I fixed it by adding the rule that dropping the cheese results in loss of ownership".[23] Even though the variant of the fable we quoted resulted from a bug in the program, it is very interesting, because it illustrates the workings of the program itself while making up a story.

5.2.3 A Few Challenges

Erik Mueller has remarked (2004, p. 308) that the several story-understanding programs that have been developed "may be characterized according to their (1) breadth of coverage, (2) depth of understanding, (3) ability to handle new stories, and (4) ability to handle real-world input such as text and speech." In particular (ibid.):

> Narrow coverage systems deal with stories about a particular domain or topic area such as management successions or terrorist incidents. Broad coverage systems deal with stories that span many domains. Shallow understanding systems build a superficial understanding of a story. The understanding might consist of the important events of the story and the roles of story characters in those events. Deep understanding systems build a deep understanding. This might include the trajectories of story characters through time and space, the emotions, goals, beliefs, desires, and intentions of characters, and the themes and morals of the story. Some systems handle only the particular stories they were designed to handle, and must be modified to handle new stories. Other systems can handle an unlimited number of new, previously unseen stories. While some systems require predicate-argument structures or edited text as input, others are able to cope with naturally occurring text or speech. A general story understanding system would be one with broad coverage, deep understanding, and the ability to handle new and real stories. So far, a system like this has not been built.

Computational formalisms for the analysis and generation of narratives (e.g., see Nissan, 2008f) have implications beyond the actual use of computers. That domain of research had interesting results to show as early as the late 1970s, was put on

---

[22] TALE-SPIN had applied to the same character – the crow – rules for interaction and negotiation between two characters. The crow got both roles in the interaction, hence the awkward effect on the generated story.

[23] Meehan (1981a, p. 220). Note that TALE-SPIN, in line with the Yale School of natural-language processing, does not handle stories by means of a story-grammar, but rather has the story developed through a hierarchy of characters' goals, plans to achieve them, subservient goals for the plans to succeed, secondary plans for achieving those secondary goals, and so forth.

the back burner, so to speak, in the late 1980s and in the 1990s, and since then has been resurgent. Some projects fall squarely within the concerns of folktale studies. Besides, sporadically some project would concern itself with humorous[24] mock-aetiological tales[25] (Nissan, 2002a). During the 1970s and 1980s, when

---

[24] There exists a discipline called *computational humour* (e.g., Hulstijn & Nijholt, 1996; Stock, Strapparava, & Nijholt, 2002; Binsted, Bergen, Coulson, Nijholt, & Stock, 2006). Various scholars in artificial intelligence and computational linguistics, especially Victor Raskin (whose linguist disciple Salvatore Attardo is also prominent in the theory of humour), Graeme Ritchie (and his disciples such as Kim Binsted), Anton Nijholt, Oliviero Stock and his collaborator Carlo Strapparava, Andrew Ortony, Akira Utsumi, and myself (I am one of the editors in the field: of two journals, and of Bejamin's book series Topics in Humor Research), are active in research into humour, trying to devise computational models capturing what it is that produces humour, or then in order to capture narrower categories, such as verbal jokes, or more in particular (which is Ritchie's case: see e.g. Ritchie, 2004), punning verbal jokes. There exist international journals in humour research, namely: *HUMOR, International Journal of Humor Research* (see http://www.degruyter.de/journals/humor/detail.cfm), and the more recently established *Israeli Journal of Humor Research: An International Journal*. Both are receptive to studies in computational humour.

[25] Bear in mind that there are narrative explanations that if two adult, competent members of advanced modern Western civilisation were to tell each other, would be taken to be humorous, because we can safely assume that both of them "know better", and that therefore the communication is *non-bona-fide* (the utterer or writer does not believe the content of what he or she is communicating), and yet this is not a communication with the intention of deceving the recipient. But in other or earlier different contexts, even that same explanation may be intended as *bona-fide* communication, and both the utterer and recipient would take it very seriously and believe it. This is for example the case of the early to high modern Western theories about the origins of languages and ethnicities, and this sometimes still persists, e.g. the modern myth of the supposedly late Indo-European "invasion" of Europe (Nissan, 2010b). Or then, consider culture-bound distrust of tomatoes (the early modern *pommes d'amour*) because of supposed toxicity, not just physiological but also (as a consequence) moral (Nissan, 2011e). Moreover, there may be explanations that obey poetic conventions, and the *alethic* value (i.e., truth value) of the communication may not be necessarily relevant (Nissan, 2008k). Such explanations may occur in *homiletics* (when not involving *dogma*) – such as in an ancient tale about how the Mediterranean Sea originated, in relation to how sinful early generations were (see Nissan, 2010 [2011]) – or then in the *belles lettres*. But the *logic of fiction* is a complex and debated issue. There are several theories of the logic of fiction. For various approaches to the logic of fiction, see Lamarque and Olsen (1994), Crittendon (1991), Walton (1990), and Woods (1974). Pollard (1997, p. 265) explains:

> Unlike real things, the entities of fiction are incomplete. While the proposition that Napoleon disliked cats is in principle decidable, the proposition that Sherlock Holmes disliked cats is not. On this latter issue, Conan Doyle's texts are silent. Furthermore, according to so-called 'classical' logic, anything whatever follows what is false. If the statements of fiction are taken as false, then what may seem perfectly acceptable inferences made by readers are rendered arbitrary: it would be as reasonable to infer from Conan Doyle's novels that the moon is made of green cheese as it would to infer that Holmes was cleverer than Inspector Lestrade.

A related issue is the emotions of readers of fiction. Consider this passage from Colin Radford's (1995, pp. 73–74) restatement of the position, he critiques, of Alex Neill (1993), who replied in Neill (1995).

> However, and as Neill observes, things are not so simple. For wouldn't many of us, and certainly the less sentimental readers and theatergoers, be surprised, shocked, even outraged

5.2 An Overview of Artificial Intelligence Approaches to Narratives

multi-paragraph stories were analysed by a computer program, there would be a tacit assumption about the narration being linear, even though this was not crucial to the methods employed. From the late 1990s, projects have been emerging, that make nonlinear narratives an explicit concern. Narratives may be *linear* or *nonlinear*, in presentation or content or both; see, e.g., Szilas (1999).

At the University of Paris 8, Nicolas Szilas published about interactive drama with nonlinearities (Szilas, 1999), and later on, with Jean-Hugues Rety he developed the *IDtension* project. It studies graph-based narrative structures, considering minimal structure for stories (Szilas & Rety, 2004). At MIT, Davenport and Murtaugh (1997) reported about the *ConTour* story-generation system. The basic unit in

---

> if we found ourselves reading a version of [Tolstoy's] *Anna Karenina* in which she lives happily ever after, a play in which the actor playing Mercutio [in Shakespeare's play *Romeo and Juliet*] refuses to die, or Nahum Tate's version of *Lear?* Does this not show that we do not *really* desire that things should be other and better for the characters, or does it not show, as I have argued [(Radford, 1975)], that we have conflicting desires?

Contrast this to Francis W. Dauer's discussion of the nature of fictional characters (Dauer, 1995). In particular, with reference to a Charlie Chaplin film and interpersonal emotions among its characters, Dauer gives a few definitions for the purposes of analysis (ibid., p. 36; the reference is to Chaplin's 1931 film *City Lights*):

> "Charlie wants the blind flower girl to see again" would be such an example. Let's say such a claim is a *referential* claim about a fictional character. On the other hand, some claims we make about fictional characters obviously are not referential claims. "Charlie is a fictional character" is the most trivial example of this – we cannot understand this in terms of how it would be with an actual person who is a fictional character. [...] Let me then say a claim about a fictional character is a *formal claim* if (a) it is not a referential claim, and (b) aside from limiting cases like "Charlie is a fictional character", it is to be understood along such lines as the function the character is playing in the work of art or its success. [... I]t seems to me that some statements about fictional characters can be given referential as well as formal readings. [...] Consider:
>
> D: Desdemona had to meet a (sic) unhappy end.
>
> If we give D a referential reading, D is to be understood in terms of some actual people having to have, or being destined to have unhappy ends. If the resulting referential claim is correct, *Othello* is in part to be understood to be about (or to be a portrayal of) people having unhappy destinies. I am reasonably certain that *Othello* is not to be understood in this way. On the other hand, D could be given a formal reading along some lines like: The integrity and coherence of the play demands that things do not turn out in the end hunky-dory for Othello and Desdemona. If we give D this sort of formal reading, which does not touch on actual world issues of fatalism or hard determinism, it seems to me that the resulting claim is correct. Thus, I suggest: D can have referential and formal readings, and while D is false or incorrect as a referential claim, it is true or correct as a formal claim. [...] To infer the correctness of the referential claim from the correctness of the corresponding formal claim is then a *fallacy*, and we might call it the *referential fallacy*.

Dauer (1995, n. 2, p. 38) mentions "Kendall Walton's suggestion of fifteen years ago that we do not really pity Willy Loman – rather our state is one where 'make-believedly' we feel pity [(Walton, 1978)]. This account of our affective reactions to fictional characters seems 'too thin' and has spawned a number of counterproposals", such as Skulsky (1980), Novitz (1980) and Neill (1991). Incidentally, emotion in theories of justice is the subject of an article by Mary Dauglas (1993).

ConTour is a video fragment, labelled with a variety of keywords. Such fragments should be combined to form a narrative, or a documentary. Besides, Kevin Brooks[26] – at MIT, under the supervision of Glorianna Davenport – researched the construction of computational cinematographic narrative and developed a software tool, called *Agent Stories,* for assisting writers in the design and presentation of "nonlinear/metalinear narratives". Cf. Maureen Thomas's (2004) introduction to narrativity, a deliverable of NM2, a project funded by the European Union. Interactive entertainment is the subject of Handler Miller (2004). Also see, e.g., Swartjes and Theune (2006). The ACM holds a series of *International Conferences on Virtual Storytelling (ICVS),* e.g., Cavazza and Donikian (2007).

There is a spectrum of possibilities, as to the extent to which one is to make a narrative's presentation, or even its content when generated, nonlinear. This applies to oralcy, written text, and video presentations as well, as for example flashbacks are an option for presentation even when relating a narrative in a conversation. At one end of the spectrum, one has just linear narratives. At the other end, one has random unfolding. The latter option is one that some teams are exploring for the purposes of interactive television: video presentations of narratives, whose actual unfolding, at given points, may branch differently in a way that may be called random, based on a pool of alternatives.

It is the middle of the spectrum that arguably yields the most interesting potential for formalisation and automation. Between the extremes (i.e., between linearity and random branching) there are intermediate situations in which how a narrative develops is more or less heavily constrained by norms pertaining to the medium, genre, style and poetic conventions, as well as the very nature of the universe depicted (the storyworld) in which the story is supposed to take place. The logic of the story requires consistency. Jeffrey Scott, the author of hundreds of scripts for animation, remarks on this (Scott, 2003, p. 47):

> For example, if you see a character with a beard in one scene and clean shaven in the next, one could assume he shaved it off — *provided* it was logical. If he's in a car, racing down a highway with a beard, then in the next scene he pulls up in the same car clean shaven, this will be illogical. However, if he had a beard one day, and the next day had no beard while on his way to an important business meeting — this *would* be logical.

One needs as well to check in the general metadata (i.e., the abstracted data about the data) of a story or a series, for example, in both the static and evolving metadata about each of the cast of characters.

5.2.4 The Task of Reconstructing the Facts

The film *Rashomon*, of 1950, was directed by Akira Kurosawa (1950) and based on a short story, *In the Forest* (1921), by Ryukonosuke Akutagawa (1892–1927).

---

[26] Brooks (1996, 1999, 2002); cf. Davenport, Bradley, Agamanolis, Barry, and Brooks (2000).

5.2 An Overview of Artificial Intelligence Approaches to Narratives

In *Rashomon,* different versions are related in turn as to how a death occurred. *Rashomon* is an example of content nonlinearity, as the story branches out into several versions of how past events are reconstructed. This is a good example of how it is specifically *explanations* which determine content nonlinearity. Each such explanation is a subnarrative which is alternative to the other explanations provided. A narrative whose goal is to explain something given is called an *aetiological* narrative. As to the universe of the global narrative of *Rashomon,* it is a universe in which ghosts may intervene and give testimony in front of a court, and this contradicts the conventions of realism, which only partly apply (if at all) to *Rashomon.*

The poetic conventions also affect the generation of explanations: these are only partly realistic (magic realism may be a better descriptor), as what makes an explanation appear *adequate* (which is not the same as *true*) is mediated by a match to the poetic conventions of the given universe. Moreover, one aspect of the film *Rashomon* is that it is a *whodunit* story. Unlike in your typical whodunit story, of the four witnesses, three (of which one is a ghost) each claim to be the perpetrator. Set in a forest near Kyoto in fifteenth-century war-torn Japan, *Rashomon* revolves around the death of a samurai. A court is called to find out. A bandit states it was he who killed him. The wife of the deceased claims it was she who did. The ghost of the deceased claims it was suicide. Then a peasant gives yet another version.

In real life, law enforcement and judiciary contexts have to refer to a set of evidence in order to reconstruct the facts of a given legal narrative. Artificial intelligence for modelling the reasoning on legal evidence is an area we are dealing with in the present book. One of the seminal projects in that domain, as early as the late 1980s, is ALIBI, for which, see above in Section 2.2.2. But it is also a story-generation program; in that domain, it was perhaps the only reported system that was not developed in North America in those years. Its input is a simplified accusation, and the tool, which impersonates the accused, has to propose an exonerating or a less liable account of the events to which the accusation refers.

Whereas the latter is not concerned with literature or literary criteria, these were paramount for the COLUMBUS model (Nissan, 2002a), in which a parodistic, archaistic literary text was analysed (manually, but using artificial intelligence techniques for story-understanding), based on mock-explanations.

Other formalisms in literary studies (with implications for other fields as well, including AI & Law), namely, representations based on *epistemic formulae,* were developed by Nissan for the manipulation of personal identities in Pirandello's play *Henry IV* (Nissan, 2002b), for the play *Slave Island* by Marivaux (Nissan, 2003a), and for a passage from a Middle English romance on Alexander the Great (Nissan, 2003b). Episodic formulae were also used in order to analyse historical narratives (Nissan, 2007b, 2008j), apocryphal historical anecdotes – actually, folktales (Nissan, 2008g), or patterns from social history (Nissan, Hall, Lobina, & de la Motte, 2004; Nissan, 2008i, 2009 [2010], 2010a).

Representations in episodic formulae do not come along, for the time being, with an automated inference engine, so episodic formulae are still only for manual analysis. There have been more mathematical approaches to narrative processing, though Honghua Gan (1994) developed a formal approach to automated story understanding, based on scripts and plans, but emphasising the role of causal relationships; Gan evisaged three cases of extension to "stepwise default theories" for story understanding: confirmation, distraction, and interference (Gan, 1994, p. 269). In fact (Nissan, 2008j, section 1.1):

> In the history of narrative processing, some approaches to narratives were formulated and discussed more mathematically than others, and this is the case of the work of Honghua Gan, e.g., in [Gan (1994)]. Earlier work had "formalized the story understanding process based on scripts and plans with stepwise default theories", that however "offer final results for understanding a specific story", but "do not provide the history of changes of partial states of any objects the story may concern. Moreover, the causal models for missing events are incomplete in script-based understanding, and even not involved in plan-based understanding" [(ibid., p. 265)]. In [Gan's paper], a default rule representation was proposed for causal relationships. "Stepwise default theories [...] los[e] inference structures from which the final result is derived", i.e., they "only give results for causal prediction in understanding a story, and there [are] no intermediate results for causal explanation and causal diagnosis" [(ibid., p. 269)]. By contrast, in frame-based systems "[t]he whole default causal chain can be linked to the concerned object frame by *dcc* links, e.g., the default causal chain for eating in the restaurant will be associated to the object frame *RESTAURANT*", and such a frame is referred to as a host frame [(ibid., p. 270)]. In [the same paper by Gan], stepwise default theories were integrated with frame-based systems, in order to provide "the history of partial state changes of agents and objects in the story by generating an understanding chain" [(ibid., p. 265)]: the complete causal model of the story is a default causal chain.

5.2.5 Grammar-Driven vs. Goal-Driven Processing of Stories: Propp's Precedent

In the *conceptual dependency* school of automated story processing that flourished at Yale University during the 1970s and 1980s, the process is driven by goals and plans (see Sections 5.8 and 5.9 below). This is in contrast to *grammar-driven* story-processing, in which the story has to match a formal grammar, or is generated by using a formal grammar. Already Vladimir Propp, in an often cited, classic work (Propp, 1928), proposed a mathematical model for thematic patterns in folktales, a model that can be taken to be a story-generation model. He applied it to the genre of the Russian folktale. It is a work that "has had epochal significance in [almost] all areas of the study of traditional literature" (Beatie, 1976, p. 39).

Two articles, respectively by Alan Dundes (1962, repr. 1975) and S.S. Jones (1979), became the foundation of the structural narratological study of folktales. *Narratology* (Onega & Garcia Landa, 1996) is associated with *structuralism*. The study of narrative themes is *thematics*. *Thematology* is the study of the evolution of a thematic series (a story, or rather the cluster of its variants) throughout a given culture, and its methodology is related to narratology. Some concepts from the structuralist approach to folktales appear in Figs. 5.2.5.1 and 5.2.5.2 and in Table 5.2.5.1. Cf., e.g., Doležel (1972), Ben-Amos (1980), Lakoff (1972).

5.2 An Overview of Artificial Intelligence Approaches to Narratives

Fig. 5.2.5.1 The telos gives meaning to the structural constant (with a deep pattern of cognitive structures mediating). The structural constant gives meaning to the motifeme, that gives meaning to the motif (with a configuration of motifs possibly mediating)

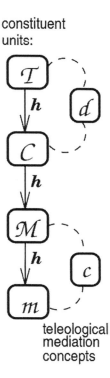

Table 5.2.5.1 Concepts involved in Fig. 5.2.5.1

m	*Motif:* how a motifeme is actualised in a given oikotype, i.e., in a given culturally specific type.[27]
c	*Configuration of motifs:* this is a teleological mediation concept.
M	*Motifeme:* this is the narrative function; it is an abstraction of a motif, occupying a place in a sequence in the skeleton of the plot of a folktale.
C	*Structural constant*
d	*Deep pattern* of cognitive structures: ideological climate, moods, emotions, tones. It is a teleological mediation concept.
T	*Telos:* this is the core idea. It is close to the deep pattern, but it is overt, rational, not as subjective. See Fig. 5.2.5.2.
h	"gives meaning to"

---

[27] In the words of Natascha Würzbach: "A motif is the concrete realisation of a fixed abstract idea, often spanning a complete narrative unit. [...] [T]he motif is a 'moveable stock device' that appears in many [historical] periods and genres. The content dimension of a motif comprises character

Fig. 5.2.5.2 The difference between the deep pattern and the telos

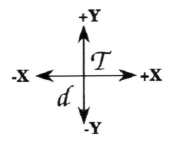

A fundamental tool in the scholarship of the folktale is the classification of tale types on the part of Aarne and Thompson (1928 and sqq. edns.). Antti Amatus Aarne (1867–1925) established a system for indexing tale-plots, which was translated from the German and enlarged by Stith Thompson (Aarne & Thompson, 1928 and sqq. edns.), with a recent update by Hans-Jörg Uther (Uther, 2004). Referring to the classification of Aarne and Thompson is the standard fare of the study of folkloric narratives. Aarne died shortly before Vladimir Propp published his ground-breaking study of the Russian folktales (Propp, 1928), which paved the way also for *story grammars* in cognitive science[28] – David Rumelhart[29] rather preferred to call them *story schemata* – and automatic story processing within AI.

Propp envisaged twenty-two tale functions, and nine more in the "preparatory section" of a tale, a part that is sometimes absent. One of Propp's tale functions is

---

('doppelganger', 'amazon') and action ('quest', 'marriage'), locality ('paradise, 'Gothic ruin'), and objects ('sword', 'rose'), temporal phases ('spring', 'night'), and dispositions ('madness', 'illness'). [...] The term 'motifeme' (Doležel, 1972) is frequently used to refer to the specific deep-structural narrative function of a motif" (Würzbach, 2005, p. 322). A motifeme is at a higher level of abstraction than the motif is, and is a concept introduced by Dundes (1962, repr. 1975). Concerning the concept of motif, see also Ben-Amos (1980).

[28] Rumelhart (1975, 1980a, 1980b, cf. 1977a, 1977b); Rumelhart and Ortony (1977).

[29] David Rumelhart is a psychologist, and has collaborated across disciplines, with Jay McClelland (psychology), Geoffrey Hinton (artificial intelligence), and Paul Smolensky (physics, artificial intelligence). Interdisciplinary collaborations are frequent in cognitive science research (Schunn, Okada, & Crowley, 1995).

transformation, such as when the hero lets his hair and beard grow exceedingly (and possibly makes himself unavailable, so that his previous self is not to be found), and then again when he has a hair cut, gets a shave, and otherwise enables *recognition*. Not always Propp's transformation function is intended as a disguise disabling recognition on the part of other characters. It is sometimes an enablement, such as when a character turns himself into a bird and flies.

Lakoff (1972) applied a parser approach to the Propp schema.[30] From the controversy concerning story grammars in cognitive science (which was influential in AI), see Black and Wilensky (1979), Rumelhart (1980b), Frisch and Perlis (1981), Wilensky (1983b), and Garnham (1983). Whereas I usually adopt goal-driven formalisms in my own work in AI, I agree that story grammars are nevertheless fairly important to how we both generate and make sense of stories. This is especially so, when a story appears to be amenable to themes and motifs from international folklore.

In his response to Black and Wilensky's (1979) critique of story grammars, Rumelhart (1980b) claimed that they had been evaluating story grammars on irrelevant grounds. He summarised their argument as follows (Rumelhart, 1980b, p. 313):

> They argue that story grammars (or story schemata as I prefer to call them) are not a productive approach to the study of story understanding, and they offer three main lines of argumentation. First, they argue that story grammars are not *formally* adequate in as much as most of them are represented as a set of context free rewrite rules which are known to be inadequate even for sentence grammars. Second, they argue that story grammars are not *empirically* adequate in as much as there are stories which do not seem to follow story grammars and there are nonstories which do. Finally, they argue that story grammars could not form an adequate basis for a comprehension model since in order to apply the grammar you need to have interpreted the story. These arguments are, in my opinion, indicative of a misunderstanding of the enterprise that I and others working on these issues have been engaged in. I believe that they are all based on a misunderstanding about what grammars might be good for and about how comprehension might occur.

Rumelhart's response stressed that problem-solving and goals are central to many stories: "Most story grammars are based around the observation that many stories seem to involve a sort of problem solving motif (cf. Mandler & Johnson, 1977; Rumelhart, 1975, 1977b; Stein & Glenn, 1979; Thorndyke, 1977)" (Rumelhart, 1980b, p. 313). Many stories, Rumelhart pointed out, set a problem for a character, and this motivates a goal: "Such stories have roughly the following structure: First, something happens to a protagonist which sets up a goal that must be satisfied. Then the remainder of the story is a description of the protagonist's problem solving behavior in seeking the goal coupled with the results of that behavior" (ibid.). Story grammars in turn, Rumelhart claimed, actually formalise the structure of such problem solving episodes (ibid., p. 314):

---

[30] In 2005 in Madrid, Peinado, and Gervás (2005b) combined case-based reasoning with an implementation of tale morphology *à la* Vladimir Propp.

In some stories there are several of these problem solving episodes, sometimes with different protagonists in the different episodes. Story grammars are, in essence, various schemes for formalizing this structure. The formalizations have usually (cf. Mandler & Johnson, 1977; Rumelhart, 1975; Stein & Glenn, 1979; Thorndyke, 1977), but not always (cf. Rumelhart, 1977b), involved the use of rewrite rules which conveniently, and generatively, capture the relationships among the various pieces of such stories.

According to Rumelhart (1980b, p. 314) the misunderstanding on the part of his critics (who are adept at the Yale school's *script* formalism) arose because their starting point was in formal language theory and what generative grammars mean there, and which to Rumelhart has little to do with why grammars are interesting in psychology:

> Black and Wilensky appear to endorse the view that a grammar is primarily a device for generating all and only the sentences of a language. That definition of grammar presupposes the view that a language is properly defined as a set of sentences and that a grammar is merely a recursive device for enumerating them. That definition, coming out of the theory of formal languages, has very little to do with why a grammar might be *psychologically* interesting. The psychologically interesting thing about a grammar is that it proposes an analysis of the *constituent structure* of a linguistic unit. There never has been, and probably never will be, a grammar of the English language which will generate all and only the sentences of English. By the same token, there never has been and probably never will be a grammar of stories which generates all and only the population of things called stories. Nevertheless, there are grammars of English (and grammars of stories) that are interesting.

Grammars "are interesting *because* they tell us what elements 'go together' to form higher elements and how one group of elements is related to another" (ibid., p. 314), and also because grammars enable the identification of analogous elements. To Rumelhart (1980, p. 315), if anything it is the script approach that is formally clumsy (and this can be easily recognised by those who recognise that historically, practitioners of artificial intelligence can be divided in two camps: the *neaties*, who are after nice formal theories, and the *messies*, who research useful devices empirically):

> Black and Wilensky appear to be so caught up in the issues of formal language theory (in which considerations of constituent structure are secondary) that they completely ignore this key issue. Instead they focus on largely technical and, from a psychological perspective, irrelevant issues. For example, they claim that most story grammars are "formally inadequate", because they lack complete self-embedding. Obviously, this cannot be an important criticism, for it is a trivial matter to add any sort of self-embedding to a system specified in a rewrite formalism. I originally employed a rewrite system *because it was so easy to express recursion* in this formalism. I created the "Old Farmer" story to illustrate the importance of recursion. In fact, one of my major objections to the other formalisms for story and event knowledge has been the clumsiness of recursion within them (e.g., recursion cannot be represented in the popular script formalism).

Moreover, Rumelhart (1977a) had stressed the interactive nature of comprehension, in the sense that comprehension identifies and exploits possibilities suggested both from top-down and from bottom-up. This is likely to find sympathetic ears in current research into story comprehension. There has recently been a resurgence of the use of story grammars on the part of some researchers, but they usually combine that device with another kind of representation as well. BRUTUS, a program making use of both frames and story grammars, generates narratives of betrayal (Bringsjord &

5.2 An Overview of Artificial Intelligence Approaches to Narratives   349

Ferrucci, 2000). Also the *Joseph* story-generation program (Lang, 2003) combines the goal-driven approach with story grammars. *Joseph* produces randomly generated natural language narratives conforming to a grammar, and that resemble Russian folktales.

Propp was concerned with the Russian folktale, and the Russian folktale is part of an international genre. At any rate, Propp was concerned with a particular genre. But Marie-Laure Ryan has pointed out: "It was the legacy of French structuralism, more particularly of Roland Barthes and Claude Bremond, to have emancipated narrative from literature and from fiction, and to have recognised it as a semiotic phenomenon that transcends disciplines and media" (Ryan, 2005, p. 344).

Chapter 1 in Scott Turner's thesis (1992, cf. 1994) about his MINSTREL story-generating program describes his chance encounter with the 1968 edition of Propp's *The Morphology of the Folktale,* and its equations. "As a computer scientist, I found this fascinating". He further remarks (Turner, 1992, p. 1): "In theory, Propp's grammar could be programmed into a computer and used to recognize folktales – provided someone first translated each folktale into Propp's notation. [...] Propp's grammar could be used to 'grow' a story from seed to completion. [...] I did eventually write a computer program that tells stories. But it tooks years, not hours, and in the end, Vladmir [sic] Propp's intriguing little grammar was nowhere to be seen". Unsurprisingly, as being Michael Dyer's supervisee, Scott Turner adopted the goal-driven technique of the Yale conceptual dependency school.

5.2.6 *Let Us Not Simplify the 1970s: A More Populated Pool of Approaches, and More Nuanced Distinctions*

It would be wrong to believe that story grammars were the only *rule-based* approach to narrative understanding. In a 1980 paper in automated story-understanding, Alfred Correira (1980), from the University of Texas at Austin, discussed "computing story trees". Parsing narrative texts was, to him, "a process of collecting simple textual propositions into thematically and causally related units" (Correira, 1980, p. 135). He adopted the concept of *macrostructures* that had been previously introduced by Kintsch and van Dijk's (1978) 'Recalling and Summarizing Stories'.

Correira (1980) also applied logic rules, expressed as *extended Horn clauses (EHC)*. The first part of the rule (what one usually refers to as the left-hand side of the rule) was, in Correira's own formalism, "the HEAD of the rule, and represents the macrostructure pattern. The second part is the PREcondition for the rule. The propositions in the precondition are the conditions which must be true, or can be made true, before Rufolo can embark on an episode of TRADINGVOYAGE" – this being from a narrative from Giovanni Boccaccio's *Decameron,* that Kintsch and van Dijk (1978) had used in their exemplification. "The third part is the EXPansion of the rule. If Rufolo goes on a TRADINGVOYAGE, then these are the (probable) actions he will take in doing so. The final part of the rule is the POSTcondition of the rule, which consists of the propositions that will become true upon the successful completion (instantiation) of the TRADINGVOYAGE rule" (Correira, 1980, p. 138).

It would be wrong to think that in the 1970s, grammar-driven or rule-driven approaches to narrative processing were in stark opposition to the goal-driven approach of the Yale school. What Rumelhart said in defence of story grammars, in his answer to the critique of story grammars in Black and Wilensky (1979), sounds like the approach of the Yale school, from which Wilensky, his critic, had come (Rumelhart, 1980b, p. 314): "The basic theme of the research on story schemata is to look at a story and to identify the goals, subgoals, the various attempts to achieve the goals, and the various methods that have been employed." It should not come as too much of a surprise to find out that to Correira, his own rules were akin to the Yale school's scripts and plans (Correira, 1980, p. 138):

> The resulting rule form is related conceptually and historically to the notion of a script as developed by Schank and Abelson (1977) (cf. Norman and Rumelhart, 1975). The precondition sets the stage for the invocation of a rule. It describes the setting and the roles of the characters involved in the rule. The expansion consists of the actions normally taken during the invocation of the rule. The postcondition is the result of these actions. When used in a script-like role, a rule is activated when its precondition has been satisfied, and its expansion can then be sequentially instantiated.
>
> A rule can also be used as a plan. A plan is a data structure that suggests actions to be taken in pursuit of some goal. This corresponds to activating a rule according to its postcondition, i.e. employing a rule because its postcondition contains the desired effect.

I quote an enumeration of methods current at the time, from Correira (1980, p. 135):

> Experiments with text processing led to such procedural constructs as frames (Minsky, 1975; Charniak and Wilks, 1976; Bobrow and Winograd, 1977), scripts and plans (Schank and Abelson, 1977), focus spaces (Grosz, 1977), and partitioned networks (Hendrix, 1976), among others. These efforts involved conceptual structures consisting of large, cognitively unified sets of propositions. They modelled understanding as a process of filling in or matching the slots in a particular structure with appropriate entities derived from input text.
>
> There have also been rule-based approaches to the text processing problem, most notably the template/paraplate notion of Wilks (1975), and the story grammars of Rumelhart (1975, 1980a, 1980b). Although both approaches (procedures and rules) have their merits, it is a rule-based approach which will be presented here.
>
> This paper describes a rule-based computational model for text comprehension, patterned after the theory of macrostructures proposed by Kintsch and van Dijk (1978). The rules are notationally and conceptually derived from the Horn clause, especially as described by Kowalski (1979). Each rule consists of sets of thematically, causally, or temporally related propositions. The rules are organized into a network with the macrostructures becoming more generalized approaching the root. The resulting structure, called the Story Tree, represents a set of textual structures.

Kintsch and van Dijk (1978) had proposed to organise a discourse as a hierarchy of macrostructures. These are essentially metapropositions. The text's sentences, clauses, or phrases are the input propositions, and this is the lowest level of discourse textual representation. "Propositions are conjoined by links of implication: if proposition A implies proposition B, then A and B are connected, and the link is marked with the strength of the connection, ranging from (barely) possible to (absolutely) necessary" (Correira, 1980, p. 136). Moreover: "The propositions and their connections reside in a text base. A text base can be either explicit, if all the implied information necessary for coherence is made explicit, or implicit, if propositions that can be assumed to be known or implied are omitted. A text is an explicit data base by itself, and all summaries of that text are implicit data bases. A college physics text would have a much more explicit text base than after-dinner conversation" (Correira, 1980, p. 136).

As to the tree structure: "As a computational entity, a macrostructure is a node in a story tree whose immediate descendants consist of the subordinate propositions by which the node is implied, and is itself a descendant of the macrostructure it (partially) implies. Every macrostructure in this tree is the root of a derivation tree whose terminals are simple propositions" (Correira, 1980, p. 136).

At this point, *summarisation* enters the picture: "Each level of the tree shares the attribute of summarizability, i.e. a summary of the text may be extracted from any level of the tree, becoming less specific as the summary level approaches the root. The lowest level summary is the original text itself; the highest level (the root) is a title for the text" (Correira, 1980, p. 136).

5.2.7 Some Computational Narrative Processing Projects from the 1970s, 1980s, 1990s, and Later

Narratives are, of course, pervasive in human life. As to scholarship about narratives, there has been growth in various realms. One of these is computer science, in a subdomain of artificial intelligence which is now called *narrative intelligence*. Beginning an article, 'Models of narrative analysis: A typology', which he published in 1995 in the *Journal of Narrative and Life History*, a clinical psychologist, Elliot G. Mishler, wrote (1995, p. 87):

> This is an exciting time for narrative researchers, a period of rapid growth in the number and variety of narrative studies in the human sciences. The analysis of narrative discourse, both written and spoken, has become a central topic for investigators in many countries, representing a wide spectrum of disciplines and diverse theoretical and methodological perspectives. The breadth of interest is manifested in the frequency of conferences and symposia, this journal, an annual series of edited volumes on narrative and life history [Josselson and Lieblich (1993)], and an accelerating stream of articles and books.

Mateas and Sengers have stated (2003, p. 1):

> By telling stories we make sense of the world. We order its events and find meaning in them by assimilating them to more-or-less familiar narratives. It is this human ability to organize experience into narrative form that David Blair and Tom Meyer call "Narrative Intelligence" [Blair and Meyer (1997)] and around which AI research into narrative coalesces.

Blair and Meyer's paper (1997) that Mateas and Sengers's passage quoted above cited appeared in a volume on automated autonomous personality agents to go with computer animation's synthetic actors. Section 5.2.15 is concerned with this subject.

Early natural language understanding programs included Terry Winograd SHRDLU (Winograd, 1972), and Roger Schank's and Christopher Riesbeck's

MARGIE (Schank, Goldman, Rieger, & Riesbeck, 1973; Schank, Goldman, Rieger, & Riesbeck, 1975). At MIT, Eugene Charniak (1972) resorted to the device whose activation is spawned and is known as *demons,* in a model of children's story comprehension. He was later to work on a frame-based language comprehension program called *Ms. Malaprop* (Charniak, 1977a, 1977b), and afterwards he developed at Brown University, in the WIMP project, a theory of *marker passing* for language comprehension (Charniak, 1983, 1986). The following is quoted from Charniak (1991):

> A recognition problem is one of inferring the presence of some entity from some input, typically observing the presence of other entities and the relations between them. We will make the common assumption that high-level recognition is accomplished by selecting an appropriate *schema* from a schema library. A schema is a generalized internal description of a class of entities in terms of their parts, their properties, and the relations between them. [...] In plan recognition, the generalized plans are schemas. [...] A crucial problem faced by schema selection is that of searching the schema library for the right schema; typically a single piece of local evidence is multiply ambiguous as to which schema it could indicate. For example, an act of getting a rope might fit into many schemas.
>
> One of the few concrete proposals to solve this problem has been *marker-passing* [...] Marker-passing uses a breadth-first search[31] to find paths between concepts in an associative network made up of concepts and their part-subpart relations. The idea is that a path between two schemas suggests which schema(s) to consider for recognition. For example, a knob instance and a hinge instance might suggest a door (instance); since there are links between the schemas door and knob and between door and hinge in the associative network (they are part-subpart relations), there is therefore a path from knob through door to hinge. Unfortunately, most marker-passing systems have found many more bad paths, suggesting incorrect schemas, than good ones [...] We will show in this paper that the good/bad ratio can be raised quite high by exploiting probability information; we realize this benefit by (cheaply) controlling the marker-passer's search, extending it in promising directions and terminating it in unpromising ones.

At Brown University, Charniak with Robert Goldman and Glen Carroll developed *Wimp3,* with a probabilistic account of marker passing for the purposes of plan recognition (Goldman, 1990; Carroll & Charniak, 1991).[32] At Berkeley, Peter Norvig developed FAUSTUS, in which a theory inference for text understanding

---

[31] *Breadth-first search* is a standard concept from artificial intelligence. I quote from Luger and Stubblefield (1998, p. 99): "In addition to specifying a search direction (data-driven or goal-driven), a search algorithm must determine the order in which states are examined in the tree or the graph." In particular,"two possibilities for the order in which the nodes of the graph are considered: *depth-first* and *breadth-first* search. [...] In depth-first search, when a state is examined, all of its children and their descendants are examined before any of its siblings. Depth-first search goes deeper into the search space whenever this is possible. Only when no further descendants of a state can be found are its siblings considered. [...] Breadth-first search, in contrast, explores the space in a level-by-level fashion. Only when there are no more states to be explored at a given level does the algorithm move on to the next level."

[32] More recent research by Charniak's team has been concerned with *conversation disentanglement* (Elsner & Charniak, 2008) and with *discourse coherence* (Elsner, Austerweil, & Charniak, 2007).

was implemented, also based on marker passing (Norvig, 1987, 1989). Again at Berkeley, Dekai Wu developed a project in automatic inference for natural-language interpretation, based on a probabilistic approach to marker passing (Wu, 1992).

Steven Rosenberg developed at MIT a news article comprehension model based on frames (Rosenberg, 1977). Wendy Lehnert developed at Yale the QUALM question answering program, embodying her novel theory (Lehnert, 1978, cf. 1977). Richard Cullingford, also at Yale, used Lehnert's program in SAM, a script-based program for automatically understanding newspaper stories (Cullingford, 1978, 1981). At Yale, Robert Wilensky developed the PAM story-understanding program, with plans and goals (Wilensky, 1978, 1981, 1982, 1983a; cf. 1980, 1983b). In 1978, Janet Kolodner was working at Yale on CYRUS, a program with episodic memory about information about the travels of the U.S. foreign secretary Cyrus Vance (Kolodner, 1984). Also at Yale, Jaime Carbonell developed POLITICS, a program impersonating persons who, holding dovish or hawkish political views from the United States, gave answers about international affairs based on two different ideological goal trees (Carbonell, 1978, 1979, 1981). Again at Yale, Gerald DeJong developed FRUMP, a program for news story skimming (DeJong, 1979); Michael Lebowitz developed IPP, an integrated understanding system with generalisation and episodic memory; and Michael Dyer developed BORIS, a story understanding system that combined MOPs (a generalisation of scripts), TAUs (thematic abstraction units), plans, goals, and emotions: it was based on behaviour ascribed to emotional responses, from which the program took its cue for understanding characters' behaviour and the story itself (Dyer, 1983a; 1983b; 1987; Lehnert, Dyer, Johnson, Yang, & Harley, 1983). In relation to that project, Dyer's supervisor, Wendy Lehnert, developed *plot units,* a somewhat more rudimentary approach relating emotions to turns in a narrative (Lehnert, 1982).[33]

Based on her positing that narratives are summarised by readers according to *affect-state patterns,* Lehnert (1982) developed a suitable representation. To her, a mental model of a narrative consists of both character acts (which may be physical

---

[33] It may come as a surprise to some, that the problem of an automated analysis of narratives simplistically ascribing a decidedly negative role to a collective actor being an ethnic group, has arisen as early as the early 1980s, in a research project. This was when Hayward Alker, Wendy Lehnert and Daniel Schneider developed a computational hermeneutic of Toynbee's reception of Christus Patiens according to the synoptic gospels (Lehnert, Alker, & Schneider, 1983; Alker, Lehnert, & Schneider, 1985; Alker, 1996). In Tonfoni (1985), Alker et al. (1985) follows an introductory article on plot units in automated narrative understanding (Lehnert & Loiselle, 1985). Lehnert had developed the plot units approach to the automated treatment of narratives. She left Yale for the University of Massachusetts in 1982, not before a more advanced approach came to fruition in Michael Dyer's PhD thesis about the BORIS system, a project in which Lehnert had an important role (Lehnert et al., 1983; Dyer, 1983a). In the publications about the computational project based on Toynbee's (and Gospels) narrative, it was admitted that, because of the need to simplify, the Jews had been given a negative role in the model. Those papers exhibited here and there some passages in anthropology, which did not alter the basic fact about which the authors possibly felt some discomfort.

or mental), and state propositions. She maintained that such states and events are recalled according to their affect. The affects were rudimentary, actually out of just three values: positive events for the acting character (+), negative events for the acting character (−), or neutral mental states (M). Links between states and events come in different kinds, according to the way they relate to one another. One kind of link is *motivation* (m): mental states can motivate events or other mental states. Another kind of link is *actualisation* (a): mental states can be actualised by events. Yet another kind of link is *termination* (t): events can terminate mental states or other events. There also is an *equivalence* link (e) between mental states and events. According to the way states and events are linked, Lehnert (1982) defined particular patterns of mental states and events as *primitive plot units*.

The *problem* primitive plot unit is represented (Fig. 5.2.7.1) as a negative event motivating a mental state:

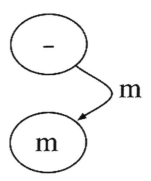

Fig. 5.2.7.1 The *problem* primitive plot unit

In the *resolution* primitive plot unit (Fig. 5.2.7.2), a positive event terminates a negative event:

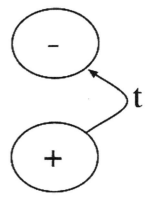

Fig. 5.2.7.2 The *resolution* primitive plot unit

5.2 An Overview of Artificial Intelligence Approaches to Narratives

In the *success* primitive plot unit (Fig. 5.2.7.3), a mental state actualises a positive event:

Fig. 5.2.7.3 The *success* primitive plot unit

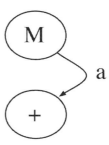

A complex plot unit for *intentional problem resolution* is as follows (Fig. 5.2.7.4):

Fig. 5.2.7.4 A complex plot unit for *intentional problem resolution*

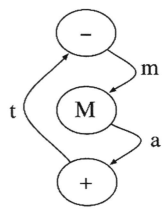

By contrast, a complex plot unit for *fortuitous problem resolution* is as follows (Fig. 5.2.7.5):

Fig. 5.2.7.5 A complex plot unit for *fortuitous problem resolution*

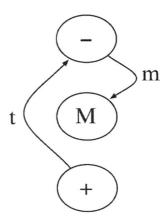

In the late 1970s and early 1980s, Roger Schank and Christopher Riesback's research group at Yale University "quickly became focused on understanding narratives. In a series of programs, they developed a theory of the knowledge structures necessary to understand narratives" (Mateas & Sengers, 2003, p. 2). "[T]hese early narrative systems fell out of favor" as "[t]hey were intensely knowledge-based", and therefore were difficult to be made more general. In my view, this is an inescapable requirement, even though you may try to improve machine learning. At any rate, the field suffered when, "as funding for AI [i.e., artificial intelligence] dried up during the AI Winter, AI research became more focused on constrained problems with clear, measurable results and immediate practical utility" (ibid.), with an agenda which "rules out the ability to work on complex phenomena such as the human use of narratives" (ibid.). "Except for occasional exceptions continuing in the Yale tradition, such as Mueller's model [(1990)] of daydreaming[34] and Turner's model of storytelling [Turner (1994)],[35] sustained work on narrative disappeared from AI" (Mateas & Sengers, 2003, p. 3).

It was not the case that work on narrative in AI had completely died out, though.[36] For example, proceedings continued to appear. Consider in particular Mark Kantrowitz's work (at Carnegie Mellon University) on GLINDA, in the *Oz* interactive fiction project (Kantrowitz, 1990). At any rate, if there has been a winter of AI research into narratives, in other areas of computer science "narrative became an influence" (Mateas & Sengers, 2003, p. 3), such as in human-computer interface design, and in hypertext research. Moreover, as the technology of virtual reality was developing, research into narratives within computing turned to embedding a narrative dimension into interactive virtual environments, with stories unfolding by interaction with human users.[37]

Projects in the automated understanding of narratives included the *OpEd* project from UCLA, of 1989, in editorial comprehension, developed by Sergio Alvarado (1990). Also at UCLA, Stephanie August developed ARIEL in 1991, for automatically understanding analogies in arguments in the text of an editorial.

---

[34] Erik Mueller's DAYDREAMER produced vindictive daydreams (related in the first person): the narrator dreams of vengeance for being rejected for a date by a famous movie star.

[35] Scott Turner's thesis (1992) is posted on the Web. Our references to pages in Turner are to his thesis, as in that report. Both Mueller's DAYDREAMER project, and Turner's MINSTREL project, were supervised by Michael Dyer. In the given period, there were other teams and other projects in story generation, e.g., Smith and Witten (1991), Okada and Endo (1992), as well as Lyn Pemberton's project (1989).

[36] At the Media Lab of the Massachusetts Institute of Technology (MIT), the Narrative Intelligence (NI) Reading Group was active during the best part of the 1990s, and continues as an e-list.

[37] E.g., Wavish and Connah (1997), Cavazza, Charles, and Mead (2002a), Riedl and Young (2004). On interactive fiction, cf. Niesz and Holland (1984). Young (2007) "set out a basic approach to the modeling of narrative in interactive virtual worlds", and "story elements – plot and character – are defined in terms of plans that drive the dynamics of a virtual environment", whereas the communicative actions (discourse elements) "are defined in terms of discourse plans whose communicative goals include conveying the story world plan's structure", with reference to the development of the Mimesis software architecture for interactive narrative. Suspense is an aspect involved.

5.2.8 Primitive Acts in the Conceptual Dependency Approach

The early 1970s saw the rise of the conceptual dependency theory of goals and actions in the United States at the University of Yale, and of Maria Nowakowska's theory of goals and actions in Warsaw, Poland. The latter theory was more mathematical, and for all its merits, it did not have much of an aftermath except in her own research, even though it was published in important forums. Those two theories could still be combined together, and could potentially be usefully complementary to each other.[38]

Let us point out some rudiments of the approach of the Yale school of natural-language processing. "A basic premise of *Conceptual Dependency* (*CD*) is that meaning arises from a combination of memory search, planning, and inference. Only a small fraction of meaning is actually conveyed directly by those lexical items which explicitly appear in a given sentence" (Dyer, 1983a, p. 379). The meaning of sentences is represented by decomposing them into primitive acts. There are eleven of them in CD theory. Each primitive act has a few case-frames associated, which hold expectations for what conceptualisations should follow. Those case-frames include: actor, recipient, object (if any), direction, and instrumental case. Here is a list of the eleven primitive acts:

ATRANS. This is transfer of possession. An examnple of this is getting some merchandise, and paying for it:

(ATRANS		(ATRANS	
ACTOR	$customer_1$	ACTOR	$newsagent_1$
OBJECT	£2.30	OBJECT	$magazine_1$
FROM	$customer_1$	FROM	$newsagent_1$
TO	$newsagent_1$)	TO	$customer_1$)

This does not necessarily involve physical transfer; for example:

(ATRANS		(ATRANS	
ACTOR	U.S.A.	ACTOR	CzaristEmpire
OBJECT	$heftyprice_1$	OBJECT	Alaska
FROM	U.S.A.	FROM	CzaristEmpire
TO	CzaristEmpire)	TO	U.S.A.)

PROPEL. This is the application of physical force. Shoving, throwing, hitting, falling, pulling, are actions that all involve propel.

PTRANS. This is the transfer of physical location. For example, if the newswagent walks over to a customer and hands over a magazine to that customer,

---

[38] The late Maria Nowakowska mentioned to me in Knoxville, Tennessee, in 1985, that the two theories are akin and were independently developed, but had a different fate. See in particular Nowakowska's 'A formal theory of actions' (1973a); *Language of Motivation and Language of Actions* (1973b); and 'Action theory: Algebra of goals and algebra of means' (1973b). See also in fn. 60 above (in the notes of Section 2.2.2.7).

who is buying it, this involves PROPEL subserving PTRANS (the newsagent moves him- or herself, and moves the magazine), itself subserving ATRANS (because of the commercial transaction).

INGEST. This is when an organism takes something from outside and makes it internal. Examples are eating, drinking, swallowing one's saliva, and smoking.

EXPEL. This is the opposite of INGEST. sweating and crying are among the examples of this primitive act.

MTRANS. This is the transfer of mental information from one individual to another, or between distinct parts of the same individual's memory. When the latter, this is involved in remembering, forgetting, learning, and recalling. When MTRANS takes place between different interlocutors instead, this is involved in such actions as talking or reading.

MBUILD. This is the primitive act of thought processes which create new conceptualisations from old ones. MBUILD is involved in realising, considering, imagining, deciding, and concluding.

MOVE. This is the movement of a body part of some animate organism. An example of this is walking, which is represented as a PTRANS, but what accomplishes that PTRANS is an instrumental MOVE of LEGS. Other examples of actions involving MOVE include waving, throwing, dancing, and jumping.

GRASP. This is the act of physically contacting an object. Usually this is accomplished by MOVE as applied to one's arm or one's hand. Actions such as holding, grabbing, or hugging involve GRASP. Grasping some notion instead does not involve GRASP, but MBUILD instead.

SPEAK. This stands for any vocalisation. The act of MTRANS is often accomplished by people by means of the SPEAK primitive act.

ATTEND. This is the act of directing a sense organ. Hearing someone or something, or listening to someone or some musical instrument, involves ATTENDing one's ears towards the sounds being made.

5.2.9 Scripts, Goals, Plans, MOPs, and TAUs in the Conceptual Dependency Approach

5.2.9.1 Goals

Conceptual Dependency theory enumerates the following kinds of goals: *satisfaction goals* (*S-goals*) as arising from the need to satisfy recurring bodily desires; *delta goals* (*D-goals*), which represent desires for a change in state, *entertainment goals* (*E-goals*); *achievement goals* (*A-goals*), which involve the long-term attainment of social status or position (e.g., A-GOOD-JOB and A-SKILL); and *preservation goals* (*P-goals*). Preservation goals are those goals which become active only when threatened; they include P-HEALTH, P-COMFORT, P-APPEARANCE, and P-FINANCES. An entertainment goal is involved, for example, when one goes to the restaurant with a friend in order to satisfy an E-COMPANY goal rather than to satisfy S-HUNGER. The change of state desired in delta goals may be mental, or physical, or of control. The latter is the case of D-CONT, i.e., the desire to gain control of something, and of D-SOCCONT, i.e., the desire to gain control of someone (e.g., in a kidnapping).

For each goal, in order to achieve it there may be a number of *plans* (each with its own preconditions which must be satisfied before the plan can be invoked). Detailed planning can be avoided, by resorting to *scripts*. These represent a large sequence of stereotypical actions, and have roles and props associated with them. For example, $MOVIE is the script about going to a movie. Actions involved include "buying a ticket, giving the ticket to the doorman, getting a ripped ticket in return, going to the candy counter, entering the theater, sitting down, watching the movie, and leaving through the doors marked 'exit'" (Dyer, 1983a, p. 383).

5.2.9.2 Scripts in Cullingford's SAM

Scripts are patterns that capture a sequence of events that can be expected to take place in a given situation, involving given kinds of characters. Unless it is explicitly stated, in a story being analysed, that things went differently, a story-understanding program based on scripts will assume that by default, the unfolding in the given situation was as per the defaults specified in the script. Scripts have roles in which characters in a story may fit, and also have props. For example, the props of the script for using the subway, $SUBWAY, include (Cullingford, 1981, p. 102): a token, money paid for a token, a turnstile, a seat on the platform, the train itself, one of the cars, a seat on the car, a strap for the patron to grasp, and the gate leading from the platform at the destination station. Roles in the subway script include (Cullingford, 1981, p. 101): a group of subway riders (patrons group: *patgrp*), the cashier, the conductor, the person controlling the train, and the subway organisation. Episodes in that same script include (Cullingford, 1981, p. 108):

E1: Patron enters station (represented as M1: patgrp PTRANS to inside station), then the alternatives E2 and E3, namely: E2: Patron goes directly to turnstile (M2: patgrp PTRANS to turnstile), E3: Patron gets a token, then goes to turnstile (M3: agent ATRANS token to patgrp). After this branching into those two alternatives, the control flow joins again, into episode E4: Patron goes through turnstile, goes to platform (M4: patgrp WAIT at platform). Next, there is the *cyclic* episode E5, which loops, because this is an episode which may happen several times in succession, the minimum being one. E5: Subway arrives (M5: trainman PTRANS subway to platform). Next, we find episode E6: Patron enters subway and sits down (M6: patgrp MOVE to seat). Next, there is the cyclic episode E7: Subway goes to a new destination (M7: trainman PTRANS subway to destination). Finally, there is episode E8: Patron leaves the station (M8: patgrp PTRANS from station).

Eventually, scripts were refined into *MOPs (Memory Organization Packages)*, which differ from scripts in that a MOP also includes character's goals in relation to the sequence of plans, and therefore helps to understand the motivational dynamics of a story. Moreover, MOPs enable abstraction: for example, a MOP for service at a restaurant can be just be a special case of a more abstract MOP, capturing the pattern of situations such that service is provided, and the customer pays later.

At the University of Yale, Richard Cullingford (1978, 1981) developed SAM (Script Applier Mechanism), a program analysing stories by identifying and applying relevant scripts, not MOPs. Even so, SAM could analyse a story such as the following, and then provide an answer to a question, and refer to the mood of the protagonist (Cullingford, 1981, p. 78):

> JOHN WENT TO A RESTAURANT. HE ORDERED A HOT DOG. THE WAITER SAID THEY DIDN'T HAVE ANY. HE ASKED FOR A HAMBURGER. WHEN THE HAMBURGER CAME, IT WAS BURNT. HE LEFT THE RESTAURANT.

When asked:

> WHY DIDN'T JOHN EAT THE HAMBURGER?

SAM was informed that John did not eat the hamburger indeed. SAM was able to explain why John did not eat the hamburger:

> BECAUSE THE HAMBURGER WAS OVERDONE.

When asked:

> DID JOHN PAY THE CHECK?

SAM provided this answer:

> NO JOHN WAS ANGRY BECAUSE THE HAMBURGER WAS OVERDONE AND SO HE LEFT THE RESTAURANT.

Cullingford (1981, p. 81) could boast that:

> SAM was a pioneering effort in story understanding, an attempt to directly confront the messy, but real, problems associated with reading connected texts, as opposed to isolated sentences. It was also the first system which brought enough knowledge to bear on a domain that certain interesting problems in summarization, question-answering and machine translation could be attacked.

SAM, as well its simplified version, MicroSAM or McSAM, were originally coded in the Lisp functional programming language. Leon Sterling and Ehud Shapiro (1986, pp. 233–236) showed how simple it is to recode MicroSAM in the Prolog logic programming language. In their own implementation (Sterling & Shapiro, 1986, pp. 233–234):

> The top-level relation is *mcsam(Story,Script)* which expands a *Story* into its "understood" equivalent according to a relevant *Script*. The script is found by the predicate *find(Story,Script,Defaults)*. The story is searched for a non-variable argument that triggers the name of a script. In our example of John visiting Leones, the atom *leones* triggers the

5.2 An Overview of Artificial Intelligence Approaches to Narratives 361

restaurant script, indicated by the fact *trigger(leones,restaurant)* [in the Prolog program]. The matching of the story to the script is done by *match(Script,Story)* which associates lines in the story with lines in the script.

Their example input was: "John went to Leones, ate a hamburger and left." By expanding the script, with defaults filled in (because they are not contradicted by the story), the output produced was:

> John went to Leones. He was shown from the door to a seat. A waiter brought John a hamburger, which John ate by mouth. The waiter brought John a check, and John left Leones for another place.

Actually, the default expectation in the restaurant script is that John paid the bill. Let us turn to how MOPs are defined for given situations. A good example is the multi-paragraph understanding program BORIS, developed by Michael Dyer (1983a). Basically, not only characters' goals and motivations, but also their emotions were quite important to the workings of BORIS. It is from displays of emotion that the system could realise whether something went wrong, some plan did not succeed, or some active goal was thwarted.

5.2.9.3 I-Links and MOPS (Memory Organization Packages) in Dyer's BORIS

Motivations and intentions of narrative characters inside the upgraded scripts, the memory organisation packages (MOPs), in Michael Dyer's BORIS are captured by so-called I-*links*. The roles into which characters fit are written at the top of a box encompassing the MOP. Under the role, the goals of that role appear in a column. Between role-columns, a column of plans appears. The goals are connected to plans by I-links.

Various kinds of I-links exist. An event can either force, or be forced by an event. An event can motivate a goal, or thwart a goal, or achieve a goal. An event can block a goal, or be realised by a goal. A goal can be thwarted by an event, or be motivated by an event, or be achieved by an event. A goal can suspend another goal, or be suspended by another goal. A goal can intend a plan, or enable a plan. A plan can realise an event, or be blocked by an event. A plan can be intended by a goal, or be enabled by a goal. No I-link exists from a plan to a plan (Dyer, 1983a, pp. 199–200). Of these I-links, "intends" is abbreviated in diagrams as *i*, "motivates" as *m*, "achieves" as *a*, "realizes" as *r*, "blocks" as *b*, "suspends" as *s*, "forces" as *f*, "enables" as *e*, and "thwarts" as *t*.

Figure 5.2.9.3.1 shows the MOP for borrowing, M-BORROW, from Dyer's BORIS. Figure 5.2.9.3.2 shows the MOP for such service that the client has to pay later. The latter MOP is quite useful in BORIS, because by customising it for the relation between customer and owner, and for the relation between customer and waiter or waitress, one can define the MOP for service at a restaurant: Figure 5.2.9.3.3 shows how. There are strands between MOPs, that link particular episodes (actually: plans) inside the MOP for a restaurant to either MOPs or scripts for kinds of service, and for a meal.

Fig. 5.2.9.3.1 The MOP (memory organization package) for borrowing, M-BORROW. Redrawn from Dyer (1983a, p. 207)

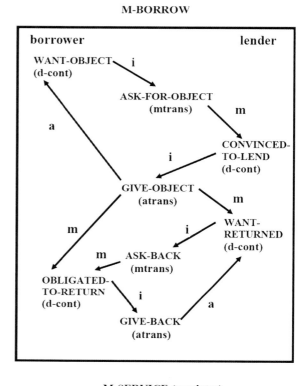

Fig. 5.2.9.3.2 The MOP for such service that the client has to pay later. Redrawn from Dyer (1983a, p. 221)

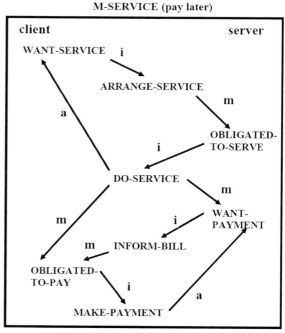

Fig. 5.2.9.3.3 Strands between MOPs: how the MOP for a restaurant is defined by means of either MOPs or scripts for kinds of service, and for a meal. Redrawn from Dyer (1983a, p. 220)

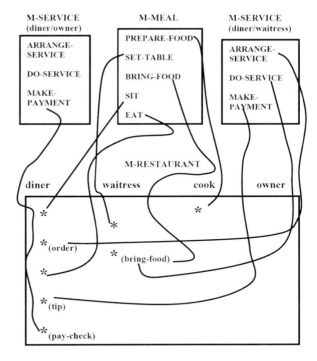

5.2.9.4 Evidence for a Divorce Case, in BORIS

The main story analysed by BORIS is DIVORCE-1, about evidence for a divorce case (Dyer, 1983a, pp. 1–5). BORIS is able to answer questions once it has analysed the first paragraph, and then again once it has analysed the second paragraph, and so forth. We omit here many of the questions and answers. The multi-paragraph story is as follows:

> Richard hadn't heard from his college roommate Paul for years. Richard had borrowed money from Paul which was never paid back. But now he had no idea where to find his old friend. When a letter finally arrived from San Francisco, Richard was anxious to find out how Paul was.
> Unfortunately, the news was not good. Paul's wife Sarah wanted a divorce. She also wanted the car, the house, the children, and alimony. Paul wanted the divorce, but he didn't want to see Sarah walk off with everything he had. His salary from the state school system was very small. Not knowing who to turn to, he was hoping for a favor from the only lawyer he knew. Paul gave his home phone number in case Richard felt he could help.
> Richard eagerly picked up the phone and dialed. After a brief conversation, Paul agreed to have lunch with him the next day. He sounded extremely relieved and grateful.
> The next day, as Richard was driving to the restaurant, he barely avoided hitting an old man on the street. He felt extremely upset by the incident, and had three drinks at the restaurant. When Paul arrived Richard was fairly drunk. After the food came, Richard spilled a cup of coffee on Paul. Paul seemed very annoyed by this so Richard offered to drive him home for a change of clothes.

> When Paul walked into the bedroom and found Sarah with another man he nearly had a heart attack. Then he realized what a blessing it was. With Richard there as a witness, Sarah's divorce case was shot. Richard congratulated Paul and suggested that they celebrate at dinner. Paul was eager to comply.

After analysing the fourth paragraph, one of the questions BORIS was asked was: "Why did Richard spill the coffee?". BORIS was able to make the causal connection, so it answered: "RICHARD WAS DRUNK." The fifth paragraph states that Paul nearly had a heart attack, but it doesn't say explicitly that he was surprised. BORIS was able to understand that the effect of what the husband saw was for him to be surprised. The question "What happened to Paul at home?" was answered: "PAUL CAUGHT SARAH COMMITTING ADULTERY." Then it was asked: "How did Paul feel?", and the answer was: "PAUL WAS SURPRISED." Next, BORIS was asked: "Why did Sarah lose her divorce case?", which informs the program that she did lose the case indeed. BORIS answered: "SARAH COMMITTED ADULTERY." Then BORIS was asked: "Why did Richard congratulate Paul?", and it gave this reply: "PAUL WON THE DIVORCE CASE." That is to say, it was considered to be foregone. Actually, such a finding in court cannot be taken for granted, before the adjudication is made. Judges would be unimpressed with a party seen to consider the conclusion foregone. But Dyer (1983a, p. 22) does point out indeed that "In DIVORCE-1 the husband wins although the characters never actually get to court." Presumably Sarah is convinced to settle without litigating, and accepts her loss. By contrast (ibid.), "In DIVORCE-2 the characters all appear in court and the husband loses." That second narrative is quoted below (Dyer, 1983a, pp. 19–20):

> George was having lunch with another teacher and grading homework assignments when the waitress accidentally knocked a glass of coke on him. George was very annoyed and left refusing to pay the check. He decided to drive home to get out of his wet clothes.
> When he got there, he found his wife Ann and another man in bed. George became extremely upset and felt like going out and getting plastered.
> At the bar he ran into an old college roommate David, who he hadn't seen in years. David offered to buy him a few drinks and soon they were both pretty drunk. When George found out that David was a lawyer, he told him all about his troubles and asked David to represent him in court. Since David owed George money he had never returned, he felt obligated to help out.
> Later, David wrote to Ann, informing her that George wanted a divorce. Her lawyer called back and told David that she intended to get the house, the children and a lot of alimony. When George heard this, he was very worried. He didn't earn much at the junior high school. David told him not to worry, since the judge would award the case to George once he learned that Ann had been cheating on him.
> When they got to court, David presented George's case, but without a witness they had no proof and Ann won. George almost had a fit. David could only offer George his condolences.

5.2.9.5 Thematic Abstraction Units (TAUs) in Dyer's BORIS

In Dyer's BORIS, thematic abstraction units (TAUs) are abstractions of situations, such that some planning and expectation failure occurs. These are situations that oftentimes are captured by an adage. For example, the situation of an employee who is unsatisfied with work conditions, seeks another job, and is offered one elsewhere, and then his original boss offers some improvement, but the employee has already made his or her mind, is captured by the adage "Closing the barn door after the horse", and corresponds to the pattern of TAU-POST-HOC (Dyer, 1983a, p. 29):

> TAU-POST-HOC
> 1   x has preservation goal G active
>   since enablement condition C unsatisfied.
> 2   x knows a plan P that will keep G
>   from failing by satisfying C.
> 3   x does not execute P and G fails.
>   x attempts to recover from the failure
>   of G by executing P.
>   P fails since P is effective for C,
>   but not in recovering from G's failure.
> 4   In the future, x must execute P when G
>   is active and C is not satisfied.

In the DIVORCE-1 story analysed by BORIS, the situation of Paul who hoped for a favour from the only lawyer he knew, Richard, an old friend who turns out to be willing to extending a helping hand, is captured by TAU-DIRE-STRAITS as well as by the adage "A friend in need is a friend indeed" (Dyer, 1983a, p. 36):

> TAU-DIRE-STRAITS
> x has a crisis goal G.
> x has experienced a planning failure
> (i.e. x can't resolve the crisis by himself).
> x seeks a friend y to be his agent
> (since y knows what plans to execute).

This TAU has the following affective expectations associated with it:

> x is uncertain whether y
>   will be able to help.
> If y agrees to help
>   Then x will have a positive
>   affect toward y
> Else x will have a negative
>   affect (possibly toward y).

5.2.9.6 Other Kinds of Knowledge Sources in BORIS

Dyer's BORIS knows about various kinds of affect. Moreover, there are such empathetic situations that a character expresses, either to himself or herself, or to another character, the reaction that the former feels concerning a goal situation affecting the second character. Such situations are represented as ACEs, i.e., Affect as a Consequence of Empathy (Dyer, 1983a, p. 121). When the interpersonal theme (IPT) is those two characters, x and y, being friends,

(IPT-FRIENDS x y)
relevant ACEs include *commiserate* or *condole,* whose representation is

    x MTRANS
       TO y
       that [goal failure (y)
           causes: x feel NEG]

as well as *felicitate* or *congratulate,* whose representation is:

    x MTRANS
       TO y
       that [goal success (y)
           causes: x feel POS]

Vice versa if the theme is (IPT-ENEMIES x y), whose relevant ACEs are gloat if the enemy experiences a goal failure, or envy or spite if the enemy experiences a goal success. Regardless of the theme, another ACE is *reassure,* whose representation is:

    x MTRANS
       TO y
       that [y should feel POS
          in spite of active goal p-goal
          or goal failure]

BORIS also includes role theme information, such as RL-TEACHER, being role theme information about teachers. When analysing some given event, BORIS searches knowledge structures associated with that role theme, when a character who is a teacher is involved (Dyer, 1983a, p. 152).

There are in BORIS knowledge structures organised like a MOP, but which are about interpersonal situations. Such is the case of IP-FAVOR. There are two roles: person-a and person-b. Here again, like in a MOP, The roles into which characters fit are written at the top of a box encompassing the MOP. Under the role, the goals of that role appear in a column. Between role-columns, a column of plans appears. The goals are connected to plans by I-links. In IP-FAVOR, person-a's goal WANT-FAVOR intends plan ASK-FOR-FAVOR (with "invoke ipt", i.e., invoke an interpersonal theme: see below).

In turn, ASK-FOR-FAVOR intends PERSUADED. At PERSUADED, there also is an incoming arrow labeled "thm" (i.e., *thematic link*), from person-b's RELATIONAL-OBLIGATION (which is treated like a goal). PERSUADED motivates plan DO-FAVOR (agency), which achieves person-a's goal WANT-FAVOR, and also motivates person-a's own RELATIONAL-OBLIGATION. When person-b's goal WANT-RETURN-FAVOR is active, it intends plan ASK-FOR-RETURN-FAVOR, which motivates PERSUADED, which is linked by "thm" to person-a's RELATIONAL-OBLIGATION, and moreover intends plan DO-RETURN-FAVOR (agency), and this in turn achieves person-b's goal WANT-RETURN-FAVOR (Dyer, 1983a, p. 282).

Interpersonal themes (IPTs) are frequent in social situations. For example, in the story about Paul's anxiety while expecting a divorce, and his getting help from

5.2 An Overview of Artificial Intelligence Approaches to Narratives

his old friend, the lawyer Richard, "Richard hadn't heard from his college roommate Paul for years" triggers in BORIS a suspension of an interpersonal theme (SUSPEND-IPT). Richard having borrowed money from Paul that then he didn't return, involves IP-FAVOR. The arrival of Paul's letter and Richard being anxious to find out how Paul was involves interpersonal communication: IP-COMM, and also the MOP for a letter, M-LETTER, is triggered. "Unfortunately, the news was not good" triggers IP-EMPATHY. Paul hoping for a favour triggers again IP-FAVOR. Paul agreeing to have lunch with Richard, after the long time they hadn't been in contact, triggers RENEW-IPT. Richard offering to drive Paul home triggers IP-FAVOR (ibid., p. 294).

Paul finding his wife Sarah with another man triggers IPT-LOVE violation, which is not the same thing as the violation of the marriage contract, which is legal rather than social. Richard congratulating Paul triggers IP-EMPATHY (ibid., p. 294). This is when it is clear that as there is an eyewitness to her adultery, other than her husband, Sarah would better settle her divorce.[39] The suggestion that the two friends should celebrate at dinner triggers IP-SOC, an interpersonal theme that takes care of the fact that interpersonal relationship change over time (ibid., p. 291). There is a cycle – Dyer called it the *Ip-cycle* (ibid., p. 292) – that starts when INIT-IPT turns the interpersonal theme into being active. Then SUSPEND-IPT may intervene, that renders it inactive. From there, RENEW-IPT may make it active again. At any rate, when an interpersonal theme is active, is may be redefined, and REDEFINE-IPT takes care of that in BORIS (ibid., p. 292).

RELs, i.e., relations, are another kind of structure: "Marriages are complex knowledge structures in that they create many social, interpersonal, affective, legal and thematic expectations. In BORIS, the relationship of marriage is represented by R-MARRIAGE, which contains both interpersonal and social dimensions" (ibid., p. 229). Two given characters, a man and a woman, may be involved in, e.g., a marriage relationship, R-MARRIAGE, whose instance will be, e.g., R-MARRIAGE0 between ANN0 and GEORGE0 (ibid., p. 188).

"The termination of the interpersonal theme IPT-LOVERS causes emotional turmoil, such as guilt and jealousy, while the termination of the marital contract

---

[39] Marital infidelity fits in another kind of legal narrative as well, namely, as motive for crime against one's spouse. Allen and Pardo (2007a, pp. 119–123) offered a critique, in terms of the *reference-class problem* (see Section 2.4 above) of how probability theory was applied to juridical proof concerning infidelity in Davis and Follette (2003, 2002). Also Friedman and Park (2003) criticised (but Allen & Pardo believe they did not go far enough) the conclusions and choice of base rates in the calculations in Davis and Follette (2002). The latter (discussing a simplified example in order to discuss a real case) purported to demonstrate quantifying the value of evidence, as illustrated on the value of a defendant's infidelity in the murder of his wife, claiming that such infidelity is not probative of whether a man murdered or will murder his wife. In the real case, the prosecution had relied heavily on motive evidence, claiming the the defendant had deliberately drowned his wife once they had fallen into the ditch. The prosecution claimed that the husband may have somehow caused the crash, and that he faked his being unconscious or unable to breathe when paramedics arrived. Davis and Follette (2003) adjusted their analysis, in reply to the criticism of Friedman and Park (2003). This however did not satisfy Allen and Pardo (2007a), who also criticised (ibid., p. 123, fn.19) Kaye and Koehler's (2003) criticism of Davis and Follette (2002).

causes legal turmoil, such as alimony and custody battles" (ibid., p. 229). *Life themes* were admittedly not dealt with in BORIS; in marriage, life-theme aspects involve courtship, engagement, the wedding, and birth and rearing of children (ibid., pp. 46, 229).

The various kinds of knowledge sources in BORIS are connected in a Knowledge Dependency Graph, as shown in Fig. 5.2.9.6.1. "Knowledge structure dependencies help in the recognition process (ibid., p. 173), as the set of links in that graph "serves as a constraint on processing effort and makes predictions concerning both processing and memory" (ibid.). There are knowledge interaction demons, but "only a portion of such demons is ever active at one time, since the number of links emanating from a given knowledge structure is rarely more than six" (ibid.). This makes the system more efficient. Two consequences of that constraint are that: "A greater amount of processing effort will be expended on those knowledge sources with the most connections in the Knowledge Dependency Graph" (ibid.), and that: "Since BORIS only checks for one fourth of all possible knowledge interactions, any story containing interactions which do not fit the ones predicted by the KS-Graph will be both a) more difficult to understand, and b) more difficult to recall" (ibid., p. 174).

"*Main scenarios* consist of settings in which the major events of the story occur" (ibid., p. 256). "*Transition scenarios* arise whenever a character moves from one main scenario to another" (ibid.). "Mental scenarios come about when

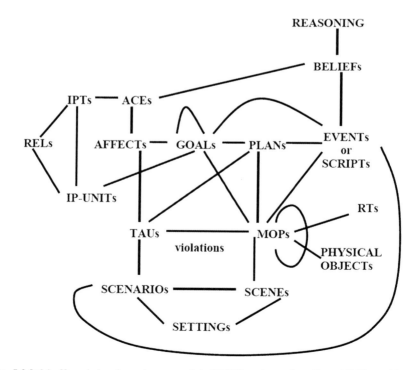

Fig. 5.2.9.6.1 Knowledge dependency graph in BORIS, redrawn from Dyer (1983a, p. 171)

5.2 An Overview of Artificial Intelligence Approaches to Narratives

two characters communicate with one another across scenario boundaries", such as when in one of the divorce stories, Richard opened Paul's letter: "the content of Paul's letter forms a mental scenario" (ibid.).

"Main scenarios organize episodes which occur within the same spatio-temporal setting. BORIS uses scene information [in] each MOP to decide when to instantiate a scenario" (ibid., p. 259). The scenes SC-OUTSIDE-COURT and SC-COURTROOM are contained in the MOP whose name is M-LEGAL-DISPUTE. When analysing one of the divorce stories, as BORIS reads "When they got to the court", the program "searches for a MOP associated with the courtroom setting. Once M-LEGAL-DISPUTE is found, BORIS instantiates a new scenario with SC-COURTROOM as one of its scenes" (ibid., p. 260). Figure 5.2.9.6.2 shows the MOP from BORIS for a legal dispute, namely, M-LEGAL-DISPUTE.

Again from BORIS, Fig. 5.2.9.6.3 shows the MOP for a lawyer representing a client; of course if the application is intended for use by a professional in the legal domain, one can be expected to take issue with the last plan, PRESENT-EVIDENCE, at the bottom of the box (it has an incoming enablement arrow). A lawyer would rather organise the evidence, which will be delivered by witnesses in court or will result from the documents (which may be pointed to from the witnesses statements), and the lawyer would eventually sum things up while eventually arguing the case. Figure 5.2.9.6.4 shows how, in BORIS, strands link the plans among three different MOPs in the legal domain.

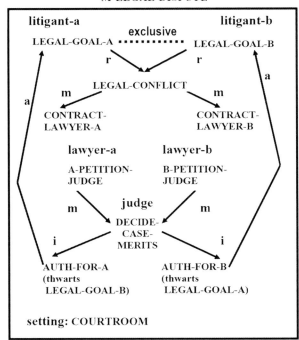

Fig. 5.2.9.6.2 The MOP for a legal dispute in BORIS, redrawn from Dyer (1983a, p. 237)

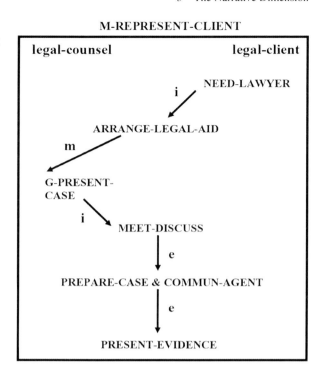

Fig. 5.2.9.6.3 The MOP for a lawyer representing a client in BORIS, redrawn from Dyer (1983a, p. 239)

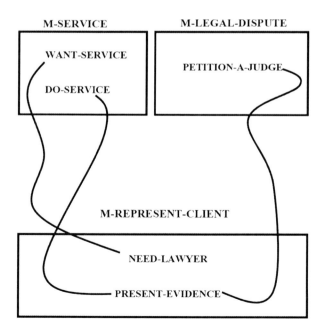

Fig. 5.2.9.6.4 Strands linking plans from different MOPs in the legal domain, redrawn from Dyer (1983a, p. 241)

5.2.9.7 Contractual Situations and Shady Deals in STARE

The STARE system was described by Seth R. Goldman, Michael G. Dyer, and Margot Flowers (1985, 1987, 1988). The computational model was of the cognitive processes involved in remembering, recalling, and applying past experiences in new situations. Issues of recalling past cases were admittedly in the context of first-year law students learning contract law. The input is one-paragraph text, describing a contractual situation. Sometimes, the situation described concerned an unlawful deal. At any rate, it was the task of STARE to determine whether or not a contract actually exists under the principles of contract law. One case is *Merchant v. Vacationer:* "O'Hara, a police officer on vacation in Florida, promises Alfred, a store owner, that he will keep an eye on Alfred's store during Alfred's lunch hour if Alfred will pay him $10. Alfred agrees to pay O'Hara $10.". Goldman, Dyer, and Flowers (1987, section 1.1) explained:

> Is there a contract in this situation? Answering this question requires (1) knowledge about social roles such as policemen, store owners, and public servants, (2) what effect being "on vacation" has for O'Hara, (3) what it means to "promise" to do something, (4) what it means "to keep an eye" on something, and (5) what it means to agree to something. In addition, there are many inferences we can make. One such inference is that O'Hara wants to earn some money while on vacation.

Merchant v. Vacationer was contrasted to *Merchant v. Copper:* "Fred, a police officer, promises Barney, a merchant who owns a store on Fred's beat, that he will keep an eye on Barney's store if Barney pays him $50 per month. Barney agrees to pay Fred $59 per month." In this other situation, something is very wrong. There is a conflict arising from Fred's actions. This policeman is extracting money from Barney, in order to do something he is already supposed to do. Another shady deal is *Witness v. Citizen:* "John promises to tell the truth in court if Mary will promise to pay John $100. Mary promises to pay John $100." This is somewhat similar to *Merchant v. Copper,* because a witness is under obligation to tell the truth, and yet this witness is extracting money from somebody, so he will say in court whatever he is going to say. In processing the input of *Witness v. Citizen,* STARE represented John's offer as follows (Goldman et al., 1987, section 1.2), based on Conceptual Dependency theory:

```
INPUT: (MTRANS ACTOR (HUMAN   NAME     John
                              GENDER   MALE)
               TO    (HUMAN   NAME     Mary
                              GENDER   FEMALE)
               OBJ   (MTRANS ACTOR Mary
                             TO    John
                             OBJ   (ATRANS ACTOR Mary
                                           TO    John
                                           OBJ   $100
                                           TIME  Future
               )            )            )
```

```
    --- result motivates -→
            (MTRANS ACTOR John
                    TO    Judge & Jury
                    OBJ  (MENT-OBJ STATUS true)
                    TIME  Future
            )
```

When generating the output, a trace of the program run is produced. The input is processed, and a type of common sense OFFER is recognized. Then demons (i.e., agents) are spawned to determine if this is a Legal OFFER. In particular, the demons activated are CHECK-OFFEROR-RIGHTS and CHECK-OFFEREE-RIGHTS. Of these, it results from CHECK-OFFEROR-RIGHTS that John already has a DUTY to tell the truth. Thus, on that count, the input fails. The indexing of this input episode is done, by using the failure of CHECK-OFFEROR-RIGHTS. During the indexing, STARE is reminded of *Merchant v. Copper*. STARE attempts to generalise from reminding. But no common features are detected. Then expectation demons from OFFER are spawned, and these demons include EXPECT-ACCEPT and EXPECT-REJECT. Then comes the end of the conceptualisation.

In *Witness v. Citizen*, STARE's decision is as follows (Goldman et al., 1987, section 1.2):

```
OUTPUT:
  DECISION: There is no contract between John and Mary.
  REASONS:  John's offer was not a legal offer because John
            already has a DUTY to tell the truth in court.
            Mary's acceptance was not legal because there
            was no preceding legal offer.
  REMINDINGS:    Merchant v. Copper
```

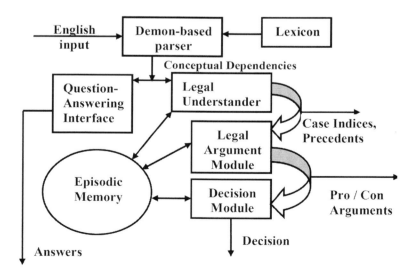

Fig. 5.2.9.7.1 The architecture of STARE (redrawn from Goldman et al., 1987)

5.2 An Overview of Artificial Intelligence Approaches to Narratives   373

STARE was reminded of *Merchant v. Copper* while processing *Witness v. Citizen*, because there is a conflicting duty for the offeror in both cases. The architecture of STARE is shown in Fig. 5.2.9.7.1, being redrawn from Goldman et al. (1987).

5.2.10 SWALE and Related Systems for Generating Explanations from Precedents

Alex Kass at Yale in the late 1980s developed SWALE, a case-based tool for understanding with explanation patterns. SWALE is a system that generates explanations for unusual death stories; its perspective within case-based reasoning is one of explaining out anomalies (Kass, 1990; Kass, Leake, & Owens, 1986). Alex Kass also developed TWEAKER and ABE, for adapting explanations in order to develop hypotheses for understanding (Kass, 1990, 1992, 1994). Ashwin Ram, at Yale in 1989, developed the AQUA project, in case-based explanation: the story understanding was driven by questions asked (Ram, 1989, 1994). Around 1990, David Leake, also at Yale, developed *Accepter*, a theory and tool for evaluating explanations (Leake, 1992, 1994). Chris Owens, also at Yale in the same period, developed *Retriever* and *Anon*, tools for indexing and retrieving planning knowledge from memory, in the perspective of case-based explanation and automated understanding (Owens, 1990, 1994).

In the book *Inside Case-Based Explanation*, edited by Schank, Kass, and Riesbeck (1994), Part I is a condensation of Schank's book (1986) *Explanation Patterns*. Part II of the book *Inside Case-Based Explanation* comprises chapters 3–9, and is an application of the theory. In particular, chapter 3 provides an overview of SWALE, because of its historical importance, as being a computer program that generates explanations by retrieving, instantiating, and adapting *explanation patterns* (*XPs* for short). Part III supplies the code, in Common Lisp, of a miniature version of SWALE. The code of the miniature is annotated.[40] Chapters 4–9 in Part II of *Inside Case-Based Explanation* describe in detail individual systems that relate to specific parts of SWALE (these, too, are covered in the code of the miniature in Part III). Of these chapters, Chapters 4 and 5 are about how to retrieve from memory relevant precedents, which here are previous explanations.

How to determine the appropriate abstraction level for the memory indices that enable case retrieval is the subject of chapter 4 of *Inside Case-Based Explanation*. Whereas highly abstract indices can be very powerful for retrieving relevant cases, how to accurately ascribe such abstract indices to an input case comes at a high cost. The information in an input case, the way it is found there, is not necessarily a good indicator for retrieval, and this is especially true when cases from a variety of domains are stored. Chapter 4, concerned with the *Anon* system for retrieving explanations, proposes that the appropriate level of abstraction for indices, so that explanations be generated for planning anomalies, is the level typically captured in

---

[40] The code of a version of SWALE in miniature, Micro SWALE, is accessible on the Web at http://www.cs.indiana.edu/~leake/cbr/code/

proverbial advice. There is a long tradition for using chunks of common sense at the level of adages (proverbs) for planning advice, when dealing with planning failures, in Roger Schank's *conceptual dependency* school of automated understanding of narratives, and this was especially the case of Michael Dyer's BORIS system, which used TAUs, i.e., thematic abstraction units (Dyer, 1983a, 1983b). Also note that at UCLA in 1991, John Reeves, supervised by Michael Dyer, developed THUNDER (Reeves, 1991): it was a program interpreting funny situations as plan failure (it was described as irony, but this is not precise, and was a misnomer indeed; rather, what thunder was concerned with was the workings of what makes stories from a given category funny).

Chapter 5 of the book *Inside Case-Based Explanation* is about the *Abby* system, in which stories about social situations are represented. The concern of chapter 5 is with the indexing vocabulary required for explanation retrieval. Much domain-specific knowledge is required. Chapter 6 is about the *Accepter* system, and is concerned with how, given an anomalous situation, to automatically evaluate the appropriateness of a retrieved candidate explanation. Such retrieved explanations are indexed under the same anomaly type as the current problem for which an explanation has to be generated. The proposed model of evaluation is context-sensitive, and based on what the current goals of the automated reasoner are. For anomaly detection and explanation, a recursive model is proposed in chapter 6 of *Inside Case-Based Explanation*.

Chapter 7 of that same book is about the AQUA system (Ram, 1994), embodying an approach to the generation of explanations that is based on a mechanism for question asking and answering. The questions are classified according to various kinds of knowledge goal of the understanding agent. The questions themselves are represented as memory structures, and they specify both knowledge requirement and the intended purpose of such knowledge once it is obtained. The model of explanation is recursive. In fact, answering can span further questions. Ashwin Ram (1994) "propose[d] the following taxonomy of knowledge goals for story understanding":

> *Text goals*: Knowledge goals of a text analysis program, arising from text-level tasks. These are the questions that arise from basic syntactic and semantic analysis that needs to be done on the input text, such as noun group attachment or pronoun reference. An example text goal is to find the referent of a pronoun.
>
> *Memory goals*: Knowledge goals of a dynamic memory program, arising from memory-level tasks. A dynamic memory must be able to notice similarities, match incoming concepts to stereotypes in memory, form generalizations, and so on. An example memory goal might be to look for an event predicted by stored knowledge of a stereotyped action, such as asking what the ransom will be when one hears about a kidnapping.
>
> *Explanation goals*: Goals of an explainer that arise from explanation-level tasks, including the detection and resolution of anomalies, and the building of motivational and causal explanations for the events in the story in order to understand why the characters acted as they did or why certain events did or did not occur. An example explanation goal might be to figure out the motivation of a suicide truck bomber mentioned in a story.
>
> *Relevance goals*: Goals of any intelligent system in the real world, concerning the identification of aspects of the current situation that are "interesting" or relevant to its general goals. An example is looking for the name of an airline in a hijacking story if the understander were contemplating travelling by air soon.

5.2 An Overview of Artificial Intelligence Approaches to Narratives

Moreover, the *explanation patterns (XPs)*, which in AQUA have four components, in AQUA were defined by Ram (1994) as follows[41]:

- *PRE-XP-NODES*: Nodes that represent what is known before the XP is applied. One of these nodes, the EXPLAINS node, represents the particular action being explained.
- *XP-ASSERTED-NODES*: Nodes asserted by the XP as the explanation for the EXPLAINS node. These comprise the premises of the explanation.
- *INTERNAL-XP-NODES*: Internal nodes asserted by the XP in order to link the XP-ASSERTED-NODES to the EXPLAINS node.
- *LINKS*: Causal links asserted by the XP. These taken together with the INTERNAL-XP-NODES are also called the internals of the XP.

> An explanation pattern is a directed, acyclic graph of conceptual nodes connected with causal LINKS, which in turn could invoke further XPs at the next level of detail. The PRE-XP-NODES are the sink nodes (consequences) of the graph, and the XP-ASSERTED-NODES are the source nodes (antecedents or premises). The difference between XP-ASSERTED-NODES and INTERNAL-XP-NODES is that the former are merely asserted by the XP without further explanation, whereas the latter have causal antecedents within the XP itself. An XP applies when the EXPLAINS node matches the concept being explained and the PRE-XP-NODES are in the current set of beliefs. The resulting hypothesis is confirmed when all the XP-ASSERTED-NODES are verified.

Chapter 8 of *Inside Case-Based Explanation* is about the TWEAKER system, embodying an approach to the adaptation of retrieved explanations. Such modification of explanations is done by selecting and applying retrieval strategies. These retrieval strategies are themselves stored in memory, and have to be retrieved. Chapter 8 is mainly concerned with classifying adaptation strategies (avoiding overly general strategies, which tend to be unreliable, or overly specific stategies, that tend to have just limited applicability), rather than how to select one such strategy that is appropriate.

- An adaptation strategy in TWEAKER may be to *generalise*. This is appropriate when (according to AQUA's classification of general causes of explanation failure) the system has encountered a *novel situation*.
- Another adaptation strategy in TWEAKER is to *substitute*. This is appropriate when the general cause of failure is having an *incorrect model*.
- Yet another adaptation strategy in TWEAKER is to *specialise*. This is appropriate when the general cause of failure is *misindexing* of knowledge stored in memory.

Chapter 9 of *Inside Case-Based Explanation* is about the *Brainstormer* system for plan adaptation (rather than the adaptation of explanations). Abstract planning advice at the level of proverbs is stored in memory, and *Brainstormer* has to apply

---

[41] Ram (1994) provided as an example XP-RELIGIOUS-FANATIC for explaining suicide bombings, and noted the interest of a story (from newspaper news from 1985) where the prospective perpetrator was not a fanatic, but was motivated by blackmail.

such advice to some planning problem at hand. This is done by resorting to a process of *lambda abstraction,* by which the given problem is restated in terms of the abstract plan vocabulary. In order to achieve this, in memory there are rules about how to recognise instances of a given abstract concept. As by redescribing one may obtain intermediate rather than final concepts, the mechanism – here, too – is recursive. The intermediate concepts are then redescribed, again via the process of lambda abstraction. Besides, as some proverbs contradict each other, one has to resolve this ambiguity by considering in detail the specific planning situation.

5.2.11 Input from Earlier Research into More Recent Research in Automated Story Understanding

In 1996, Michael Cox from Georgia Tech in Atlanta reported (Cox, 1996a) about Meta-AQUA. It involved introspective multistrategy learning, and an empirical study of TALE-SPIN stories. Cox (n.d., section 5.2) remarked:

> Each anomaly in a story represents a source of knowledge discrepancy for Meta-AQUA and a potential explanation target. For each anomaly up to three points are awarded: one point for identifying that a question needs to be posed, a second for providing any explanation, and a third for matching the "correct" explanation as enumerated by an oracle. With this or any like function, the evaluator should generate a real number between 1 and 0. Then to normalize the explanation criterion with performance (given a performance measure also between 1 and 0), it is sufficient to calculate performance/(2–explanation). [...]. Without the incorporation of self-explanation into the overall performance measure, many metareasoning implementations can simply optimize performance first and then sprinkle on a bit of meta-sugar after the fact.

The project of Cox was in story understanding, whereas TALE-SPIN had been a fable-like story generator (Meehan, 1976, 1981a, 1981b) from Yale University's conceptual dependency school. During the 1990s, also at Georgia Tech, the ISAAC model (and functional theory) of creative reading was developed by Kenneth Moorman (1997; cf. Moorman & Ram, 1994).

Cox's research is into metacognition in computation, self-aware cognitive agents, and learning strategies under reasoning failure.[42] The level of doing is the *ground level.* The level of reasoning is the *object level.* The level of metareasoning is the *meta-level.* The ground level provides the object level with *perception.* The object level provides the ground level with *action selection.* The meta-level *controls* the object level, but is *monitored* by it as well.[43] Cox (2007b, section 1) explained:

> If the reasoning that is performed at the object level and not just its results is represented in a declarative knowledge structure that captures the mental states and decision-making

---

[42] Cox (1994, 1996a, 1996b, 2005, 2007a, 2007b). Cox and Raja (2007), Cox and Ram (1999).

[43] In the conclusions, Cox (2007b) lists some hard problems for building autonomous agents endowed with metareasoning, including the *Homunculus Problem:* "How can we effectively control metareasoning without substituting yet another computational layer above the meta-level?"

5.2 An Overview of Artificial Intelligence Approaches to Narratives

sequence, then these knowledge structures can themselves be passed to the meta-level for monitoring. For example the Meta-AQUA system [Cox & Ram (1999)] keeps a trace of its story understanding decisions in structures called a Trace Meta-eXplanation Pattern (TMXP). Here the object-level story understanding task is to explain anomalous or unusual events in a ground-level story perceived by the system. Then if this explanation process fails, Meta-AQUA passes the TMXP and the current story representation to a learning subsystem. The learner performs an introspection of the trace to obtain an explanation of the explanation failure called an Introspective Meta-eXplanation Pattern (IMXP). The IMXPs are used to generate a set of learning goals that are passed back to control the object-level learning and hence improve subsequent understanding. TMXPs explain *how* reasoning occurs; IMXPs explain *why* reasoning fails.

Unfortunately these meta-explanation structures are so complicated that, although they have been shown empirically to support complex learning, they cannot be easily understood by humans. Indeed before I demonstrate the Meta-AQUA system to others, I often spend twenty minutes reviewing the TMXP and IMXP schemas, so that I can answer questions effectively. However I claim that all metareasoning systems share this characteristic. The kinds of recursive processing an agent must do to perform metareasoning (e.g., within the metacognitive loop of [Anderson & Perlis (2005)]) and the types of knowledge structures used to support metareasoning (e.g., the introspective explanations in [Raja & Goel (2007)] or [Fox & Leake (2001)]) produce a severe cognitive demand on even the most sophisticated observer. What is required is the implementation of an infrastructure to support interactive explanation of an agent's own reasoning.

Apart from Cox's Meta-AQUA, another project that resorted to concepts from much older research, is the resurrection of Lehnert's (1982) plot units in a project reported about by Appling and Riedl (2009). Their project is in *plot summarisation:*

> We are developing a system to learn from readers how to automatically reason about plot unit summarization involved in single character narratives. These stories are aggregations of temporally ordered *events*. There are however events that different readers might leave out if they were summarizing a story to another person. Taking into account this nature, and that of plot units i.e. their implicit summarization, it inherently follows that not all events of a story should necessarily be kept in a summary. That is, only the most important events would be kept to preserve the high-level principles of the original story and these should correspond to Lehnert's complex plot units. As we build a corpus of stories to train our plot units system with we used the notion of story *interpretations* as another useful abstraction that allows our system to work with different views of a single story, these result in unique subsets of events from an original story. We focus on learning and reasoning on the level of interpretations but unabridged stories are also supported.

For that purpose, Appling and Riedl (2009) resort to probabilistic machine learning techniques:

> Since the primary work in this paper is the identification of representations that can be used for learning to summarize plots we are interested in the class of machine learning frameworks dealing with probabilistic graphical models. These frameworks can model sequential domains in an accessible and tractable way, important for achieving useful results in a short amount of time. Concerning plot units, they have many interesting properties: temporality, event relatedness, and interpretability. These are properties that can be easily exploited

by probabilistic graphical models such as Hidden Markov Models,[44] Markov Random Fields,[45] and Conditional Random Fields [...]

For a given story, a story graph is constructed, and areas within the graph may provide alternative interpretations. This is something that already Tapiero, den Broek, and Quintana (2002) have discussed: the mental representation of narrative texts as networks, and the role of necessity and sufficiency in the detection of different types of causal relations. The purpose of that study was "to determine how the perceived strength of 4 types of causal relations (physical causality, motivation, psychological causation, and enablement) is affected by causal properties (i.e., necessity and sufficiency) and by distance in the text surface structure".

5.2.12 *Other Systems for Automated Story Understanding*

A former student of Michael Dyer, Erik Mueller (1998, 1999a), reported about *ThoughtTreasure,* involving plans, goals, emotions, grids, and simulation.[46] Also Mueller (1999b, 2002) dealt with story understanding. In 2003, then based at IBM Research, Mueller (2003, 2004a, 2004b, 2006, 2007) reported about a model-based story-understanding program, the model being constructed through multiple representations. Event calculus was the main representation, and satisfiability was a major concern of the project.

At the University of California at Berkeley, Srinivas Narayanan (1997) developed KARMA, a narrative-understanding model concerned with understanding metaphor and aspect, making use of *x-schemas.* Lynette Hirschman of MITRE developed *Deep Read,* a reading comprehension system (Hirschman, Light, Breck, & Burger,

---

[44] "Hidden Markov Models (HMM) are probabilistic finite state automata that model the probabilities of a linear sequence of events. In a HMM, one only knows a probabilistic function of the state sequence through which the model passes. Given a training corpus in which the information is sequentially structured and which is manually annotated, efficient algorithms learn the probabilities of all transitions and emissions" (Stranieri & Zeleznikow, 2005a, Glossary).

[45] Basically, a *Markov random field* is an undirected graph, that is to say, the edges between pairs of nodes are not arrows. Each node in a MRF can be in any of a finite number of states. The state of a node statistically depends upon each of its neighbours (i.e., those nodes to which the given node is connected by an edge), and upon no other node in the graph. A *propagation matrix,* symbolised as ψ, respresents the dependency between a node and its neighbours in the given MRF. Each case $\psi(i, j)$ in the matrix has a value which is equal to the probability of a node *i* being in state *j* given that it has a neighbour in state *i*. If an assignment of states to the nodes in a MRF is given, then by using the propagation matrix it is possible to compute a likelihood of observing that assignment. The problem of inferring the maximum likelihood assignment of states to nodes, where the correct states for some of the nodes are possibly known beforehand, is solved by those using MRFs by resorting to heuristic techniques.

[46] A quite useful resource, and one to which the present treatment of automated story processing owes much, is Erik Mueller's website (http://xenia.media.mit.edu/~mueller/storyund/storyres.html) on automated story understanding or generation.

1999). Machine learning[47] was applied to question-answering for reading comprehension tests, in a system from Singapore, *Aquareas,* reported about by Ng, Teo, and Kwan (2000). Ellen Riloff and Michael Thelen (2000), from the University of Utah, reported about a rule-based question answering system for reading comprehension tests.

The physical world in which narratives unfold was the concern of a spatio-temporal model from France, reported about by Gerard and Sansonnet (2000). It was a model for the representation of situations described in narrative texts that had to be analysed automatically. This was also a concern in Mueller (2007), an article about the modelling of space and time when understanding automatically narratives about restaurants.

At the University of Edinburgh, Harry Halpin under the supervision of Johanna Moore developed a system for plot analysis resorting to both symbolic semantic analysis and statistical analysis. The representation was the event calculus, and a method called *latent semantic analysis (LSA)* was used. The tool was a plot advice agent (Halpin, 2003; Halpin & Moore, 2010).

In 1989, the EL/Epilog/Ecologic project was developed by Lenhart Schubert and Chung Hee Hwang at the University of Alberta and the University of Rochester, in collaboration with Boeing. Episodic logic was applied to natural-language understanding (Schubert & Hwang, 1989, 2000). Kathleen Dahlgren and others at the University of Western Ontario in collaboration with IBM in 1989 developed KT, in which a logic-based knowledge representation was applied to commonsense reasoning for understanding texts automatically (Dahlgren, McDowell, & Stabler, 1989). Around 1990, TACITUS was developed by Jerry Hobbs and others at SRI in California; it resorted to a logic-based knowledge representations, and to weighted abduction, a concept related to explanation being generated as inference to the "best" explanation,[48] and quantified by means of weights (Hobbs, Stickel, Appelt, & Martin, 1993).

In 1993, Palmer, Passonneau, Weir, and Finin (1993) from Unisys reported about the KERNEL text understanding system, involving complex interaction between system modules. In 1995, Stuart Shapiro and William Rapaport from the State University of New York at Buffalo (Shapiro & Rapaport, 1995) reported about *SnePS/Cassie,* a "computational reader of narratives" handling beliefs and using a representation in terms of propositional semantic networks.

In 1993, Golden and Rumelhart (1993), from the University of Texas at Dallas and from Stanford, reported about a model working in situation-state space, and being a parallel distributed processing model of story comprehension and recall. Work by David Rumelhart[49] was historically important for cognitive and computational models of *story recognition* (Rumelhart, 1975, 1980a, 1980b), just as it was

---

[47] For *machine learning,* see e.g. Mitchell (1997).

[48] See Section 2.2.1.6 above.

[49] David Rumelhart is a psychologist, and has collaborated across disciplines, with Jay McClelland (psychology), Geoffrey Hinton (artificial intelligence), and Paul Smolensky (physics, artificial intelligence).

for *parallel distributed processing* (Rumelhart, Smolensky, McClelland, & Hinton, 1986c).

Recall from episodic memory is the task of REMIND, developed by Trent Lange and Charles Wharton at UCLA (Lange & Wharton, 1992). It involved spreading activation, inferencing, and disambiguation. Importantly, the application of connectionism (neural networks) to story-understanding emerged in those years. Charles Dolan developed at UCLA the CRAM project (Dolan, 1989), in which comprehension involved morals, and whose workings resorted to *tensor manipulation networks*. Also see the various articles collected in a volume, *Connectionist Natural Language Processing*, edited by Noel Sharkey (1992), and which I reviewed (Nissan, 1997d). Importantly, story-processing was involved, as Michael Dyer, at UCLA, had meanwhile turned to combining symbolic (old-fashioned AI) with neural processing while processing narratives; e.g., see Dyer (1991a, 1991b, 1995), Lee, Flowers, and Dyer (1992), and Dyer, Flowers, and Wang (1992). Trent Lange developed in 1989 at UCLA, under Dyer's supervision, the ROBIN project, that carried out inferencing in a connectionist networks for the purposes of narrative understanding (Lange & Dyer, 1989). Risto Miikkulainen, supervised by Dyer at UCLA, developed DISCERN, combining scripts with connectionism (Miikkulainen & Dyer, 1991; Miikkulainen, 1993). Nenov and Dyer (1993, 1994) presented a combined neural and procedural model of language learning.

In 1992, Mark St. John of Carnegie Mellon University presented the Story Gestalt model, combining scripts and connectionism for the purposes of the automated understanding of narratives (St. John, 1992). In 1995–1999, at the University of Chicago, Langston, Trabasso, and Magliano (1999) were working on a connectionist model of narrative comprehension, being a modified *construction-integration model*. Frank, Koppen, Noordman, and Vonk (2003), from Tilburg, Nijmegen, and the Max Planck Institute for Psycholinguistics, described a connectionist system carrying out knowledge-based inferences in story comprehension. The connectionist approach of this *Distributed Situation Space (DSS)* model was self-organising maps. A microworld was involved, and the representation was in a situation-state space.

5.2.13 Automated or Interactive Story Generation

Let us turn to making up a story interactively, with the help of a computer program. A conference session presentation in 2005 stated (Lönneker, Meister, Gervás, Peinado, & Mateas, 2005)[50]:

> Currently, story generators enjoy a phase of revival, both as stand-alone systems or embedded components. Most of them make reference to an explicit model of narrative, but the approaches used are diverse: they range from story grammars in the generative vein to the conceptually inspired engagement-reflection cycle. Real-life applications include the generation of a set of plot plans for screen writers in a commercial entertainment environment, who could use the automatically created story pool as a source of inspiration, and the generation of new kinds of interactive dramas (video games).

---

[50] By Birte Lönneker, also see Lönneker (2005) and Lönneker and Meister (2005).

5.2 An Overview of Artificial Intelligence Approaches to Narratives   381

Resolving a story while interacting is a problem, and influences how much freedom users are given (see, e.g., Sgouros, 1999). Cesare John Saretto (2001, p. 3) pointed out:

> Let us consider an interactive detective story. The audience member is playing the role of a detective. The author intends for a crucial clue to be delivered to the player by a mobster near the end of the story. However, the mobster in question is also one of a group of mobsters who beat up the detective earlier in the drama for meddling where he didn't belong. During the beating, the player proves more skilled at defending himself than the author intended. He manages to draw his gun and mortally wound the mobster who is to later deliver the critical clue. Without the clue, the player will very possibly never be able to solve the case. If the author had intended for the resolution of his story to convey a message or moral, that resolution may never be reached, and the author's message will be lost. Indeed if the story being told was more educational in nature rather than entertaining, a loss of the message would defeat the purpose of telling the story. With no author present to fix a broken interactive narrative, the audience member become actor may quickly find himself in a boring and inconsistent universe without any hope of a meaningful resolution to the story. To avoid this situation we must answer two questions: where do we draw the line between the will of the user and the author's intended story, and how do we police such a line, once it is drawn?

The goal of providing animated life-like characters, so-called "believable embodied agents", in computer interfaces (as "embodied conversational characters") or virtual environments, has been quite conspicuously providing motivation for an increase in research into the simulation of emotion within computer science, and this in turn is important for processing narrative properly. "The time is ripe for AI to reengage narrative", Mateas and Sengers claim in an editorial capacity (Mateas & Sengers, 2003, p. 4). In fact, on occasion some paper in computational processing of narratives has appeared on the pages of the *Artificial Intelligence* journal, in the first decade of the new century (Callaway & Lester, 2002). Charles Callaway and James Lester (2001) had already reported about the *StoryBook* story-generation system.

It has been claimed that "[a]utomatic narrative generation systems can be classified as character-centric and author-centric techniques"; the former "tend to develop narratives with strong character believability but weak coherent plot lines", whereas "[a]uthor-centric systems tend to develop narratives with strong plot coherence but weak character believability" (Riedl, 2003).[51]

---

[51] Mark Riedl, who claimed that much, tried to derive benefits from both techniques in a narrative generation system called Actor Conference. See Riedl (2003), where Riedl "informally evaluate[d] several narrative generation systems". Character-based interactive storytelling was the subject of Cavazza, Charles, and Mead (2001), Cavazza, Charles, and Mead (2002b). Riedl, Saretto, and Young (2003) were concerned with an approach for managing the interaction of human users with "computer-controlled agents in an interactive narrative-oriented virtual environment". Because of the requirement, for such systems, that "the freedom of the user to perform whatever action she desires must be balanced with the preservation of the storyline used to control the system's characters", they proposed *narrative mediation,* a technique "that exploits a plan-based model of narrative structure to manage and respond to users' actions inside a virtual world. We define two general classes of response to situations where users execute actions that interfere with story structure: accommodation and intervention. Finally, we specify an architecture that uses these definitions to monitor and automatically characterize user actions, and to compute and implement responses to unanticipated activity."

Historically, automated story-generation programs were inaugurated by TALE-SPIN, developed by James Meehan at Yale University, and involving the setting and achievement of goals and plans, and working by simulation (Meehan, 1976, 1981a, 1981b). Already Sheldon Klein's *Automated Novel Writer* (Klein, 1973) simulated the effects of generated events in the narrative universe.[52] That program used to generate crime stories (murder mysteries). It focused on generating proper sentences. The kind of approach to story-generation embodied in Klein's program is now called *author-centric,* but it had some *character-centric* sides to it as well. (By contrast, Meehan's TALE-SPIN focused on the characters, the goals they were given, and their rational behaviour. Meehan's characters could have one out of thirteen different emotional states, and their current emotional state affected the choices they were making.)

Author-centric features of Klein's program includes the fact it contained a set of rules about how events affect characters. Those events combine to generate a plot, and in every such plot, one out six available murder events occurs. There was little variation, because the scenarios were governed by a rigid structure. The character-centric aspect of Klein's program is that each character was assigned a numerical value for some traits. Based on past events, and on those character attributes, the program used to make choices concerning which events would occur. The following is a sample output from Klein's program:

JAMES WAS VERY RICH.
CLIVE WAS IMPOVERISHED.
CLIVE WANTED MONEY.
THE BUTLER WAS RELATED TO JAMES.
CLIVE THOUGHT THAT CLIVE INHERITED THE MONEY.
CLIVE KNEW THAT JAMES DRANK A MILK.
CLIVE POISONED THE MILK.
JAMES DRANK THE MILK.
JAMES WENT TO BED.
JAMES DIED.
THE OTHERS THOUGHT THAT JAMES WAS ASLEEP.
THE BUTLER RETURNED THE BOTTLE.
RONALD AWAKENED.
RONALD GOT UP.
RONALD THOUGHT THAT THE DAY WAS BEAUTIFUL.

---

[52] As early as 1963, Sheldon Klein published about the computer coding of English words (Klein & Simmons, 1963a), and syntax and the computer generation of coherent discourse (Klein & Simmons, 1963b). Until he retired in 2003, Sheldon Klein was professor of both computer science and linguistics at the University of Wisconsin at Madison. He has researched analogical reasoning models (e.g., Klein, 2002), the generation of 3D virtual reality worlds using a meta-linguistic system, which can be configured to model a variety of theoretical linguistic models. It could be configured either as a machine translation system, or as a natural language interface to application command languages. Klein also researched the role of Boolean groups and analogy in complex behavioral systems, including the representation of categorial grammars.

RONALD FOUND JAMES.
RONALD SAW THAT JAMES WAS DEAD.
RONALD YELLED.
THE OTHERS AWAKENED.
THE OTHERS RAN TO RONALD.
THE OTHERS SAW JAMES.
EVERYONE TALKED.
HEATHER CALLED THE POLICEMEN.
HUME EXAMINED THE BODY.
DR. BARTHOLOMEW HUME SAID THAT JAMES WAS KILLED BY POISON.

In 1983 at the University of Exeter, Masoud Yazdani reported about ROALD, an event generator in a fictional world of stories, also resorting to goals and simulation (Yazdani, 1983). Also in 1983, at Columbia University in New York, Michael Lebowitz reported about UNIVERSE, a story-generator making use of person frames, stereotypes, and memory of past events. Plots generated by UNIVERSE are for a never-ending soap-opera. In UNIVERSE, like in Sheldon Klein's program, each character was assigned a numerical value for some traits, but the approach to story-generation was author-centric. In 1984, William Chamberlain and Thomas Etter reported about the Racter project, in which syntax directives were resorted to in order to generate nonsensical sentences, such as "The policeman's beard is half constructed" (Racter, 1984).[53]

Erik Mueller's DAYDREAMER produced vindictive daydreams, related in the first person (Mueller & Dyer, 1985a, 1985b; Mueller, 1987, 1990). Such daydreams were "in reaction to being rejected for a date by a famous movie star. Daydreaming differs from storytelling largely in the number and types of problem constraints. One can daydream a ray gun that makes noisome children vanish; to use such a ray gun in a story would require some clever justification" (Turner, 1992, at section 13.3, p. 368). Whereas a daydream "can jump from topic to topic at the daydreamer's every whim", in contrast "a story must provide a constant and recognizable framework for the reader's understanding" (ibid., p. 369). Mueller and Dyer (1985a) explained:

DAYDREAMER is composed of:

- a **scenario generator** consisting of a *planner* (Fikes & Nilsson, 1971; Meehan, 1976) and *relaxation rules*,
- a **dynamic episodic memory** (Tulving, 1972; Kolodner, 1984) of experiences used by the scenario generator,
- a collection of *personal goals* (Maslow, 1943; Schank & Abelson, 1977) and **control goals** which guide the scenario generator,
- an **emotion component** in which daydreams initiate, and are initiated by, emotional states arising from goal outcomes, and
- **domain knowledge** of interpersonal relations and common everyday occurrences.

---

[53] A website about Racter exists: "Racter FAQ", at http://www.robotwisdom.com/ai/racterfaq.html

Starting in 1987 up to 1990, three prototypes of ALIBI were developed under my own direction (see Section 2.2.2 above). ALIBI impersonates somebody trying to exonerate himself from a charge, by offering an exonerating explanation for the facts observed and listed in the charge. For example, robbery is blamed on an accident and on misunderstanding. I was quite interested in narrative-processing programs, but was soon convinced (by the comments of an important scholar at an international conference) that the project yielded promise in the domain of AI & Law. It is fair to say that ALIBI was a constrained kind of story-generation program: what is generated is exonerating explanations which are themselves narratives: ALIBI has oftentimes been referred to as a program making up excuses, but in fact in real life a person may give an exonerating explanation that is quite true, regardless of how believable it sounds at first).

ALIBI was first reported about in 1989. That was also the year when *Oz* was launched at Carnegie-Mellon University in Pittsburgh, PA, and when at Yale University, Natalie Dehn, who already in 1981 had published about story-invention (Dehn, 1981), produced the definitive presentation of her *Author* system (Dehn, 1989). *Author* was based on reconstructive and dynamic memory. As to *Oz,* this is a tool for interactive drama. The intention was that stories generated would have rich characters, as this is known to be something from which traditional storytelling media draw their emotional power. *Oz* works with goals and emotions. Joseph Bates, Scott Reilly, and Bryan Loyall worked on that project, among others. See, e.g., Smith and Bates (1989), Bates, Loyall, and Reilly (1992), Reilly (1996), Loyall (1997), as well as Kantrowitz (1990). In Canada, at the University of Calgary, in 1992 Tony Smith and Ian Witten reported about TAILOR (Smith & Witten, 1992). TAILOR was a planner in story space (Phillips & Huntley, 1993). In 1993, Melanie Anne Phillips and Chris Huntley reported about the *Dramatica* project, embodying a theory of story.[54] In the early 1990s, at the University of California in Los Angeles, Scott Turner developed a famous story-generation program, MINSTREL. We are going to discuss it in Section 5.2.16.

Formal scenarios are the foundation of Boris Galitsky's *Scenario Synthesizer,* developed at Rutgers University (Galitsky, 1998, 1999). Like with Anthony Jameson's system, IMP, from the early 1980s (Jameson, 1983), the purpose of what Galitsky's program does is to control buyer's impression. But in Galitsky's program, it is narratives that are generated, whereas IMP only answered questions. At North Carolina State University, Charles Callaway developed the *Author/Story Book* project; his program plans sentences for narrative prose generation, and resorts to a functional systemic grammar (Callaway, 2000; Callaway & Lester, 2001, 2002). Stories about Little Red Riding Hood are generated. In their BRUTUS project, Selmer Bringsjord and David A. Ferrucci resorted to both frames and story grammars. BRUTUS generates narratives of betrayal (Bringsjord & Ferrucci, 2000).

In the late 1990s at MIT, under the supervision of Glorianna Davenport, Kevin Michael Brooks (1996, 1999, 2002) developed the *Agent Stories* project. It

---

[54] See the Dramatica werbsite, at http://www.dramatica.com/

5.2 An Overview of Artificial Intelligence Approaches to Narratives

resorted to story agents in order to author story pieces, resulting in a *metalinear cinematic narrative*. Brooks has researched the construction of computational cinematographic narrative and developed a software tool, called *Agent Stories*, for assisting writers in the design and presentation of "nonlinear/metalinear narratives" (cf. Davenport et al., 2000).

Automated story-generation projects from the 2000s include MEXICA, developed by Pérez y Pérez and Sharples (2001), as well as Liu and Singh's MAKEBELIEVE (2002), and Mark Owen Riedl's FABULIST. The latter pays attention to both plot coherence and character believability (Riedl, 2004; cf. Riedl, 2003; Riedl & Young, 2004). Riedl, Rowe, and Elson (2008) presented "two intelligent support tools for the authoring and production of *machinima*. Machinima is a technique for producing computer-animated movies through the manipulation of computer game technologies. The first system we describe, *ReQUEST*, is an intelligent support tool for the authoring of plots. The second system, *Cambot*, produces *machinima* from a pre-authored script by manipulating virtual avatars and a virtual camera in a 3D graphical environment."

Heather Barber and Daniel Kudenko (2008) described the GADIN system (the acronym stands for *Adaptive Dilemma-based Interactive Narratives*). The method was claimed to be suitable for "any domain which makes use of clichéd storylines". The particular application was "within the children's story domain of a dinosaur adventure". GADIN "automatically generates interactive narratives which are focused on dilemmas in order to create dramatic tension. The user interacts with the system by making decisions on relevant dilemmas and by freely choosing their own actions". Barber and Kudenko (2008)

> introduce[d] the version of GADIN which is able to create a finite story. The narrative finishes – in a manner which is satisfying to the user – when a dynamically determined story goal is achieved. Satisfaction of this goal may involve the user acting in a way which changes the dispositions of other characters. If the user actions cause the goal to become impossible or unlikely then they cause the story goal to be re-selected, thus meaning that the user is able to fundamentally change the overall narrative while still experiencing a coherent narrative and clear ending.

At the University of Paris 8, Nicolas Szilas and Jean-Hugues Rety have developed the *IDtension* project. It studies graph-based narrative structures, considering minimal structure for stories (Szilas & Rety, 2004). Szilas had already published about interactive drama with nonlinearities (Szilas, 1999). Interactive drama was the subject of Brenda Laurel's dissertation of 1986 (Laurel, 1986), and of Weyhrauch's dissertation of 1997 (Weyhrauch, 1997). Several dissertations about automated story-generation have been discussed in the Netherlands in the 2000s; for example a master's thesis by Douwe Terluin (2008), supervised by Rineke Verbrugge at the University of Groningen, was concerned with how to separate paragraphs in generated stories, by using discourse structure. Michael Mateas explains (2005):

> The alternative to the story graph is story management. The first story manager was proposed by Brenda Laurel in her thesis on interactive drama (Laurel), and further developed by AI research groups exploring interactive narrative. A story manager replaces the graph structure with a policy for story event selection. The author still creates the nodes of the story

graph, where nodes represent story events such as scenes or individual character actions (depending on the granularity of global agency). However, rather than manually linking the nodes, that author instead creates a selection policy for story events; story events are activated as a function of the history of the story so far and the actions performed by the player. The story policy implicitly defines a story graph; theoretically, one can imagine unrolling the policy into a graph by recording the story function's response to all possible inputs (story histories + player action). The whole point of the story management approach, however, is to keep the graph implicit. By implicitly specifying graphs via a story policy, authors can create interactive stories that would be impractical to explicitly specify as graphs, and can thus create experiences with rich global agency.

The motivation for devising *story management* as an alternative to *story graphs* is in order to provide human players with *global narrative agency*. This has to be understood within the framework of the controversy concerning whether there should be a predefined narrative inside interactive computer games (Mateas, 2005):

> For some designers and theorists, interactive story worlds are a holy grail of game design (e.g. Murray, Crawford), while for others narrative is antithetical to interactive experiences, destroying the high-agency, procedural potential of games (e.g. Eskelinen, Frasca). The heart of the tension between games and narrative lies in player agency. A player is said to have agency when she can form intentions with respect to the experience, take action with respect to those intentions, and interpret responses in terms of the action and intentions. Those who argue against narrative games point to the predetermined or predestined nature of narrative; strong narrative structures have complex sequences of cause and effect, complex character relationships and sequences of character interactions. Since player interaction can at any moment disrupt this narrative structure, the only way to maintain the structure is to remove or severely limit the player's ability to effect the structure. This eliminates so-called 'global' agency, forcing the player down a predetermined path. Thus ludologists argue that if narrative must inevitably mean a diminishment in player agency, it should not be used in game design.

Mateas pointed out that when he was writing that much, in 2005, extant story-based computer games appeared to be conforming with the *ludologist* position, in that "the story structure is completely fixed, or has an extremely simple branching structure. The player has local agency, that is, can move around the environment and interact with objects and non-player characters, but the narrative structure is a linear sequence of cut scenes unlocked during the gameplay" (ibid.).

Mateas (2005) contrasted two approaches to story management.[55] Mateas and Stern (2003) had developed *Façade,* an interactive drama whose story manager was *beat-based,* in the sense of *dramatic beats* as understood by McKee: beats are the smallest units of dramatic value change. "The desired story is modeled by one or more story value arcs (in *Façade,* the tension story value), and by declarative knowledge represented on each beat" (Mateas, 2005). By contrast, Bates (1992) and Weyhrauch (1997) had first defined the *search based drama manager (SBDM)*. In the latter, a player's activity can cause *Player Moves* to happen. These are abstract plot points that depend upon the player's activity. The player experiences the world through a sequence of Player Moves. A Player Move is recognised

---

[55] Apart from *Façade* and the SBDM approaches, yet another approach to story management was adopted in the IDA system by Magerko and Laifo (2003).

5.2 An Overview of Artificial Intelligence Approaches to Narratives

once the concrete activity accomplishes a plot point. That recognition in turn will cause the drama manager to project all possible future histories of Player Moves and System Moves. An evaluation function enables the drama manager to select its own next move: the SBDM, having recognised a Player Move, "evaluates the resulting total histories with the evaluation function, and backs these evaluations up the search tree (in a manner similar to game-tree search) to decide which system move to make next that is most likely to cause a good total story to happen" (Mateas, 2005).

In fact, the SBDM's task is to carry out *System Moves,* i.e., such actions that would encourage or obviate a Player Move. This can be displayed concretely by moving things around. But it can also consist of changing the goals of characters. "System Moves give the SBDM a way to warp the world around the player so as to make certain Player Moves more or less likely. Besides the System Moves, the author also provides the SBDM with a story-specific evaluation function that, given a complete sequence of Player and System Moves, returns a number indicating the 'goodness' of the story" (Mateas, 2005).

At the Universidad Complutense of Madrid, from 2004 a team has been active which comprises Federico Peinado, Pablo Gervás and others in the development of story-generation programs. They been dealing with creativity issues in story plot generation (Peinado & Gervás, 2005a). They applied ontologies to story-generation, when they reimplemented Scott Turner's originally Lisp-coded MINSTREL (see Section 5.2.16 below) in the formal semantics of the OWL Web ontology language (Peinado & Gervás, 2006a).[56] They also developed a description logic ontology[57] for the generation of fairytales (Peinado, Gervás, & Díaz-Agudo, 2004). They applied case-based reasoning (CBR) to story plot generation (Gervás, Díaz-Agudo, Peinado, & Hervás, 2005; Díaz-Agudo, Gervás, & Peinado, 2004). Moreover, they resorted to CBR in an implementation, called *ProtoPropp,* of tale morphology à la Vladimir Propp (Peinado & Gervás, 2005b). "A case-based reasoning process is defined to generate plots from a user query, with two important phases: retrieval of old stories, and adaptation to build a new one. The user query specifies an initial setting for the story, and the ontology is used to measure during the generation process the semantic distance between concepts specified by the user and those that appear in the texts" (ibid.).[58]

---

[56] Some projects from the 2000s that are not mentioned here are surveyed in Dov Winer's (in press) 'Review of Ontology Based Storytelling Devices'.

[57] To ontologies, a popular technology during the 2000s, we devote to it Section 6.1.7.3 below.

[58] Peinado and Gervás explain (2005b): "The ProtoPropp application considers a plot generation problem in terms of Proppian functions, and a solution to that problem in terms of the assignment of a conceptual representation of the plot of a story. This involves transcribing existing folk tales into conceptual representations of their contents and associating them with elements of Proppian morphology. This is done by resorting to a formalized knowledge base of concepts, organised into a taxonomy, which explicitly includes the relations between them. Such a knowledge base, following current terminology in AI, is referred to as an *ontology* (Gruber [1993, 1995]). The use of explicit conceptual knowledge to guide the CBR process characterises *Knowledge Intensive* CBR (Díaz-Agudo & González-Calero, 2003)."

They have delved into narratology models for adoption in artificial intelligence (Gervás, Lönneker-Rodman, Meister, & Peinado, 2006). They have worked on automated customisation of such characters in the stories that are not themselves players, based on the temperament of the players (Gómez-Gauchía & Peinado, 2006). They have worked on role-playing games, with a plot-centric interface (Leon, Peinado, Navarro, & Cortiguera, 2008), while also developing character-based automated storytelling (Peinado, Cavazza, & Pizzi, 2008); cf. Peinado and Gervás (2004, 2007). They have dealt with the evaluation of story-generation programs (Peinado & Gervás, 2006b). They have researched remote control for storytelling environments (Peinado & Navarro, 2007). In 2007, Peinado and Gervás were claiming (2007, p. 196):

> Specially during past decade, research on Interactive Digital Storytelling (IDS) has been growing relatively fast. Many papers about this topic are published each year in any of the conferences and journals that accept this kind of scientific contributions (from specific but also general fields such as Computer Entertainment and Education, Multimedia Systems, Artificial Intelligence, etc.). Some theoretical proposals have been described around the same idea: computational models for automatic control of an interactive narration.

Applying to IDS concepts from *role-playing games* (*RPGs*) was proposed, e.g., by Louchart and Aylett (2003).[59] Peinado and Gervás (2007) proposed a preliminary formalisation of "of a well-known theory, what we called the Game Master (GM) paradigm. This theory claims that the richer and more intuitive metaphor of an automatic director for IDS applications is a human GM controlling a role-playing game. This paradigm, sometimes [...] overlooked, is a particular instance of the more general 'centralized approach' to IDS management" (ibid., p. 197). Extant computational approaches to IDS are "widely different" (ibid.). Some proposed approaches are based on emergent behavior of *non-player characters* (*NPCs*); these achieve dramatic goals. Other appraches are centralised, in that they give more responsibility to a central dramatic planning algorithm. There exist intermediate solutions that add "controllable NPCs to a centralized planner for achieving story goals or adopting a mixed approach, with a centralized director and a set of semiautonomous agents. There are also standalone dramatic planners that control the most important narrative elements, like characters or the whole fictional world" (ibid.).[60]

Figure 5.2.13.1 shows a schema,[61] redrawn from figure 1 in Lönneker and Meister (2005), of the architecture of a hypothetical ideal *Story Generator Algorithm* (*SGA*). Birte Lönneker and Jan Christoph Meister, from the University

---

[59] From the same team, cf. Aylett, et al. (2008): "Nowadays, the video gaming experience is shifting from merely realistic to believable", but "the behaviour of the computer driven player and non-playing characters is often poor when compared to their visual appearance." Aylett et al. (2008) "present[ed] a robotics inspired behavioural AI technique to simulate characters' personalities in an multi-award winning commercial video game."

[60] Concerning story generation, also see Ogata (2004).

[61] Concerning "histoire domain" vs. "discours domain", bear in mind that in narratology, the *story* is called *histoire* in French and фабула (*fabula*) in Russian, whereas the *discourse* is called *récit* (or sometimes *discours*) in French and сюжет (*syužet*) in Russian. The French or Russian terms are sometimes used in discussions in English or in other languages as well.

5.2 An Overview of Artificial Intelligence Approaches to Narratives

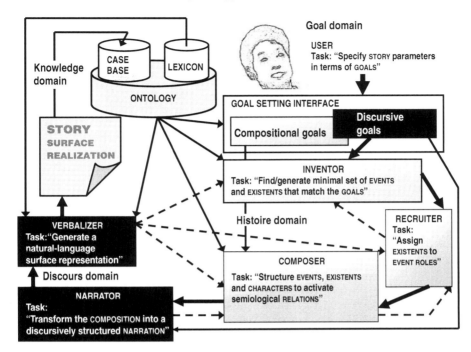

Fig. 5.2.13.1 A schema, redrawn from fig. 1 in Lönneker and Meister (2005), of the architecture of a hypothetical ideal *Story Generator Algorithm* (*SGA*)

of Hamburg, were focusing on the theoretically oriented tasks. Their approach is discussed in detail in a book by Meister (2003).

5.2.14 eChronicle Systems

There is a direction of research that goes by the name *eChronicle systems*. *E-chronicles* are sometimes found on the Web. Sometimes, some organisation just chose the name for its newsletter, but the term *e-chronicle* denotes something more specific: in an *e-chronicle repository,* a mass of thematically related events is listed. It stands to reason that suitable computer tools would process that wealth of information. In the words of the Paris-based scholar Gian Piero Zarri (2011):

> An 'eChronicle' system can be defined in short as way of recording, organizing and then accessing *streams of multimedia events* captured by individuals, groups, or organizations making use of video, audio and any other possible type of sensors. The 'chronicles' gathered in this way may concern any sort of 'narratives' like meeting minutes, conference records, wedding videos, surveillance videos, football games, visitor logs, sales activities, 'lifelogs' obtained from wearable sensors, etc. The technical challenges, here, concern mainly the ways of *aggregating the events into coherent 'episodes' and of providing access to this sort of material at the required level of granularity*. A unifying indexing system employing an event-based domain model is used in general to introduce a *conceptual layer* onto the *metadata layer* proper to each repository. Note that i) the users of the eChronicle repositories

are not concerned with the original data sources, and ii) that *exploration, and not 'normal' querying*, is the predominant way of interaction with these repositories.[62] [...] The solution (NKRL) [proposed by Zarri][63] for the 'intelligent' management of (non-fictional) narratives can be considered as a *fully-fledged eChronicle technique* [...]. In NKRL, however, a fundamental aspect of this language/environment concerns the presence of powerful *'reasoning' techniques* – an aspect that is not taken into consideration sufficiently in depth in eChronicles that are mainly interested in the accumulation of narrative materials more than in the 'intelligent' exploitation of their inner relationships.

Arguably such techniques go the extra mile to meet some of the requirements of textual data mining (see Chapter 6, this volume). In 'Multimedia electronic chronicles', a "Media Vision" column in *IEEE Multimedia* in July 2003, Ramesh Jain began by mentioning LifeLog, a new project that the Defense Advanced Research Projects Agency (DARPA) was going to start,[64] and that it gave rise to controversy because of privacy issues. "LifeLog is about recording everything that a person does using video, audio, and other sensors [...] The goal is to • record all this data, • organize it so that it becomes easy to analyze the activities of this person, • review the person's activities as needed, • detect patterns, and, • organize the information so that the LifeLogs of different people can interact with each other." This was supposed to "facilitate routine tasks like coordinating meetings by considering not only calendars but also individual preferences inferred by these systems and thus provide 'cognitive assistants' to people for organizing their activities" (Jain, 2003, p. 112). Jain began a section headlined "From logs to e-chronicles", by remarking (ibid.):

> Many organizations keep detailed logs of events. Rumor has it that many corporations keep a log of every keystroke made by their employees. And, it's widely believed that government agencies in many countries log all events, including telephone conversations, of suspected criminals – in most cases without the subject's knowledge. These activities are hardly surprising because for decades detectives have reported the activities of enemies as well as loved ones.
>
> So what does all this have to do with multimedia research and practice? I believe that multimedia is at the center of a newly emerging field: multimedia electronic chronicles, or e-chronicles. An e-chronicle records events using multiple sensors and provides access to this data at multiple levels of granularity and abstractions, using appropriate access mechanisms in representations and terminology familiar to application users.

The idea was that: "A well-designed e-chronicle will maintain all detailed records, while providing summaries of important events as well as access to events at the required level of granularity" (Jain, 2003, p. 111).[65] There were precedents: "Many variants of e-chronicles have already appeared and are being used. Data warehouses, video surveillance systems, meeting recording systems, sensor networks, and even blogs are early forms of e-chronicles." (ibid.). Jain concluded with a challenge: "I

---

[62] Publications dealing with eChronicle systems include, e.g., Güven, Podlaseck, and Pingali (2005), and Westermann and Jain (2006).

[63] NKRL has been discussed in several papers by Zarri over the years, as early as 1996 (Zarri, 1996), but see now his book (Zarri, 2009).

[64] http://www.darpa.mil/baa/baa03-30.htm

[65] Sic. Jain's column (2003) started on p. 112, but continued on p. 111.

5.2 An Overview of Artificial Intelligence Approaches to Narratives

challenge the multimedia research community to contribute their ideas and solutions to e-chronicles".

A sidebar in Westermann and Jain (2007, pp. 20–21) explains these things differently, and *life logs* have become a common noun (whereas LifeLog had been the proper name of a DARPA project):

> *EChronicles* are information systems for documenting real-world events via multiple media or other suitable sensor data. EChronicles offer tools that let users interactively explore, visualize, and experience the course of events at different levels of granularity. Real-world events and their characteristics form the central units of interest in eChronicles_and not media and their metadata as in traditional multimedia content analysis, databases, and metadata formats. Experimental eChronicles have been implemented for a diverse range of domains, including the chronicling of tennis matches, or meetings. *Life logs*, another emerging application, aim to permanently record and document people's activities with media and other sensor data, so that users can go back, review, and explore important events in their lives. Life logs can be considered a subcategory of eChronicles. As with eChronicles, the notion of events is central to life logs. Some life log applications record the daily life events of people with wearable sensors; others record all that media users produce and activities they perform on their computers and relate both media and activities to real-world events, such as that obtained from user calendars.

For example, Jain, Kim, and Li (2003) described a tool for eChronicles, as applied to meetings.[66] Data from user calendars are used in the life log discussed by Gemmell, Lueder, and Bell (2003). "Events appear in multimedia presentation formats, programming frameworks, and databases, as well as in next-generation multimedia applications such as eChronicles, life logs, or the Event Web. A common event model for multimedia could serve as a unifying foundation for all of these applications" (Westermann & Jain, 2007, p. 19).

According to Ramesh Jain: "The concept of 'event' can serve as the fundamental organizational principle for multimedia systems", and "you can combine events in many ways to define other (compound) events" (Jain, 2008, p. 47). When discussing the need for a common multimedia event model, Westermann and Jain (2007, p. 22) provide this example:

> Media independence is necessary to establish a base model that suits many applications. Often, events might exist that aren't documented by media. A soccer eChronicle, for example, might contain high-level composite events, such as a league season, that consists of subevents, such as the individual matches in the season. Although the subevents might be extensively documented by media, the composite event might not be directly documented by media at all.[67]

---

[66] Ramesh Jain's team has also dealt with eChornicles in Westermann and Jain (2006a, 2006b) and in Kim, Gargi, and Jain (2005).

[67] Westermann and Jain (2007, p. 22) also claim that "real-world events can't be made properties of individual media. In the soccer eChronicle, many different media might describe a match event: the video streams from the different cameras capturing the match from different perspectives, the audio streams from the microphones capturing the stadium roar, photographs of the match highlights, the edited video finally broadcast, newspaper reviews, and so on. It isn't reasonable to tie the match event's existence to any one of those media. It also isn't reasonable to duplicate the event's description with each medium's description."

To Jain, three aspects of events should be defined explicitly. These are: information about the event, experiences related to the event, and the event's structural and causal relationships with other events (ibid., p. 48). "Because of emerging digital-media devices and technology, we're now in a position to develop the EventWeb" (ibid., p. 46). Moreover (ibid.):

> Creating EventWeb will require developing technology to produce events using heterogeneous media elements, represent each event as a node, and then create explicit links between events and between events and information on the current Web. EventWeb organizes data in terms of events and experiences and allows natural access from users' perspectives. For each event, EventWeb collects and organizes audio, visual, tactile, textual, and other data to provide people with an environment for experiencing the event from their perspective. EventWeb also easily reorganizes events to satisfy different viewpoints and naturally incorporates new data types – dynamic, temporal, and live. [...] People can use an Event Markup Language to post their events and related information and experiential data in the form of photos, audio, videos, and textual data. An EML will also provide an environment for expressing and creating relationships among events. Combining this language with event capture and a media-processing tool will help users identify events of interest in the EventWeb.[68]

Jain's conceptions of complex events and capturing experiences is apparently independent of, yet resonates with something one comes across in philosophy. A philosopher from Purdue University, Michael Jacovides (2010a, p. 141), argues[69]

> that experiences are complex events that befall their subjects. Each experience has a single subject and depends on the state or the event that it is of. The constituents of an experience are (or underlie) its subject, its grounding event or state, and everything that the subject is

---

[68] The concept is starting to have an impact in, for example, the design of computer models for engineering. Ashit Talukder, who has been developing a tool for cyclone tracking (Panangadan, Ho, & Talukder, 2009), describes (Talukder, 2010) what is, among the other things, an application of Jain's concept to machine vision and decision support; "event-based multimedia stream data processing and representation solution is presented for large scale geographically distributed phenomena", such as cyclones or oil spills, phenomena that are to be automatically detected from raw untagged image streams (Talukder, ibid.). Satellite data on the cyclone eye are annotated (Ho & Talukder, 2009). Ontologies have been developed for representing and annotating video-events (François, Nevatia, Hobbs, & Bolles, 2005). It must be said, however, that event-based spatiotemporal data models had long been known: for example, Donna Peuquet, and Niu Duan described (1995) an application to the temporal analysis of geographical data.

[69] Also see Jacovides (2010b), in which it is accepted, following John Dewey (1929, chapter 1), Crispin Sartwell (1995), Charles Travis (2004), and William Alston (2005), that experiences do not "represent" anything. Jacovides remarks (2010a, p. 142): "Some might be interested in this question for the same reason that historians of ideas are interested in drawing out consequences of unlikely doctrines in Plotinus or Leibniz. Others might be more sympathetic to the possibility that experiences don't represent, but want to have certain doubts resolved. For example, they might worry that a nonrepresentational account of experiences can't explain how experiences justify beliefs. For such readers, my project might serve as proof of concept. More optimistically, my account of experiences as nonrepresentational events might be so attractive that it helps justify the doctrine that experiences don't represent. I am myself convinced that experiences (ordinarily so-called) do not represent, and what follows is my best attempt to give a positive account of what they actually are."

5.2 An Overview of Artificial Intelligence Approaches to Narratives

aware of during that time that's relevant to the telling of the story of how it was to participate in that event or be put in that state. The experience occurs where the person having the experience is. An experience of an event or state occurs when that event or state makes a difference to its possessor's conscious life, where this difference is either a matter of really knowing what's happening or merely a matter of being affected.

Jacovides explains as follows the difference between experiences and objects, and how they are related (Jacovides, 2010a, p. 143):

> Red is a quality, but not a quality that most events can have. Explosions and flashes may be exceptions, but they are unusual events that seem to lack substrata. The fact that experiences can't be red just goes to show that experiences are ordinary events in this regard. A party can't be red, not even a party at a firehouse where all the guests wear red pants. In order to investigate the intrinsic qualities of experiences, we ought to examine qualities that ordinary events can bear. Parties can last until three in the morning. Parties can be drunken, exciting, or enjoyable. Can experiences last until three in the morning? Can they be drunken, exciting, or enjoyable? Yes, of course.
>
> Almost all events depend on at least one enduring object. Explosions and flashes again might be counterexamples, but I'll set them aside. Most events are complex in that they depend on more than one enduring object. These involved objects are agents from which the event arises, patients that the events befall, or neither agents nor patients, but nevertheless participants in the event. The officiant is an agent in a wedding. The bride and groom are both agents and patients. The surroundings and the guests participate in one way or another.

Of shared experiences, Jacovides claims (2010a, p. 144):

> Strictly speaking, an experience will happen to at most one subject. We do talk about shared experiences, and I take such locutions seriously. In the end, however, I think that shared experiences are, at most, higher-order complex events that overlap the more basic personal experiences. If Jack and Jill walk up a hill they share an experience. Even so, Jack's experience might be pleasant while Jill's is unpleasant. I infer that Jack's experience is, at some level, a distinct experience from Jill's.
>
> One might object to the lesson I draw from Jack and Jill: "here's an alternative construal: their experience might be pleasant to Jack but unpleasant to Jill. This is consistent with its being one experience." I'm not inclined to go that way. It seems to me that being pleasant is an intrinsic feature of experiences, at least at the root level. Since being intrinsically pleasant is incompatible with being intrinsically painful for basic experiences, Jack and Jill can't be having the very same basic experiences, though we might try to construct collective experiences out of their individual ones.
>
> There are degrees of commonality in experience and the proper analysis of these degrees might require appeal to particular facts about particular objects, events, or occasions. If Jack and Jill walk up a hill at the same time, they share an experience in a stronger sense than if they walk up the hill on different days or if they walk up different hills. [...]

Bearing in mind what philosophers have to say about events and experiences may enhance, with a rigorous framework, such event-based computing that caters to human experience (as opposed, e.g., to models in computer image recognition within scientific computing). In particular, this appears to be interesting for the design of eChronicles.

5.2.15 Virtual Embodied Agents

There exists an important body of research into automated autonomous personality agents to go with computer animation's synthetic actors. This is related to computer scientists' research into the simulation of emotions.[70] Anton Nijholt's team is active in researching embodied, animated conversational agents. These are also called *avatars*. Nijholt (2002) surveyed the state of the art in that domain, in affective computing, and in verbal and nonverbal interaction, "with the aim to see whether it is useful for embodied conversational agents to integrate humor capabilities in their internal model of intelligence, emotions and interaction (verbal and nonverbal) capabilities" (Nijholt, 2002, p. 101). Nijholt and his colleague Mariët Theune are also active in story generation by intelligent agents (e.g., Theune, Faas, Nijholt, & Heylen, 2003; Oinonen, Theune, Nijholt, & Heylen, 2005; Oinonen, Theune, Nijholt, & Uijlings, 2006).[71] Nijholt further remarked (2002, p. 105):

> Embodied conversational agents (ECAs) have become a well-established research area. Embodied agents are agents that are visible in the interface as animated cartoon characters or animated objects resembling human beings. Sometimes they just consist of an animated talking face, displaying facial expressions and, when using speech synthesis, having lip synchronization. These agents are used to inform and explain or even to demonstrate products or sequences of activities in educational, e-commerce or entertainment settings.

At the Stanford University, Barbara Hayes-Roth directed the *Virtual Theater* project (Hayes-Roth & Robert van Gent, 1997). The following is quoted from an article in which I joined forces with a collaborator of hers, in order to enhance my own ALIBI model of a cognitive agent seeking exoneration[72]:

> In a Virtual Theater application, synthetic actors are provided that can interact with each other and with users to create interactive stories in a textual or graphical environment. Each synthetic actor portrays a character defined by the designer of the application. The definition of a character includes abstract characteristics such as a personality, a repertoire of actions that he or she can perform, a set of interpersonal relationships, and an abstract script that the actor can follow. A synthetic actor is able to improvise its behavior according to the character that it portrays and the directions it receives from other actors, users, or an abstract script. Synthetic actors can be completely autonomous or avatars directed by users. So, a user can actively influence an interactive story by the directions he or she gives to his or her avatar.

---

[70] See, e.g., an overview in section 6 of Cassinis, et al. (2007), and a complementary overview of other aspects in Nissan et al. (2008), Nissan (2009b, 2009c). An important step was the AbMaL model, introduced by Paul O'Rorke and Andrew Ortony (1994), and modelling the emotions in story-understanding, with a representation by means of situation calculus. Also see Marvin Minsky's *The Emotion Machine,* whose chapter 6 is concerned with story-understanding (Minsky, 2002).

[71] At http://hmi.ewi.utwente.nl/showcases/The%20Virtual%20Storyteller one can access a publication list of The Virtual Stroyteller project from Anton Nijholt and Mariët Theune's team at the University of Twente (Enschede, The Netherlands). For example, the doctoral dissertation of Ivo Swartjes (2009) is accessible there.
Also see http://redcap.interactive-storytelling.de/authoring-tools/virtualstoryteller/

[72] From an earlier draft (entitled 'Legal Evidence: The Dramatis Personae Approach') of Nissan and Rousseau (1997).

5.2 An Overview of Artificial Intelligence Approaches to Narratives

This is historically distinct from "synthetic actors" as known from sophisticated 3D animation – regardless of a story plot other than motion or displays of emotion – but complete with facial expressions, gait, and wrinkled cloth: such "synthetic actors" were developed by Nadia Magnenat Thalmann and Daniel Thalmann,[73] with characters "Marilyn" [Monroe] and "Elvis" [Presley].) Eventually, the concepts were technically merged, and have become familiar to the broad public through the online *Second Life*.

One of the applications of the *Virtual Theater* was *Cybercafe* (Rousseau, 1995). It contained[74]

> an autonomous actor playing the role of a waiter, and an avatar portraying a customer. The user-interface contains two windows: one presenting the actions that a user can select for his or her avatar, and one textually describing how the story unfolds in the current context. A user can direct his or her avatar by selecting buttons corresponding to actions that can be performed by the customer in the current context. Actions performed by any actor are displayed by a text animator in a window containing the description of the interaction.

An important feature was that characters behaved opportunistically, improvising according to the situation at hand (ibid.):

> The Cybercafe is based on local improvisation, which means that all characters decide their behavior relying on the current state of the world and the actions that they can perform. Reasoning on mental states is quite simplified in the system. Possible states of the world, that can be considered as potential goals, and transitions between those states are modeled using state machines. Actions that an actor can perform to realize the transitions correspond to its abilities. A synthetic actor knows a list of irrelevant actions for each potential state. For instance, a character who is seated cannot sit neither walk. An individual that is standing cannot stand up. Some state machines can involve more than a character in the transitions; e.g., the state machine that models the interaction between the waiter and the customer when the latter orders involve both agents. Both actors have a copy of the state machine dealing with the situation and can detect when a transition is effective, although the transition is not realized by one of their actions. It allows them to cooperate.

For all of the improvisation, characters had personality traits impinging upon their respective behaviour (ibid.):

> The main focus of [...] work with the Cybercafe is the expression of personality traits through the behavior. No matter their personality, characters of the Cybercafe follow an abstract scenario defined in terms of a series of actions and cues specified at an abstract level. A cue is an action of a given type performed by another actor. For the waiter, a script could be as simple as "Perform an action till you want to stop and want to wait for a cue from the customer". Being called by a customer would be an example of cue. Transitions specified in state machines also define parts of a scenario.

---

[73] For example, a very effective image of successive stages of motion appeared in 1993 on the cover of issue 4(3) of the journal edited by the Thalmanns, *The Journal of Visualization and Computer Animation*. See Magnenat Thalmann and Thalmann (1991a); also section 2 in Magnenat Thalmann and Thalmann (1991b). Refer as well to Magnenat Thalmann and Thalmann (1996, 2001).

[74] The quotation is from an earlier draft (entitled 'Legal Evidence: The Dramatis Personae Approach') of Nissan and Rousseau (1997).

The goal of providing animated life-like characters, *believable embodied agents,* in computer interfaces (as *embodied conversational characters*) or virtual environments has been quite conspicuously providing motivation for an increase in research into the simulation of emotion within computer science. For example, a paper collection edited by Prendinger and Ishizuka (2004) is devoted to tools, affective functions, and applications in relation to life-like characters. Another paper collection on embodied conversational characters was edited by Cassell, Sullivan, Prevost, and Churchill (2000).

At the Massachusetts Institute of Technology, Bryson and Thórisson (2000) proposed[75] a *character architecture* called *Spark of Life (SoL).* The following is quoted from Bryson and Thórisson (2000, p. 58):

> Much research into agents for entertainment concentrates on the problem of combining the concept of a script with the notion of autonomous, reactive characters [...].[76] Our constructive narrative approach eliminates this problem by changing the top level creative design from a *script* to a *cast of characters*. This simplifies the task of the player by removing the need for character addition, substitution, alteration, or removal. It has the penalty of removing a substantial element of narrative structure: a sequential order of events. However, this problem has already been addressed by the creators of role-playing and adventure games. Their solution is that plot, if desired, can be advanced by knowledgeable characters, found objects, and revealed locations. Structure is produced through the use of geographic space as well as character personality. Personality traits such as loyalty, contentment or agoraphobia can be used to maintain order despite a large cast of autonomous characters, by tying particular characters to particular locations. Developing such characters requires an agent architecture powerful enough to support this complexity. It also requires sufficient modularity to allow reasonably quick construction of behaviour patterns. [...]

---

[75] The forum in which Bryson and Thórisson (2000) 'Dragons, Bats and Evil Knights: A Three-Layer Design Approach to Character Based Creative Play' appeared was the journal *Virtual Reality*, published by Springer-Verlag. Bryson and Thórisson's *Spark of Life* is "an architecture for complex characters capable of multi-modal real-time dialogue with humans, and [in their paper they also presented] some of [their] experiences from using these techniques on a large-scale industrial VR [i.e., Virtual Reality] project at LEGO" (ibid., p. 69). "A constructive narrative is creative on several levels. In designing a creative experience, the goal is to provide both interesting media for expressing the content to be recombined, and tools that facilitate the recombination. If the media itself includes active creators, in our case agents that autonomously create situations and social dynamics, then the user has the opportunity to engage in truly complex constructive play. This kind of creative experience is currently only afforded to writers of drama, corporate managers, and public policy makers. However, creating an environment for such play takes considerable artistic and technical skill and planning. We have described how a creative environment with constantly changing stories and adventures can be developed using artificial intelligence and design techniques thart exploit and express the creativity of the designers. Tne intelligent agents in these environments [...] embody the rules and knowledge both invented and learned by their designers" (ibid.).

[76] Citing Hayes-Roth and van Gent (1997), Lester and Stone (1997), André, Rist, and Müller (1998).

5.2.16 Story-Generation with MINSTREL

Scott Turner's MINSTREL story-generation program is driven by author goals, and also character's goals are important. An important aspect of MINSTREL is that it applied what in AI is known as "case-based reasoning", i.e., reasoning from precedent. MINSTREL develops stories by trying to recall pertinent elements from stories already in its repertoire.[77] This is one of the reasons Turner's project should be of interest to folktale studies. In order to make precedents usable, MINSTREL resorts to "creative heuristics", called Transform-Recall-Adapt Methods (TRAMs). "In addition to a process model of author-level problem-solving, MINSTREL implements four important classes of author-level goals and plans: (1) Thematic, (2) Dramatic, (3) Consistency, and (4) Presentation. MINSTREL uses these goals and plans to tell a number of short stories in the King Arthur domain".[78] "When MINSTREL tells a story, its primary goal is to illustrate a particular story theme. MINSTREL's story themes are stereotypical planning situations, which can often be summarized by an adage [...]".[79] "By limiting MINSTREL to Planning Advice Themes, we are able to address many of the issues in telling theme-based stories without the need to create a general theory of themes".[80]

For instantiating the main character's role, MINSTREL would choose (either at random, or by being given a hint) a hermit, or a knight, or a princess, or a king.[81] Turner analysed imperfections in a story resulting as output, *The Proud Knight*[82]:

> Once upon a time, a hermit named Bebe told a knight named Grunfeld that if Grunfeld fought a dragon then something bad would happen. Grunfeld was very proud. Because he was very proud, he wanted to impress the king. Grunfeld moved to a dragon. Grunfeld fought a dragon. The dragon was destroyed, but Grunfeld was wounded. [Two errors:] *Grunfeld was wounded because he fought a knight. Grunfeld being wounded impressed the king.*

---

[77] Turner (1992, p. 377): "[I]n the MINSTREL model of episodic memory, individual episodes can be recalled only if the recall indices are unique or nearly so. If a set of recall indices matches more that a few episodes, then memory can only recall generalizations about those episodes. To recall a particular episode, the recall indices must be *elaborated* until they uniquely specify an episode. [... T]he MINSTREL model of creativity focuses a great deal of effort on efficient and directed search of episodic memory for knowledge that can be used for invention. [...] The purpose of MINSTREL's model of memory and MINSTREL's concentration on the directed, efficient search for useful knowledge is to limit the size and scope of knowledge that MINSTREL must process in order to be creative".

[78] From Turner's (1992) thesis abstract.

[79] Turner (1992, section 6.1., p. 155). By contrast, in Dyer's BORIS multi-paragraph story understanding program (e.g., Dyer, 1983a), an adage corresponds to a "thematic-organisation unit" (TAU) that is a pattern resorted to in order to *understand* a story. In BORIS, this is related to plan failures. Later on, Dyer tried to model also jokes, based on these.

[80] Turner (1992, section 6.1., p. 156).

[81] Turner (1992, pp. 412, 417).

[82] The story is in Turner (1992), p. 412, Fig. 15.18. The analysis is ibid., on p. 412 ff.

Turner's italics identify what he consider to be erroneous, namely, Grunfeld's being wounded twice (the second time, by a knight), and the king being impressed by injuries. Turner showed how this problem occurred and was solved. "After it has been determined that Grunfeld is wounded in the fight with the dragon, MINSTREL checks to see if it knows anything further about woundings that it should add to the scene".[83] Using two creativity heuristics, MINSTREL recalls the episode *Knight Fight:* "In order to impress the king, a knight killed a dragon, thwarting the dragon's goal of staying alive". As MINSTREL did not manage "to recall a scene in which some state thwarts a knight's goal of protecting his health", MINSTREL applied a creativity heuristic that generalises a character, so the knight was generalised to another violent character, 'monster', of which a dragon is a particular case. Then, MINSTREL tried to recall something about a monster's goal of health preservation being thwarted. Yet, as it knew about a dragon having been killed, rather than just wounded, also the new specification of the problem produced no resulting recall. Then, a creativity heuristic "that modifies a thwarting state to a similar, related state" was applied to the specification, modifying the monster's (i.e., the generalised knight's) wounding to death, and MINSTREL recalled a precedent being a dragon's death from the episode *Knight Fight.*

This was adapted to the story being generated, "by changing the dragon's death back to wounding", and the monster (i.e., the generalised violent character) back to a knight. "Unfortunately, the modified episode has with it the remainder of the original 'Knight Fight' episode, in which the knight fights the dragon and impresses the king", and thus extraneous scenes were added to the story being generated, "resulting in the scenes in which Grunfeld fights another knight" – the knight from *Knight Fight* who killed the dragon onto which *The Proud Knight's* knight had been mapped – "and in which Grunfeld's injury impresses the king", because in *Knight Fight* the king was impressed by the death of the dragon onto which *The Proud Knight's* knight had been mapped.[84] Turner explains that the heuristic of finding a similar thwarting state performed an incorrect adaptation step: it "was able to correctly adapt the thwarting state", but "was unable to correctly adapt the extraneous scenes";[85] it should have removed the portion it didn't manage to adapt. Once that correction to the software was made, a correct version of *The Proud Knight* was generated. Another, similar story, *The Proud King,* was generated by recalling *The Proud Knight.* After being wounded while fighting a dragon, King Arthur wants to protect his health, so he becomes a hermit (i.e., a non-violent character).[86]

---

[83] Turner (1992, p. 413).

[84] Turner (1992, p. 413).

[85] Turner (1992, p. 414).

[86] Also within his discussion, in Turner (1992, section 15.5.2), of MINSTREL's performance, Turner related about a failed attempt to generate a story for the moral "Pride goes before a fall". What was generated, was the story *The Proud Hermit* (Turner, 1992, p. 411, figure 15.17): "Once upon a time there was a hermit. Someone warned him not to pick berries, but he went ahead and picked them anyway. Nothing happened". Turner does not envisage considering this a successful antistory. Rather, he explains why *The Proud Hermit* was a failure. MINSTREL had chosen for

5.2 An Overview of Artificial Intelligence Approaches to Narratives

5.2.17 Environments For Storytelling

I am going to exemplify environments for storytelling. Marina Umaschi Bers (2003) discusses various narrative tools she designed for them to be used by children. One of the tools she discusses is SAGE. She wrote (2003, p. 115):

> SAGE is an authoring environment for children to create their own wise storytellers to interact with by telling and listening to stories. Children can engage with SAGE in two modes: 1) by choosing a wise storyteller from a library of already existing characters and sharing with him or her what is going on in their lives. The sage storyteller "listens" and then offers a relevant tale in response, and 2) by designing their own sages...

In SAGE, the computation module parses the user's story, expands extracted nouns and verbs through a hierarchical semantic lexical reference system, and then, based on the augmented keywords, it "perform[s] a match between the user's personal story and an inspirational story in the database", in that they deal with the same themes (Umaschi Bers, 2003). This is different from Dyer's BORIS story understanding program (Dyer, 1983a) proposing an adage to match the thematic abstraction unit (TAU) – a chunk of narrative structure – in the parsed narrative (Dyer, 1983a, cf. Dyer, 1983b, 1987; Lehnert et al., 1983). SAGE does not capture the narrative structure. "Our earliest research showed that children engaged deeply with sages that we had designed, such as a Hasidic Rabbi and a Buddhist scholar" (Umaschi Bers, 2003, p. 116, citing Umaschi, 1996).[87]

---

the main character the hermit role. "MINSTREL's next step is to instantiate the prideful act. [...] To do this, MINSTREL uses episodic memory to recall a typical action by the hermit, and uses this to instantiate the prideful act. In this case, MINSTREL recalls a scene in which a hermit picks berries in the woods. At this point, MINSTREL bogs down. MINSTREL cannot invent any bad consequences of picking berries. So MINSTREL is unable to fill in the 'fall' portion of 'Pride goes before a fall', and the story fizzles. [...] Being unable to continue a story because of a bad decision earlier in the storytelling is a common problem for MINSTREL. MINSTREL has a very limited planning model, and no effort was made to give MINSTREL plans for retracting bad solutions, or for recovery from decisions that resulted in a large number of failed goals". These limitations of MINSTREL stem from its being a doctoral project. Technology was already in existence for devising quite sophisticated planning models, and backtracking from a bad decision is commonplace in planning programs from AI.

[87] In an "extract from a conversation log between a ten year old and the Hasidic Rabbi" (Umaschi Bers, 2003, p. 116), the child relates difficulties with studying math and other subjects. The artificial character replies by quoting a somewhat remote adage, followed by an explanation: "The Gerer Rabbi said: 'Exile contains redemption within itself, as seed contains the fruit [the unquote sign is missing here, in Umaschi's paper]. Right work and real diligence will bring out the hidden reward". The character asks the child whether he sees the point, and the child replies: "yes, so now I see that I just have to keep on trying no matter what" (ibid., p. 117). It is the user's own human intelligence that puts the meaning in the output of SAGE's pattern matching. Motivation plays a part in such success; a pilot study was conducted by using SAGE – an identity construction environment – for therapeutic purposes with chronically ill children: to young cardiac patients, using SAGE was "a way of coping with cardiac illness, hospitalizations, and invasive medical procedures" (ibid.).

Incidentally, about the opening of the response from the artificial agent in SAGE; "The Gerer Rabbi": which one? i.e., which holder of the title? the current one? or the first one, Israel Meir Alter of Gur, the Hasidic author of *Chiddushei HaRim* and the founder of the dynasty of Gur

Umaschi Bers (2003) also discusses *Kaleidostories,* a web-based identity construction environment which guides children in the generation of a personal online portrait with Self narratives, and in choosing or creating role models (ibid., pp. 118–121). Yet another software environment described by Umaschi Bers is *Zora,* "a 3D multi-user environment that provides the tools for young users to create a virtual city" (ibid., p. 121).

Rui Prada, Isabel Machado, and Ana Paiva (2000) reported about TEATRIX, a virtual environment for story generation. TEATRIX is a learning environment. The intended users are children, who engage in interactive story-generation collaboratively, in three phases: the story set-up (the child chooses which scenes and, next, characters to include in a story), story creation, and story writing. Stories generated and performed by the children are stored as a movie, and other children can review the movie, editing it or annotating it. In TEATRIX, acting (a child impersonates one of the characters), reading and writing were merged into a single environment. Characters have a name, a social stereotype (e.g., an old lady), and a role, and these are predefined. Only six different roles are allowed, in TEATRIX. As to scenes in TEATRIX, these are predefined spatial locations, and they have some décor, as well as exits that connect them to other scenes.

The application of models of narrative to digital interactive games has been described as "Ludology meets narratology" by Mateas and Stern (2005).[88] In fact, current work on interactive games, also and especially in industry, resorts both to advanced computer animation or virtual reality techniques, and increasingly to models of narrative or specifically of storytelling.

Brandon Rickman's *Dr. K–* "project is an attempt to create a fabricated narrative environment, an environment where nothing exists except that which is visible to the user" (Rickman, 2003, p. 131). "The user is presented with a screen of text", which states a place and some scenery. As a result of user interaction, in which the user selects with a mouse some element out of those presented on the screen, the screen updates, e.g. with some action on the part of some character (ibid.). "This operation is analogous to an audience continually asking questions to a storyteller while the storyteller performs" (ibid.), and he or she "can provide a direct answer, or be evasive in a number of ways" (ibid., p. 132). In a given situation, the user may click on "Some scenery", to make it more specific. "There are four structural elements in Dr. K–. There are props, scenes, actors, and actions" (ibid.). "A prop element is a piece of scenery, a self-contained object or environmental component" (ibid., p. 133). "A prop that is the focus of the user's attention tends to flux into a

---

(Góra Kalwaria)? Perhaps the child wouldn't bother anyway. At any rate, *Tales of the Hasidim,* the renowned popularistic collection by Martin Buber (1878–1965) of Hasidic anecdotes and aphorisms (Buber, 1947), includes – in the chapter devoted to that founder of Gur Hasidism – an anecdote appropriate for the user's predicament as related by Umaschi Bers: the anecdote from Buber recommends perseverance indeed, yet concludes disconsolately, which in the context is not the thing the child needs to hear. Information about Hasidic dynastic genealogies can be found, e.g., in the *Encyclopaedia Judaica* (published in Jerusalem by Keter, 1972), Vol. 1, pp. 160–167.

[88] Also see Mateas (2001), a longer version of which is Mateas (2004).

5.2 An Overview of Artificial Intelligence Approaches to Narratives

more specific state. Props that have been neglected by the user tend to revert to more archetypical state. Thus it is possible that a rug, after a period of activity, may revert to *cloth. But if the user then focuses on the *cloth, it may transform into a curtain" (ibid.). "A scene element is a named location, a construction of place. Scenes are defined by the collection of props that they archetypically contain" (ibid., p. 134). "Scenes are never the direct focus of the user", and "are a byproduct of user interaction" (ibid.); during exploration by the user, "[u]pon reaching a certain threshold [...] the scene transforms to a more focused state" (ibid.). "Actors are much like props, but they can be mobile or autonomous" (ibid.). "There is one major pitfall to avoid when creating a fabricated world: the repeated generation of unparseable nonsense" (ibid., p. 140). To "maintain some level of comprehensibility" (ibid.) of this virtual reality project (even though it is merely based on screens of rudimentary text), it "can be presented within a theatrical setting", "the story engine is tuned so that there will be some sense of progression" (ibid., p. 141), and there "is the choice of specific subject material for the story" (ibid., p. 140). Rickman's "Dr. K– is constructed around the historic account of William Burke and William Hare in 1820s Edinburgh" (ibid., p. 140): they "made a living by killing people and selling the bodies to an anatomy school" (ibid., p. 140). "This should not be considered a backstory, however. It exists more as a background motif", and users "may recognize some of [Burke and Hare's] elements within the narrative", rather than finding their actual story (ibid., p. 140).

Michael Mateas (pers. comm., 2 May 2006) described a project of his as follows:

> Regarding ABL (A Behavior Language), my reactive planning language for authoring autonomous characters, it's not so much a language within which you author story structure but a language for defining the moment-by-moment decision-making logic of real-time autonomous characters. In Facade (available for download at www.interactivestory.net) the AI architecture includes both the ABL-based autonomous characters, and a separate component, the drama manager, that is responsible for maintaining the narrative flow and dramatic arc (there's also the natural language processing subsystem, but that's not specifically relevant to story and character). On Façade, see in Section 5.2.13 above.

Let us say something specific about technologies to support children's play with narratives, i.e., the kind of tools that Umaschi Bers has been developing. At the Media Laboratory of the Massachusetts Institute of Technology, Cassel and Ryokai (2001) have been concerned with the development of tools that support children's fantasy play[89] and storytelling. Their *StoryMat* is "a system that supports and listens

---

[89] Cassel and Ryokai stated (2001, pp. 171–172): "One common form of storytelling among young children is fantasy play. We can define this kind of spontaneous play by the fact that the children's language and actions are both the process and the product of their fantasy play. For example, a child who is holding a block tells her playmate, 'Pretend this is a train, OK?' Children demonstrate in this language a sense of possibility – the concept of 'what might be' [...]. Through their language and their action they create the world in which they are playing. Fantasy play, which can include role-playing, dressing-up, and storytelling with objects such as stuffed animals, allows children to explore different possibilities in their life without the risk of failure and frustration from unexpected events. Pretense gives children a unique opportunity to explore their own emotional arousal [...] and also an opportunity to experiment with possible interactions and relationships

to children's voices in their own storytelling play, whether they are playing collaboratively, or without a playmate. StoryMat offers a child-driven, story-listening space by recording and recalling children's narrating voices, and the movements they make with their stuffed animals on a colourful story-evoking quilt." (Cassel & Ryokai, 2001, p. 169). "Hayes-Roth's Improvisational Puppets System [...] provided an environment where children could play-act by using personality-rich characters. By manipulating the characters on the computer screen like puppets, children explored different character actions and reactions. Hayes-Roth and her colleagues found that although children are able to construct stories collaboratively both with peers and parents, they engaged in more open-ended play with their peers than with adult partners." (Cassel & Ryokai, 2001, p. 172).[90] "Most commercial applications in the domain of tangible personal technologies for children are variants on dolls, with increasingly sophisticated repertoires of behaviours. Microsoft Actimates' 'Barney' and Mattel's 'Talk with Me Barbie'® have embedded quite sophisticated technology into familiar stuffed animals and dolls. These toys, however, deliver adult-scripted content with thin layers of personalisation, and do not engage children in their own fantasy play. In both cases the toy is the speaker and the child is firmly in the position of listener." (Cassel & Ryokai, 2001, p. 173). This is not the case with StoryMat: "Our philosophy is that good technology for children supports child-initiated and child-driven play." (ibid.). In fact (ibid., pp. 176–177):

> StoryMat is a soft, quilt-like play mat with appliquéd objects such as houses and roads. It provides an under-determined play space for children to tell their own stories on, and yet it is an active participant in their play since it records and recalls their stories. [...] As far as the child is concerned, StoryMat functions entirely independently of a computer or keyboard, thus allowing pre-literate children to engage with the system. When children tell their stories with a toy of StoryMat, their narrating voices and the associated movements of the toys are recorded. The recorded story is then compared with other stories told by children who have visited the mat previously. One of the past stories, that shares a similar pattern (specifically, the length of the story, the pattern of the path the toy took, and the identity of the toy) with the present story is recalled on the mat, as a moving shadow of the toy with its narrator's voice. This, in turn, provides an opportunity for the child to continue the themes of the story she heard by telling her own new story. The child may tell her subsequent story by coming up with a creative solution to the story she just heard. Or she may continue telling her own story and incorporate some story elements from the story she just heard. In this sense, StoryMat is a kind of imaginary playmate, but who also mediates natural collaboration between a child and her peer group. [...] In addition to providing a larger-than-themselves interface, this particular kind of quilt serves as a unique interface for collaborative storytelling. Objects sewn on the mat are story-evoking: paths going in different directions, trees, houses and fields of contrasting colours. These objects serve as "story starters" for children, yet they are under-determined enough to be transformed into any objects children imagine them to be.

---

among humans [...]. As such, fantasy play fulfills an important purpose in children's emotional and social development."

[90] Citing Hayes-Roth and van Gent (1997) – actually, a pre-publication technical report was cited – and Huard and Hayes-Roth (1996).

5.2.18 Bias in Narrative Reporting, and Nonlinear Retelling

The challenge of representing narrative according to different perspectives, and in particular, as reported by different, ideologically biased sources, has been responded to, within artificial intelligence. The problem of how to capture capabilities of reporting a story according to partisan goals, and of understanding a story so told, has been handled by some scholars.

One of the last narrative programs from the 1980s conceptual-dependency school while it was still based at the University of Yale, namely, Eduard Hovy's PAULINE, was a milestone in modelling the generation of partisan reports on the same events.[91] For example, it would report about a demonstration held on campus, from the viewpoint of the university's authorities, and from the viewpoint of one of the demonstrators.

ABDUL/ILANA was a tool from the early 1980s, also developed by computational linguists. It was an AI program that used to simulate the generation of adversary arguments on an international conflict (Flowers, et al., 1982). In a disputation with adversary arguments, the players do not actually expect to convince each other, and their persuasion goals target observers.

In a different perspective on different partisan sources – the perspective of belief revision as applied to an idealised computational modelling of the making of opinions during the progressive delivery of evidence in court – Dragoni and Nissan (2004) have taken into account how the degree of credibility of the different persons who provide different items of information is dynamically affected by how some information they supplied comes to be evaluated. See Section 2.1.2 above.

A distinction is to be made between bias in conversation, and bias in presenting a narrative. In this and in the next paragraph, we exemplify those two situations. Already the early 1980s saw an AI program, IMP, give misleading information while avoiding outright lies (Jameson, 1983). That project addressed the relation between truth and manipulative presentation. IMP may try to mislead on purpose, without actually lying. A dialogue system, it impersonates a real estate agent, trying to rent moderately priced furnished rooms on the Hamburg market. Well-informed about the market, IMP assumes that the customer possesses the same general information, against which the customer assesses the qualities of the room considered. The program tries to convey a good impression about the goods, and about itself as well. It would not volunteer damaging information, unless a direct, specific relevant question is made. IMP has a goal of maintaining a neutral image of itself and an impression of completeness for its own answers; on occasion, it reportedly simulated insulted surprise if an intervening question by the customer seems to imply (by detailed questioning) that IMP is concealing information.[92] Also the purpose

---

[91] Hovy (1987a, 1987b, 1988a, 1988b, 1988c, 1988d, 1991, 1993).

[92] In contrast to IMP, that does not lie, but just tries to conceal information that would militate against its interests, at the present state of the art of AI there is an active field concerned with modelling such deceptive communication that agents deliberately try to deceive their interlocutors by conveying false content (rather than just withholding inconvenient information, like in IMP).

of Boris Galitsky's *Scenario Synthesizer*, developed at Rutgers University (Galitsky, 1998, 1999), is to control buyer's impression.

Narrative, and in particular, nonlinear narrative, are central to the following. Domike, Mateas and Vanouse (2003)[93] describe *Terminal Time*, which "is a history 'engine': a machine which combines historical events, ideological rhetoric, familiar forms of TV documentary, consumer polls and artificial intelligence algorithms to create hybrid cinematic experiences for mass audiences" (Domike et al., 2003, p. 155) that in turn respond, which is measured by a device connected to a computer, allowing the "program to create historical narratives that attempt to mirror and often exaggerate their biases and desires" (ibid.). "Although dominant in popular media today, the cookie-cutter documentary is just one form of historical documentary" (ibid., p. 156): "each program has a distinct dramatic arc, a beginning, middle and an end. The rhetorical structure [...] invariably involves a crisis situation, a climax, and a clear resolution" (ibid.), offering just one interpretation of history. "Overall the tone set is one of progress" (ibid.).

Terminal Time explores the early Soviet filmmaking's "Kuleshov effect", by which: "The one who controls the order[ing of visual data], controls the message" (ibid., p. 157). "Expressive AI views a system as a performance. Within a performative space, the system expresses the author's ideas" and is viewed "as a communication between author and audience" (ibid., p. 167). *Terminal Time*'s software architecture consists of the following major components: "knowledge base, ideological goal trees [...][94] rule-based natural language generator, rhetorical devices, and a database of indexed audio/visual elements primarily consisting of short digital movies and sound files containing music" (Domike et al., 2003, p. 168).

5.2.19 Self-Exoneration with ALIBI, in the Perspective of Narrative Inventiveness

We have already discussed my own ALIBI system in Section 2.2.2 above. ALIBI receives as input an accusation, and its output explains it out, seeking to deny or at any rate minimise liability. The discussion in Section 2.2.2 was in the context of our presentation of computational approaches to reasoning about a criminal charge and to explanations. Nevertheless, it makes sense to also consider ALIBI a story-generator.[95] In fact, there is nothing in ALIBI that refers to the (episodic) memory

---

For example, at the 2000 Autonomous Agents Conference there was a Workshop on Deception, Fraud and Trust in Agent Societies. See s.v. 'Deception' in this book's subject index.

[93] Also see Mateas, Domike, and Vanouse (1999).

[94] Citing Jaime Carbonell's thesis about POLITICS (1979). Also see Carbonell (1978, 1981).

[95] Already in the early stages of the ALIBI project, I entertained the long-term aim that this project would be eventually also contributing to automated story-generation of an explanatory kind. In 1986, I finished the implementation of my own PhD project, ONOMATURGE, which provided with a simple definition, generated and proposed Hebrew candidate neologisms, and ranked them according to a calculated estimate of their respective psychosemantic transparency to speakers of the language (e.g., Nissan, 1987d, 2000b). My initial plans when defining the ONOMATURGE

5.2 An Overview of Artificial Intelligence Approaches to Narratives

that the suspect (who is impersonated by ALIBI) must already have about his or her past at the time when the events ascribed to that character took place.

ALIBI takes as an input an accusation (expressed either as logical predicates, or, which is the case of ALIBI2, in simple natural language). It decomposes the actions referred to in the input, developing a hierarchy in which, e.g., 'stealing' is considered as 'taking' in given circumstances. The deontic (moral or legal) factors are separated from the action, but (in ALIBI3) track is kept, so that relative degree of liability can be computed. This is done when the planner constructs another tree, which is meant to provide an explanation for the events related, which is alternative to the accusation, and either aims at complete exoneration, or (in ALIBI3) as a second best, for diminished liability.

Processing has the program recursively decompose the actions in the input, into a tree of actions, down to elementary, atomic actions. Moreover, as mentioned, actions are stripped of their deontic connotation. It's up to the system to concoct such a plan where that act of taking fits in a way that is legitimate for the defendant. Generating the justification corresponds to a reconstitution of actions into a different tree. Then the terminal actions in the *decomposition tree* are differently reconstituted into alternative explanations (each corresponding to a *recomposition tree*) that eliminate or minimise liability.

In one of the stories, a man is accused of having shot and wounded a jeweller, while robbing him. One effect of 'wounding' is that the wounded jeweller was unable to take care of his property. This is exploited by an excuse ALIBI makes (if an excuse it is, rather than the factual truth). It states that, having shot the jeweller accidentally, the defendant did take away property, but it was in order to look after it and then return it. Another effect of 'wounding' is that the wounded jeweller needed medical aid.

The defendant may supplement his excuse by claiming he *ran* away, in order to get such help for the jeweller. 'Armed threat' is an interpretation involving the effect of holding a weapon and possibly pointing it (which happens to be at somebody who then feels threatened), but ALIBI may try to admit to physically holding the object (which happens to be a weapon), while denying the intentions ascribed (of threatening an interlocutor who is therefore a victim), possibly implying an inadequacy of the defendant at realising the interlocutor's interpretation of the situation. Actually, one excuse ALIBI tries, is that the defendant was carrying the weapon for an innocent purpose, and, possibly forgetting about its presence, was innocently talking to the victim, and was unaware the latter acted by feeling threatened. *Mens rea* is denied.

---

project and bringing it from Italy to Israel were that I would eventually also develop a computational model of folk-etymological reasoning about words (something that, historically in the modern era, has had an impact on neologisation by loanword nativisation within language planning for various languages, including Hebrew, as eventually shown in his 2000 Oxford thesis by the linguist Ghil'ad Zuckermann [2000, cf. 2003, 2006]). Also when doing ALIBI, my long-term hopes were that by developing a mechanism for finding explanatory trajectories, this would eventually contribute to computational modelling of folk-etymological processes. With Zuckermann and Yaakov HaCohen-Kerner, at the long last I am working on the latter project, which is called GALLURA. The aim is to generate aetiological tales of a folk-etymological kind.

Whereas in general ALIBI may generate "alibis" that sound reasonable, the explanations it gives for the story mentioned here is ludicrous: the result is unintended humour.[96] Arguably this is because the circumstances included in the charge are damning, and the suspect (through the artificial cognitive agent impersonating that suspect) finds it very difficult to extricate himself.

ALIBI1 was implemented in the Prolog programming language during the academic year 1987–1988, under my supervision, by two by two *Expert Systems* and *Prolog* students I had been teaching at Ben-Gurion University of the Negev in Beer-Sheva, Israel, namely, Tsvi Kuflik and Gilad Puni. Kuflik is at present (2011) on faculty at the Management Information Systems Department of the University of Haifa. In ALIBI2, implemented in 1989, the semantics was reorganised in a format inspired by case-grammars. ALIBI2 could accept an input in simple English (a sequence of sentences, each with just one clause, and without the need to process personal pronouns). ALIBI2 was implemented by two students of the *Computational Linguistics* course I was teaching, Roni Salfati and Yuval Shaul, by reusing code from ALIBI1.

ALIBI3 was implemented in 1990, and involved a recoding in the Lisp programming language, but more importantly, instead of just aiming at such explanations that would seek total exoneration, failing that ALIBI3 would provide such explanations that would at any rate minimise liability. ALIBI3 was implemented as an undergraduate project by Auni Spanioli, under my supervision. Moreover, a somewhat related prototype, SKILL, was implemented in 1990 in Prolog as an undergraduate project by Fadel Fakher-Eldeen. Justifying poor behaviour was extended to areas other than in the legal domain: skill in performing at some task was judged according to common-sense knowledge (including widespread prejudices, e.g. that adult women, unlike little girls, are often expected to be able to cook well) about the task, on classes of performers, and on the environment. The discussion in Nissan and Rousseau (1997) is about how to endow ALIBI with reasoning about complicity; see in Section 2.2.2.7 in the present book.

5.2.20 Crime Stories, Mediation by the Media, and Crime Fiction: Any Lesson to Be Learnt in Computer Models?

5.2.20.1 Criminal Investigation and Criminal Trials Within the Remit of Literary Studies

Laurance Donnelly (2003, p. 8) pointed out:

> The origins of Forensic Geology can probably be traced to the publication of *Sherlock Holmes* in the late 19th century. For instance, Dr Watson observed how Holmes could recognize different soils on clothing, and from their colour and consistency could identify what part of London they came from [...] Other Victorian writers of fiction also made reference to the use of geology in solving crimes. For instance, Thorndyke [...] described red-brown

---

[96] Intended humour, though discouraged in litigants, is sometimes put to use by judges in the courtroom. See Hobbs (2007).

loam containing chalk fragments and foraminifera (microfossils) on a suspect's clothing. This was identified as being characteristic of the Cretaceous Chalk at Gravesend in Kent. It was at this locality where a body was subsequently located in a dene hole (a prehistoric flint mine). Although fictitious, these demonstrated an understanding of how geology might be used to solve crimes.

It is quite interesting that Edmond Locard, a pioneer of several disciplines within forensic science, published a book in criminalistics that, as stated in its title, *La Criminalistique à l'usage des gens du monde et des auteurs de romans policiers,* was catering to the authors of detective novels (Locard, 1937).

The early modern *belles lettres,* international folklore, and even late antique homiletical literature, all know variants of a story about a perspicacious observer who manages to reconstruct past events by observing circumstances, typically including traces of passage on a route. Rosoni remarks (1995, p. 279) that Voltaire's cogent argument against probabilities as applied to circumstantial proof is in contradiction with the eminently circumstantial logic of Voltaire's *qua* novelist in *Zadig.* (Let us recall in passing that in the front material of *Zadig,* its appeal is claimed even to such readers who dislike novels. The plot of the pseudo-Oriental tale is laden with events where parties with opposite claims are pitted against each other. Moreover, Voltaire himself consigned the two parts of the novel to different publishers, cashing from both yet denying both their entitlement to the novel in full.) In Babylon, the righteous Zadig is accused of having stolen the King's horse and the Queen's pet bitch. Zadig proposes an investigation line of hypotheses by which he had recognised the footprints and other marks left by the two animals in the sand (Nissan, 2001b).

A Persian proverb states: "'Did you see a camel?' 'No'." Haïm (1956) also provides a free translation: "Say that you did not see the camel, and relieve yourself of all commitments", and proceeds to explain by means of an anecdote (ibid., pp. 275–276):

> A wise man, popularly identified with the famous poet *Sa'di,* was crossing the desert. On seeing the footprints of a camel, he knew that a camel had been passing before him. Further on, when he came to a lucern-field, he noticed that only one side of the field had been grazed, and guessed that the camel must have been blind in one eye. In the vicinity also he saw the trace of a camel's kneeling-place, as well as the footprints of a woman, which made him think that the rider, who had been a woman, must have caused the camel to kneel in that spot for a rest.* [Haïm, ibid.: *The anecdote has been, and is capable of being expanded by other details dealing with traces and conjectures, which contribute nothing subservient to the purpose.] At this juncture a man came up to *Sa'di,* and asked him whether he had seen a camel in the neighbourhood. *Sa'di* furnished the interrogator with all the foregoing signs and details, whereupon the man, who seemed to be the camel's owner, began to beat the innocent poet, who he thought had stolen the beast and kept the woman. In this way *Sa'di* committed himself by using his perspicacity, whereas if, in reply to the man who asked him whether he had *seen* the camel, he had only said, 'No', he would have been relieved of such a commitment. [...] The reason that the anecdote is connected *Sa'di* is based on the following verse: [...] *i.e.* How long dost thou allow to be beaten by the camel-drivers, O *Sa'di?* Thou couldst have ignored the matter from the beginning, and said, "No", in reply to the question, "Have you seen a camel?" It would seem as if *Sa'di* had personally experienced the trouble described in the anecdote, but the verse in question seems altogether spurious, and must have been invented by the vulgar to justify the belief that it was *Sa'di* who originated the pvb. At any rate the story is very old. (ibid., pp. 275–276).

There is a variant of the camel track story, in an Italian book of 1557: *Peregrinaggio di tre figliuoli del re di Serendippo* (i.e., 'The Wanderings of Three Sons of the King of Serendip', i.e, Sri Lanka), itself being based, through an Armenian author, on the Persian-language *Hasht Bihisht* (*Eight Paradises*, 1302) by a poet, Khosrau, who was himself based in India. A Dutch forensic pathologist, Pek van Andel, of the University of Groningen, mentioned the *Serendippo* precedent in an article (van Andel, 1994) about serendipity, a concept the word for which was coined and defined by Horace Walpole on 28 January 1758. (Van Andel is the expert whose report disproved the accepted view in the Netherlands' Ballpoint Case – a few chapters in Malsch and Nijboer (1999) discuss that case – thus leading to the overturning of the sentence. Namely, he proved that it cannot be that the victim's head was shot a ballpoint pen through her right eye into the left lobe of the brain with a small crossbow, according to a confession ascribed to the defendant, who was the victim's son. Van Andel's results were the outcome of his own shooting ballpoint pens into the eye sockets of dead human bodies, by using a small crossbow: it turned out that the pen would come apart on impact against the back of the socket.)

As far as I know, the earliest version of the camel track story is to be found in *Lamentations Rabbah,* a Jewish homiletic work about the theme of the biblical book of *Lamentations* (for this variant of the story, cf. Hasan-Rokem, 1996, p. 61). There is a parallel passage (discussed by Hasan-Rokem, ibid., pp. 69–73) in the *Babylonian Talmud,* tractate *Sanhedrin,* 104ab (i.e., on both sides of folio 104). The passage in the latter concerns two prisoners taken by a Roman slaverer on Mt. Carmel. He overhears them as they tell each other that they had been preceeded, on the same road, by a camel that was blind in one eye, was carrying on the one side a wineskin, and on the other side one containing oil instead, and so forth. (MS Munich has a longer story, in which the two are able to discover, by a kind of reasoning that is implausible to a modern mind, that their master was the illegitimate child of a professional male dancer, and he eventually discovers that this was true.) In the version from *Lamentations Rabbah,* the circumstances are somewhat different.

Thus far in the present Section 5.2.20.1, we have been considering stories about some clever character who is able to reconstruct events from traces. This is central to detective stories, yet is quite distinct from literature about crime. "Browse a bookstore, writes Mark Seltzer, and you will find a healthy shelf labeled 'Crime'. Besides it may be a smaller, seedier shelf labeled 'True Crime'. The first is popular crime fiction, the second crime fact" – in the words of the publisher's blurb for Seltzer (2006), a book that analyses cultural factors in the blurring of the distinction between fiction and real event.

Let us turn to narratives about courtroom settings in films. "[C]inematic trials make much of such situations where extremely unfortunate circumstances [are in place], in the evidence as gathered, as well as in its handling in court. Norman Rosenberg (1994) is concerned with fiction and analyses, indeed, the filmic representations of court trials. He acknowledges the practical inescapability of our adopting a positivist attitude to evidence, even when aware of its limitations. Literary studies have been impinging on the law literature, especially from North America, increasingly in recent years, to the joy of some, the dismay of others" (Geiger, Nissan, & Stollman, 2001).

5.2 An Overview of Artificial Intelligence Approaches to Narratives

Moreover, lawyers as characters in fiction do not necessarily appear with a focus on the logic of a particular trial. The biographical element may be overriding. For example, there had been lawyers in William Faulkner's family, as wells as among his friends."It is hardly surprising, therefore, that Faulkner's narratives are replete with legal characters. Watson recounts more than a scene of these, spotlighting Gavin Stevens, who plays a prominent role for three decades in works ranging from *Sanctuary* to *The Mansion*" (Labor, 1994).

Clues: A Journal of Detection, published by Heldref Publications (Helen Dwight Reid Educational Foundation, in Washington, DC) is the only U.S. scholarly journal on mystery and detective fiction. Whereas such fiction is in print, television, and films, the journal itself published academic essays and nonfiction book reviews. Crime investigation is a central theme, but from the viewpoint of literary and film studies. The first volume of *Clues* was published in 1980.

A prominent psychologist, Amina Memon, included this passage in her 2008 course handouts for the course in *Psychology, Law and Eyewitness Testimony* at the University of Aberdeen:

> I have never recommended a "fiction" writer before but to get a good insight into the course as a whole, you might want to read a John Grisham book – *The Innocent* – it's actually based on a real case where an innocent person was wrongly convicted – based on flawed evidence, questioning techniques and unethical investigative procedures including confession evidence inappropriately obtained. Grisham also refers to DNA exoneration evidence (the innocence project, see above for website).[97]

Computing and computer security have made inroads in this domain, too. Consider *heist films,* i.e., such films whose plot is woven around a group of people trying to steal something (if, in particular, it is a comic film, then it is called a *caper movie*). For example, in the 1964 heist film *Topkapi* (directed by Jules Dassin, starring Melina Mercouri, Peter Ustinov, Maximilian Schell, and Robert Morley, and based on Eric Ambler's 1962 novel, *The Light of Day*), the object to be stolen was a bejewelled dagger from Istanbul's Topkapi Museum. In a memorable scene, the gang lowers one of its members, by means of a rope held by Ustinov, into a museum hall, down from the ceiling. When during the 1990s another film was made, in which there also was a scene (clearly inspired by *Topkapi*) with a gang member being lowered down from the ceiling, what was being stolen was data from a personal computer. This reflects how conspicuous, as well as glamorous, computing has become.

Semiologists Thomas Sebeok and Jean Umiker-Sebeok have developed a comparison of the inference method of Sherlock Holmes and Peirce's abductive reasoning.[98]

Bear in mind that the reasoning about a murder story can be quite apart from the reasoning associated with crime investigation, or even with detective stories. Take late antique and medieval traditions woven upon Scriptural narratives (possibly

---

[97] She was referring to http://www.innocenceproject.org/ This is a website that documents real life cases of miscarriages of justice. Junkin (2004) discussed the case of the first death-row inmate exonerated by DNA evidence.

[98] That work by the Sebeoks has been translated in several languages (Sebeok & Sebeok, 1979, 1980, 1981, 1982a, 1982b, 1983, 1989, 1994).

filling gaps where Scripture itself is silent). A short communication by Breeze (1992) in a journal in English studies pointed out that within a medieval Christian tradition on the *Genesis* narrative of Cain and Abel, the narrative variant that has it that Cain used a camel jawbone to kill Abel is distinctive of Irish sources, as opposed to the other variant (from texts more broadly co-territorial within the British Isles, i.e., also from Great Britain) that maintains that Cain's tool to that effect was the jawbone of a donkey.

This detail is an evident product of narrative contamination from the story of Samson, who used the jawbone of a rather freshly deceased donkey (thus not fully skeletonized and dry) to kill several of his enemies. The same topic of Cain's murder weapon in relation to Samson's use of a jawbone was dealt with by Barb (1972).

In this example, the kind of reasoning that matters is the difference between narrative variants as related to *stemmatology,* i.e., the dependency hierarchy between texts, or families of manuscripts (and early printed editions). In the given example, the geography of the manuscripts also matters. Stemmatology is due to the fact that manuscripts had to be copied, and even though copyists did not necessarily manage to be precise when copying, and for that matter did not even abide by a code of practice requiring that copies be exact, this is a far cry from creative intrusion into what they were copying. Unless a misreading is involved, it's no mere copying inexactitude when a tradition maintains that Cain used a camel jawbone instead of the jawbone of an ass.

Howe et al. (2001) described "using programs designed for biological analysis of sequence evolution to uncover the relationships between different manuscript versions of a text", i.e., for the purposes of stemmatology (van Reenen & van Mulken, 1996): diagrams of phylogenetic analysis are used, in order to represent manuscript affiliation in a *stemma* (or stemmatological tree), which shows how manuscripts are clustered with respect to a supposed original. Stemmatological trees are not what is new about the method; it is the application to stemmatology of software originally intended for biology, that was novel.

5.2.20.2 When Life Imitates Art

It does happen that a detective story appears to have inspired an actual crime, and investigators may use this as supplementary circumstantial evidence, which is not necessarily for the court, but rather for their own dynamics of forming an opinion while carrying out the investigation. In a newspaper in Orlando, Florida, Michael McLeod (1991), writing in the Sunday supplement of the *Orlando Sentinel,* reported about the case, from Alturas, Polk County, of George Trepal. This man, a computer expert, was married to Diana, an orthopaedic surgeon, and both of them were active members of Mensa, the social club whose member must have a high I.Q. (supposedly a reliable indicator of high intelligence). Their neighbours were working-class Parearlyn "Pye" Carr, his second wife, Peggy, and their teenager children or stepchildren. In 1988, Pye had received a threat in the mail a few months before his wife, a son and a stepson, fell ill. This turned out to be thallium poisoning, and Peggy became comatose, was eventually disconnected from life support, and died in March 1989. Thallium, an outlawed substance, is a heavy metal once

5.2 An Overview of Artificial Intelligence Approaches to Narratives 411

found in rat poison. The note Pye had received said: "You and your so-called family have two weeks to move out of Florida forever or else you all die. This is no joke."

Thallium was found in cola bottles that the Carr family was drinking. As it eventually turned out during the investigation, it was George Trepal who had placed the tainted bottles on the Carrs' doorstep. As mentioned, three members of the family developed symptoms of poisoning, and for Peggy the outcome was fatal. There was a history of altercations between the two families. The Carrs played loud music, whereas George Trepall would not tolerate the noise of a television set, and his wife would watch TV at a friend's.

Diana and George Trepall used to stage annually a murder mystery at a hotel: some participants would play out a murder, while others tried to solve the whodunit. George used to research the scripts written by his wife. After the Trepals moved houses (as Diana moved to a medical practice in another town), a small brown bottle was found at their Alturas house and it tested positive for thallium. In the Trepals' new home, police discovered a homemade collection of information on poisons. And the wife's collection of murder mysteries included *The Pale Horse* by Agatha Christie, a tale of a series of murders by thallium poisoning.

In 1975, George Trepal had been convicted in Charlotte, North Carolina, for conspiracy to manufacture amphetamines for a drug ring. He was also known to have tried to poison a person: "Trepal had once smeared a homemade hallucinogen on a refrigerator handle when he suspected someone of stealing his roommates' food – hoping the culprits would absorb the drug through their skin" (McLeod, 1991, p. 138). The police hadn't mentioned in interviews with the media the threat note that Pye Carr had received. An undercover agent signed up for the Trepals' mystery weekend, and in a brochure she was handed to introduce participants to the weekend, there was this passage: "When a death threat appears on the doorstep, prudent people watch what they eat. Most items on the doorstep are just a neighbor's way of saying, 'I don't like you. Move out or else.'" (McLeod, 1991, p. 139). This text is similar to the text of threat note that Pye Carr received, and also dovetails with the poison found in the cola bottles left on the Carrs' doorstep.

Clearly *The Pale Horse* by Agatha Christie being found where the Trepals lived was not a prominent item in the evidence, but it reinforced the coherence of the hypothesis that George Trepals was to blame. The evidence against George Trepals was entirely circumstantial, but overwhelming. He was found guilty of Peggy Carr's murder and condemned to death by a Florida court.

5.2.20.3 The *JAMA* Model: Modelling an Outcry for Failing to Prosecute. On the Impinging Cultural Effects of a Repertoire of Former Narratives

In the JAMA model (only partly implemented as a program),[99] a sample legal narrative is analysed, of a hate murder crime and the way in public perception the

---

[99] See Geiger et al. (2001), Nissan (2001b), Nissan and Dragoni (2000). The JAMA project is the starting point of Geiger et al. (2001), Nissan (2001c), and a section in Nissan and Dragoni (2000); cf. Nissan and Martino (2004b, pp. 197, 199). The full-fledged JAMA architecture (only

inquiry was handled. In the JAMA project, an attempt was made – while emulating, in so doing, some of the knowledge sources that Michael Dyer had used in his BORIS story-understanding program (Dyer, 1983a) – public or media reactions to the murder by arson of a homeless Somali refugee in Rome, Ahmed Ali Giama. He was burned to death as he was sleeping on a bench in a public park. Eyewitnesses identified the suspects, who were nevertheless released without being prosecuted.[100]

Whereas at present there are a few Somalis who are notable in the professions in Italy (especially medicine), around 1980 Somalis in Italy were almost invariably, and at any rate always as far as the public could see, at the lowest rung of society. And yet, this was not necessarily a reflection of a lack of education: some of them had been, it seems, professionals, or teachers. In the evening of 22 May 1979, the chilling murder of Ahmed Ali Giama (Jama) had taken place in Rome, and the victim had been reported to have had both professional qualifications, namely, as a lawyer in Somalia and as a teacher in that same country, and yet he was homeless in Italy. (Apparently he had been a law student at the University of Kiev.) Giama was reported to have been an opponent of Siad Barre's dictatorship; at any rate, he had eventually become a homeless exile in Rome.

On 22 May 1979, Giama was sleeping on a bench in a park, being the churchyard (*sagrato*) of Santa Maria della Pace, near Piazza Navona. A group of persons burnt him alive. There was the testimony of a group of persons who, because of their professions, would have been expected to be quite cogent, and yet, the suspects were released without being prosecuted.[101] Later on there was a trial ending in their

---

partly implemented) is about how a cultural repertoire of narratives (from both collective historical memory, and fiction) contributes to shaping the reception by public opinion of a crime story, and how law enforcement handles or mishandles it. The discussion leads to an examination of concepts of narrative improbability, as well as to considerations about the legal "doctrine of chances" (see in the Glossary). Also relevant is how the mass media report about crime; see Schlesinger and Tumber's book (1994) *Reporting Crime: The Media Politics of Criminal Justice*.

[100] I recall mentioning this case to an Italian examining magistrate in December 1999, and he was startled and quite uncomfortable at the mention. Public opinion in Italy (where I was raised, and lived from 1965 and 1983) disliked the release of the suspects. Magistrates, too, when not in a professional capacity are members of the public.

[101] Nissan, analysing the outrage in the media concerning the Giama case and to the outcome of the investigation, wrote as follows (Geiger et al., 2001, in the abstract):

> Apparently in the same racist crime category as the case of [Black 18-year-old student] Stephen Lawrence's murder ([by a gang of white youths, while he was waiting at a bus stop] in [Eltham in the London borough of] Greenwich on April 22, 1993), with the ensuing [and enduring] controversy in the U.K., the Jama case (some twenty years ago) stood apart because of a very unusual element: the eyewitnesses identifying the suspects were a group of football referees and linesmen eating together at a restaurant, and seeing the sleeping man as he was set ablaze in a public park nearby. Professional background as witnesses-cum-factfinders in a mass sport, and public perceptions of their required characteristics, couldn't but feature prominently in the public perception of the case, even more so as the suspects were released by the magistrate conducting the inquiry. There are sides to this case that involve different expected effects in an inquisitorial criminal procedure system from the

5.2 An Overview of Artificial Intelligence Approaches to Narratives 413

conviction, but later on they were acquitted on appeal. The following is quoted from Geiger et al. (2001):

> One day, as he was asleep an a bench in a public park in Rome, covered with newspaper sheets, somebody (a group of perpetrators) set fire to these newspaper sheets, and Jama found his death in the flames. There was a public outcry in the country, and an inquiry was of course carried out. (There was an outcry in Somalia, too: President Barre rode a nationalistic wave, and had a state funeral organized for Jama.) There had been eyewitnesses to the crime: a party of soccer referees and linesmen who had been eating outside a restaurant nearby. They identified the suspects: a group of youngsters (one of them a woman). These happened to be from the Parioli neighbourhood. Eventually, the inquiring magistrate released them, declaring to the media: "Sono bravi ragazzi" ("They are nice young fellows"). New outcry. In a context where in the public eye, the institutions would often come under scrutiny (on occasion, the judiciary also giving rise to controversy, or even the target of violence from some quarters), that public statement made right after the release by the magistrate conducting the inquiry sounded quite ambivalent: was that the conclusion, or a premise?[102]

Continent, where an investigating magistrate leads the inquiry and prepares the prosecution case, as opposed to trial by jury under the Anglo-American adversarial system.

In the Lawrence case in London, too, nobody was ever convicted. Eventually, this led to a recognition that there was institutional racism in the police. Moreover, it is significant that about fifteen years after the murder, at the time London's chief police commissioner Ian Blair was dismissed by London's new mayor Boris Johnson, while referring to the Lawrence case Ian Blair stated that the case was treated the way such cases occurring amid the working class are treated. This claim in turn involved race and class stereotyping, because the Lawrence family was Black, but middle class. Being Black was their sectorial identity within British society, but the statement chief of the London Metropolitan Police gave in the interview, was clear evidence of his considering Black people in London as being *en bloc* part of the working class. Therefore, to Sir Ian Blair being Black was not only a sectorial identity within society, but also a class identity. Contrast this perception to the social realities researched in Daye's (1994) *Middle-Class Blacks in Britain*.

[102] Furthermore, Nissan had written in that same article (Geiger et al., 2001):

> In lay perception, the eyewitnesses were both unusual and formidable: football referees and linesmen. More eagle-sighted or lynx-eyed that *that* sort? (Not that losing teams' fans would agree that these are infallible, on the playing grounds. But here you got a [meeting] of "focal" kinds of events: football, tearful drama, and political nasties.) There was the "glaring" element, when one is to match this to a repertoire of narration styles for a judiciary theme. (Never mind the [farces] of Dario Fo, but the football referees as dismissed witnesses sounded like they were lifted from a play by Bertolt Brecht, a still fairly popular author during those years.)
>
> On the face of it, it's quite an extralegal perspective on the given legal narrative. Yet, realising what is involved in lay perceptions of it is all-important (not just for countries with a jury, which wasn't the case of Italy at the time, and the case had never gone to court in the first place), if we are to provide a common-sense backdrop that is credible for more technically legal models.
>
> Again: what is special about the Jama murder is the character evidence about the witnesses – these appear to almost be too good to be true [...] – and the character evidence about the suspects. These were young adults, males and one female, from fairly well-to-do families from a given residential neighbourhood [namely, the Parioli]. Such a neighbourhood background was at best ambivalent on the face of it, in what could be expected at the time to be the public perception (and indeed it [was the widespread perception in the

It must be said however that the public perception was in response to exposure by the information media,[103] and these in turn paid due attention to the case after authoritative personalities (including the Pope) had shown the way. In the context of a discussion of Somali–Italian relations during the 1970s, the following is stated about the Giama case in Giovagnoli and Pons (2003, p. 407, my translation)[104]:

> It was an act of extreme and ferocious racism, expressing the creeping refusal and fear on the part of a segment of Italian society, at a time when the phenomenon is incipient of immigration from Africa, mostly from Italy's former colonies and from the Maghreb. Responses at senior levels were several, and indignant. The [Communist] mayor [Giulio Carlo] Argan [an art critic on good terms with the Vatican] condemns the crime as an infamy, and asks to be permitted to pay tribute to Ali Giama's body by paying visit. But Somalia's diplomats do not accept any interference, and obtain that the body be sent to Somalia by June the 2nd. Besides, on the day following the crime, the Pope visited a parish at the centre of Rome, and this attracted attention upon the crime, thwarting the risk that the press would pass it under silence. All four perpetrators were identified, tried, and sentenced to serve a total of 61 years in prison, at the Assizes in Rome, but later on they were acquitted. Such an outcome did definitely not help to improve relations between Italy and Somalia.

In the crime narrative which inspired the JAMA project, the crime had not just any witness. While he was sleeping on a bench in a park, covered with newspapers,

---

> event]). In fact, in the given European capital where the crime and ensuing inquiry took place, the conspicuous presence of young far-right extremists from that particular neighbourhood motivated these being labelled with the name for its inhabitants [i.e., *pariolini*]. In the given period, the term was known in the nationwide political lexicon to be a descriptor with that denotation.

[103] I personally recall that when I gave a talk at a conference in Birmingham, on 17 April 2000, and mentioned the Giama narrative and the JAMA project, a prominent AI & Law scholar in the audience remarked that such racist episodes happen all the time. Just a few days afterwards, as I was back in London, there was a (minor) news item in the broadcasted media about a Black woman suffering a racist attack in Birmingham of all places: she was doused in petrol and burnt, but at the time had survived her burns. BBC Radio 4 did not give those news much prominence.

[104] In the following, the original text is given, from Giovagnoli and Pons (2003, p. 407; fn. 38 cites Del Boca, 2001 [1987], vol. 4, pp. 497–498):

> Un altro drammatico episodio ostacola la ricomposizione dei rapporti italo-somali. Il 22 maggio 1979, di sera, viene barbaramente ucciso a Roma un giovane somalo, Ahmed Ali Giama, ex studente di legge presso l'Università di Kiev, dato alle fiamme da alcuni sconosciuti mentre dormiva sul sagrato della chiesa di Santa Maria della Pace, nelle vicinanze di piazza Navona. È un gesto di estremo e feroce razzismo, che esprime il rifiuto e la paura striscianti in una parte della società italiana, in un momento in cui comincia ad affacciarsi il fenomeno dell'immigrazione africana, proveniente in gran parte dalle ex colonie e dall'Africa maghrebina. Le reazioni ad alto livello sono diverse e sdegnate. Il sindaco Argan lo condanna come un infame crimine e chiede di poter salutare la salma di Ali Giama con un atto di riverenza. Ma la diplomazia somala non accetta interferenze e ottiene il rimpatrio della salma per il 2 giugno. Inoltre, nel giorno successivo all'episodio, una visita del papa a una parrocchia del centro di Roma attira l'attenzione al misfatto ed evita che esso passi sotto silenzio sulla stampa. I quattro aggressori, tutti identificati, processati e condannati a 61 anni complessivi di carcere dalla Corte d'assise di Roma, vengono poi assolti. Questa conclusione certamente non appiana gli attriti.

the victim was burnt alive. The event was seen by a group of soccer referees and linesmen, who were dining at a restaurant nearby. They identified a group of young men and a woman, but these were eventually released, causing an outcry. One of the background generalisations that were in effect, is that soccer referees and linesmen are eagle-eyed,[105] and within the tragedy, it was fortunate that such eyewitness testimony was available. Nevertheless, the examining magistrate concluded otherwise and did not prosecute. Incidentally, in eyewitness psychology there is a pattern by which a very confident witness may be overconfident and wrong. The public reaction however was, quite justifiably, that the case should have gone to court.

What is peculiar and awkward indeed about the eyewitnesses, is that they were football referees. But they were together, and presumably talking to each other, which presumably may have influenced how they recollected what they saw. Public expectations about the reliability of the visual acuity of such sports professionals are involved (the crime event was unrelated to either a sports event or sport-related violence, so that it was a striking coincidence that such very special eyewitnesses were available). That "even" with such testimony the case did not even go to court, lent itself to interpretations based on cultural factors and expectations. The point of selecting the particular narrative, the Jama murder and inquiry, is in that the awkward elements in it arguably help to shed light on more commonplace events. There are sides to this case that involve different expected effects in an inquisitorial criminal procedure system from the Continent, where an investigating magistrate leads the inquiry and prepares the prosecution case, as opposed to trial by jury under the Anglo-American adversarial system.

In the JAMA prototype, the attempt was made to approach the given case from the point of vantage of narrative models from AI; the difference with respect to narrative processing from the 1980s is in that not only situational social commonsense knowledge is represented, but also drawing on a more specifically cultural (literary) repertoire. The perpetrators were positively identified (but some legal psychologist may say that all too confident witnesses who were together may be wrong), by a singular kind of witnesses: a group of football referees and linesmen, who were partying together at a restaurant close by. At the stadium, these are professional witnesses-cum-factfinders. That such witnesses happened to be available when Jama was murdered, is almost "too good to be true". (The blessing-in-disguise situational pattern was applied, to a story involving the availability of a witness, in a natural-language processing approach to narrative understanding, Dyer's book (1983a) on BORIS). Nevertheless, the investigating magistrate released the suspects, instead of prosecuting them.

In the *JAMA* project, what is of interest is how public perceptions of this were likely to be shaped in terms of public attitudes (trust or mistrust) to institutional justice, partly based on experience from previous cases reported about in the media, or even on a literary repertoire (e.g., Bertolt Brecht's plays: the extreme details in

---

[105] Except, that is, when the football referees decides against the team of which you are a supporter yourself.

the actual Jama story, such as the professional profile of the witnesses, reminds of Brecht, as popularly perceived in the 1970s, notwithstanding Brecht being far from a humanitarian).[106] A software architectural schema as designed was presented in Nissan and Dragoni (2000). The schema is redrawn in Fig. 5.2.20.3.1.

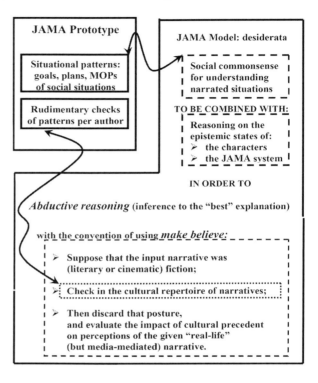

Fig. 5.2.20.3.1 The architecture of JAMA, and unimplemented desiderata

---

[106] Bertolt Brecht's ethics is illustrarted by the following. Brecht's *The Measures Taken,* a play from 1930, offered a Marxist-Leninist precept of departing from conventional moral (and even from an immediate, superficial understanding of Marx's alternative to the "bourgeois" sense of good and evil: [Marxian] good is whatever brings about the dictatorship of the proletariat, and [Marxian] evil is whatever obstacles it). In the play, revolutionaries who came to China in order to stir up a revolution kill one of their own, who out of compassion repeatedly helped the poor, for all to see. Their rationale is that his behaviour would have caused them to be detected. In *The Measures Taken* (which Arthur Koestler, who first was a Zionist at a socialist commune in the Galilee, then a fashionable reporter for the Western media, then a Communist in the Soviet Union, and finally an anti-Communist, called the most revealing work of communist art), three members of the underground cell kill and eat their fourth comrade, to avoid starving, then justify this to their superior. "Through his actions, the man had weakened their position by committing four crimes: pity, loyalty, dignity and righteous indignation, all violations of the true communist's code. The superior endorses the murder: 'He who fights for communism has of all the virtues only one: that he fights for communism.' The chorus in the play, speaking for Brecht, intones: 'Sink into the mud, embrace the butcher, but change the world: It needs it.' For the future freedom of mankind, they eliminated their colleague's freedom and his life as well." The wording is that of Toronto author, journalist, broadcaster, and editor Robert Fulford (2005).

5.2.20.4 Episodic Similarities vs. Character Similarities

It is important to realise the difference between situational similarities between patterns of social behaviour (such as the ones captured in MOPs or the ones captured in TAUs in Dyer's BORIS program: see Section 5.2.9 above), and similarity between how events unfolded in what could be expected to be a fairly peculiar manner in a particular episode (this is something that in BORIS is represented in its *episodic memory* for each given narrative it analyses). Coincidences do happen, so that episodic similarity would result even for peculiar sequences of events. Or then, there may be correlates, yet not such strong correlates as the one that enable you to capture service at restaurants in a MOP for restaurants.

It is also important to realise the difference between

- the JAMA model seeking similarities of a narrative from the news to either collective memory in a given society, or in its pool of prominent items in its literary or theatrical or cinematic shared legacy, as being part of the cultural heritage,
- and on the other hand, the situation of seeking similarities between given individuals from real life and characters in a piece of fiction, with the latter characters possibly drawing inspiration from the former persons.

A distinction is to be made between a given person typifying some feature, and a given person as a source of inspiration of some fictional character. William Amos is the author of *The Originals: Who's Really Who in Fiction* (Amos, 1985). This peculiar dictionary of literary characters pinpoints and explains the supposed identity of the persons from real life who are assumed to have inspired a given character in a work of fiction. In the introduction, Amos remarks (ibid., pp. xiii–xv):

> Tolstoy's use of relatives as models was obvious to his family, yet he noted how sorry he would be should anyone think he intended to depict any real person. In denying his use of Leigh Hunt as 'Harold Skimpole', Dickens added deviousness to duplicity, privately revelling in his portrait's accuracy, publicly disavowing all resemblance and averting his victim's wrath by publishing favourable profiles elsewhere. Maugham denied basing a character on Hugh Walpole, only to admit the identification once his model was dead. [...] If unadorned, drawn-from-life portrayal succeeds only with walking-on parts, and models for major characters are transformed into the author's own creation after the first couple of paragraphs, are originals really necessary? Listen long enough to writers and you might conclude that their models are inconsequential to the point of irrelevance. Certainly, the readers' guessing games which originals inspire are for authors a great irritant. For Proust, they were particularly vexing. His habit of combining several people's traits in a single character meant that as many as half-a-dozen different identifications could be partially correct, but none could be entirely right [...]. Balzac complained of the impertinence of more than seventy women who claimed to be his 'Foedora'. [...] In 1910 a libel action established that where there was evidence that some people might reasonably believe a plaintiff was the person referred to, it was immaterial that the writer never intended to refer to him. The minefield thus created for authors has prompted Graham Greene to recall a firm of solicitors who in the 1930s specialised in cross-checking characters' names with entries in the London telephone directory. The rarer the name, the greater the risk [...]. Happily, these hazards have been reduced by the [England and Wales] Defamation Act of 1952. No longer can the innocent novelist be so easily convicted of libelling a person unknown to him; but publishers must establish

either that the words were not defamatory or that no reference to the plaintiff was intended and no circumstances were known by which he or she might be thought to be referred to. They are also required to withdraw offending material [...].

Around 1990, coming out of a classroom, a professor of literary studies at Bar-Ilan University (Israel) found me waiting for him outside, and after we greeted each other, he told me: "Do you know? Amos Oz has used your name, *Ephraim Nissan*, for the protagonist of his latest novel". "I wasn't aware of that. I hope he didn't traduce me". "Oh, no! That character is sort of half-a-Messiah". "I need that like a hole in the head". "Who reads those novels anyway?"

Unfortunately, however, later on a newspaper supplement carried a *précis* of the novel, naming the protagonist and describing his awkwardness. By chance, novelist Oz was academically affiliated with the university (and campus) where I had previously earned a PhD in computer science, but I wasn't acquainted with him. There are five or six men with the same first name, 'Ephraim', and family name, 'Nissan', in the country's electoral lists. This is an example of similarities of characters confined to homonymy, but in his getting the name there may have been a causal link (namely, that the novelist came across my name in writing and he liked the sound, or that he overheard it at the cafeteria on campus).

5.2.21 *Mathematical Logic and Crime Stories from CSI: Crime Scene Investigation^{TM}: Löwe, Pacuit and Saraf's Representation, Building Blocks, and Algorithm*

A mathematical representation of stories has been devised by logician Benedikt Löwe of the Institute for Logic, Language and Computation of the University of Amsterdam, the Department of Mathematics of the University of Hamburg, and the Institute of Mathematics of the University of Bonn, along with Eric Pacuit from the Department of Computer Science of Stanford University, and eventually also Sanchit Saraf, from the Department of Mathematics and Statistics, Indian Institute of Technology, Kanpur. Löwe made an important statement about the way his ideas about narratives developed, in an email of 24 September 2009 sent from New York to Yuri Gurevich with copies to Eric Pacuit of the Department of Philosophy of the University of Stanford, Andreas Blass at the University of Michigan, computer scientist Nachum Dershowitz at the University of Tel-Aviv, and Rohit Parikh at the City University of New York, a text that has further circulated:

> there have been two completely disjoint entry points into the area of formalization of stories: One of them was my interest in dynamic logic and the ideas to represent stories as models of dynamic epistemic logic (or more general logics). This was prompted by discussions with Andres Perea at LOFT 2004, and then developed eventually (via various intermediate steps) into the paper published in the *Australasian Journal of Logic* with Eric [Pacuit. This is the paper Löwe & Pacuit (2008)]. The other one was my work on 'practice-based philosophy of mathematics' and my strong belief that the formalization of proofs in whatever proof system is not the real story about what these proofs are. I was intrigued by an idea of Robert Thomas who stressed the similarity between proofs and narratives. In the end, Thomas gave

5.2 An Overview of Artificial Intelligence Approaches to Narratives

up this idea (I talked to him about this in Hatfield last July [2009] at a conference about mathematical proof), but I had this feeling that if you understand proofs as narratives *and* you have a formal means to characterize the structure of narratives, this might give some approximation of our notion of identity of proofs. However, we got stuck in the "a formal means to characterize the structure of narratives" part – this seems to be much more complicated than we originally thought, and decades of research in narratology do not seem to help much.

Löwe and Pacuit (2008) begin by pointing out that the process by which logic and artificial intelligence had grown apart was being reversed fin recent years: "logic overcame its traditional focus and started to study phenomena of interaction and interactive reasoning. This is best represented in the research area called *Logic and Games* in which logicians used dynamic techniques in order to study behaviour in game and communication situations and in what Parikh calls *Social Software*[107] [Parikh (2002)].[108] These new developments allowed logicians to provide theoretical insight in the general project of understanding reasoning processes in multi-agent situations." (ibid., p. 163). "One particular interesting encounter between logic and game theory is the use of belief revision techniques in the sense of [Gärdenfors

---

[107] This is not to be confused for computer software used for social interaction. Here is a definition from the Wikipedia entry for "Social software (social procedure)": "In philosophy and the social sciences, *social software* is an interdisciplinary research program that borrows mathematical tools and techniques from game theory and computer science in order to analyze and design social procedures. The goals of research in this field are modeling social situations, developing theories of correctness, and designing social procedures. Work under the term social software has been going on since about 1996, and conferences in Copenhagen, London, Utrecht and New York, have been partly or wholly devoted to it. Much of the work is carried out at the City University of New York under the leadership of Rohit Jivanlal Parikh, who was influential in the development of the field." Social procedures are analysed, and they are examined for fairness, appropriateness, correctness, and efficiency.

The same Wikipedia entry explains: "For example, an election procedure could be a simple majority vote, Borda count, a Single Transferable vote (STV), or Approval voting. All of these procedures can be examined for various properties like monotonicity. Monotonicity has the property that voting for a candidate should not harm that candidate. This may seem obvious, true under any system, but it is something which can happen in STV. Another question would be the ability to elect a Condorcet winner in case there is one. Other principles which are considered by researchers in social software include the concept that a procedure for fair division should be Pareto optimal, equitable and envy free. A procedure for auctions should be one which would encourage bidders to bid their actual valuation – a property which holds with the Vickrey auction. What is new in social software compared to older fields is the use of tools from computer science like program logic, analysis of algorithms and epistemic logic. Like programs, social procedures dovetail into each other. For instance an airport provides runways for planes to land, but it also provides security checks, and it must provide for ways in which buses and taxis can take arriving passengers to their local destinations. The entire mechanism can be analyzed in the way in which a complex computer program can be analyzed. The Banach-Knaster procedure for dividing a cake fairly, or the Brams and Taylor procedure for fair division have been analyzed in this way. To point to the need for epistemic logic, a building not only needs restrooms, for obvious reasons, it also needs signs indicating where they are. Thus epistemic considerations enter in addition to structural ones. For a more urgent example, in addition to medicines, physicians also need tests to indicate what a patient's problem is."

[108] Cf. Pacuit and Parikh (2007), Pacuit (2005), Parikh (2001), Pacuit, Parikh, and Cogan (2006).

(1992)] as a means of analysis of games. The game-theoretic analysis of rationality and the study of belief revision have in common that they have a normative hue; they are concerned with questions of what constitutes rational behaviour and what would be quality measures for rationality." (ibid.). Löwe and Pacuit (2008) however take a different route (ibid., p. 163):

> we develop a formal and abstract framework that allows us to reason about behaviour in games with mistaken and changing beliefs leaving aside normative questions concerning whether the agents are behaving "rationally"; we focus on what the agents *do* in a game. In this paper, we are not concerned with the reasoning process of the (ideal) economic agent; rather, our intended application is *artificial* agents, e.g., autonomous agents interacting with a human user or with each other as part of a computer game or in a virtual world. Arguably, when such agents interact, the underlying epistemic and rationality assumptions are much less important than the *actual* reasoning process used by the agents.

Löwe and Pacuit (2008) gave a story of mistaken beliefs ("in the style of a TV drama"): "The reader can imagine that this is the outline of a script. The reasoning processes referred to in the story can be made visible to the audience by monologues (Walter talking to himself in his car) or by conversations with some *confidant* or *confidante*." (ibid., p. 164). Then they proceeded to give the definitions for their formal system and how to use this setting to get a *backward induction solution*.[109] Next, they applied their semantics to the story of the example, and analysed it.

Löwe, Pacuit, and Saraf (2008) use "a simple algorithm for analyzing stories in terms of belief states" that had been developed in Löwe and Pacuit (2008), "to analyse actual stories from a commercial TV crime series, and identify a small number of building blocks sufficient to construct the doxastic game structure of these stories." (Löwe, et al., 2008, abstract). The TV crime series is *CSI: Crime Scene Investigation*™. They explained (ibid., Introduction):

> Whereas in [Löwe & Pacuit (2008, sec. 4)], the algorithm was used to fully analyze a fictitious story about love and deceit, in this paper, we focus on actual stories commercially produced for television broadcasting in this paper. In a descriptive-empirical approach we

---

[109] Here is a definition (http://en.wikipedia.org/wiki/Backward_induction): "*Backward induction* is the process of reasoning backwards in time, from the end of a problem or situation, to determine a sequence of optimal actions. It proceeds by first considering the last time a decision might be made and choosing what to do in any situation at that time. Using this information, one can then determine what to do at the second-to-last time of decision. This process continues backwards until one has determined the best action for every possible situation (i.e. for every possible information set) at every point in time. In the mathematical optimization method of dynamic programming, backward induction is one of the main methods for solving the Bellman equation. In game theory, backward induction is a method used to compute subgame perfect equilibria in sequential games. The only difference is that optimization involves just one decision maker, who chooses what do at each point of time, whereas game theory analyzes how the decisions of several players interact. That is, by anticipating what the last player will do in each situation, it is possible to determine what the second-to-last player will do, and so on. Backward induction has been used to solve games as long as the field of game theory has existed. John [von] Neumann and Oskar Morgenstern suggested solving zero-sum, two-person games by backward induction in their *Theory of Games and Economic Behavior* (1953), the book which established game theory as a field of study."

5.2 An Overview of Artificial Intelligence Approaches to Narratives

investigate their common structural properties based on a formalization in our system. The doxastic tree structures associated to the stories allow natural definitions of formal properties and complexity that can be further used to classify story types. The results of this paper show that from a large number of possible formal structures, commercial crime stories only use a very small number of doxastically simple[110] basic building blocks ([as shown in Löwe et al. (2008, section 2.4)]).

As opposed to Löwe and Pacuit (2008), in Löwe et al. (2008) *event nodes* were explicitly used. These are "nodes in which none of the agents makes a decision, but instead an event happens. Structurally, these nodes do not differ from the standard *action nodes*, but beliefs about events are theoretically on a lower level (of theory of mind) than beliefs about beliefs." (ibid., section 2.1).

To reconstruct the stories, the need for eight building blocks was identified (ibid., section 2.4). "The trivial building blocks are just events or actions that happen with no reasoning at all": these are called "doxastic blocks of level -1. We denote them by Ev if it is an event, and by Act(**P**) if it is an action by player **P**. Typical examples are random events or actions where agents just follow their whim without deliberation." (ibid.) But "being represented by a building block of level -1 does not mean that the *discourse* of the story shows no deliberation: in fact, even in our investigated stories we find examples of agents discussing whether they should follow their beliefs (i.e., perform a higher level action) or not, and finally decide to perform the action without taking their beliefs into account. These would still be formalized as blocks of level -1." (ibid.).

In the *tree diagrams* showing *building blocks*, a pair of adjacent squares indicates whose move in the game it is. The move could be of either a player, or an event. Refer to Fig. 5.2.21.1. If **X** is an event, i.e., if **X**=**E**, then this is the building block of an event, Ev, but if **X** is a player, then the diagram represents Act(**X**), i.e., action by player **X**.

If in a tree diagram there are more than one pair of adjacent squares, each pair of adjacent squares indicates whose move in the game it is. Sometimes the move is that of an event, rather than of a player, and then the node is an event node rather than an action node. Players symbols are indicated in boldface. Agents are assumed to be introspective, in the sense that agents are aware of their preferences and iterations thereof.

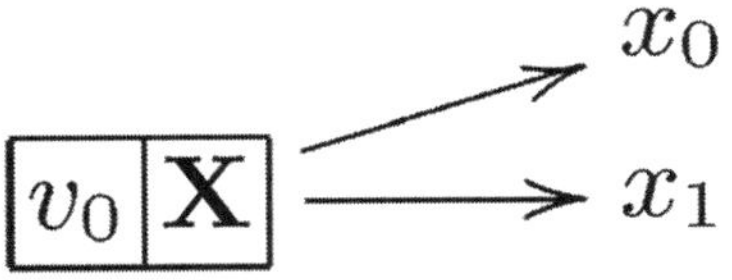

Fig. 5.2.21.1 A tree diagram and a formula of either an event (if **X** is an event), or a player's action (if **X** is a player), according to Löwe et al. (2008, section 2.4)

$$S(v_0, \varnothing)(\mathbf{X}) = (x_1, x_0)$$

---

[110] "Doxastically simple" means simple, as far as belief is concerned. The context is that of the logics of belief.

T is the game tree, and t_i is a terminal node of that tree; v_i is a nonterminal node of the tree. S is a state, and it is followed by a parenthesis containing two arguments (a node, and a list containing nil, or one player, or two players), and then another parenthesis containing a player. This is followed by an equal sign, followed by an ordering of nodes. If one of the nodes is nonterminal, is means that what precedes it is preferred over every outcome of that nonterminal, and that every outcome of that nonterminal is preferred over everything that follows the nonterminal.

There is a way to represent a situation the way it objectively is in reality: $S(t, \emptyset)$ is the *true state of affairs* at position t. For state S, the S-true preference of player **P** at position t is the ordering that equals $S(t, \emptyset)(\mathbf{P})$. For example, $S(v_0, \emptyset)(\mathbf{P}) = (t_1, t_0)$ means that the S-true preference of **P** at nonterminal node v_0 is equal to the ordering by which terminal node t_1 is preferred over terminal node t_0.

$S(t, \mathbf{P})$ stands for player **P**'s belief at position t. Moreover, the following notation is used in order to express *nested beliefs,* i.e., the belief of a player about the belif of another player. If **A** and **B** are players and there is a state description $S(t, \mathbf{B})$, then $S(t, \mathbf{AB})$ stands for **A**'s belief about $S(t, \mathbf{B})$.

"The next level of basic building blocks are those that have reasoning based on beliefs, but not require any theory of mind at all, i.e., building blocks of level 0. The two fundamental building blocks here are *expected event* (ExEv(**P**)) and *unexpected event* (UnEv(**P**))" (ibid., section 2.4). Refer to Fig. 5.2.21.2.

The same tree diagram represents either an expected event, whose formula is:

$$\text{ExEv}(\mathbf{P}): \quad S(v_0, \emptyset)(\mathbf{P}) = (t_1, t_0);$$
$$S(v_0, \mathbf{P})(\mathbf{E}) = (t_1, x);$$
$$S(v_1, \emptyset)(\mathbf{E}) = (t_1, x)$$

or otherwise an unexpected event, whose formula is:

$$\text{UnEv}(\mathbf{P}): \quad S(v_0, \emptyset)(\mathbf{P}) = (t_1, t_0);$$
$$S(v_0, \mathbf{P})(\mathbf{E}) = (t_1, x);$$
$$S(v_1, \emptyset)(\mathbf{E}) = (x, t_1)$$

This is read as follows: "Moving beyond zeroth order theory of mind, we now proceed to building blocks that require beliefs about beliefs. There are two such building blocks used in our stories, *Unexpected Action* (UnAc(**P,Q**)) and *Collaboration gone wrong* (CoGW(**P,Q**))" (ibid.). See the tree diagram of an unexpected action in Fig. 5.2.21.3. The formula corresponding to an unexpected action is:

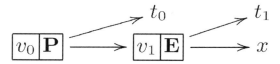

Fig. 5.2.21.2 The tree diagram of either an expected event or an unexpected event, depending on the accompanying formula (Löwe et al., 2008, section 2.4)

Fig. 5.2.21.3 The tree diagram of an unexpected action (Löwe et al., 2008, section 2.4)

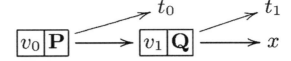

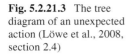

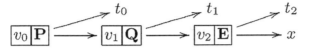

Fig. 5.2.21.4 The tree diagram of collaboration gone wrong (Löwe et al., 2008, section 2.4)

$$\text{UnAc}(\mathbf{P},\mathbf{Q}): \quad S(v_0, \emptyset)(\mathbf{P}) = (t_1, t_0);$$
$$S(v_0, \mathbf{P})(\mathbf{Q}) = (t_1, x);$$
$$S(v_1, \emptyset)(\mathbf{Q}) = (t_1, x)$$

"There is an obvious analogue of ExEv(**P**) at this level that would be called *Expected Action*" (ibid.). By contrast, Fig. 5.2.21.4 shows the tree diagram of collaboration gone wrong, and its corresponding formula is:

$$\text{CoGW}(\mathbf{P},\mathbf{Q}): \quad S(v_0, \emptyset)(\mathbf{P}) = (t_1, t_0);$$
$$S(v_0, \mathbf{P})(\mathbf{Q}) = (t_2, t_1);$$
$$S(v_1, \emptyset)(\mathbf{Q}) = (t_2, t_1);$$
$$S(v_0, \mathbf{P})(\mathbf{E}) = (t_2, x);$$
$$S(v_0, \mathbf{PQ})(\mathbf{E}) = (t_2, x);$$
$$S(v_1, \mathbf{Q})(\mathbf{E}) = (t_2, x);$$
$$S(v_2, \emptyset)(\mathbf{E}) = (x, t_2)$$

"Finally, we move to the building blocks that use second order beliefs. In our stories, there are only three such building blocks. One of them (in the story *The corrupt judge*) is slightly more complicated due to a component of incomplete information in the story" (ibid.). "The other two building blocks are *Betrayal* (Betr(**P,Q**)) and *Unsuccessful Collaboration with a Third* (UnCT(**P,Q,R**))" (ibid.). Figure 5.2.21.5 shows the tree diagram of betrayal, and its corresponding formula is:

$$\text{Betr}(\mathbf{P},\mathbf{Q}): \quad S(v_0, \emptyset)(\mathbf{P}) = (x, t_0);$$
$$S(v_0, \mathbf{P})(\mathbf{Q}) = (t_2, t_1);$$
$$S(v_1, \emptyset)(\mathbf{Q}) = (t_2, t_1);$$
$$S(v_0, \mathbf{PQ})(\mathbf{P}) = (t_2, x);$$
$$S(v_1, \mathbf{Q})(\mathbf{P}) = (t_2, x);$$
$$S(v_2, \emptyset)(\mathbf{P}) = (x, t_2)$$

By contrast, Fig. 5.2.21.6 shows the diagram of unsuccessful collaboration with a third – "Again, as with UnAc(**P,Q**) and UnEv(**P**) = UnAc(**P,E**), we see that

Fig. 5.2.21.5 The tree diagram of betrayal (Löwe et al., 2008, section 2.4)

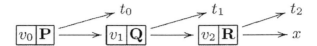

Fig. 5.2.21.6 The tree diagram of unsuccessful collaboration with a third (Löwe et al., 2008, section 2.4). Each pair of adjacent squares indicates whose move in the game it is: it's **P**'s move at nonterminal node v_0 and it's **Q**'s move at nonterminal node v_1 and it's **R**'s move at nonterminal node v_2

Collaboration gone wrong is the special case of *Unsuccessful Collaboration with a Third* where the 'third' is an event." (ibid.) – and we can see that much indeed from the formula of unsuccessful collaboration with a third; the formula is:

$$\begin{aligned}
\mathsf{UnCT}(\mathbf{P},\mathbf{Q},\mathbf{R}): \quad & S(v_0, \emptyset)(\mathbf{P}) = (t_2, t_0); \\
& S(v_0, \mathbf{P})(\mathbf{Q}) = (t_2, t_1); \\
& S(v_1, \emptyset)(\mathbf{Q}) = (t_2, t_1); \\
& S(v_0, \mathbf{P})(\mathbf{R}) = (t_2, x); \\
& S(v_0, \mathbf{PQ})(\mathbf{R}) = (t_2, x); \\
& S(v_1, \mathbf{Q})(\mathbf{R}) = (t_2, x); \\
& S(v_2, \emptyset)(\mathbf{R}) = (x, t_2)
\end{aligned}$$

"These building blocks can be stacked." (ibid.). It must be said that this kind of approach with building blocks bears a strong resemblance to structural narratology as initiated by Vladimir Propp in the Soviet Union in the late 1920s (Propp, 1928), and which become popular among scholars in English speaking countries in the late 1950s. What is novel in Löwe and Pacuit's formalism is the sound and elegant mathematics, complementing the idea of building blocks. They combined their application to games of logic, with lessons drawn from the state of the art of structuralist narratology. They actually pay much attention to the distinction between the formal structure of a story (this component is called *story* in narratology) and its presentation (in narratology, this component is called *discourse*).[111]

Löwe et al. (2008) analysed ten stories. "Half of our stories involves basic building blocks of at most level 1." (ibid., section 4). Figure 5.2.21.7 shows the tree diagram by whose means Löwe et al. (2008, appendix) formalised the story *Faked*

---

[111] Löwe, Pacuit and Saraf (2008) even go to the extent of pointing out that in narratology, the *story* is called *histoire* in French and фабула (*fabula*) in Russian, whereas the *discourse* is called *récit* (or sometimes *discours*) in French and сюжет (*syužet*) in Russian. This is useful, as those other terms are also used sometimes in other languages.

5.2 An Overview of Artificial Intelligence Approaches to Narratives

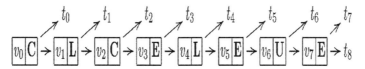

Fig. 5.2.21.7 The tree diagram given in Löwe et al. (2008) for episode 3 of the story *Faked Kidnapping*, where the agents are Chip Rundle, C, Laura Garris, L, and the CSI unit, U

Kidnapping, which is one of the stories only involving basic building blocks of the simpler kinds. This story was formalised as

Betr(C,L); UnEv(C); UnEv(L); Act(U); Ev

That is to say, betrayal occurs between Chip Rundle and Laura Garris, then an unexpected event affects each of them, the CSI unit intervenes, and then there is an event.

The formula of that same story as given by Löwe et al. (2008, appendix) is as follows:

$S(v_0, \emptyset)(\mathbf{C}) = (t_3, t_2, t_0, t_1); S(v_2, \emptyset)(\mathbf{C}) = (t_3, t_2); S(v_2, \mathbf{C})(\mathbf{E}) = (t_3, v_4);$
$S(v_0, \mathbf{C})(\mathbf{L}) = (t_2, t_1, v_3); S(v_0, \mathbf{CL})(\mathbf{C}) = (t_2, v_3); S(v_1, \mathbf{L})(\mathbf{C}) = (t_2, v_3);$
$S(v_2, \emptyset)(\mathbf{L}) = (t_2, t_1, v_3); S(v_3, \emptyset)(\mathbf{E}) = (v_4, t_3);$
$S(v_1, \emptyset)(\mathbf{L}) = (t_5, v_6); S(v_4, \emptyset)(\mathbf{L}) = (t_5, t_4); S(v_5, \emptyset)(\mathbf{E}) = (v_6, t_5);$
$S(v_6, \emptyset)(\mathbf{U}) = (v_7, t_6); S(v_7, \emptyset)(\mathbf{E}) = (v_7, t_8)$

Löwe et al. (2008, section 3.4) recognise that "the narrative sometimes does not allow us to uncontroversially choose the formalization. The dual problem to this is that the *discourse* is often much richer than the structure necessitates. In particular, there is information that may not be relevant, but could be included in the story." Moreover, they recognise (ibid., section 2.3) that "in actual stories (as opposed to stories invented for the purpose of formalization [...]), we cannot expect to have full states. Instead, we'll have some information about players' preferences and beliefs that is enough to run the algorithm described in § 2.2." Löwe et al. (2008, section 3.2) proposed to mimic imperfect or incomplete information by event games.

In order to exemplify this, they proposed this narrative: "Detective Miller thinks that Jeff is Anne's murderer while, in fact, it is Peter. Miller believes that Jeff will show up during the night in Anne's apartment to destroy evidence and thus hides behind a shower curtain to surprise Jeff. However, Peter shows up to destroy the evidence, and is arrested." They conceded that one could opt to formalise as an imperfect or incomplete information game, from game theory. They nevertheless preferred to formalise that story by resorting to an event node $v2$ representing "Peter turns out to be the murderer", as shown in the tree diagram of Fig. 5.2.21.8. Also refer to the accompanying key list (Table 5.2.21.1) and to the formula (Table 5.2.21.2).

Fig. 5.2.21.8 The detective thinks the wrong person is the murderer, but then catches the right one (Löwe et al. 2008, section 3.2). A key list appears in Table 5.2.21.1

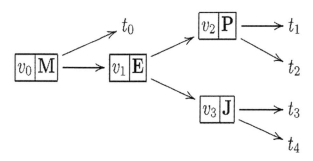

Table 5.2.21.1 Key list for Fig. 5.2.21.8

M	Detective Miller
J	Jeff
P	Peter
v_1	"Peter turns out to be Anne's murderer".
t_1	"Jeff is the murderer, returns to the apartment and is caught".
t_2	"Jeff is the murderer and does not return to the apartment".
t_3	"Peter is the murderer, returns to the apartment and is caught".
t_4	"Peter is the murderer and does not return to the apartment".

Table 5.2.21.2 Formula for Fig. 5.2.21.8

$S(v_0, \mathbf{M})(\mathbf{E}) = (v_3, v_2)$	Miller believes that Jeff will turn out to be the murderer.
$S(v_3, \mathbf{M})(\mathbf{J}) = t_3;$ $S(v_1, \emptyset)(\mathbf{E}) = (v_2, v_3)$	Peter is the actual murderer.
$S(v_2, \emptyset)(\mathbf{P}) = (t_1, t_2)$	Peter in fact plans to return to the apartment.

Concerning the adequacy of the representation of that story, Löwe et al. claim (2008, section 3.2):

> While this structure adequately describes the motivation of Miller and his surprise about catching someone who was not the suspect, it is unable to motivate why Peter chooses to go to the apartment. However, we found that for the chosen stories from the series *CSI: Crime Scene Investigation*™, the impact on the adequacy of our formalizations was relatively minor. One of the reasons is that "strictly go by the evidence" is one of the often repeated creeds of the CSI members, prohibiting the actors from letting beliefs influence their actions.

And in a footnote: "A consequence of this is also that the investigators play only a minor rôle in our formalizations, often occurring in event nodes, and rarely making any decisions."

We rephrase discursively the algorithm from Löwe et al. (2008, section 2), and renounce here the considerably more formal setting and symbolism of their original definitions and discussion. The assumption is that the players will follow the *backward induction solution*. Then it is possible to analyse the game (which here is a story), and predict its outcome, once we are given a tuple comprising four elements:

5.2 An Overview of Artificial Intelligence Approaches to Narratives

a finite set of players, the tree (being a finite set of nodes and the edges relating them), a moving function (i.e., whose move it is, at every node of the tree), and the set of states.

In order to carry out the analysis, a set of labellings is constructed, from the tree to the set of its terminal nodes. That labelling represents the subjective belief, relative to the set of player symbols, of the outcome of the game if it has reached the node t. For example (here, we are modifying the original notation from the paper), let us notate labels as $\mathsf{label}_{\mathsf{state}}(\mathsf{node})$. If the *subjective labelling* which we notate as $\mathsf{label}_{\mathsf{state}(\mathbf{A})}(\mathsf{t})$ is equal to t_k where t_k belongs to the set of terminal nodes of the tree, then player **A** believes that if the game reaches t, the eventual outcome is t_k.

The labelling algorithm is as follows. If t is a terminal node, then assign t as value to label_W for all states W. "In order to calculate the label of a node t controlled by player **P**, we need the **P**-subjective labels of all of its successors." (ibid.). Said otherwise: if t is a node of the tree, and it is **P**'s move at node t, and we fix a state W, then we can define label_W as follows: find the W-true preference of player **P**, that is, the ordering that equals $W(t, \phi)(\mathbf{P})$. The consider the labels $\mathsf{label}_{W(\mathbf{P})}(t')$ for all such nodes t' that belong to the set of immediate successors of t in the tree, and pick that node which is the maximal of these,[112] say, t^*. Then assign t^* as value to $\mathsf{label}_W(t)$.

This procedure has to be carried out until all *subjective labellings* are carried out, it is possible to compute the true run of the game. That is to say, the true run can be read off recursively. Remember that the subjective labellings are terminal nodes, and if the node is, say, t_k then player **A** believes that if the game reaches t, the eventual outcome is t_k. As the subjective labellings are terminal nodes, then for state S and for each t such that the moving function is $\mu(t) = \mathbf{P}$ (that is to say: the move is of player **P**, at position t), there is a unique node t' that belongs to the set of immediate successors of t in the tree, such that

$$\mathsf{label}_{S(\mathbf{P})}(t') = \mathsf{label}_S(t)$$

In order to compute the true run of the game (i.e., of the story), start from the root of the tree, and then take at each step the unique successor determined by $\mathsf{label}_S(t)$ until you reach a terminal node. (Of course, in a tree there is only one path between every two nodes of the tree.)

5.2.22 Other Approaches

Ontologies are a technology that has received much attention during the 2000s (we devote to it Section 6.1.7.3 below). Ontologies are playing an increasing role in

---

[112] For example, in the ordering $S(v_0, \emptyset)(\mathbf{C}) = (t_3, t_2, t_0, t_1)$, which is the first state description in the formula for the story *Faked Kidnapping* we had considered, the maximal node is t_3 because it precedes all other nodes listed.

story-generation programs. We have omitted treatment of such ontology-based tools in the present overview, but some such projects from the 2000s that are not mentioned here are surveyed in Dov Winer's (in press) 'Review of Ontology Based Storytelling Devices'. At any rate, the resurgence during the 2000s of automated narrative processing, after the "AI winter" of the 1990s – when artificial intelligence shied away from open-textured problems like those which that story-processors of the late 1970s and of the 1980s had tried to tackle – has especially affected story-generation software, rather than story-understanding tools. This is in relation to the development of computer games having conspicuously entered the computer science academic curriculum during the 2000s.

Note moreover that formalisms for communication and for representing narratives keep emerging. We are not going to delve here into the so-called "Leibnizian spatio-temporal representation" proposed by Katai, Kawakami, Shiose, and Notsu (2010), but it is worthwhile to signal it. By contrast to Newton's view that space and time are independent, Leibniz defined them as referring to each other, and this view is combined by Katai et al. (2010) with C. S. Peirce's existential graphs, as well as with *occurrence nets,* the latter being a variant of *Petri nets,* a widespread formalism for temporal organisation. This representational framework is applied to communication between characters within the plot of a particular play.

In the next section, Section 5.3, we are going to turn to *episodic formulae,* a formalism introduced by myself in the early 2000s. It is a method of capturing various facets of a narrative plot, and is partly indebted to the conceptual dependency theory from the late 1970s and 1980s.

5.3 Episodic Formulae

5.3.1 Instances of a Method of Representation for Narratives and Legal Narratives

Like oftentimes with information technology, shallower processing may yield practical tools, whereas the ambition of in-depth analysis may have for the time being confine itself to theoretical work done on paper. This applies, for example, to whether we can expect AI tools for supporting legal evidence to capture in depth a legal narrative. See Fig. 5.3.1.1.

In Section 5.2 I provided an overview of computational representation and processing of narratives. The technique presented in the present Section 5.3, instead, is for the time being intended for manual analysis, even though it will hopefully be eventually become a representation translatable into a lower-level representation that can be run on the computer. It owes a debt to the conceptual-dependency school (Schank, 1972), which we have considered in Section 5.2.8, and which between the mid-1970s and mid-1980s used to be based at the University of Yale (e.g., Schank & Riesbeck, 1981). Actually, one of the examples of the BORIS computer tool

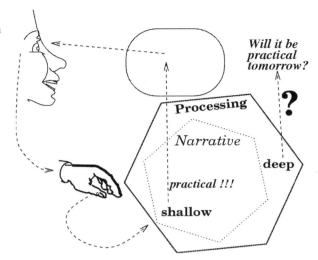

Fig. 5.3.1.1 Practical concerns, versus the ambition of deeper models

answering questions after parsing and making sense of multi-paragraph text, was (as we have seen in Section 5.2.9) about a man who goes home with a friend, and discovers his wife in flagrant adultery; the friend who happens to be the eyewitness happens to be what according to previous plans would have had to be the lawyer representing him (Dyer, 1983a).

This section is concerned with a particular method that has been applied to several narratives, including legal narratives and identification evidence. I developed a notation in formulae for capturing various kinds of elements of a narrative. By means of such *episodic formulae,* notions which can be represented include beliefs, perceptions, communication, testimony, intentionality, purposeful action, identity, taking roles, physical possession, ownership, and other such concepts. Several of the narratives to which the method was applied were especially concerned with individual (or sometimes, kind-) identity and identification. Whereas the context mostly was the application of AI to law, with particular attention to evidence, nevertheless the sample narratives in a few of the resulting publications were from literary texts:

- the plot of the play *Henry IV* by Pirandello (Nissan, 2002b), in which identity relations are quite complex: a modern man having fallen off a horse at a historical pageant, comes to believe he is a medieval emperor (always at the age of 26, around the time he humiliated himself at Canossa), and about twenty years afterwards, having recovered his sanity, yet still posturing as the emperor, he provokes and kills his former rival in love, whom he suspects of having caused his accident;
- the play *L'Ile des esclaves* (*Slave Island*) by Marivaux, where a central notion is usurped identity: two couples, the former masters, the other lone their servants, are shipwrecked, and the judicial authority on the island on whose shores they landed decree that they must switch their identities, and therefore their

social status. Nissan (2003a) sets this situation into formulae, and also develops a classification of situations of false personation, including from the legal viewpoint;
- from a Middle English romance about Alexander the Great, who is recognised by Queen Candace in India notwithstanding his assumed identity. Nissan (2003b) developed for this a formalism, which includes the notions of action, enlisting support, assumed identity, counterdeception, and recognition based on visual evidence from a portrait.

For one of the narratives analysed (Nissan et al., 2004), the context was the analysis of policy-making within the *WaterTime* project, and the application was to a narrative about the privatisation of a city water system, and its eventual remunicipalisation in the wake of proven corruption on the part of a mayor. Among the other things, such concepts as *privatisation* and *graft* were set into formulae, and for comparison purposes, so was the concept *tax-farming* (a king of old who having received payment from a private individual, would grant the exploitation of resources in some region in the form of privatised tax collection or taxation, was by this very act not violating the law, unlike some modern administrator who concludes a corrupt contract).

Nissan (2001d) applied the same formal method for representing competing claims of identification in the so-called "Smemorato di Collegno" amnesia case, which divided Italian public opinion in two camps during the late 1920s. The same man was claimed by two different women, each claiming he was her husband. Nissan (2003d) develops an analysis in formulae for two cases:

- the feveroles case: of litigation in England after a firm, who had received an order for feveroles, inquired with its own supplier about what *feveroles* means, and having been told they are horsebeans, ordered and was supplied with horsebeans, only to discover it was misled, because it was supplied with feves, and horsebeans can be feves, fevettes, or feveroles, the latter being the most costly kind;
- the Cardiff Giant case: a hoax in New York State, from around 1870. The Cardiff Giant was an alleged petrified antediluvian man, whose alleged discovery was made public in October 1869. It had actually been carved on the initiative of George Hull, a cigar-maker, who sold shares of the Giant property to three Syracuse businessmen. The syndicate displayed the Giant, and Hull refused an offer to purchase or rent it, made by Phineas Taylor Barnum (1810–1891), who is currently especially known in connection with the circus that he eventually established in 1871. Barnum had a copy of the Giant made, and then exhibited it, claiming it was the original, bought from Hull's investors, and that by then these were exhibiting a copy. In December 1869, both "giants" were being exhibited in New York City. The Hull-led syndicate sued Barnum for calling his copy "genuine" and their original a "fake". Under oath, on February 2, 1870, Hull revealed his original hoax. The court ruled that Barnum could not be sued for calling the Cardiff Giant a fraud when it actually was a fraud, and the case was dismissed.

5.3 Episodic Formulae

Nissan (2003c) proposes a formal representation (which I reworked into Section 5.3.3 below) for the controversy concerning the Meinertzhagen bird collection, about which some claimed (with a forensic test apparently confirming this) that at least one specimen had been restuffed and relabelled. Such a situation makes for interesting formulae. Nissan (2007b), about the MURAD subproject of the AURANGZEB project (itself part of the PLOTINUS umbrella project, a sequel to the earlier analyses), analyses a historical episode from a war of succession in northern India during the 1650s.

The eventual winner of that war, Aurangzeb, deceives Murad, who is his brother and sulking ally in their fight against the other brothers. Murad is hosted at Aurangzeb's camp, dined and wined into sleep, and then put in fetters once his bodyguard is overpowered and his own weapons are taken away from his side. The main notions are beliefs, goals, plans, and deception. Some complex situations are coded into instances of Toulmin's structure for arguments. (Also note that a model of betrayal is incorporated in BRUTUS, an automated story-generation system described by Bringsjord and Ferrucci (2000). BRUTUS has sophisticated, yet domain-specific abilities as a narrator, producing concrete narratives.)

Nissan (2008j) introduced the similar formalism for the AJIT subproject of the AURANGZEB project. The AURANGZEB project is specifically concerned with combining episodic formulae with argument structure data (in particular, Toulmin's). One can see this in the set of formulae developed for the Murad narrative, as well as in the set of formulae intended to capture the Ajit narrative. The latter is as follows.

The Raja of Marwar, Jaswant Singh (or Jasavantasingha), Maharaja of Jodhpur (b. 1625, r. 1638, d. 1678) – the Hindu ruling monarch of Marwar, from the Rathor or Rathore clan of the Rajput military community that had long been in the service of the Muslim Mughal imperial dynasty – had perished because of that hardships of the winter at his command post near the Khyber Pass in December 1678, and this had been after his only son had also perished. This was during a war they were both fighting in Afghanistan, in the service of Aurangzeb, in order to repel some invading Afghan tribes (Eraly, 2004, p. 418). Because of tributes unpaid, Aurangzeb proceeded to make Jaswant's debt good from the dead Jaswant's personal assets. Aurangzeb had the principality of Marwar put under direct imperial administration.

For a while, Aurangzeb toyed with the idea of appointing Indra Singh as successor to Jaswant, in order to divide the Rathors. Following Jaswant's death, among possible claimants for his throne the strongest was Indra Singh (a grandson of Jaswant's elder brother), but he was not acceptable to most Rathors in the elite of Marwar. Once Aurangzeb learned that two of Jaswant's wives were pregnant, he agreed to wait for the birth of the babies. Two sons were born. Ajit was born first. Aurangzeb ordered the two babies and their respective mothers seized, so that he would maintain them at his court in Delhi, and so that the children would be raised under his supervision. His preferred daughter, Zebunnisa, was in charge of educating the child who had been seized, and who, so Aurangzeb was made to believe, was Ajit, the heir to Jaswant's throne. Importantly, the two boys would be raised in Aurangzeb's own religion, and this was unacceptable to the Rathor dynasty of Marwar.

What had actually happened, was that the Rathors, under the leadership of Marwar's able politician, Durgadas (1638–1718), had exchanged the two babies and the two women. The female attendants were made to dress up and posture as though they were Jaswant's wives. The real queens were dressed like men, and fled with Jaswant's babies, together with a contingent of Rajputs. Aurangzeb's imperial officers had seized the wrong persons. When the imperial officers went to seize the queens and the princes, the Rajputs fought as if they were indeed fighting to defend their royal family, and many were killed. It is the account of Khafi Khan that the historian Eraly adopts at this point (Eraly, 2004, p. 421). Other accounts exist, of this episode and of the ruse of the Rajput in order to avoid Ajit being seized, but Khafi Khan's is the account in which all elements fall in place and make sense. This is the account that is represented in our formulae, as well as common sense about being obliged or not feeling under obligation, such as when both Jaswant and his son died in the service of Aurangzeb.

A guerrilla war ensued: the plains of Marwar had been occupied by imperial troops, with Rathor bands based on the hills or the desert, emerging and harrassing them from time to time. Eventually Aurangzeb left Rajasthan to wage war on Deccan in the south of India. Durgadas sought refuge in the Deccan, but in 1687 he returned to Marwar, and brought Ajit Singh, eight years old then, out of concealment. Thus, the Rathors of Marwar made it known that the real Ajit was under their control. Aurangzeb refused to concede that much. It was only once, in the late 1690s, Durgadas did Aurangzeb an important favour, that the Emperor became reconciled to Durgadas and to Ajit. When Ajit wed a bride from another royal family, it became clear that he was the real Ajit indeed. The marriage itself, into another royal family, removed all doubt about Ajit's identity. Instead of making Ajit the ruler of Marwar, he was given another territory to rule, and the compromise was accepted (until after Aurangzeb's demise).[113]

Using episodic formulae along with Toulmin's data structure for arguments proved useful, for representing the Ajit narrative, and opposite viewpoints concerning Aurangzeb's motives when dealing with Marwar found expression in the handy representation of the argumentation. Episodic formulae enabled analysing the narrative at a finer grain than it would have been possible if only a representation for arguments had been used, as applied to natural language propositions.

Episodic formulae were also developed in Nissan (2008b), analysing a perhaps apocryphal anecdote about the emperor Tamerlane. He invited three painters in turn, and commissioned from each, his own portrait. The first painter painted the king as a very handsome man, and Tamerlane had him beheaded, to punish him for his excessive flattery. The second painter represented the king realistically, if one means by that: warts and all. Tamerlane had him beheaded, as he found it intolerably offensive to see himself represented with hideous features. The third painter portrayed the king in the act of shooting an arrow, and did so "realistically", yet without revealing

---

[113] Nissan (2009b) is an article in the humanities, developing a full-fledged discussion of a side story that appears in Nissan (2008j).

5.3 Episodic Formulae

the physical defects, because the posture was such that these would not be apparent. How did the third painter portray Tamerlane? In fact, in order to shoot the arrow from his bow, Tamerlane was kneeling down, so one would not notice that one leg was shorter. To aim, Tamerlane shut an eye, so one could not tell out the squint which affected his eyes (because you need to see both of them open, to tell out). This way, the life of the third painter was saved.

This story of Tamerlane and the three painters involves fairly complex epistemic structures of belief and intentionality, and these are involved in the characters' reasoning about the human body of one of them, and about the depiction of that body in a portrait (i.e., in a given kind of representation). Tamerlane shares with the three painters all of them being instances of the kind 'human being'. Nevertheless, Tamerlane doesn't possess the specific skills associated with the kind 'painter', and contracts out to painters the task of painting his portrait. Tamerlane, being an instance of the kind 'absolute ruler', of which there only is (at most) one in a given polity, possesses a very high degree of authority on all other agents within the polity, and they in turn not only do not possess authority on him (except his doctor, if he considers him authoritative and follows his advice), but also hardly can resist his orders. Therefore, it is extremely dangerous for them to provoke his susceptibility, which is both affected by emotion, and is rational at the same time. He does not need to be concerned about the same in the reverse relation (unless he does so to so many and to such a degree, that the polity would rebel as well as his own otherwise obedient army).

It is important to stress that when we represent the anecdote about Tamerlane and the three painters by means of episodic formulae, we are making no claim of automatable processing. It would have been a different story, had we been representing the narrative in terms of *event calculus,* or *situation calculus,* or extensions of these. These are representations at a lower level, yet ones that are rigorous and computable. Developing a translation of at least a subset of the language of episodic formulae into an extension of either event calculus or situation calculus is a desideratum, and it is unclear to what extent such an effort would be successful.

The article (Nissan, 2008g) about the TIMUR model (the representation in episodic formulae of the anecdote about Tamerlane) appeared in a robotics journal, and it is especially considering this, that is remarkable that it resorted to notions familiar to folklorists, from the study of folktales. The article argues for the importance of providing an explicit treatment for the narrative dimension of social interaction, even when this takes place in a society of embodied agents: not only among animated avatars in a virtual environments, but even in a society of robots. There are some approaches in narrative inquiry (such as ones from the study of folktales, including, but not only, *story grammars*) that may be useful for capturing situational patterns. These are quite useful when there is a stock repertoire of narrative functions.

Nissan (2008g), the article about the TIMUR model, which iself is about agents reasoning about their own or each other's body, appeared in the same journal issue as Nissan (2008h), a survey about embodied artificial agents (either robots, screen avatars, i.e., animated characters in computer interfaces) that reason about agents' bodies (e.g., *metamorphic robots,* i.e., *self-reconfiguring* robots), as well as about such software that incorporates a model of the human body.

Another model, resorting to both episodic formulae and block schemata as familiar for representing feedback in *systems & control* research (from engineering or cybernetics), was described in Nissan (2008e, 2009 [2010], 2010a), in the *Journal of Sociocybernetics* as well as in a journal in the history of ideas. Nissan (2008i) is about a social pattern, whereas the papers Nissan (2009 [2010], 2010a) are about a particular episode that exemplifies it, and that was analysed by means of episodic formulae. All three articles articles are about social narratives of compulsory signs (medieval or later) of group identity disclosure, imposed by an authority interested in fostering prejudice and imposing patterns of exclusion effectively.

The analysis "is applied to the core pattern of such social dynamics of prejudice, that takes the form of forcing members of a dyspreferred group to wear a sign of recognition. Moreover, block schemata are given, that show feedback on the attitudes of society, based on the goals of a malevolent authority. The phenomenon has occurred several times throughout history: e.g., the Jewish badge in medieval Europe, or under Nazi rule, as well as for Hindus under Taliban rule in Afghanistan. We begin by situating such an episode in the history of the Mongol Il-Khanid kingdom [comprising Iran and Iraq]. The earliest precedent was under the Abbasid Caliphate. In 1831, the badge was still imposed in Modena, by a ruler who provided the model for Stendhal's *La Chartreuse de Parme*" (from the abstract of Nissan, 2008e).

The specific narrative analysed in Nissan (2009 [2010], 2010a) is from the final years of the 19th century in Teheran. Nissan (2010a) develops a discussion mainly within the humanities, whereas Nissan (2009 [2010]) provides the formulae for the same narrative. What makes it especially interesting for analysis in terms of a goal hierarchy as represented by means of episodic formulae, is that the representative of a French educational philanthropic organisation (the Alliance Israélite Universelle) sought to have the red patch imposed on Jews replaced with the badge of his own organisation, thus intending to subvert the humiliating purpose with which the compulsory sign disclosing affiliation in the given faith community had been imposed in 1897.

Nissan (2007c, forthcoming a) analyses episodes from two criminal cases. At a trial in Newcastle, the defence counsel claimed that his dog had eaten a video tape that was vital evidence; he was able to obtain copy of the video evidence later on during the same hearing (see Section 3.2.4 above). This is analysed by structuring arguments about how to interpret this, using Wigmore Charts (a technique we have seen in Section 3.2). The second case considered is the series of trials against Sofri and others for the murder, in 1972, of a police chief in Milan (the case is very controversial). In response to the defence requesting the material evidence (garments worn by the victim when he was shot, the bullet, and a car), the prosecution claimed that the material evidence was no longer available, as mice in the storehouse had destroyed it. This is analysed by using episodic formulae the kind of formalism to which the present Section 5.3 is devoted.

Figure 5.3.1.2 underscores the contrast between blue-sky research, and practical projects, within the experience of the present author.

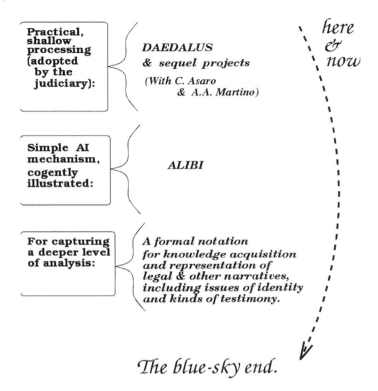

Fig. 5.3.1.2 A spectrum of goals, in projects in which the present author was involved

5.3.2 The Notation of Episodic Formulae

In the following, the symbols available for use in episodic formulae are defined. Readers interested in using these symbols in formulae can obtain them from myself, including (which I typically do) in order to incorporate individual symbols as an .eps file inside LaTex code (I can also provide contextual nuggets of LaTex code, or then samples). I can be contacted by email at ephraimnissan@hotmail.com for that purpose, or for any professional communication.

In episodic formulae, temporal relations include the ones shown in Table 5.3.2.1.

Standard logical operators we are going to use in Section 5.3.3 include the ones shown in Table 5.3.2.2.

Also the standard operators on sets, namely, intersection and union, are in use (for example, in order to define as agent the union of individual characters or sets of characters). See in Table 5.3.2.3.

We adopt the standard mathematical notation by which binary infix operators such as "and", "or", "intersection", and "union", that are usually placed between two arguments, such as shown in Table 5.3.2.4, can become a prefix operator, placed before a set of arguments. For example:

Table 5.3.2.1 Temporal relations used in episodic formulae	≺	precedes	≻	succeeds
	⪯	precedes or equals	⪰	succeeds or equals
	≻≻	much later than		

Table 5.3.2.2 Logical operators used in episodic formulae	∧	and
	∨	or (inclusively, i.e., either or both)
	¬	not
	∀	for all
	∃	there exists
	∄	there exists no...

Table 5.3.2.3 Set-theoretical operators used in episodic formulae	∩	intersection
	∪	union
	∈	is a member of the set...
	⊂	is contained in the set...
	⊃	contains
	∅	empty set

Table 5.3.2.4 An example of binary infix operators	$S_1 \cap S_2$	intersection of sets S_1 and S_2
	$p_1 \wedge p_2$	proposition p_1 and proposition p_2

5.3 Episodic Formulae

$$\bigwedge_{i=1}^{N} p_i \equiv p_1 \wedge \ldots \wedge p_N$$

The following is in the standard notation of *set theory*. Curly braces enclose a set. Sometimes there is a vertical line after an initial symbol with a generic subscript, as in the following example:

$$\left\{ \wp_i \middle| \begin{array}{l} (\wp_i \text{ is-a } bird) \wedge \\ \wedge (\wp_i \text{ is } stuffed) \end{array} \right\}$$

This formula means: "a set of such elements, that each element is a bird and is stuffed". The subscript identifies any of those members, whereas the specific values will be from 1 upwards, up to the cardinality (i.e., the number of elements) of the given set. As to "is" and "is-a" as being infix binary operators (that is to say, they each follow the subject and precede its predicate), these are standard in *semantic networks* from artificial intelligence.

In episodic formulae, whenever the symbol for an agent appears as a subscript to the symbol for a verb, that agent is to be taken as the subject of the action expressed by that verb. If, instead, an agent (or an inanimate concept) appears as the subscript of a noun, then the referent is to be understood as an instance of the concept named, which belongs to the concept symbolised by the subscript.

Symbols specific of our episodic formulae notation includes those shown in Table 5.3.2.5. A notation for "crumpled", i.e., discarded relations between proposition was also defined. See Table 5.3.2.6. Episodic formulae express ability, permissibility, and agency as shown in Table 5.3.2.7.

The notation shown in Table 5.3.2.8 is about belief. We don't distinguish between belief and knowledge, but see Abelson (1979) concerning the differences. Abelson listed seven differentiating features. The notation shown in Table 5.3.2.9 is about characters' goals. For a character realising something (conceiving of an idea), as well as for making a hypothesis, in episodic formulae we have the symbols shown in Table 5.3.2.10.

We have symbols for perception in episodic formulae (the character giving testimony is identified by a subscript to the symbol, whereas the time is indicated by a superscript to the same symbol). See Table 5.3.2.11. In contrast, Table 5.3.2.12 comprises symbols for kinds of giving testimony (here, too, the character giving testimony is identified by a subscript to the symbol, whereas the time is indicated by a superscript to the same symbol).

Only quite few further symbols were defined, and that was in order to express that given affective attitudes are felt by some given character (which, like for all other symbols defined above, can be indicated by means of a subscript to the symbols, and that can be not necessarily an individual character, but as well a collective character, such as society, or its ruling group).

Table 5.3.2.5 Symbols specific of episodic formulae

Symbol	Description
$\left(\mu_a^b \ whatever\right)$	Agent **a** communicates to agent **b** *whatever*. If the latter is followed by an exclamation mark, then this communication is an order.
$\left(\text{has}_x \ \text{[}\lambda\text{]} \ y\right)$	Agent **x** is the legal owner of **y**.
$\left(\text{has}_x \ \text{[}\phi\text{]} \ y\right)$	Agent **x** has the physical possession of **y**.
$\boxed{m}\!\!\Rightarrow$	The proposition which is on the left side eventuated, and this **motivated** the eventuation of the proposition which is on the right side.
$\overline{m}\!\!\Rightarrow$	The proposition on the left side (if eventuated) **would motivate** the eventuation of the proposition on the right side.
$\boxed{\text{enb}}\!\!\Rightarrow$	The proposition which is on the left side eventuated, and this **enabled** the eventuation of the proposition which is on the right side.
$\overline{\text{enb}}\!\!\Rightarrow$	The proposition on the left side (if eventuated) **would enable** the eventuation of proposition on the right side.
$\boxed{c}\!\!\Rightarrow$	The proposition which is on the left side eventuated, and this **caused** the eventuation of the proposition which is on the right side.
$\overline{c}\!\!\Rightarrow$	The proposition on the left side (if eventuated) **would cause** the eventuation of proposition on the right side.
$\boxed{\text{rf}}\!\!\Rightarrow$	The proposition which is on the left side eventuated, and this **reinforced** the eventuation of the proposition which is on the right side.
$\overline{\text{rf}}\!\!\Rightarrow$	The proposition on the left side (if eventuated) **would reinforce** the eventuation of proposition on the right side.
$\boxed{}\!\!\Rightarrow$	The proposition which is on the left side eventuated, and this **includes** the eventuation of the proposition which is on the right side.

5.3 Episodic Formulae

Table 5.3.2.6 "Crumpled" relations

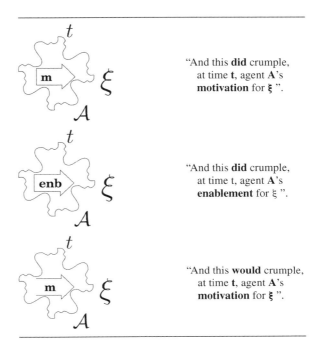

"And this **did** crumple, at time **t**, agent **A**'s **motivation** for ξ ".

"And this **did** crumple, at time t, agent **A**'s **enablement** for ξ ".

"And this **would** crumple, at time **t**, agent **A**'s **motivation** for ξ ".

Table 5.3.2.7 A notation for ability, permissibility, and agency

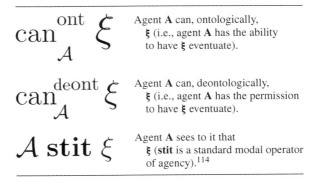

Agent **A** can, ontologically, ξ (i.e., agent **A** has the ability to have ξ eventuate).

Agent **A** can, deontologically, ξ (i.e., agent **A** has the permission to have ξ eventuate).

Agent **A** sees to it that ξ (**stit** is a standard modal operator of agency).[114]

---

[114] On the *stit* operator, see Horty and Belnap (1995). The *stit* operator was introduced by Belnap and Perloff (1988). In an article applied to a legal narrative, Perloff (2003) shows how a modal logic of agency with a *stit* operator (*stit* stands for "sees to it that") can be concretely applied in legal analysis. Whereas it used to be the case, in logic-based accounts of agency, that analysts would focus on actions rather than on agents (i.e., the actors that carry out actions; not necessarily "police agents"), Perloff shows that "stit theory puts the agent at the center of the action".

Table 5.3.2.8 A notation for belief

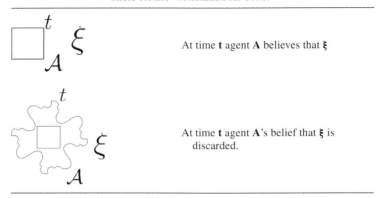

At time **t** agent **A** believes that **ξ**

At time **t** agent **A**'s belief that **ξ** is discarded.

Table 5.3.2.9 A notation concerning characters' goals

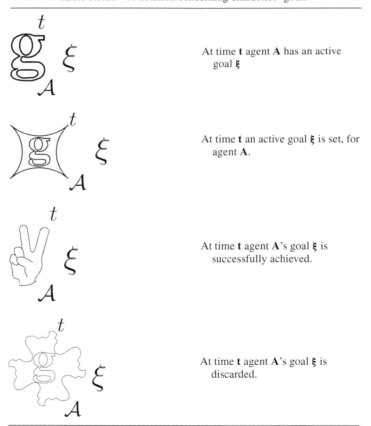

At time **t** agent **A** has an active goal **ξ**

At time **t** an active goal **ξ** is set, for agent **A**.

At time **t** agent **A**'s goal **ξ** is successfully achieved.

At time **t** agent **A**'s goal **ξ** is discarded.

5.3 Episodic Formulae

Table 5.3.2.10 A notation for realisation, or conceiving of an idea

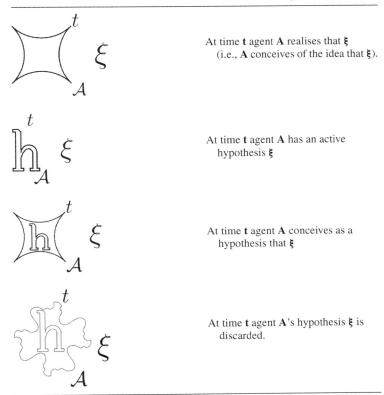

At time **t** agent **A** realises that **ξ**
(i.e., **A** conceives of the idea that **ξ**).

At time **t** agent **A** has an active hypothesis **ξ**

At time **t** agent **A** conceives as a hypothesis that **ξ**

At time **t** agent **A**'s hypothesis **ξ** is discarded.

In particular, the following notation expresses hope, despair, and the like. The following is the notation for hope:

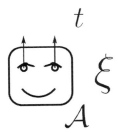

Table 5.3.2.11 A notation for perception

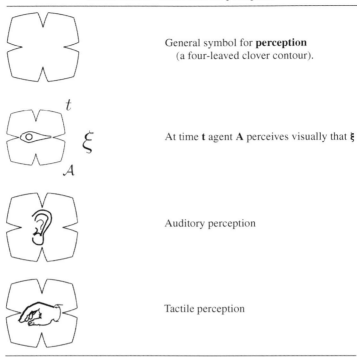

General symbol for **perception** (a four-leaved clover contour).

At time **t** agent **A** perceives visually that ξ

Auditory perception

Tactile perception

The symbol for dread is similar to the symbol for hope:

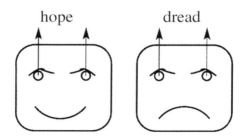

5.3 Episodic Formulae 443

Table 5.3.2.12 A notation for kinds of giving testimony

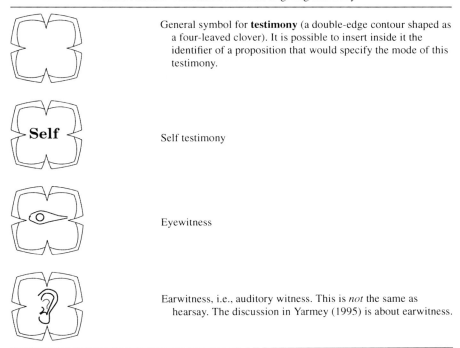

(clover symbol)	General symbol for **testimony** (a double-edge contour shaped as a four-leaved clover). It is possible to insert inside it the identifier of a proposition that would specify the mode of this testimony.
(clover with "Self")	Self testimony
(clover with eye)	Eyewitness
(clover with ear)	Earwitness, i.e., auditory witness. This is *not* the same as hearsay. The discussion in Yarmey (1995) is about earwitness.

Whereas hope and dread are about the future, despair and relief are post-event emotions. The symbols for these are as follows:

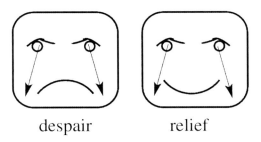

despair   relief

In episodic formulae, also symbols for prejudice are available. In order to indicate that At time **t** agent **A** has a positive, or very positive, or negative, or very negative prejudice towards ξ the following four notations are available:

$$\boxed{+}_A^t \xi, \quad \boxed{\boxed{+}}_A^t \xi, \quad \boxed{-}_A^t \xi, \quad \boxed{\boxed{-}}_A^t \xi$$

Typically one would only use a subset of all these symbols. One may argue that one could go on defining new symbols, and that there would be no end to it. Nevertheless, experience with applying this notation to several narratives has shown that the technique converges. There is no risk of going on defining more and more symbols. For sure, it would be possible to replace words (names of predicates) for the graphic symbols. The advantage of the graphics (notwithstanding such preference being subjective) is that the episodic formulae tend to look compact, and one can relatively quickly make sense of what is on the page, whereas with verbal strings identifying standard predicates or modal operators, one is forced to read line by line.

5.3.3 An Example: From Suspects and Allegations to Forensic Testing of the Stuffed Birds of the Meinertzhagen Collection

5.3.3.1 The Background, and the Narrative Represented

In Lipske's words (1999), "A British soldier, spy and noted amateur ornithologist in the early part of this century", Richard Meinertzhagen,[115] died at age 89, a week

---

[115] Biographies in book form of Col. Richard Henry Meinertzhagen include Cocker (1990), Capstick (1998), and Lord (1971). A radio broadcast by the journalist Mark Cocker (2000) took on board the negative picture of Meinertzhagen as an ornithologist that has been recently emerging. A biography by Brian Garfield (2007) presents the man as a fraud. Garfield is, among the other things, "the author of novels that have been made into Hollywood movies (including *Hopscotch* and *Death Wish*)", and "a former president of the Mystery Writers of America". The summary of Garfield's book claims: "Tall, handsome, charming Col. Richard Meinertzhagen (1878–1967) was an acclaimed British war hero, a secret agent, and a dean of international ornithology. His exploits inspired three biographies, movies have been based on his life, and a square in Jerusalem is dedicated to his memory. Meinertzhagen was trusted by Winston Churchill, David Lloyd George, Chaim Weizmann, David Ben Gurion, T. E. Lawrence, Elspeth Huxley, and a great many others. He bamboozled them all. Meinertzhagen was a fraud. Many of the adventures recorded in his celebrated diaries were imaginary, including a meeting with Hitler while he had a loaded pistol in his pocket, an attempt to rescue the Russian royal family in 1918, and a shoot-out with Arabs in Haifa when he was seventy years old. True, he was a key player in Middle Eastern events after World War I, and during the 1930s he represented Zionism's interests in negotiations with Germany. [This was at the time when Britain allowed into Palestine a fraction of the Jews trying to leave Nazi Germany.] But he also set up Nazi front organizations in England, committed a half-century of major and costly scientific fraud, and – oddly – may have been innocent of many killings to which he confessed (e.g., the murder of his own polo groom – a crime of which he cheerfully boasted, although the evidence suggests it never occurred at all), while he may have been guilty of at least one homicide of which he professed innocence. [...]". Some of the research by Garfield in his biography of Meinertzhagen has however been questioned in Storrs Olson (2008), in an ornithology journal.
Among the claims made by Garfield (2007, p. 209), there is plagiarism. To say it with Wikipedia (at http://en.wikipedia.org/wiki/Richard_Meinertzhagen): "As the author of numerous taxonomic and other works on birds, and possessing a vast collection of bird and bird lice specimens, Meinertzhagen was long considered one of Britain's greatest ornithologists. Yet his magnum opus, *Birds of Arabia* (1954), is believed to have been based on the unpublished manuscript of another naturalist, George Bates, who is not sufficiently credited in that book." Based on Garfield (2007, p. 68), Wikipedia also points out: "In the east African Kenya Highlands in 1905, Meinertzhagen

after the June 1967 Six Day War,[116] was long credited with creating one of the world's best private collections of Old World bird specimens".[117] In 1993, *Ibis,* the journal of the British Ornithologists' Union, published an article, actually an exposé by Alan Knox (1993), which "suggested, however, that labels on some of his birds were fraudulent" (Lipske, 1999). "The benefits to be gained from museum collections depend implicitly upon the accuracy of the information associated with the specimens and the correct interpretation of those data [...] Collectors and dealers have often been suspected of fabricating data for a variety of reasons, but proven cases have been documented only rarely. [...] This paper examines one such case" (Knox, 1993, p. 320). It has already been observed (in an informal forum) that the exposé, with "a case of fraud examined" in its title, must have been startling to the unsuspecting reader given the nature of papers usually published in *Ibis;* it happened to be sandwiched between more innocent material in the July 1993 issue, namely, Theo Meijer's 'Is the Starling *Sturnus vulgaris* a determinate layer?' (pp. 315–319), and a comment note by T. R. Birkhead, M. T. Stanback and R. E. Simmons, 'The phalloid organ of buffalo weavers *Bubalornis*' (pp. 326–331).

The following is quoted from Knox (1993, p. 320):

> Richard Meinertzhagen (1878–1967) was the last of the great British bird collectors. Over his lifetime he amassed thousands of bird skins and countless other natural history specimens. In 1954 his birds were transferred to the then British Museum (Natural History), now known as the Natural History Museum (NHM). The collection was the largest — nearly 20,000 skins — acquired by the Museum in the last 75 years. It was technically superb, containing many excellently prepared skins with neat hand-written labels. The collection consisted primarily of Palearctic birds and as such was exceptionally complete. However, it was, and remains, deeply flawed.

Knox (ibid.) remarked that during his lifetime, Meinertzhagen "was regarded with suspicion by many of his contemporaries. Charles Vaurie, for example, was very unhappy about his behaviour. In a letter to F. E. Warr he wrote, 'I can cay [*sic* in Knox, but read: say] *upon my oath* that Meinertzhagen's collection contains skins *stolen* from the Leningrad Museum, the Paris Museum, and the American Museum of Natural History.... He also removed labels, and replaced them by others to suit

---

crushed a major revolt by murdering the Nandi Orkoiyot (spiritual leader) Koitalel Arap Samoei who was leading it. He shot Koitalel, who had come to negotiate, on 19 October 1905, while shaking his hand." Posthumous claims of scientific misconduct against Meinertzhagen have also resulted in some farfetched speculations. Again Wikipedia, based on Garfield (2007, p. 172), states: "Meinertzhagen's second wife, the ornithologist Anne Constance Jackson, died in 1928 at age 40 in a remote Scottish village in an incident that was ruled a shooting accident. The official finding was that she accidentally shot herself in the head with a revolver during target practice alone with Richard. There is speculation that the shooting was not an accident and that Meinertzhagen shot her out of fear that she would expose him and his fraudulent activities."

[116] Richard Meinertzhagen was born on 3 March 1878, the scion of a merchant-bank dynasty with an international reputation, and died on 17 June 1967.

[117] Bird taxidermy is the subject of Farber (1977), Peter (1999), Harrison (1964, revised 1976), and Gutebier, Schmidt, and Rogers (1989), whereas Horie and Murphy (1988) is more generally on the taxidermy of vertebrates.

his ideas and theories'".[118] Knox states that while examining specimens of Redpolls (*Carduelis flammea*) from the Meinertzhagen collection, he "noted other discrepancies" (Knox, 1993, p. 320) other than such that had previously pointed out and reported by another scholar, Phillip Clancey. "In order to clarify this, I [i.e., Knox] re-examined all the Meinertzhagen redpolls at the Natural History Museum" (Knox, 1993, p. 320). Crucial damning evidence was then provided by Rasmussen and Prŷs-Jones (2003).

In addition to what Knox (1993) and Lipske (1999) state concerning Meinertzhagen – and I think it's important that I mention this because of the very fact that the prescription was so extreme – consider that a proposal was made, at the time, that Meinertzhagen's bird collection be destroyed; this understandably elicited a response of incredulity: after all, even conceding that the collection was problematic or worse, nevertheless any specimen from that given collection could be readily identified, or made identifiable, as coming from the Meinertzhagen collection, so such a measure, which would only have been appropriate had it been devised to stem the spread of an epidemic or anyway of contamination of the data, could safely be deemed to have been, if applied, punitive rather then useful, and what is more, punitive even to the detriment of usefulness for the historical record. That such a proposal had been made at all, makes it sensible that recollections arose of other instances of animosity toward Meinertzhagen – and this in a context unrelated to ornithology.

Knox however provides a reasonable explanation of how specimens from the collection were, as though, spreading contamination, because their original association with the Meinertzhagen collection was being lost owing to misplacing (this, in turn, ought to make one wonder about sloppy practices, and even about a problem with credibility that is not confined to the Meinertzhagen collection). The following is taken from Knox (1993, p. 323):

> With the rumours and suspicions that surrounded Meinertzhagen during his lifetime, there was some concern at the acceptance of the collection at the NHM (Cocker, 1990). Indeed, J. D. Macdonald, the head of the Bird Room at the time, is reported to have said that the collection should have been burned (Cocker, 1990, p. 274). After the collection passed to the Museum, it was intended that it should be kept separate from the main collection [...]. For many years these were separate drawers marked "Meinertzhagen specimens", but, with the passage of time, most of the specimens have been incorporated into the main collection.

The admission made in the latter quotation identifies an important component in the questionability of the information associated with specimens.[119] Table 1 in Roberts,

---

[118] Knox, quoting from the letter by the well-known ornithologist Charles Vaurie, points out: "(letter quoted in Cocker, 1990, p. 274)".

[119] A dismembered collection, when information enabling reconstruction of the original constitution of the original collection or of recipient collections, let alone the loss of the track through which a given specimen went through, is also the subject of a case from archaeology, described in this note. For comparison, consider the following situation. Dore and Vellani (1994) discuss a subset of items from the inventory of archaeological findings at a museum in Bologna; those items are of local Celtic origin. Most findings were made during excavations in the 1870s. Stefania Vellani's section in Dore and Vellani (1994) focuses on two glass bracelets, several bronze buckles, and so forth. Special problems arose concerning the ascription of the bracelets to a major collection that

5.3 Episodic Formulae

Elphick, and Reed (2009) lists "Types of errors in sightings that can occur even with 'verifiable' physical evidence". One type of error is "Interpretation errors of labels", for example because of "difference in British vs. American dating whereby 11 March 2007, could be recorded as either 11/3/07 or 3/11/07", or then because of "abbreviation of the year to the last two digits". A second kind of error is "Interpretation errors of specimens", for example "recent rediscovery of the polecat (*Mustela putorius*) in Scotland resulted from surreptitious translocation rather than a persisting population (Solow, Kitchener, Roberts, & Birks, 2006)". A third kind of error is "Labeling of location errors" (this includes: "spatial and temporal imprecision", "transcriptional errors", "insufficient knowledge by the end users of location names used by collector; changes in geographical names", or then "gradual loss of data and accumulated errors of the type mentioned above with increasing age of specimen as they pass through many hands", "labeling with the center where the specimens were accumulated or shipped rather than the collection locality; assumed origin of the specimen by curators", and then again, "curators substituting original labels for their own, making it impossible to verify spelling, handwriting, or original data").

---

had been put together and then donated by an artist, Pelagio Palagi. In Haevernick's typological classification, she had stated that these pieces had belonged to the Palagi collection, and that no data were extant as to the place where they had been discovered, as Vellani points out (Dore & Vellani, 1994, pp. 43–44). Nevertheless, "[t]he very ascription [to the Palagi collection] was the first problem to face: in fact, only one of the bracelets, the one tagged IT 767, still carried the inventory tag 'Palagi', which is the only distinctive sign of certain association with that collection" (ibid., p. 44, my translation from Italian).

The museum inventory was also found to only ascribe one of the bracelets to the Palagi collection. Moreover, the handwritten inventory ascribed to Edoardo Brizio (from around 1871) was found to make no mention of glass bracelets. In contrast, in the inventory of the Palagi Milan house (turned into a museum, prior to the transfer to Bologna in 1860) – that inventory was recovered in the Bologna museum archive – both bracelets were found to be listed (Dore & Vellani, 1994, p. 44). A second problem, one which remained unsolved, was that of the determination of where did the items come from, before joining the Palagi collection (ibid.). Furthermore (ibid., my translation).

In fact, after its acquisition on the part of the Bologna city council in 1860, [the Palagi collection was dismembered, and no exhaustive inventory was made. Membership in this important collection was simply entrusted to the inventory tags, which unfortunately are all too perishable. Moreover, the loss of the provenience data is a gap shared by many of the objects belonging to the Palagi collection, especially when it comes to material of documentary interest such as these bracelets. Blame for this loss is probably to be apportioned to Palagi himself, if E. Gerhard, the well-known German archaeologist who had become a consultant and buyer on Palagi's behalf, talking about the collection even before the artist's death, could state: "At various times, he augmented (...) his collection with new findings, yet he never had these eventuate in public awareness or any publications, so of most of them, by now, the place of provenience is unknown"

Still, Vellani hypothesised a provenience broadly located in Lombardy or Piedmont, as Palagi "was especially attentive to findings which took place in those areas where he himself stayed for a long time" (ibid., my translation). Vellani also suggests that perhaps in the future, better understanding may come into being of such artifacts in Italy, and that this could enhance the standing of her hypothesis.

Moreover, the same table lists "Specimen misidentification once in a collection": this is "known as Elvis taxa (Erwin & Droser, 1993)". There also is "Deliberate fraud through planting of specimens in the field": "most notably, Prof. J. W. Heslop Harrison in an attempt to increase evidence for his theory that the island of Rum was a refugium (Pearman & Walker, 2004)". Next in the table, there is "theft and relabeling": "most notorious example, Richard Meinertzhagen (Rasmussen & Prŷs-Jones, 2003)". And finally, there is "misrepresentation for commercial purposes". This is the case of "Victorian orchid collectors who, on occasion, gave erroneous geographic origins to protect their sources".

At any rate, during the 1990s (I recall), one would come across some defence of Meinertzhagen in ornithologists' semiformal printed forums. Nevertheless, after 1997 the controversy gained momentum. The Forest Spotted Owlet (*Athene blewitti*, of which *Heteroglaux blewitti* is a synonym), which had long been thought to be extinct, was rediscovered in India. In the following, I quote from an unsigned paper (Anon., 2001) that appeared in the *Deccan Herald* of Bangalore, India, on Sunday, October 14, 2001, and is posted at that newspaper's website. The paper begins as follows: "The rediscovery of a bird which is supposedly extinct is of course a dramatic occasion; and this happened in the case of the Jerdons or Double-banded Courser in Andhra Pradesh. One significant fact which emerges when a rare bird is rediscovered is that we become aware of the importance of micro-habitats for saving an endangered species. It was only because the famous naturalist T[homas] C[averhill] Jerdon (perhaps the first of the genre in India" as his work was published in the middle decades of the nineteenth century, including Jerdon (1847) and his classic, Jerdon (1862–1864)), "described the bird and its habitat so accurately that the continuing attempts to rediscover it succeeded". In the final part of the paper, the case that is of interest for our present purposes is dealt with:

> Another case of a bird which had disappeared for many years but was rediscovered recently is of the forest spotted owlet (Athene blewitti). The bird had not been seen for the past 113 years inspite of ornithologists searching for it in the forests on the banks of the Narbada where the species was last seen. As in the case of Jerdons Courser, the search finally succeeded, and on 25th November 1997, three Americans (one of whom was Ben King, well-known in India for his useful book: *A Field Guide to the Birds of South East Asia*) found the birds in the foothills of Satpura Mountains near Shahada in Maharashtra. Before this sighting the only information relating to these birds, endemic to India, was on the basis of seven specimens collected as long ago as 1880. One of the researchers from the BNHS [i.e., the Bombay Natural History Society] who is attempting to gather information about the provenance and the ecology of these birds is Parah Ishtiaq. A problem she faces is to distinguish males from females, as there is no difference in the outward appearance of males and females. Also, the birds apparently look rather similar to the common spotted owlets (Athene brama), but experienced ornithologists can tell them apart by the difference in their facial markings. Some time ago I received an excited call from a lady in Indiranagar saying that her son, a keen birder, had discovered this bird in Bangalore and had taken a photograph. I was quite sure that the photo he had taken was of the common spotted owlet and so it turned out to be. Fortunately, the calls of the two species are very different. The spotted owlets only screech, while its rarer cousin has a modicum of a "song". By tape recording the calls of these birds and broadcasting them in likely habitats, and from the response received, the research team is able to make a reasonable estimate of the number of birds that exist. But all this effort at rehabilitating an endangered species will fail if the environment

5.3 Episodic Formulae   449

of these birds continues to be eroded; and on this front the news is alarming. Parah Ishtiaq writes, "Pamela (Rasmussen) and I went to Taloda in search of the forest owlet. Around 5000 hectares of the plains forest had recently been clear-felled to serve as a rehabilitation site for people displaced by the Sardar Sarovar Dam. About 500 families now live in this area and use the forest resources". Unfortunately then, this endangered species is still in danger.

The Bangalore newspaper article then turned to the Meinertzhagen controversy:

> Incidentally, this bird is associated with one of the most disgraceful attempts by an ornithologist of international standing, claiming to have seen it in the wild, and producing a specimen as incontrovertible evidence, while in fact all that he did was to steal a specimen from the Museum of Natural History in Kensington London and submitting it again as a new find.

Then readers were told: "This was (to the shock of the ornithologists of the world)", the famous Meinertzhagen, "who in his lifetime was a highly respected naturalist." Next, some tribute is given to the man. The late dean of Bombay ornithologists "Salim Ali[120] has some interesting things to say about this dashing and courageous soldier who during the First World War, managed to deceive his enemies in many ingenious ways". But: "It was fortunate for [this soldier and scholar] and his friends that his fraudulent tendencies were discovered only many years after his death".

As can be readily seen, the newspaper is taking the hypothesis about ornithological fraud on the part of Meinertzhagen as a given, even though the formulation (in line with the style of Indian English prose) is somewhat old-fashioned in, among the other things, its moderate and deferent formulations. Also, note that whereas Lipske (1999), whose own text was published in a popularisation forum of the Smithsonian Institution, understandably emphasises the role of the latter's staff[121] (see below), the Bangalore-based, Mysore-owned newspaper especially conveys the experiences of local ornithologists or bird watchers.

Details of how Rasmussen and her colleagues came to develop and probe into the hypothesis that some specimens in Meinertzhagen's bird collection, and in particular the stuffed specimen of the Forest Spotted Owlet – Fig. 5.3.3.1.1(a) is an old depiction of the species; Fig. 5.3.3.1.1(b) is more accurate – is not authentic, but is rather a camouflaged older specimen that was stolen, then restuffed and relabelled, will be represented information in episodic formulae in a subsequent section.

One of the Smithsonian Institution Research Reports is an informal, popularistic account by Michael Lipske (1999) of the rediscovery in India, by ornithologist

---

[120] An explanation is in order, concerning the reference to Salim Ali: "To many people, Salim Ali and Indian Ornithology were almost synonymous" (Perrins, 1988, p. 305). "The work for which he will be most widely remembered was the ten-volume work (written with S.D. Ripley *The Handbook of the Birds of India and Pakistan* (1968–74). He was in the process of re-writing this important work at the age of 90; the first five volumes have been published" from 1978 (Perrins, ibid., p. 306).

[121] Prof. Pamela C. Rasmussen of the Michigan State University (MSU) earlier was a researcher at the Smithsonian. She was born in 1958, and earned her Ph.D. from the University of Kansas in 1990. While remaining a Research Associate at the Smithsonian Institution, in 2011 she was Assistant Professor at the MSU Department of Zoology, and Assistant Curator of Mammalogy & Ornithology at the MSU Museum.

Fig. 5.3.3.1.1 (a) A painting from 1891 of the Forest Spotted Owlet (*Athene blewitti*), rediscovered by Pamela Rasmussen. The original graphics is in colour[122] (b) A more accurate depiction of the same species

Pamela Rasmussen of the U.S. National Museum of Natural History, of the already mentioned Forest Spotted Owlet (*Athene blewitti*), a bird that had long been thought to be extinct. Lipske wrote: "Seven stuffed skins in a handful of museums were all that seemed to remain of a species that several experts had crossed off as extinct". After living individuals of the given owlet species "had gone unseen by any scientist for 113 years", "one morning in 1997" Rasmussen "gazed, only half trusting her eyes at" an individual of that very bird species, perched on a tree in western India (more individuals were found later on): "the forest owlet that Rasmussen had sought for two weeks from one side of India to the other" (Lipske, 1999).[123] Lipske further stated:

---

[122] An explanation given at http://en.wikipedia.org/wiki/File:Athene_blewitti.jpg (which is where the image now appears: it was uploaded in 2008 into the Wikimedia Commons by Jim F. Bleak) states: "Until recently, the best illustration of the Forest Owlet was this one, which appeared in *The Scientific Results of the Second Yarkard Mission*, published in 1891. The illustration has several inaccuracies: the cheek patches are too dark and the breast is too barred; the belly, lower flanks, and undertail coverts should be completely white, not marked; the bands in the wing should be whiter; and the bill should be larger."

[123] The Wikipedia entry http://en.wikipedia.org/wiki/Pamela_C._Rasmussen explains: "She rediscovered the Forest Owlet *Athene blewitti*, which had not been seen since 1884, in western India [(Rasmussen & Ishtiaq, 1999; Rasmussen & King, 1998)], previous searches by S. Dillon Ripley, Salim Ali and others having failed because they relied on fake documentation from Richard Meinertzhagen [(Ripley, 1976; Rasmussen, 1998)]". Further relevant citations include Gallagher (1998), Oehler (2009), Seabrook (2006), Dalton (2005), and Weidensaul (2002).

5.3 Episodic Formulae

To find out, she visited Britain's Natural History Museum in London, where most of Meinertzhagen's collection of tens of thousands of birds now resides. Working with ornithologists there, she examined the colonel's unique India specimens. "Each was either clearly fraudulent or highly suspicious", Rasmussen says.

She discovered that Meinertzhagen had done some of his most successful bird hunting not in the wild but in the museum's specimen cabinets. He was known to boast of his collection's "unique perfection", she says. "One of the reasons that it was uniquely perfect was because he was stealing the best specimens" from other collectors' museum contributions.

With Robert Prys-Jones, head of the Bird Section at Britain's Natural History Museum, Rasmussen established that hundreds of Meinertzhagen specimens were birds he filched; some he restuffed and then relabeled with false information. Of all the ornithological treasures the colonel stole, the rarest was India's forest owlet. Cracking the case required sophisticated detective work.

Rasmussen had found that, of seven known specimens of the owlet in museums, only one was said to have been collected in this century-in 1914 by Meinertzhagen. Most of the others had been collected in the 1880s by James Davidson, a British official and bird enthusiast stationed in western India.

Lipske (1999) goes on to relate how Rasmussen and her colleagues carried out examinations of the suspicious items:

Working with ornithologist Nigel Collar of BirdLife International in England, Rasmussen examined the Meinertzhagen owlet at the British Museum. Both experts could see that original stitching and stuffing had been removed from the skin and that new stuffing had been inserted and the bird resewn. Closer study of the specimen and X-ray photographs of it revealed characteristic preparation touches unique to Davidson, a self-taught worker with one-of-a-kind methods for handling bird skins.

Fairly certain that Meinertzhagen's owlet actually had been collected by Davidson, the ornithologists still wanted more evidence. Even though the bird had been restuffed, Rasmussen remembers hoping "maybe, just maybe, there will be a fiber or something somewhere that will tie it to Davidson". Luckily, there was.

Inside a wing, stuffed around a joint, there remained some raw cotton that had turned yellow from fat. Checking the wing of an owl of another species Davidson collected in India, the sleuths found what looked like similar cotton. They sent both samples to the Federal Bureau of Investigation in Washington, D.C., where forensic tests indicated that the two bits of cotton were virtually identical.

"That, along with other clues, just basically put the nail in the coffin", Rasmussen says, noting the improbability that Meinertzhagen would have had access to the same kind of rough cotton Davidson used 30 years earlier. The owlet was a previously unknown, fifth Davidson specimen, presumably stolen from Britain's Natural History Museum by Meinertzhagen and decades later returned to it as part of the colonel's rich collection.

To make things clearer, we recapitulate this narrative of the Meinertzhagen bird collection controversy in Figs. 5.3.3.1.2, 5.3.3.1.3, and 5.3.3.1.4.

News of the alleged fraud were divulged indeed to the broad public in Anglo-Saxon countries, for example, in a BBC Radio 4 broadcast by Mark Cocker (2000). Willingness to believe that Meinertzhagen may have been motivated to practice deception, and may have been able to achieve it successfully, in a scholarly field (which is of course highly reprehensible) has been, no doubt, reinforced (if not inspired) by the fact that Meinertzhagen was, and is, much admired for his performance in military intelligence. That is an area in which deception is considered a virtue. Before turning to the development of a formalism, the following will give

Fig. 5.3.3.1.2 A recapitulation of the Meinertzhagen bird collection controversy (part a)[124]

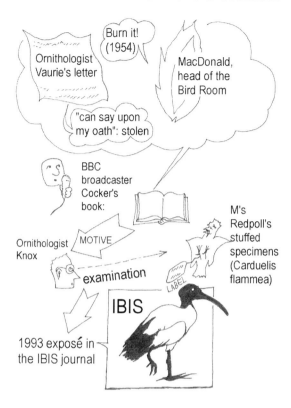

a flavour of the kind of exploits in which Meinertzhagen applied ruse in order to achieve military goals.[125]

---

[124] Facial resemblance is not guaranteed. For one thing, Mark Cocker looks like he has all his hair intact, when seen in front.

[125] During the first World War, Meinertzhagen took part in "the British expeditionary force attempting to conquer German East Africa. Assigned to intelligence duties, he displayed a talent for deviousness that he would later put to resounding effect" during the British invasion of the Ottoman empire from Egypt; an example of his deeds in intelligence while posted in Kenya is, he claimed, as follows: "The most effective agent working for the Germans, he soon learned, was" a Near Easterner "too elusive to capture" (Rabinovich, 1997). Meinertzhagen however "thought of another way of neutralizing him. He wrote a letter to the Arab thanking him for information about German dispositions – information which had in fact been picked up by wireless intercept". In order to frame the spy in the eyes of his German bosses, Meinertzhagen "requested more details in the letter and included 1,500 rupees. He then sent it off with one of his own men whom he had reason to believe would be bumbling enough to be caught by the Germans. Word was received shortly thereafter that the [addressee of the letter] had been tried and shot" (Rabinovich, 1997). In 1917, on the front advancing from the Sinai peninsula, Meinertzhagen "was appointed head of the intelligence section at the forward British headquarters" and "[i]t was in this capacity that he achieved his greatest renown. [...] With the war in France stalemated, British prime minister David Lloyd George had asked for Jerusalem as a morale-boosting Christmas present for the nation, and

5.3 Episodic Formulae

Fig. 5.3.3.1.3 A recapitulation of the Meinertzhagen bird collection controversy (part b)

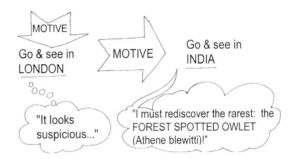

[commander Gen. Edmund] Allenby was determined to give it. The plan adopted by Allenby consisted of simultaneous thrusts at Gaza and Beersheba, with the Turks to be misled about which was the main blow" (ibid.). It was then that Meinertzhagen "began to prepare his grand deception. He asked his sister, Mary, in England to supply him with a letter to an imaginary husband, supposedly a staff officer serving at Allenby's headquarters, announcing the birth of their baby. He himself began constructing this imagined persona from forged 'evidence'. This included a notebook filled with observations and vague messages, an agenda for a meeting at Allenby's headquarters, some notes about a code, a telegram announcing a reconnaissance around Beersheba and orders for an attack on Gaza" (ibid.). And then:

> Stuffing all this into a haversack which he sprinkled with fresh blood, Meinertzhagen rode out on horseback on October 12 toward the Turkish lines near Beersheba. A Turkish mounted patrol duly spotted him and gave chase, but reined in after a mile. To reawaken their interest, Meinertzhagen dismounted and opened fire. The Turks resumed the chase at a gallop. At one point, Meinertzhagen lurched in his saddle as if hit and dropped the haversack together with his rifle, canteen and field glasses before making his getaway. The Turks and their German advisers took the bait. The faked plans showed that the British were planning a reconnaissance toward Beersheba and a main attack on Gaza. The Turks deployed their forces accordingly. Allenby massed artillery before Gaza as if in confirmation, but sent a large force on a night march toward Beersheba. Australian horsemen swept into the town before the Turks could destroy its wells. With the Turks thrown off balance by this flank attack, Allenby now began to drive against Gaza, which fell on November 16.

Fig. 5.3.3.1.4 A recapitulation of the Meinertzhagen bird collection controversy (part c)

5.3.3.2 Preliminaries of the Formal Representation for the Stuffed Birds Case: Formulae About Meinertzhagen and His Bird Collection

In my notation, a superscript on the left side of the symbol of a time-point stands for a time unit whose granularity is as per the *grainsize* indicated in the superscript itself (e.g., **d** for day, **y** for year, and so forth). The symbol formed from the symbol for the time-point as augmented with the left-side superscript for *granularity*,[126] is a symbol for a time-interval containing the given time-point. Let us introduce these symbols for times, accounting for grainsize. See Table 5.3.3.2.1.

We are now ready for representing in a formula the years of birth and of death of Richard Meinertzhagen:

$$({}^{y}t_{\mathcal{M}}^{\alpha} = 1878) \wedge ({}^{y}t_{\mathcal{M}}^{\omega} = 1967)$$

Meinertzhagen is often credited with this so-called Haversack Ruse. It was depicted in the 1987 film *The Lighthorsemen*.

[126] As time-granularity is important in the representation as introduced here, it is of interest to signal Bettini, Jajodia, and Wang (2000), a book on time granularities and how they are processed in representations from computer science, in particular from the viewpoints of database design, of

5.3 Episodic Formulae

Table 5.3.3.2.1 Symbols for time, accounting for grainsize

t^α	the time of the birth of the person indicated as a subscript.
t^ω	the time of the death of the person indicated as a subscript.
$t^\alpha_\mathcal{M}$	the time of the birth of Richard Meinertzhagen.
$t^\omega_\mathcal{M}$	the time of the death of Richard Meinertzhagen.
$^y t^\alpha_\mathcal{M}$	the year in which Richard Meinertzhagen was born.
$^y t^\omega_\mathcal{M}$	the year in which Richard Meinertzhagen died.

We need a proposition to state that since birth, there existed Richard Meinertzhagen, and that he was a person, and a male:

$$\text{At } t,\ t \succeq t^\alpha_\mathcal{M}: \begin{pmatrix} \exists\ \mathcal{M}\ \wedge \\ \wedge\ (\mathcal{M}\ \textbf{is-a}\ person)\ \wedge \\ \wedge\ (\mathcal{M}\ \textbf{is}\ male) \end{pmatrix}$$

From his birth to his death, Richard Meinertzhagen was alive and was British:

$$\text{At } t,\ t^\alpha_\mathcal{M} \preceq t \preceq t^\omega_\mathcal{M}: \begin{pmatrix} (\mathcal{M}\ \textbf{is}\ alive)\ \wedge \\ \wedge\ (\mathcal{M}\ \textbf{is}\ British) \end{pmatrix}$$

From a given point in time, which was much later than his birth date, until his his retirement from the army, which was much earlier than his death, Richard Meinertzhagen was a colonel[127]:

$$\text{At } t,\ t^\alpha_\mathcal{M} \lll t^c_\mathcal{M} \preceq t \preceq t^r_\mathcal{M} \lll t^\omega_\mathcal{M}:\ (\mathcal{M}\ \textbf{is-a}\ colonel)$$

---

constraint reasoning, and of automated knowledge discovery. Also see Bettini, Wang, and Jajodia (2002). We are going to discuss formal models of time in Section 8.4.2.3.

[127] Richard Meinertzhagen retired from the army in 1925. Afterwards he was a retired colonel.

Table 5.3.3.2.2 Some relevant times and institutions

$t^{\delta}_{\mathcal{M}}$	the time when the Natural History branch of the British Museum obtained Meinertzhagen's bird collection. This is the point in the time (not the year) of the collection's physical (and accessibility) transfer to the Natural History branch. Possibly, this was a time interval, but for our present purposes, we treat this time as though it was a point along the time axis.
$yt^{\delta}_{\mathcal{M}}$	the year when the Natural History branch of the British Museum obtained Meinertzhagen's bird collection.
$\mathfrak{M}'$	the Natural History branch of the British Museum.
$\mathfrak{M}''$	the Natural History Museum.

The year was: $yt^{\delta}_{\mathcal{M}} = 1954$

There was another point in time, also much later than his birth date, when Richard Meinertzhagen became an ornithologist, and such he remained until his death:

$$\text{At } t,\ t^{\alpha}_{\mathcal{M}} \prec\prec t^{b}_{\mathcal{M}} \preceq t \prec t^{\omega}_{\mathcal{M}}: \quad (\mathcal{M} \text{ \textbf{is-a} } ornithologist)$$

In his lifetime, he published autobiographical material, which was more than once, at times in his life which occurred when he had already attained the rank of colonel:

$$\text{At } t^{i},\ t^{c}_{\mathcal{M}} \prec t^{i} \prec t^{\omega}_{\mathcal{M}}: \quad (\text{publish}_{\mathcal{M}}\ memoirs^{i}_{\mathcal{M}})$$

It was in the year 1954 that Meinertzhagen's bird collection was acquired by, and transferred to, what by then was Natural History branch of the British Museum, and was only later to become the Natural History Museum. Let us define some notation for the case at hand; see Table 5.3.3.2.2.

The next formula states that at a point in time during the lifetime of Richard Meinertzhagen (this was earlier than his death, and wasn't earlier than his becaming an ornithologist), there had been in existence an evolving bird collection associated with him, whose stage of evolution is identified by points in time, and of which he had both the legal ownership (represented by a hand containing the letter lambda), and the physical possession (represented by a hand containing the letter phi). The latest stage in the collection's evolution we are considering (as though it remained static thereafter) is the one identified by the superscript being delta:

5.3 Episodic Formulae

$$\text{At } t,\ t_{\mathcal{M}}^{b} \preceq t \prec t_{\mathcal{M}}^{\delta}\colon \left(\exists\ BirdCollection_{\mathcal{M}}^{t}\right) \wedge$$
$$\wedge \left(\text{has}_{\mathcal{M}}\ \boxed{\lambda \Rightarrow}\ BirdCollection_{\mathcal{M}}^{t}\right) \wedge$$
$$\wedge \left(\text{has}_{\mathcal{M}}\ \boxed{\varphi \Rightarrow}\ BirdCollection_{\mathcal{M}}^{t}\right).$$

Moreover:

$$\text{At } t,\ t \succeq t_{\mathcal{M}}^{\delta}\colon \left(\exists\ BirdCollection_{\mathcal{M}}^{\delta}\right) \wedge$$
$$\wedge \left(\text{has}_{\mathfrak{m}}\ \boxed{\varphi \Rightarrow}\ BirdCollection_{\mathcal{M}}^{\delta}\right) \wedge$$
$$\wedge \left(\exists \mathfrak{m}' \Rightarrow (\mathfrak{m} = \mathfrak{m}')\right) \wedge$$
$$\wedge \left(\exists \mathfrak{m}'' \Rightarrow (\mathfrak{m} = \mathfrak{m}'')\right).$$

This paragraph describes in words the previous formula. Up to when (at least) the physical possession of the bird collection was transferred, it was Meinertzhagen who used to have both the physical possession and the legal ownership of the collection, which had been undergoing various stages since when Meinertzhagen (by then already an ornithologist) started it. Following the transfer of the physical possession of the collection (as in the latest stage at which it was while in Meinertzhagen's possession), the collection was in (at least) the physical possession of either the Natural History branch of the British Museum, or the Natural History Museum, whichever that same evolving entity, the recipient of the collection, was.

This way, we accommodate the fact that it was what by then was the Natural History branch of the British Museum, that received the collection, and that eventually the hosting museum was to become the Natural History Museum. Starting at the transfer point in time, which was in 1954, the Meinertzhagen bird collection was to remain (let us assume it for the sake of simplicity) in its latest evolution stage, and this during what was left of his lifetime, and thereafter as well. That is to say, the way in which he had left it at his death. That much is represented in the next formula. (In particular, let us agree that we consider the bird collection merely as a set, and that every stage is characterised by the extension of the set, i.e., by which items were members in that set).

$$\text{At } t,\ t \succeq t_{\mathcal{M}}^{\delta}\colon \left(BirdCollection_{\mathcal{M}}^{t} = BirdCollection_{\mathcal{M}}^{\delta}\right)$$

A more refined version of our formal representation would continue to assign the value of t to the superscript of the symbol for the bird collection, in order to be able to refer to whatever physically and perceptually happened to the collection, since it was originally stored in clearly identified drawers, until when "most specimens have been incorporated into the main collection" at the Museum (Knox, 1993, p. 323).

From 1954, which was thirteen years before Meinertzhagen's death, his bird collection was accessible to a set of persons identified by the given point in time at which the accessibility state is considered:

$$\text{At } t, \quad t \succeq t^a \succ t^\delta_\mathcal{M} : \left(\begin{array}{c} BirdCollection^\delta_\mathcal{M} \text{ is} \\ accessible\text{-}to(\mathcal{B}^t) \end{array} \right)$$

5.3.3.3 A Notation for Biographies

The present Section 5.3.3.3 can be safely skipped, by those readers only interested in following the formalism for the controversy concerning Meinertzhagen's bird collection. The more mathematically minded, however, may find in Section 5.3.3.3 an embryo for a more refined formalisation of biographies. In order to represent a biography, in Nissan (2002b) I introduced this notation, when I developed a formalism for capturing some information from the plot of Pirandello's play *Henry IV*.[128]

Let *biographical context* be symbolised by a hollow M. Let Richard Meinertzhagen's biographical context at time t be represented by the symbol

$$\mathcal{M}^t_\mathcal{M}$$

Let is be defined by *mutual recursion*, as follows. Let it be formulated as a doubleton, whose two members are "entourage" (or "milieu") and "history", that is to say: the subset of people of Meinertzhagen's entourage at time t, who (by then) are individually known to Meinertzhagen; and the history of Meinertzhagen at time t. It is expected that a person is, by default, aware of his or her own biographical context: at the given point in time, the given person is aware of his or her current milieu, as well as of his or her history, which in turn, among the other things, comprises the same person's past milieu states.

---

[128] After a horse fall at a historical pageant, the protagonist of *Henry IV*, whose own days are those of Pirandello, believes he is the eleventh-century emperor of Germany around the time of his penance at Canossa. The people in his entourage are complacent, and he lives his delusion for about twenty years. He "maps" the persons from his life onto characters from the standard historiographical account of the emperor Henry IV. Unbeknown to his entourage, the protagonist has meanwhile recovered, and knows who he actually is. He eventually tells some visitors, then, even though he didn't premeditate to take the life of the man he considers responsible for causing his horse fall, he wounds him mortally. Onlookers are divided in their opinions: is he sane? The protagonist is now to posture as though he is not, forever.

5.3 Episodic Formulae

The "entourage" member of that doubleton is symbolised as

$$Q^t_M$$

The "history" member of that doubleton is symbolised as

$$h^t_M$$

and is itself a doubleton, as shown in second formula in the following:

$$\begin{cases} \mathcal{M}^t_M \equiv \langle Q^t_M, h^t_M \rangle \\ h^t_M \equiv \langle \hat{e}^t_M, \mathcal{M}^{\hat{t}}_M \rangle \end{cases}$$

There is a double recursion, because the left-hand part of the first formula is defined by means of the left-hand part of the second formula, whereas the left-hand part of the second formula is defined by means of the left-hand part of the first formula.

In the doubleton for "history", the second member – that is

$$\mathcal{M}^{\hat{t}}_M$$

– is the latest past biographical context of the same agent, so that biographical context is defined recursively. By our convention:

$$\hat{e}^t_M \equiv e^t_M - e^{\hat{t}}_M$$

just as:

$$\hat{e}^{\hat{t}}_M \equiv e^{\hat{t}}_M - e^{\hat{\hat{t}}}_M$$

That is to say, the e surmounted by the hat stands for a set (of events in which the given individual is knowingly involved) resulting from a difference of two sets, and having occurred in the latest interval of time since the biographical context had last changed: the e surmounted by the hat stands for an increment with respect to the latest earlier point in time when the biographical context was different, whereas without the hat, the symbol e stands for a cumulated set:

$$e^t_A \equiv \hat{e}^t_A \bigcup_{\tau = t^\alpha_A}^{\hat{t}(b.d.i.)} \hat{e}^\tau_A$$

where $b.d.i.$ is defined as:
$b.d.i \equiv$ "by discrete increments as in the definition of $\hat{t}$ vis-à-vis t."
By our definition:

e^t_M — the set of such current events (here, conventionally, from birth on) that involve the person Richard Meinertzhagen, provided that the latter was aware of them.

$\hat{e}^t_M$ — the increment of the events set from time double-hatted t until time single-hatted t.

As a subset of e^t_M we need include Meinertzhagen's state of relations with Q^t_M (his then current entourage). In e^t_M other elements possibly are events of the Self alone, either physiological (such as sudden illness), or mental (some thoughts that occurred to the given individual). Likewise, for

$$\mathcal{M}^\tau_M \, , \ Q^\tau_M \, , \text{ and } h^\tau_M \, ,$$

a lifelong trajectory of states (as a set of sets) can be reconstituted. Now, let us depart from the treatment given in Nissan (2003c), and specialise this notation for subsets of the biographical context, of the entourage, and of the biographical history, so that, given a person y, only such persons who are (or were) y's social superiors would be members in the subset of the entourage, and only events pertaining to y's relations with them would appear in the subset of the history. For this purpose, we introduce a variant of the hollow-M symbol, namely, a soaring (or, using a term from heraldry: essorant) hollow-M symbol to indicate the subset of the biographical context which is about y's social superiors:

5.3 Episodic Formulae

Here, too, we have a definition resorting to a mutual recursion:

$$\begin{cases} \mathcal{M}_y^t \equiv \langle \,^{\text{soc}^+}Q_y^t, \,^{\text{soc}^+}h_y^t \rangle \\ \,^{\text{soc}^+}h_y^t \equiv \langle \,^{\text{soc}^+}\widehat{e}_y^t, \mathcal{M}_y^{\widehat{t}} \rangle \end{cases}$$

where:

$$\,^{\text{soc}^+}Q_y^t \equiv \left\{ x \,\Big|\, \left(x \in Q_y^t \right) \land \left(x \overset{\text{soc}}{>} y \right) \right\}$$

Let us go back to the formalism in Nissan (2003c). At time t during Meinertzhagen's life, the people in set

$$Q_{\mathcal{M}}^\tau$$

were in Meinertzhagen's entourage, and were individually known to him at that time. At various times, Meinertzhagen's interaction with individuals, the content of that interaction, and his and theirs respective personalities motivated – that much is known and uncontroversial about Meinertzhagen's biography – feelings that were either friendly of hostile to Meinertzhagen himself. As a matter of fact, Richard Meinertzhagen is known to have stirred strong feelings toward himself: of admiration or dislike or both, but, typically, he was the kind of person that was either very much liked, or very much disliked.

Let us define two sets of persons belonging to Meinertzhagen's milieu at a given time:

$$\exists Q_{+\mathcal{M}}^t, \quad \exists Q_{-\mathcal{M}}^t, \quad \left(Q_{+\mathcal{M}}^t \bigcup Q_{-\mathcal{M}}^t \right) \subseteq Q_{\mathcal{M}}^t$$

$$\exists t, \quad \begin{pmatrix} \left(q \in Q_{\mathcal{M}}^t\right) \land \\ \land \begin{pmatrix} \exists \tau, \tau \succeq t, \\ \text{At } \tau: \\ (\text{likes}_q \, \mathcal{M}) \end{pmatrix} \end{pmatrix} \Leftrightarrow \left(q \in Q_{+\mathcal{M}}^\tau\right)$$

$$\exists t, \quad \left(\wedge \begin{pmatrix} (q \in Q^t_{\mathcal{M}}) \wedge \\ \begin{pmatrix} \exists \tau, \tau \succeq t, \\ \text{At } \tau : \\ (\text{dislikes}_q \mathcal{M}) \end{pmatrix} \end{pmatrix} \right) \Leftrightarrow (q \in Q^\tau_{-\mathcal{M}})$$

The two sets of persons thus defined,

$$Q^\tau_{+\mathcal{M}} \quad \text{and} \quad Q^\tau_{-\mathcal{M}} \, .$$

are of people who became acquainted with Meinertzhagen at some time t in his life and thus belonged to his entourage at least at the time of that first contact, and who since, at any rate at time τ, had respectively harboured good feelings or bad feelings towards him. Notice that it makes sense for such sets to be defined even if τ happens to be after Meinertzhagen's death. Those two sets of persons are not necessarily disjoint, as some people may have mixed feelings at a given moment; moreover, at different times a given person may entertain a positive view and a hostile view of another given person. Thus, it *may* happen that the intersection of those two sets is other than the empty set, at points in time that may even be the same:

$$\exists t', \quad \exists t'', \quad \left(Q^{t'}_{+\mathcal{M}} \bigcap Q^{t''}_{-\mathcal{M}} \right) \neq \emptyset$$

and perhaps so even for $t' = t''$

as the very same persons may belong to the opposite camps at the same time. In fact, it would just be a simplification if we were to consider those two sets as being the intersections of Meinertzhagen's entourage with, respectively, his friends and his foes. At any rate, at given times t, there exist two (evolving) sets:

$$\exists \mathit{friends}^t_{\mathcal{M}}, \quad \exists \mathit{foes}^t_{\mathcal{M}}$$

and whereas both sets can be expected to have a subset contained in

$$Q^\tau_{\mathcal{M}}$$

some members of the two sets have not been known to Meinertzhagen personally. Both sets constitute instances of cumulation. Both sets persist in time beyond the time of Richard Meinertzhagen's death, and at any rate their respective membership can be considered to be fluid. For example, this or that person's being a member in his set of friends or his set of foes at a given time. Moreover, attitudes need

5.3 Episodic Formulae   463

not be so crisp. They may as well be different in different domains: given individuals may have modified their appreciation of Meinertzhagen *qua* bird collector since the publication of arguments disproving his integrity in that role, but may perhaps retain their opinion of him as a spy master. Meinertzhagen is sometimes claimed to have been self-aggrandising in his memoirs. It is not unconceivable that

$$\exists \kappa, \ \exists \mathfrak{P}, \ \mathfrak{P} \text{ is-a } person,$$

$$\kappa \subset \text{content}(memoirs^i_M),$$

$$\exists t, \ \left(\text{At } t: \ \left(\text{read}_{\mathfrak{P}} \ \kappa\right)\right) \ \boxed{m}\!\!\Rightarrow$$

$$\boxed{m}\!\!\Rightarrow [foes^t_M := (foes^{t-1}_M \cup \mathfrak{P})] \boxed{m}\!\!\Rightarrow$$

$$\boxed{m}\!\!\Rightarrow \left[\begin{array}{l} \text{At } t+n: \\ \text{criticize}_{\mathfrak{P}} \ (integrity_M \ (\text{make}_M \ form(memoirs^i_M))) \end{array}\right]$$

where := is the symbol of value assignment to a variable, familiar to computer programmers. The formula means that there exists some person (symbolised as a hollow **r**), and there exists part of the content of any of Richard Meinertzhagen's autobiographical writings, and there exists a time when the person mentioned earlier read that part of Meinertzhagen's own memoirs, and that motivated that reader to join the set of Meinertzhagen's foes (that is to say, the reader had not been among those hostile to Meinertzhagen prior to that moment), and this developing a hostile attitude towards Meinertzhagen motivated that reader, at some later time, to criticise Meinertzhagen's integrity in how Meinertzhagen wrote his memoirs.[129]

---

[129] And indeed, some have harshly criticised Meinertzhagen's diaries on formal grounds, such as suggesting that entries were rewritten or transplanted at a given data whereas they were written later on. Yet, the very motivation for the degree to which the criticism was damning perhaps was not always independent of Meinertzhagen's attitudes as displayed in the content of the diaries, vis-à-vis the critic's own opinions. It must be borne in mind that memoirs or even diaries that authors publish, usually are not to be held by the same standards of verifiability based on the evidence that can be expected in police inquiries, or, then, of records of laboratory tests, or, then again, of records of the handling and disposal of hazardous material (in the 1990s, there was a scandal in the U.K. concerning fake recording of the disposal process of nuclear waste). The documentary side is merely one of the things that make autobiographical texts, memoirs, or even diaries, interesting and worth of publication by a trade publisher. Tampering with the text, inserting reconstructions from memory, may be motivated on literary grounds. Unless special claims are made by an author for the text having been recorded at the time it happened, and only at that time, in order to prove something, some rewriting or supplementing would not normally affect the integrity of the text, other than in the eyes of some Draconian beholder, perhaps of one willing to assume an author's intent to deceive unless proven otherwise. Generally speaking, it happens sometimes that somebody takes exception to text in somebody else's diaries being completed from memory at a later date, or, then, makes much, by way of discredit, of editorial intervention in diaries – something that is routine in the publishing industry (charges of editing are something that, e.g., was invoked at a time by detractors of Anne Frank's diaries, which is an example of how an explicit argument may not necessarily be the main point of the argument being made).

In concepts "memoirs" and "diary", a crucial role is played by testimony about the Self, which in my notation is represented as:

$$\underset{\mathcal{M}}{\overset{t_2}{\text{Self}}} [\text{At } t_1, \ldots]$$

or, more generally, this way:

$$\underset{\mathcal{M}}{\overset{t_T}{\text{Self}}} \bigwedge_{i=1}^{N} [\text{At } t_i, \ldots]$$

The notation introduced in the present Section 5.3.3.3 will not appear in the rest of the formalism about the Meinertzhagen narrative, which is because of what I select, out of the narrative, for representation here.

5.3.3.4 Formalising the Allegations About Meinertzhagen's Stuffed Birds

For the purposes of formalising the allegations concerning some stuffed birds in the Meinertzhagen bird collection, let us stick henceforth to excerpts from a text from the Smithsonian Institution Research Reports, an informal, popularistic account by Michael Lipske (1999) of the rediscovery in India, by ornithologist Pamela Rasmussen of the U.S. National Museum of Natural History, of the Forest Spotted Owlet (*Athene blewitti*), a bird that had long been thought to be extinct.

"Seven stuffed skins in a handful of museums were all that seemed to remain of a species that several experts had crossed off as extinct". After living individuals of the given owlet species "had gone unseen by any scientist for 113 years", "one morning in 1997" Rasmussen "gazed, only half trusting her eyes at" an individual of that very bird species, perched on a tree in western India (more individuals were

---

Still, hypothesising intent to deceive, and success at deceiving, is not so surprising when one considers that Meinertzhagen was, and is, admired for his role in military intelligence during the First World War. The line of reasoning would go as follows: Meinertzhagen's talent for deception, which he exploited to a good effect in his capacity of managing military intelligence in a given region during that war, would enable him, and indeed even tempt him, into application in some other field. Moreover, if we are to believe Meinertzhagen's published allegation that Lawrence of Arabia, his friend notwithstanding their political views being opposite in important respects, had admitted to him that he bluffed in his own published autobiographical material, this may have one ask after all, by analogy, whether Meinertzhagen didn't likewise indulge, at least sometimes, in taking some liberties with the factual truth while offering a public image of himself. Both of them had attained mythical status, owing to self-reports of daring and highly adventurous feats; that one of these two celebrities was ascribing to the other one the admission that much of his published memoirs was bluff, was something conducive to something like that being suspected (as well) of the one making the claim.

5.3 Episodic Formulae

found later on): "the forest owlet that Rasmussen had sought for two weeks from one side of India to the other".

In the narrative at hand, let us symbolise the individual human characters as follows:

$\mathcal{M}$ The deceased bird collector and master spy.
$\mathcal{R}$ Living ornithologist Pamela C. Rasmussen.
$\mathcal{C}_1$ First group of $\mathcal{R}$'s colleagues.
$\mathcal{C}_2$ Second group of $\mathcal{R}$'s colleagues.

In the following formula,

$$t_\circ, \quad {}^d t_\circ, \quad \text{and} \quad {}^y t_\circ$$

respectively are the time of the given event, the day on which it took place, and the year in which this happened.

$$e_1 \equiv \begin{bmatrix} \text{At } t_\circ, \\ t_\circ \subset \text{morning}({}^d t_\circ) \subset {}^y t_\circ \\ {}^y t_\circ = 1997 : \\ \left(\underset{\mathcal{R}}{\boxed{}}{}^{t_\circ} \left(\begin{array}{l} \beta \wedge \\ \wedge (\beta \text{ is } alive) \wedge \\ \wedge (\beta \text{ is-a } bird) \end{array} \right) \right) \wedge \\ \wedge \left(\underset{\mathcal{R}}{\bigcap}{}^{t_\circ} (\beta \in Athene\_blewitti) \right) \end{bmatrix}$$

The previous formula states that at a given time in the morning of a day in 1997, Rasmussen visually perceived an individual bird which, as she could see, was alive, and which, at that very time, she realised belonged to the species *Athene blewitti*.

Apart from the temporal relations we have been using thus far, a shorthand using

over the line for a time interval with "precedes or equals", on both sides is used in the next formula. Let us first describe in words what the formula states: there is a given set of places (even far away from each other), all of them being in India, and during the entire temporal interval T (which corresponds to the period starting as early as two weeks earlier than the sighting of the living member of *Athene blewitti*, and as late as a given number of days later on), Rasmussen was in India with an active goal, and for all those places in the list, there was a time when Rasmussen was in that place. Rasmussen's active goal during that visit was such that for a non-empty set of individual birds, and for two non-empty sets of time-points, (of which temporal sets the first one is a subset of the interval T) at some point in time (belonging to the first temporal set) Rasmussen would visually perceive any of the individual birds in the bird-set and see it is alive, and then at some identical or subsequent point in time she would know that the given individual bird belongs to the species *Athene blewitti*.

$$\exists Places, \; Places \subset India,$$

$$Places = \{\ldots, \gamma_1, \ldots, \gamma_2, \ldots\},$$

$$\text{far}(\gamma_1, \gamma_2), \quad \forall t, \; t \subset T,$$

$$T \equiv \left({}^d t_\circ - 2 \text{ weeks} \; \vdash\!\!\!-\!\!\!\dashv \; {}^d t_\circ + n \text{ days} \right),$$

$$(\text{At } t: \; \mathcal{R} \text{ in } India) \wedge \left(\underset{\mathcal{R}}{\overset{t}{\text{\Large\ding{43}}}} G_1 \right) \wedge$$

$$\wedge \begin{bmatrix} \forall \gamma_f, \quad \gamma_f \in Places, \\ \exists \tau \; \tau \subset T, \\ \left(At \; \tau: \quad \mathcal{R} \text{ in } \gamma_f \right) \end{bmatrix},$$

where

$$G_1 \equiv \begin{bmatrix} \exists \{b_i\}, \; \exists \{t_{j_1}\}, \; \exists \{t_{j_2}\}, \\ \{t_{j_1}\} \neq \emptyset, \; \{t_{j_2}\} \neq \emptyset, \\ \{b_i\} \neq \emptyset, \; (\{t_{j_1}\} \subset T) \wedge \\ \wedge \; \forall t_{j_1}, \; \forall t_{j_2}, \; t_{j_1} \preceq t_{j_2}: \\ \left(\underset{\mathcal{R}}{\overset{t_{j_1}}{\text{\Large\ding{170}}}} (b_i \wedge (b_i \text{ is alive})) \right) \wedge \\ \wedge \left(\underset{\mathcal{R}}{\overset{t_{j_2}}{\square}} (b_i \in Athene\_blewitti) \right) \end{bmatrix}$$

The next formula states that the bird-sighting event actually took place, and that this caused Rasmussen goal of having such bird-sightings to be achieved. It is followed by another formula, stating that up to that moment, during her visit to India, that same goal hadn't been achieved as yet.

$$\text{At } t_\circ: \; e_1 \; \boxed{\text{c}}\!\!\!\Rightarrow \; \underset{\mathcal{R}}{\overset{t_\circ}{\text{\Large\ding{43}}}} G_1$$

5.3 Episodic Formulae

$$\text{At } t, \ (t \subset T) \wedge (t \prec t_\circ): \quad \neg \left(\underset{\mathcal{R}}{\text{✌}}^t G_1 \right)$$

In the next formula, we first define a temporal span whose starting point and whose ending point belong to vastly different grainsizes; in fact, the interval starts one generation earlier than Rasmussen obtaining the eventful bird-sighting, and ends just before the day of that particular event. The formula also states that there existed, during the given time interval, a set whose cardinality (i.e., whose number of members) was seven, and which consisted of stuffed specimens of the species *Athene blewitti*, those specimen being at some museum.

$$\text{At } t, \ (t_o - 1 \ generation) \prec t \prec {}^d t_o:$$

$$\exists S, \quad |S| = 7,$$

$$S \equiv \left\{ \text{🕊}_i \ \middle| \ \text{🕊}_i \begin{array}{l} (\text{🕊}_i \in Athene\_blewitti) \wedge \\ \wedge \ (\text{🕊}_i \text{ is } stuffed) \wedge \\ \wedge \ (\text{🕊}_i \text{ is in } m) \wedge \\ \wedge \ (m \text{ is-a } museum) \end{array} \right\}$$

In 113 years, no scientist had seen a living individual of *Athene blewitti* and published a report of that sighting:

$$\forall t^*, \quad t^* \subset \tau, \quad \tau \equiv ({}^y t_\circ - 113 years \vdash\!\!\!\dashv {}^y t_\circ),$$

$$\not\exists \sigma, \quad (\sigma \text{ is-a } scientist) \wedge$$

$$\wedge \ \underset{\sigma}{\text{📖}}^{t^*} (b_k \wedge (\text{At } t^*\!: b_k \text{ is } alive)) \wedge$$

$$\wedge \left[\left(\square_\sigma (b_k \in Athene\_blewitti) \right) \begin{array}{c} \text{At } t, \ t^* \preceq t \preceq t_\sigma^\omega: \\ \text{📨} \end{array} (publish_\sigma \ \pi_1) \right]$$

$$\pi_1 \equiv \left[\wedge \underset{\sigma}{\text{📖}}^t \left(\begin{array}{l} \exists b_k \wedge (b_k \in Athene\_blewitti) \wedge \\ \text{At } t^*\!: \exists b_k \wedge \\ \wedge (b_k \text{ is } alive) \end{array} \right) \right].$$

At an advanced stage of a multi-year project, Rasmussen and her colleagues are pursuing the goal of their publishing a *Field Guide to Birds of India*, the plan enacted for that purpose being: their preparing the *Field Guide to Birds of India*. (Let us symbolise the latter as *F*.) We represent this as follows:

$$\forall t, \quad t \subset \Theta, \quad \textbf{most-of}(\Theta) \prec T,$$

$$T \equiv ({}^{y}\vartheta_1 \vdash\!\!\!\dashv {}^{y}\vartheta_2), \quad {}^{y}\vartheta_1 \neq {}^{y}\vartheta_2,$$

$$\left(\mathcal{G}^{t}_{\mathcal{R}\cup\mathcal{C}_1} \ G_2\right) \wedge \left(\text{pursue}_{\mathcal{R}\cup\mathcal{C}_1} \ G_2\right)$$

$$G_2 \equiv \left(\text{publish}_{\mathcal{R}\cup\mathcal{C}_1} \ F\right)$$

$$\text{plan}_1(G_2) \equiv \left(\text{prepare}_{\mathcal{R}\cup\mathcal{C}_1} \ F\right).$$

Now, let us describe the event of the 1993 exposé in *Ibis*; remember that an event of communication is symbolised by means of the message itself being preceded by a prefix μ whose subscript refers to the originator of the message, and whose superscript (if there is one) refers to the addressees (or recipient) of the message. The next formula states that at a given time during 1993, *Ibis*, which is a journal, published a particular article which, starting from its publication time, was conveying such information which contained this other bit of information: namely, that there exists a set of stuffed bird specimens, that set being a subset of the Meinertzhagen bird collection, and such that there exists a set of such labels which are part of the given specimen (from the given set of bird specimens), and which convey information that is false.

$$[\text{At } t_E, {}^{y}t_E = 1993: (\text{publish}_{Ibis} \ E)] \wedge$$

$$\wedge (E \ \textbf{is-a} \ article) \wedge (Ibis \ \textbf{is-a} \ journal) \wedge$$

$$\wedge (\text{At } \tau, \tau \succeq t_E: \ \mu_E \varepsilon) \wedge (\varepsilon' \subset \varepsilon)$$

Lipske (1999), who was first describing Rasmussen's rediscovery of the owlet species *Athene blewitti* in India, turns to some background information:

> Coming nose to beak with the long-absent species required days of difficult hunting along forest paths and stream beds. But before leaving for India, Rasmussen had already picked her way down another trail that led through a jungle of scientific deception.
> She had been in the final stages of preparing a field guide to birds of the Indian subcontinent (a project initiated by Smithsonian Secretary Emeritus S. Dillon Ripley), when she read an article that raised questions about the accuracy of bird records made by Col. Richard Meinertzhagen. A British soldier, spy and noted amateur ornithologist in the early part of this century, Meinerthagen (who died in 1967) was long credited with creating one of the world's best private collections of Old World bird specimens.
> The 1993 article suggested, however, that labels on some of his birds were fraudulent. This was unsettling news for Rasmussen. There were more than a dozen kinds of birds for which Meinertzhagen was the only collector claiming to have found that species in India. "I had to know whether to include all these taxa" in the field guide or rule them out as Indian birds, she says.

5.3 Episodic Formulae

The next formula represents the knowledge that upon reading the exposé in *Ibis*, Rasmussen realised that ε' (i.e., that there are stuffed birds in the Meinertzhagen collection whose labels convey false information) is something running counter (this is symbolised by a lightning-like arrow) her and her colleagues' goal G_2, and this in turn provided motivation for her to set for herself yet another goal, G_3:

$$\varepsilon' \equiv \begin{bmatrix} \exists \Sigma, \\ \Sigma \equiv \left\{ \ell_i \mid \begin{array}{l} (\ell_i \text{ \textbf{is-a} } bird) \wedge \\ \wedge \; (\ell_i \text{ is } stuffed) \end{array} \right\}, \\ \Sigma \subset BirdCollection^\delta_{\mathcal{M}}, \; \exists L, \\ L \equiv \left\{ \lambda_j \mid \begin{array}{l} (\lambda_j \text{ \textbf{is-a} } label) \wedge \\ \wedge \; (\lambda_j \subset \ell_j \in \Sigma) \wedge \\ \wedge \; (\mu_{\lambda_j} \; info_j) \wedge \\ \wedge \; (info_j \text{ \textbf{is false}}) \end{array} \right\} \end{bmatrix}$$

At t, $t \succeq t_E$, $t \subset$ **final-stages-of** (Θ):

$(\text{read}_{\mathcal{R}} \; E) \; \boxed{\text{c}}\!\!\Rightarrow \left(\Box_{\mathcal{R}}(\mu_E \; \varepsilon') \right) \boxed{\text{c}}\!\!\Rightarrow$

$\boxed{\text{c}}\!\!\Rightarrow \left(\bowtie^t_{\mathcal{R}} (\varepsilon' \Longrightarrow G_z) \right) \boxed{\text{m}}\!\!\Rightarrow \left(\bowtie^t_{\mathcal{R}} G_3 \right)$

Let *ForEx* stand for *ForensicExamination*.

$$G_3 \equiv \left(ForEx^{taxidermy}_{\mathcal{R} \cup \mathcal{C}_2} \; \Psi \right)$$

Lipske (1999) continues his account as follows:

> To find out, she visited Britain's Natural History Museum in London, where most of Meinertzhagen's collection of tens of thousands of birds now resides. Working with ornithologists there, she examined the colonel's unique India specimens. "Each was either clearly fraudulent or highly suspicious", Rasmussen says.
>
> She discovered that Meinertzhagen had done some of his most successful bird hunting not in the wild but in the museum's specimen cabinets. He was known to boast of his collection's "unique perfection", she says. "One of the reasons that it was uniquely perfect was because he was stealing the best specimens" from other collectors' museum contributions.
>
> With Robert Prys-Jones, head of the Bird Section at Britain's Natural History Museum, Rasmussen established that hundreds of Meinertzhagen specimens were birds he filched;

some he restuffed and then relabeled with false information. Of all the ornithological treasures the colonel stole, the rarest was India's forest owlet. Cracking the case required sophisticated detective work.

Rasmussen had found that, of seven known specimens of the owlet in museums, only one was said to have been collected in this century — in 1914 by Meinertzhagen. Most of the others had been collected in the 1880s by James Davidson, a British official and bird enthusiast stationed in western India.

Lipske goes on to relate how Rasmussen and her colleagues carried out examinations of the suspicious items:

> Working with ornithologist Nigel Collar of BirdLife International in England, Rasmussen examined the Meinertzhagen owlet at the British Museum. Both experts could see that original stitching and stuffing had been removed from the skin and that new stuffing had been inserted and the bird resewn. Closer study of the specimen and X-ray photographs of it revealed characteristic preparation touches unique to Davidson, a self-taught worker with one-of-a-kind methods for handling bird skins.
>
> Fairly certain that Meinertzhagen's owlet actually had been collected by Davidson, the ornithologists still wanted more evidence. Even though the bird had been restuffed, Rasmussen remembers hoping "maybe, just maybe, there will be a fiber or something somewhere that will tie it to Davidson". Luckily, there was.
>
> Inside a wing, stuffed around a joint, there remained some raw cotton that had turned yellow from fat. Checking the wing of an owl of another species Davidson collected in India, the sleuths found what looked like similar cotton. They sent both samples to the Federal Bureau of Investigation in Washington, DC, where forensic tests indicated that the two bits of cotton were virtually identical.
>
> "That, along with other clues, just basically put the nail in the coffin", Rasmussen says, noting the improbability that Meinertzhagen would have had access to the same kind of rough cotton Davidson used 30 years earlier. The owlet was a previously unknown, fifth Davidson specimen, presumably stolen from Britain's Natural History Museum by Meinertzhagen and decades later returned to it as part of the colonel's rich collection.

The following formula states that the set we call Ψ and which as stated in the previous formula, was to be subjected to taxidermic examinations, is constituted of all such stuffed bird items from the Meinertzhagen collection which according to their label originated in India, and which represent a species or subspecies (whichever taxon is minimal, i.e., if there are subspecies of the given bird species, then we are looking for representatives of those subspecies indeed, rather than merely – which is more general – of their species), provided that there is no independent evidence from other collections, deemed trustworthy, which include such an item with a label also stating that the given individual bird was collected in India. This was the narrower set of stuffed birds to be examined, for the purposes of ascertaining that the given species or subspecies could be listed in the field guide as being present in India indeed.

$$\Psi \equiv \left\{ \psi \;\middle|\; \begin{array}{l} f_1(\psi, \Omega) \wedge f_2(\Omega), \\ \forall \Omega, \; (\Omega \text{ \textbf{is-a} } bird) \wedge \\ \wedge \; \Omega = \min \left\{ \begin{array}{l} species(bird), \\ subspecies(bird) \end{array} \right\} \end{array} \right\}$$

5.3 Episodic Formulae

$$f_1(\psi, \Omega) \equiv \begin{bmatrix} (\psi \text{ is-a } \Omega) \wedge \\ \wedge \; (\psi \text{ is } stuffed) \wedge \\ \wedge \; (\psi \in BirdCollection_{\mathcal{M}}^{\delta}) \wedge \\ \wedge \; \left(\mu_{\lambda_\psi} (\psi \text{ is-from } India) \right) \end{bmatrix}$$

$$f_2(\Omega) \equiv \begin{bmatrix} \not\exists \xi, \, (\xi \text{ is-a } \Omega) \wedge \\ \wedge \; (\xi \text{ is } stuffed) \wedge \\ \wedge \; \exists z, \exists \lambda_\xi, (\xi \in BirdCollection_z) \wedge \\ \wedge \; \left(\mu_{\lambda_\xi} (\xi \text{ is-from } India) \right) \\ \wedge \; \left(\Box_{\mathcal{R} \cup \mathcal{C}_2} \begin{pmatrix} BirdCollection_z \\ \text{is } trustworthy \end{pmatrix} \right) \end{bmatrix}$$

As seen earlier,

$$G_3 \equiv \left(ForEx_{\mathcal{R} \cup \mathcal{C}_2}^{taxidermy} \Psi \right)$$

We state that the very ability of, and permissibility for, Rasmussen and Prŷs-Jones, that G_3 would eventuate, motivated an event:

$$\text{can}_{\mathcal{R} \cup \mathcal{C}_2}^{ont, \, deont} G_3 \; \boxed{\mathbf{m}}\!\!\!\Longrightarrow e_2$$

This event was that Rasmussen and her second set of collaborators arranged for that forensic examination to be carried out:

$$e_2 \equiv \left[\text{make}_{\mathcal{R} \cup \mathcal{C}_2} \; ForEx_{\mathcal{R} \cup \mathcal{C}_2}^{taxidermy} \; \Psi \right]$$

$$(e_2 \cup \varepsilon') \; \boxed{\mathbf{m}}\!\!\!\Longrightarrow (\mu_{\mathcal{R}} \; \varepsilon'')$$

where

$$\varepsilon'' \equiv \begin{bmatrix} \forall \psi, \ \psi \in \Psi, \\ (\psi \text{ is "clearly fraudulent"}) \lor \\ \lor \ (\psi \text{ is "highly suspicious"}) \end{bmatrix}$$

Rasmussen and her collaborators claimed ε'''

$$\mu_{\mathcal{R} \cup \mathcal{P}} \ \varepsilon'''$$

where ε''' is defined as follows:

$$\varepsilon''' = \begin{bmatrix} \exists X, \ \exists Y, \ Y \subset X \subset BirdCollection_{\mathcal{M}}^{\delta}, \\ X \equiv \{x_u\}, Y \equiv \{y_v\}, \forall x_u, \forall y_v, \\ \begin{bmatrix} \text{steal}_{\mathcal{M}} \ x_u; \\ \varepsilon_1'''(x_u) \land (\mathcal{M} \text{ stit } \varepsilon_2'''(y_v)) \end{bmatrix} \end{bmatrix}$$

$$\varepsilon_1'''(x_u) \equiv \begin{bmatrix} \text{remove}_{\mathcal{M}}(Old(Label(x_u))); \\ \text{stick}_{\mathcal{M}}(Current(Label(x_u))) \end{bmatrix}$$

$$\varepsilon_2'''(y_v) \equiv \begin{bmatrix} \text{remove}(Old(Stitching(y_v))); \\ \text{remove}(Old(Stuffing(y_v))); \\ \text{insert}(New(Stuffing(y_v))); \\ \text{sew}(New(Stitching(y_v))) \end{bmatrix}$$

It's Meinertzhagen who sees to it that the removal of the old stitching and stuffing and their replacements are carried out; yet, we omit the subject subscript from the strings for the relevant verbs, as it is immaterial whether it was Meinertzhagen himself who (allegedly) carried out those operations, or (less likely) somebody else doing that discreetly on his behalf at his behest.

The supposed motivation for ε''' is the desire (ascribed to Meinertzhagen and more generally associated with stealing and camouflaging of stolen goods) to enact such a situation that it would not be known, other than to the culprit, that he has undue possession of the specimen he actually flaunts as being in his possession (or in the possession of whomever eventually receives from him that specimen, or the entire collection). In particular, it should not be known that of the specimen he has in his possession he is not the legal owner. Moreover, and more in particular,

5.3 Episodic Formulae

it should not be known that the item is the same that unduly disappeared from the possession of the legitimate owner. To obtain the desired constellation of epistemic states in the outside world, it was necessary to give the stolen item a new identity. Should even the legitimate owner see the stolen specimen, because of the camouflaging the owner would no longer be able to recognize it as one that disappeared from his possession.

As seen in the formula for ε''', let us define:

x_u	the stolen specimen if it is to be relabelled, and more particularly:
y_v	if moreover the stolen specimen is to be both restuffed and relabelled.
x'_u	the relabelled item once the camouflaging was carried out.
y'_v	the restuffed and relabelled item once the camouflaging was carried out.

We can rewrite the accusers' allegations as follows:

$$\mu_{\mathcal{RUP}}\left(\wedge\left(\left(\underset{\mathcal{M}}{\text{\LARGE{☞}}} \pi_1\right) \overset{\text{m}}{\Longrightarrow} \varepsilon'''\right)^{\varepsilon''' \wedge \pi_0 \wedge}\right)$$

$$\pi_0 \equiv \left[\text{has}_O \overset{\lambda}{\Longrightarrow} x_u\right]$$

$$\pi_0 \Rightarrow \pi'_0$$

$$\pi'_0 \equiv \left[\text{has}_O \overset{\lambda}{\Longrightarrow} x'_u\right]$$

In the latter, we are simplifying with respect to a situation in which the legal ownership of the set of specimens to which the stolen specimen belonged, may meanwhile have changed, and in complex ways for that matter. Also for the sake of simplicity, I am omitting some temporal references.

$$\pi_1 \supset \pi_2 \supset \pi_3$$

$$\pi_2 \equiv \begin{bmatrix} \forall p,\ (p\ \textbf{is-a}\ person),\ p \neq \mathcal{M}, \\ \textbf{if}\ \left(\underset{p}{\text{⋈}}^{t}\ x'_u\right) \\ \textbf{then}\ \neg\ \underset{p}{\square}^{t}\ \pi'_0 \end{bmatrix}$$

$$\pi_3 \equiv \begin{bmatrix} \textbf{if}\ \left(\underset{O}{\text{⋈}}^{t}\ x'_u\right) \\ \textbf{then}\ \neg\ \underset{O}{\square}^{t}\ \pi'_0 \end{bmatrix}$$

Now, we can go ahead and represent likewise this other information: "Closer study of the specimen and X-ray photographs of it revealed characteristic preparation touches unique to Davidson" (Lipske, 1999), which I already quoted earlier. Realization of these peculiarities in the preparation of the specimen, motivated the goal of more testing: "Rasmussen remembers hoping 'maybe, just maybe, there will be a fiber or something somewhere that will tie it to Davidson'. Luckily, there was" (Lipske, 1999). The evidence found was "[i]nside a wing, stuffed around a joint", namely, "there remained some raw cotton that had turned yellow from fat. Checking the wing of an owl of another species Davidson collected in India, the sleuths found what looked like similar cotton". This in turn prompted the goal of having the cotton samples examined by a qualified laboratory. Which was at "the Federal Bureau of Investigation in Washington, DC, where forensic tests indicated that the two bits of cotton were virtually identical" (Lipske, 1999). This, to Rasmussen's own satisfaction, was proof enough: "'That, along with other clues, just basically put the nail in the coffin', Rasmussen says, noting the improbability that Meinertzhagen would have had access to the same kind of rough cotton Davidson used 30 years earlier", which of course is an assumption. This is not a legal case that went to court, but rather an event that tilted the balance in a controversy about the history of science that had implications for ongoing ornithological research.

Formal representation of this would make use of my notation for motivation, goal setting, goal satisfaction (i.e., goal achievement), perception, realisation, and so forth. In the following, I rather prefer to develop a representation for another side of the narrative at hand. It is *hypothesis formation*, for which we have already seen a notation.

Let us also introduce a set of propositions symbolised by a π with a numerical superscript instead of a subscript (which we had used in the formulae thus far). First of all, we want to state that according to what is known to *standard historiography* (which we symbolise by a capital Greek upsilon) Meinertzhagen was a "master of deception" in a given domain, espionage, and that for that reason he won acclaim.

5.3 Episodic Formulae

Υ standard historiography (up to and excluding Rasmussen's findings).

$\Box_{\mathcal{M}}^{-1} \Upsilon$ Meinertzhagen's standard historiographical image; i.e., whatever is known to standard historiography about him (up to and excluding Rasmussen's findings).

$$\pi^1 \subset \Box_{\mathcal{M}}^{-1} \Upsilon$$

$$\pi^1 \equiv \begin{bmatrix} \mathcal{M} & \textbf{is-a} & \text{``master of deception''} \\ & \textbf{in-domain} & \text{espionage}^{\text{military}} \end{bmatrix}$$

where

$$(p_o \textbf{ is-a ``master of deception''}) \Longrightarrow$$
$$\Longrightarrow (p_o \textbf{ is } habitually(successfully(very(deceitful))))$$

$$\pi^1 \xrightarrow{\boxed{\textbf{m}}} \pi^2$$

$$\pi^2 \equiv [\text{acclaim}_\Upsilon \; \mathcal{M} \; \textbf{qua} \; \pi^1]$$

It is both permissible (i.e., deontically possible) for Meinertzhagen (in the historical perspective of his own country), and ontologically possible for him (he had the ability for that to happen), to be (or have been) a master of deception in military espionage:

$$\pi^3 \equiv \left(\text{can}_{\mathcal{M}}^{\text{ont, deont}} \pi^1 \right)$$

$$\left[\pi^3 \xrightarrow{\boxed{\textbf{m}}} \pi^4 \right]$$

$$\left[\pi^3 \xrightarrow{\boxed{\textbf{rf}}} \pi^6 \right] \equiv \pi^7$$

where the arrow in the latter formula stands for "and this reinforced". The next formula is about a hypothesis being formed, and the one after that is about it being a standing hypothesis.

$$\pi^4 \equiv \left(\boxed{h} \left(\pi^9 \right) \right)$$

$$\pi^6 \equiv \left(h \ \pi^8 \right)$$

Meinertzhagen's very abilities tempted him, notwithstanding the thing he was able to do being impermissible:

$$\pi^8 \equiv \left[\begin{array}{c} (\text{can}_{\mathcal{M}}^{\text{ont}} \ \pi^9) \ \wedge \\ \wedge (\text{ is-tempted}_{\mathcal{M}} \rightleftharpoons (\neg \text{can}_{\mathcal{M}}^{\text{deont}} \ \pi^9)) \end{array} \right]$$

Proposition π^8 states that Meinertzhagen was both able to, and illegitimately tempted to, see to it that proposition π^9 is true. Motivation of the hypothesis π^9 arising, and π^8 (an extant hypothesis) being reinforced, are things that may have been verified independently: either, or both of them concomitantly. Thus:

$$(\pi^5 \wedge \neg \pi^7) \vee (\pi^7 \wedge \neg \pi^5)$$

$$\pi^9 \equiv [\text{be}_{\mathcal{M}} \ successfully(deceitful) \ \textbf{qua} \ D]$$

where, according to the situation (the controversy about the Meinertzhagen bird collection, or the controversy about Meinertzhagen's memoirs):

$$D \in \left\{ \begin{array}{c} diarist, \\ birdcollector \end{array} \right\}$$

That is to say, **D** stands for *diarist* or for *birdcollector*. Literally, D belongs to a set which comprises *diarist* and *birdcollector*.

5.4 Bex's Approach to Combining Stories and Arguments in Sense-Making Software for Crime Investigation

An interesting project in AI & Law that tries to combine stories and arguments in sense-making software for crime investigation, was reported about (Bex, et al., 2007) by a team from the Dutch universities of Groningen (Floris Bex, Bart Verheij,

5.4 Bex's Approach to Combining Stories and Arguments in Sense-Making...

Henry Prakken) and Utrecht (Susan van den Braak, Herre van Oostendorp, Gerard Vreeswijk, and again Henry Prakken). Eventually, having moved to the University of Dundee in Scotland, Floris Bex has published in book form a formal hybrid theory of how to relate arguments, stories, and criminal evidence (Bex, 2011).

As stated by Bex et al. (2007, p. 145):

> A formal model is proposed that combines AI formalisms for abductive inference to the best explanation and for defeasible argumentation. Stories about what might have happened in a case are represented as causal networks and possible hypotheses can be inferred by abductive reasoning. Links between stories and the available evidence are expressed with evidential generalisations that express how observations can be inferred from evidential sources with defeasible argumentation. It is argued that this approach unifies two well-known accounts of reasoning about evidence, namely, anchored narratives theory and new evidence theory. After the reasoning model is defined, a design is presented for sense-making software that allows crime investigators to visualise their thinking about a case in terms of the reasoning model.

The visualisation component of the architecture envisaged by Bex et al. (2007) is called *AVERs*, and was "implemented as a web front-end to an SQL database. A case can be represented visually through multiple views; in this paper we will focus on the two graphical views, that is, the evidence view and the story view" (section 6 ibid.). Ideally, they wanted to design a more sophisticated tool than such *investigative analysis software* for organising and visualising the evidence in the practice of crime investigation, as the British tool HOLMES 2 (short for *Home Office Large Major Enquiry System*),[130] and *Analyst's Notebook*,[131] this other tool offered by the British firm i2, as well as like the experimental tool from the Netherlands, BRAINS, reported about by van der Schoor (2004). Moreover, Bex et al. (2007) were building upon the remarkable record of some of the authors in research into argumentation within AI & Law, and they also wanted to relate their project to approaches from legal scholarship to legal narratives, and they specifically considered the *new evidence theory* (citing Anderson & Twining, 1991,[132] and Schum & Tillers, 1991) and the *anchored narrative theory* (citing Wagenaar et al., 1993).

There is no evidence in the paper of awareness of qualms among some scholars about Bayesianism in models of legal evidence. Nevertheless, Bex et al. (2007)

---

[130] http://www.holmes2.com/holmes2/index.php

[131] http://www.i2.co.uk/Products/Analysts Notebook/default.asp

[132] An extensively revised edition – Anderson, Schum, and Twining (2005) – of Anderson and Twining's textbook on evidence and proof (1991) has appeared in 2005. Anderson et al. (2005) "is a rigorous introduction to the construction and criticism of arguments about questions of fact, and to the marshalling and evaluation of evidence at all stages of litigation. It covers the principles underlying the logic of proof; the uses and dangers of story-telling; standards for decision and the relationship between probabilities and proof; the chart method and other methods of analyzing and ordering evidence in fact-investigation, in preparing for trial, and in connection with other important decisions in legal processes and in criminal investigation and intelligence analysis" (from the publisher's blurb).

propose a model likely to be well received by both the Bayesians and the skeptics in the controversy about probability in law. This is because the model of Bex et al. (2007) is based on causal networks[133] and on logic, without resorting to probabilities (even though arguably these could be added, should one wish to). All in all, unsurprisingly, the model of Bex et al. (2007) is very close to the kind of modelling of argumentation as being applied to narratives, from the respective (and sometimes joint) oeuvre of Henry Prakken, Floris Bex, Bart Verheij, and Susan van den Braak.

Bex et al. (2007) concede that both *explanation* and *prediction,* both of them familiar tasks from artificial intelligence, are important in crime investigation,[134] but admittedly, in the given paper, they confined themselves to only model explanation, as far as stories are concerned. They envisaged also addressing prediction in future research. They considered physical causation, mental causation, and the defeasibility of reasoning with causal information.[135]

Their own approach was to combine reasoning from cause to effect[136] and reasoning from effect to cause. They combined *abductive* reasoning[137] and *modus-ponens*-style reasoning[138]: "while the construction of stories to explain the available evidence is modelled as abductive reasoning with networks of causal generalisations, source-based reasoning about evidence is modelled as modus-ponens-style reasoning with evidential generalisations" (section 3 in Bex et al., 2007).

---

[133] Incidentally, in psychology, *causal attribution* in cognitive processes and beliefs is the subject of Hewstone (1989).

[134] "Both forms of reasoning are, of course, of prime importance in reasoning about evidence, whether story- or argument-based. Often an attempted proof that a certain crime took place is constructed by saying that an observed fact (the evidence) holds since something else (the crime) happened which caused it. Such an explanation can then be tested by predicting what else must have been caused by the crime if it has taken place and by trying to find evidence concerning the predicted facts" (from section 2.2 in Bex et al., 2007).

[135] "Clearly, reasoning with causal information is defeasible in several ways: causal generalisations may have exceptions (striking a match will cause fire except if the match is wet) and observed evidence may be explained by several alternatives (the grass is wet since it rained or since the sprinkler was turned on)" (from section 2.2 in Bex et al., 2007).

[136] "A reason not to represent all causal information from effect to cause has to do with the fact that crime investigators very often draw time lines and causal-network-like structures. Since we want to build software for supporting crime investigators, we want to support this habit. This explains why for our purposes representing all causal information from effect to cause is less desirable" (from section 3 in Bex et al., 2007). By contrast, the reason given for not only representing causation from cause to effect is about witness testimony: "the relation between a witness testimony and its content must be represented as causal generalisations, in which the witness testimony is regarded as caused by something else. One possible cause of a witness testimony is, of course, the truth of the event to which the witness testifies" (ibid.). Nevertheless, the witness may have been hallucinating, or at any rate is wrongly believing that he or she saw something. Or then, the witness may have reasons to lie. Cf. Thagard (2005).

[137] We discussed abductive reasoning in Section. 2.2.1.6 in this book.

[138] When *modus ponens* is applied, in we must see one premise as an *antecedent,* another as a *conditional* and the conclusion is the *consequent.* This is the classical Aristotelian *syllogism.*

5.4 Bex's Approach to Combining Stories and Arguments in Sense-Making... 479

Bex et al. (2007, section 4) adopted a causation network graphic approach along with an example from Bex, Prakken, and Verheij (2006), in which different diagrams represent the prosecution's story and the defence's story about a case of burglary.[139] Arrows stand for causation or sequence inside a rectangular contour with rounded angles. From outside the contour, arrows (standing for support or for refutation, e.g. from testimony, or from an argument about the testimony) may enter the contour and point to this or that box, which in turn stands for a narrative element.[140] For example, based on testimony from various witnesses about what they heard, the defence claims that the witnesses did not hear a loud bang, and this provides refutation for the causal expectation that there should have been a loud bang, had the prosecution's story be true.[141] Bex et al. explained (2007, section 4):

> The reader may find some of the causal or evidential generalisations in this example weak or far-fetched. However, this is not a problem for our approach. The very idea of our sense-making system (which it shares with, for example, Wigmore's charting method) is that it is the user of the system who is responsible for carefully testing the quality of his stories and arguments. The software should support the user in this critical process; it should not itself automatically generate sensible stories and arguments.

The most important part of the approach developed in Bex et al. (2007) is the fomalism. "General knowledge is in our approach expressed with two sets G_C and G_E of *causal* and *evidential* generalisations. Logically, we formalise both types of generalisations in the same way, with a special conditional connective) which only satisfies the modus ponens inference rule" (Bex et al., 2007, section 5.1). Out of many formal and computational accounts of abductive reasoning that are available in artificial intelligence, Bex et al. (2007, section 5.2) proposed a simple one. They defined an *abductive framework* as a tuple $A_C = (G_C, O, F, X)$ is the *causal theory*, and is a set of causal generalisations. O stand for the the *observations*, is a set of ground first-order literals, and does not have to be consistent. F is either a subset of O, or the entire set O. F is the set of the *explananda*, and is a consistent set of first-order literals. "They are the observations which have to be explained", whereas the observations not in F do not strictly have to be explained but explaining them does make an explanation better". As to X, it is the set of the *explanantia*; that is to say, X "s

---

[139] Burglary is also the subject of Oatley, Zeleznikow, Leary, and Ewart (2005), in a *link analysis* perspective.

[140] "The part of the figure within the large rounded box represents the causal network corresponding to the prosecution's story. The four small grey boxes outside the causal network are pieces of testimonial evidence. With the evidential generalisation 'a witness usually speaks the truth' they can be used to build arguments to support nodes inside the causal network" (from section 4 in Bex et al., 2007).

[141] Andrew King is the defendant, and the Zomerdijk family house is where an attempted burglary is claimed to have taken place. Here is part of the prosecution story: "Because it is dark, King does not see the toy lying on the floor. King hits the toy, causing it to make a sound which causes the dog to give tongue. King hears the dog and runs outside, closing the door behind him. Mr. Zomerdijk hears the toy and the dog. He goes to the bedroom and sees King running away through the closed garden door."

the set of all ground literals occurring in the antecedent of some causal generalisation in G_C and instantiated with some term in" the union set of G_C and O. Let $\vdash$ stand for logical implication according to the set of all deductive inference rules extended with modus ponens for $\Rightarrow$. An *explanation* in terms of A_C is a set $H \subseteq X$ of hypotheses such that for each *explanandum* $f \in F$ it holds that the explanation implies that *explanandum* (that is, that $H \vdash f$) and that the explanation does not imply something false (that is, that $H \nvdash \bot$).

Admittedly, as the approach in Bex et al. (2007) is purely qualitative, in order to compare alternative explanations resorting to probability distributions over H is not applicable (as stated in section 5.2 ibid.). Therefore, Bex et al. (2007) adopted a simple *ordering* on explanations: "if H' is better than H on the observations explained and not worse on the observations contradicted, or if H' is better on the observations contradicted and not worse on the observations explained, then H' is better than H. If they are equal on both criteria, then they are equally good overall. In all other cases they are incomparable" (from section 5.2 ibid.; they also expressed this ordering in formulae). Moreover, "combining abduction with argumentation allows a refinement of this preference relation" (ibid.). Bex et al. (2007, section 5.3) defined a *logic for defeasible argumentation*,[142] the application being as a "logic for reasoning with evidential generalisations. Since such generalisations allow for exceptions, this logic must be nonmonotonic."[143] Their choice was as follows (ibid.):

> In our case the classical inference rules are those of standard first-order logic while the only defeasible inference rule is the modus ponens rule for the $\Rightarrow$ connective. Undercutters to this defeasible version of modus ponens are formalised as arguments for the conclusion $\neg$ valid(g) where g is the name of the generalisation to which modus ponens is applied.[144]

The qualitativeness of the approach, from which its avoidance of a probabilistic representation follows, would arguably make the method quite interesting for the Bayesian skeptics among legal scholars,[145] without however antagonising the legal Bayesians (as the latter could possibly insert a probabilistic component in the argumentation module). Another formalism that the Bayesian skeptics ought to look into, as they are likely to come to like it very much, is the model for arguments and critical questions concerning legal narratives, as proposed by Bex et al. (2009), and which we already considered in Section 3.4.4.4.

---

[142] Carbogim, Robertson and Lee (2000) presented a comprehensive survey of defeasible argumentation. In this book, we have dealt with *defeasibility* in Sections 3.3 and 3.9.1. "Nonmonotonic reasoning, because conclusions must sometimes be reconsidered, is called *defeasible;* that is, new information may sometimes invalidate previous results. Representation and search procedures that keep track of the reasoning steps of a logic system are called *truth maintenance systems* or TMS. In defeasible reasoning, the TMS preserves the consistency of the knowledge base, keeping track of conclusions that might later need be questioned" (Luger & Stubblefield, 1998, p. 270). See, e.g., Antoniou (1997) and Antonious (2000), as well as, in an AI & Law context, Antoniou, Billington, and Maher (1999).

[143] See a definition of *monotonic* vs. *nonmonotonic* reasoning in fn. 93 in Chapter 2.

[144] $\neg$ valid(g) means "g is not valid".

[145] See above in Sections 2.4 and 5.1.

5.5 Persuasion Stories vs. Arguments

In a poster paper at a workshop on story-processing, Bex and Bench-Capon (2010) combined the narrative dimension with multiagent persuasive argumentation.[146] They noted that "in a context of persuasion[147] people will often tell a story (i.e. a sequence of events caused or experienced by actors) rather than give an argument based on conditional rules. For example, teaching a child not to lie is easier done by telling the story of *The Boy Who Cried Wolf* than by presenting an argument that one should not tell lies in circumstances where there is no gain in telling the lie because this will demote the value of honesty and consequently people will not believe you when you do tell the truth" (ibid., p. 4). Being persuaded by a story into accepting a norm involves identification: "A story does not persuade by imparting explicit rules or values, but instead by having an agent identify with the situations or actors in a story" (ibid., p. 4).

In their brief position paper, Bex and Bench-Capon (2010) stated their "aim to explore the role of stories in persuasion, particularly in the context of value-based practical reasoning with agents" (ibid., p. 5). Questions they ask include: "*What is the structure of a story?*", "*When is a story persuasive for a particular agent?*", "*Given an agent and his knowledge of different stories, how does an agent choose an action?*", "*What is the relation between arguments and stories in the context of practical reasoning?*" (ibid., p. 5).

---

[146] Section. 6.1.6 in this book is about multiagent systems. Bear in mind that it is not merely the case that argumentation could be modelled by means of multiagent systems. It is also the case that effective management of multiagent systems may require negotiation between autonomous agents, and therefore research into computational models of argumentation is beneficial for research into multiagent systems within computer science. At any rate, within AI & Law there has been research on modelling argumentation among antagonistic agents by means of multiagent systems. Artikis, Sergot, and Pitt (2003) presented a theoretical and computational framework for the executable specification of *open multiagent computational systems*. These "are composed of heterogeneous and possibly antagonistic software entities. Characteristic features are limited trust and unpredictable behaviour. Members of such systems may fail to, or even choose not to, conform to the norms governing their interactions. It has been argued that systems of this type should have a formal, declarative, verifiable, and meaningful semantics." (ibid., p. 12).

[147] For a treatment of AI modelling of persuasion in court, see e.g. Bench-Capon (2003a, 2003b).

Printed by Publishers' Graphics LLC